"Finally, an economics textbook that puts people before business!"

Richard Easterlin, *Professor Emeritus of Economics at the University of Southern California*

"The real world seldom operates like the diagrams in economics textbooks. Often left out are that human beings often act irrationally, markets have rules, and models typically began with the assumption of 'all else being equal.' John Komlos provides a welcome and much needed real-world look at the dismal science in his Critique of Pure Economics. In plain language that even high school seniors can grasp, Komlos shows the wishful thinking that infects standard economic texts and builds his case with empirical facts."

David Cay Johnston, *Pulitzer Prize-winning author of* The Fine Print: How Big Companies Use "Plain English" to Rob You Blind *and of the New York Times bestseller,* Perfectly Legal: The Covert Campaign to Rig Our Tax System to Benefit the Super Rich—and Cheat Everybody Else

"The 'Great Recession' which began in 2008 was not anticipated by economists, and they remain divided about the remedies. Economics requires a re-think, but this is proving hard. In this excellent book, John Komlos makes a start: he shows what parts of theory remain useful, and which ones have been falsified by experience. He highlights what the new theory will need to explain. Most importantly, he shows that it is necessary to start from current economics in order to reform it. Fluently written, accessible, and highly recommended as a corrective to standard textbooks."

Avner Offer, *Emeritus Fellow of All Souls College, University of Oxford, Fellow of the British Academy*

"Komlos's provocative book at once brings together and creatively synthesizes a great deal of work critical of conventional economics and lays out the broad contours of an alternative approach that the author calls humanistic economics. Komlos's book is timely and relevant. The author includes excellent discussions of income and wealth inequality, the cultural contradictions of capitalism, and green environmental accounting, as well as an entire chapter on the financial sector (a sector often omitted entirely in introductory classes) and the sector's role in the Great Recession."

Peter Coclanis, *Director of the Global Research Institute at the University of North Carolina at Chapel Hill*

"A wonderful book, a manifesto, written in a style that is easy to follow. Highly innovative and a must-read, especially but not only for students who are new to economics. John Komlos has given us a valuable tool that we can use to enrich our teaching and open the minds of our students. We owe him our thanks. More, we owe him our students' patronage."

Gerald Friedman, *Professor of Economics, University of Massachusetts, Amherst*

"John Komlos has given us a very useful companion text to the standard introductory economics version. Students would do well to read the two together. In fact, anyone who has taken introductory economics and had it shape their thinking about the world would benefit from learning about the issues raised in this book."

Dean Baker, *Senior Economist, Center for Economic and Policy Research*

"John Komlos provides an important complement to—and corrective for—the standard Economics 101 textbook. This book clearly explains why free markets are far from perfect and, indeed, do not exist in the vast majority of the modern economy. Instead of fetishizing economic efficiency, Komlos explains why economics should focus on creating a better society and helping all of us live more fulfilling lives."

James Kwak, *Professor of Law, University of Connecticut, co-author of*
13 Bankers: The Wall Street Takeover and the Next Financial Meltdown

"This book is a must-read, not only for economic students and professors who teach economics, but for psychology, sociology, political science, history, and philosophy students and professors as well. That is, it is a must-read for anyone who wishes to understand the discipline of economics and the way in which it has contributed to the conservative/neoliberal economic, social, and political policies that have guided us to the dysfunctional social and political systems we find ourselves in the midst of today."

George H. Blackford, *formerly University of Michigan-Flint,*
Contributions to Political Economy *(2019), 1-2*

"Komlos uses a literary style that empowers the reader with information and in-depth discussion of topics of current interest from the repercussions of the financial crisis to the rise of populism. The book is full of creative ideas and the author achieves his goal of presenting a realistic approach to introductory economics."

Andres F. Cantillo, *Kansas City Kansas, Community College,*
Australasian Journal of Economics Education *Volume 16, Number 1, 2019*

"This book is aimed at the introductory level and grounds its presentation in a lot of helpful stylised facts to connect to the real world. It contrasts the mainstream approach with many important heterodox insights in order to help readers to get a more realistic and multifaceted picture of economic relationships."

Torsten Niechoj, *Rhine-Waal University of Applied Sciences,*
Kamp-Lintfort, Germany, and FMM Fellow, European Journal of Economics and Economic Policies: Intervention, *Vol. 17 No. 1, 2020*

"This book explains a tremendous amount of how economies like the U.S. function in recent years. In doing so, it integrates conventional economic analysis with wide ranging socio-economic analyses and the thoughtful insights of the author on many topics related to how economies function or do not function well. At the very least, he has gone a long way in showing how economies can become a more important and different discipline than it has been. I highly recommend his text for many students of economics."

John F. Tomer, *Emeritus Professor of Economics, founding*
member of the Society for the Advancement of Behavioral Economics
(SABE), Society and Economy

"John Komlos's book has the sense and sensibilities for building up an economy that works for the 99%, not just the 1%."

Annavajhula J.C. Bose, *Shri Ram College of*
Commerce, India, Ecotalker blog

FOUNDATIONS OF REAL-WORLD ECONOMICS

The 2008 financial crisis, the rise of Trumpism, and the other populist movements which have followed in their wake have grown out of the frustrations of those hurt by the economic policies advocated by conventional economists for generations. Despite this, textbooks remain frozen in time, continuing to uphold traditional policies as though nothing has happened.

Foundations of Real-World Economics demonstrates how misleading it can be to apply oversimplified models of perfect competition to the real world. The math works well on college blackboards but not so well on the Main Streets of America. This volume explores the realities of oligopolies, the real impact of the minimum wage, the double-edged sword of free trade, and other ways in which powerful institutions cause distortions in mainstream models. Bringing together the work of key scholars like Kahneman, Minsky, and Schumpeter, this textbook takes into consideration the inefficiencies that arise when the perfectly competitive model is applied to the real world dominated by multinational oligopolies. The third edition has been updated throughout, bringing in new material on the financial crises, the rise of populism, racism, inequality, climate change, and the Covid-19 pandemic.

A must-have for students studying the principles of economics as well as micro- and macroeconomics, this textbook redresses the existing imbalance in economic teaching as John Komlos focuses on the paradigm of humanistic economics.

John Komlos is Professor Emeritus of Economics and of Economic History at the University of Munich, Germany. He has also taught at universities such as Harvard, Duke, UNC-Chapel Hill, the University of Vienna, and the Vienna School of Economics and Business. In 2003, Komlos founded the field of *Economics & Human Biology* with the journal of the same name, and through his research realized the limitations of conventional economic theory and has been an ardent advocate of humanistic economics.

FOUNDATIONS OF REAL-WORLD ECONOMICS

What Every Economics Student Needs to Know

Third Edition

John Komlos

Routledge
Taylor & Francis Group

NEW YORK AND LONDON

Designed cover image: Guillermo del Olmo / Shutterstock

Third edition published 2023
by Routledge
605 Third Avenue, New York, NY 10158

and by Routledge
4 Park Square, Milton Park, Abingdon, Oxon, OX14 4RN

Routledge is an imprint of the Taylor & Francis Group, an informa business

First edition published by M.E. Sharpe 2014

First edition published by Routledge 2015
Second edition published by Routledge 2019

Library of Congress Cataloging-in-Publication Data
Names: Komlos, John, 1944–author.
Title: Foundations of real-world economics : what every economics student
needs to know / John Komlos.
Description: Third edition. | New York, NY : Routledge, 2023. |
Includes bibliographical references and index.
Classification: LCC HB171.5 .K643 2023 | DDC 330–dc23/eng/20220914
LC record available at https://lccn.loc.gov/2022044709

ISBN: 978-1-032-00484-6 (hbk)
ISBN: 978-1-032-00172-2 (pbk)
ISBN: 978-1-003-17435-6 (ebk)

DOI: 10.4324/9781003174356

Typeset in Interstate
by codeMantra

Access the Support Material: www.routledge.com/9781032001722

CONTENTS

FIGURES

TABLES

ILLUSTRATIONS

PREFACE TO THE THIRD EDITION

> We must grant to markets what belongs to markets—and retain for people what rightfully belongs to them.
>
> —The author

The motivation for conceiving of the first edition of *Foundations* originated a dozen years ago in the wake of the financial crisis, as it became evident that mainstream economists, who dominated the profession, were caught utterly unprepared for it. They had to improvise to avoid a Chernobyl-like meltdown of the economy.[1] Like millions of others, Queen Elizabeth famously wondered in amazement "Why did nobody notice," the coming of such a stupendous catastrophe?[2] It became obvious that we were witnessing the failure of "zombie neoliberalism"[3] and that a paradigm shift was desperately needed to face the challenges of the new century. The text focused "on the neglected issue of the discrepancy between current economic scholarship and the simplistic, methodologically flawed, outdated, and irrelevant economics we too often teach undergraduates."[4] The aim was to reveal the mistaken theories, covert assumptions, overlooked facts, trivialized exceptions, and the accumulating evidence contradicting the mainstream canon.[5] The new paradigm proposed was "humanistic economics" or "capitalism with a human face," a hybrid of the Nordic Model and of the social market economy.[6]

The message was well received. One reviewer pointed out that "this book is a must-read for anyone interested in reforming the discipline of economics to create a more just society and to promote human development."[7] Another said that "everyone who teaches undergraduate economics should read *Foundations of Real-World Economics*."[8] Another reviewer thought that: "it is trained mainstream economists, not introductory-level students, who should take the time to read, and reflect upon, this book."[9]

Several translations[10] and scores of positive reviews later a new edition was necessitated by the turbulence of the intervening years. These brought into ever sharper focus that the neoclassical paradigm, based on Milton Freedman's and Friedrich Hayek's[11] ideology of market fundamentalism had led to policy failures of historic proportions.[12] The second edition included the topics usually covered in introductory economics courses plus an expanded discussion of globalization and the financial crisis.

The continual deterioration of the social and political order made three additional chapters necessary in this edition. Economics students should know about the economic causes of the unimaginable rise in populism; they should know how false economic theories led to fallacious economic policies, thereby fostering a disillusionment among a large group of men left behind. Feeling mistreated, they revolted against entrenched elites and overthrew the establishment in 2016, a process that culminated in the ferocious Bastille-like uprising on January 6, 2021 (see Chapter 15).[13]

Moreover the Black Lives Matter movement made it difficult to ignore the plight of minorities usually overlooked in mainstream economic courses. In fact, Blacks and Hispanics practically never appear in Econ-101 courses. Students should also know that economics treats discrimination with kid gloves and learn about the appalling disadvantages of those born on the wrong side of the tracks. So, Chapter 16 examines the racist subtext hidden deep within the mainstream's canon.

Then came the Covid-19 pandemic and economists had to scramble again to meet the challenges of a high-impact low-probability event that challenged the very existence of millions of people. The lessons learned from the pandemic is that basic needs are much more important than economists were willing to acknowledge and that fail-safe strategies such as in airplane design should be incorporated into the economic canon so that the very existence of the economic system is not threatened periodically (see Chapter 17). With these three new chapters the student should be able to comprehend the current state of the economy and how we got to this point.

Some of the reviewers suggested that I mention who the intended audience is. I wrote the book for *anyone* who wants to gain essential understanding of how a *real* market economy works and how it can be transformed so that it becomes inclusive. Humanistic economics puts the human element at center stage rather than inanimate abstract concepts like gross domestic product. How do people feel in the economy becomes the key issue rather than how much people earn in the economy. So obviously this should be interesting for students taking introductory courses but also includes their professors who are open-minded enough to notice that mainstream economic theory does not work well in the real world and are looking for alternative ways to approach the subject. The audience also includes graduate students who are looking for new topics and ideas to explore. They will find the extended footnote references useful. This could be helpful at the start of a research project. As several reviewers mentioned, this is an "honest" rendering of the economy without equivocating or trying to whitewash the dual nature of the real-existing economy. It does not focus on theoretical markets but on real-existing ones. Although several reviewers criticized the hundred-dollar words I use, I was able to use the textbook successfully in introductory courses.

The thesis of this volume is that the only way out of the West's current dilemma is through a paradigm shift toward a Capitalism with a Human Face.[14] Humanism means that the economy should work for everyone and not only for the select few. This can be accomplished only if we discard the failed assumptions of mainstream economics and instead of analyzing imaginary markets, we base our theories on evidence gleaned from the real world. Consequently, the book has been used also as a counterweight to conventional economics textbooks so that students gain pluralist insights about the actual economy.

Such a comprehensive paradigm shift will not be easy since there is a political world-view behind the mainstream's interpretation of the discipline and vested interests with deep pockets supporting the status quo. Nonetheless, we must discard a failed ideology,[15] because as long as our minds are trapped in the dogma of neoclassical economics, sketched eloquently on academic blackboards, we will be unable to attain a society in which everyone is flourishing.

Notes

1 John Cassidy, "After the Blowup. Laissez-Faire Economists Do Some Soul-Searching—and Finger-Pointing," *The New Yorker*, January 11, 2010.

2 Dimitris Chorafas, "Queen Elizabeth II and the Economists," in *The Changing Role of Central Banks* (Palgrave Macmillan, 2013), pp. 15-36.

3 Neoliberalism advocates for free-market capitalism, deregulation, and small government. Felicia Wong, "Build Back Better Meets the Spooky Season: Zombie Neoliberalism Creeps into the Negotiations," Roosevelt Institute, October 21, 2021; Thomas Palley, *Neoliberalism and the Road to Inequality and Stagnation: A Chronicle Foretold* (Edward Elgar, 2021).

4 Benjamin Balak, "Book Review" of the second edition, *Political Studies Review* 19 (2021), 3: NP3-NP4.

5 Tony Lawson, *Essays on the Nature and State of Modern Economics* (Routledge, 2015).

6 Julie Nelson, *Economics for Humans*, 2nd edn. (University of Chicago Press, 2018); Torben Andersen et al., *The Nordic Model: Embracing Globalization and Sharing Risks* (The Research Institute of the Finnish Economy, 2007).

7 Rhys Manley, "Book Review," *Journal of Human Development and Capabilities* 21 (2020), 2: 209-210.

8 Michael Ash, "Book Review," *Basic Income Studies* 15 (2020), 2.

9 John Foster, "Book Review," *Economic Record* 95 (2019), 311: 514-516.

10 Translated into Chinese, German, Hungarian, Romanian, and Russian.

11 Milton Friedman, *Capitalism and Freedom* (University of Chicago Press, 1962); Milton Friedman and Rose Friedman, *Free to Choose* (Harcourt Brace, 1979); Friedrich Hayek, *The Road to Serfdom* (University of Chicago Press, 1944).

12 Adair Turner, *Economics After the Crisis: Objectives and Means* (MIT Press, 2012); Assaf Razin, *Understanding Global Crises* (MIT Press, 2014), p. 5, suggests that most theorists consider the pre-crisis consensus a mistake.

13 Donald Trump's inciting pre-insurrection speech: https://www.rev.com/blog/transcripts/donald-trump-speech-save-america-rally-transcript-january-6.

14 Samuel Bowles and Wendy Carlin, "What Students Learn in Economics 101: Time for a Change," *Journal of Economic Literature* 58 (2020), 1: 176-214.

15 Anonymous, "Efforts to Modernise Economics Teaching Are Gathering Steam," *The Economist*, March 20, 2021.

1 Welcome to Real-World Economics

Earth provides enough to satisfy every man's need, but not every man's greed.

—Mahatma Gandhi[1]

The financial crisis and the Covid-19 pandemic illustrated vividly how markets often go haywire; yet, mainstream textbooks remain unchanged, failing to convey the fundamental flaws and Achilles' heels of the free-market system.[2] These limitations resulted in so much accumulated frustration with a system that skewed its benefits to a select few and left too many people far behind, scrambling to eke out a bare existence, that it culminated in the rise of far-right populism and a threat to democracy itself. Yet, academics and politicians continue to sing the praises of abstract markets as if they had descended straight from heaven while maintaining a conspiracy of silence about the fact that without extravagant government bailouts the whole capitalist system would have collapsed. In a panic, only central banks could print trillions of dollars or euros to avoid utter calamity.

The doctrinaire approach to the teaching of economics is illustrated by the arrogant assertion that, "we know that markets work." That was hardly evident in 2008 or in 2020. In reality, they only do so within an appropriate *institutional framework*, with appropriate government *oversight*, and they not only work inefficiently frequently but tend to tip the stream of benefits toward a few insiders.[3] Hence, we should explore and delineate clearly the circumstances that prevent real markets from working as well as their theoretical counterparts and suggest remedies for their failings.[4] The ideological commitment to *"market fundamentalism,"* which led to the excessive reliance on markets in public policy, has brought us to our current precarious political and social polarization. I hope the present volume will rectify this misconception and improve the understanding of real-existing economies by presenting a real-world perspective as opposed to the fantasy world of mainstream textbooks.[5]

Alan Greenspan's post-meltdown confession that he made a ghastly error in believing in—and aggressively preaching—market deregulation demonstrates vividly the miscalculations of the fundamentalist approach to economics. Congressman Waxman asked if he had been wrong; Greenspan responded:

> I made a mistake in presuming that the self-interest of organizations, specifically banks ... were such that they were best capable of protecting their own shareholders and equity in the firms .... The problem here is [that] something which looked to be a very solid edifice and indeed a critical pillar to market competition and free markets did break down and ... that ... shocked me. I still do not fully understand why it happened.[6]

DOI: 10.4324/9781003174356-1

History is replete with people caught unaware by such ideological blinders. Greenspan made two *inexcusable* mistakes in that short statement: (1) inanimate abstractions like firms cannot have self-interest. They have employees who have their own self-interest in mind and the interest of those employees and the interest of the owners of the firm are often not well aligned (see Section 8.2). (2) Moreover, a banks' management cannot assess the impact of their activities on the rest of the financial system, since they only see their own balance sheet, not those of other banks. The oversight of the whole system was Greenspan's responsibility. Only he could assess the *systemic risks*: how the bankruptcy of one bank and the default on its obligations create a cascade of defaults throughout the financial system (see Section 14.1).[7] Systemic risk arises because the banks are interlinked.[8] So, Greenspan was negligent in abrogating this responsibility.

Congressman Waxman continued: "You had an ideology …. this is your statement: 'I do have an ideology. My judgment is that free competitive markets are by far the unrivaled way to organize economies.'" Greenspan's answer was not very convincing: "Yes, I found a flaw … in the model that I perceived … how the world works." Waxman: "In other words, you found that your view of the world, your ideology, was not right." Greenspan: "Precisely. That's precisely the reason I was shocked."[9]

Greenspan should not have been shocked. One did not need a PhD to realize that housing prices were off the charts and that it made no economic sense because incomes were not increasing (see Figure 14.2). It would not have been difficult to realize that increasing demand was not logical without an increase in incomes. Yet, Greenspan and Benjamin Bernanke, his successor in 2006, chose to ignore this critical evidence, since they were blinded by their ideology that markets were infallible. *Ideology immune to empirical evidence becomes dogma.* So, they were trapped by their own ideology.

1.1 My Credo: It's Not the Economy—It's How People Feel in the Economy![10]

My worldview is progressive, democratic, and *humanistic*.[11] Instead of focusing on production and consumption, I concentrate *on how flesh-and-blood people feel in the real-existing economy*.[12] That is a crucial difference because mainstream economics equates consumption with well-being, which is easily refuted (see Chapter 2). Instead, humanistic economics aims to improve the *quality of life* and to restructure the economy to increase *life satisfaction* for everyone because there are better ways to measure well-being than in terms of money. The goal should be to catch up to Finland in educational attainment, to Switzerland in happiness, to Norway in longevity, and to Denmark in equality, rather than growing the economy.[13] These countries have demonstrated how to improve human flourishing, so they can provide guidance. All students (graduate and undergraduate) must know this.

Economic analysis should begin with empirical evidence, as the natural sciences, rather than with assumptions.[14] Evidence should be at the core of the discipline since "economics is supposed to be an inquiry into the world, not pure thinking."[15] Hence, it should not rely on axioms and derive theorems based on them using deductive logic. Instead, it should start with data, and build theories based on that evidence using inductive logic. It should also be open to *falsification*,[16] but it holds these axioms with such religious faith that they become doctrine and are therefore insensitive to evidence contradicting them.[17] Yet, human beings are not inanimate objects whose trajectory can be described accurately by mathematical formulas. Unlike planets, they can and do change direction. Isaac Newton, one of the greatest scientists, admitted as much in 1720: "I can calculate the movement of the stars, but not the madness of men."[18]

We need theories that are valid not only on academic blackboards[19] but also in concentrated areas of poverty like Cleveland's 44115 zip code area (with a median household income of $15,034).[20] Mainstream economic theory does not work so well there as it does on Park Avenue in New York City (10282 zip code) (with a median household income of $250,000)—four times the national median.[21]

Instead of revering income, humanistic economics stresses values that enhance human dignity and promote *mass flourishing*.[22] "Flourishing can be understood as a state of living in which all aspects of a person's life are good, including, ... happiness and life satisfaction, physical and mental health, meaning and purpose, character and virtue, and close social relationships."[23] Flourishing can be promoted by universal healthcare, universal educational opportunities from kindergarten through college, guaranteed basic needs, minimal stress, and a widespread safety net. Those are the basic ingredients of a *thriving society*.

Humanistic economics also advocates the minimization of pain and anxiety. *Homo oeconomicus*, the idealized construct of mainstream economics, feels no pain or stress or anxiety. Conventional economics assumes that utility cannot become negative. Hence, the current economic system treats the anguish of disadvantaged groups with an indifference that borders on negligence. These include children attending dysfunctional schools in dysfunctional neighborhoods growing up in dysfunctional families, the working poor who are unable to find their bearings in the new economy transformed by the IT revolution and globalization, those trapped in a culture of poverty, or displaced union workers experiencing downward social mobility. They are sentient beings and ought not be treated like inanimate objects without feelings.

The quest for the good life is as old as philosophy itself. Aristotle argued 2350 years ago that the essence of a good life was understanding the world around us. This book is about understanding the fundamental nature of today's economy as it actually works rather than the way it is *imagined* in academic classrooms. Change should start with understanding. My focus is on how real human beings actually live and feel. An abstract concept like the Gross Domestic Product, the total output of an economy, is a number that does not reveal how people feel in that economy. Hence, *GDP should not be equated with welfare* (see Section 7.13).

Moreover, we should be aware of the tyranny of averages, because average income or average GDP per capita are not the same as life satisfaction actually experienced by human beings living in that economy. Those statistics conceal how the income or GDP is distributed in the society which is crucial to understanding how much welfare is being generated. The increasingly uneven distribution of income is crucial, since it created much disaffection and consequently has become a potent political force ripe for manipulation (see Chapter 15).[24]

The pre-Covid-19 common wisdom was that "the economy is in good shape."[25] However, this was a major mistake because (1) it is a misuse of averages and completely disregards the distribution of benefits; and (2) what really matters is if the people living in the economy are in good shape. Gallup polls indicate that this is not the case in the US (see Chapter 2).[26]

Furthermore, I believe that our starting point should not be Adam Smith's *Wealth of Nations* (1776), but his *Theory of Moral Sentiments* (1759), in which Smith asserted forcefully that we possess an innate empathy toward our fellow human beings.[27] Moreover, *ethical principles of fairness* are part of our nature.[28] We ought not expunge these notions from the economics canon. Hence, I believe that mass flourishing can be achieved only in a *just society*, one in which compassion is more important than efficiency (see Section 5.7).[29] Even arch-conservative Republican Alan Greenspan, an ardent advocate of free markets, realized that the perception that the economy is *just* is an essential prerequisite of sustaining Capitalism:

> [y]ou cannot have the benefits of capitalist market growth without the support of … virtually all of the people; and if you have an increasing sense that the rewards of capitalism are being distributed unjustly, the system will not stand.[30]

Well, he was right, it was not standing very firmly on January 6, 2021.

1.2 Humanistic Economics, the New Paradigm

Humanistic economics is not an oxymoron. It implies that a more just capitalism is possible, embedded in a truly democratic society that enables people to live their daily lives with less anxiety, less conflict, less inequality, less insecurity, less manipulation, less pain, less poverty, less stress, less uncertainty, no unemployment, and less fear that their lives could spiral out of control in the next recession. This *Capitalism with a Human Face* would also increase ethical behavior, increase educational attainment, increase the health of the population, increase intellectual satisfaction, allow more leisure time, enable people to love and respect one another, improve social relationships, and enable the attainment of a moral life easier.[31] This is not utopian theorizing. It has been largely achieved in Switzerland, in Scandinavia, and is close to the social-market economy of Germany and Austria, and to the welfare states of other Western European countries.[32] These countries have the highest quality of life in the world.[33] My constructive agenda is to demonstrate that humanistic economics should be the new paradigm for organizing our economic thinking. By emphasizing that consumption ought not to be the goal of a meaningful life, humanistic economics differs fundamentally from the mainstream (Table 1.1). Human beings are *not* "economic agents." The mainstream's emphasis on income often conflicts with human values. "Capitalism with a human face" would enable everyone to live fulfilled lives. John Maynard Keynes said as much:

Table 1.1 The differences between humanistic and mainstream economics

		Humanistic economics	Mainstream economics
1	Start of analysis	Evidence	Axioms
2	Begins with	Children	Adults
3	Logic used	Inductive	Deductive
4	Sister disciplines	Included	Excluded
5	Human Psychology	Behavioral	Rational
6	Mathematics	Minimal	Extensive
7	Markets	Just	Free
8	Government's role	Substantial	Minimal
9	Pain/stress	Minimize	Omitted
10	Utility function	Interdependent	Independent
11	Goal	Quality of life	Consumption
12	Distribution	Important	Unimportant
13	Basic needs	Paramount	Omitted
14	Relative income	Important	Omitted
15	Opportunity	De facto	De Jure
16	Power	Important	Omitted
17	Species	Homo sapiens	Homo oeconomicus

I think that capitalism, wisely managed, can probably be made more efficient for attaining economic ends than any alternative system yet in sight, but that in itself it is in many ways extremely objectionable. Our problem is to work out a social organization which shall be as efficient as possible without offending our notions of a satisfactory way of life.[34]

The common wisdom erroneously equates economic growth with rising living standards (see Section 7.13). However, surveys categorically contradict this proposition. The growth fetish-ism disregards not only the pollution it causes but also other negative externalities associated with growth, such as stress and insecurity. Furthermore, focusing on growth disregards the distribution of its benefits: economic growth has not benefited the destitute, the uneducated underclass, or the underemployed. *Despite 250 years of economic growth since the Industrial Revolution, discontent is more widespread than ever* because income has concentrated at the top 1 percent. It is amazing how much dissatisfaction the $23 trillion US economy produces (see Chapters 2 and 15).[35] In 2019, merely 55 percent of US adults considered themselves "thriving" while the rest were "struggling" (41 percent) or "suffering" (4 percent).[36] This economy is ineffi-cient at producing contentment for some 150 million of its citizens. Consequently, by disregard-ing the distribution of income and the stress generated by the economic system, free-market aficionados have led us astray.

Another important issue is that humanistic economics considers *de jure* equal opportunity insufficient for a *just economy* without *de facto* equal opportunity. Wealth is a privilege because it provides opportunities to those who possess it. Babies born into poor families have less chance of living a fulfilled life than those born into wealthy ones. Hence, their future develop-ment diverges, depending on their initial endowment. Such random allocation at the start of life cannot possibly be the basis of a good society. Our goal ought to be to create a just society in which children have *de facto* equal opportunity, not just in theory, and those who are born at a disadvantage can be compensated by society for their initial bad luck (see Section 5.7).[37]

The aim of this volume is to provide a critical framework that helps us understand the actu-ally existing economy—and how the mistakes of the conventional canon have landed us in our current divisive predicament (see Chapter 15). The book also provides a guide to a humanistic economy to which we should aspire and serves as a counterweight to conventional textbooks which instill in students full confidence in the benefits of the free-market system. Such confi-dence is unwarranted. After all, markets are human inventions; they do not deserve our blind faith. So, this book advocates a new paradigm: *Capitalism with a Human Face*.

1.3 A Primer on Blackboard Economics

"What do George Akerlof, Kenneth Arrow, Daniel Kahneman, Paul Krugman, Thomas Schelling, Herbert Simon, Robert Shiller, Joseph Stiglitz, Richard Thaler, and Oliver Williamson have in common?" would make a great Econ-101 question except for the fact that the contributions of these Nobelists are typically omitted from mainstream textbooks or relegated to obscure foot-notes. Instead of emphasizing their critical ideas, these textbooks hype a free-market nirvana whose validity does not extend beyond the classroom.

Hence, millions of students taking Econ-101 fail to grasp essential aspects of *real-existing* markets in the hyper-globalized world of the twenty-first century. Rather, they learn a caricature of the economy at a level of abstraction that creates a fantasy world and distorts their vision: how inefficient! These textbooks perpetuate a stereotype that markets are efficient, thereby automatically leading to a blissful life. The students fail to grasp that these are abstract hypo-thetical markets in Alice-in-Wonderland economies, not in the real world. Conventional textbooks sing praises to the immense achievements of the market system, disregarding inconvenient evidence contradicting their claims like the skyrocketing *"deaths of despair"* by the underprivi-leged, the millions in jail who were rejected by the legal labor market, or the inequality-fueled rise of populism against the entrenched elites who control the system.

Super rationality reigns in this utopian kingdom inhabited by *homo oeconomicus* with suf-ficient brain power to know every detail of the economy and are therefore not satisfied with anything less than *maximizing their welfare*. These consumers possess perfect understanding of the nuances in contracts in small print; they have perfect foresight from the beginning of their lives onward and are not inhibited by the challenges of information overload because information is available freely, instantaneously, and a cinch to understand. They are neither manipulated nor tempted, so they have complete control over their desires. They avoid bouts of irrational exuberance. Welcome to the *pseudo-science* of mainstream economics.[38]

Theirs is a caricature of human nature and of real-existing markets. The mainstream over-looks emotions and that habit and the unconscious mind play a substantial role in our decisions (see Chapter 4). Thus, it overlooks the path-breaking work of Sigmund Freud on the unconscious mind which is not only a source of many of our desires, but frequently comes into conflict with our rational thoughts.[39] Overlooking this leads economic policy makers astray. After all, if peo-ple are rational, there is no need for *consumer protection* from predatory mortgages. Yet, much of our reasoning is rationalizing our unconscious thoughts. By putting an enormous faith in the power of reason, mainstream economics reveals its *pre-Freudian* essence.

Moreover, in the mainstream's fantasy world there are no brands, so goods have no quality dimension, and product choice becomes a no-brainer: two slices of generic pizza, or three? There are no traps, no false promises, no stress, so buyers need not be on their guard in this idyllic economy. There are no regrets, no need for human judgment or intuition, no emotion, no real uncertainty, hence no mistakes, and no need to worry about lawyers' fees or other enforce-ment or transaction costs. Indeed, there is no society at all, no children, no gender, no glass ceilings, no class, hence no lower class, no power, hence no power imbalances, and neither space nor race, and hardly any time dimension. In this imaginary world consumers are not swayed by advertisements or by other people's consumption.

Producers also inhabit this make-believe economy. They also know everything about con-sumers' wants and their demand for the firms' products, so they can maximize their profits with ease. Actually, the textbook firms are Mom-and-Pop operations, not modern multinational cor-porations. They are so small and there are so many of them that they are *price takers*; they must accept the market price, unable to influence it at all (see Chapter 6). This *"perfect competition"*[40] is still the default model although obviously "most industries are now dominated by a small number of large firms."[41] There are no shareholders in these models or board of directors, no CEOs who maximize their own income rather than that of distant shareholders (see Chapter 8). These firms do not advertise to persuade consumers to buy their products, much less collude with others, deceive, or game the system.[42] Lobbyists are an extinct species, so there is no politi-cal process that can serve the interests of the high and mighty.[43] Problems are posed in terms of a single decision without antecedents and without fundamental uncertainty and without further implications in subsequent periods. In fact, time hardly plays a role in this static world since sequential decisions are neglected.[44]

Laws are in place, so we can disregard how they came into being or what advantages they provide to those already influential. Laws are not broken, and people do not take advantage of their counterparty's lack of information and hence there are no enforcement costs for contracts. So, oversight would be a waste of effort. Everything runs smoothly—there are no opportunities to finagle, no conflicts, let alone wars. Basic needs have given way to benign wants. Free markets are efficient, hence above morality, so questioning their *laissez-faire* premise would be a waste of ethical scruples. However, the mainstream fails to note that this is also a value judgment implying that efficiency is more valuable than sustainability, justice, reducing stress, or eliminating poverty.[45] Hence, questions of fairness are supposedly superfluous.

Moreover, the system is in perpetual *equilibrium*, meaning that supply equals demand in all markets; so, there is no need to worry about bubbles or crisis. Well-being is measured in terms of money, but there are no rich or poor so there is no hunger, therefore the system is democratic: one dollar, one vote. The fact that some consumers own more dollars than others is their birthright, so there is no need to waste time discussing that in reality some do have many more votes. These are the basic elements of *positive neoclassical economics*, at least on the blackboard. But there is nothing positive about the axioms upon which these propositions are based and the inconvenient truth is that they are based on value judgments and have little to do with the actual economy as it exists today full of too-big-to-fail banks and supranational mega-corporations with global reach who operate mostly above democratic oversight. Actually, the canon hides the fact that free markets have never ever existed in the real world because they cannot possibly exist in a social vacuum.[46]

The mentality of conventional economists is rooted in the much simpler Smithian world of the eighteenth century without its moral sensibilities.[47] That is like trying to understand atomic physics with Newton's laws instead of quantum mechanics. Hence, the dominant *neoliberal economic theory is anachronistic*—inadequate to meet the challenges of the crisis-ridden world of the twenty-first century. "Ivory tower" economists are experiencing a paradigm paralysis that blocks their ability to evaluate their canon critically.[48] They are inflexible, unable to think outside of the abstract framework they have created because alternative perspectives are inconceivable to them. They refuse to give up the simplistic assumptions of an imagined economy inhabited by implausible super-rational agents—*Übermenschen*—Supermen—devoid of emotion, without any sense of community, whose only identity is that of being consumers, or producers with hardly any interaction among them.[49] In contrast, humanistic economics is about flesh-and-blood people.

1.4 A Paradigm Shift Is Long Overdue

Our long-range goal should be to provide a thorough empirical foundation for the discipline, while our proximate goal is to demonstrate that the mainstream canon is woefully misleading and therefore a paradigm shift is absolutely necessary away from the current dominance of neoclassical economics and toward humanistic economics.[50] For economics to be relevant, it must become more realistic and work for the benefit of Everyman and not only for the top 1 percent.[51]

Today, economic policy is of paramount importance. The White House has the Council of Economic Advisers and the National Economic Council; the legislative branch's Congressional Budget Office has 235 employees; the Department of Commerce has the Bureau of Economic Analysis with 500 employees; the Bureau of Labor Statistics employs 2,500; the Bureau of the

Census also collects economic data and employs 5,600 people. So, lots of effort is expended on understanding the economy. Hence, it behooves us to discard false theories.

Mainstream economics has been unable to create an inclusive economy in which most people felt good about their life.[52] Mainstream economics steered us straight into the biggest economic crisis in 75 years, and the political crisis was not far behind (see Chapters 14 and 15).[53] Mainstream economics misjudged the severe impact of globalization on the lives of low-skilled workers (see Chapter 13). Mainstream economics misunderstood the impact of inequality on the social and political systems. These errors add up to an extraordinary set of policy blunders.[54] Hence, a paradigm shift is long overdue.[55] That is the proximate reason for writing this book. Without these blatant blunders I would certainly not have done so.

Instead of chasing the elusive "American Dream" in a "treadmill" economy with a few winners and many losers, we should focus on creating a more *harmonious economy* with a creative, decent, dignified, enjoyable, satisfactory, secure, sustainable, and peaceful life, one that is not based on excessive consumption, instant gratification, and cutthroat competition—one that is less materialistic.[56] For the first time ever, we have the possibility of achieving a quality of life that eluded our predecessors without struggling to achieve ever more material goods.[57] That is the essence of *humanistic economics*.

The emphasis on competition in economics is based on *Social Darwinism*—the survival of the fittest. Supposedly, competition brings forth more of the best products and best performance. But we already have enough material goods. We no longer need to strive for more. What we need more of is contentment. We could all live comfortably, given our level of productivity. Materialism is insatiable and therefore ultimately cannot satisfy because it just makes us want more. Rather, we need to rein in our appetite, our greed, and have a mindset that is less concerned with success measured by money and status and be able to enjoy more of what we already possess.[58] Instead of growing the economy, we need psychological, spiritual, and moral growth. However, for that, we need a new economic paradigm appropriate for the twenty-first century. The Canadian Institute of Wellbeing defines well-being thus:

> The presence of the highest possible quality of life ..., focused on ... good living standards, robust health, a sustainable environment, vital communities, an educated populace, balanced time use, high levels of civic participation, and access to and participation in dynamic arts, culture and recreation.[59]

In short, well-being is not identical with GDP or income (see Section 10.10).[60] A good life in Capitalism with a Human Face should include the *minimizing* of anxiety, inequality, insecurity, pain, poverty, stress, unemployment, and *maximizing* ethics, intellectual satisfaction, health, leisure time, social relationships, love, respect, and a moral life.[61] President Jimmy Carter implied as much:

> [t]oo many of us now tend to worship self-indulgence and consumption. Human identity is no longer defined by what one does, but by what one owns. But we have discovered that owning things and consuming things do not satisfy our longing for meaning.[62]

However, his warning fell on deaf ears: "[Carter] totally ignored the fact that the country's dominant institutions—corporations, advertising, popular culture—were instrumental in promoting and sustaining the hedonistic ethic."[63]

The reader should not misunderstand. I am not advocating abolishing markets or creating an immense leviathan and am resolute about protecting freedoms enunciated in the Universal Declaration of Human Rights. However, I have a wider conception of liberty than libertarians.

Freedom is more than the absence of legal restraint to act. Crucially, it has to encompass Amartya Sen's notion of *capability*: the *ability* to act.[64] It includes the "freedom from want" and the "freedom from fear" emphasized by President Franklin Roosevelt: "Liberty requires opportunity to make a living—a living decent according to the standard of the time, a living which gives man not only enough to live by, but something to live for."[65] That includes, furthermore, the ability to live without the anxiety generated by a high-stress economy, so we should not have to worry about our job or pension disappearing, being defrauded, or paying medical bills or college tuition. The UN's Declaration of Human Rights includes these freedoms:

> Everyone has the right to a standard of living adequate for the health and well-being of himself and of his family, including food, clothing, housing and medical care and necessary social services, and the right to security in the event of unemployment, sickness, disability, widowhood, old age or other lack of livelihood in circumstances beyond his control.[66]

My conception of a good life also includes the freedom to live without the feeling of relative deprivation from seeing the lifestyles of the profligate rich and famous. One should also be free to develop one's personality autonomously rather than having it imposed by media magnates and influencers. In addition, developing one's character without the interference of the profit motive of multinationals is an essential aspect of true freedom.[67] We would then not be inculcated from the get-go with the fundamental elements of consumerism.

Furthermore, I also believe that many markets work well some of the time, and a few markets work well most of the time, but *no market works well for long without adequate oversight*. This is a crucial insight. So, we must verify if specific markets at a specific time really accomplish what is expected of them and, if not, we should improve their performance so that we can function better in them. I am an enthusiastic supporter of those markets that enable individuals to exercise their creativity, autonomy, and individuality without psychological manipulation or coercion and without interference from influencers peddling conformity, and predatory lenders fishing for gullible people, but my support is contingent on *empirical verification*. We should not ignore evidence contradicting the orthodox canon. If markets are suboptimal or even harmful, we must retain the right to reform them. This is also the essence of humanistic economics. Crucially, we, the people, should remain the masters of markets, and not vice versa.[68] Moreover, their benefits should be widely dispersed. So, markets are not above moral judgment.

Actually, there is a continuum of socio-economic systems, ranging from market fundamentalism to socialism. I advocate finding that constellation of institutional arrangements at the golden mean between the two extremes that can provide a fulfilled life for all. However, I do not believe that we need to "grow the economy" to achieve this. Rather, we should create a fairer economy that can sustain future generations, eliminate discontent, and minimize insecurity and *minimize suffering*, mental and physical.

Ernst Schumacher, a pioneer environmental economist, had a similar vision: "The most striking thing about modern industry is that it requires so much and accomplishes so little. Modern industry seems to be inefficient to a degree that surpasses one's ordinary powers of imagination."[69] By being "inefficient," he meant that the economy generates so little life satisfaction despite high average income and despite using so much resources. He continued: "the aim should be to obtain the maximum of well-being with the minimum of consumption." Thus, our goal should be to improve our sensibilities and *consumption skills* so that we can improve our lives by obtaining

more gratification with less consumption.[70] That is, become smarter, more autonomous consumers immune to instant gratification.

1.5 Real-World Economics Is Superior

The recognition is increasing that "the progress of economic science has been seriously damaged,"[71] because "[m]odern economics is sick. Economics has increasingly become an intellectual game played for its own sake and not for its practical consequences for understating the
economic world."[72] Consequently, there is a widespread effort to reform the discipline. This
includes "Rethinking Economics,"[73] an international movement committed to "building a better
economics."[74] On the 500-year anniversary of Martin Luther's *95 Theses*, it posted "33 Theses
for an Economics Reformation" on the entrance of the London School of Economics, arguing
that "within economics, an unhealthy intellectual monopoly has developed."[75] The manifesto is
practically identical to humanistic economics.[76]

Similarly, the editors of the journal *Capitalism and Society* are explicit in their criticism of
the "otherworldly neoclassical school ... using mathematics to model unrealistic assumptions":[77]

> Today's established economics–the economics dominant in classrooms, banks, and govern-
> ments–misconceives the modern economy. This disconnect has consequences for how we
> understand history, how we make policy, and how we view capitalism. Its explanations fail
> and mislead at important junctures in modern history. Until economics is grounded on the
> basic character of modern economies ... it limits and distorts our view.[78]

However, the groundswell of rejection of mainstream models has not been adequately represented in academic classrooms or in policy.[79] There is a veritable iron curtain protecting the
power centers of neoliberal ideology that maintain its dominance in all top journals crucial for
promotion and admittance into departments that shape the future of the discipline.[80] Even today
most research papers published in prestigious journals begin with unrealistic assumptions.

No less an authority than Nobelist, Joseph Stiglitz, declared–prematurely in 2009–that
"neoliberalism as a doctrine, market fundamentalism is dead:"[81]

> This September has been to market fundamentalism what the fall of the Berlin Wall was
> to communism. We all knew that those ideas were flawed, that free market ideology didn't
> work; we all knew that communism didn't work, but these were defining moments that
> made it clear that it didn't work ... America really has a system ... of corporatism corporate
> welfarism ... under the guise of free market economics. And it is that mixture, which was
> fundamentally flawed, incoherent, was intellectually bankrupt.from the beginning, that has
> been shown not to work.[82]

Nonetheless, the popular textbooks remain unchanged. This is hardly a benign oversight. It has
immense consequences, since it influences the media, political discourse, and the mindset of
the voting citizenry. No wonder that many believe, "much of what economists do nowadays is
a waste of time."[83]

1.6 Simple Is for the Simple-Minded

The argument that a simple overview suffices to lay the foundations in Econ-101 before students learn more sophisticated aspects of the discipline, is blatantly false. It sells the students

far too short. Oversimplification leads to the distortion of reality beyond recognition, deceives students, and blends into indoctrination. If the straight-talking Nobel Prize-winning physicist, Richard Feynman (1918–1988) were still with us, he would concur that such caricatures should not persist in academia. In his 1974 commencement address at the California Institute of Technology, he beseeched students to practice "scientific integrity," "utter honesty," and to "lean over backwards" so as not to "fool ourselves."[84] I believe this holds also for teachers of economics. Economists should be held to the same ethical standards as other professionals.[85] From the start, students must learn about the limitations of real markets as opposed to theoretical ones for four reasons:

1. Half-truths do not belong in academia: not in the beginning or at the end of a program; omitting crucial aspects like Herbert Simon's theory of satisficing or behavioral economics is not living up to Feynman's standard of being "utterly honest."[86]
2. It is much more efficient to learn economics properly the first time than to have to correct it subsequently. It is extremely difficult to unlearn something once one is socialized into accepting the main tenets of the discipline without learning about their real-world limitations. The human mind is not so flexible: once the neural networks are in place, they are tedious to rewire.[87]
3. The more "sophisticated" ideas of imperfect markets are not so complicated and can be taught successfully at the introductory level. Neglecting them, dubbed "imperfections" or *"frictions,"* and focusing instead on perfectly competitive markets distorts economic theory to such an extent that students leave the course "convinced of the righteousness of neoclassical economics and the necessity of deregulation and the reduction of taxes," i.e., with a fundamentally misleading caricature of the real existing economy.[88]
4. Most students of Econ-101 do not continue to study economics; so, they never learn the more nuanced models and are therefore convinced for the rest of their lives that markets work perfectly well without government interference. This influence played a substantial role in political developments by supporting an ideology tilted toward the free-market worldview. Thus, students should not be deceived and the distinction between theoretical and actual markets clarified from the start. Admittedly, instructors are expected to cover a considerable amount of material in Econ-101. Nonetheless, quality ought not be sacrificed for quantity: it is more important that students are not deceived and get a balanced view of the real-existing economy.

1.7 "It's Only a Model!" Is Deceiving

The reliance on mathematics in economic models does not make economics into a rigorous science because the methodology has many drawbacks.[89] These include "sins of omission": complex social and political processes cannot be captured accurately in a few equations. Consequently, many relevant issues are omitted, which leads to "narrow methodological biases," and "epistemological insularity," the isolation from other social sciences.[90] Simple models are unrealistic conceptualization of a complex economy with thousands of variables and interacting components. So, simplification renders many models harmful, as became obvious during the 2008 crisis.

Consider also that some critical issues can only be approximated. Obviously, extreme inequality can destabilize a democratic political system, but the precise relationship between the two variables cannot be described mathematically. Yet, if economists omit political destabilization from their thinking about inequality, they are committing a critical error. Thinking about such issues requires approximation based on intuitive judgment. Teachers are doing their students a disservice if they allow them to leave their classroom without understanding that the political implications of such issues as inequality.

Because of such systematic oversight, simplified blackboard models are applied casually to real-world situations erroneously and lead to *disastrous* policies. The perfectly competitive model, the workhorse of mainstream economics, is invariably misapplied because it is irrelevant in today's economy (see Chapter 9). This is an immense flaw because it led to destructive policies. For example, Greenspan's and Bernanke's application of simple Econ-101 textbook models to the complex financial sector, while ignoring the warning signs before 2008, had catastrophic consequences (see Chapter 14). Similarly, economists omitted in their mathematical equations the ominous political forces that were unleashed by globalization, with similarly disastrous results (see Chapter 15).

Hence, the economics profession is responsible, in the main, for how ill-informed the public, the media, and politicians are about real-world economics. Economists have failed miserably to "bend over backwards" by clearly explaining the limitations of blackboard models. It is insufficient to mention the assumptions at the beginning of the semester and assume that the students remember them years later when they assume responsible positions by becoming newspaper editors, radio commentators, small-town mayors, or political activists, and choose among political candidates based partly on dubious economic models, remembering that free markets are supposedly efficient.[91] This failure has immense deleterious implications for society and its political system. Hence, we must clarify when *blackboard models are not applicable to real-world phenomena*. Without such emphasis most textbooks fail to provide adequate guidance to understanding the real-existing economy.

Thus, the deficiencies of Econ-101 have become a powerful political force as citizens become vulnerable to simplistic sound bites: "competition will lead to growth," "the free market is efficient," "lowering taxes will create jobs," "government is not the solution to our problems, government is the problem,"[92] "we are adults, we do not need consumer protection." To avoid such stereotypical political slogans becoming common wisdom, academics must avoid half-truths before the students are indoctrinated into thinking that competitive free markets miraculously provide the answers to all real-world economic problems.

Yet, economists often argue that unrealistic models are acceptable if their predictions are useful. However, mainstream economics fails miserably in this respect. For instance, typical models predicted that our life satisfaction would increase as real per capita gross national product rose by a factor of 3.5 in the US since 1950. Yet, that prediction is falsified by the inconvenient truth that the share of adults who are happy remained unchanged in the intervening half-century.[93] If anything, it has declined. Hence, the importance of money is obviously overvalued by economists.

Yet another example is Greenspan's prediction that deregulation would increase the efficiency of the financial sector, but that prediction was falsified when financial markets imploded in 2008. Similarly, Bernanke predicted that the subprime mortgage problem would not "drive the economy too far from its full employment path."[94] Yet, this Princeton star macroeconomist was dead wrong: two years later the official unemployment rate reached 10 percent, and the actual unemployment rate was closer to 17 percent.[95] Economists also predicted that globalization would increase prosperity. Instead, it increased the number of have-nots and provided fodder for populism. Economists blundered by predicting that a financial crisis would not occur although there were enough warnings that people in authority disregarded.[96] Despite these mistakes there is no rush to scrap falsified theories in order to put economics on the right track in order to avoid such blunders in the future.

In sum, the failure of economic theory to provide reasonable predictions to the major challenges of our time is essentially a travesty. The argument has been falsified innumerable times that economists can predict accurately even with unrealistic models. Thus, the conclusion is warranted that:

> mainstream economists nowadays might not be particularly good at predicting financial crashes, facilitating general prosperity, or coming up with models for abating climate change, but when it comes to establishing themselves in positions of intellectual authority, unaffected by such failings, their success is unparalleled. One would have to look at the history of religions to find anything like it.[97]

Why this is the case is the subject of this volume.

1.8 Takeaways

The financial crisis of 2008 and the subsequent rise of populism demonstrated the failure of economic theories to grasp the full implications of their policies in the real world. In mainstream classrooms, markets are described as self-regulating institutions that work efficiently without government oversight. However, the devastation of the crisis, together with the upswell of discontent associated with a level of inequality not seen since the Robber Barons of a bygone era demonstrated convincingly how economists were blindsided by events. Theirs was not a minor error but a failure of historic proportions.

Trumpism captured the frustration of the electorate with free-market principles that dominated policies since the trickle-down theories of Reaganomics. Two hundred counties flipped from Obama to Trump in the 2016 election because of the anxiety linked to *downward social mobility* and the devastation that mismanaged globalization brought to the Rust Belt, to small towns, and to rural America.

Yet, textbooks remain unchanged, failing to convey the fundamental shortcomings of the free-market system as well as the ways in which social, political, and economic processes are intertwined. This chapter points to the weaknesses of the current economy and argues that only "Capitalism with a Human Face" can lead to a flourishing society.

Questions for Discussion

1   Do you agree with Alan Greenspan that everyone has an ideology?
2   What is your ideology and how does it compare to the ideology of a typical American?
3   Do you think that the assumptions made in economics textbooks about the behavior of individuals and firms are sufficiently realistic to be appropriate and useful in their application to the real world, or do you think that they are oversimplifications?
4   Do you think that a value-free economics is possible?
5   Do you think it is useful to distinguish between basic needs, wants, and conspicuous consumption?

6   Do advertisements or fashion trends influence your consumption habits?
7   Do you think that ethical considerations are as important as economic efficiency?
8   Do you think that consumerism should be the dominant culture? What about instant gratification, keeping up with the Joneses, conspicuous consumption?
9   Do markets always function well and increase our quality of life or do they frustrate many and exclude some?
10 Can you think of instances when you were disappointed by a salesperson, or deceived, or defrauded, or someone took advantage of your lack of knowledge or experience?
11 Does society have the right to control market activity?
12 Do you expect professors to follow Feynman's admonition to be "utterly honest"?
13 Are you more satisfied with your life than were your parents or grandparents?
14 Do you think that reducing the conspicuous consumption of the rich through higher taxes would improve the supply of public goods such as schools and infrastructure in the United States?
15 Do you know someone who voted for Donald Trump? Why did he/she vote for him?

Notes

1   In the public domain. https://www.reuters.com/article/us-gandhi-works/gandhi-works-to-go-public-60-years-after-his-death-idUSTRE50418A20090105.
2   Diane Coyle, *What's the Use of Economics? Teaching the Dismal Science After the Financial Crisis* (London Publishing Partnership, 2012); Bradford DeLong, "Economics in Crisis," *The Economists' Voice* 8 (2011) 2: 1-2; David Colander, "Why Economics Textbooks Should, But Don't, and Won't, Change," *European Journal of Economics and Economic Policies: Intervention* 12 (2015), 2: 229-235; Joseph Stiglitz, "On the Market for Principles of Economics Textbooks: Innovation and Product Differentiation," *Journal of Economic Education*, 19 (1988), 2: 171-182.
3   Robert Nelson, *Economics as Religion: From Samuelson to Chicago and Beyond* (Pennsylvania State University Press, 2002).
4   Dani Rodrik, *Economics Rules: The Rights and Wrongs of the Dismal Science* (Norton, 2016).
5   Ariel Rubinstein, "Comments on Economic Models, Economics, and Economists: Remarks on Economics Rules by Dani Rodrik," *Journal of Economic Literature* 55 (2017), 1: 162-172.
6   "Waxman to Greenspan: Were You Wrong?" YouTube video, 5:05, posted by "NancyPelosi," October 23, 2008; www.youtube.com/watch?v=txw4GvEFGWs.
7   This was pointed out by Daniel Kahneman, "Reflection on a Crisis," @ 18 minutes. https://www.youtube.com/watch?v=LjGl6bZF6zs.
8   Javier Bianchi, "Overborrowing and Systemic Externalities in the Business Cycle," *American Economic Review* 101 (2011), 7: 3400-3426.
9   "Waxman to Greenspan: Were You Wrong?" op. cit.
10 Paraphrasing Bill Clinton's campaign slogan of 1992.
11 Mark Lutz and Kenneth Lux, *Humanistic Economics: The New Challenge* (Bootstrap Press, 1988); George Brockway, *The End of Economic Man: An Introduction to Humanistic Economics* (Norton, 1991); Wilhelm Röpke, *A Humane Economy: The Social Framework of the Free Market* (Henry Regnery, 1960).
12 Reema Patel et al., *Building a Public Culture of Economics* (RSA, 2018); https://www.thersa.org/; Joe Earle et al., *The Econocracy: The Perils of Leaving Economics to the Experts* (Manchester University Press, 2016).
13 Giorgos Kallis et al., *The Case for Degrowth* (Polity Press, 2020); Kate Raworth, *Doughnut Economics: Seven Ways to Think Like a 21st Century Economist* (Chelsea Green Publishing, 2017).

14 "Our criticism of the accepted classical theory of economics has consisted not so much in finding logical flaws in its analysis as in pointing out that its tacit assumptions are seldom or never satisfied, with the result that it cannot solve the economic problems of the actual world." John Maynard Keynes, *The General Theory of Employment, Interest and Money* (Macmillan, 1936), Chapter 24.

15 The mainstream is guilty of "cultural barbarism," and "historical ignorance." Deirdre McCloskey, *The Secret Sins of Economics* (Prickly Paradigm Press, 2002).

16 Karl Popper, *Conjectures and Refutations: The Growth of Scientific Knowledge* (Harper & Row, 1963); Donald McCloskey, "The Rhetoric of Economics," *Journal of Economic Literature* 31 (1983), 2: 482–504.

17 Eugene McCarraher, *The Enchantments of Mammon: How Capitalism Became the Religion of Modernity* (Harvard University Press, 2019).

18 Wikipedia, "South Sea Company."

19 Nobelist Ronald Coase dubbed unrealistic models "blackboard economics." *The Firm, the Market, and the Law* (University of Chicago Press, 1988), p. 19.

20 Median income is that of the typical household. Half are below and half are above the median.

21 "Income by Zip Code," https://www.incomebyzipcode.com/search.

22 Edmund Phelps, *Mass Flourishing: How Grassroots Innovation Created Jobs, Challenge, and Change* (Princeton University Press, 2013), p. 273.

23 Tyler VanderWeele, "On the Promotion of Human Flourishing," *Perspective PNAS* 114 (2017), 31: 8148–8156; https://www.pnas.org/content/114/31/8148. https://opportunityinsights.org/; Harvard has a program in human flourishing: https://hfh.fas.harvard.edu/; Yale offers a course on the good life: https://news.yale.edu/2021/04/14/how-gain-sense-well-being-free-and-online.

24 Heather Boushey, *Unbound: How Inequality Constricts Our Economy and What We Can Do about It* (Harvard University Press, 2019).

25 Martin Feldstein, "The U.S. Economy Is in Good Shape," *The Wall Street Journal*, February 21, 2016; https://www.wsj.com/articles/the-u-s-economy-is-in-good-shape-1456097121.

26 Gallup, "U.S. Life Evaluation," www.gallup.com/poll/151157/life-evaluation-weekly.aspx; https://news.gallup.com/poll/315614/record-drop-life-ratings-partially-rebound.aspx.

27 Vernon Smith and Bart Wilson, *Humanomics: Moral Sentiments and the Wealth of Nations for the Twenty-First Century* (Cambridge University Press, 2019).

28 "How selfish ... man may be supposed, there are evidently some principles in his nature, which interest him in the fortune of others, and render their happiness necessary to him, though he derives nothing from it except the pleasure of seeing it." Adam Smith, *The Theory of Moral Sentiments* (A. Millar, 1759), I.I.1.

29 Amartya Sen, *The Idea of Justice* (Penguin, 2010).

30 "Alan Greenspan on Income Inequality," YouTube video, posted by "johnklin," September 28, 2007, @ 2:36. www.youtube.com/watch?v=oqx88MyUSck.

31 Zero unemployment is also advocated in William Dugger and James Peach, *Economic Abundance: An Introduction* (Routledge, 2009).

32 Peter Hall and David Soskice, *Varieties of Capitalism* (Oxford University Press, 2001).

33 Of the nine happiest countries in the world five are in Scandinavia. The others are Switzerland, the Netherlands, Austria, and New Zealand. https://happiness-report.s3.amazonaws.com/2020/WHR20_Ch2_Statistical_Appendix.pdf; Figure 7. The ranking of the most livable cities is similar: https://world-happiness.report/ed/2020/cities-and-happiness-a-global-ranking-and-analysis/.

34 John Maynard Keynes, *The End of Laissez-Faire: The Economic Consequences of the Peace* (Hogarth Press, 1926).

35 Richard Easterlin, "The Economics of Happiness," *Daedalus* 133 (2004), 2: 26–33.

36 Gallup, "U.S. Life Evaluation," op. cit.

37 Some people are luckier in the choice of their parents than others. John Komlos, "Income Inequality Begins at Birth and These Are the Stats that Prove It," *PBS Newshour*. www.pbs.org/newshour/making-sense/plight-african-americans-u-s-2015/.

38   YouTube video, "Richard Feynman on Pseudoscience," https://www.youtube.com/watch?v=tWr39 Q9vBgo.

39   Sigmund Freud, *The Unconscious* (Penguin Classics, 2005), first published as *Das Unbewußte* in 1915.

40   Perfect competition occurs when there are a very large number of buyers and sellers so that no one can influence the market price of a homogeneous product. There are no barriers to entry into the industry. No one has market power, so everyone is a price taker, accepting the market price.

41   John Harsany, "Games with Incomplete Information," Nobel Lecture, December 9, 1994.

42   David Cay Johnston, *Free Lunch: How the Wealthiest Americans Enrich Themselves at Government Expense and Stick You with the Bill* (Portfolio Books, 2007).

43   David Cay Johnston, *Perfectly Legal: The Covert Campaign to Rig Our Tax System to Benefit the Super-Rich—and Cheat Everybody Else* (Portfolio Books, 2003).

44   Joan Robinson, "Time in Economic Theory," *Kyklos* 33 (1980), 2: b219-b229.

45   Jeffrey Sachs, *Building the New American Economy: Smart, Fair, and Sustainable* (Columbia University Press, 2017).

46   William Dugger, "Dugger's Theorem: The Free Market Is Impossible," *Journal of Economic Issues* 39 (2005), 2: b309-b324.

47   "[T]he basic psychological assumptions on which mainstream (neoclassical) economics is based—though they have long since been disproved by actual psychologists—have colonized the rest of the academy, and have had a profound impact on popular understandings of the world." David Graeber, "Against Economics," *The New York Review of Books*, December 5, 2019.

48   Ha-Joon Chang, *23 Things They Don't Tell You About Capitalism* (Bloomsbury Press, 2011); Philip O'Hara, "Principles of Institutional-Evolutionary Political Economy - Converging Themes from the Schools of Heterodoxy," *Journal of Economic Issues* 41 (2007), 1: 1-42; see also the journal *Real-World Economics Review*.

49   Stephen Marglin, *The Dismal Science: How Thinking Like an Economist Undermines Community* (Harvard University Press, 2010).

50   Thomas Kuhn, *The Structure of Scientific Revolutions* (University of Chicago Press, 1962).

51   Robert Reich, *Saving Capitalism: For the Many, Not the Few* (Knopf, 2015).

52   Edmund Phelps, *Designing Inclusion: How to Raise Low-End Pay and Employment in Private Enterprise* (Cambridge University Press, 2003).

53   Irene van Staveren, *Economics After the Crisis: An Introduction to Economics from a Pluralist and Global Perspective* (Routledge, 2015).

54   Michael Sandel, "Populism, Liberalism, and Democracy," *Philosophy & Social Criticism* 44 (2018), 4: 353-359; here p. 354.

55   Steven Keen, *The New Economics: A Manifesto* (Polity, 2021); Sam de Muijnck and Joris Tieleman, *Economy Studies: A Guide to Rethinking Economics Education* (Amsterdam University Press, 2021); Geoffrey Schneider, *Microeconomic Principles and Problems: A Pluralist Introduction* (Routledge, 2019); Robert Samuelson, "It's Time We Tear Up Our Economics Textbooks and Start Over," *Washington Post*, June 23, 2019; Gerald Friedman, *Microeconomics: Individual Choice in Communities*, 4th edn. (Kendall Hunt Publishing, 2018); Andrew Mearman et al., "Whither Political Economy? Evaluating the CORE Project as a Response to Calls for Change in Economics Teaching," *Review of Political Economy* 30 (2018), 2: 241-259; The CORE Team, *The Economy: Economics for a Changing World* (Oxford University Press, 2017), https:/Core-Econ.Org/the-Economy/?Lang=En.; Anonymous, "The Teaching of Economics Gets an Overdue Overhaul," *The Economist*, September 23, 2017; Stuart Birks, *Rethinking Economics: From Analogies to the Real World* (Springer, 2015); Jamie Morgan, "Necessary Pluralism in Economics: The Case for Heterodoxy," *Royal Economic Society Newsletter*, no. 167, October 2014, pp. 16-19; https://www.res.org.uk/uploads/assets/uploaded/d0f470de-3d71-40db-92aa8d77b543b361.pdf; Rod Hill and Tony Myatt, *The Economics Anti-Textbook* (Zed Books, 2010); see also *International Journal of Pluralism and Economics Education*.

56 B.F. Skinner thought that a good life was "a life of friendship, health, art, a healthy balance between work and leisure, a minimum of unpleasantness, and a feeling that one has made worthwhile contributions to one's society." Wikipedia, "B.F. Skinner."

57 Amartya Sen and Martha Nussbaum, *The Quality of Life* (Oxford University Press, 1993).

58 In Pope John Paul II's socio-economic encyclical, *Centesimus annus* (1991), both private property and the organization of labor unions are included among a variety of fundamental human rights.

59 "What Is Wellbeing?" https://uwaterloo.ca/canadian-index-wellbeing/what-wellbeing.

60 Joseph Stiglitz et al., *Mismeasuring Our Lives: Why the GDP Doesn't Add Up* (New Books, 2010); Marc Fleurbaey and Didier Blanchet, *Beyond GDP: Measuring Welfare and Assessing Sustainability* (Oxford University Press, 2013).

61 Zero unemployment is also advocated in William Dugger and James Peach, *Economic Abundance: An Introduction* (Routledge, 2009).

62 David Shi, *The Simple Life: Plain Living and High Thinking in American Culture* (University of Georgia Press, 2007), p. 272.

63 Ibid.

64 Amartya Sen, *Rationality and Freedom* (Harvard University Press, 2002).

65 Franklin D. Roosevelt, "Speech Before the 1936 Democratic National Convention," Philadelphia, June 27, 1936.

66 Article 25 (1948); www.un.org/en/universal-declaration-human-rights/.

67 This is congruent with the classical conception of liberty: "Society cannot exist, unless a controlling power upon will and appetite be placed somewhere; and the less of it there is within, the more there must be without. It is ordained in the eternal constitution of things, that men of intemperate minds cannot be free. Their passions forge their fetters." Edmund Burke, *Letter to a Member of the National Assembly* (Dodsley, 1791), pp. 68-69.

68 This was also demanded by the "Occupy Wall Street" movement.

69 Ernst Schumacher, *Small Is Beautiful: Economics as If People Mattered* (Harper Torchbook, 1973).

70 Tibor Scitovsky, *The Joyless Economy: An Inquiry into Human Satisfaction and Consumer Dissatisfaction* (Oxford University Press, 1976); Harvey Leibenstein, *Beyond Economic Man: A New Foundation for Microeconomics* (Harvard University Press, 1976).

71 McCloskey, *Secret Sins*, op. cit.

72 Mark Blaug, "Ugly Currents in Modern Economics," *Options Politiques*, September 1997, pp. 3-8.

73 www.rethinkeconomics.org/.

74 Dani Rodrik, *Economics Rules: The Rights and Wrongs of the Dismal Science* (Norton, 2016); Samuel Decker et al., *Principles and Pluralist Approaches in Teaching Economics: Toward a Transformative Science* (Routledge, 2019); Frank Stilwell, *Political Economy: The Contest of Economic Ideas*, 3rd edn (Oxford University Press, 2011); Jeffrey Madrick, *Seven Bad Ideas: How Mainstream Economists Have Damaged America and the World* (Vintage, 2015); "Heterodox Economics Newsletter," https://www.heterodoxnews.com/HEN/home.html; Jonathan Aldred, *Licence to Be Bad: How Economics Corrupted Us* (Allen Lane, 2019); Paul Krugman, "The Dismal Science," *The New York Times*, September 25, 2014; The International Confederation of Associations for Pluralism in Economics, https://icape.org.

75 Andrew Simms, "The New Reformation: 33 Theses for an Economics Reformation, December 12, 2017, http://www.newweather.org/2017/12/12/the-new-reformation-33-theses-for-an-economics-reformation/; David Boyle and Andrew Simms, *The New Economics: A Bigger Picture* (Earthscan, 2009); Editors, "What's Wrong with the Economy—and with Economics?," *The New York Review of Books*, March 14-15, 2015; the CORE Team, *The Economy*, op. cit.

76 The Institute for New Economic Thinking has similar aims: http://www.ineteconomics.org; https://economicpluralism.org/; http://othercanon.org/; http://nature-economy.de/.

77 Michael Lind, "The Strange Career of Paul Krugman," *Tablet*, November 22, 2021.

78   www.degruyter.com/view/j/cas.

79   Bart Nooteboom, *Uprooting Economics: A Manifesto for Change* (Edward Elgar Publishing, 2019); Jamie Morgan, "The Contemporary Relevance of a Cambridge Tradition: Economics as Political Economy, Political Economy as Social Theory and Ethical Theory," *Cambridge Journal of Economics* 40 (2016), 2: 663-700.

80   Lorenzo Ductor et al., "On the Influence of Top Journals," *Cambridge Working Papers in Economics* CWPE2029, 2020; James Heckman and Sidharth Moktan, "Publishing and Promotion in Economics: The Tyranny of the Top Five," *Journal of Economic Literature* 58 (2020), 2: 419-470; Kevin Hoover and Andrej Svorenčík, "Who Runs the AEA?" Duke University CHOPE, Working Paper 2020-12.

81   YouTube video, "Joseph Stiglitz - 'Market Fundamentalism Is Dead,'" November 10, 2008. www.youtube.com/watch?v=x_2-Tv2GPs0.

82   Ibid.

83   Deirdre McCloskey, "The Trouble with Mathematics and Statistics in Economics," *History of Economic Ideas* 13 (2005): 85-102.

84   Richard Feynman, "Cargo Cult Science," *Engineering and Science* 37 (1974), 7: 10-13.

85   George DeMartino, *The Economist's Oath: On the Need for and Content of Professional Economic Ethics* (Oxford University Press, 2011); Wilfred Dolfsma and Ioana Negru, *The Ethical Formation of Economists* (Routledge, 2021); Kenneth Boulding, "Economics as a Moral Science," *The American Economic Review* 59 (1969), 1: 1-12.

86   Herbert Simon, "Rationality in Psychology and Economics," in Robin Hogarth and Melvin Reder (eds.), *Rational Choice: The Contrast Between Economics and Psychology* (University of Chicago Press, 1986); Amos Tversky and Daniel Kahneman, "Judgment under Uncertainty: Heuristics and Biases," *Science*, New Series 185 (1974), 4157: 1124-1131.

87   B.F. Skinner, *Science and Human Behavior* (Free Press, 1965), pp. 62-71.

88   Rhys Manley, "Book Review," *Journal of Human Development and Capabilities* 21 (2020), 2: 209-210.

89   Paul Romer, "Mathiness in the Theory of Economic Growth," *American Economic Review: Papers & Proceedings* 105 (2015) 5: 89-93; Erica Thompson and Leonard Smith, "Escape from Model-Land," *Economics*, 13 (2019), 40: 1-15.

90   George Akerlof, "Sins of Omission and the Practice of Economics," *Journal of Economic Literature* 58 (2020), 2: 405-418; Marion Fourcade et al., "The Superiority of Economists," *Journal of Economic Perspectives* 29 (2015), 1: 89-114; here p. 91.

91   Daniel Saunders, "The Impact of Neoliberalism on College Students," *Journal of College and Character* 8 (2007), 5: 1-9.

92   Ronald Reagan, Inaugural Address, January 20, 1981, https://www.presidency.ucsb.edu/documents/inaugural-address-11.

93   Richard Easterlin, "Happiness and Economic Growth – The Evidence," in Wolfgang Glatzer et al. (eds.), *Global Handbook of Quality of Life* (Springer, 2015), pp. 283-299.

94   YouTube Video, "Bernanke Was Wrong." www.youtube.com/watch?v=INmqvibv4UU&t=2s.

95   St. Louis Fed, series UNRATE and U6RATE.

96   "The collapse of the housing bubble will lead to a loss of between \$1.3tr and \$2.6tr of housing wealth," Dean Baker, "The Run-up in Home Prices: A Bubble," *Challenge* 45 (2002), 6: 93-119.

97   Graeber, "Against Economics," op. cit.

2 The Evidence
Markets Are Neither Omniscient Nor Omnipotent

> The true measure of any society can be found in how it treats its most vulnerable members.
>
> —Mahatma Gandhi[1]

If the US incarceration was not the highest in the world, if the homicide rate were on par with European levels, if poverty had been eliminated, if the opioid epidemic had not occurred, if people would not be killing strangers in large numbers, if the suicide rate had not increased, if life satisfaction were higher, if inequality would not have risen, if life expectancy had not declined, if the health-care system were more efficient, if everyone could afford to go to college, if the financial crisis had not started on Wall Street, if mental health had not deteriorated, if the obesity rate had not increased, if the national debt were declining, if global warming was not threatening, if the Rust Belt had not been created, if jobs were not exported in large numbers, if populism had not become a key factor in the political arena, if there had been no insurrection on January 6, 2021, in other words, if the society were made up of thriving and happy people as the economists had predicted would be the case in a growing economy, believe me, I would certainly not have written this book. This chapter presents the evidence on all these problems that have their roots in faulty economic theories.

2.1 Markets Are Not Created by Divine Power

According to conventional wisdom, free markets are infallible, pristine, and endowed with supernatural powers. However, in reality, they are neither natural nor emerge spontaneously out of disorder. In other words, they are not created by a deity.[2] Rather, they are man-made institutions and are only as good as the rules (institutional, moral, and legal) that govern the behavior of market participants. The historical record shows that *markets generally implode without adequate oversight*—as in 2008—by an authority that enforces these rules. Hence, markets can be formed and reformed to suit our purposes to improve our lives. They should not be idolized. They are a means to an end and not an end in themselves. The market system is with us, for better or for worse; a world without it is unimaginable but we should be vigilant and not become subservient to it.

Markets have succeeded at producing a super-abundance of goods, raising life expectancy, and creating miracles in science, engineering, transportation, medicine, communication, and information technology. These remarkable achievements notwithstanding, the system fails

DOI: 10.4324/9781003174356-2

to satisfy because *markets have Achilles' heels that detract substantially from their ability to increase the well-being of the population.* Moreover, in important ways we have regressed. We have significant deficits in mental and physical health, deficits in our ability to cope with stress, difficulties saving for a rainy day, are unable to determine a comfortable work-life balance, unable to prevent global warming, and incapable of creating an inclusive economy. We should grow psychologically, improve self-control, enable everyone to share in prosperity, and acquire habits that support a virtuous life. So, the emphasis on material progress is short-sighted. We should also consider that immense poverty and deprivation continue to haunt the US and the globe.[3] In short, we must reject the notion that "market mechanisms are the primary instruments of achieving the public good."[4]

2.2 Running the Economy "Hot"

The common wisdom is that free-market capitalism "has been an enormous success."[5] However, this is short-sighted. It ignores the widespread conviction that "we live in a broken nation ... The stench of national decline is in the air."[6] Such sentiments would have been unimaginable before the financial crisis and it would be inconceivable in a prosperous society with a thriving citizenry, because the enormous social and political problems stem directly from the structure of the economic system, the way it distributes the wealth it creates, and the ways in which multitudes are marginalized from birth.[7] The emphasis on free markets has been misplaced because they are incapable of ameliorating the social problems they create.[8] They are incapable of creating a good society. That is not their function.

Yet, market aficionados contend that we should separate the social, political, and economic issues. However, such compartmentalization is arbitrary and harbors a misguided value judgment, because these aspects of life are intricately intertwined and influence each other.[9] The social sciences are a seamless web; attempts to separate them creates confusion. Welfare is the joint product of social, political, and economic conditions.

Capitalism can be organized in an extremely individualistic manner, as in the US—everyone for himself/herself—or it can integrate collectivist elements, as in the Western European welfare states—all for one and one for all, at least as far as basic needs are concerned. The emphasis on individual rights produces a highly competitive, insecure, and unbalanced system, as in the US with high anxiety and frustration whereas the emphasis on safety produces a low-pressure system, as in Scandinavia, which incorporates institutions that lead to a more relaxed lifestyle. One of the many shortcomings of mainstream economics is the utter *disregard of stressors* that are the ingredients of a high-pressure *winner-take-all* economy in which competition, output, and freedom are the indicators of success instead of security, safety, leisure, and peace of mind.

2.3 The Downside of a High-Pressure Capitalism

A high-pressure economy runs at full throttle. The emphasis in such an economy is on generating income, disregarding its effect on the quality of life. Mankiw summarizes the mainstream philosophy succinctly: "A country's standard of living depends on its ability to produce goods and services."[10] He fails to mention the impact of maximizing production on mental and physical health, on safety, on a wholesome work-life balance, on excessive risks, on uncertainty, on anxiety, on crime, or on human flourishing. Yet, running the economy "hot" fosters the accumulation of stress until people feel unwell, although the economy is producing an incredible amount of goods and services, more precisely, $23 trillion's worth.[11]

Hence, rampant social, political, and economic challenges accumulate because of the inequitable distribution of schooling, employment, income, and wealth. Consequently, there is *no quality-of-life indicator for which the US is ranked favorably in international comparison.*[12] In all such indicators, the US rank is inferior to those of other developed nations. This is the case with health, including mental health,[13] life expectancy, life satisfaction, educational attainment, incarceration rate, crime rate, and children's welfare.

The US has slipped into 18th place on the world's *happiness ranking*, having fallen further behind developed countries (Figure 2.1).[14] Hence, concentrating on income is misplaced because it does not translate into a flourishing society (see Section 7.13).[15] Note that all countries higher than the US on the happiness scale have universal medical care and higher tax rates. Obviously, the security of the safety net is very important to people. Worry is not part of economists' toolkit, but it nonetheless subtracts from the subjective evaluation of well-being. In the US, 32 percent of adults worried "a lot,"[16] and 55 percent experienced stress (in 2018), one of the highest rates in the world, an increase of 9 percentage points since 2008.[17] In contrast, the Scandinavian versions of capitalism are exemplary at providing for a thriving democratic society that supports its members in case of need.

Because of the lack of opportunity for the less-skilled and less-educated, despair has been accumulating for decades in the US. The anxiety-ridden working class feels trapped in hopelessness and often strikes out with desperate acts of frustration. Consequently, the *homicide rate* in the US is 10 times as high as in Norway, where marginalization is reduced substantially by state-provided safety nets (Table 2.1).[18] There were 20,000 murders in the US in 2020 and an additional 39,000 injuries due to gun violence.[19]

Frequent *mass killings* provide further evidence that "people who were actively and poisonously alienated–were ... *explosively* distrustful. Explosive distrust is ... an aggressive animosity and an urge to destroy."[20] There were 434 such shootings in the US in 2019 and 614 in 2020.[21] This is not an isolated phenomenon; it indicates that people are alienated by the socio-economic system and turn against it through random acts of violence. Never before in human history have people murdered strangers without an obvious reason. Typical motives were monetary gain, vengeance, jealousy, or were politically motivated. This new development is an ominous evidence of the fraying of the social contract, the invisible glue that binds societies together.[22]

The *incarceration rate* is another symptom of social malaise. It is six times as high in the US than in Canada (Table 2.2). This is evidence that people are unable to find their place in the

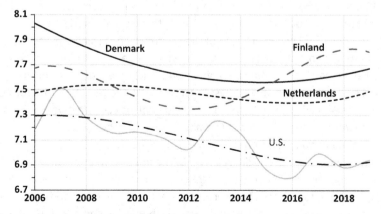

Figure 2.1 International comparison of the Happiness Index
Source: https://worldhappiness.report/ed/2020/#appendices-and-data "Data for Table 2.1."

Table 2.1 The US homicide rate per capita as a multiple of the rate in selected countries, 2018

Country	Rate	Country	Rate
Norway	10.6	Germany	5.2
Italy	8.7	Denmark	4.9
The Netherlands	8.5	Sweden	4.6
Switzerland	8.5	UK	4.1
Spain	8.0	France	4.1
Ireland	5.7	Finland	3.0

Source: https://dataunodc.un.org/content/data/homicide/homicide-rate.

Table 2.2 The US incarceration rate as a multiple of the rate in selected countries, 2018

Country	Rate	Country	Rate
Japan	16.6	Norway	8.3
Finland	12.4	Italy	6.6
Denmark	10.5	Austria	6.4
The Netherlands	10.1	Canada	6.2
Switzerland	8.6	Spain	5.3
Germany	8.4	UK	4.8

Source: https://dataunodc.un.org/data/prison/persons percent20held percent20total.

legal labor market. The wealthy are not usually involved in street gangs. In 2018, there were 2.1 million inmates in jail, the highest rate in the developed world![23] With 5 percent of the world's population, the US has one-fourth of its prisoners.[24] This has political consequences since many ex-felons are not allowed to vote. As a feedback effect, criminality increases anxiety in society, thereby diminishing the quality of life further. Few economists acknowledge that this problem is indicative of the failure of the educational system to prepare young adults for the labor market.

Additionally, few economists admit that the "hot" economy leaves too many people struggling. *Endemic poverty* is brutal in its unforgiving insecurity.[25] In 2019, 39.5 million Americans were considered poor but including those who were slightly above the poverty line, the number barely keeping their head above water increases to 52 million.[26] The poverty rate among US children—at 18.2 percent—is six times as high as in Denmark (Figure 2.2). One reason for this high rate is that the share of *single-parent* families with children has tripled from 7.4 percent in 1950 to 30.1 percent in 2019 and nearly half of the children living in single-parent households are poor.[27] In 2020, 18 million children (27 percent) lived in single-parent households, implying that they are not likely to be able to obtain the college education needed in the knowledge economy, one that would be a path to the middle class.[28] This does not bode well for the future of human capital formation (see Section 7.4). The solution of *humanistic economics is to eliminate poverty and create top-notch schools throughout the land.*

Moreover, too many poor children live in *slums* that deprive them of an adequate start in life, particularly in education and socialization that are important for economic mobility.[29] Even the kindergarten they attend impacts children's life chances.[30] The free market does not provide a level playing field for children trapped in dysfunctional neighborhoods with dysfunctional school systems and the concomitant poverty trap such environments foster.[31] That constrains their future potential and is an immense waste of human resources.

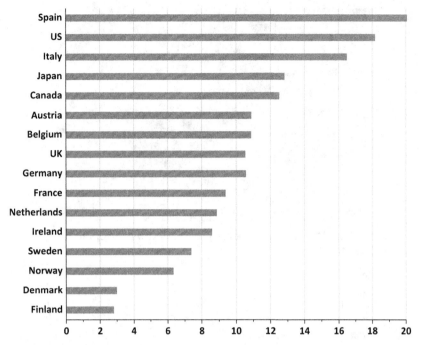

Figure 2.2 Poverty rate among children below age 18, 2016
Source: OECD Family Database, Part 4. Child outcomes CO2.2.C, https://www.oecd.org/els/family/
database.htm.

No other rich country neglects the fate of future generations comparably. According to UNICEF, the *welfare* of US children slipped from 26th place in 2013 to 36th place in 2020 behind middle-income countries like Hungary.[32] Six million children are reported for maltreatment to US agencies annually,[33] and 1,840 children died from maltreatment in 2019.[34] US pre-term birth rates are closer to those prevailing in developing countries than in Europe.[35] A teenager in Mississippi is 15 times more likely to give birth than her counterpart in Switzerland.[36] Similarly, the US was ranked in 33rd place to be a mother.[37] The top five countries are all in Scandinavia with low infant mortality and high maternal health. All these problems are rooted in the economic system that increases the cost of children's upbringing and offers inadequate government support for poor families.

No wonder US children are lagging far behind their counterparts around the globe in *educational attainment*: 15-year-olds have placed 14th in reading, 19th in science, and 38th in mathematics.[38] This embarrassing performance does not bode well for the ability of the United States to compete in the information age. The mediocre quality of the US educational system reflects the public's anti-government attitude and its reluctance to provide adequate funding for it. Consequently, *public goods* like quality schools are scarce. John Kenneth Galbraith's contrast of "private affluence" with "public squalor" is much more evident today than it was in the 1950s when he first noticed it.[39]

In addition, *homelessness* has been on the rise. In January 2020 (pre-Covid) 580,000 people were homeless, of which 226,000 were unsheltered; 57 percent were minorities and 8 percent were veterans.[40] Moreover, 1.4 million people experienced homelessness at some time during 2018, including 500,000 families with children.[41] This is unconscionable in a rich society.

Illustration 2.1 The market treats poor children cruelly. How will history judge us?
Credit: iStock.com/AvailableLight.

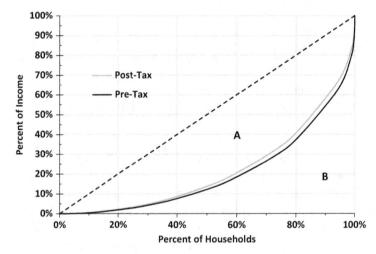

Figure 2.3 Cumulative income distribution, US, 2018
Source: https://www.irs.gov/statistics/soi-tax-stats-individual-statistical-tables-by-size-of-adjusted-gross-income.

All of these social problems have their root in the extreme level of *inequality* in the US The *Gini coefficient* is one of the many ways to measure inequality. In Figure 2.3 the diagonal depicts the line of perfect equality. Along it 10 percent of the population earns 10 percent of total income, 20 percent earns 20 percent of total income, and so forth. Hence, the farther is the actual distribution—the Lorenz curve—from this diagonal, the more unequal is the income distribution. Figure 2.3 shows two Lorenz curves: for pre-tax and post-tax incomes in 2018. They are close to each other, implying that taxes did not change the distribution significantly.

The area between the diagonal and the Lorenz curve is denoted by (A) and the total area of the triangle is (A+B), then the Gini index is $\frac{A}{A+B}$. The US income distribution, based on tax returns, is extremely unequal. The post-tax (disposable) income of all those in the bottom 60 percent of the income distribution made up only 20 percent of total income (Figure 2.3). That implies that the top 40 percent earned 80 percent of total income. Moreover, the richest 1 percent also earned 20 percent of total income. (The top 1 percent's share is calculated from the top down.)[42] So, the top 1.5 million taxpayers earned as much money as the bottom 90 million taxpayers. Checks written by these ultra-rich could go far to alleviate the misery described above. Among developed countries, the US has the largest Gini coefficient—the most unequal income distribution (Figure 2.4).

No wonder there is so much discontent, frustration, and suffering: the left tail of the income distribution has a disproportionate impact on the social and political system. The median income of the lowest 20 percent of the income distribution—the poorest 64 million people—was just $18,000 in 2019, barely enough to keep body and soul together.[43]

Bankruptcies are further indication of the precarious lives people live and their difficulties to meet their obligations, often because of medical expenses.[44] There are about 800,000 bankruptcies annually; these have nearly doubled per capita since 1980.[45] The nine million homeowners who lost their home between 2006 and 2014 contributed to the sense of betrayal felt by the lower-middle class.[46]

Other problems with the quality of life in the US include the harassment of consumers.[47] Telemarketers scammers are ubiquitous, related even to the Coronavirus stimulus checks and during the financial crisis there were criminals who offered "bogus" help to save homes from foreclosure.[48] In 2014, 18 million people in the US experienced identity theft; in 2018, 23 million people had such experiences.[49]

Moreover, the US is the only rich country without *universal health insurance*. Because of the Affordable Care Act (2010) the number of uninsured declined from 45 million (17 percent) to 27 million by 2016 (11 percent).[50] However, the Trump administration reversed this trend, and the number of uninsured increased by 2.2 million. Some 60 percent of the uninsured are from

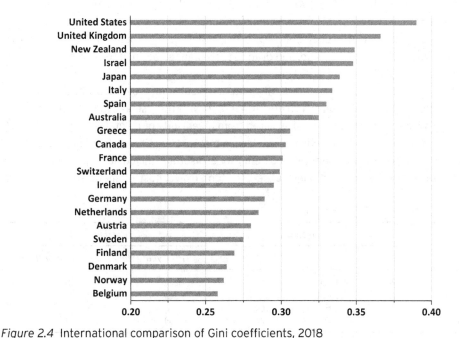

Figure 2.4 International comparison of Gini coefficients, 2018
Note: For some countries the latest data available is for 2017.
Source: https://stats.oecd.org/Index.aspx?DataSetCode=IDD#. OECD Statistics, Social Protection and Well-Being, Income Distribution and Poverty.

minority groups; the highest rates are among Hispanics (20 percent), American Indians (22 percent), and Blacks (11.4 percent).

Additionally, in 2019, 10.5 percent of households (35 million people) in one of the richest countries in the world lived with *food insecurity*. The rate was higher among households with children (13.6 percent), among female-headed households (29 percent), African Americans (19 percent), and households below 185 percent of the poverty threshold (27.6 percent), which for a family of four was $48,000.[51]

Another consequence of economic insecurity is the use of antidepressants as a coping strategy for stress, hopelessness, and loneliness.[52] We maintain a modicum of social stability only with their use.[53] The use of such drugs has jumped by 65 percent in 15 years,[54] implying that increased incomes failed to gratify.[55] A remarkable 213 million prescriptions for such drugs were dispensed in 2010 in the US.[56]

The opioid epidemic resembles the use of the drug "Soma" in the dystopian novel, *Brave New World* (1931). Its purpose in the novel was social control, while today the widespread use of *addictive drugs* like fentanyl is associated with running the economy under high pressure. Marijuana is the mass drug of choice since it relaxes and induces a euphoric mental state (Table 2.3). It is being legalized extensively for "recreational uses." Some 31 million people used marijuana during the month prior to the survey.

The association with stress becomes apparent considering that in wake of the economic crisis (between 2007 and 2009) the *annual* rate of increase in marijuana use tripled from 700,000 individuals to 2.1 million and stayed high thereafter, increasing again after 2016 to 2.9 million.[57] By 2019, 57 million people used drugs during the previous year and that is one-fifth of the population above the age of 12.[58] Thus, the accelerating rate of drug use is associated with the additional anxiety induced by the Great Recession and the election of Donald Trump. Economists neglect the mental strain associated with being evicted, becoming unemployed, and coping with economic uncertainty, and insecurity, but the reality is different.[59] Of course, *homo oeconomicus* has no emotions but human beings do, and drug use is a manifestation of the anxiety generated by precarious quality of life.

The high-pressure economy, coupled with extensive substance use and abuse, led to an immense number of *mental health* problems in tandem with the rise in economic insecurity.[60] In 2019, 51.5 million adults (20 percent) suffered from an episode of mental illness (Table 2.4).[61] This high incidence is a clear indication of the fragile mental condition of the population. These are diagnosed cases of mental, behavioral, or emotional disorders including: depression, bipolar disorder, phobia, anxiety disorder, panic, obsessive-compulsive, posttraumatic stress, anorexia

Table 2.3 Drug use in the US, 2019 (millions)

Drug	Used ever			Used in 2019	
	2002	2019	Increase (%)	Past year (%)	Past month (%)
Marijuana	94.9	127.1	32.2	48.2	31.6
Cocaine	33.9	41.4	7.5	5.5	2.0
Heroin	3.7	5.7	2.0	0.7	0.4
Hallucinogens	31.9	44.1	12.2	6.0	1.9

Source: Substance Abuse and Mental Health Services Administration, "2019 National Survey of Drug Use and Health," https://www.samhsa.gov/data/release/2019-national-survey-drug-use-and-health-nsduh-releases, Table 7.1A.

nervosa, hallucinations, delusions, or suicidal thoughts but exclude substance use disorders.[62] Between 2008 and 2019, the number of episodes increased by 29 percent; younger adults, and minorities increased the most (Table 2.4). Among the four million youth who received some mental health service, most cases were for depression, anxiety, and suicidal tendencies.[63] The economic burden of depression surpassed $210 billion.[64]

The incidence of *mental illness* did not change much between 2008 and 2015 with the exception of young adults (ages 18-25), who experienced a 0.5 percentage points annual increase (Table 2.5). However, after 2016, all ethnic groups experienced a marked acceleration in incidence. Teenagers were also affected. Self-inflicted injuries among girls doubled between 2007 and 2020.[65] This is a horrible report card on the US *quality of life*. Mental health continued to deteriorate during the Covid-19 pandemic.[66]

These adverse developments are tolerated at a time of unimaginable affluence with 724 billionaires in the US enjoying a combined wealth of an astronomical $4.4 trillion.[67] Jeff Bezos

Table 2.4 Number of adults who experienced a mental illness episode in the past year, 2019 (thousands)

	2008	2019	Change	
			Increase	(%)
All	39826	51495	11669	29
18-25	6099	9930	3831	63
26 or older	33727	41565	7838	23
Male	14778	19758	4980	34
Female	25048	31737	6689	27
White	28286	34967	6681	24
Black	4314	5174	860	20
AIAN	163	260	97	60
Asian	1300	2100	800	62
2 or more races	666	1390	724	109
Hispanic	4855	7440	2585	53

Notes: Age 18 and above. AIAN is American Indian/Alaska Native
Source: Substance Abuse and Mental Health Services Administration (SAMSHA), 2020. "2019 National Survey of Drug Use and Health." https://www.samhsa.gov/data/release/2019-national-survey-drug-use-and-health-nsduh-releases, Table 10.1A.

Table 2.5 Rate of change of the percent of adults affected by mental illness

	Percentage per annum	
	2008-2015	2016-2019
Age 18-25	0.5	1.9
Men	0.1	0.5
Women	0.0	0.8
White	0.1	0.7
Black	-0.2	0.5
Asian	-0.2	0.6
Hispanic	-0.2	0.9
All Adults	0.0	0.7

Source: Substance Abuse and Mental Health Services Administration (SAMSHA), 2020. "2019 National Survey of Drug Use and Health." Table 10. https://www.samhsa.gov/data/release/2019-national-survey-drug-use-and-health-nsduh-releases, 1A and Table 10.1B.

heads the list with $200 billion. His wealth increased by $100 billion between 2017 and 2021. In addition, there were 500,000 taxpayers, who earned more than $1 million in 2018 (with an average (after-tax) income of $2.4 million).[68] Thus, 0.3 percent of taxpayers earned a combined $1.8 trillion, or 15 percent of the total personal income in the US. Put another way, half a million taxpayers earned as much as the poorest 80 million. Does this economy sound like a free-market nirvana? The answer is obvious, but there is more to consider.

2.4 Decline in Life Expectancy Reveals the Diminution of the Quality of Life

Demographic developments are significant from an economic perspective because they reveal subtle aspects of the quality of life that conventional monetary indicators bypass. Life expectancy is an excellent proxy indicator since it is a function of the quality and affordability of medical care from gestation through the life course. It is also a function of the quality and quantity of nutrition, pollution, crime, stress, water quality, addiction to alcohol or drugs, diseases, medical schools, availability of physicians, family structure, family planning, work-life balance, and much more. Thus, it is an omnibus indicator of countless essential aspects of life that are otherwise obscure. Moreover, life is a good in itself.

Hence, the *decline in life expectancy* in the US relative to rich countries beginning in 1984 and the absolute decline since 2015 are powerful indications that a high-pressure economy is unable to deliver essential elements of a good life for a substantial share of the population (see Figures 15.4 and 17.1). Babies born in 1980 lived merely seven months less than those born in rich countries and the US was still ahead of the UK and Germany. However, it began to lag behind suddenly under the Reagan administration and by 1988 it was 17 months behind. By 2019, US life expectancy was closer to that of Cuba and Costa Rica, whose average incomes are miniscule. Furthermore, US white teenagers were twice as likely to perish than their G7 counterparts, while Black twenty-somethings were four times as likely not to celebrate their 30th birthday.[69] While the decline in life expectancy *relative* to the G7 countries began in 1984, the *absolute* decline began in 2015 and among those without a BA the *absolute* decline began in 2011, despite improvements in medicine.[70] This is unquestionably among the most disturbing developments since 1980, because it is an objective indicator of the health of the population and of the ability of the political system to respond to these challenges.[71] It is a robust thermometer capable of capturing the essence of general welfare.

The assertion of influential economists that "the US economy is in good shape,"[72] is contradicted by all the above developments as well as by the dystopian phenomenon that annually 150,000 Americans escaped the pain of economic life through suicide, opioid overdose, or alcoholism.[73] Ignoring these *deaths of despair* reflects mainstream economists' myopia and is evidence of the failure of neoliberal policies, since people would not kill themselves or others in droves in an economy in which they are flourishing.[74] The per capita overdose deaths in the US are 14 times as high as in Switzerland (Table 2.6).

Drug overdose deaths have been increasing rapidly during the era dominated by neoliberal economic policies. There were "merely" 6,000 drug overdose deaths in the US in 1980 but the numbers rose to 52,000 by 2015, i.e., an increase by an astonishing factor of 8.5 and continued to rise.[75] In 2021, they reached 100,000 for an unfathomable cumulative total of nearly one million.[76] The upshot is a "shocking increase in midlife mortality" among white American men

Table 2.6 The US drug overdose deaths as a multiple of the rates in selected countries, 2018

Country	Rate	Country	Rate
Switzerland	14	Denmark	5
Germany	13	Ireland	5
The Netherlands	11	UK	4
Austria	8	Norway	4
Spain	8	Sweden	3
Finland	6		

Source: United Nations, "Mortality" https://dataunodc.un.org/data/drugs/Mortality.

without a college education, a strictly American phenomenon. This has not happened before in a developed country in peacetime. Blacks and Hispanics were mostly immune to this epidemic since they were used to being at the bottom of the totem pole, and therefore did not experience the pain of downward social mobility as less-educated white men did.

While mass killers aggress society, addiction and suicide imply self-aggression. The cumulative total deaths of despair in the twenty-first century was "greater than the total number of Americans who died in the two world wars."[77] The policy failures that led to this unprecedented level of psychological distress illustrates the deep crisis of a high-pressure capitalism (Section 2.2). After all, there is nothing worse for self-esteem than the loss of economic status and social isolation brought about by a decline in social status.[78]

The rudimentary safety net proved insufficient and the healthcare system was woefully inefficient:

> The organization of the American healthcare system is a disaster for the harm it does to health, but even more because it is draining the livelihoods of Americans in order to make a rich minority richer. Pharmaceutical companies are reaping enormous profits from their patients' addictions, and from pricing strategies that deny ordinary people access to decades-old medical advances.[79]

Material deprivation was not the only factor in the accumulation of despair.[80] Mental health of those marooned at the bottom of the social pyramid deteriorated also because of isolation and loneliness:

> because less educated men are less marriageable, the problems in the labor market are not only making them worse off materially but also depriving them of all the benefits that marriage brings ... married people live longer, are healthier, and are more satisfied with their lives ....[81]

The dissolution of these traditional social structures of support left a crippling void. The family was gone, union jobs were gone, neighborly love was gone, the churches were irrelevant for most, the government looked away, and the gig economy did not provide sufficient income stability to be successful in the marriage market. The fraying of the social contract meant that for the have-nots in distress there was nothing to grasp onto except a bottle, a trigger, or a hypodermic needle. Suicide was not the sole response to despair. Others turned to populism or mass murder in Las Vegas, bombing in Nashville, or storming of the Capitol. These are all manifestations of a deep malaise signifying an unprecedented and widespread emotional emptiness.

2.5 Markets Have Numerous Limitations

In exceptional circumstances markets accomplish what is expected of them. They help entrepreneurs produce what consumer want at reasonable prices. However, without adequate regulation under most real-world conditions they are inefficient, are not inclusive, and cause a myriad of social and political problems.[82] So, laissez-faire should not be the default model. Instead, the default model should be that markets need strict oversight. It is hard to think of markets that are self-regulating except those on the blackboard.

Markets are inefficient if credible *information* is costly to acquire or challenging to understand, if there is real *uncertainty* involved that requires judgment, if the outcome is remote in time, if the product is *intangible* like safety, if *children* are involved, if *power* is unequal between counterparties, as in the case of monopsony,[83] if the *quality* of the product is difficult to ascertain, if production is concentrated in oligopolies[84] or monopolies,[85] if *transaction costs* are significant, if there are *externalities*,[86] if the burden can be passed onto *future generations*, if the consumer can be manipulated using "psychological engineering,"[87] or if market outcomes are *unethical*. Economists call these factors *imperfections* (or frictions) and because they are ubiquitous, real-world markets are practically always *inefficient*. These are all critical issues that affect our lives in crucial ways. Models that disregard them and instead rely on perfectly competitive markets are not applicable in the real world.

For example, the Nobelist Kenneth Arrow established eons ago that private health-care markets are inefficient, because of the "existence of uncertainty in the incidence of disease and in the efficacy of treatment."[88] In addition, there is virtually no price competition in medical care; *asymmetric information*[89] is omnipresent and favors physicians as authority figures; the American Medical Association limits the number of doctors, driving up the price of health care (see Section 9.5); people have biased predictions of their future health-care needs; and hospitals often have *monopoly power*. Furthermore, health insurance is so expensive that 11 percent of the US population (in 2019) is without insurance. Besides, insurers can surprise customers with fine print that enables them to deny coverage when it is needed. Under such conditions, market outcomes are inefficient. Yet, policy-makers continue to apply the perfectly competitive model to the health-care market.

That the US population is the least healthy among developed nations, although it spends the most on medical care is evidence that its system is the most inefficient.[90] Life expectancy at birth ranks 31st in the world (Figure 2.5), but health-care expenditure is twice the median of rich countries (Figure 2.6). Paying more and getting less for it is the definition of inefficiency. In contrast, people are healthier and live longer in countries in which there is government-sponsored universal health insurance. Health care in Canada costs $5,400 per-capita, while Americans spend twice as much ($11,100) but live two years less. If the US adopted Canada's system, each household would save $14,700 annually. How inefficient! The waste is $1.8 trillion dollars, close to the after-tax profits of US corporations (pre-Covid).[91]

The median life expectancy in the rich countries with a combined population of nearly 700 million was 81.8 years in 2018, 3.1 years above that of the US at 78.7 years (Figure 2.5). *The US is an outlier* considering how much it spends on health care and how little it gets for it (Figure 2.7). Something must be awry with the market system if a service that is so expensive delivers such inferior outcomes. The takeaway is that competition is an ineffective mechanism to achieve adequate health care at affordable prices without extensive government oversight.

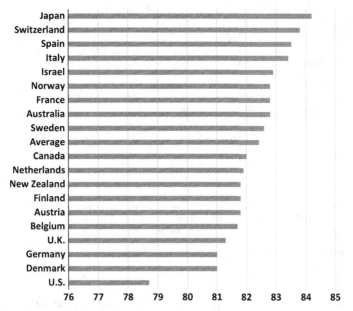

Figure 2.5 Life expectancy at birth, 2018
Source: Health Status, Life Expectancy, OECD, Statistics, https://stats.oecd.org/Index.aspx.?

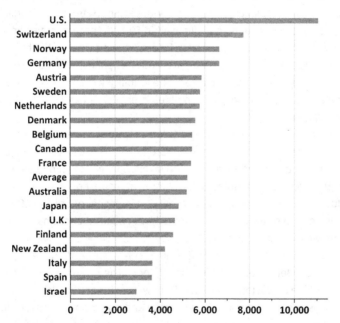

Figure 2.6 Per capita health-care expenditures, US dollars, 2019
Note: Average excludes US
Source: Health Care Expenditures, 2019 OECD, Statistics, https://stats.oecd.org/Index.aspx

Other deficient aspects of markets include *inadequate long-range planning* because the incentive structure is biased toward the present. Markets are also inefficient at producing an education policy that provides broad-based, quality education. Markets were not designed for that purpose because children do not have agency and are incapable of choosing their school system.

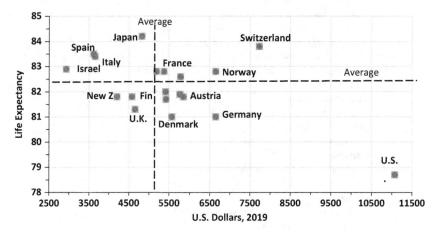

Figure 2.7 Life expectancy at birth vs health-care expenditures per capita
Source: see Figures 2.5 and 2.6.

Moreover, markets are ineffective at providing safe products since *safety* is a difficult-to-ascertain intangible attribute and because consumers tend to have a psychological bias toward the present–*present biasedness*. Hence, safety often does not seem worth its cost in the short run since safe products are costlier and their benefits are both uncertain and in the future. For instance, a high-rise apartment building collapsed in Florida three years after an engineer recommended repairs "in the immediate and near future."[92] The threat to the building was ambiguous but the expense was obvious and immediate, and the repairs were consequently postponed until disaster struck and 97 people were killed. The inability to confront climate change has the same psychological basis. Spending on intangibles is challenging especially in the presence of the urge for *immediate gratification*.

Price competition also thwarts the provisioning of safety. For example, seat belts in automobiles were hardly used until they were mandated in 1968.[93] Of course, we are now so used to them that we buckle up automatically. Another example is providing safe baby cribs, which seems like a simple product to manufacture. Yet, only after dozens of babies suffocated did the Consumer Product Safety Commission mandate the safe design of cribs in 2011. Producers were impeded from selling safe cribs, because it would have required coordination among them that price competition was incapable of providing.[94]

The incompetence of businesses at provisioning safety is also demonstrated by such disasters as Union Carbide's deadly gas leak in Bhopal, India, the grounding of the *Exxon Valdez* oil tanker in Alaska, and the explosion aboard the Deepwater Horizon oil-drilling disaster in the Gulf of Mexico. Such disasters caused immense suffering and environmental degradation.

2.6 The "Achilles' Heel" of Markets

The inconvenient truth is that markets have "Achilles' heels"–vulnerable characteristics–that interfere with their smooth functioning and detract from their ability to efficiently improve the quality of life. These deficiencies are intrinsic problems–like bounded rationality (Chapter 4), imperfect and asymmetric information (Chapter 5), unequal power between counterparties (Chapter 5), social interactions (Chapter 5), conspicuous consumption (Chapter 5), monopolies and oligopolies (Chapter 6), transaction costs (Chapter 8), opportunistic behavior (Chapter 8), imperfect foresight (Chapter 8), pollution (Chapter 11), fragility of finance (Chapter 14), discrimination (Chapter 15), planning for tiny-probability huge-impact events (Chapter 17)—that are associated with the workings of *real existing* markets as opposed to imaginary ones, preventing them from being as efficient as they are on blackboards.

These Achilles' heels are market imperfections. However, they are far from being as benign as those terms might imply. Furthermore, they are regularly omitted from conventional courses and not only introductory ones, although they are influential in determining the way markets work. Overlooking them implies that millions of students leave their economics courses having focused on "complete markets" without imperfections, and which run like clockwork.

Hence, economists have been ignoring the "elephant in the room." Actually, *the US economy's performance is mediocre in improving the quality of life*: health, peace of mind, happiness, longevity, security, safety, education, social mobility, children's welfare, and human development are all inferior compared to other developed nations. Mainstream economists ignore those aspects that do not fit into their dogma: the millions incarcerated for lack of opportunity in the legal labor market, the hopelessness that drives people to reach for sedatives, the accumulation of anger that leads people to kill strangers, the slums that stymie children's development, the poverty trap, the greed of the superrich, the falling life expectancy, the unfair economic policies that lead to populist movements, or the lack of preparedness to confront an epidemic. They conveniently disregard all this evidence contradicting the fantasy world that exists only in their imagination.

Hence, *progress has been much more tentative than mainstream economists concede*, and it has been limited to half the US population.[95] We could have done much more to improve the quality of life of Everyman on Main Street, given our immense wealth. However, the focus of economists and politicians has not been on making sure that the population was flourishing but on growing the economy. They did not understand that *well-being is multifaceted and should not be equated with growth of GDP*.

2.7 The Best Government Is Not the One That Governs Least

Government should not be disparaged because markets and governments complement each other.[96] Government does many things more efficiently than markets, including building the interstate highway network, providing health care for seniors, guaranteeing Social Security, which has taken care of citizens effectively for almost a century.[97] Government-sponsored basic research brought about the IT revolution and funded medical discoveries.[98] Markets are incapable of creating the market's institutional structure, which includes the political system, ideology, law, and unwritten norms that determine the behavior of market participants. Markets would not function well without appropriate institutions. Thus, government is indispensable. To be sure, it needs to be effective. But the colloquial slogan, "that government is best which governs the least" is patently false.[99] That doctrine, according to Franklin D. Roosevelt, makes government seem indifferent to the plight of humankind.[100] Governments have to adjust to the size and complexity of the economy and those needs of the people which markets are incapable of fulfilling adequately.

Moreover, there were crucial moments when financial markets would have imploded without sufficient government aid, and giants like GM and Chrysler desperately needed to be resuscitated with state funds. We also need central banks to be the *lender of last resort* to maintain the stability of the financial system. In short, there are good reasons not to sing hymns to free markets unconditionally.[101] Markets did not achieve our current level of wealth by themselves and could not have done so. It was a partnership of individual and community effort.

Markets are institutions just like governments, and, like governments, they should also be under our control. Markets are not sovereign; we are. We, the people, retain the ultimate right in a democratic society to determine what our goals are and how to accomplish them. Some of those goals should be left to markets while others should be determined through our political representatives or other nonmarket institutions. Although some people vilify it, the government is we. It represents our collective will—our collective interest—which we cannot adequately enforce as individuals.

Admittedly, influential vested interests have co-opted institutions that stymied government's ability to act in the public interest.[102] Otherwise it is difficult to comprehend the transfer of trillions of dollars from 99 percent of the population to the top 1 percent.[103] The economic system as currently constituted has led to such concentration of wealth that our democracy is being turned into a plutocracy (see Section 15.1).[104] For example, the carbon industry has successfully generated a misguided effort to minimize the threat of global warming,[105] the National Rifle Association has prevented a ban on military-style assault rifles, and Wall Street has resisted stringent financial regulation and has weakened the Consumer Financial Protection Bureau.[106]

Markets are incapable of providing effective protection of consumers, children, the environment, the weak, the poor, minority rights, public goods, guarantee bank deposits, or the interests of future generations. Markets would sell cigarettes and alcohol to children. It was not until government regulation that cigarette smoking was cut in half in the US. If allowed, markets would even reinstitute slavery.

Another responsibility of government is to maintain the balance of power within the economy. An unregulated market is not truly free, if monopoly exists, or parties have markedly different access to information, or if one party has much more power than its counterparty. Such "free" markets would not be truly free for those who do not enjoy those advantages. Without adequate government oversight, power accumulates in the hands of the few and only government can prevent such imbalances.

In addition, governments must establish and continuously reform the institutions within which the economy functions. Property rights are defined and protected by government and so is the legal system with its enforcement mechanisms. Markets were incapable of ending discrimination against African Americans and enabling them to purchase coffee at a lunch counter of their choice or to sit where they liked on buses and trains. People had to sacrifice their lives before the rights of desegregated markets were achieved in housing, banking, and employment.[107] The government must provide a safety net.[108] It is the collective responsibility of society to come to the aid of those who are unable to meet their basic needs through no fault of their own. Helping them is not only charitable but also ensures social stability. Hunger, envy, relative deprivation, or longing for the "American Dream," as Hillary's "deplorables" so forcefully demonstrated in November 2016 and in January 2021, can generate a lot of political instability.

Additionally, we need government's help in case of emergencies caused by natural disasters as the Covid-19 pandemic revealed (see Chapter 17). In such cases, even those who otherwise espouse a deep-seated mistrust of government turn unabashedly to it for bailouts without seeing any hypocrisy in it.[109] Moreover, there is no real difference between a natural catastrophe and a disease striking an individual. Both are random events. Why can't the same model of relief be applied to those who are struck by cancer or another debilitating disease?

2.8 Morality Should Take Precedence over Markets

Being human inventions, markets ought not take precedence over our moral values.[110] Markets are part of our ethical system, and we should organize them so that they do not hurt people and distribute the fruits of the economy equitably. If markets do us harm, then we, the people, ought to retain the right to make alternative arrangements and take collective action to stop the pain caused by markets. Market outcomes ought not be above ethical considerations.[111] Selling babies might be efficient from an economic viewpoint, but we find such markets morally reprehensible. Moreover, there are many valuable socio-economic goals that markets are incapable of achieving, like providing for an equitable distribution of rewards, because even a small early advantage can generate substantial subsequent benefits. So, in principle we ought not rely on markets to create a moral socio-economic framework for us and when they do not lead to satisfactory outcomes, they should be modified.

2.9 Economics Is a Social Science, Not a Natural Science

The mainstream completely disregards other disciplines, contrary to accepted scientific practice. Yet, the social sciences are like a seamless web: *all truths are linked to one another*. Truth in psychology must be valid in economics also. Would chemists overlook results from physics? Certainly not! Neglecting sister social sciences is a recipe for failure. Nonetheless, economists systematically disregard the principles of psychology, sociology, and political science. Social

Illustration 2.2 The market did not give Rosa Parks the option to sit anywhere on the bus
Credit: By permission of the Montgomery County Judge of Probate.

psychology, for example, frames the problem of human action in terms of group dynamics. However, such interaction effects as groupthink, herding behavior, conspicuous consumption, status seeking, and consumption norms, are overlooked by mainstream economists, although economic activity obviously takes place in a society and within a political system and not among isolated individuals.[112]

Furthermore, economics is not based on controlled experiments as the natural sciences.[113] Instead, economics begins by assuming that people are rational and maximize their utility, although four Nobel Prizes were awarded for showing that this is impossible for mortals.[114] This approach is like the methodology of medieval philosophers who would argue about "how many angels can dance on the head of a pin." St. Thomas Aquinas, for example, assumed that God was perfect, infinite, and immutable.[115] This was a reasonable starting point for him to imagine the nature of God. Similarly, economists imagine perfect competition in frictionless markets and build the discipline around such implausible assumptions.

Economists disregard that these assumptions are not a reliable guide to good science (see Table 1.1). After all, for a couple of thousand years after Aristotle it seemed logical that heavier objects fall faster than lighter ones until Galileo falsified this assumption. Hence, experiments and experience are a more reliable guide to the real economy than mathematical theorems based on logical deductions from controversial premises.

Moreover, their assumptions are *not open to falsification* and incongruous results, that contradict the assumption of rationality are ignored.[116] Consider the "ultimatum game:" a two-player experiment. Player (1) receives $100, provided she shares it with Player (2). Player (1) decides how much to share. However, if Player (2) rejects the offer, then nobody keeps any money! If both players were rational, selfish, and maximizing, then Player (1) would offer a small amount, say $1, to Player (2) because $1 is greater than zero so Player (2) should accept it rather than receiving nothing. However, this logical inference is contradicted in experiments. Instead, Player (2) consistently rejects a share less than one-third and often the split is closer to 50-50.[117]

The results of this experiment blatantly falsify the assumption that people are selfish, guided by reason, and maximize utility. Instead, they reveal the importance of *emotion*, empathy for others, and the feeling of revulsion at being treated unfairly. Decisions are also mediated by hormones that trigger emotional responses, rather than pure reason. In short, our feelings of justice guide our interaction with others and our willingness to cooperate. These results, replicated innumerable times, in various cultures, contradict the rational-agent model but have been censured from mainstream textbooks. "Economists in recent decades have perhaps too easily dismissed such irrationality."[118]

2.10 Ideology Is Unavoidable and Pervasive in Economics

Ideology plays a major role in the social sciences. They cannot be free of preconceived notions "because the understanding of a 'social' experience itself is always fashioned by ideas that are in the researchers themselves."[119] Evading the issue of ideology in both theory and policy advice is a severe shortcoming of mainstream economics. Textbooks ignore the issue completely. However, as Greenspan emphasized, it is impossible to organize our thoughts without making fundamental assumptions, and these depend on our mindset, world-view, intuition, and intellectual commitments. In turn, these influence the rest of the ideas derived from them including the conclusions.

Hence, economics cannot be purged of ideology; the economists' political, moral, emotional, and philosophical inclinations–*conscious and unconscious*–are reflected in their assumptions and thus in how they structure their thinking and understanding of the world.[120] Much of that ideology is colored by their political philosophy. Contrary to received wisdom, economics cannot become rigorous until it is based on verifiable empirical evidence, instead of unfounded axioms, and cease being obsessed with utility maximization, refuted a very long time ago (see Chapter 4).

Ideology is like a heuristic that enables us to get along in a complex world full of intractable uncertainties. It helps when we must make decisions with limited information and are unable to understand fully the intricate network of interconnectedness among numerous variables. It is our rule of thumb for action.

The pervasiveness of ideology is why there are so many different schools of thought in economics–Austrian, behavioral, evolutionary, feminist, heterodox, institutional, Marxist, monetarist, neoclassical, New-Keynesian, Post-Keynesian, radical, and socialist–and that is why economists do not have coherent advice on the most important issues of the day.[121]

2.11 Takeaways

While markets can be useful, they are not omniscient; they are man-made institutions with innumerable shortcomings. This chapter presents overwhelming empirical evidence that high-pressure capitalism has not led to a good life for a substantial share of the US population. The contrast between Jeff Bezos buying a $500 million yacht and his warehouse employees who have difficulty keeping their head above water demonstrates the large divide between the haves and the have-nots. The evidence of the impact of misguided policies includes the incarceration rate, the mental health crisis, mediocre schools, the decline in life expectancy, underemployment, the opioid crisis, homelessness, endemic poverty, the persistence of slums, environmental deterioration, decaying infrastructure and that only half of the population is thriving. This is the nature of a $23 trillion dual economy. If deregulation had not culminated in the financial crisis, if globalization had led to a thriving society, if the numerous tax cuts had not created an obscene level of inequality, if young men were not killing toddlers for the first time in history, if the January 6th insurrection had not occurred, in short if the US were a thriving society, there would be no need to replace neoliberal economics with humanistic economics.

Questions for Discussion

1   Do you think that the "starving the beast" strategy has been successful? Is it moral?
2   Do you think that the social ills of the United States such as poverty and crime are rooted in the way the economic system distributes income and wealth?
3   How is it possible that so many people are struggling in the United States, one of the richest countries in the world?
4   Why is it that health care is so incredibly costly in the United States, yet the free market is unable to provide better health for the population than in the welfare states of Western Europe?
5   Why is there so much poverty in the United States?
6   Would you favor increasing taxes or decreasing military spending to lessen the poverty rate, improve the infrastructure, or invest in education and innovation?

7   Discuss: The quality of life in the United States is very good; people just do not appreciate what they have.

8   What are the differences between the quality of life, living standards, income, and gross domestic product (GDP)?

9   Discuss: Market outcomes based on competition ought not be questioned. They are above moral considerations.

10   Do you think people act rationally all the time, most of the time, some of the time, or none of the time?

11   What is the difference between the unemployed and the underemployed?

12   What kind of a labor market would you devise if you were deciding behind a "veil of ignorance," that is, not knowing where in the labor market you would end up?

13   If children are not responsible for choosing their parents, why should they inherit the living standards of their parents?

14   Is it fair to have such a high level of inequality as in the US?

15   Should market outcomes be questioned from an ethical viewpoint?

16   What do governments do well? And do not say nothing...

17   Have you been tricked or entrapped into buying something you regretted?

18   Have you or someone you personally know been defrauded?

19   What essential services are markets not particularly good at providing?

20   What products are not provided by markets?

21   What does the "Achilles' heel" of markets refer to?

22   Should we set ourselves the goal of catching up with Canada in life expectancy and with Finland in educational attainment?

23   Do you know what your health insurance coverage is in the case of hospitalization?

24   Have you accepted a contract on the internet without reading all of it?

Notes

1   In the public domain. https://www.reuters.com/article/us-gandhi-works/gandhi-works-to-go-public-60-years-after-his-death-idUSTRE50418A20090105.

2   "For the past quarter century we have worshiped the 'free' market as an ideology rather than for what it is—a natural product of human social evolution and a set of economic tools with which to construct a just and equitable society." Peter Whybrow, "Dangerously Addictive: Why We Are Biologically Ill-Suited to the Riches of Modern America," *The Chronicle of Higher Education*, March 13, 2009.

3   For a heart-breaking story, read: Terrence McCoy, "After the Check Is Gone," *The Washington Post*, October 6, 2017.

4   Michael Sandel, "Populism, Liberalism, and Democracy," *Philosophy & Social Criticism* 44 (2018), 4: 353-359; here p. 354.

5   Lawrence Summers, "Why Isn't Capitalism Working?" *Reuters*, January 9, 2012. Summers was the Director of the National Economic Council under President Obama.

6   David Brooks, "America Is Having a Moral Convulsion," *The Atlantic*, October 5, 2020.

7   Douglas Almond and Janet Currie, "Killing Me Softly: The Fetal Origins Hypothesis." *Journal of Economic Perspectives* 25 (2011), 3: 153-172.

8   Robert Reich, *The Common Good* (Knopf, 2018); Jean Tirole, *Economics for the Common Good* (Princeton University Press, 2017).

9   John Komlos, "How Reaganomics, Deregulation and Bailouts Led to the Rise of Trump," *PBS Newshour*, April 25, 2016. www.pbs.org/newshour/making-sense/column-how-reaganomics-deregulation-and-bailouts-led-to-the-rise-of-trump/.

10 Gregory Mankiw, *Principles of Economics*, 8th edn. (Cengage, 2018), p. 15.

11 Recently, the expression "running the economy hot" is used to imply that the economy is running at full employment, close to potential GDP, without reducing Keynesian stimulus measures. This is not the meaning of the term being used here.

12 Angus Deaton and Paul Schreyer, "GDP, Wellbeing, and Health: Thoughts on the 2017 Round of the International Comparison Program," NBER Working Paper 28177.

13 "The Americans are much sicker than the English." James Banks et al., "Disease and Disadvantage in the United States and in England," *Journal of the American Medical Association* 295 (2006), 17: 2037-2045.

14 https://worldhappiness.report/ed/2020/social-environments-for-world-happiness/, Figure 2.1.

15 https://happiness-report.s3.amazonaws.com/2020/WHR20_Ch2_Statistical_Appendix.pdf, p. 39.

16 Alyssa Davis, "US Daily Worry Easing, but Still Up Since Trump Election," Gallup-Sharecare Well-Being Index, August 4, 2017.

17 Julie Ray, "Americans' Stress, Worry and Anger Intensified in 2018," Gallup, April 25, 2018; https://news.gallup.com/poll/249098/americans-stress-worry-anger-intensified-2018.aspx.

18 United Nations Office on Drugs and Crime, *Statistics*; https://data.unodc.org/.

19 https://www.gunviolencearchive.org/past-tolls.

20 Brooks, "America is Having a Moral Convulsion," op. cit.

21 Wikipedia, "List of Mass Shootings in the United States in 2020."

22 Brian Epstein, "How Many Kinds of Glue Hold the Social World Together?" in Mattia Gallotti and John Michael (eds.), *Social Ontology and Social Cognition* (Springer, 2014), pp. 41-55.

23 And another 4.4 million people are on probation. Their numbers have been declining, however. Bureau of Justice Statistics, "Correctional Populations in the United States," https://www.bjs.gov/content/pub/pdf/cpus1718.pdf.

24 Christopher Hartney, "US Rates of Incarceration: A Global Perspective," www.nccdglobal.org/sites/default/files/publication_pdf/factsheet-us-incarceration.pdf.

25 Jessica Semega et al., "Income and Poverty in the United States: 2019," *Current Population Reports*, P60-270, 2020.

26 Craig Benson, "Poverty: 2018 and 2019," *American Community Survey Briefs*, September 2020; Tables 1 and 5; https://www.census.gov/content/dam/Census/library/publications/2020/acs/acsbr20-04.pdf.

27 US Census Bureau, Data, Historical Families Tables, Table FM-1, "Families by Presence of Own Children under 18: 1950 to Present," https://www.census.gov/data/tables/time-series/demo/families/families.html.

28 US Census Bureau, Data, Historical Families Tables, Table FM-3, "Average Number of Own Children Under 18 Per Family by Type of Family: 1955 to Present," https://www.census.gov/data/tables/time-series/demo/families/families.html.

29 Raj Chetty et al., "The Effects of Exposure to Better Neighborhoods on Children: New Evidence from the Moving to Opportunity Experiment," *American Economic Review* 106 (2016), 4: 855-902; Dolores Acevedo-Garcia, et al., "The Geography of Child Opportunity: Why Neighborhoods Matter for Equity," January 2020; https://www.diversitydatakids.org/sites/default/files/file/ddk_the-geography-of-child-opportunity_2020v2_0.pdf?_ga=2.139372723.1882290790.1621556092-355995447.1621556092.

30 Raj Chetty et al., "How Does Your Kindergarten Classroom Affect Your Earnings? Evidence from Project Star," *Quarterly Journal of Economics* 126 (2011), 4: 1593-1660.

31 ACLU, "School-To-Prison Pipeline," https://www.aclu.org/issues/juvenile-justice/school-prison-pipeline.

32 UNICEF, Innocenti Report Card 11, p. 2 and Report Card 16, p. 11. On another index, the US ranked 43rd. Save the Children, "Global Childhood Report 2020," p. 3; https://www.savethechildren.org/content/dam/usa/reports/advocacy/global-childhood-report-2020.pdf.

33 Childhelp, "National Child Abuse Statistics & Facts." www.childhelp.org/child-abuse-statistics/.

34 Children's Bureau, US Department of Health and Human Services, "Child Maltreatment, 2019" (2021), p. xii; https://www.acf.hhs.gov/cb/research-data-technology/statistics-research/child-maltreatment.

35 Christopher Howson et al. (eds.), *Born Too Soon: The Global Action Report on Preterm Birth* (WHO, 2012).

36 "[T]een childbearing is so high in the United States because of underlying social and economic problems. It reflects a decision ... to 'drop-out' of the economic mainstream ... because they feel they have little chance of advancement." Melissa Kearney and Phillip Levine, "Why Is the Teen Birth Rate in the United States So High and Why Does It Matter?" *Journal of Economic Perspectives* 26 (2012), 2: 141-166.

37 Save the Children, "State of the World's Mothers 2015," https://www.savethechildren.org/content/dam/usa/reports/advocacy/sowm/sowm-2015.pdf.

38 In 2018; Wikipedia, "Programme for International Student Assessment."

39 John Kenneth Galbraith, *The Affluent Society* (Houghton Mifflin, 1958).

40 US Department of Housing and Urban Development, "Part 1: The 2020 Annual Homeless Assessment Report to Congress," March 18, 2021; https://www.hud.gov/press/press_releases_media_advisories/hud_no_21_041.

41 US Department of Housing and Urban Development, "Part 2: The 2018 Annual Homeless Assessment Report to Congress," September 2020; https://www.huduser.gov/portal/sites/default/files/pdf/2018-AHAR-Part-2.pdf.

42 Note that 99 percent of the population has 80 percent of the income. That means that 1 percent of the population has 100 - 80 percent = 20 percent of total income (Figure 2.3).

43 Federal Reserve, *Bulletin*, 106 (September 2020) No. 5, https://www.federalreserve.gov/publications/files/scf20.pdf, p. 7.

44 Juliet Schor, *The Overspent American: Why We Want What We Don't Need* (Harper Perennial, 1999).

45 US Courts, "Bankruptcy Statistics," https://www.uscourts.gov/statistics-reports/analysis-reports/bankruptcy-filings-statistics/bankruptcy-statistics-data.

46 Includes those who were foreclosed, bank repossessions, or sold their home via a distress sale; National Association of Realtors. Laura Kusisto, "Many Who Lost Homes to Foreclosure in Last Decade Won't Return," *Wall Street Journal*, April 20, 2015; https://www.attomdata.com/news/market-trends/foreclosures/attom-data-solutions-2020-year-end-u-s-foreclosure-market-report/.

47 "Ripoff Report," has thousands of stories about scams: www.ripoffreport.com/reports/specific_search/internet.

48 https://www.irs.gov/newsroom/irs-issues-warning-about-coronavirus-related-scams-watch-out-for-schemes-tied-to-economic-impact-payments; Jennifer Schultz, "Top Consumer Complaints in 2009," *New York Times*, July 27, 2010.

49 Bureau of Justice Statistics, "Press Release," September 27, 2015. www.bjs.gov/content/pub/press/vit14pr.cfm; "Victims of Identity Theft, 2018," https://bjs.ojp.gov/content/pub/pdf/vit18_sum.pdf.

50 Kaiser Family Foundation, "Key Facts about the Uninsured Population," November 6, 2020; https://www.kff.org/uninsured/issue-brief/key-facts-about-the-uninsured-population/; Anon, "Commonwealth Fund Affordable Care Act Tracking Survey, February to March 2018," May 2018; www.commonwealthfund.org/publications/surveys/2018/may/commonwealth-fund-affordable-care-act-tracking-survey-february-march.

51 US Department of Agriculture, "Interactive Chart: Food Security Trends." https://www.ers.usda.gov/topics/food-nutrition-assistance/food-security-in-the-us/key-statistics-graphics/#foodsecure.

52 Arthur Brooks, "How Loneliness Is Tearing America Apart," *The New York Times*, November 23, 2018.

53 Robin Marantz Henig, "Valium's Contribution to Our New Normal," *The New York Times*, September 29, 2012.

54 E.J. Mundell, "US Antidepressant Use Jumps 65 Percent in 15 years," *Medical Reporter*, August 15, 2017.

55 Antidepressant use increased from 5.8 percent of the population in 1996 to 10.1 percent in 2005. The increase in nine years was from 13.3 to 27.0 million persons. Mark Olfson and Steven Marcus, "National Patterns in Antidepressant Medication Treatment," *Archives of General Psychiatry* 66 (2009), 8: 848-856.

56 Wikipedia, "Antidepressant." Ramin Mojtabai, "Increase in Antidepressant Medication in the US Adult Population Between 1990 and 2003," *Psychotherapy and Psychosomatics* 77 (2008), 2: 83-92.

57 SAMSHA, Table 7.1A.

58 SAMHSA, Tables 1.1A and 1.1B.

59 People "are always struggling to interpret the 'news,' to understand the implications for the future." Joseph Stiglitz, "Economic Fluctuations and Pseudo-Wealth," NBER Working Paper 28415, January 2021, p. 3.

60 Eric Tucker et al., "Man Who Fatally Stabbed Pentagon Officer Had Troubled Past," Associated Press, August 4, 2021; Binbin Yu et al., "Trends in Depression Among Adults in the United States, NHANES 2005-2016," *Journal of Affective Disorders* 263 (2020): 609-620; Ramin Mojtabai et al., "National Trends in the Prevalence and Treatment of Depression in Adolescents and Young Adults," *Pediatrics* 138 (2016), 6: 1 -10; Mark Olfson et al., "National Trends in the Outpatient Treatment of Depression," *Journal of the American Medical Association* 287 (2002): 203-209; Steven Marcus and Mark Olfson, "National Trends in the Treatment for Depression from 1998 to 2007," *Archives of General Psychiatry* 67 (2010): 1265-1273.

61 SAMSHA, Table 9.1A.

62 According to SAMHSA, "Appendix A: Key Definitions for the 2019 National Survey on Drug Use and Health."

63 SAMSHA, Table 9.4A.

64 Paul E. Greenberg et al., "The Economic Burden of Adults with Major Depressive Disorder in the United States, 2005 and 2010," *Journal of Clinical Psychiatry*, 76 (2015), 2: 155-162; here p. 159.

65 Matt Richtel, "'It's Life or Death': The Mental Health Crisis Among US Teens," *The New York Times*, April 23, 2022.

66 Tara Parker-Pope et al., "Why 1,320 Therapists Are Worried About Mental Health in America Right Now," *The New York Times*, December 16, 2021; CDC, "Children & Mental Health: Part One," https://www.cdc.gov/nchs/pressroom/podcasts/2021/20210514/20210514.htm.

67 Billion is a thousand million. Kerry Dolan et al. (eds), "The Richest in 2021," *Forbes*, https://www.forbes.com/billionaires/.

68 US IRS, "SOI Tax Stats–2018," https://www.irs.gov/statistics/soi-tax-stats-individual-statistical-tables-by-size-of-adjusted-gross-income.

69 Steffie Wolhandler et al., "Public Policy and Health in the Trump Era," *Lancet*, 397 (2021): 705-753.

70 Anne Case and Angus Deaton, "Mortality Rates by College Degree Before and During Covid-19," NBER Working Paper no. 29318.

71 Steven Woolf and Laudan Aron (eds.), *US Health in International Perspective: Shorter Lives, Poorer Health* (National Academy of Sciences, 2013).

72 Martin Feldstein, "The US Economy Is in Good Shape," *The Wall Street Journal*, February 21, 2016; Mary Daly, "Raising the Speed Limit on Future Growth," *FRBSF Economic Letter*, April 2, 2018; John Williams, "Looking Back, Looking Ahead," *FRBSF Economic Letter*, January 23, 2017; John M. Berry, "Yellen's Swan Song," *The International Economy*, Winter 2017; Gregory Mankiw, "Will the Economy Re-Elect Trump? Should It?" *The New York Times*, February 28, 2020.

73 Anne Case and Angus Deaton, *Deaths of Despair and the Future of Capitalism* (Princeton University Press, 2020), p. 113.

74 Jeffrey Sachs, "America's Illusions of Growth," *Project Syndicate*, May 14, 2019.

75 Josh Katz, "Drug Deaths in America Are Rising Faster Than Ever," *The New York Times*, June 5, 2017.

76 CDC, "Drug Overdose Deaths," https://www.cdc.gov/nchs/pressroom/nchs_press_releases/2021/20211117.htm; https://www.cdc.gov/drugoverdose/data/statedeaths.html.

77 CDC, "Drug Overdose Deaths," https://www.cdc.gov/drugoverdose/deaths/index.html.

78 Case and Deaton, *Deaths of Despair*, op. cit., p. 100.

79 Ibid., p. 262.

80 Ibid., pp. 67, 94, 101, 102, 270.

81 Ibid., p. 169; David Autor et al., "When Work Disappears: Manufacturing Decline and the Falling Marriage Market Value of Young Men," *American Economic Review: Insights* 1 (2019), 2: 161-178.

82   Richard Wilkinson and Kate Pickett, *The Inner Level: How More Equal Societies Reduce Stress, Restore Sanity and Improve Everyone's Well-Being* (Penguin Press, 2019).

83   A monopsonist is a large firm that has the power to influence the wage it pays to its employees (see Section 9.3).

84   An oligopoly is a market dominated by a few large firms so that the individual firms can set the price of its product strategically (see Section 6.3).

85   A monopoly is a single seller of a product that is free to choose its price (see Section 6.3).

86   Externalities are costs (like pollution) passed onto other parties that are not part of the activity creating the externality.

87   Anonymous, "Are Video Games Really Addictive?" *The Economist*, January 1, 2022.

88   Kenneth Arrow, "Uncertainty and the Welfare Economics of Medical Care," *American Economic Review* 53 (1963), 5: 141-149.

89   Asymmetric information is when one party to a transaction knows more about the product or contract than the counterparty.

90   Angus Deaton, "Income, Health, and Well-Being Around the World: Evidence from the Gallup World Poll," *Journal of Economic Perspectives* 22 (2008), 2: 53-72; here p. 68.

91   St. Louis Fed, series CPATAX.

92   https://www.townofsurfsidefl.gov/docs/default-source/default-document-library/town-clerk-documents/champlain-towers-south-public-records/email-records/email-related-2018-structural-field-survey-report.pdf?sfvrsn=aa311194_2.

93   Ralph Nader, *Unsafe at Any Speed: The Designed-In Dangers of the American Automobile* (Grossman, 1965).

94   "Crib Information Center," US Consumer Product Safety Commission.

95   Raj Chetty et al., "The Fading American Dream: Trends in Absolute Income Mobility Since 1940," *Science* 856 (2017), 6336: 398-406.

96   Daron Acemoglu and James Robinson, *The Narrow Corridor: States, Societies, and the Fate of Liberty* (Penguin Press, 2019); Oliver Williamson, *Markets and Hierarchies: Analysis and Antitrust Implications* (The Free Press, 1975).

97   Walter Euken, *The Foundations of Economics: History and Theory in the Analysis of Economic Reality* (Springer, 1950).

98   Mariana Mazzucato, *The Entrepreneurial State: Debunking Public vs Private Sector Myths* (Public Affairs, 2015).

99   This phrase, attributed to Henry Thoreau, is a staple in Republican politicians' slogans. Joshua Gillin, "Mike Pence Erroneously Credits Thomas Jefferson with Small Government Quote," *POLITIFACT*, September 21, 2017.

100 "Franklin D. Roosevelt's Address Announcing the Second New Deal," http://docs.fdrlibrary.marist.edu/od2ndst.html.

101 Joseph Stiglitz, *Freefall: America, Free Markets, and the Sinking of the World Economy* (Norton, 2010).

102 Lobbying spending in the US reached $3,000 million annually in 2008 and has been above that since. Statista, https://www.statista.com/statistics/257337/total-lobbying-spending-in-the-us/.

103 Simon Johnson, "The Quiet Coup," *The Atlantic*, May 2009.

104 Charles Ferguson, *Predator Nation: Corporate Criminals, Political Corruption, and the Hijacking of America* (Crown Business, 2012).

105 Chris Mooney, *The Republican War on Science* (Basic Books, 2005).

106 Christopher Witko et al., *Hijacking the Agenda: Economic Power and Political Influence* (Russell Sage Foundation, 2021).

107 Three civil rights activists were brutally murdered in 1964 in Philadelphia, Mississippi. Wikipedia, "Murders of Chaney, Goodman, and Schwerner."

108 Helen Epstein, "Left Behind," *The New York Review of Books*, March 26, 2020.

109 Joseph Stiglitz, "Learning from Harvey," *Project Syndicate*, September 8, 2017:

> In responding to the hurricane [Harvey]—and in funding some of the repair—everyone turns to government, just as they did in the aftermath of the 2008 economic crisis … it is ironic that this is now occurring in a part of the country where government and collective action are so frequently rebuked. It was no less ironic when the titans of US banking, having preached the neoliberal gospel of downsizing government and eliminating regulations that proscribed some of their most dangerous and anti-social activities, turned to government in their moment of need.

110 Roshnee Ossewaarde-Lowtoo, *Reviving the Love for Economic Justice* (Lexington Books, 2021).

111 Michael Sandel, *What Money Can't Buy: The Moral Limits of Markets* (Farrar, Straus and Giroux, 2012); Peter Rona and Laszlo Zsolnai (eds.), *Economics as a Moral Science* (Springer, 2017).

112 David Riesman et al., *The Lonely Crowd: A Study of the Changing American Character* (Yale University Press, 1961); Lee Ross and Richard Nisbett, *The Person and the Situation: Perspectives of Social Psychology*, 2nd edn. (Pinter & Martin, 2011).

113 Ariel Rubinstein, "A Sceptic's Comment on the Study of Economics," *The Economic Journal* 116 (2006): C1-C9.

114 Herbert Simon (1978), Daniel Kahneman (2002), Robert Shiller (2013), and Richard Thaler (2017).

115 Wikipedia, "Thomas Aquinas."

116 Edward Chamberlin, "An Experimental Imperfect Market," *Journal of Political Economy* 56 (1948), 2: 95-108; "*Utility* is a metaphysical concept of impregnable circularity; *utility* is the quality in commodities that makes individuals want to buy them, and the fact that individuals want to buy them shows that they have *utility*." Joan Robinson, *Economic Philosophy* (Penguin Books, 1962), p. 48.

117 Martin Nowak et al., "Fairness Versus Reason in the Ultimatum Game," *Science* 289 (2000), 5485: 1773-1775.

118 Joseph Stiglitz, "Economic Fluctuations and Pseudo-Wealth," NBER Working Paper no. 28415, January 2021, p. 29.

119 Wikipedia, "Frankfurt School."

120 Steven Rappaport, "Abstraction and Unrealistic Assumptions in Economics," *Journal of Economic Methodology* 3 (1996), 2: 215-236.

121 Nick Wilkinson, *An Introduction to Behavioral Economics: A Guide for Students* (Palgrave Macmillan, 2007); Marc Lavoie, *Post-Keynesian Economics* (Palgrave Macmillan, 2007); Richard Wolff and Stephen Resnick, *Contending Economic Theories: Neoclassical, Keynesian, and Marxian* (MIT Press, 2012); Kenneth Boulding, *Evolutionary Economics* (Sage, 1981).

3 The Nature of Demand

> The impotence of man moderating and checking the emotions I name bondage, for, when a man who is prey to his emotions, he is not his own master ... he is often compelled, while seeing that which is better for him, to follow that which is worse.
>
> —Baruch Spinoza[1]

We demonstrated above that the US economy provides an inadequate quality of life for half of its population. In this chapter we explain that the fundamental reason for this is that mainstream economics creates a fantasy world made up of hypothetical markets that misleads, and this has dire consequences for the formulation of economic policy and the way the economy functions. We discuss the psychology of consumption, overlooked in standard textbooks, which is crucial to understanding the extensive frustration within the system.

3.1 The Post-Scarcity Economy

A conventional assumption is that we live in a world of scarcity. This implies misleadingly that our desires are infinite, although they are not innately endless and depend fundamentally on external influences. In fact, except for the obvious basic needs, our wants are primarily culturally constructed. They are not fixed at birth: we are not born with a desire for iPhones. In other words, the feeling of scarcity is artificially induced.

To associate the developed world, overflowing with goods, with pervasive scarcity is a misuse of the concept. On the contrary, abundance reigns and a goodly share of the population is satiated. Our stores are filled to the brim and our closets are cluttered with stuff we hardly use and never really needed. However, firms induce desires in consumers to buy more, using psychological manipulation techniques. So, the feeling of scarcity is artificially induced in people through advertisements and influencers.[2] The challenge is not scarcity but the distribution of income. Actually, what is scarce today is security, stress-free leisure time with family and friends, decent jobs, trust, respect for one another, and public goods like excellent schools, reliable infrastructure, and safe neighborhoods. If our desires are man-made and not natural, we should consider their origin within the economic system.

3.2 Tastes Are Endogenous, Contrary to Conventional Assumptions

Consumer sovereignty is the mainstream doctrine according to which consumers dictate what and how much businesses produce. This is supposedly democratic since they "vote" with their

DOI: 10.4324/9781003174356-3

dollars to channel production so as to satisfy their desires (Figure 3.1). This is an incorrect characterization, because dollars are not equally distributed: some people are born with a lot more of such "votes" than others, so the process cannot possibly be democratic: the wants of the wealthy consumers dominate.[3]

Moreover, sovereignty implies that consumers are in charge of the economy's destiny since, according to the dominant dogma, *tastes are determined outside of the economic system: they are assumed to be exogenous*. Consequently, tastes are of no concern to mainstream economists. They are assumed to be given. If people would not demand stuff, firms would not produce it. So, the conventional claim is that our wants are satisfied, and everyone is happy (Figure 3.1).

However, this model is patently false. There is *no evidence whatsoever* that tastes are exogenous, i.e., that wants are determined before individuals enter the economy and that their choices are guided by their innate desire for products, like iPhones. This is nonsensical, since obviously we do not wait till we reach adulthood to enter the market as consumers and corporations influence our desires in profound ways through their ubiquitous advertisements practically from the very beginning of our life.[4] Corporate expenditures on advertisement were about 1 percent of the GDP between 1950 and 1980 but rose to 1.3 percent by 2017, reaching $300 billion annually (Figure 3.2).[5] Contrary to mainstream's claim, tastes are *endogenous, i.e., determined within the economic system*, except for basic needs, genetically determined: food, clothing, shelter, and health care.

Consequently, mainstream economic theory is essentially *adult economics*: it skips the crucial first two decades of life during which our psyche and *subconscious mind* develop. Nobody enters the economy as an adult with fully developed tastes. Instead, we enter it at birth and our

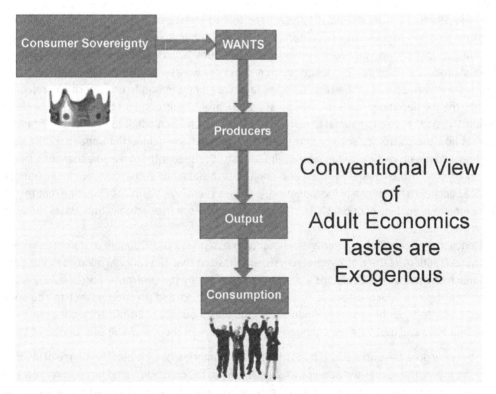

Figure 3.1 Conventional view of consumer sovereignty: tastes are supposedly exogenous

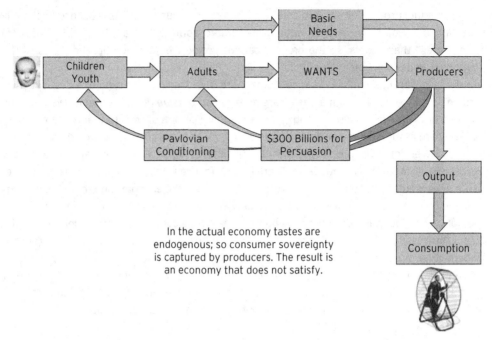

Figure 3.2 Tastes are determined within the economic system in the real world

thinking is influenced by that economy throughout our growing years (Figure 3.2).[6] Hence, by the time people reach adulthood, they have experienced an extended process of habit formation because Madison Avenue–the epicenter of the advertising industry–influences their emotions by inundating them with powerful messages using cultural icons who compel them to buy their clients' products.[7] *Through this socialization process people assimilate the dominant culture* in which they learn to mimic the tastes, values, and consumption habits of celebrities projected across the media. Under such intense pressure, children are groomed to grow up to become acquisitive and reliable consumers.[8] Instead of prudence, children adapt to *instant gratification*. That is how the consumer society developed and corporations gained the upper hand by supporting a *dominant culture* suitable for their interests. Consequently, to assume that consumers are in control of their tastes, values, and choices is misleading. In the current circumstances choice becomes a "pretense of individualism."[9] Thus, a seemingly harmless assertion that tastes are exogenous enables economists to overlook a crucial issue that actually invalidates many of their theories.

Hence, the concept of *consumer sovereignty is essentially pre-Freudian and pre-Pavlovian.* Sigmund Freud, the father of psychoanalysis, emphasized that the rational mind does not control much of what we do. Decisions are often directed not by the prefrontal cortex but by emotions and desires, which originate in the *unconscious mind* and are not subject to the laws of logic. These thought processes induce feelings and thoughts that influence our actions in profound ways and motivate us, although we are unaware of their origin. Freud suggested that:

> Not only does the unconscious mind hide buried memories, but it is also the source of instinctive drives, like sexual and aggressive ones. Although the conscious mind has no direct access to the content of the unconscious, our actions are strongly affected by that content.[10]

Illustration 3.1 Starting analysis with adults is a major error of mainstream economics
Credit: Shutterstock, 1595488672.

The importance of the unconscious mind is well known in cognitive psychology.[11] The manipulation of *children's unconscious* by the media lays the foundation for a culture of hyperconsumerism. That cannot be undone by rational processes once the child reaches adulthood since the unconscious is not accessible through introspection.[12] Hence, the solution of humanistic economics is to protect the development of children's unconscious from business influence.

Conditioning is another important psychological marketing principle also ignored in conventional economics, although it is crucial.[13] Ivan Pavlov discovered that dogs could be taught to respond involuntarily to any stimulus. Feeding dogs while simultaneously ringing a bell made the dogs associate the stimulus (ringing bell) with food. After a while they began reflexively to salivate in response to hearing the bell even *without* the food. This is also true for humans and is a significant part of habit formation that influences behavior, although we are unaware of it.

Advertisers take advantage of conditioning by depicting young good-looking people in fashionable attire smiling and enjoying themselves drinking a brand of soft drink. We involuntarily associate that soft drink with enjoyment and covet it. This is classical conditioning. We may choose to buy a six-pack without thinking about it, and yet to an outside observer the purchase would appear like a rational decision. Such marketing strategies are both demeaning and exploitative since they appeal subliminally to difficult-to-control primordial desires and take advantage of our psychological limitations. Our choices often lead to buyer's remorse, as advertisers entice consumers into buying products that they subsequently regret having purchased.

Another conditioning technique is reinforcing behavior by rewarding it. That is why there are so many *reward programs* like frequent-flyer miles, free gifts, and premiums. The conditioning starts early: fast-food chains present toys to toddlers to condition them to want the food at those eateries long after they received the toys.[14] Cigarette companies give samples to youth. "The firearms industry has poured millions of dollars into a broad campaign to ensure its future by getting guns into the hands of children."[15] Parents are unable to shield children from this multibillion-dollar effort at conditioning. Reward points for using credit cards have also been very effective means of enriching banks which earn money at practically every purchase we make.

Freud and Pavlov are ignored completely by mainstream economists because their discoveries undermine the assumption upon which neoclassical economics rests, namely the rational-agent model, according to which *homo oeconomicus* cannot be manipulated, is objective about its wants, is super-rational, and is in perfect control of its desires. This is an unforgivable fallacy in conventional economics with grave consequences for the discipline and for policy.

To grow up in a culture with asymmetric power to influence social media means that we become fixated on material aspects of life and our psychological and moral development is stymied. There are hardly any advertisements about the aspects of life that are unprofitable to the business world including frugality, patience, circumspection, to save for a rainy day, to practice moderation, to exercise self-control, and appreciate the free things in life like nature, or visit the public library, to relax with friends, avoid envy, not to imitate the rich and famous, to appreciate that we are healthy and not hungry, to be kind to our fellow travelers on this Earth without being greedy.[16] Consequently, we are free to choose our cola drink, but we are deprived of a basic right to develop our own character–*utility function*–autonomously, without such overbearing corporate interference. However, we are unaware of this overarching influence on our character because we are so accustomed to it.[17]

This is a major hindrance to our ability to enjoy life, because new desires are implanted in us as soon as the old ones are satisfied. Contentment is unprofitable. No wonder that the typical American is overweight, indebted, and mostly discontented. We did not choose to become so. This culture was imposed upon us by powerful profit-seeking corporations. This state of *unfreedom* is an immense contradiction for a nation in which the popular culture holds freedom supreme.[18] In sum, consumer sovereignty is a mirage in the real existing economy (Figure 3.2). The result is an economy that fails to satisfy:

> The "yawning void, an insatiable hunger, an emptiness waiting to be filled," that [Christopher] Lasch identified as animating the typical narcissist of the 1970s has grown only deeper ... The Great Recession was supposed to portend ... a recalibration of our lifestyle, and usher in a new era of making more of less. But the pressures that drive the dysregulated American haven't abated ... Wall Street is resurgent, and unemployment is still high. For too many people, the cycle of craving and debt that drives our treadmill existence simply can't be broken.[19]

Consumer protection could protect the individuality and subconscious of children from the conditioning of mega-corporations by limiting their power to implant the habit of acquisition of must-have products. Aldous Huxley, known for his prophetic dystopian novel *Brave New World* (1931), which warned the world of the dehumanizing forces of totalitarianism, recognized the significance of protecting children. He saw presciently that the threats to our individualism and freedom can come from big business, not just from governments. He noted astutely that Madison Avenue discovered that the shortest way to the parents' bank account is through their children:

> Today's children walk around singing ... commercials ... this whole question of children ... is a terribly important one because children are quite clearly much more suggestible than the average grownup; and ... all the propaganda [is] an extraordinarily powerful force playing on these children, who, after all, are going to grow up and be adults quite soon ... The

children ... in the United States are "television and radio fodder" ... after all, you can read in the trade journals the most lyrical accounts of how necessary it is, to get hold of the children because then they will be loyal brand buyers later on.[20]

We have not evolved to be able to handle today's affluence gracefully. According to psychiatrist Peter Whybrow, "Human beings grew up under frugal circumstances. They don't know how to manage affluence."[21] He shows that there is

a dangerous misfit emerging between our consumer-driven culture and the brain systems that evolved to deal with privation 200,000 years ago. Absent of any controls—cultural or economic constraints—we are easily hooked on our acquisitive pleasure seeking behaviors.[22]

In short, human biology is ill equipped to cope with the demands of "the 24/7, global, information-saturated, rapid-fire culture we ... have come to crave."[23]

3.3 Basic Needs Should Have Priority

Mainstream economists consider demand exclusively in terms of "wants," although we should distinguish between three sources of consumer demand, depending on the type of goods involved (necessities, comforts and social necessities, and luxuries):

1. Basic needs are necessary for biological survival and are genetically controlled.[24] These include food sufficient to avoid hunger, safe drinking water to relieve thirst, healthy shelter to protect from the elements, clothing appropriate for weather conditions, and medical care to maintain health; we would perish without these goods and services.
2. Comfort goods are necessary for survival in the society. They are a precondition for a dignified life in a particular society, like an automobile in most areas in the US, because of the shortage of public transportation. Access to education, computers, the internet, and telephone are also in this category, as we cannot function effectively without them in a modern society. These goods enhance one's capability to function with self-respect within the society in which we live.[25]
3. Luxury goods are not necessary for life, either biologically or socially; they are demanded (a) because of an acquired taste (soft drinks); or (b) because consumers are manipulated psychologically into wanting them (the latest iPhone); or (c) in order to *signal* social status by virtue of their exclusiveness (a Mercedes).[26] These are also called Veblen goods[27] or positional goods. *Conspicuous consumption* is unique because it confers social status and thereby creates a negative externality: envy. The share of these types of goods in total expenditure has increased from 20 percent in 1901 to 32 percent in 1950 to 50 percent by 2003.[28] People flaunt their wealth in order to attain *social status*, so these goods are highly visible. To show off one's savings deposit balances is not considered socially appropriate. Flaunting has its cultural norms.

The distinction among these three types of goods is crucial to understanding the fundamental differences between the consumption of bread, health care, a used car, and a new BMW. The Covid-19 pandemic demonstrated vividly the life-and-death significance of basic needs (see Chapter 17). To conflate these three types of goods merely as consumption misses this crucial point.

In rich countries, the necessities of life make up a small share of total expenditures. Hence, the conventional assumption that "wants" are "unlimited" is by no means warranted for goods in groups (1) and (2), especially since storage is costly. A principle of Humanistic Economics is to *prioritize satisfying basic social and physical needs* for everyone. In other words, goods in groups (1) and (2) ought to take priority over goods in group (3). As the humanistic psychologist Erich Fromm affirmed, "the unconditional right of everyone to have a sufficient material basis to live a dignified human life ... a man has the same right as a dog has to live and not to starve."[29] Basic needs are finite: the size of the stomach is limited as is the amount of clothing we need.

Free markets cannot lead to a good life since markets are not content with producing goods to satisfy the needs in groups (1) and (2) and devote $300 billion per annum to coax consumers into coveting goods corporations want them to buy. This is the foundation of the treadmill existence in the developed world. For instance, the market share of Virginia Slims' cigarettes grew enormously by using an "aspirational image" which "co-opted women's liberation slogans to build a modern female image."[30] In contrast, the Marlboro Man was a rugged individualist projecting an ultra-masculine image and became one of the most successful brands world-wide.[31] "The Marlboro Man was strong, powerful. He never speaks. He's so tough."[32] Its sales increased 300 percent after the ad debuted in 1955. Inconveniently, it killed some 2.3 million people by 2005 in the US alone and probably another 1.6 million in the subsequent ten years.[33] However,

Illustration 3.2 Drink to contentment. Most people who drink colas do not look this sophisticated. One bottle has 41 grams of sugar. For a woman, the recommended daily intake of non-naturally occurring sugar is 25 grams! No wonder two-thirds of American adults are overweight or obese

Credit: iStock.com/travelif.

Illustration 3.3 The Marlboro Man represents the macho rugged individualism of the dominant American ideology. Marlboro's supposedly transformative experience killed millions of men by causing cancer

Credit: From the collection of Stanford Research into the Impact of Tobacco Advertising (tobacco.stanford.edu).

the managers and shareholders of Phillip Morris earned billions through this effective marketing strategy. What price success!

In sum, humans develop a Pavlovian conditioned response to advertisements so effectively that they are not conscious of their dependence. Corporations are able to dominate by creating fads and exploiting human psychological weaknesses to induce consumers to buy their products. Otherwise, we would be much more frugal, and our wants would be considerably more modest. Corporations' $300 billion per annum expenditure is a persuasion bombshell—four times as much as the amount spent on computers in 2016.[34]

Humanistic economics advocates an improvement in the quality of life by emancipating ourselves from these influences to become self-actualizing individuals according to Maslow's hierarchy of needs: people who enjoy autonomy in personal development, who are rich in spirit, creative and wise enough not to depend on influencers to tell them how to live.[35] Until de facto consumer sovereignty is established, free markets cannot lead to a fulfilled life for most people, because businesses profit from persuading us to be greedy, but as greed has no satiation, greedy people experience a vicious circle of incessantly chasing new desires implanted in them without being satisfied. Fixation on material needs cannot gratify in the longer term because such persons are blocked from further psychological and moral development. They are hindered from seeking meaning in life in intangibles rather than in material goods, although there is an unlimited supply of good feelings that can be generated from the beauty of nature, from self-respect, lasting friendships, loving relationships, and spiritual connectedness.[36]

Consider furthermore, that three of the eight Millennium Development Goals of the United Nations pertain to health: child health, maternal health, and combating diseases. In the UN

Declaration of Human Rights, mothers and children are singled out for being "entitled to special care and assistance." Consequently, we need to make sure that the distribution of income suffices to provide for the basic needs and dignified life of everyone.

The neglect of basic needs by the mainstream economists has major consequences, because it has led to the toleration of deprivation and ill health among the disadvantaged, while the new elites are spending obscene amounts frivolously on conspicuous consumption unabashedly, like $2 million on a birthday party.[37] Should not a baby's health have priority over children's playhouses costing $250,000,[38] or a $300 million yacht, [39] or the 310,000 breast augmentation procedures performed in the US annually?[40] We should surely ask whether the invisible hand is working properly if an actor like John Travolta has two jet airplanes parked in his back yard. Does Mitt Romney really need an elevator for his car at his La Jolla beach house?[41] Instead of being sovereigns, consumers willingly conform to business interests since they are socialized into the dominant ideology of consumption, instant gratification, and being oblivious to the extreme degree of income inequality. If the wealthy had to pay higher taxes, they would not be able to afford such frivolous lifestyles, and we could afford more mental health facilities so that the number of mass shootings would be reduced.[42]

3.4 The Invisible Hand Is Often Invisible Because It Is Not There[43]

Adam Smith's famous metaphor of the invisible hand is a shorthand for the self-regulating mechanism of the market; it implies that the actions of selfish individuals will benefit society as though guided by an "invisible hand." The coordination of competitive markets compels self-interested producers and consumers to increase social welfare. According to the common wisdom the "invisible hand works its magic."[44] They continue to emphasize the metaphor although many economists received Nobel Prizes decades ago for stressing that markets fail to improve social welfare in numerous circumstances, including in case of imperfect information, and since imperfect information is ubiquitous, markets are usually inefficient.[45] This should be the default model. Stiglitz has warned repeatedly that the metaphor is inappropriate.[46]

Hence, the invisible hand metaphor is deceptive in today's world. Smith was describing an eighteenth-century economy in which the quality of products was easily ascertained. No significant information problems existed. Moreover, the butcher bought bread from the baker and the baker bought meat from the butcher, for decades. Not only had they known one another since childhood but their parents did also. They attended the same church and were present at each other's major life events: marriages, baptisms, and burials. Under such circumstances, *opportunistic behavior* was frowned upon. Obviously, the butcher would not have gained by selling inferior-quality meat, neither would the baker have benefited by short-changing the butcher. They would have been discredited for life if they engaged in opportunistic behavior.

Moreover, eighteenth-century businessmen were much more likely to believe in the Ten Commandments than today's businessmen, and consequently would have been much less likely to deceive others because of the fear of God. There was no sense in risking ending up in purgatory.

In Smith's time, there was no small print, the products were simple, and transactions were based on repeated face-to-face exchange within the confines of a village community with a sense of permanence. There was strong social pressure to restrict opportunistic behavior: deceivers and the greedy would have been ostracized. In contrast, in today's impersonal economy Dick Fuld, who bankrupted Lehman Brothers, is not ostracized at all, and heads an asset management firm with 16 employees and $200 million in assets. He still earns a several-million-dollar salary, and his net worth of $250 million should suffice to maintain his luxurious lifestyle.[47] We should not let an eighteenth-century metaphor dominate our current thinking of how markets work. Mortgage-backed securities in a globalized world are so complex and so opaque that none of the conditions of that Smithian world pertains to them. Thus, the Smithian world is hardly a useful guide to today's economy.[48] *Asymmetric information* is key to understanding the modern economy.

The Meltdown of 2008 is an example of how individual and group interests diverge despite competition. The interest of Angelo Mozilo, CEO of Countrywide Financial, a major culprit in the subprime mortgage crisis, was not aligned with those of his customers, shareholders, or of society.[49] His net worth is still $600 million despite all the damage he did to the economy.[50] The net worth of others whose firms disappeared in the Meltdown include (in millions) Roland Arnall, Ameriquest ($1,500); Jon Corzine, MF Global ($350); Dick Fuld, Lehman Brothers ($250); John Thain, Merrill Lynch ($100); James Cayne, Bear Stearns ($100). However, many of their customers and investors lost everything, and additional millions were hurt severely through the loss of their jobs and pensions by their reckless behavior.[51] Even Alan Greenspan, former Chairman of the Federal Reserve, who allowed the crisis to accumulate, has a net worth of $10 million. In other words, the financial aristocracy was largely immune to the calamity—none of them lost their place in the top 1% percent—while society paid dearly. The "invisible hand" was nowhere to be seen.

Actually, deception has been integrated into the typical business model. Scandals are incessant.[52] Enron, Arthur Anderson, Volkswagen (emission scandal), Wells Fargo (employees opened more than 2 million bogus checking and credit card accounts), are household names associated with corporate crimes. Goldman Sachs paid a $550 million penalty for defrauding investors on one of its bonds (collateralized debt obligations). (Of course, that was not a big deal for a firm that made $13,000 million profits the previous year.) AIG agreed to pay $725 million in a fraud case.[53] These firms knew much more about the financial products they were selling than did their buyers, and they took advantage of asymmetric information. Thus, invoking Smith's butchers and bakers as stand-ins for twenty-first-century turbo-capitalism is silly.

3.5 The Magic of Competition Is Not an Elixir

Competition has a positive connotation in western culture because we have perfect markets in mind, which are rare in the modern economy. Competition supposedly eliminates inefficient firms and ensures that the best products are produced. However, competition in the real word is insufficient for a good economy, especially if complex transactions are involved, when quality is difficult to ascertain, in the presence of asymmetric information, or if the market is dominated by oligopolies, as is the case today. Competition will also hinder cooperation and not create or enforce safety standards. So, competition does not work its "magic" outside of the classroom when these ubiquitous factors are present, and government needs to provide oversight to ameliorate the market's shortcomings.

Competition can also become a race to the bottom especially when an intangible attribute like risk is involved in the transaction. The reason is that risk is difficult to ascertain and easy to hide. Hence, money managers who obtained a high return before the 2008 crisis by taking excessive risks were at a competitive advantage vis-à-vis their more prudent colleagues who earned a lower return. Since risk was hidden from investors, most flocked to high-return money managers, putting the prudent ones out of business. That process led to high returns temporarily with excessive risk-taking until the system imploded.

When competition becomes brutal, unscrupulous businesspeople may be the ones that thrive temporarily.[54] Countrywide Financial was initially a decent mortgage originator. However, when subprime mortgages became popular, it began to lose market share around 2000 and its CEO, Angelo Mozilo, jumped on the bandwagon and started selling millions of predatory mortgages, preying on gullible people. He confessed in an email: "In all my years in the business, I have never seen a more toxic product."[55] Yet, that did not deter him from marketing and profiting from it. CNN named him one of the ten biggest culprits of the financial crisis.[56]

Competition is also not magical if the costs are conditional on uncertain future events. Thus, credit card companies can tempt with gimmicks like rock-bottom teaser interest rates that last a few months, with amazing reward programs with cash back, and deceptive points, hoping to penalize customers heavily with subsequent late fees. Fierce competition in the credit card market has not lowered penalties, however. They are still stuck at $36. The reason is that the companies do not want to advertise a lower penalty fee because they want to avoid drawing the customer's attention to them. They want those fees to remain hidden and focus on the tempting aspects of their offer.

Until the Credit Card Act of 2009 stopped the practice, credit card companies were also allowed to charge customers for overdrawing their account with a hefty $35 penalty.[57] Even after the legislation, some companies are charging usurious interest rates originally hidden from consumers.[58] Banks earn a walloping $100 billion in credit card fees, leaving many consumers deeply indebted.[59] Americans are inundated with 3.3 billion pieces of mail annually and have 670 million credit cards. Some $3.8 trillion is charged on credit cards annually. Consumers paid an interest rate of 17 percent on $1.1tr in outstanding balances in 2018 when the "risk-free" Treasury rate was 2.8 percent.[60]

Government oversight is also needed for products related to health and safety since markets are incapable of providing safe products without regulation. Suppose ground beef manufacturers put labels on their product stating "We guarantee that this beef has only 1 million *E. Coli* bacteria per pound. We'll give you thousand dollars if you get sick." Would people buy it? Probably not, because consumers do not know—and do not want to be reminded—that *E. Coli* invariably exist in ground beef, and they do not know what the FDA's approved limit is. All they want to know is that the ground beef is safe to eat if cooked properly, but the company could not convince us to trust it in a credible way. So, labeling is not a reliable substitute for government inspection and regulation.

Hence, competition is not a magical elixir. It is not a sufficient condition for market outcomes to be satisfactory. Relying on competition to create an efficient economy reflects the ideology of social Darwinism. However, in a high-pressure economy, it becomes such a cutthroat contest for survival that it generates much consternation and leads to the accumulation of frustration instead of a good life.

3.6 Consumerism Was Not Our Choice

Consumerism was imposed upon us by the business world.[61] Shopping became the national pastime and hunting for bargains became an addictive mania.[62] Consumerism weighs heavily on society because it induces us to sacrifice personal relationships in the process of obtaining material goods, and we subject ourselves to longer work hours to acquire things we are persuaded to buy. In addition, we mortgage the living standards of future generations in the process. The outcome is a stressful existence.[63]

Under normal circumstances, the emotional, reward-seeking, selfish, "myopic" part of our brain is checked and balanced in its desirous cravings by our powers of cognition—our awareness of the consequences, say, of eating too much, or spending too much. But after decades of never-before-seen levels of affluence and endless messages promoting instant gratification, Whybrow says, this self-regulatory system has been sidetracked. The "'orgy of self-indulgence' that spread in our land of no-money-down mortgages ... has disturbed the 'ancient mechanisms that sustain our physical and mental balance'."[64]

We did not choose to be this way. Rather, our brain and nervous system have been reconfigured by commercial interests. We want to belong; we want to be part of the society, and through shopping we reaffirm our sense of belonging. Hence, habitual shopping becomes an end in itself, a substitute for satisfying psychological needs of belonging, being respected, to develop intimate relationships, and to have a sense of accomplishment.[65] However, consumption is an inferior substitute for gaining respect, so consumerism leads to an anxious life in a high-stress society.

The corporate world has promoted a culture in which people obtain these psychological rewards through shopping which increases corporate profits rather than from activities that are not monetized—enjoying nature, music, reading, or spending time with family and friends. The result is that "our emotional life has become impoverished."[66] Consequently, "despite our material riches what eludes many Americans, beyond a good night's sleep, is a genuine sense of fulfillment—a sense of being in harmony with others and oneself."[67] Consequently,

> we consume everything with voracity. Behind this consumptive frenzy, lies an inner vacuity, an incapacity of people to be autonomous, to be truly productive citizens and unique selves. The perennial challenge is to imagine an alternative existence for ourselves—one that is ever more intelligent, humane and compassionate ... There is ... a sense of depression, a sense of loneliness.... very often, overeating and overbuying are the results of states of depression or intense anxiety.[68]

What we feel as freedom is, to a large extent, the freedom to buy or to consume; to say: "I want this cigarette. I want this car. I want this thing rather than another."[69] Precisely because many of the competing brands are not actually very different, the individual feels the great power of being free to choose.

Fromm urged us to regain

> the right to be oneself ... We live in ... [a] Western industrialized society ... which creates a ... type of Man whom one could call *homo consumens*, the consumer Man ... He devotes his life to producing things and consuming things.[70]

And in the process he is losing his human nature and becoming an object to be manipulated—"not much more than a mechanism."[71]

We were so preoccupied with the threat of big government controlling our lives that we were blindsided by the threat of other institutions amassing power, Madison Avenue, Wall Street, Hollywood, Silicon Valley, and mega-corporations that slowly but incrementally did just that: encroached on our freedoms, manipulated our individuality, and invaded our privacy.[72] Enter the IT revolution and suddenly we are much closer to Huxley's and Orwell's dystopian vision. "Big Brother Is Watching You" not only through surveillance by the state but also by Facebook, Amazon, and Google.[73] They collect and store data on every click we make on the internet and exploit our psychological vulnerabilities and incentivize us to consume.

Facebook also classifies our political views into a spectrum from liberal to conservative and granted access to Cambridge Analytica, a political consulting firm, to 87 million confidential data. Analytica used the information to target voters with personal ads to support the election of Donald Trump. This is true unfreedom: welcome to *1984*. The role of social media in the assault on Congress of January 6th was also substantial.

The mainstream contends that increasing the number of products available in markets increases welfare, because it enhances consumers' choices. However, the proposition overlooks the fact that choosing between products takes time, effort, and increases the possibility of confusion. Therefore, increasing the number of options imposes search costs on consumers, and these could exceed the benefit of the additional option, thereby decreasing welfare.[74] A typical grocery store carries dozens of varieties of balsamic vinegar and olive oil. Brand differences are often minor: tests have revealed, for example, no difference among gasoline brands.[75] After a point, choice leads to confusion and excessive transaction costs. Shopping under such circumstances is challenging.

In contrast, Schumacher argued that less is more:

> A Buddhist economist would consider... [the conventional] approach excessively irrational: since ... the aim should be to obtain the maximum of well-being with the minimum of consumption ... [the] essence of civilisation [is] not in a multiplication of wants but in the purification of human character.[76]

3.7 The Market Has Hidden Magnification Mechanisms

Magnification mechanisms include first-mover advantages because markets' *winner-take-all* (losers-lose-all) design amplifies the benefits of being ever-so-slightly earlier at producing something than a competitor. For instance, the Linux operating system is supposedly better than Windows but came on the market later. Due to first-mover-advantages, the wealth of Bill Gates is 2,600 times as much as the creator of Linux, Linus Torvalds. Due to the design of markets the great wealth amassed by the top 1 percent is way out of proportion to their contribution to the economy (and society). The larger implication for society is that the amplification mechanism leads to a misallocation of resources: people earn more than warranted by their economic contribution.

This mechanism also works in other types of contests. For example, Mark Spitz became world famous and a household name for winning seven gold medals in the 1972 Olympics. In the 100-meter freestyle he was less than 0.5 second faster than the second-place finisher whose name has been forgotten. In the 200-meters race, he was 0.1 second faster. Spitz' net worth is $20 million. The others have nothing. Again, Spitz was ever-so-slightly better to win the competition, but his benefits were way out of proportion to the split-second advantages. That is the idea of the magnification mechanism.

There is an additional source of inefficiency caused by the fortunes amassed by the winners. They signal a tantalizing prize potentially available to a lucky person. So, the same emotions that make poor people purchase lottery tickets lead them to the fantasy that they, too, might strike it rich like Bill Gates. The enormous size of the prize generates unrealistic optimism and many overestimate the probability of success while accepting their lower status in life in the meanwhile.[77] The eventual outcome is disappointment instead of contentment. In sum, the unrealistic demonstration effect of such jackpots induces a misallocation of human resources into activities with a low probability of success and ends in frustration of the losers that can easily boil over into anger directed against the system.

3.8 Variations in Cognitive Endowment

Human cognitive endowment is heterogeneous. This poses an additional challenge for orthodox economics as textbooks quietly assume the opposite, namely, that people are homogeneous and have the same *intelligence quotient (IQ)*, so they are all equally capable of solving the complex problems in today's global economy. However, this is obviously fallacious: both cognitive ability and economic literacy vary enormously.[78] The IQ of a population is normally distributed with mean of 100, 16 percent is below 85, and 16 percent is above 115, implying that the latter group can think much faster, has a larger working memory, and can solve problems more accurately than the former. Moreover, the higher IQ group gains additional advantages during their youth because they become better educated. This double advantage provides enormous opportunities for deception and manipulation of the low-IQ group by the high-IQ group. Humanistic Economics does not disregard this crucial psychological fact.

These advantages have significant consequences in real markets because businesses can afford to hire the smartest to entrap those with low cognitive skills. That is one important reason why extensive consumer protection is essential for a good economy. *Caveat emptor*—let the buyer beware—is not symmetric; it disadvantages consumers by putting additional burden on them. This is one reason for the *poverty trap*. Buyers and sellers should be treated equally under the law.

The smart entrapped and exploited the weaknesses of their less-well-informed clients frequently during the subprime-mortgage debacle. The counterparties were not equally informed about the transaction and were not equally capable of understanding the terms and risks involved since various complex stipulations were incomprehensible to them. In fact, most of the important products purchased nowadays involve contracts that are complicated and challenging to understand. That is why the U.S. Congress created the Consumer Financial Protection Bureau.[79] As Elizabeth Warren, who was in charge initially, warned, "The time for hiding tricks and traps in fine print is over."[80]

3.9 Genetic Endowment Influences Human Behavior

Genetic endowment influences many personal characteristics that, in turn, influence consumers.[81] Such attributes include cognitive ability, although the social environment also plays a crucial role. Twin studies indicate that education and earnings are affected both by genes and by the social environment.[82] The emergent field of "genoeconomics" postulates that economic outcomes (income, wealth, education) are "about as heritable as many medical conditions."[83]

Our genetic code is an essential aspect of human nature and is therefore a crucial determinant of economic success.[84] A burgeoning literature shows that many of our choices are actually not the outcome of conscious cognitive processes alone but are influenced considerably by our genetic endowment and its interaction with the environment.[85] "Variation in a surprisingly wide range of behaviors is substantially influenced by genetic differences."[86] For instance, the heritability of the degree of risk aversion is estimated to be about 45 percent.[87] The role played by genetics in such attributes as IQ, educational attainment, lifetime earnings, empathy, and aspects of our personality like impatience, will power, self-control, attention span, and risk taking may be as great as the role played by cultural norms.[88] Hence, rational choice is an inappropriate assumption since genetic endowment is so influential: "in much of what we think, feel and do, we march to ancient drummers."[89] Thus, in many respects, our prefrontal cortex is not in control of our decisions. Biology influences human behavior significantly: "in order to understand the human condition, it is necessary to accept that we do have instincts."[90] *Homo oeconomicus* is a caricature of flesh-and-blood human beings.

3.10 Neuroeconomics Discovers Some Economic Secrets

The brain is made up of 100 billion neurons which communicate with each other using chemical signals. Economists have begun to explore how these neural networks affect economic behavior and the field of neuroeconomics was born. It examines the biological origins of market activity using functional magnetic resonance imaging, which registers blood flow in the capillaries of the brain and thereby identifies neurons firing electrochemical signals.[91]

These experiments reveal flaws in the standard theory of utility maximization: brain activities show that the hard-wired circuits in the rational part of the brain postulated by standard decision theory are not always activated. The brain also uses other processes. For instance, if the choice is between two alternatives, one of which is certain while the other is risky, the processing takes place in a different part of the brain than when both alternatives are risky.[92] Amazingly, parallel processors are used for different tasks, and reasoning of the prefrontal cortex is not always in control. This also explains why emotions sometimes override logic. "Brain mechanisms combine controlled and automatic processes, operating using cognition and affect [emotion] … Reason has its hands full with headstrong passions and appetites."[93] Neuroeconomic experiments also confirmed the importance of the social brain in other-regarding preferences, "pro-social behavior including trust, altruism, reciprocity, empathy, generosity, or concern for equity."[94] This innovative research program will undoubtedly reveal many more secrets "and perhaps even transform economics completely in the future."[95]

3.11 Takeaways

Neoclassical economists assume arbitrarily that people's decision-making apparatus, their taste, and utility function, are exogenous to the economic system. In other words, economists are not concerned about the determination of consumers' taste during the first two decades of life. They buy iPhones because they like them and the reason they like them has allegedly nothing to do with other people buying them or the fact that Apple Inc. has spent billions in order to inundate them with advertising about it on social media. This theory, called methodological individualism, is pre-Freudian and pre-Pavlovian and is among the most retrograde aspects of mainstream economics. It enables the profession to disregard basic needs which were obviously extremely important during the Covid pandemic. It enables them to disregard the first two decades of life which are crucial from a developmental viewpoint. After all, that is when our unconscious mind and character can be most effectively manipulated by influencers working for powerful corporations. It also enables economists to conflate necessities with conspicuous consumption. An economic system in which consumers are manipulated will not lead to a flourishing society because it leads to a treadmill existence of unfreedom. Consumers are not allowed to remain sovereign over their desires and lose the ability to control their consumption, evinced by their indebtedness and by the lack of ability to control their appetite.

Questions for Discussion

1   Do we live in an age of scarcity?
2   Can you give examples of firms trying to condition you to buy their product?
3   Can you give examples of firms trying to influence your unconscious so you'll buy their product?
4   Do you think seeking status is worthwhile?
5   Have you bought something to impress your peers?
6   Are your purchases influenced by Madison Avenue, by Hollywood, by influencers, or by Silicon Valley?
7   Do you know anyone who copies what celebrities wear?
8   Does keeping up with the Joneses lead to a satisfactory life?
9   Do you think that conspicuous consumption is socially acceptable?
10 Can you name some Veblen goods?
11 Do you think that a BMW is a basic need?
12 Is there a difference between alleviating a toothache and buying a luxury yacht?
13 Do you think that basic needs, including health care, should be available to everybody in society?
14 What do you think of a tax on frivolous products such as plastic surgery undertaken for reasons of vanity? Or luxury yachts bought for display?
15 Do you know people who are maxed out on their credit cards?
16 Do you know people who charge products frivolously on their credit cards?
17 Do you think people spend similarly when paying cash or paying with a credit card?
18 Do you think that mothers and babies should be entitled to health care?
19 How much credit card debt do you or your parents have? What did they spend it on?
20 Have you ever regretted purchasing something or signing a contract?

Notes

1   Baruch Spinoza, *Ethics*, Part IV, "Of Human Bondage, or the Strength of the Emotions" (1677; Trans. R.H.M. Elwes, 1883).
2   It is not moral to subject people to such pressure, according to Vance Packard, *The Hidden Persuaders* (David McKay, 1957).
3   Tibor Scitovsky, "On the Principle of Consumers' Sovereignty," *American Economic Review* 52 (1962), 2: 262–268.
4   John Kenneth Galbraith, *The New Industrial State* (Houghton Mifflin, 1967).
5   Shane Greenstein, "The Economics of Digitization," *NBER Reporter* 2, July 2020.
6   "[C]hildren Are Active Participants in Markets." John List et al., "How Experiments with Children Inform Economics," NBER Working Paper no. 28825, May 2021.
7   Andrea Dworkin and Catharine MacKinnon, *Pornography and Civil Rights: A New Day for Women's Equality* (Organizing Against Pornography, 1988).
8   Businesses are exploring ways to influence our dreams: https://thehustle.co/are-advertisers-going-to-infiltrate-our-dreams/.
9   Wikipedia, "Theodore Adorno."
10 Peter Gray, *Psychology*, 4th edn. (Worth, 2002), p. 17.
11 Louis Augusto, "Unconscious Knowledge: A Survey," *Advances in Cognitive Psychology* 6 (2010): 116–141.

12   Juliet Schor, *Born to Buy: The Commercialized Child and the New Consumer Culture* (Scribner, 2005).

13   Philip Kotler and Gary Armstrong, *Principles of Marketing*, 17th edn. (Prentice Hall, 2017).

14   Lara O'Reilly, "McDonald's Slapped Down for Focusing Its Happy Meal Advertising on the Toy and Not the Food," *Business Insider*, May 15, 2015.

15   Mike McIntire, "Selling a New Generation on Guns," *The New York Times*, January 26, 2013.

16   Exceptions are organizations like Adbusters that opposes addictive consumerism.

17   Seeing this need to learn about being able to live a happier life, Yale University is now offering a course on the subject. David Shimer, "Yale's Most Popular Class Ever: Happiness," *The New York Times*, January 26, 2018.

18   "[M]ost men and women will grow up to love their servitude." Aldous Huxley, *Brave New World* (Chatto and Windus, 1931).

19   Judith Warner, "Dysregulation Nation," *The New York Times*, June 18, 2010; https://www.nytimes.com/2010/06/20/magazine/20fFOB-WWLN-t.html.

20   "Mike Wallace Interviews Aldous Huxley," May 18, 1958, YouTube video, www.youtube.com/watch?v=HSx91KiNyFU; transcript: www.cuttingthroughthematrix.com/articles/Mike_Wallace_interviews_Aldous_Huxley_May_18_1958.html.

21   Peter Whybrow interview with *Charlie Rose*, March 18, 2005, and October 12, 2015. https://charlierose.com/videos/10351.

22   Ibid.

23   Peter Whybrow, *American Mania: When More Is Not Enough* (Norton, 2005), book cover.

24   Robert Allen, "Absolute Poverty: When Necessity Displaces Desire," *American Economic Review* 107 (2017), 12: 3690–3721.

25   Amartya Sen, *Commodities and Capabilities* (North-Holland, 1985).

26   Boston Consulting, "The New World of Luxury," December 2010; https://image src.bcg.com/Images/BCG_The_New_World_of_Luxury_Dec_10_tcm55-115341.pdf.

27   Thorstein Veblen, *The Theory of the Leisure Class: An Economic Study of Institutions* (Macmillan, 1899).

28   U.S. Department of Labor, Bureau of Labor Statistics, *100 Years of U.S. Consumer Spending: Data for the Nation, New York City, and Boston, August 3, 2006.* www.bls.gov/opub/uscs/report991.pdf.

29   It is the "right of each man to unfold as an individual and as a human being." Erich Fromm, "The Automaton Citizen and Human Rights," www.fromm-gesellschaft.eu/images/pdf-Dateien/2008a-1966-e.pdf. Erich Fromm, *The Sane Society* (Routledge, 1956); Erich Fromm, *The Art of Loving* (Harper & Row, 1956).

30   Benjamin Toll and Pamela Ling, "The Virginia Slims Identity Crisis: An Inside Look at Tobacco Industry Marketing to Women," *Tobacco Control* 14 (2005), 3: 172–180; https://tobaccocontrol.bmj.com/content/14/3/172.

31   "Honey, I Blew Up the Marlboro Man," *Tobacco Control* 1 (1992), 4: 300–303; https://tobaccocontrol.bmj.com/content/1/4/300.

32   However, "the three actors who played the Marlboro Man died of lung cancer." Katie Connolly, "Six Ads That Changed The Way You Think," *BBC News*, January 3, 2011.

33   Andrew Hyland et al., "Happy Birthday Marlboro: The Cigarette Whose Taste Outlasts Its Customers," *Tobacco Control* 15 (2006), 2: 75–77; https://tobaccocontrol.bmj.com/content/15/2/75.

34   Douglas Galbi, "U.S. Advertising Expenditure Data," *Purple Motes*, September 14, 2008. In contrast, the value of motor vehicle output was $540 billion. U.S. Department of Commerce, Bureau of Economic Analysis, *Income and Product Accounts Tables:* Table 1.2.5. Gross Domestic Product by Major Type of Product; https://apps.bea.gov/iTable/iTable.cfm?reqid=19&step=2.

35   Abraham Maslow, "A Theory of Human Motivation," *Psychological Review* 50 (1943): 370–396.

36   Mihaly Csikszentmihalyi, *Flow: The Psychology of Optimal Experience* (Harper, 2008). Martin Seligman, *Flourish: A Visionary New Understanding of Happiness and Well-Being* (The Free Press, 2012).

37   Dennis Kozlowski, former CEO of Tyco International, spent $2 million on his wife's birthday party but ended up serving 6.5 years in jail for fraud. Kia Makarechi, "What Happens After You Serve Your White-Collar Prison Sentence?," *Vanity Fair*, March 2, 2015.

38   Kate Murphy, "Child's Play, Grown-Up Cash," *The New York Times*, July 20, 2011.

39   Robert Frank, "Baccarat Meets Bomb-Proof Glass on the High Seas," *The Wall Street Journal*, April 23, 2010.

40   The number of breast augmentation procedures has tripled since 1997. The American Society for Aesthetic Plastic Surgery, "Cosmetic Surgery National Data Bank Statistics, 2016," pp. 10, 11, 23. www.surgery.org/sites/default/files/ASAPS-Stats2016.pdf.

41   Ashley Parker, "For Romney, a Four-Car Garage with Its Own Elevator," *The New York Times*, March 27, 2012.

42   John Komlos, "How Raising Taxes on the Rich Could Prevent Mass Shootings," *PBS Newshour*, September 2, 2015. www.pbs.org/newshour/making-sense/face-mass-murders-case-universal-mental-health-insurance/.

43   Joseph Stiglitz, "Information and the Change in the Paradigm in Economics," *American Economic Review* 92 (2002), 3: 460–501.

44   Gregory Mankiw, *Principles of Economics*, 8th edn. (Cengage, 2018), p. 9.

45   Bruce Greenwald and Joseph Stiglitz, "Externalities in Economies with Imperfect Information and Incomplete Markets," *Quarterly Journal of Economics* 101 (1986): 229–264.

46   Joseph Stiglitz, *The Price of Inequality* (Norton, 2012), p. 112.

47   He maintains his mansion in Greenwich, CT, with annual taxes of $70,000. Justin Baer and Gregory Zuckerman, "Branded a Villain, Lehman's Dick Fuld Chases Redemption," *The Wall Street Journal*, September 6, 2018. See also: Celebrity Net Worth, "Richard Fuld Net Worth." www.celebritynetworth.com/richest-businessmen/wall-street/richard-fuld-net-worth/.

48   Peter Whybrow, *The Well-Tuned Brain: The Remedy for a Manic Society* (Norton & Company, 2016).

49   He was fined $67 million for fraud, but Bank of America paid for it since it took over his bank. Gretchen Morgenson, "Lending Magnate Settles Fraud Case," *The New York Times*, October 15, 2010.

50   Celebrity Net Worth, "Angelo Mozilo," "Richard Fuld," "John Thain," and "James Cayne." Dennis Hevesi, "Roland Arnall, Mortgage Innovator, Dies at 68," *The New York Times*, March 18, 2008.

51   Some 140 banks failed in 2009 and another 157 in 2010. Wikipedia, "List of Bank Failures in the United States (2008–Present)."

52   *Fortune* Editors, "The Biggest Business Scandals of 2020," *Fortune*, December 27, 2020 is an annual column.

53   Stephen LeRoy, "Is the 'Invisible Hand' Still Relevant?" *FRBSF Economic Letter* no. 14, May 3, 2010.

54   David Brooks, "Why Our Elites Stink," *The New York Times*, July 12, 2012.

55   Gretchen Morgenson, "How Countrywide Covered the Cracks," *The New York Times*, October 16, 2010.

56   "Celebrity Net Worth." Wikipedia, "Angelo Mozilo," Condé Nast Portfolio ranked Mozilo second on their list of "Worst American CEOs of All Time."

57   The Act protects consumers in a myriad of ways from the chicanery of credit card companies. One example:
     Requires a card issuer, upon receipt of payment, to apply amounts in excess of the minimum payment amount first to the balance bearing the highest rate of interest, and then to each successive balance bearing the next highest rate of interest, until the payment is exhausted.
                          (U.S. Congress, House, *Credit Card Act of 2009*, HR 627, 111th Congress,
                                                      1st session, January 6, 2009)

58   James Kwak, "When a 79.9% APR Is Good?" *The Baseline Scenario*, January 8, 2010. Deceptive practices are not efficient, because they enrich some at the expense of others without their consent.

59   Hannah Rounds, "Average Household Credit Card Debt in America: 2017 Statistics." www.magnifymoney.com/blog/news/u-s-credit-card-debt-by-the-numbers628618371.

60   Board of Governors of the Federal Reserve System, "Report to the Congress on the Profitability of Credit Card Operations of Depository Institutions," July 2019.

61   Vance Packard, *The Naked Society* (David McKay, 1964).

62   Shirley Lee and Avis Mysyk, "The Medicalization of Compulsive Buying," *Social Science and Medicine* 58 (2004), 9: 1709–1718.

63   Whybrow, *The Well-Tuned Brain*, op. cit.

64   Warner, "Dysregulation Nation." op. cit.

65   Wikipedia, "Erich Fromm."

66   Ibid.

67   Peter Whybrow, *Get Satisfied: How Twenty People Like You Found the Satisfaction of Enough* (Easton Studio Press, 2007).

68   Erich Fromm, "Homo Consumens," YouTube video, posted by "Q&A projects," www.youtube.com/watch?v=VeaWHrFrXFO.

69   Mike Wallace interview: Erich Fromm, May 25, 1958.

70   Ibid.

71   Ibid.

72   John Komlos, "Another Road to Serfdom," *Challenge: The Magazine of Economic Affairs*, 59 (2016), 6: 491–518.

73   Roger McNamee, *Zucked: Waking Up to the Facebook Catastrophe* (Penguin Press, 2019); Jonathan Tepper and Denise Hearn, *The Myth of Capitalism: Monopolies and the Death of Competition* (Wiley, 2018).

74   "Barry Schwartz: The Paradox of Choice," YouTube video, 20:23, posted by "TEDtalksDirector," January 16, 2007.

75   Elisabeth Leamy, "Generic vs. Brand-Name Gas: Are They Different?" *ABC News Good Morning America*, March 24, 2007.

76   Ernst Schumacher, *Small Is Beautiful: Economics as if People Mattered* (Harper Torchbook, 1973).

77   Paul Rogers, "The Cognitive Psychology of Lottery Gambling: A Theoretical Review," *Journal of Gambling Studies* 14 (1998), 2: 111–134.

78   William Dickens, "Cognitive Ability," in Steven Durlauf and Lawrence Blume (eds), *The New Palgrave Dictionary of Economics*, 2nd edn. (Palgrave Macmillan, 2008).

79   A fine of $210 million was levied on Capitol One. Ben Protess, and Jessica Silver-Greenberg, "Consumer Watchdog Fines Capital One for Deceptive Credit Card Practices," *The New York Times*, July 18, 2012.

80   Elizabeth Warren, "Fighting to Protect Consumers," The White House Blog, September 17, 2010.

81   Arthur Robson, "The Biological Basis of Economic Behavior," *Journal of Economic Literature* 29 (2001): 11–33; Aysu Okbay et al., "Genome-Wide Association Study Identifies 74 Loci Associated with Educational Attainment," *Nature* 533 (2016): 539–542.

82   Paul Taubman, "The Determinants of Earnings: Genetics, Family, and Other Environments: A Study of White Male Twins," *American Economic Review* 66 (1976), 5: 858–870.

83   Daniel Benjamin et al., "The Promises and Pitfalls of Genoeconomics," *Annual Review of Economics* 4 (July 2012): 627–662; Daniel Barth et al., "Genetic Endowments and Wealth Inequality," *Journal of Political Economy* 128 (2020), 4: 1474–1522.

84   Michael Zyphur et al., "The Genetics of Economic Risk Preferences," *Journal of Behavioral Decision Making* 22 (2009): 367–377.

85   Deirdre Barrett, *Supernormal Stimuli: How Primal Urges Overran Their Evolutionary Purpose* (Norton, 2010); Terence Burnham, "High-Testosterone Men Reject Low Ultimatum Game Offers," *Proceedings of the Royal Society B* 274 (2007), 1623: 2327–2330.

86   William Dickens, "Behavioural Genetics," in Steven Durlauf and Lawrence Blume (eds), *The New Palgrave Dictionary of Economics*, 2nd edn. (Palgrave Macmillan, 2008). Guang Guo et al., "The Integration of Genetic Propensities into Social-Control Models of Delinquency and Violence Among Male Youths," *American Sociological Review* 73 (2008), 4: 543–568.

87   Jonathan Beauchamp et al., "Molecular Genetics and Economics," *Journal of Economic Perspectives* 25 (2011), 4: 1–27.

88 Jere Behrman and Paul Taubman, "Is Schooling 'Mostly in the Genes'? Nature-Nurture Decomposition Using Data on Relatives," *Journal of Political Economy* 97 (1989), 6: 1425–1446; David Cesarini et al., "Genetic Variation in Preferences for Giving and Risk Taking," *The Quarterly Journal of Economics* 124 (2009), 2: 809–842.

89 Whybrow, *American Mania*, op. cit., p. 57.

90 Edward Wilson, "Evolution and Our Inner Conflict," *The New York Times*, June 24, 2012; Edward Wilson, *The Social Conquest of Earth* (Norton, 2012).

91 Daniel Serra, "Decision-Making: From Neuroscience to Neuroeconomics," *Theory and Decision* (2021), 91: 1–80.

92 John Dickhaut et al., "The Impact of the Certainty Context on the Process of Choice," *Proceedings of the National Academy of Sciences of the United States of America* 100 (2003): 3536–3541.

93 Colin Camerer et al., "Neuroeconomics: How Neuroscience Can Inform Economics," *Journal of Economic Literature* 43 (2005), 1: 9–64.

94 Serra, "Decision-Making," op. cit., p. 62.

95 Ibid.

4 *Homo Oeconomicus* Is Extinct
The Foundations of Behavioral Economics

I see the Right, and I Approve it too,
Condemn the Wrong—and yet the Wrong Pursue.
—Ovid[1]

Economists' gravest mistake is clinging obstinately to a fictional rational species called *homo oeconomicus*, although psychologists are unanimous in asserting that it has nothing to do with *homo sapiens*.[2] Psychologists should know since they study the human mind with experiments. In this chapter we abandon this one-dimensional caricature of human beings and stress, instead, the importance of discarding the rational-agent utility-maximizing model. We proceed by examining the mind of real flesh-and-blood people and demonstrate some of their biases.[3] We also explore the importance of *intuition, emotion, and status seeking* in economic behavior.[4]

4.1 Utility Maximization Is Anachronistic Economics

The conventional assumption is that people are rational, know their self-interest, and therefore maximize their utility, subject to their budget constraint.[5] Rational choice is the use of reasoning to achieve optimal ends in an objective manner logically, without emotion, reflex, habit, intuition, instinct, the subconscious, or conditioning. Thus, on the blackboard, consumers obtain the most satisfaction possible from the money they spend.

However, maximization in the real world is not a cinch because: (1) consumers must have *perfect knowledge* of the attributes of all goods and cannot be confused about the quality of the products offered; they understand completely the legal implications of the fine print in contracts; (2) they must *know their own utility function*—so they can arrange all goods in order of their preference; they must know which goods will yield more utility and what is best for them; this sounds easy but it isn't in the presence of incomplete information, uncertainty or in sequential decisions, especially if the impact of the decision is in the distant future; (3) they should not choose randomly: their *preferences must be stable*; they must choose with reason, thinking through their needs and wants, with full knowledge of prices and quantities they desire; emotion should not overwhelm their ability to reason; and (4) their preferences must be consistent; *transitivity* requires that: (a) if they like hamburgers more than hot dogs, and (b) hot dogs more than grilled cheese sandwiches, then, transitivity requires that (c) they like hamburgers more than grilled cheese sandwiches. Whether they like hamburgers more than hot dogs, and hot

DOI: 10.4324/9781003174356-4

Illustration 4.1 Virginia Slims' successful marketing appealed to feminists by combining imagery
of glamour, freedom, independence, emancipation, empowerment, slimness, and
attractiveness. It increased smoking among teenage girls and killed hundreds of
thousands of women. The message was designed to bypass the prefrontal cortex
Credit: From the Collection of Stanford Research into the Impact of Tobacco Advertising (tobacco.stanford.edu).

dogs more than grilled cheese sandwiches is up to them. But once these two statements hold,
the third statement is not up to them: rationality requires that they like hamburgers more than
grilled cheese sandwiches; (5) based on these premises, consumers can maximize their utility,
i.e., do what is the very best for them.

The reasons behind these conditions are understandable: consumers must know the quality and prices of all goods to make a reasoned choice. With *imperfect information*, they could
not maximize their utility. The above assumptions are popular, because of their simplicity, and
many eloquent mathematical models follow from them on the blackboard. An economy in which
consumers maximize their utility and firms produce under perfect competition is efficient and
inhabited by happy consumers whose needs are satisfied, provided there are no negative externalities like pollution. In addition, such an imaginary economy is politically desirable since it is
democratic: everyone produces and consumes as they please and ideologically accentuates
freedom of choice and methodological individualism. Consequently, the privileged also support neoliberal economics financially since it accepts their dominant position in society. So why
would we intervene in consumers' choices? Why should the government care how consumers
spend their money?

While these assumptions work well on blackboards, they are inappropriate in the real world
because:

1.   Consumers cannot possibly know most of the prices and quality of goods in an economy;
     so imperfect information prevails which requires *judgment*.

2. Consumers do not always know what they want: they are often conflicted and uncertain about their choice; this is different than being indifferent, which means that they like one thing as much as another. *Uncertainty* means that consumers can vacillate, not knowing what to choose; this is especially true for goods with multidimensional characteristics like safety, speed of delivery, convenience, or aesthetic appeal; consumers can become catatonic in such cases.

3. To recognize one's self-interest in a complex world is not obvious. It takes much learning, self-knowledge gained through observation, introspection, experience, and self-control to choose wisely. Humans are not automatons. They have to acquire consumption skills and to make decisions without all the necessary information using their own judgment. Under real-life circumstances, preferences can become unstable.

4. Transitivity does not always hold because people can be inconsistent. Faced with a choice between x and y, people sometimes choose x and sometimes choose y. This is *preference reversal:* "such inconsistencies are observed even in the absence of systematic changes in the decision maker's taste which might be due to learning … therefore the observed inconsistencies reflect inherent variability or momentary fluctuation in the evaluative process."[6] Given these obstacles, maximization is not possible for mortals.

There is an additional problem associated with *Arrow's impossibility theorem*, according to which, preferences cannot be aggregated in a consistent way within a group or a society. A unique procedure does not exist that would create a consistent aggregate demand curve. This is an essential challenge to the supply and demand analysis of conventional economics and is a fundamental problem in welfare economics and social choice theory.[7] For example, suppose the family has three members, Jack, Jill, and Joan. Jack prefers oranges to apples to grapes (Oranges>Apples>Grapes) while Jill's preferences are: Apples>Grapes>Oranges, and Joan's are Grapes>Oranges>Apples. What is the preferred ordering for this group? There isn't one: Jack and Joan like oranges more than apples, Jack and Jill like apples more than grapes, while Jill and Joan like grapes more than oranges. So, there is no majority for any of the three items: 2 prefer oranges, 2 apples, and 2 grapes. Absent an authority, Arrow proved that there is no way out of this dilemma.

However, textbook examples are always super-simple and never involve decisions with real uncertainty, deception, power, imperfect information, ambiguity, vagueness, or the possibility of manipulation. Textbook examples never require judgment because they are limited to choices between two straightforward alternatives: a single decision among well-known generic goods without a time dimension and without qualities like reliability, safety, durability, or attractiveness. Surely, you know if you prefer hot dogs to grilled cheese sandwiches at the prevailing price. Then a self-interested consumer should be able to choose satisfactorily without confusion. However, our wants and needs are at times fuzzy.[8] Real people are unsure, hesitate, and must decide within a time constraint. That's not a snap. Besides, typical consumers are puzzled with complex products and might not know if they should buy a condominium now, or a house, or wait until a more opportune time, and instead look for an apartment to rent.

Hence, the textbook "no brainers" are deceptive: they conceal that the manner in which simple decisions are made are not generalizable to complex ones that require a sequence of decisions, or involve judgment, real uncertainty, or emotions, and if the quality of the product is difficult to ascertain. That was precisely Greenspan's mistake. He followed Econ-101 logic and thought that selling mortgage-backed securities was like selling cereal and did not need government oversight (see Chapter 14). Applying the perfectly competitive model to the financial system was careless thinking.

Actually, he was irresponsible, because contrary to Econ-101, all real markets (as opposed to imaginary ones) need government oversight to various degrees. Even the cereal market is governed by regulations of the Food and Drug Administration.[9] Thus, decisions pertaining to complex products like mortgages, insurance, cell phone contracts, apartment leases, and investments are qualitatively different from buying generic products.[10] Generalizing from simple examples to complex ones is a major shortcoming of conventional economics with unfortunate consequences for consumers' welfare. The fantasy world of *homo oeconomicus* is odious because it implies that consumer protection is superfluous, thereby thwarting many consumers' ability to navigate smoothly through an extremely complex economy. Without protection too many consumers fall prey to unscrupulous marketing techniques as we witnessed with the predatory lending practices prior to the Meltdown of 2008.[11]

4.2 Optimization Is Impossible for Humans

Every psychologist knows that human beings are not always rational and are incapable of maximizing their utility in a coherent manner.[12] Nobel Prize-winning economist, Amartya Sen, discredited *homo oeconomicus* by arguing that "the purely economic man is indeed close to being a social moron."[13]

The human brain has many limitations and biases. We are often unaware of why we desire something, as the reasons are hidden from our conscious thought processes or are rooted in evolutionary physiology. Our attention span is limited, we experience information overload, become impatient, or act impulsively. Moreover, the human brain has great difficulty processing information involving the calculation of probabilities: we do not understand the laws of probability. Often there is insufficient time to think about decisions carefully, i.e., to sort out the relevant information from irrelevant ones and to assess the reliability of the information. These are some reasons why reaching an optimum decision continues to elude us and explains why we frequently make mistakes and regret the decisions we have made.

Most decisions require human judgment under conditions of radical uncertainty: "the important events that animate life are rare and fundamentally unpredictable."[14] Real uncertainty, when the probability of future outcomes is unknowable poses a formidable challenge to rational decision-making. Hence, few of our decisions are rational. They are guided mostly by our unconscious mind, by wishful thinking, faith, intuition, emotion, or are based on judgment. The subprime mortgage crisis demonstrated how much harm results if people misunderstand and misprice risk.

4.3 The Imperfections of the Human Brain

None of our body components is perfect. Do we see as well as an eagle, or smell as well as a dog? The human brain is also imperfect.[15] It is a product of evolution, as are all other organs, and evolution does not produce perfection. Evolution did not eliminate either the "blind spot" in our eyes or color blindness. Good enough to survive and reproduce is good enough for evolution. Evolution did not make us into Superman and Superwoman, as academic economists imply.

Our brain is much more complex than economists admit. It is made up of many specialized modules, which sometimes work together well but at other times hold contradictory beliefs, vacillate between polar opposites, and violate strongly held moral beliefs.[16]

> The human brain is a hybrid: an evolved hierarchy of three-brains-in-one. We have a reptilian "lizard" brain, which controls our bodily functions like our breathing and heart muscles. Around this primitive core developed ... the limbic cortex ... the early mammalian brain, which is the root of kinship behavior and nurturance.[17]

The expansion of this part of the brain culminated in the development of our species' unique prefrontal lobes, where reasoning takes place. It makes reasoning possible, but that does not imply that it is in control all the time.

If the process of making choices in our self-interest were easy, our society would not be in such disarray (see Chapter 2). There would not be so many who are discontented with their lives, struggling, unhappy, depressed, addicted, dependent on antidepressants, wantonly killing people, or behind bars. If this is the best we can do maximizing utility, our brain must not be such a reliable guide to action.

Our hormones, genetic make-up, nervous system all stand in the way of making rational decisions:

> [W]e remain driven by our ancient desires. Desire is as vital as breathing ... [but] when the brain's reward circuits are overloaded or unconstrained, then desire can turn to craving and to an addictive greed that co-opts executive analysis and common sense.[18]

Thus, the prefrontal cortex is not always in control. Our craving for sweets, for instance, provided an evolutionary advantage millennia ago when calories were scarce. But evolution did not provide hormones to switch off such desires, because that was unnecessary in the past characterized by endemic food shortages. Thus, when combined with advertisements of corporations seeking revenue from selling sweet drinks and food, our uncontrollable cravings induce a diabetic epidemic. That is why two-thirds of the US population became overweight or obese. This highlights the absurdity of the rational agent utility-maximizing model and its real-world consequences. The belief in that model leaves consumers unprotected against powerful corporations and leads to widespread health problems. Thus, human beings have not become optimal decision-makers through evolution. It is not useful to consider rationality as a binary characteristic: "Human behavior ... requires a fluid interaction between controlled and automatic processes ... We naturally tend to exaggerate the importance of control."[19]

4.4 Bounded Rationality Should Be the Default Model

More than half a century ago, Nobelist Herbert Simon demonstrated the limits of rationality: *utility maximization is impossible* for human beings. Yet, economics textbooks ignore the universally recognized principle that "psychology and economics provide wide-ranging *evidence* that bounded rationality is important."[20] Actually, it should be the default model in economics, because "[b]ehaviour cannot be invented in the armchair."[21]

The utility function is an abstraction; it does not really exist, as does our ability to feel temperature. Being unable to optimize an imaginary utility function does not mean that we are incompetent, but a computer-like calculation is beyond the brain's capability. Off the blackboard, the human mind has extensive limitations that prevent it from attaining optimum ends, including imperfect information of a product's price and quality, limited intelligence to understand nuances in contracts, unknown probabilities of future events, limited attention spans, lapses in memory, being distracted by irrelevant issues, forgetting to ask relevant questions, being unreasonably trusting, being subject to peer pressure, flaws in reasoning due to habit, jumping to illogical conclusions, information overload, misinterpreting evidence, emotions interfering with logical thinking, or being misled by shrewd counterparties. If we are harried or under stress, we may not be able to concentrate on understanding crucial properties of a product or the nuances of a contract. All this can lead to confusion, misinterpretation, or misjudgment, far from an optimum decision.[22] The causes of bounded rationality are innumerable; moreover, sequential decisions—like planning for a career—are infinitely more complicated than a single decision.

Consumers never have complete information in making complicated decisions. Generating information about alternatives and understanding them form a lengthy process requiring time, money, patience, effort, and perseverance. Because of these formidable obstacles called *transactions costs*, reaching an optimum decision remains a pipedream. Choice in today's complex economy is like solving an intricate puzzle. Buying health insurance, obtaining a mortgage, or negotiating a labor contract are not comparable to the no-brainer examples in textbooks, particularly if the counterparty hides crucial conditions in small print using obscure legal terms. Complex choices involve a problem-solving process requiring intelligence and human judgment. With limited cognitive capacity, the human mind is incapable of reaching the optimum in finite time. This problem burdens poor people excessively, because they lack the resources to do extensive searching and lack the social networks to help them.

Furthermore, companies increase the cognitive burden by limiting transparency with extremely complicated offers structured differently from competitors so that comparison becomes impractical. Their strategy, designed by psychologists, works because its opaqueness softens competition and limits the possibility of making an informed rational decision. In such cases, consumers generally use a *rule of thumb* to decide.[23]

Mega-corporations devote considerable money to outsmart consumers who have limited time to solve a complicated problem. In contrast, insurance companies hire an army of full-time math wizards and psychologists to construct the most effective way to take advantage of the customers' cognitive limitations. In short, corporations have the upper hand and can outmaneuver consumers as they have much more resources at their disposal to create a market structure to their benefit. That means power to manipulate consumers.

Consider the drug plans offered for Medicare Part D (Figure 4.1). No mortal could ascertain which plan is best. Under such circumstances one must simplify using a rule of thumb: "I'll take the most expensive policy" or "I'll choose as my friend suggested." Insurance companies make the offer in this obscure manner to make it difficult to understand the details so that competition would not eliminate their profit.[24]

4.5 Satisficing Is More Realistic than Optimizing

In the mid-1950s, Herbert Simon demonstrated that people search for a satisfactory solution to their problem instead of the best possible solution—because that is unattainable.[25] This method of making decisions is called *satisficing*. Given the brain's limitations in processing information,

	AARP MedicareRx Preferred (PDP) (S5820-007-0)							
	Estimated Annual Drug Costs: [?]	Monthly Premium: [?]	Deductibles: [?] and Drug Copay/ Coinsurance: [?]	Drug Restrictions: [?]	Drug Coverage: [?]	Estimated Annual Health and Drug Costs: [?]	Overall Plan Rating: [?]	
☐	$1,670	$33.40 Drug: $33.40 Health: N/A	Annual Drug Deductible: $0.00 Health Plan Deductible: N/A Drug Copay/ Coinsurance: $7 - $81, 33%	N/A	All Your Drugs on Formulary: N/A No Gap Coverage	$4,800 Includes $3,138 for Original Medicare	★ ★ ★ ✦ 3.5 out of 5 stars	Enroll

	First Health Part D Premier (PDP) (S5768-039-0)							
	Estimated Annual Drug Costs: [?]	Monthly Premium: [?]	Deductibles: [?] and Drug Copay/ Coinsurance: [?]	Drug Restrictions: [?]	Drug Coverage: [?]	Estimated Annual Health and Drug Costs: [?]	Overall Plan Rating: [?]	
☐	$1,752	$37.00 Drug: $37.00 Health: N/A	Annual Drug Deductible: $150.00 Health Plan Deductible: N/A Drug Copay/ Coinsurance: $10, 15% - 32%	N/A	All Your Drugs on Formulary: N/A No Gap Coverage	$4,900 Includes $3,138 for Original Medicare	★ ★ ★ ✦ 3.5 out of 5 stars	Enroll

	Humana Enhanced (PDP) (S5884-066-0)							
	Estimated Annual Drug Costs: [?]	Monthly Premium: [?]	Deductibles: [?] and Drug Copay/ Coinsurance: [?]	Drug Restrictions: [?]	Drug Coverage: [?]	Estimated Annual Health and Drug Costs: [?]	Overall Plan Rating: [?]	
☐	$1,807	$46.00 Drug: $46.00 Health: N/A	Annual Drug Deductible: $0.00 Health Plan Deductible: N/A Drug Copay/ Coinsurance: $7 - $74, 33%	N/A	All Your Drugs on Formulary: N/A Call plan for details	$4,950 Includes $3,138 for Original Medicare	★ ★ ★ 3 out of 5 stars	Enroll

Figure 4.1 Medicare Part D options confuse

the constraints of time and of finances, the harried lives we live, the large amount of information needed for a reasoned decision, and the complexity of the problems to be solved, we are content with finding a good-enough solution (given our level of aspiration). Given bounded rationality, trying to reach the optimum is impossible and it would get us bogged down in everyday life, frustrate us, and lead to paralysis. Hence, satisficing is much more realistic than the utility-maximizing model.[26]

A critical consequence of the satisficing model is that the sequence in which choices are made in real time influences the outcome, whereas in the maximizing model with perfect information it does not. Let us consider the two models in a thought experiment. The choice at a supermarket is not between two items, as in the textbooks, but among 25,000 items, and our cognitive capacity fails to handle that amount of information. Hence, upon entering the store, customers know neither all the goods being offered for sale nor their prices, thereby violating a basic precondition of optimization. Hence, maximization is unrealistic, and we resort to shortcuts to accomplish our goals: we satisfice, meaning, we seek an acceptable solution to alleviate hunger.

We choose an aisle and the products come into view sequentially. Our early choices influence our subsequent decisions. We might see some fried chicken in the deli department and buy some for dinner. Yet, if we see pizza on sale subsequently, we will not buy it, because it would take too much effort to return the chicken to the deli section. Social norms prevent us from leaving the chicken fingers in the pizza section and take the pizza instead. However, if we had chosen the pizza aisle first, we would have bought it instead of the chicken. In short, we were not confronted with a fixed set of alternatives as we entered. We had to search in real time and space, and we did succeed in satisfying our goal of buying something for dinner.

We satisficed rather than optimized, because with the limited time, effort, and information available, our choice for dinner was influenced by the happenstance of choosing one aisle of the supermarket instead of another, and it was not easily reversable.[27] Moreover, it would have been too time-consuming to first find all the available alternatives before making a choice. In the presence of transaction costs associated with searching with a time constraint, we were unable to choose the best possible dinner, but we did buy a good-enough dinner.

In other words, an optimum decision is a snap in a classroom but not in real-world situations when transaction costs are associated with searching and the choice entails a sequence of decisions under uncertainty with limited information. Although this is a common problem for real human beings, such examples are missing from textbooks. The concept of satisficing is anathema to mainstream economists because it contradicts the eloquent theorems of neoclassical economics. It does not conform to models of optimization by rational fully-informed economic agents with perfect foresight.

4.6 Biases and Wonders of Intuition

Behavioral economists Daniel Kahneman, Amos Tversky, and Richard Thaler superseded bounded rationality by demonstrating *decades ago* that intuition plays a major role in our thinking, and that the rational part of the brain is not in complete control of our actions. In other words, the prefrontal cortex supervises our intuitive decisions lightly.[28] They call this way of thinking *System 1* (intuition) and *System 2* (reasoning).[29] Thoughts that originate in System 1 are fast, spontaneous, automatic, effortless, associative, impulsive, and difficult to control or modify. They are not voluntary and include biases that lead to systematic mistakes.[30] In contrast, operations of System 2 are slow, deliberate, conscious, flexible, rule-based, effortful, and analytic.

Faced with many unknowns in evolutionary time, humans were selected for the ability to make split-second decisions automatically without deliberate thinking.[31] In ambiguous situations the ability of the brain to make decisions spontaneously with limited information was useful for survival. So, humans adapted the ability to take advantage of intuitive thinking. This ability is still useful because we often must make quick judgments to reduce the heavy load of solving problems with incomplete information in an uncertain environment without becoming catatonic.

The brain also has difficulties assessing probabilities accurately. Other limitations include having insufficient self-control, we can become confused, and prioritize the present without giving the future sufficient consideration. What 20-year-old thinks seriously about her retirement income? Our genetic disposition, including our instinct for survival and our potent sex drive, also often override our rational self. In sum, psychological experiments suggest that human beings are incapable of being consistently coherent, rational, and exercising perfect self-control.

Real-life problems differ from exam questions, because for the latter we know that a solution exists, whereas for real-life problems that is not true. "People are not accustomed to thinking hard, and are often content to trust a plausible judgment that comes to mind."[32] In such cases, System 1 at least provides a tolerable solution, even if it is frequently erroneous.

Thus, choices are not necessarily an outcome of reasoning; rather, intuition frequently plays an essential role. We habitually rely on System 1's plausible judgments, which are prone to systematic error, and System 2 is incapable of monitoring it properly or overriding its judgments: *System 2 supervises System 1 only lightly.*

Ignoring behavioral economics makes mainstream economics textbooks anachronistic: *homo sapiens* are incapable of maximizing an imaginary utility function. They are susceptible to errors in judgment especially in decisions involving real uncertainty, when the probability distribution of the occurrence of an event is unknowable.[33]

4.7 Heuristics Help Avoid Becoming Catatonic

Computationally convoluted complex decisions with limited information are daunting and, with limited time, overload System 2. Should I quit my current job and look for a better one? In cases of radical uncertainty people rely on *heuristics*—rules of thumb—to decide. That ability provided an evolutionary advantage: becoming catatonic could have become fatal. So, we learned to substitute a related, but easier, problem for the inaccessible one, called *attribute substitution*. The mind makes an information-processing shortcut—an intuitive judgment overcomes ambiguity.

The substituted problem is easily accessible, perhaps because of prior experience. One solves a problem one is capable of solving. Evolution did not favor those who became stuck on a problem. The substitution is done intuitively, so we are unaware of it, since System 2 is not in control. The use of heuristics is one of the many sources of cognitive biases. Thus, rationality is frequently beyond the reach of mortals.[34]

4.8 Three Biases of the Human Mind: Framing, Accessibility, and Anchoring

We do not always react identically to the same information. *Our choices depend critically on how the options are presented or "framed."* Framing effects are important in how the unconscious mind reacts to a situation. Emotionally, it makes a difference if we hear that out of 100 people 90 survive a medical operation, or if we learn that 10 out of 100 die. The information is identical, but the emotional response varies, depending on whether we focus on surviving or dying. This is not rational but emotional. Framing effects would not affect *homo oeconomicus*.

Framing can lead to illogical preference reversals.[35] This is important in consumer behavior because it implies that decisions depend on how choices are presented. Preference reversals, associated with words with emotional content like loss or gain, contradict the consistency requirement of rationality. Of course, marketers know this and frame their advertisements by relentlessly circumventing System 2. It also implies that humans can be manipulated by targeting their emotion. Since Americans watch 2-3 hours of TV daily[36] and spend two hours on the internet, Madison Avenue has abundant opportunities to suppress System 2, and influence our subconscious. Neuromarketers are studying psychological engineering to influence us more effectively.[37]

Behavioral economists have documented through decades of experimenting that the reasons we are prone to logical fallacies is that *intuition overrides the rules of logic*. For instance, people are willing to pay more for a life insurance policy that pays in case of terrorist attack while traveling than for one that pays in case of death from any cause, although it is clear upon reflection that the probability of the second scenario exceeds that of the first: it pays in case of death from terrorist attack and from other causes. However, framing the offer in terms of terrorism triggers emotions that lead to ignoring basic principles of probability. Thus, the threat from a low-probability event, like a terrorist attack, is disproportionally magnified whereas the threat from a higher-probability event is attenuated.

For another example, consider the following description of a person: "Linda is 31 years old, single, outspoken, and very bright. She majored in philosophy. As a student, she was deeply concerned with issues of discrimination and social justice, and also participated in anti-nuclear demonstrations." Almost everyone rated the probability that "Linda is a bank teller and is active in the feminist movement" higher than the probability that "Linda is a bank teller."[38] This "conjunction fallacy" occurs because we intuitively *anchor* our thoughts on Linda's feminism and its significance is magnified out of proportion. The focus on this attribute draws attention away from the obvious fact that if she is a feminist bank teller, she must be a bank teller as well, i.e., the probability that she is a feminist bank teller cannot exceed the probability that she is a bank teller.

Additionally, some attributes of objects are more *accessible* than others. The average length of lines in Figure 4.2 is determined instantaneously by our perceptual system, because the average is a *"natural assessment."* However, the sum of the length of those lines is not similarly accessible instantaneously. We need effort to compute it using System 2. It is not a natural assessment.

Furthermore, *context affects accessibility*. What do you see in Figure 4.3a? The middle object looks like the letter B. Now consider Figure 4.3b. Most people see 13. Because the context differs, our perceptual system interprets the same ambiguous middle object differently. The

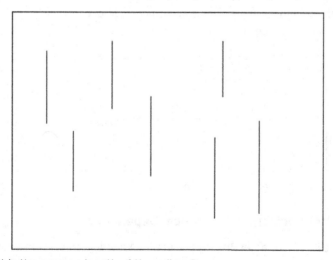

Figure 4.2 What is the average length of these lines?

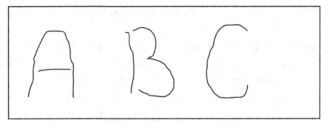

Figure 4.3a (a) Context matters in case of ambiguity

surroundings help the mind to overcome ambiguity. This psychological principle is important in judging the quality of products and is generally exploited by the advertising industry. It makes people vulnerable to manipulation. In contrast, *homo oeconomicus* is not vulnerable to ambiguity and cannot be manipulated.

For instance, if buying a car, we immediately see the condition of the outside. However, the attributes of its engine and performance are not immediately ascertainable. It takes deliberate effort to assess them. Knowing that appearance and context matter, car advertisements often sway consumers' emotions using images of power, sex, and celebrities to divert our attention away from other attributes. These natural assessments are registered automatically in the perceptual system without our consciously thinking about it, that is, without intention or effort. The use of anchoring and framing in advertisements is prevalent.

Preferences are affected by irrelevant features of advertisements, like attractive models standing next to a car. The enticing image is easily accessible and is unconsciously associated with the automobile without our being aware of it. Accordingly, Madison Avenue attempts to shift the decision from a rational one to an emotional one. This also contradicts the rational-agent model because *homo oeconomicus* would not be affected by irrelevant features like a celebrity promoting a product.

Anchoring occurs when people focus and rely on some information more than appropriate in making decisions and consequently overlook other important aspects. That is how "teaser rates" manipulated people to sign mortgages they did not completely understand. By stressing low initial mortgage rates, customers' perception of the risks of variable rates were reduced. Mortgage brokers used anchoring extensively in the predatory lending schemes that contributed to the subprime mortgage crisis.[39]

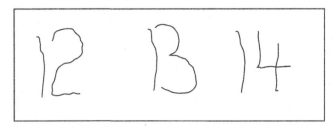

Figure 4.3b (b) Context matters in case of ambiguity

4.9 The Utility Function Is Reference-Dependent

Are changes or levels more accessible to our brain? According to conventional theory, utility is determined by the *amount* (level) of consumption. To *homo oeconomicus* a given amount of cereal induces a certain amount of satisfaction, regardless of prior levels of cereal consumption.

A weekly salary of $1,000 yields a certain level of satisfaction in *homo oeconomicus* regardless of what its salary was last week. Period. The accustomed level of income or consumption is inconsequential. The social norm and others' consumption are also irrelevant.

However, this presumption is clearly false, being incompatible with human psychology. Experiments reveal that our valuation of something depends on a reference value (basic needs excluded). The satisfaction generated by the absolute magnitude (level) of wealth, income, or consumption is much more difficult for humans to evaluate than changes in those variables. The brain can gage changes easier than levels because we become accustomed to current levels of consumption (adapted). Thus, *perception is reference-dependent* because the reference level is the measuring scale. Hence, the *utility function of real people is interdependent*, i.e., a person's utility depends on the consumption of others as well as on prior levels of consumption.[40] However, the utility function of *homo oeconomicus* is independent of everyone else's consumption.[41]

To demonstrate the significance of *relative incomes*, consider first the conventional approach. The expected utility function of a *risk-averse* individual is concave (Figure 4.4). Consider two possible outcomes, A and B with equal probability. Suppose $A = \$0$, $B = \$100$. Then the expected value of the *gamble* is:

$$E(C) = \tfrac{1}{2}B + \tfrac{1}{2}A = \$50$$

on the x-axis, and the expected level of utility is

$$\tfrac{1}{2}U(B) + \tfrac{1}{2}U(A)$$

on the y-axis.

In contrast, suppose income is $C = \$50$ with *certainty*. Notice that U(C) (the utility of $50) with certainty exceeds the gamble's expected utility although its expected value is also $50. For a risk-averse individual the gamble provides less utility because it is uncertain:

$$U(C) > \tfrac{1}{2}[U(B)+U(A)]$$

although on average:

$$C = \$50 = E(C) = \tfrac{1}{2}(B+A) \text{ in both scenarios}$$

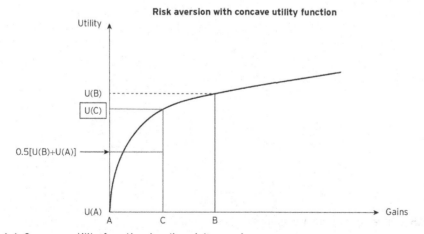

Figure 4.4 Concave utility function implies risk aversion

Consequently, the stress associated with not knowing if income will be $0 or $100 detracts from utility. This is the logic behind insurance markets. People are willing to pay to avoid uncertain outcomes. To reiterate, $50 with certainty generates more utility than a gamble whose expected value is also $50.

In contrast, the utility function of a *risk-seeking* individual is *convex* (Figure 4.5). The gamble in this case is the same as above, except now this person enjoys the excitement associated with risk. Consequently, in this case, the utility of the gamble exceeds that of C with certainty:

$$U(C) < \tfrac{1}{2}U(B) + \tfrac{1}{2}U(A)$$

For this person, an income of $50 with certainty is less attractive than a gamble whose expected value is $50 (Figure 4.5). This person would not buy insurance. However, most people are risk averse and not risk seeking.

The importance of the distinction between levels and changes in income or wealth is illustrated by the following example. Suppose Cathy learns that her investment of $4 million declined in value to $3 million. In contrast, Susan learns that her wealth increased from $1 million to $1.1 million. Who is happier? According to conventional analysis, Cathy is happier, because her level of wealth still exceeds Susan's wealth (Figure 4.6). So, if Cathy were of the specie *homo oeconomicus*, her utility level would be higher since the utility of $3 million exceeds that of $1.1 million. However, that does not adequately reveal the emotions generated in human beings after losing $1 million or after gaining 0.1 million dollars.[42] Hence, the conventional analysis contradicts common sense: obviously, Susan is happier. Humans differ from *homo oeconomicus*: they have feelings. So, Cathy's loss makes her feel miserable, whereas Susan's gain makes her jubilant. This illustrates the reference dependence of the utility function.

4.10 Prospect Theory Is the Future Foundation of Economics

Prospect theory reformulates the above problem in terms of gains and losses (Figure 4.7). Instead of the one-quadrant models above, the utility function of prospect theory consists of two quadrants (quadrants 2 and 4 are disregarded).[43] Moving along the x-axis to the right of the origin is considered a gain in dollars and moving up along the y-axis is considered an increase in

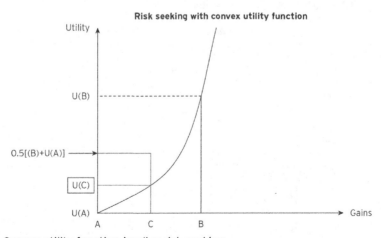

Figure 4.5 Convex utility function implies risk seeking

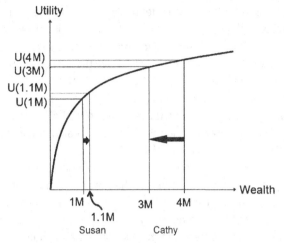

Figure 4.6 Changes in utility and wealth of two investors according to the conventional model

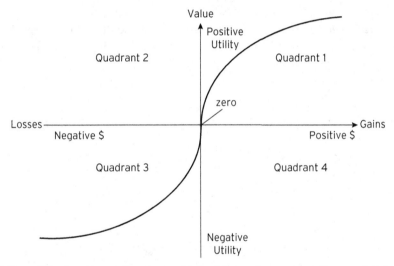

Figure 4.7 The utility function defined on gains and losses in prospect theory of Behavioral Economics

utility. In contrast, moving to the left of the origin on the x-axis is a loss in dollars, and moving down from the origin is a decrease in utility.

In prospect theory, the starting level of wealth (income) is at the origin, i.e., corresponds to zero. Quadrant 1 is reserved for gains. It is like the conventional utility function except the x-axis is *not calibrated in terms of levels of wealth* (income) but in terms of gains from the current value at the origin. Losses are depicted as negative values in quadrant 3 as in the Cartesian coordinate system. The greater the loss, the farther is one to the left of the origin. The utility function in quadrant 3 has the same convex shape as the risk-seeking utility function of Figure 4.5 except that it is calibrated in terms of losses rather than in absolute values. In Figure 4.5 the x-axis has increasing values toward the right. The function of quadrant 3 in Figure 4.7 also has the x-axis increasing toward to right (they are becoming less negative). Hence, Figure 4.5 and the function in quadrant 3 of Figure 4.7 are identical except that the origin of Figure 4.5 is not shown in Figure 4.7 but is at the south-east corner of quadrant 3. Consequently, the utility function of quadrant 3 in Figure 4.7 is risk seeking in losses like the convex utility function in Figure 4.5. The difference is that in Figure 4.7 the x-axis is above the utility function and the y-axis is to the right of the function whereas in Figure 4.5 they are below and to the left respectively. Starting at –$1 million on the x-axis of Figure 4.8 and moving toward the origin would be considered a gain (less negative), just as moving toward the right along the x-axis in Figure 4.5 is a gain. Similarly, moving from *U(–1M)* upward along the y-axis is increasing in utility (less negative), just as moving upward in Figure 4.5 is a gain in utility.

Experiments reveal a kink at the origin in Figure 4.7. The slope of the function at the origin in quadrant 3 is about twice as steep as the slope of the function in quadrant 1 (in absolute value). Losses in this range decrease welfare much more than gains increase it. Gains and losses do not compensate one another; they are not symmetric because of *loss aversion*: people have a stronger preference for avoiding losses than they do for acquiring gains. A gain of $2 is needed to compensate the negative feelings generated by the loss of $1. Put another way, losses are about twice as powerful as gains in generating emotions. This is the *endowment effect*: once people possess something, they want to hold onto it compulsively.[44]

Using prospect theory, the commonsense result is obtained that Susan feels better than Cathy (Figure 4.8). Because Susan has a gain of $0.1 million, her utility function is in quadrant 1, putting her utility into the positive range:

U(+0.1M)

Cathy's loss of $1 million, puts her utility into quadrant 3 and her level of utility is in the negative range on the y-axis:

U(–1M)

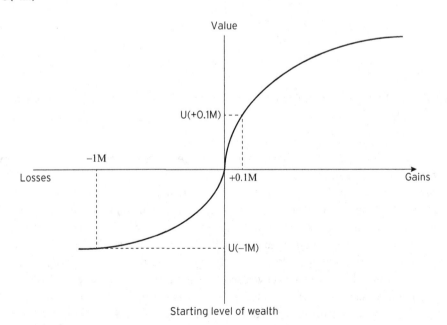

Figure 4.8 Comparison of Cathy's and Susan's utility, according to prospect theory

Therefore, Susan is happier than Cathy regardless of their initial wealth level since Susan's utility is higher on the y-axis after her gain

U(+0.1M)> U(-1M)

Susan's gain generates positive utility whereas Cathy's loss generates negative utility (regret). The value of a gain obviously exceeds that of a loss. So, prospect theory yields the common-sensical result.

In a sense, behavioral economists did for economics what Einstein's theory of relativity did for physics. Before Einstein, people thought that time was constant and immutable. He showed that it was relative. Similarly, behavioral economists showed that utility is not a constant function of the level of wealth (income). Levels are not the conveyors of utility; rather, changes in those levels are. Consequently, when we first purchase a product our level of utility spikes, but with time we become accustomed to it, and our satisfaction diminishes. We adapt to its use. In short, a reference point plays a major role in determining the amount of utility we obtain from an object. Thus, utility ought not be divorced from emotion, and emotion is triggered by changes. Conventional consumer theory is unrealistic because it ignores the pain of losses and the regret of mistakes. Behavioral economists catapulted economics from eighteenth-century certitude to twentieth-century relativity.

A choice between two options provides another example of the advantages of prospect theory: option 1 is a loss of $75 with certainty, while option 2 is a gamble with 50 percent chance of losing $200 or 50 percent chance of gaining $50. The expected value of the second option is the same as that of option 1: a loss of $75 since

$$\tfrac{1}{2}(-\$200)+\tfrac{1}{2}(\$50) = \tfrac{1}{2}-\$100+\$25 = -\$75$$

Which option would a typical risk-averse investor prefer? Standard utility theory suggests that they should prefer the less risky option 1 (Figure 4.9).

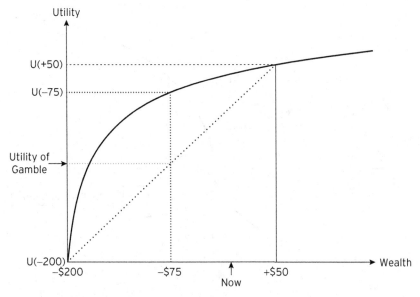

Figure 4.9 Conventional comparison of two options

The utility of the gamble is halfway between U(+50) and U(-200). The diagonal dotted line indicates where the halfway point is on the y-axis.[45] Evidently, the utility of -$75 with certainty [U(-75)]—option 1—exceeds the utility of the gamble (the utility of the expected value of -$75—option 2—i.e., with the uncertain outcome):

U(-$75)>½U(+$50)+U(-$200)

So, one would expect risk-averse people to choose option 1.

However, experiments falsify this model. Most people choose option 2, the gamble, which is inconsistent with risk aversion and implies that in this case most people are risk seeking in losses since with option 2 they might lose much more than the $75 loss of option 1.[46] A reason for the anomaly is that people's attention is focused excessively on the possible gain of $50 magnifying it out of proportion, while discounting the probability of a much greater loss of $200.

However, the choice of option 2 becomes obvious in prospect theory. The certain loss generates a loss of utility in the negative region of the y-axis U(-$75) (Figure 4.10). The utility of the gamble (option 2) has to be compared to U(-$75). In order to calculate that utility, note that the gain of $50 in quadrant 1 yields positive utility on the y-axis: U(+$50). Since the probability of its occurrence is 50 percent, its contribution to expected utility is half as much:

½*U(+$50)

Next, the loss is depicted in quadrant 3 where -$200 generates U(-$200).[47] Since the probability of its occurrence is also 50 percent, its contribution to expected utility is half as much:

½*U(-$200).

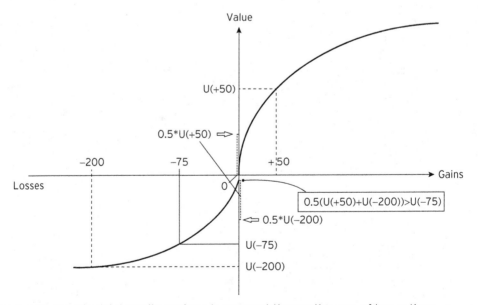

Figure 4.10 Experimental results conform to prospect theory: the case of two options

The sum of the two expected utilities:

½U(-$200)+ ½U(+$50)

is the total utility of the gamble (option 2). So, we add half of the utility of the $50 gain to half of the negative utility of the $200 loss and obtain a point close to the origin, i.e., well above the utility of the $75 loss with certainty:

½[U(-$200)+U(+$50)]>U(-$75)

No wonder most people choose option 2 that includes the possibility of a very large loss: prospect theory confirms experimental evidence and predicts that people will choose to gamble rather than accept the certain loss of $75.

Thus, a basic counterintuitive prediction of prospect theory is that while people are risk averse in gains, they are *risk seeking in losses*. Such inclination was surely part of the reason for the excessive risk taking during the financial crisis of 2008. Risk seeking in losses also explains the $9 billion loss in 2012 of a JPMorgan trader, dubbed "The London Whale."[48] The risks investors accept for possible gains are disproportional to the possible losses. This realization is an important reason for the regulation of financial markets. Behavioral economics replaces the naïve psychology of rational agent models with a more psychologically informed view of human decision-making.

4.11 Behavioral Economics Opens Up New Vistas

Behavioral economics encompasses the role of heuristics, psychological biases, framing effects, anchoring, and emotion to understand the decision-making of flesh-and-blood human beings. It also helps devise strategies by which individuals are allowed to make their own choices, but the choices are framed so that they are *nudged* into choosing the wise option, for example, to start saving early for retirement.[49] This is *"libertarian paternalism."* The wise choice can be elicited, for instance, by making it the default option.

The mispricing of risk and bubbles in housing and in stock prices in the run-up to the 2008 financial crisis is another example of its concerns. Behavioral finance recognizes that mistakes are caused by overconfidence, overreaction to price movements, speculation, inappropriate expectations, and herding behavior. These can create positive feedback loops leading to bubbles and crashes.

Asset bubbles cannot be understood in the conventional supply and demand model. In that framework an increase in the price of a product will cause investors or consumers to demand less of the product, while firms will want to supply more (Figure 4.11). The excess supply induces pressure in the market to lower prices and the initial equilibrium is restored. This is the conventional *negative feedback loop*: the *market is self-regulating*. This model reassured Greenspan and Bernanke to remain complacent about the doubling of house prices prior to the crash of 2008. They did not learn behavioral finance.

While the conventional model is suitable in most retail markets, it is inappropriate for assets that can be transferred readily and whose price-dynamics are associated with expectations and speculation. The reason is that if prices increase from their initial equilibrium value P0 by chance, then investors might form exaggerated expectations that they will continue to increase (Figure 4.12). Expectation of price increases means that investors would realize capital gains

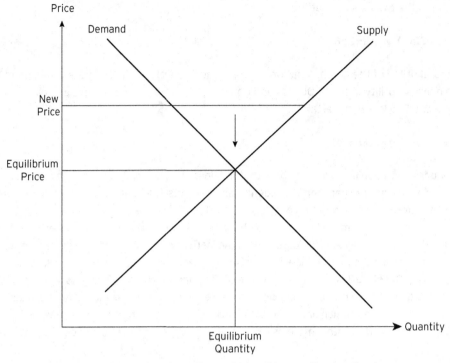

Figure 4.11 Conventional demand and supply analysis with negative feedback

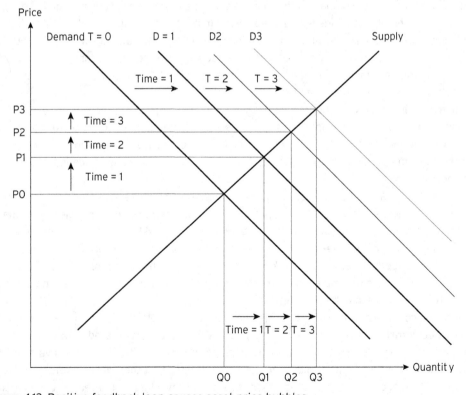

Figure 4.12 Positive feedback loop causes asset price bubbles

which makes that asset more profitable to hold. Thus, the change in expectations shifts the demand curve to the right to D1, establishing a new equilibrium at P1, Q1. As additional investors realize the lucrative nature of these expected capital gains, the demand curve continues to shift to D2, D3, etc., thereby creating a *positive feedback loop* that contributes to further price increases P2, P3, etc. This process can continue until the market runs out of gullible speculators, and expectations change, followed by a collapse of prices. Such errors create large inefficiencies and negative externalities, as in 2008 (see Chapter 14).

4.12 Takeaways

Contrary to overwhelming psychological evidence, mainstream economists continue to assume that people are rational and can maximize their welfare. This view is also contradicted by all the survey evidence which show that our well-being has not improved at all, although consumption has increased substantially. Our mind is not a super-computer; we are not Superman or Superwoman. In the real world we must make complex decisions with imperfect information when the outcome is uncertain, and the repercussions of those decisions extend well into the future. Under such circumstances we are unable to maximize a theoretical utility function, and must rely on our intuition or a rule of thumb to decide, or alternatively copy the action of others to avoid becoming catatonic, often unbeknownst to us, guided by our unconscious mind beyond the control of our prefrontal cortex. In such cases we generally satisfice, i.e., we seek a satisfactory solution, one that is good enough but may not be the best conceivable. However, satisficing frequently leads to mistakes. In addition, a wrong choice may snowball and lead to several other bad decisions entrapping people in poverty. Behavioral economics must become the theoretical foundation of a humanistic economics replacing the utility-maximizing rational-agent models.

Questions for Discussion

1. Is it fair to take advantage of or profit from the ignorance of others?
2. What is the difference between optimizing and satisficing?
3. Would you describe your shopping as satisficing or optimizing?
4. Were you conditioned to want some products?
5. How much of what you buy is based on rational choice?
6. Were you ever influenced by advertisement to buy a product? Were you satisfied with that product thereafter or did you find that it was different than what you supposed?
7. Did you ever experience being very happy with a new product but after a while you got used to it and began to take it for granted?
8. Have you ever been influenced by what celebrities wear?
9. Do you sometimes choose randomly when the choice is too difficult?
10. Have you ever bought something just because your friend had it?
11. Do you think consumer protection is superfluous or often necessary?
12. Why do you think so many people are depressed or have other mental health issues?
13. Do you crave sweets? Can you withstand the temptation?
14. Why do you suppose so many people are unable to control their weight?
15. Do you think that people choose to be obese or overweight?
16. Do you order some things in a restaurant while in company just not to be different?
17. Do search costs sometimes prevent you from buying the best product available?

18. How do you decide when you are uncertain about the quality of a product?
19. Are you making plans for your retirement income?
20. Have you ever made a decision that was right for you, but which led to other choices that were less palatable? Hint: see path dependence or sequential choice in Chapter 8.
21. Is buying a shoe the same kind of a decision as going to the doctor for chest pain?
22. Can you give an example when you made a decision based on intuition?
23. Are some of your tastes similar to that of your parents?
24. Why should one get paid for being born smart?
25. Do you think that predatory loans should be prohibited?
26. Do you buy things that you know are not good for you?
27. Have you ever bought something guided by your emotions?

Notes

1 Ovid, *Metamorphoses* (ad 8), p. 203. Ovid was a Roman poet.
2 Richard Thaler, "From *Homo Oeconomicus* to *Homo Sapiens*," *Journal of Economic Perspectives* 14 (2000), 1: 133-141; Edward Cartwright, *Behavioral Economics*, 3rd edn. (Routledge, 2016).
3 Richard Thaler, *Misbehaving: The Making of Behavioral Economics* (Norton, 2016); Richard Thaler, "Behavioral Economics: Past, Present, and Future," *The American Economic Review* 106 (2016), 7: 1577-1600.
4 Vance Packard, *The Status Seekers* (David McKay, 1959).
5 Another problem is that most budget constraints are not fixed. Soft budget constraints lead to problems that stem from indebtedness.
6 Amos Tversky, "Intransitivity of Preferences," *Psychological Review* 76 (1969), 31-48; here p. 31; Kenneth May, "Intransitivity, Utility, and the Aggregation of Preference Patterns," *Econometrica* 22 (1954), 1: 1-13.
7 "Arrow's Theorem," in *Stanford Encyclopedia of Philosophy*. Available at: www.plato.stanford.edu.
8 Lotfi Zadeh, "Fuzzy Logic and Approximate Reasoning," *Synthese* 30 (1975): 407-428.
9 There are 1160 links referring to regulations, www.fda.gov/.
10 My internet bill was raised repeatedly without my knowledge. It was probably in the fine print of the contract I signed without reading it.
11 Jessica Sberlati, "Countrywide Commercial 3," YouTube, October 26, 2007.
12 The assumption of rationality is a "nonstarter," according to Kahneman. Links to his lectures are available at: www.princeton.edu/~kahneman/.
13 Amartya Sen, "Rational Fools: A Critique of the Behavioural Foundations of Economic Theory," *Philosophy and Public Affairs* 6 (1977), 4: 317-344; here p. 336.
14 Joseph Stiglitz, "Economic Fluctuations and Pseudo-Wealth," NBER Working Paper no. 28415, January 2021, p. 29.
15 Daniel Kahneman et al., *Noise: A Flaw in Human Judgment* (Little, Brown Spark, 2021).
16 Robert Kurzban, *Why Everyone (Else) Is a Hypocrite: Evolution and the Modular Mind* (Princeton University Press, 2011).
17 Peter Whybrow, "Dangerously Addictive: Why We Are Biologically Ill-Suited to the Riches of Modern America," *The Chronicle of Higher Education*, March 13, 2009.
18 Peter Whybrow, *American Mania: When More Is Not Enough* (Norton, 2005).
19 Colin Camerer et al., "Neuroeconomics: How Neuroscience Can Inform Economics," *Journal of Economic Literature* 43 (2005), 1: 9-64.
20 John Conlisk, "Why Bounded Rationality?" *Journal of Economic Literature* 34 (1996), 2: 669-700; Erik Anger, "We're All Behavioral Economists Now," *Journal of Economic Methodology* 26 (2019), 3: 195-207.

21 Reinhard Selten, "Features of Experimentally Observed Bounded Rationality," *European Economic Review* 42 (1998): 413-436.

22 Herbert Simon, *Models of Bounded Rationality* (MIT Press, 1982).

23 A rule of thumb is a short-cut procedure derived from experience or custom that enables one to find a satisfactory approach to a specific problem when (1) too little information is available; (2) when there is insufficient time to consider all important aspects of the problem that could influence the decision; or (3) when it is impractical, impossible, or too costly to find a better solution. The procedure is like an educated guess or using common sense, but can often be deceiving, far from optimal, and can also lead to stereotyping and prejudice.

24 There are organizations that can help consumers make reasoned decisions, like AARP, but these influence only a tiny fraction of our consumption decisions.

25 Herbert Simon, "A Behavioral Model of Rational Choice," *Quarterly Journal of Economics* 69 (1955): 99-118.

26 Daniel McFadden, "Free Markets and Fettered Consumers," *American Economic Review* 96 (2006), 1: 3-29.

27 With the internet, some planning and comparison shopping might well improve, but at the same time firms collect a humongous amount of information on consumers that enables corporations to manipulate them.

28 Thaler, "Behavioral Economics: Past, Present, and Future," op, cit.

29 Daniel Kahneman, *Thinking, Fast and Slow* (Farrar, Straus and Giroux, 2011).

30 Dan Ariely, *Predictably Irrational: The Hidden Forces That Shape Our Decisions* (HarperCollins, 2008); "Dan Ariely: The Upside of Irrationality," www.youtube.com/watch?v=vsBq-FayrDY.

31 Malcolm Gladwell, *Blink: The Power of Thinking Without Thinking* (Little, Brown, 2005).

32 Daniel Kahneman, "Maps of Bounded Rationality: Psychology for Behavioral Economics," *American Economic Review* 93 (2003), 5: 1449-1475; here p. 1450.

33 Wikipedia, "List of Cognitive Biases" has more than 100 biases.

34 Nobel Prize, "Prize Lecture by Daniel Kahneman," www.nobelprize.org/mediaplayer/?id=531.

35 Amos Tversky and Richard Thaler, "Anomalies: Preference Reversals," *Journal of Economic Perspectives* 4 (1990), 2: 201-211.

36 Daniel Hamermesh, *Spending Time: The Most Valuable Resource* (Oxford University Press, 2019), p. 11.

37 "If pitches are to succeed, they need to reach the subconscious level of the brain, the place where consumers develop initial interest in products, inclinations to buy them and brand loyalty," Natasha Singer, "Making Ads That Whisper to the Brain," *The New York Times*, November 13, 2010.

38 Kahneman, "Maps of Bounded Rationality", op. cit., p. 1462.

39 YouTube, "Countrywide Commercial 3," https://www.youtbe.com/watch?v=Ei5OrV-CmHg.

40 Ted O'Donoghue and Charles Sprenger, "Reference-Dependent Preferences," in Douglas Bernheim et al. (eds.), *Handbook of Behavioral Economics: Applications and Foundations* (Elsevier, 2018), pp. 1-77.

41 Thomas Schelling, *Micromotives and Macrobehavior* (Norton, 1978).

42 One might argue that the utility of two persons are not comparable. But then one can also think of this example as Cathy in two different scenarios. Besides, why do we have representative agent models if people are not comparable? The literature on microfoundations of macroeconomics is based on the idea that there is a typical person (see Section 10.6). If there is a typical person, there can be two typical persons. Moreover, we also aggregate incomes of different people to assess national income. Macro models use representative firms. It appears that when it is convenient to do so, economists assume that there is a typical person who represents the whole society and therefore they do compare utility functions across individuals, but when it is inconvenient to do so, they reject the possibility.

43 Quadrant 2 is disregarded because the utility function would imply that a loss in wealth would increase utility and quadrant 4 would imply that gains in wealth would decrease utility. This is nonsensical.

44 Daniel Kahneman et al., "Anomalies: The Endowment Effect, Loss Aversion, and Status Quo Bias," *Journal of Economic Perspectives* 5 (1991), 1: 193-206.

45   This is the case since -$75 on the x-axis is halfway between -$200 and +$50.

46   The experiment has been repeated with many different combinations of numbers. People are risk seeking if negative prospects are involved: "the majority of subjects were willing to accept a risk of 0.8 to lose 4,000, in preference to a sure loss of 3,000, although the gamble has a lower expected value." Daniel Kahneman and Amos Tversky, "Prospect Theory: An Analysis of Decisions Under Risk," *Econometrica* 47 (1979), 2: 263-291; here p. 268.

47   The convex utility function in quadrant 3 implies that while U (-$200)< U (-$75) in the negative range of the y-axis, the utility of the $200 loss is only slightly below the utility associated with the loss of $75. The value gained from the 50 percent chance of gaining $50 overcompensates for this small difference.

48   This was the largest single trading loss in recorded history. However, there are 20 other trades with losses greater than $1 billion. Wikipedia, "List of Trading Losses."

49   Richard Thaler and Cass Sunstein, *Nudge: Improving Decisions About Health, Wealth, and Happiness* (Yale University Press, 2008).

5 Taste-Makers and Consumption

> Manipulation ... fails to respect people's autonomy and is an affront to their dignity.
> —Cass Sunstein[1]

Chapters 3 and 4 established that the mainstream economic canon contradicts standard scientific practice for a multitude of reasons: it begins with arbitrary assumptions that contradict experimental evidence; it disregards the research findings of sister disciplines; it overlooks an array of important aspects of the real-existing economy such as transaction costs; it relegates imperfect information to an epiphenomenon. The flaws are too numerous to mention. Additionally, it is replete with hidden value judgments that do not assign sufficient urgency to equity, sustainability, or the welfare of future generations. Hence, the canon is biased in favor of laissez-faire markets, disregarding contradictory evidence. In this chapter we continue to discuss further flaws of blackboard economics that omit crucial aspects of the economy like *power imbalances*, sociological aspects, cultural influences, and our innate desire for fairness.

5.1 Interdependent Utility Function Should Be the Default Model

Conventional economic theory presumes that individual consumer preferences are independent of each other. From this it follows that consumers' demand for goods varies only if their own income changes or the price of goods change, but not if their neighbor's consumption changes. Thus, neoclassical theory omits both interaction effects among consumers, envy, and manipulation of desires. This is an inexplicable oversight because people have strong *other-regarding preferences* called *interdependent utility*. They are also concerned with what others think of their consumption.[2]

   Consumption is influenced significantly by social norms, habits, customs, and such emotional motives as status seeking, snobbism, keeping up with the Joneses, bandwagon effects, and herding behavior.[3] Consumption invariably occurs within a social context; one seldom consumes in isolation. As society became more affluent, interdependent utility functions became more prominent.[4] There are many more consumption externalities now than there were a century ago, and many distinguished economists argued in vain that *relative consumption* and *relative incomes* matter significantly.[5] Consumers copy the buying habits of their peers and influencers and care about what others think of their consumption. This is particularly relevant for luxury or *positional goods*—ostentatious display of social status to impress others—the consumption of such products create externalities as they affect others. This is ignored in mainstream economics.

DOI: 10.4324/9781003174356-5

Illustration 5.1 Consumerism overwhelms. Madison Avenue makes consumption seem as though it leads to a good life. it does not. It often leads to frustration and indebtedness.

Credit: iStock.com/tobiasjo.

Interdependent utility functions are important since utility depends on reference values like past consumption, social norms, or consumption of peers.[6] Positional goods signal social position (prestige) and thereby affect the way others feel and consume. This is a negative externality. *Status seeking* implies that consumers spend more on positional goods than on products not seen publicly.[7] This is a distortion and decreases social welfare because it creates a hedonic treadmill: the quest for status is futile from the perspective of the whole society since it is a *zero-sum game*. If one climbs in the hierarchy, others descend in relative terms. Status seeking probably has an evolutionary basis as people with high status had a higher probability of surviving and reproducing.[8]

Some positional goods are in fixed supply. Hence, economic growth does not lead to an increased supply of such products. The number of apartments on 5th Avenue overlooking Central Park is limited and the number of acceptances into Ivy League universities will also not increase with economic growth.

The fashion industry is an example of how the demand for clothing is manipulated. Using Madison Avenue, magazines and influencers, the fashion industry creates a bandwagon effect that makes consumers feel uncomfortable if they do not conform to the current dress code.[9] They feel anxious about being ostracized.

The increased competition for status is the likely reason why people are working as much in 2019 as in 1982 (34.0 hours per week).[10] In order to keep up with the social norm, people works long hours. Moreover, nowadays the typical household has two workers in the labor force whereas a generation ago one worker sufficed to maintain a family of four. Because leisure is a normal good, one would expect that people would enjoy more of it with increasing income. Instead, the consumption of leisure has not increased in the US and working hours per family rose, because household income failed to keep pace with the social norms set by the superrich. Households had to provide more labor to keep up with social norms.

Hence, progressive taxation, which counters the exaggerated competition for status and hence the purchase of positional goods, increases social welfare, contrary to conventional theory. Keeping up with the Joneses—in search of the elusive American Dream—leads to an epidemic of stress, overwork, and accumulation of debt without fulfillment.[11] Humanistic Economics supports welfare-enhancing government regulations that foster safety, savings, health, leisure activity, holidays, and consumption taxes on luxury goods.

5.2 The Economy Is Embedded in a Society

The economy does not exist in a vacuum and ought not be separated from its social context.[12] Yet, society is omitted from standard economics: super-individualistic economic theory—*methodological individualism*—assumes that people do not influence one another through their economic activity. However, the truth is that we are not Robinson Crusoes: behavior in society is highly structured by cultural expectations, institutions, social norms, and how we can remain esteemed members of the society.[13] These influence our value system, which calibrates our aspirations, constrains our choices, and channels our actions like the legal system and institutional structure do.[14] Practically none of our decisions are autonomous since "No man is an island."[15]

To avoid becoming outcasts, people tend to conform to the attitudes, mores, and accepted behavior of their society.[16] Consequently, they learn how to act to be accepted, what they should consider important in their lives, and how they can gain power and respect within the social order.[17] They follow fashion trends to belong. The rules are complex: the color coordination must be right, and skinnier lapels or an inch shorter hemline can stymie a job interview.

We learn the terms on which we are accepted by our peers. If they idolize money, we are more likely to devote our lives to its acquisition than if they hold spirituality in higher esteem and consider money less important. Thus, cultural values and norms have a major influence on our attitudes even if we have internalized them so much that we are not conscious about them. The values are ingrained in our subconscious. Belonging gives us a sense of security. We copy the behavior of role models. If people in our reference group shop frequently, we are more likely to become compulsive shoppers.[18] If drug dealers are the conspicuous consumers in the neighborhood, one might be drawn to illegal activity. Social pressure can be overcome only with determination.[19] That is how the culture of consumption is propagated from generation to generation. We order differently in a restaurant when we are alone than when we are with friends. In sum, group interaction is a crucial element of economic activity.

The discipline of social psychology and economic sociology—disregarded by neoclassical economists—concentrate on analyzing the ways in which the social structures, institutions, and culture shape our character, mindset, habits, and tastes.[20] Its findings are that small-scale societies differ considerably from industrialized populations, and Western societies differ from non-Western societies in a vast number of domains: cognition, social decision-making, altruism, norms of civic cooperation, and moral judgment.[21] To be sure, there are feedback effects so that a society's dominant character influences institutions and culture. Hence, human character is malleable and the way we interpret the world is endogenous to the socio-economic system. These findings deviate markedly from methodological individualism of mainstream economics.

Stampedes at Walmart stores are examples of herding behavior. One person starts running and it becomes contagious, sometimes resulting in injury; people have been trampled to death.[22] People lose their individuality in a crowd: normal inhibitions evaporate, and people act as a "faceless" member of a group.

Gender roles are also socially constructed. Until the 1960s, married women were primarily homemakers. With the equal rights social movements, women's labor force participation increased strikingly (Section 11.10). In 1950 just 20 percent of married women with children worked, whereas by the twenty-first century nearly 70 percent did.[23] Such enormous change is not the result of utility maximization but required a revolution in social norms and peer pressure.

5.3 The Culture Industry Has a Crucial Economic Function

Culture is the software of our mind for interpreting the world; it is a system of symbolic codes, the totality of mental constructs that includes our values, thinking habits, beliefs, customs, traditions, assumptions, and social interactions.[24] Culture is the lens through which we see our society, a set of attitudes, and mental reflexes that gives meaning to our life, and defines our identity as members of a society.[25] The collection of cultural characteristics influences the society's political and institutional structure and, with feedback effects, constrains the economic system but can also foster its development, depending on the mind's flexibility.[26] It has a substantial influence on all aspects of the economy, including entrepreneurship, risk taking, and propensity to innovate.[27]

A shared value system is part of culture, like the way we define property rights, and the degree to which we hold it sacred. What is fair and acceptable behavior all fall within this realm.[28] We are expected to adhere to social norms to remain respected members of society. Thus, the extent to which we can be trusted to keep our word or are willing to subvert the intentions of ambiguous contracts, is also an integral part of the culture that fosters or hinders economic activity.[29] Our adherence to religious or moral precepts also belongs here. For instance, by advocating honesty, the Ninth Commandment of the Old Testament promoted trust, lowered transaction costs, and thereby increased efficiency and fostered economic development.[30]

The extent to which society allows deviations from truth influences such factors as the kinds of advertising and packaging that are allowed in markets. The toleration of inequality, poverty, discrimination, racism, the work ethic, degree of impatience, respect of laws, willingness to bear risk, and the definition of gender roles are all part of culture. How much redistribution is acceptable to society?[31] In short, all economic decisions have cultural components. Hence, culture is a key aspect of economic activity.[32] In other words, the economy and culture are inextricably intertwined.[33]

Markets are unable to create social norms such that they perpetuate themselves. Daniel Bell argued that the culture created by capitalism generated a need for instant gratification which gradually eroded the Protestant work ethic that was fundamental to its success. The challenge is:

> [M]anaging a complex polity when the values of the society stress unrestrained appetite. The contradictions ... in contemporary capitalism derive from the unraveling of the threads which had once held the culture and the economy together, from the influence of the hedonism which has become the prevailing value in our society.[34]

The constant search for pleasure crowds out effortful work, savings, investments, virtuous character with the public interest at heart. This market-driven culture disparages frugality and instead propagates the ideology that consumption leads to a good life. It is difficult with a "porno-pop culture that is now all about us," to sustain capitalism as the ethic of hard work erodes.[35] Consequently, the dynamism of capitalism generates the seeds of its own demise: it cannot perpetuate itself without the cultural anchors that were responsible for its success.

Christopher Lasch was another critic of the super-charged market-driven *culture industry of post-industrial capitalism* that created a pathologically narcissistic personality type.[36] He observed that people's sense of identity and self-worth had diminished. The corporate world trivializes unprofitable aspects of life, including ethical scruples. It would not profit from people with a strong sense of identity, firm self-respect, and strong will power. That person would not be a compulsive and impulsive shopper easily swayed and tempted to consume. However, corporations do profit from the developmentally stymied with limited self-control so that they are vulnerable to influencers, crave the latest gadgets, succumb to new fashion fads, spend money recklessly, and disregard the needs of future generations. These spendthrifts are good for corporate balance sheets since they can extract the last dollar available on their credit cards.[37]

> To live for the moment is the prevailing passion—to live for yourself, not for your predecessors or posterity. We are fast losing the sense of historical continuity, the sense of belonging to a succession of generations originating in the past and stretching into the future.[38]

Lasch's words are even more relevant today. Our elites have lost the meaning of prudence, of setting reasonable limits on our appetite, of defending cultural values like delayed gratification and responsible leadership.[39] Instead of providing guidance, our elites have failed to defend the work ethic and a culture of prudence and surrendered leadership to those vested interests who would profit from our carelessness: the mega-corporations. Culture has been set free of its moorings and allowed to drift in the direction of money-making with people needing constant external validation through the sense of control gained as consumers.

5.4 The Ascendency of Impatience

Patience is an essential aspect of economic culture since it has a major influence on the savings rate, investments, and through that long-run economic performance. Today's decisions have ripple effects over time; inter-temporal choices depend on how much we value the future. Our propensity to discount the future is learned early in life and is subject to influences from the business community, which has an incentive to broadcast a message that pressures us to be impatient. There is a conflict between the need for savings for a sustainable future and the propensity of corporations to focus on short-term profitability that induces consumers to spend frivolously. Hence, without consumer protection to counter corporate influence, the likelihood is that impatience will dominate the culture of capitalism. That is the primary reason for the rise of indebtedness, both public and private, and the spread of an unhealthy lifestyle.

5.5 The Determination of Fairness Ought Not to Be Delegated to Markets

Humans have an intense *sense of fairness*, an inherent belief that some actions are just while others do not conform to the ethical beliefs of society. Fairness implies the adherence to social norms like reciprocity, an equitable distribution of resources, goods, or income.[40] This disposition is due partly to innate human nature and partly socially constructed and learned.[41] For instance, most people agree that price gouging is unfair, especially in the case of a natural disaster.[42] When the price of a drug for treating parasitic infection was raised from $13.50 to $750, the outcry was universal.[43] Such price gouging was branded "morally bankrupt."[44] In short, some market outcomes are ethically unpalatable. Humanistic economics advocates the incorporation of the concept of fairness into the discipline.

5.6 Justice Is More Important than Efficiency

Efficiency is an integral part of the mainstream's value system. The market economy is suppos-edly efficient. Production is efficient: firms produce optimally the right amount of goods; more could not be produced with the given amount of inputs. Consumption is also efficient: people know what they want, and more satisfaction could not be obtained from their income. Nobody could be made better off without making someone worse off. This is the Pareto condition: also called *Pareto optimality* or *Pareto efficiency*. However, this is a questionable conception of effi-ciency because it implicitly accepts the current distribution of income: on these terms, slavery was also efficient because the slaves' well-being could not be improved without making their captors worse off. So, an efficient system may well be unjust. This conception of efficiency is not always useful in policy considerations because it is often a prescription for preserving the status quo even if the status quo is unfair. Consequently, a rule requiring that a policy make nobody worse off is advocating for leaving things as they stand.

The Pareto conceptualization of efficiency is not value-neutral. Humanistic economists would rather emphasize sustainability, morality, fairness, justice, equality, or satisfying everyone's basic needs instead. After all, innumerable people have made the ultimate sacrifice for justice. I know of no one who did the same for efficiency. The conventional definition of efficiency must be wrong if we consider it efficient for Victoria's Secret to produce million-dollar bras costing $133 million since it began,[45] while children in slums lack access to a decent education and decent health care.[46] Accepting these distortions as efficient is a value judgment without moral foundations.

5.7 The Rawlsian Just Economy

John Rawls argued that a just society is one which anyone would be willing to enter at ran-dom without knowing any of their attributes.[47] He maintained that the judgments we make now about the allocation of the society's benefits are biased because we know our current endow-ments: abilities, intelligence, talent, education, looks, inherited wealth, family background, skin color, gender, income, wealth, and socio-economic status. This knowledge obviously sways our judgment. Of course, if we know that we are smart, talented, and have access to education, we would support a meritocracy based on education. So, the standard conceptualization of merit disregards the inconvenient truth that it is mostly based on luck of birth when the fundamen-tal aspects of these characteristics were determined.[48] Therefore, we should devise a *thought experiment* that constructs a society such that we would be willing to enter it at random.[49]

To construct a just society from scratch, we must design it without these biases. That can be conceived only in the "original position," behind a *"veil of ignorance,"* without knowing what our characteristics would be in the society after we enter it. Since people are generally risk averse, they would not accept a *social contract* if they were at risk of landing at the bottom of the *social pyramid*. If we entered the society at random without knowing beforehand any of our attributes, we would most likely create an economy that would be close to egalitarian. Risk-averse people would not design an economy that distributed income based on the random allocation at birth or the *"genetic lottery."* Designing the economy behind a veil of ignorance, we would maximize the welfare of the least advantaged to ensure that we would not end up *marginalized* or in utter destitution.

For example, Bill Gates chose his parents well, since his father was a prominent lawyer and his mother, the daughter of a wealthy banker, was on the board of directors of a bank. They were sufficiently wealthy to send him to an exclusive private preparatory school where he could learn to use a mainframe computer, a rare privilege in 1969. He also benefited from the basic research sponsored by government that induced the IT revolution and he was lucky that IBM's negotiations with another potential provider of a PC operating system failed. Thereafter IBM approached Gates, who ultimately provided them with MS-DOS, although he did not write most of the program himself.[50] He served primarily as a middleman. And the connection to IBM was also based on privilege since it was through his mother's association with IBM's president that he gained the opportunity to provide the operating system in the first place.

Obviously, Gates was born smart, but so were millions of others who were not born into such privilege. Moreover, his achievements are by no means proportional to his amassed wealth of $130,000,000,000, that is, $130 billion (2021). Yet, Bill no doubt thinks that he is a self-made man and deserves his 66,000 square-foot estate. Clearly, the lucky few foster the myth of meritocracy to justify their privileges.[51] However, that alleged meritocracy is in reality based on the happenstance of having been born into the right family with the right talents.

The descendants of Sam Walton undoubtedly have no qualms about inherited wealth. They surely think they deserve $235 billion although they did not do anything for it.[52] Stephen Curry undoubtedly thinks he deserves the annual salary of $44 million and is not likely to attribute his talents to his genes, his father's coaching—his father was also a basketball star—and concede that he really doesn't deserve that much money.

Jeff Bezos ($185 billion) also chose his parents well, since they gave him $300,000 to support his business in the beginning.[53] Mark Zuckerberg's mother was a psychiatrist and father was a dentist. They were wealthy enough to send him to Phillips Exeter Academy, where tuition is as much as the median household income. Half the population could not pay that tuition even if they had no other expenses whatsoever. His parents had money left over to hire a software developer to tutor him.[54] His current wealth is $129 billion.

These are among the richest men in America, all were born into privilege and are not a self-made man of myth. In a Rawlsian just state, they would not have accumulated their current riches. It was the way in which their life began and unfolded and the way the legal institutions functioned that protected their patents that granted rights that enabled them to amass their fortune. In short, the market magnified their gains based on first-mover advantages out of proportion to their contribution to social welfare.[55] That is the *magnification mechanism* of a winner-take-all economy.

5.8 We Are Not Completely Selfish

Altruism is being concerned about the welfare of others and considering "the interests of other persons, without the need of ulterior motives."[56] *Homo sapiens* are typically selfish to some extent but being self-interested is not a binary attribute.[57] This is confirmed in experiments in which people reveal their degree of selfishness by the way they divide a windfall between two players. The person originally in possession of the money usually retains about 60 percent of it and shares 40 percent with the opponent. This implies that we are not completely selfish but care about our gain in proportion to that of others.[58]

Moreover, people are vengeful toward those who betray their expectation of *pro-social* behavior. People have other-regarding preferences that include *reciprocity, altruism,* aversion to inequality, spitefulness toward *free riders,* and people care about what others earn within their firm.[59] So, there is a culturally dependent continuum of selfishness. We are capable of self-sacrifice for the benefit of strangers or for an intangible cause.[60] Neuroscientists have shown that people are hard-wired for empathy and act altruistically even if they do not derive benefit from it.[61] I think human nature is about two-thirds selfish.

Evolutionary biologists have demonstrated that human nature is not only competitive but also has cooperative elements. We could not have survived living in families, tribes, or societies if we were entirely egoistic: "social skills evolved when natural selection favored increased in-group prosociality over aggression in late human evolution."[62] Evolution selected characteristics which predisposed humans to care about the welfare of other members of their tribe.[63] People cooperate with genetic strangers. Those who disregarded group interests and failed to defend them against outsiders were ostracized and had difficulty surviving. So, those who cared for the welfare of the group had a higher probability of passing on their genes to the next generation.

This is the concept of multilevel selection in evolution: "hereditary social behavior improves the competitive ability not of just individuals within groups but among groups as a whole." Thus, people have an "intense, obsessive interest ... in other people":

> [there is an] overpowering instinctual urge to belong to groups ... Competition among groups ... promoted altruism and cooperation among all the group members. It led to group-wide morality and a sense of conscience and honor ... To yield completely to the instinctual urgings born from individual selection would dissolve society.[64]

Furthermore, hunting in groups required cooperation and hunting big game implied sharing as the best strategy, because the meat obtained was too much to consume by the hunter alone. Thus, except for a handful of psychopaths, altruism is hard-wired into our DNA so that self-centered utility maximization is not in our nature and is therefore unrealistic from the start. There is research on neural activity that suggests as much.[65] Our universal sense of fairness must have its roots in such evolutionary selection processes based on altruistic commitment to a group.[66] In sum, humans survived as members of a group and not as individuals. Focusing on individuals is a major weakness of conventional economics.[67]

Adam Smith knew that human nature is altruistic to some degree without regard to its own advantage. He recognized that we are interested in the fortunes of others and feel compassion for the misery even of strangers.[68] We "derive sorrow from the sorrow of others" even on the big screen.[69] Brain research identified "mirror neurons" that fire when we see others in distress, as though it were our own experience. Thus,

> Smith (and Hume before him) had identified sympathy as a pervasive feature of human nature by the power of introspection ... There is now ample evidence that there is a deep reason for Smith's intuition ... Sympathy has a basis in the way the brain works.[70]

The mainstream's disregard of this crucial aspect of human nature is clearly flawed.[71]

5.9 The Distinction Between Positive and Normative Economics Is a False Dichotomy

Mainstream economists distinguish between positive economics, which is supposedly objective, a rigorous analysis of the economy, and normative economics, which pertains to what the economy ought to be. They claim that the former is value-free while the latter involves value judgments. However, the distinction is artificial, because mainstream economists include many assumptions in positive economics that actually involve value judgments (see Table 1.1). What issues one considers positive economics depends on cultural norms and requires an ethical system. For instance, economists assume that people are rational, although psychologists have proven beyond a reasonable doubt that people are incapable of being rational. Thus, the deliberate disregard of the results of scientific research in sister disciplines is itself ideological and cannot be considered rigorous science. Moreover, accepting the prevailing distribution of wealth in theorizing about efficiency implies a value judgment. It is not anchored in objectivity.

Not distinguishing between basic needs and conspicuous consumption is also a subjective value judgment. The mainstream considers the assumption that wants are unlimited to be positive economics, whereas others consider it to be part of a culturally determined value system. There is no empirical evidence that humans are innately insatiable. Rather, such attributes are learned through socialization. The hostility of American textbooks toward the government is another ideological aspect of mainstream economics. That world-view does not consider the need for consumer protection from powerful business interests, although government protection of consumers has yielded such successes as halving the number of cigarette smokers; that would have been impossible without government policy. In sum, positive economic theory is far from being rigorous or value-neutral.

5.10 Expected Utility vs. Realized Utility

Conventional utility maximization obscures another problem: it rarely distinguishes between expected and realized utility. It assumes that if consumers purchase a pizza for $16.30 they received at least $16.30 worth of utility from it because they paid for it, so, they must have thought it was worth that much. However, this inference disregards that consumers paid for the pizza prior to consuming it. Hence, the correct description of the purchase is that at the time of the transaction they *expected* to receive at least $16.30 worth of satisfaction, but upon consumption the satisfaction might be less than the amount anticipated. Consequently, we need to distinguish between *expected and realized utility*. The amount consumers spend might not correspond to the level of experienced satisfaction from their purchase. This is yet another reason why income ought not be equated with welfare.

Consumers make systematic mistakes in forecasting utility generated by purchases such as not distinguishing between the initial level of utility obtained from a good and future levels of utility. When deciding, consumers generally do not account for adaptation and do not anticipate accurately the rate at which utility depreciates over time. Hence, consumers exaggerate the effect of purchases on their long-run satisfaction. There are also biases in how we remember experiences. Economists emphasize the experience of consumption but disregard that anticipation and remembering also generate utility. People usually undervalue these aspects of consumption in their decisions. An ice cream cone consumed a year ago most likely no longer provides any satisfaction. However, last year's vacation is still fresh in our memory and the slow rate of decay in the satisfaction it continues to generate is not given sufficient weight at the time the decision is made. Forecasting the rate of diminution of utility obtained from consumption is a systematic error consumers make in their decisions.

5.11 Imperfect Information Is Ubiquitous and Crucial to Understanding the Real Economy[72]

Textbooks imply that the price of a product is all the information needed for a rational decision about its purchase. This is true only in trivial cases. However, in the real world, obtaining accurate information about critical attributes of a good or service is costly, difficult, takes effort, and is frequently out of reach. Stiglitz emphasizes that:

> [t]he economics of information has constituted a revolution in economics ... upsetting long-standing presumptions, including that of market efficiency, with profound implications for economic policy. Information failures are associated with numerous other market failures, including incomplete risk markets, imperfect capital markets, and imperfections in competition, enhancing opportunities for rent seeking and abstract form of domination.[73]

According to Stiglitz and Akerlof, who should know since they received Nobel Prizes (2001) for their research on information economics, *imperfect information* is widespread and "even a small amount of information imperfection could have a profound effect on the nature of the equilibrium."[74] Since decisions are almost always made with incomplete information, efficient or optimal outcomes are rarely attainable in practice.[75] Hence, the default model should be that markets are generally inefficient without proper oversight. Yet, textbooks maintain a conspiracy of silence about the inconvenient truth that markets characterized by incomplete information, asymmetric information, and uncertain information are inefficient. Instead, they do a Pinocchio for claiming that "markets usually lead to efficiency,"[76] or that "markets have remarkable efficiency properties."[77]

The obstacles to possessing accurate information include not only the cost of acquiring it in money and effort but also the fact that producers obscure and manipulate information so as to make certain attributes more accessible than others and hide some information altogether.[78] Given asymmetric information between counterparties, and given the unequal distribution of wealth, education, and cognitive abilities, the free market provides ample opportunities for sellers to take advantage of buyers' inexperience, naiveté, lack of education, and knowledge.[79] This leads to *opportunistic behavior* and inefficient consumption and impinges on welfare.

The subprime mortgage crisis is an example of an inefficient outcome caused by asymmetric information because bankers knew far more than borrowers about the riskiness of adjustable-rate mortgages (see Chapter 14). Likewise, those who created exotic securities that subsequently became toxic, knew much more about the product than the investors who bought them, and such opportunistic behavior had grave consequences. Goldman Sachs had to pay $650 million penalty for taking advantage of asymmetric information.

The invisible hand does not lead to efficient outcomes in the presence of imperfect information.[80] Producers have more information about their products than consumers, and it is unreasonable to put all the burden of acquiring adequate information on the buyer. Not to deceive each other should be a mutual obligation. Consequently, consumer protection is warranted. Producers should not be allowed to deceive consumers. In the presence of asymmetric information, government-mandated dissemination of information would lower transaction costs and improve the buyer's ability to make an informed, satisfactory decision. The neglect of asymmetric information is not a trivial oversight in Econ-101! Humanistic economics advocates for truthful advertising. It would raise consumer satisfaction considerably.

5.12 Signaling in Case of Imperfect Information

Signals generate information. In markets with imperfect information, signals, like college diplomas, provide information as a substitute for unobservable characteristics.[81] Students attend college not only to learn but also to demonstrate to future employers that they have the intelligence and perseverance to complete an extensive educational program. Credentials are interpreted as credible signals that employers believe are positively correlated with unobservable attributes they value: reliability, work ethic, competence, flexibility in novel situations, and willingness to cooperate. In markets with imperfect information, the diploma has value beyond the value of acquired knowledge. It signals the possession of intangible attributes. A title like professor or the prestige of a university has similar value as a signal of invisible traits.

Hence, workers with a high school or college diploma earn disproportionately more than those who left school shortly before graduation, although the additional knowledge gained during the missing time is not essential for the job. Therefore, the additional effort of obtaining the credential is inefficient from the perspective of the aggregate economy because those students could have performed on the job as well without the diploma. The additional money spent on obtaining the credential and generating the signal is wasted and inefficient from an economic point of view, since the investment did not lead to increased productivity. However, with imperfect information the students are incapable of demonstrating their productivity any other way; the diploma substitutes for that information and signals a bundle of desirable capabilities. Consequently, for students, the diploma is a valuable investment because they will earn a higher wage with it. Thus, there is a divergence between private and social returns to signaling.

Another kind of signal is generated when firms sell products below cost so consumers believe that they have the low prices on everything. Such loss-leader strategies entice consumers to frequent that store but are inefficient for the consumers because their decision is not based on complete knowledge of all prices. Prices on other products offered by the firm might be higher; hence, their total purchases may cost more than at other firms. Signaling social status through *conspicuous consumption* is another type of inefficient consumption. It is an expensive way to let others know one's place in society.

Illustration 5.2 What is one without a mansion and a yacht? The lifestyle of the superrich and super-famous includes conspicuous consumption. It is rampant at a time when tens of millions are deprived of the basic human right of a decent education and decent health care

Credit: iStock.com/mariakraynova.

5.13 Time-Inconsistent Preferences

Decisions at different times can be inconsistent with one another. Preferences might change over time. This can affect decisions requiring self-control, such as weight loss, saving for retirement, or procrastination. You might choose a piece of cake for dessert and regret it by the time you're finished eating it for not having resisted the temptation.

Mainstream economists assume that people discount the future because it is less important than the present.[82] Rational choice requires that people use exponential discounting to assess the value of future utility. For instance, at a discount rate of 5 percent, the receipt of $1 a year from now is worth $0.95 today. The difference of 5 cents is payment for waiting a year for the $1. *Exponential discounting is time-consistent* because the discount rate is constant regardless of the length of time involved. Thus, having to wait two years for $1 means that it would be valued today at (0.95*0.95)=$0.9025 as it continues to lose 5 percent of its value every additional year of waiting. So, $1 ten years from now is worth 60 cents today at the compounded annual discount rate of 5 percent, and the amount continues to lose 40 percent of its value every subsequent 10 years. So, the rate of decay in the value is constant. Hence, $1 fifty years from now should be worth 60 cents 40 years from now (Figure 5.1).

However, exponential discounting is falsified in experiments: the rate of discount declines over time.[83] Instead, people use *hyperbolic discounting*. They have *time-inconsistent preferences*. Both exponential and hyperbolic discounting yield about the same value of $1 discounted 10 years from now—about 60 cents. However, while the rate of depreciation is a constant for the exponential discounting for all time, the hyperbolic discounting loses only 18 percent of its value during the 10-year interval between 30 and 40 years and then 15 percent between 40 and 50 years. This implies that waiting 10 years today means a lot to people but waiting 10 years 40 years from now is less important. This is time-inconsistency.

Present-biased preferences mean that people are myopic when looking into the distant future; 40 and 50 years from now appear quite close together, so with hyperbolic discounting people do not discount that difference at the same rate they would discount ten years closer to the present. The fact that waiting 10 years today is important but waiting 10 years 40 years from now is less important, is inconsistent with standard models of rational choice, because preferences are time-dependent. This is an important cognitive bias because it induces people to save too little for retirement or to borrow too much on credit cards. *Homo oeconomicus* uses exponential discounting while *homo sapiens* use hyperbolic discounting.

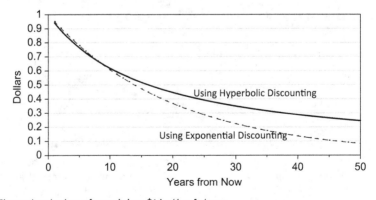

Figure 5.1 The value today of receiving $1 in the future

This myopia is another reason for consumer protection in transactions involving time. Young workers are generally not thinking of their retirement income. Thus, government, through taxation, can guarantee that some income will be available for everyone upon retirement. Otherwise, people who lack foresight could experience hardship and create negative externalities for society by becoming a burden on the community upon retirement, for example. Hyperbolic discounting also complicates problems associated with assessing probabilities. What is the probability that one will become disabled, contract one of the 200 different kinds of cancers, or will need long-term care insurance 30 years from now? We are generally biased toward the present and therefore tend to discount excessively such improbable events in the future. Yet, the government officials can calculate these probabilities accurately and compel us to buy insurance for such improbable high-impact events.

5.14 Takeaways

We did not choose to become an instant-gratification society. We did not want to become an indebted and overweight nation. However, we have gradually internalized the commercial culture to such an extent that we are no longer aware of its impact on our psyche or the extent to which the dominant ideology deprives us of our autonomy, individuality, and thereby makes us unfree. This is a major infringement on our right to develop our human potential without excessive corporate influence.

Yet another major oversight in economics is the disregard of the ethical nature of production, consumption, and income distribution. Conventional economists stress efficiency and economic growth but overlook that human beings have an intense and intrinsic sense of fairness, an inherent belief that some actions are just while others do not conform to the ethical beliefs of society. They pretend to be value-neutral by advocating the dominance of the free market. But morality should not be delegated to markets! Instead, we must strive to make the economy conform to our value system and create a just economy, as advocated by humanistic economists. This chapter describes how such a just economy would be designed from scratch.

Questions for Discussion

1   Do you think that freedom of speech should be extended to corporations? Should they be treated like people?
2   Do you think that power corrupts, including power that comes from wealth?
3   Do you think we should reduce the amount spent on the military and increase the amount spent on education?
4   Do you think that teachers should earn as much as CEOs?
5   What do you think Aldous Huxley would think of our society today? And Thomas Jefferson?
6   Explain what Joseph Stiglitz meant when he described our economic system as socialism for the rich and capitalism for the rest of us.
7   Do you think that you are in charge of your utility function?
8   Which has the greater influence on our mindset: TV or the internet?
9   Do you know anyone who has been deceived by the fine print in a contract?
10   To what extent do you think advertisements infringe on our ability to live our life as we want to?

11   Do you know any compulsive shoppers?

12   Should advertisements aimed at children under the age of 12 be prohibited, as in Norway?

13   Why do you think Americans save so much less today than they did a generation ago although their income is higher?

14   Why do you think Americans enjoy much shorter vacations than Europeans?

15   To what extent are you influenced by the consumption of others?

16   Do social and cultural norms influence your consumption?

17   How is our culture influenced by the market forces of capitalism?

18   Do you think the American Dream is within reach of most people?

19   To what extent do you think people are altruistic?

20   Do you think that a sense of fairness is innate in human nature or is it learned in the process of growing up?

21   Do you think it is more important to have an efficient society or a fair one?

22   Is the current distribution of wealth efficient or fair?

23   What do you think would be a reasonable definition of efficiency?

24   What kind of a wealth distribution would you envision?

25   Can you think of waste in the economy?

26   Which is more important: efficiency or justice?

27   Is it moral to take advantage of or profit from the ignorance of others?

28   What kind of a society would you create if you were to begin to construct it from scratch?

29   Do you agree that "too big to fail" banks should be too big to exist?

30   Do you agree with Erich Fromm that we are consumption-crazy?

Notes

1   "Fifty Shades of Manipulation," *Journal of Marketing Behavior* 1 (2016), 3–4: 213–244.

2   Samuel Bowles, "Endogenous Preferences: The Cultural Consequences of Markets and Other Economic Institutions," *Journal of Economic Literature* 36 (1998), 1: 75–111.

3   Thorstein Veblen, *The Theory of the Leisure Class: An Economic Study of Institutions* (Macmillan, 1899).

4   "How many people ruin themselves by laying out money on trinkets of frivolous utility?" Adam Smith, *The Theory of Moral Sentiments* (A. Millar, 1759), IV.I.6. www.econlib.org/library/Smith/smMS.html.

5   Robert Frank, *Choosing the Right Pond: Human Behavior and the Quest for Status* (Oxford University Press, 1985); Robert Frank, "The Demand for Unobservable and Other Nonpositional Goods," *American Economic Review* 75 (1985), 1: 101–116.

6   James Duesenberry, *Income, Saving, and the Theory of Consumer Behavior* (Harvard University Press, 1949).

7   Aron O'Cass and Emily McEwen, "Exploring Consumer Status and Conspicuous Consumption," *Journal of Consumer Behaviour* 4 (2004), 1: 25–39.

8   Arthur Robson, "The Biological Basis of Economic Behavior," *Journal of Economic Literature* 29 (2001): 11–33.

9   Solomon Asch, "Opinions and Social Pressure," *Scientific American* 193 (1955): 31–35; Harvey Leibenstein, "Bandwagon, Snob, and Veblen Effects in the Theory of Consumers' Demand," *Quarterly Journal of Economics* 64 (1950), 2: 183–207.

10   St. Louis Fed, series AVHWPEUSA065NRUG.

11   John Edwards et al. (eds.), *Ending Poverty in America: How to Restore the American Dream* (New Press, 2007).

12   Karl Polanyi, *The Great Transformation: The Political and Economic Origins of Our Time* (Rinehart, 1944).

13 Brian Epstein, *The Ant Trap: Rebuilding the Foundations of the Social Sciences* (Oxford University Press, 2015).

14 Pierre Bourdieu, *Outline of a Theory of Practice* (Cambridge University Press, 1977).

15 John Dunne, *Meditation XVII*, 1624.

16 "Anybody who is not like everybody, who does not think like everybody, runs the risk of being eliminated," José Ortega y Gasset, *The Revolt of the Masses* (Allen & Unwin, 1932).

17 Nellie Bowles, "To Fit into Silicon Valley, Wear These Wool Shoes," *The New York Times*, August 11, 2017.

18 The Shulman Center for Compulsive Theft, Spending & Hoarding, "Shopaholics Anonymous." www.shopaholicsanonymous.org/; Wikipedia, "Shopaholic."

19 Solomon Asch, "Opinions and Social Pressure," *Scientific American* 193 (1955): 31-35.

20 Eli Finkel and Roy Baumeister (eds.), *Social Psychology: The State of the Science,* 2nd edn. (Oxford University Press, 2019); Richard Swedberg, *Principles of Economic Sociology* (Princeton University Press, 2007).

21 Joseph Henrich et al., "The Weirdest People in the World?" *Behavioral and Brain Sciences* 33 (2010): 61-135; Ernst Fehr and Simon Gächter, "Altruistic Punishment in Humans," *Nature* 415 (2002), 6868: 137-140.

22 "Wal-Mart Worker Killed in Black Friday Stampede," www.youtube.com/watch?v=f5EU4GRudvc.

23 Sharon Cohany and Emy Sok, "Married Mothers in the Labor Force," *Monthly Labor Review* 130 (2007), 2: 9-16.

24 Talcott Parsons, *The Social System* (Free Press, 1951); Ann Swidler, "Culture in Action: Symbols and Strategies," *American Sociological Review* 51 (1986), 2: 273-286.

25 Pierre Bourdieu, "The Forms of Capital," in John Richardson (ed.), *Handbook of Theory and Research for the Sociology of Education* (Greenwood, 2016), pp. 241-258.

26 Daron Acemoglu and James Robinson, "Social Equilibria: A Framework," NBER Working Paper no. 28832, May 2021; https://www.nber.org/conferences/economics-culture-and-institutions-spring-2021.

27 Ernst Fehr and Karla Hoff, "Introduction: Tastes, Castes and Culture: The Influence of Society on Preferences," *Economic Journal* 121 (2011), 556: F396-F412.

28 Clifford Geertz, *The Interpretation of Cultures* (Basic Books, 1973).

29 Francis Fukuyama, *Trust: The Social Virtues and the Creation of Prosperity* (Free Press, 1995).

30 Bert Hoselitz, "Non-economic Barriers to Economic Development," *Economic Development and Cultural Change* 1 (1952), 1: 8-21.

31 Max Weber, *The Protestant Ethic and the Spirit of Capitalism* (Unwin Hyman, 1930). Originally published in 1905.

32 Lawrence Harrison and Samuel Huntington (eds.), *Culture Matters: How Values Shape Human Progress* (Basic Books, 2000).

33 Luigi Guiso et al., "Does Culture Affect Economic Outcomes?" *Journal of Economic Perspectives* 20 (2006), 2: 23-48.

34 Daniel Bell, *The Cultural Contradictions of Capitalism* (Basic Books, 1976), pp. 21-22.

35 Ibid., p. 51.

36 Christopher Lasch, *The Culture of Narcissism: American Life in an Age of Diminishing Expectations* (Norton, 1979).

37 Robert Frank, *Luxury Fever* (Princeton University Press, 1999).

38 Christopher Lasch, "The Narcissist Society," *The New York Review of Books*, September 30, 1976.

39 Christophe Hayes, *Twilight of the Elites* (Crown, 2012).

40 Golnaz Tabibnia and Matthew Lieberman, "Fairness and Cooperation Are Rewarding: Evidence from Social Cognitive Neuroscience," *Annals of the New York Academy of Sciences* 1118 (2007): 90-101.

41 Peter Corning, *The Fair Society: The Science of Human Nature and the Pursuit of Social Justice* (University of Chicago Press, 2011).

42 During Hurricane Irma the price of an airline ticket increased from $547 to $3200. Justin Sablich, "Airlines Face Criticism Amid Irma Price-Gouging Complaints," *The New York Times*, September 9, 2017.

43   Andrew Pollack, "Drug Goes from $13.50 a Tablet to $750, Overnight," *The New York Times*, September 20, 2015.

44   The price of EpiPen, an anti-allergy injection, soared from $103 to $608. Ben Popken, "Mylan Execs Gave Themselves Raises as They Hiked EpiPen Prices," *CNBC News*, August 23, 2016.

45   Sally Holmes, "$133 Million in Bras: The Complete Evolution of the Victoria's Secret Fantasy Bra," *Elle*, November 28, 2016.

46   Kate Murphy, "Child's Play, Grown-Up Cash," *The New York Times*, July 20, 2011.

47   John Rawls, *A Theory of Justice* (Harvard University Press, 1971).

48   Michael Sandel, *The Tyranny of Merit: What's Become of the Common Good?* (Farrar, Straus and Giroux, 2020).

49   This bears some resemblance to Immanuel Kant's dictum of the "categorical imperative": act as you would like all others to act. It is also similar to the golden rule, a tenet that is part of all major religions, including the Old Testament: do unto others as you would have them do unto you. If you are unwilling to enter a society, you should not want others to live in it either.

50   Wikipedia, "Bill Gates."

51   Jen Webb et al., *Understanding Bourdieu* (Allen & Unwin, 2002).

52   Ashley Fetters and Heather Kelly, "Meghan and Harry Are Becoming Your Typical American Mega-Celebrities," *The Washington Post*, May 4, 2021.

53   Wikipedia, "Jeff Bezos."

54   Wikipedia, "Mark Zuckerberg."

55   Mark Zuckerberg's history is similar. He basically expropriated the idea for Facebook from fellow students.

56   Thomas Nagel, *The Possibility of Altruism* (Clarendon Press, 1970), p. 79.

57   In evolutionary biology, altruism is defined in terms of one organism raising another organism's reproductive success at the expense of its own.

58   Richard Thaler, "Anomalies: The Ultimatum Game," *Journal of Economic Perspectives* 2 (1988), 4: 195-206.

59   Colin Camerer, *Behavioural Game Theory: Experiments in Strategic Interaction* (Russell Sage Foundation, 2003).

60   James Andreoni et al., "Altruism in Experiments," in Steven Durlauf and Lawrence Blume (eds.), *The New Palgrave Dictionary of Economics*, 2nd edn. (Palgrave Macmillan, 2008).

61   Ernst Fehr and Bettina Rockenbach, "Human Altruism: Economic, Neural, and Evolutionary Perspectives," *Current Opinions in Neurobiology* 14 (2004), 6: 784-790.

62   Brian Hare, "Survival of the Friendliest: *Homo sapiens* Evolved via Selection for Prosociality," *Annual Review of Psychology* 68 (2017): 155-186.

63   Ernst Fehr et al., "Egalitarianism in Young Children," *Nature* 454 (2008): 1079-1083.

64   Edward Wilson, "Evolution and Our Inner Conflict," *The New York Times*, June 24, 2012.

65   Dharol Tankersley et al., "Altruism Is Associated with an Increased Neural Response to Agency," *Nature Neuroscience* 10 (2007): 150-151.

66   Samuel Bowles and Herbert Gintis, *A Cooperative Species: Human Reciprocity and its Evolution* (Princeton University Press, 2011).

67   However, social norms influence the degree to which we become altruistic. Experiments reveal that women are more altruistic than men. Rachel Croson and Uri Gneezy, "Gender Differences in Preferences," *Journal of Economic Literature* 47 (2009), 2: 1-27.

68   Adam Smith, *The Theory of Moral Sentiments* (A. Millar, 1759), I.I.1.

69   Alexander Field, *Altruistically Inclined? The Behavioral Sciences, Evolutionary Theory, and the Origins of Reciprocity* (University of Michigan Press, 2002).

70   Aldo Rustichini, "Introduction. Neuroeconomics: Present and Future," *Games and Economic Behavior* 52 (2005): 201-212.

71   Daniel McFadden, "The New Science of Pleasure," NBER Working Paper no. 18687, February 2013.

72   Imperfect information means that the individual deciding about a product or contract does not know all the relevant information about it at the time of purchase.

73   Jean Tirole, "Market Failures and Public Policy," *The American Economic Review* 105 (2015), 6: 1665–1682.

74   Joseph Stiglitz, "Information and the Change in the Paradigm in Economics," *American Economic Review* 92 (2002), 3: 460–501: here p. 461.

75   Joseph Stiglitz, "The Revolution of Information Economics: The Past and the Future," NBER Working Paper no. 23780, September 2017.

76   Paul Krugman and Robin Wells, *Economics*, 3rd edn. (Worth Publishers, 2013), p. 16.

77   Paul Samuelson and William Nordhaus, *Economics*, 19th edn. (McGraw-Hill/Irwin, 2009), p. 164.

78   "Artificial intelligence is going to be able keep track of our moods in the near future using social network and take advantage of this information to be able to manipulate us even more effectively." Fabon Dzogang et al., "Circadian Mood Variations in Twitter Content," *Brain and Neuroscience Advances* 1 (2017), doi: 10.1177/2398212817744501.

79   "Amazon will pay delivery drivers a settlement of $61.7 million after a Federal Trade Commission probe found it appropriated tips from its Amazon Flex drivers over two-and-a-half years. Amazon used the tips earned by Flex drivers – hourly workers who do not receive any benefits and make deliveries in their own vehicles – to pay their wages." *Democracy Now*, February 3, 2021.

80   Joseph Stiglitz, "The Invisible Hand and Modern Welfare Economics," NBER Working Paper no. 3641, March 1991.

81   Michael Spence, "Job Market Signaling," *Quarterly Journal of Economics* 87 (1973), 3: 355–374.

82   Some people do not discount the future at all, because they look forward to the pleasures of tomorrow. Anticipation can also provide utility, generally overlooked.

83   Shane Frederick, George Loewenstein, and Ted O'Donoghue, "Time Discounting and Time Preference: A Critical Review," *Journal of Economic Literature* 40 (2002).

6 Oligopolies and Imperfect Competition

We have so far focused on consumption and turn next to examine production. Conventional economics claims that production is also efficient because the theories concentrate on perfectly competitive markets which assumes that innumerable firms produce the same homogeneous product. There are no brands in such markets since goods are generic (Figure 6.1). So, *product differentiation*, and differences in quality do not exist and advertising generic goods would make no sense.

The product price in such markets is determined by aggregate supply and demand. Since there are innumerable competing tiny firms, all firms are *price takers*–no firm has power to influence price. Hence, the demand for every firm's product is *perfectly elastic*: the demand

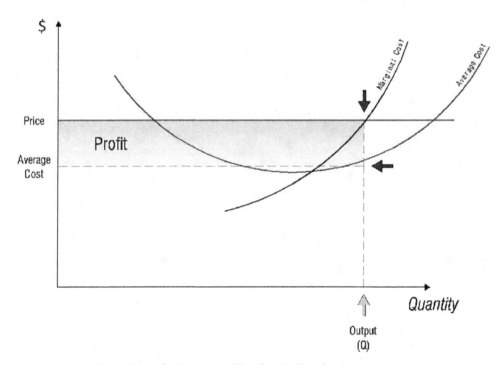

Figure 6.1 Production of a perfectly competitive firm in the short run

DOI: 10.4324/9781003174356-6

curve is the market price (Figure 6.1). Firms produce Q amount of goods where *marginal cost*, the additional cost of producing an extra unit, is equal to the price (MC = P). Since MC is rising, an additional unit of output beyond Q would cost more to produce than the price and the firm would lose money on the extra output. However, at Q, the average cost is lower than the price, so the firm is earning a profit = Q*(Price - Average Cost).

This is a short-run equilibrium because other entrepreneurs are attracted by these profits and will enter this market since there are *no barriers to entry*. The entry of new firms into the sector lowers the price of the product through competition and increases average cost of production since the new firms are competing for raw materials and labor used in this industry. This process will continue until in the long run equilibrium profits are dissipated and the firms just break even at a new market price (MC = P = AC) (Figure 6.2). Consequently, firms are producing efficiently at the minimum unit cost and have just enough revenue to stay in business. There are no profits. Profits have been competed away and there is no reason for new firms to enter this sector. These are crucial features of perfectly competitive markets.

There is nothing wrong with this model in an Alice-in-Wonderland economy. However, to focus on this model is fundamentally misguided because the perfectly competitive market structure is *irrelevant* in today's economy as far as consumers are concerned. It is still valid in wholesale

MARGINAL COST vs AVERAGE COST

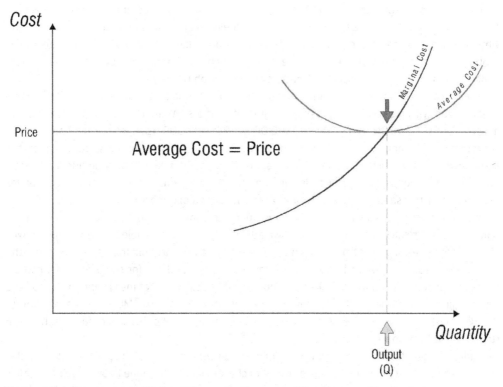

Figure 6.2 In long-run equilibrium of a perfectly competitive firm, profits disappear

markets for homogeneous raw materials like Kansas wheat or West Texas Intermediate crude oil. However, practically no consumer good is produced today under perfect competition.

Instead, most industries are dominated by a handful of firms called *oligopolies*. Such markets are characterized by *imperfect competition*. Oligopolies are not price takers but *price makers*—similarly to monopolies—and set prices for their products to their advantage, and many have sufficient power to set wages and also manipulate consumer demand through advertisements and *planned obsolescence*. Moreover, they influence the political process so that they gain further market power. Competition among oligopolies and monopolies does not result in an efficient outcome stressed by the mainstream. Instead, they do earn profits because of barriers to entry into the industry, deregulation, strategic behavior, or collusion.[2] Moreover, they are not producing the socially optimum amount of goods. They obtain a high price for their product by *limiting production*. This is inefficient from society's viewpoint. This chapter focuses on imperfect competition and how it differs from the perfectly competitive model.[3]

6.1 Multinationals Instead of Mom-and-Pop Operations

Conventional textbooks describe a firm as an individual decision-maker, analogous to the consumer, also assumed to be a sole decision-maker. There is a shoemaker and a seamstress near me who own their businesses and work alone. Theirs would be such a textbook firm, but such firms are a negligible part of the economy. Most businesses are hierarchical, authoritarian organizations within which the *visible hand of management* replaces the invisible hand of the market.[4] Thus, their structure resembles other bureaucratic institutions like government agencies.

The firm is not organized internally as a market. It is based on a command structure like the military. This contradicts the beneficial effects of free markets. If free markets were so efficient, why do firms not use that mechanism internally to organize their production. The answer is probably that a free market internal to the firm—in which each employee would become an independent contractor—would increase transaction costs prohibitively.

A corporation is not a person and does not make decisions as an individual. Rather, it is an organization with managers employing a legion of workers: Walmart: 2.2 million, Amazon: 1.3 million; FedEx: 600,000, Home Depot: 500,000, UPS: 480,000, IBM: 350,000.[5] The efficient coordination of employees within such mega-corporations is nearly impossible because the actual owners of the firms, the shareholders, are far away and cannot provide adequate oversight. The inefficiency in large firms is compensated by the gains obtained through *economies of scale*, lower transaction costs, *network externalities*, and oligopoly profits.[6]

Such giant enterprises employ too many people with conflicting goals to be able to optimize. Some employees shirk; others seek their own advantage. It is not feasible to align the incentives of each employee with that of the owners of the firm, the shareholders, especially since the employees presumably want to do the best for themselves and not for the owners. Of course, managers provide oversight, but effective monitoring is costly, sometimes prohibitively so. And who monitors the managers? The board of directors are also distant. Money managers before the 2008 crisis took excessive risks to increase their immediate bonuses disregarding the long-run effects on the shareholders.

Additional obstacles to optimization include the uncertainty about future demand and disruptive technologies affecting the firm. Those in charge have only vague knowledge of changes in demand in response to variations in the price it charges for its product. They have only subjective notions of their competitors' response to various scenarios. Hence, profit maximization is not within their reach. Managers are unable to control the actions of other firms.

The best they can do is to *satisfice with bounded rationality* (see Section 4.5). Like consumers, firms adapt rules-of-thumb (*heuristic rules*) to find an acceptable solution to their problems. The mark-up rule is one such rule by which the selling price is calculated by multiplying the cost of the product by a constant factor.

Groupthink in authoritarian organizations can prevent employees from independent thinking and critically evaluating the ideas of their colleagues.[7] Groupthink can easily lead to dysfunctional group dynamics as alternative perspectives are suppressed. Both Greenspan and his successor Ben Bernanke failed to understand the potentially destabilizing effects of *systemic risk*[8] prior to the Meltdown but the thousand PhD economists working for the Fed accepted their reasoning without question.[9]

6.2 The Illusion of Perfect Competition

Most students take away from Econ-101 that competition guarantees efficient markets. That formulation also reverberates in the media. Hence, it is important to understand that *competition is not sufficient to bring about socially efficient outcomes*. Oligopolies have many strategies to avoid the perfectly competitive outcome. They *differentiate their products* as a form of nonprice competition. Fashion brands like Louis Vuitton, Gucci, and Dior are oligopolies and have monopoly rights to manufacture products with their name, and their designs are protected by law. They compete but they nonetheless earn monopoly profits although their products are close substitutes for one another. That is the nature of competition among monopolies and oligopolies.

EpiPen, an injection used to treat emergency allergy reactions, is an example of oligopoly pricing. Heather Bresch was CEO of Mylan, a drug maker which acquired the rights to produce this 50-year-old drug. Through various machinations she was able to lobby Congress to make the product available in schools, thereby gaining an 85 percent market share while increasing EpiPen's price from $100 to $600 between 2007 and 2016. Sales jumped to $1.5 billion and her annual salary increased from $2.4 million to $19 million.[10] Her father, Joe Manchin, was governor of West Virginia and later Senator and a spoiler of the Democratic Party's agenda. That helped her to obtain connections to politicians. So political power and corporate power are intertwined.[11] The company earned monopoly profits, Bresch received a windfall, and the politicians received their share of profits at the consumers' expense. This is the way the invisible hand works in reality.[12]

Yet, textbooks continue to pretend otherwise and misled millions of students until market fundamentalism became the *dominant ideology*. The distorted formulation has immense real-world consequences like the deregulation of the financial sector (Chapter 14), destabilizing the political system (Chapter 15), perpetuation of racism (Chapter 16), and being unprepared for the Covid-19 pandemic (Chapter 17).

6.3 Imperfect Competition: Oligopolies, and Monopolies

Oligopolies are quasi-monopolistic enterprises although they have competition, because they mostly have exclusive rights to sell their products. They strategize to outsmart their competitors and their price-setting tactic resembles that of a monopoly. For instance, Apple is an oligopoly because there are other producers of computers and smartphones. Nonetheless, they have a monopoly right to sell iPhones through their patents. While iPhones do compete vigorously with Samsung's Galaxy, and many other smartphones, and have "only" 20 percent market share, Apple's pricing design successfully generated super-profits of $49,000 million *annually* on average between 2012 and 2020. Thus, oligopolies have sufficient market power to set their product price strategically because of their large market share, like a monopolist (Figure 6.3).

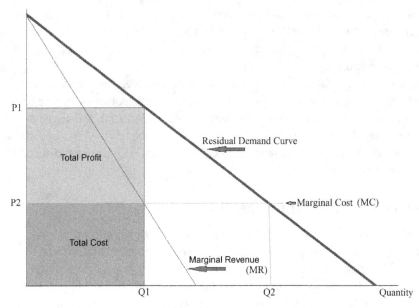

Figure 6.3 Profit of a monopolist (without fixed costs)

Oligopolies and monopolies do not have supply curves! They are large relative to the market, have market power, and sell unique branded products.[13] Apple begins its strategy by guesstimating the residual demand curve for iPhones, given the worldwide market for smartphones, and given brand loyalty which influences the extent to which other smartphones might be substituted for iPhones at a given price. The residual demand curve for iPhones is given by the market demand minus the sales of all other smartphones at prevailing prices. With these factors in mind, Apple estimates the price, P1, that will yield most profits (Figure 6.3). Apple is satisficing since the estimated residual demand curve is imprecise and the reactions of its competitors are imperfectly anticipated.

So, considered in real time, the introduction of iPhone12 began with an announcement of its price. The quantity sold would be determined subsequently; Apple will supply as many iPhones as demanded over time at the price P1. If it chose the price well, the quantity demanded will be about Q1, yielding near-maximum profits (Figure 6.3). So, iPhones do not have a supply curve.

Apple calculates its optimal price like a monopolist. It estimates the *marginal revenue* curve given its residual demand curve estimate. This is the additional revenue obtained from lowering the price incrementally by $1. As the price is lowered, the demand for iPhones increases. Total revenue is price times quantity; the marginal revenue (MR) is the amount by which total revenue increases as price is lowered. When this additional revenue is less than the marginal cost (MC) of producing iPhones, Apple will not increase its profits by lowering the price further. Thus, the optimal price is P1 and the optimal quantity of iPhones it expects to sell is Q1, where MC = MR (Figure 6.3).

If it were to decrease price below P1, for instance, to P3, its profits would decline (Figure 6.4). It would sell more iPhones at Q1+X but at a lower price P3. The top rectangle is the amount by which profits would decline because Apple must decrease the price on all iPhones. There would be additional profits also because sales increase by X. However, the additional profit designated by the rectangle [X*(P3 – MC)] is smaller than the loss in profit given by the rectangle [Q1*(P1 – P3)]. Hence, aggregate profits would decline at P3. Thus, Apple chooses P1 where MR = MC. Beyond Q1, MR<MC.

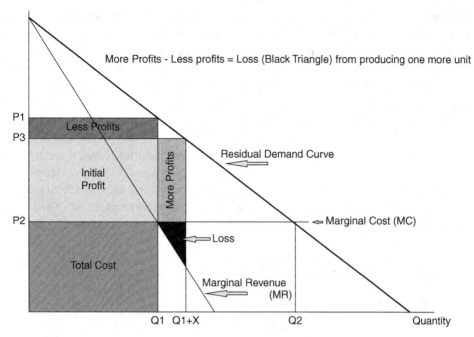

Figure 6.4 Optimal profit of a monopolist

Apple does not compete with price but differentiates its product with unique styling, appealing features, and by creating a hype through marketing, thereby enhancing the prestige value of a new iPhone protected by copyright law.[14] To stay ahead of the competition, it brings out a new model annually: it has introduced 29 models as of July 2021 with much theatrics.[15]

This strategy is optimal from Apple's point of view but suboptimal from society's perspective, because of the high prices fewer consumers afford iPhones than would be socially optimum (Q2). Hence, oligopolies and monopolies are *inefficient* from the society's view point. The social optimum is obtained where MC = P2. Until quantity Q2 the willingness of consumers to pay for iPhones exceeds the marginal cost of producing it. Hence, more consumers would like to buy the product until Q2. Apple iPhone 11 Pro Max cost about $500 to make.[16] Add $200 for research and marketing and the cost is still far below the $1,100 price for the smaller storage size version. The 200 million iPhones sold in 2020 contributed half of the firm's revenue of $274 billion.[17] Of the worldwide profits from smartphones, Apple's share was 66 percent in 2019, Samsung was second at 20 percent.

Blackboard economists argue that over time competitors will enter such markets until the supernormal profits of oligopolies are eliminated. However, they never mention how long that will take. Their predictions are refuted by real-world experience. Existing firms deter competitors from entering the market using advertising as a barrier to entry to force potential competitors to make large lump-sum investments for an uncertain venture. They may never gain sufficient market share to make the investment worthwhile. New competitors have not dared to challenge Apple's annual supernormal profits of $40–$60 billion.[18] Moreover, it has purchased 120 tech companies to squelch competition.[19]

Another form of imperfect competition is *spatial monopoly*, like gas stations since they have a monopoly on selling at a certain location. Yet, there is vigorous competition, so some of them earn small profits. Nonetheless, it is an inefficient form of market organization because there are too many gas stations and none of them is used at full capacity, leading to a misallocation of resources which could be put to other uses. The Walgreens near me is empty much of the time. Spatial monopolies dominate much of the retail sector: drugstores, restaurants, supermarkets, and department stores; they are very competitive, usually not great profit makers, and are inefficient. Walmart is an exception: it is a spatial monopoly that does make steady profits 11,000 stores worldwide earn it about $20,000 million profit annually.[20]

The super monopoly profits are also made by big pharma that delivers to the drugstores, the oil companies that deliver to the gas stations, tech giants, and financials (Table 6.1). Pharmaceuticals claim that the exorbitant prices they charge are used for research and development, but that is only half true because shareholders and CEOs also take a goodly share of the monopoly profits. From 2006 through 2015, the 18 drug companies listed in the Standard & Poor's 500 index spent a combined $516 billion on buybacks and dividends but only $465 billion on research and development.[21] And this does not include the billions spent on CEO's bloated

Table 6.1 Profits of US oligopolies, 2020 (billion dollars)

Company type	Name	Profit (billion dollars)
Big Tech	Apple	55
	Microsoft	39
	Google	34
	Intel	21
	Facebook	18
	Cisco	12
	Oracle	11
Pharma	Pfizer	16
	Johnson	15
	Novartis	12
	Merck	10
Communications	Verizon	19
	AT&T	14
	Comcast	13
Oil	Shell	16
	Exxon	14
Other	Berkshire Hathaway	81
	United Health	14
	Visa	12
	Disney	11
Retail	Walmart	15
	Amazon	12
	Home Depot	11
Finance	JPMorgan	36
	Bank of America	27
	Wells Fargo	20
	Citigroup	19
	Fanie Mae	14

Sources: "The World's Most Profitable Companies," https://asian-links.com/gdp/most-profitable-companies, "Charting America's Most Profitable Companies," https://howmuch.net/articles/top-50-most-profitable-companies-in-the-us-2020.

salaries and bonuses. In 2020, the top 15 pharma executives received total compensation of $450 million with the median salary in the $20–30 million range although good-enough managers could be found for a tiny fraction of these amounts.[22]

Government subsidies are another way to enhance profits; the fossil-fuel industry, for instance, receives annually $20 billion in government subsidies,[23] while banks received loans from the Fed at near-zero interest rates (2009–2015 and 2020–2022).[24] It is difficult not to make profits that way: profits in finance were $531 billion (2021).[25]

Thus, the default model of industrial organization should be oligopolies and monopolies in which all profits are not competed away, rather than the perfectly competitive Mom-and-Pop firms. Mainstream economists would ascribe these profits to returns to entrepreneurship but there were no entrepreneurs in the above list of companies merely employees, *agents* of the shareholders. Alternatively, they would assign it to the rewards of risk taking, but there is no evidence for that either. That is merely creative accounting, a refusal to think beyond the dogma and a pretext to obscure the reality that these oligopolistic and monopolistic profits are not being competed away. Profits by any other name are still profits.

Oligopolists' output is limited by the quantity demanded of its product and not by the increasing marginal cost of production. Most mega-corporations have constant cost of production; that is, marginal cost is generally constant, because of unemployment, underutilization of capital stock, and globalization made the labor force of the whole world available for production. Consequently, multinationals can expand production without incurring rising costs of their inputs. Hence, constant marginal and average costs should be the default model. Since price generally exceeds marginal or average cost, most oligopolies earn profits.

6.4 Prices Are Signals

According to the mainstream, prices have an *allocative function* to distribute goods to those who value the product the most. However, they fail to add that the ability to afford those prices also depends on income and therefore the poor are often at a disadvantage since they are priced out of some markets like education, health care, and housing. There are many nuances to consider. Oligopolies like Apple employ the best psychologists to determine a winning pricing strategy for its iPhone, the "single most profitable product on the planet."[26] Over time, Apple used a two-pronged strategy: (1) to increase the price of its basic iPhone in small increments; and (2) to introduce a higher-priced more impressive version simultaneously in order to test the residual demand for its smartphones. It realized that lowering price would be a losing strategy because the perception that it was a conspicuous consumption good would be damaged permanently and, moreover, it would create a price war with its rivals whereby both would squander profits. Competing with price would be a losing gambit.

The original price of iPhone was $500 in 2007. Next year's model was $600, and the price remained unchanged for three years. Then, in 2011 Apple tested the market by bringing out a model with more features, the 4S, and raised its price to $650.[27] Between 2011 and 2014, prices remained unchanged, then Apple introduced the next generation at the old price but employed the second prong of its strategy by bringing out a "Plus" version for $100 extra. This enabled it to have a better idea of its residual demand curve and the degree of consumer loyalty. So, the 6 Plus became $750 in 2014 and remained at that price the following year. Apple followed the same game plan with the next two versions 7 and 8, except that the price of 8 was raised by $50 to $800 in 2016.

In 2017, Apple deviated from its prior approach by bringing out a new model the X, with its price increasing by $200 to $1,000. This was important because the previous price increases were limited to $50-$100. So, the X version tested the resistance of its followers to the $1,000 ceiling while the two other versions it introduced in 2017, the 8 and 8 Plus were priced at $800. That was playing it safe since those customers who resisted the $1,000 barrier would have the option of buying a new version at a lower price similar to those of previous years. The strategy was psychologically perfect, so that kind of multifaceted pricing became the norm: in 2018, the XS Max was priced $100 higher at $1,100. Once the $1,000 barrier was broached that became the standard price for the next generation's top version. In 2019, Apple introduced the Pro designation: 11 Pro cost $1,000, and the 11 Pro Max started at $1,100. The price remained unchanged for the 12 Pro and the 12 Pro Max. The iPhone 13 is still selling for $800 in 2022 and the iPhone 13 Pro Max for $1,100.

Hence, Apple's *brilliant* tactic was to devise a strategy careful and psychologically well balanced, over the course of 15 years to ascertain how much the market would bear at each step in the process of raising the iPhone's price, until it eventually broached the $1,000 mark with its flagship version. It was a mixed strategy of addressing different market segments with the base price increasing from $500 in 2007 to $800 in 2020. It introduced multiple versions at the same time to test the accuracy of its estimate of the residual demand curve, the loyalty of its followers and their willingness to pay, and also to get the fans accustomed to the higher prices. That is the perfect strategy of a smart oligopolist engaging in monopolistic competition. There is no evidence at all of price competition. Instead, each year Apple introduce new gimmicky features called "bells and whistles" in the colloquial. That is the way they defended their profits and defied the theoretical prediction that in the long run competition dissipates profits. This has been falsified in the smartphone market.

Another reason why Apple was so successful in outsmarting the competition is that it is difficult for consumers to evaluate the offers because quality has so many dimensions that it is impractical for them to ascertain what exactly they are paying for. That is why the designation "Pro" and "Max" is used to make some aspects of the iPhone easily *accessible* to the consumers.

> [Its success] is directly a product of the savvy way Apple has designed and marketed the device to produce global lust ... the iPhone is in many ways a 'Veblen good,' ... a product whose high price actually increases its desirability ... the iPhone is a status symbol.[28]

Yet another aspect of price setting strategies of oligopolies is to manipulate perceptions to make their products more desirable, for instance, by pretending that the price of a shirt has just been lowered. *Homo oeconomicus* would not be influenced by such tactics but would consider whether the shirt would increase their utility by at least as much as the price. The price of the shirt yesterday is immaterial to that consideration but not for human beings. They are susceptible to falling prey to such strategies because the brain's ability to assess value is reference-dependent (see Section 4.9). The price alone does not determine the decision to buy or not, the change in price is crucial.

Thus, oligopolies devote much effort in garbling prices and instead entice customers by focusing consumers' attention on the attractive, easily accessible, aspects of their offer and concealing the less attractive ones. They use anchoring and framing strategies to focus on how much will be *saved* by purchasing a product rather than highlighting its actual price; they give the monthly instalment price rather than the total cost. They pretend that the price was just lowered in order to anchor the customer's attention on a prior higher price of the product to generate the impression that it is worth more. Firms set deadlines on discounts so that consumers feel they have limited time to take advantage of the lower price; they offer two for the price of one while inventory lasts; final day of sale offers and flash sales; they offer teaser rates like 0 percent financing for the first three months; they obscure the length of the contract or automatic renewals until canceled. Another finagling strategy is to put unsavory information into small print in the contract while the "teaser" interest rates are in large print. The list of psychological gimmicks, traps, and deceptions is long, but the salient insight is that firms hire the smartest linguists, lawyers, and psychologists to do their utmost to manipulate the consumer and make comparison shopping challenging. That is why, for example, the weight of cereal boxes is not uniform and why the easily accessible attribute, the size of the cereal boxes, is much larger than the product inside would warrant.

Collusion, such as among some oil-producing states joined in a *cartel* known as OPEC, is another strategy to gain profits. While there is still competition with producers not in the cartel, OPEC's price is determined administratively and is an important determinant of market price. OPEC considers how much they should charge, given expected response of other suppliers in the market and then they calibrate their supply to that price. In short, the causation is not from supply to price, but from price to supply.

Consider also that most banks charge \$33–\$37 for overdrawing a checking account, which is pure profit.[29] The reality is that competition does *not* lower this price because the CEOs know that if they were to lower the penalty, the rival banks would match the competition and the new equilibrium would be lower fees for everyone, thus decreasing profits. They know that price wars are futile.[30] This is tacit collusion.[31]

Quantity demanded is determined not only by current prices but also by the history of prices because those influence price expectations. Higher prices today do not always lead to a decline in the quantity demanded. Suppose the price of a good has been rising. One might interpret the current increase in price as a signal that prices will continue to rise and therefore buy even more of the good now to avoid higher prices in the future (see Figure 4.12). That is how bubbles develop in asset markets. Or suppose that the price of a good falls: one might interpret that as an indication that it will continue to decline and buy less of the good now and wait until it falls again. So, the relationship between price of a good and the quantity demanded depends also on expectations.

The conventional assumption is that one price will prevail in a market at the intersection of supply and demand. However, this is not true in case of *price discrimination*, another market imperfection. While it might increase welfare in some cases, for instance, granting discounts to youth on airplane travel, it is often used to extract more money from consumers. Generally, price discrimination penalizes those at the lower end of the income distribution because it is strategically designed to be more expensive for those who have less knowledge about the good or service in question, who cannot afford to seek additional information, or who do not understand fully the implications of signing a contract. It takes considerable effort to elude the surcharges of business strategies intended to ensnare customers. Price discrimination often exploits disadvantaged minority groups who might possess less social capital and therefore might have to pay a higher price to obtain the necessary information to make an informed decision.

A phone company that offers customers a lower price after they decline to accept their initial offer is an example of price discrimination. Price discrimination also exists with cell phone contracts. Companies deliberately complicate the offer, so it becomes difficult to compare the various plans. Companies also try to outsmart customers by using so-called "decoys," higher-priced products they are not really trying to sell. The strategy is to make the lower-priced version appear more appealing in comparison to it. The specialists designing such programs and contracts have a lot more information than the typical consumer and are therefore able to outsmart them. Humanistic economists believe that price discrimination should be regulated to ensure that it serves the public interest.

"In the early days of the Internet there was [hope] that ecommerce would lead to greater price transparency."[32] Instead, firms "keep prices in algorithm-fueled motion," extracting extra profits by personalized pricing—charging prices depending on the buyer's physical location, time of use, or other attributes.[33] Purchasing an airline ticket, I noticed that the price depended on the portal from which I accessed the company's website! That is price discrimination.

Allowing prices to ration basic necessities like health care has a moral aspect to it as well. It is inhumane to see famine amidst plenty, deprivation amidst unfathomable extravagance, for which conspicuous consumption would be an understatement. In 2021, 30 million people were at risk of famine in Africa;[34] this is a contrast with supermodel Linda Evangelista's request that the French billionaire François Henri-Pinault pay child support for their then 4-year-old son of $46,000 *monthly*.[35] Louis Vuitton's website features "most coveted" shoes selling for $2,000, and dozens of handbags carried a price tag above $4,000,[36] while a mother killed her children because of financial desperation.[37] Every day one learns about such inhumane discrepancies: while Jeff Bezos enjoys an 11-minute joy ride in space for $5,500 million, he squeezes his workers to the subsistence limit.[38] And Richard Branson is selling tickets to space for a mere $250,000 and 600 people, including Lady Gaga, Tom Hanks, Justin Bieber, and Elon Musk have already reserved a place. The logical inference is that a winner-take-all, losers-lose-all economy is unable to prevent excesses. Humanistic economists advocate setting commonsense limits on disparities in income and opportunity.

6.5 Disequilibrium Is the Norm

The conventional view is that the immutable law of supply and demand implies that equilibrium—where supply equals demand—exists in all markets at all times. Yet, it is unclear what mechanism would enable markets to reach such an equilibrium, and it is never *ever* specified how long it would take to reach it. Equilibrium is actually not easy to reach. Price depends on two crucial variables often absent from conventional supply and demand models: location and time. We do not always have the time to wait for the market to reach equilibrium. Hungry people do not have time to wait for the price of bread to decline until they can afford it.

In the presence of information and transaction costs it is challenging to match buyers and sellers; decentralized markets do not have a straightforward mechanism to accomplish this. Some models imagine a hypothetical auctioneer who calls out prices and quantities by trial and error until total quantity supplied matches total quantity demanded and thus the market-clearing price (and equilibrium) are established. The auctioneer would have to have the authority to prohibit buying and selling until the equilibrium price is reached, otherwise, if people would start buying before equilibrium is reached, prices would fluctuate. There would not be a unique equilibrium price for the product. However, such figment of the imagination is unrealistic since the auctioneer would either have to be compensated, driving an inefficient wedge between prices paid and prices received, or be a benevolent dictator, which would not be consistent with the mainstream's view that people are selfish.[39]

This is a conundrum, because price discovery is a more complex process than economists imagine, implying that the coordinating power of the market's price mechanism is not magical at all.[40] Competition is insufficient to bring about an equilibrium between supply and demand.

If one adds information and transaction costs to the model, one finds that there can be multiple equilibrium prices in a market.[41] There was no indication in, say, 1900, that medical costs in Europe and the US would diverge substantially. Medical costs in the US would not have become twice that of Europe if the American Medical Association and the insurance companies had not gained so much political power to influence the institutional structure of the health-care system. Current prices of medical services in the US could have been the same as in Europe if institutions, vested interests, and lobbies had developed differently.

The process of matching buyers to sellers can also have fatal consequences: at a Walmart's "Black Friday" "doorbuster" sale in 2008, products priced as "loss leaders"—items sold below cost—caused a stampede in which a person was trampled to death.[42]

Would General Motors and Chrysler have filed for bankruptcy if matching supply and demand were easy? It is not trivial because producers and consumers are not in the same place at the same time, and because middlemen are involved; furthermore, there is a considerable time lag between the onset of production and the sale of the product. Thus, producers have a formidable information problem and must forecast uncertain demand and anticipate market developments well in advance. This is hardly trivial. Consequently, there is constant volatility of demand and inventory cycles, leading to turbulence in the labor market, generally impacting the quality of life.

6.6 Adverse Selection Is an Information Problem

In standard transactions, the price of a product is proportional to its quality. However, in the presence of asymmetric information, the seller might know more about the quality of a product than the buyer. Then the seller could withhold critical information and some buyers may choose the product with the lower price without knowing that it was also of lower quality. In such cases the high-quality product might disappear from the market completely. This is the gist of *adverse selection* in the presence of asymmetric information. This occurs in *many* complex exchanges, including credit markets, used car markets, and insurance markets.[43]

Moreover, if insurers set a price for health insurance with a given level of coverage based on the average health of the population, then less healthy individuals will find the insurance more attractive and will be more likely to buy it than healthy ones. The insurance company does not know everything about the applicants' health so the applicant can withhold information. Consequently, the average health of those insured will be lower than the average health of the whole population. Hence, the company will incur higher costs than expected, inducing it to raise the price of insurance. The increased price, in turn, will cause more of the healthier people to discontinue their insurance. So, the insurance company will have an "adverse selection" of customers, the less healthy ones. This vicious circle could lead to *market failure*: a spiral of price increases, leading to the collapse of the insurance market as an increasing number of customers find it unattractive to buy insurance. In such cases, government-mandated insurance may be the only way to reduce adverse selection and improve the efficiency of this market.

Thus, adverse selection can occur if buyers and sellers have different information about an important aspect of a transaction. Selectivity can occur about quality of a used car or the health of a buyer of health insurance. Then one party to the exchange might benefit from hiding information from their counterparty: in the case of used cars, the seller; in the case of the health insurance, the buyer. Such exchanges are inefficient because both counterparties are not fully knowledgeable about the transaction.

6.7 Theories of Strategic Behavior

Game theory pertains to strategic behavior in groups in which there are interaction effects among the actors.[44] The business world has many aspects that mimic a repeated game with rules, strategies, and uncertainty about the response of other players. In deciding on a course of action oligopolists need to consider the reaction of their counterparties to that action and adjust it accordingly. In the game of chess, players have to form expectations about the probability of the opponent's next steps. Similarly, Apple formulates its pricing strategy based on its subjective evaluation (based on historical experience) of what Samsung's reaction will be and how that response would affect its profits. Anticipating that if it were to lower the prices of iPhones, Samsung would follow a "tit-for-tat" strategy by lowering its prices as well, Apple avoids risking a "price war" and a downward spiral of prices (Section 6.4). In this *duopoly* game Apple's dominant strategy is to maintain prices and avoid lowering them.

There are non-cooperating games, zero-sum games, but collusion is also possible, such as among major oil producers. However, the members of the OPEC cartel also face a dilemma since each would benefit if they could produce more oil at the high prices set by the cartel. Nonetheless, they have been cooperating/colluding since 1960, because they all anticipate the reaction of the other cartel members who would follow suit and the profit of all members would diminish in a price war. These concepts can be applied in many aspects of the business world.

6.8 The Influence of Corporate Power: Economic, Political, and Social

Power is the ability to control the action or thought of others. That *wealth translates directly into political power* has been known through the ages, because wealth provides irresistible incentives for politicians to act on behalf of affluent supporters. Power influences every aspect of the economy: institutional structure, legislation to further enhance economic benefits through lobbying, cultural norms, and buying habits. They all increase profits and diminish the agency of the average consumer. Hence, it is amazing that power is overlooked in mainstream economics.

Admittedly, power does not exist in perfectly competitive markets since they are characterized by countless sellers producing a generic product, with innumerable consumers. Power does not exist in such markets since producers are price takers and earn no profits in long-run equilibrium (see Section 6.1). The focus of Econ-101 on perfectly competitive markets enables it to neglect the crucial consequences of the unequal distribution of power.[45] However, this should not be the default model, because power tends to concentrate in oligopolies and monopolies. *This is a fundamental although neglected law of free-market economics.* Concentration of wealth and power is bad for democracy because democracy is based on the dispersion of power.[46]

Big business avoids perfectly competitive markets like the plague and usually finds ways of doing so. This was true for the "Robber Barons," in the late-nineteenth century: with the expansion of railroads, finance, petroleum, and steel, a new wealthy class gained prominence using questionable business practices to make their fortunes. The new elite of the digital age are no different: Zuckerberg bought up 92 rivals to squash competition in the bud to reap monopoly profits;[47] Google bought up 243 firms, Microsoft 247, Amazon 108, and Apple 120.[48] Limited competition means that these firms can expand their power and can earn near-monopoly profits.

President Dwight Eisenhower warned the nation about the "unwarranted influence" of the "military-industrial complex," and the "potential for the disastrous rise of misplaced power."[49]

Since then, corporations have extended their influence over society through the financial sector, big tech, and increased their sway over government.[50] Political and economic power was transferred from Main Street to mega-multinationals and to oligarchs to a hitherto inconceivable extent.[51]

The problem begins with the fiction that corporations are legal persons. This makes sense for conducting business. However, it is preposterous to consider businesses as persons permitted to influence political activity. To extend the political rights of individuals to an abstract entity with extensive financial resources is harmful for democracy. The First (1791) and the Fourteenth (1868) Amendments of the Constitution were intended to guarantee rights of free speech to flesh-and-blood human beings. They had nothing to do with corporations. Humanistic economics advocates limiting the activities of corporations strictly to economic matters and excluding them from the political sphere. Because businesses do not have vocal cords they cannot speak and therefore the First Amendment should not apply to them. Moreover, when employees speak for corporations, the implication is that flesh-and-blood individuals have multiple voices in society: both as their real selves and as spokespeople for an inanimate entity. This violates the principle of one person, one vote and is contrary to democratic principles as it brings about a skewed distribution of power.

In the current situation, corporate profits are leveraged into political and social power with immense feedback effects on the economic structure and its institutions. Countrywide Financial, a mortgage bank, bribed several Members of Congress by giving them low-interest mortgages.[52] The Supreme Court has intensified the power imbalances by an incomprehensible twist of the English language, conceptualizing money as speech in its 2010 *Citizens United* decision, in which it interpreted the First Amendment to imply that corporations can spend an unlimited amount of money on political campaigns. Obviously, money is not speech, and the First Amendment says absolutely nothing about money. Nonetheless, this twisted decision has permitted big money to play a huge role in elections.[53] Corporations do not have to disclose their contributions even to their shareholders, the owners of the firms.[54]

Thus, oligopolies like Goldman Sachs and JPMorgan Chase have considerable clout to manipulate regulations to their benefit.[55] Power enables *vested interests* to expand and further skew economic advantages in their favor by rewriting the rules governing market activity so that their initial advantages lead to further political power which, in turn, increases their privileges and advantages.[56] This becomes a vicious circle of power, privilege, and profit-hoarding, leading to the diminution in political influence of Everyman on Main Street.[57] Clout is the main reason why corporate taxes as a percentage of profits have declined markedly (Figure 6.5). In the twenty-first century alone, it dropped significantly from 25 percent to 9 percent of profits, that contributes the US endemic budget deficit!

Corporate clout has also brought about substantial deregulation.[58] For instance, the financial sector by itself spent $2.7 billion on lobbying from 1999 to 2008, to gain further advantages.[59] The pharmaceutical industry spent $150 million lobbying Congress in 2016 alone.[60] Through such lobbying it was able to prohibit Medicare from bargaining with pharmaceuticals over drug prices. Consequently, this regulation alone enabled it to reap additional monopoly profits of $20 billion annually.[61] Total corporate spending on lobbying amounts to a dizzying $3,000 million annually. Some corporations have dozens of lobbyists working for them. They can thus be at every relevant committee meeting. No wonder Congress is held in such low esteem that it was attacked on January 6. Its approval rating in December 2020 was at 15 percent.[62]

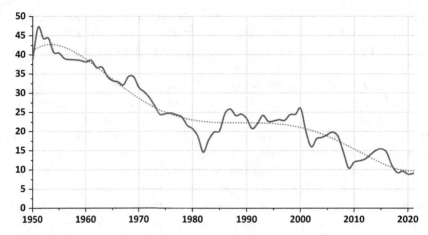

Figure 6.5 Corporate taxes as a percentage of profits
Source: St. Louis Fed, series A053RC1Q027SBEA and B075RC1Q027SBEA.

Obviously, the unemployed, the homeless, and the minimum wage workers, have no lobbyists in Washington and no money to make campaign contributions. Without countervailing power,[63] the laws governing the market's organization could not remain balanced for long:[64] "Nationwide state and local subsidies for corporations totaled more than $70bil in 2010."[65] The financial sector was bailed out with trillions of dollars of taxpayers' money in 2008/2009 while homeowners on Main Street received nothing from the establishment (see Chapter 14).

6.9 Takeaways

By ignoring the role of imperfect information, mainstream economists argue that efficient production is a cinch: firms combine the factors of production efficiently, if unions and governments do not interfere. There are no profits in the long run so income distribution is a no-brainer: employees and employers receive their just rewards, so there is no conflict and no need to moralize about the distribution of income.

The perfectly competitive model is the mainstay of mainstream theories. It might apply to Mom-and-Pop operations, but such models are anachronistic in a world in which supranational mega-corporations dominate. Oligopolies and monopolies take advantage of their market power and do not produce the socially efficient amount of goods at the socially efficient price. They differ from the profitless firms insofar as they charge super-high prices, have power to manipulate consumers and depress wages, take advantage of asymmetric information to trap consumers, practice opportunism, and, in contrast to perfectly competitive firms, make immense profits that they use to enhance their political and economic power further by financing an army of lobbyists, political action committees, and think tanks. Corporate (after tax) profits reached $2.6 trillion in 2021, having jumped 37 percent from the previous year, not seen since 1950. Apple led the pack with a dizzying $95 billion.

Questions for Discussion

1   Can you give some examples of businesses wasting the time of their consumers?
2   Has your boss ever been impolite to you?

3   Do you think that charging $36 for overdrawing a bank account is close to the bank's marginal cost of taking care of that account or is the bank taking advantage of a fine print in the agreement and earning pure profit on that charge?

4   Is the price of pizza the same everywhere in your town?

5   Is there any product whose price is uniform throughout your town?

6   Do you know of any perfectly competitive firms where you live?

7   What do you think about the concentration of power in the hands of large corporations?

8   Do you know how much profit Apple earns on an iPhone?

9   What do you think the difference is between the iPhone 13 Pro, iPhone 13, iPhone SE, and iPhone 12?

10   Can you tell the difference between an original Louis Vuitton handbag and an imitation?

11   Do you think that Goldman Sachs' $13 billion profit in 2010 (based on taxpayer subsidies) was legitimate?

12   How much money do you estimate you waste in a year?

13   Have you ever been deceived by unscrupulous marketing strategies?

14   Do you think there should be laws so that Angelo Mozilo would have to forfeit his wealth for the great damage he did to the American economy? What about Dick Fuld?

15   Do you think there should be a right to employment?

16   How many prices do you remember?

17   Do you think that innovation is always good for us?

18   Can you give examples of products with planned obsolescence?

19   Do you think that competition leads to consumer satisfaction?

20   Did you ever see shirking where you worked?

21   Does the "invisible hand" always guarantee satisfactory solutions to our problems?

22   Will the profits of Apple Inc. ever be competed away?

23   What are some differences between firms in the textbooks and firms in the real economy?

24   Do you ever get confused by all the products you see in a supermarket?

25   Do you know anyone who was deceived by his/her cell phone contract?

26   Did you make a rational choice in buying your cell phone?

27   Did you ever make a mistake in buying a product?

28   Have you ever been prey to some opportunistic behavior?

Notes

1   Adam Smith, *An Inquiry into the Nature and Causes of the Wealth of Nations* (W. Strahan and T. Cadell, 1776), Book I, Chapter V.

2   Joan Robinson, *The Economics of Imperfect Competition* (Macmillan, 1933).

3   Edward Chamberlin, *The Theory of Monopolistic Competition: A Re-Orientation of the Theory of Value* (Harvard University Press, 1933).

4   Alfred Chandler, *The Visible Hand: The Managerial Revolution in American Business* (Belknap Press, 1977).

5   The United States Defense Department has 2 million employees.

6   *Economies of scale* mean that the cost of production falls with larger output, within a certain range but not indefinitely. *Network externality* means that the existence of a product, firm, or service makes it easier or cheaper for the subsequent producer to produce or for consumers to use the product. For example, the early adoption of the Windows operating system made it attractive for the next consumer, because information about the product was readily accessible.

7 William Whyte, "Groupthink," *Fortune*, March 1952, 114–117. Whyte emphasized that in the corporate ethic, employees' individuality becomes subservient to the group ideology. Groupthink becomes a rationalized conformity to enhance their position in the organization. Vance Packard, *The Pyramid Climbers* (David McKay, 1962).

8 These are risks associated with a domino effect in the financial sector in which banks' commitments are interlinked. The solvency of one bank depends on the solvency of all other banks. Thus, the bankruptcy of Lehman Brothers would have caused the whole house of cards to collapse without taxpayer bailouts.

9 "[Bernanke] rarely challenged Greenspan. He wouldn't have gotten into that club if he didn't go along … Mr. Greenspan ran a tight ship, and he didn't fancy people spouting off with their own views." John Cassidy, "Anatomy of a Meltdown," *The New Yorker*, December 1, 2008.

10 Wikipedia, "Heather Bresch."

11 William Dugger, *Corporate Hegemony* (Praeger, 1989); Christopher Leonard, *Kochland: The Secret History of Koch Industries and Corporate Power in America* (Simon & Schuster, 2019).

12 The deregulation of the electricity market in Texas cost consumers $28 billion compared to traditional utilities. Tom McGinty and Scott Patterson, "Texas Electric Bills Were $28bil Higher Under Deregulation," *The Wall Street Journal*, February 24, 2021.

13 John Harsany, "Games with Incomplete Information," *The American Economic Review* 85 (1995), 3: 291–303.

14 Wikipedia, "iPhone."

15 CNBC Television, "Apple CEO Tim Cook: Today We Are Bringing 5G to iPhone," https://www.youtube.com/watch?v=oZzFaVetoTo.

16 Rachel Brown, "The Cost of Making an iPhone," *Investopedia*, March 27, 2020.

17 Apple Inc. "Annual Report to the U.S. Securities and Exchange Commission, for the Fiscal Year Ended September 26, 2020."

18 Statista, https://www.statista.com/statistics/267728/apples-net-income-since-2005/.

19 Wikipedia, "List of Mergers and Acquisitions by Apple."

20 Walmart Inc. "2020 Annual Report."

21 William Lazonick et al., "US Pharma's Financialized Business Model," Institute for New Economic Thinking, Working Paper 60, July 13, 2017.

22 Fraiser Kansteiner, "The Top 15 Highest-Paid Biopharma CEOs of 2020," FiercePharma, May 24, 2021.

23 https://www.greenpeace.org/usa/ending-the-climate-crisis/everything-you-need-to-know-about-fossil-fuel-subsidies/.

24 St. Louis Fed, series INTDSRUSM193N.

25 BEA, "Table 6.16D Corporate Profits by Industry," https://apps.bea.gov/iTable/iTable.cfm?reqid=19&step=3&isuri=1&1921=survey&1903=239#reqid=19&step=3&isuri=1&1921=survey&1903=239.

26 Thomas Frohlich and Alexander Hess, "America's Most Profitable Products," *24/7 Wall Street*, June 9, 2014.

27 Always referring to the least expensive model. Wikipedia, "iPhone"; Emil Protalinski, "iPhone Prices from the Original to iPhone X," *@EPro*, September 12, 2017.

28 Farhad Manjoo, "Apple's iPhone Keeps Going Its Own Way," *The New York Times*, September 9, 2015.

29 Spencer Tierney, "Overdraft Fees: What Banks Charge," nerdwallet.

30 Smriti Chand, "Pricing Determination under Oligopoly Market." www.yourarticlelibrary.com/economics/pricing-determination-under-oligopoly-market-economics/28916/.

31 Anna Maria Andriotis and Andrew Ackerman, "Overdraft Fees Enrich Banks, and the Biden Administration Wants Less of That," *The Wall Street Journal*, December 11, 2021.

32 Daisuke Wakabayashi, "Does Anyone Know What Paper Towels Should Cost?," *The New York Times*, February 26, 2021.

33 Based on the IP address of the computer, the difference was about 10 percent. "A Tale of Two Prices," *The Wall Street Journal*, December 24, 2012.

34 Nadifa Mohamed, "A Fierce Famine Stalks Africa," *The New York Times*, June 12, 2017; https://internationalmedicalcorps.org/emergency-response/famine-risk/.

35 Evangelista has a net worth of $18 million. www.therichest.com/celebnetworth/celeb/model/linda-evangelista-net-worth/. Robert Frank, "How Does a Four-Year-Old Spend $46,000 a Month?" *The Wall Street Journal*, August 3, 2011. Kathleen Elkins, "21 Outrageous Ways the Super Rich Spend Their Money," *Business Insider*, July 27, 2015.

36 https://us.louisvuitton.com/eng-us/women/shoes/iconic-shoes/_/N-1o3cray?page=2. Stephanie Clifford, "Even Marked Up, Luxury Goods Fly Off Shelves," *The New York Times*, August 3, 2011.

37 She received a 35-year sentence. Robbie Brown, "Mother in South Carolina Killed 2 Children, Police Say," *The New York Times*, August 17, 2010.

38 Kevin Dugan, "Everything to Know about Tuesday's Blue Origin Space Launch with Jeff Bezos," *Fortune*, July 19, 2021; Jodi Kantor et al., "Inside Amazon's Employment Machine," *The New York Times*, June 15, 2021.

39 Sanford Grossman and Joseph Stiglitz, "On the Impossibility of Informationally Efficient Markets," *American Economic Review* 70 (1980), 3: 393–408.

40 F.H. Hahn, "Auctioneer," in Steven Durlauf and Lawrence Blume (eds.), *The New Palgrave Dictionary of Economics*, 2nd edn. (Palgrave Macmillan, 2008).

41 Peter Diamond, "Unemployment, Vacancies, Wages," *American Economic Review*, 101 (2011), 4: 1045–1072.

42 CBS, "Store Worker Trampled, Dies," November 28, 2008, www.youtube.com/watch?v=7aUwmsi6Wc0. Walmart was fined the ridiculously low sum of $7,000 by OSHA. Dave Jamleson, "Walmart Has Finally Stopped Fighting The $7,000 Fine for a Worker's Death on Black Friday in 2008," *Huffington Post*, March 19, 2015. Searching for "Black Friday Chaos," brings up many scenes of violence, a horrific reflection on Western civilization.

43 George Akerlof, "The Market for 'Lemons': Quality Uncertainty and the Market Mechanism," *Quarterly Journal of Economics* 84 (1970), 3: 488–500.

44 John von Neumann and Oscar Morgenstern, *Theory of Games and Economic Behavior* (Princeton University Press, 1944). The book was immediately recognized as "one of the major scientific achievements" of its time. Arthur Copeland's book review in the *Bulletin of the American Mathematical Society* 51 (1945): 498–504. See also *The New York Times* review of the book: https://www.nytimes.com/1946/03/10/archives/mathematical-theory-of-poker-is-applied-to-business-problems-gaming.html.

45 Thomas Piketty, *Capital and Ideology* (Harvard University Press, 2020).

46 William Domhoff, *Who Rules America?* (Prentice-Hall, 1967); www2.ucsc.edu/whorulesamerica/power/wealth.html.

47 Wikipedia, "List of Mergers and Acquisitions by Facebook." Sheera Frenkel and Cecilia Kang, *An Ugly Truth: Inside Facebook's Battle for Domination* (Harper, 2021).

48 Wikipedia, "List of Mergers and Acquisitions by Amazon," "List of Mergers and Acquisitions by Microsoft," "List of Mergers and Acquisitions by Alphabet."

49 "Eisenhower Warns Us of the Military Industrial Complex," YouTube video. www.youtube.com/watch?v=8yO6NSBBRtY; James Ledbetter, "What Ike Got Right," *The New York Times*, December 13, 2010.

50 Franklin Roosevelt warned us about "industrial dictatorship" imposing wages on working people and about "economic royalty" expropriating other people's money. www.austincc.edu/lpatrick/his2341/fdr-36acceptancespeech.htm.

51 "The Military-Industrial Complex Rides Ever Higher," Tom Engelhardt, "Junta Lite: How Generals and Billionaires Took over Trump's Militarized America," *The Guardian*, March 1, 2017.

52 Wikipedia, "Countrywide Financial Political Loan Scandal."

53 Shane Goldmacher, "Dozen Megadonors Gave $3.4bil, One in Every 13 Dollars, Since 2009," *The New York Times*, April 20, 2021; also: https://www.issueone.org/wp-content/uploads/2021/04/Issue-One-Outsized-Influence-Report-final.pdf.

54   Thus, CEOs can spend the owners' money and even lobby against the interests of their shareholders without them knowing it. Mike McIntire and Nicholas Confessore, "Groups Shield Political Gifts of Businesses," *The New York Times*, July 8, 2012.

55   Mancur Olson, *The Logic of Collective Action: Public Goods and the Theory of Groups* (Harvard University Press, 1971).

56   Economists can be also captured by wealth; see the award-winning film, *Inside Job*; https://www.youtube.com/watch?v=bYm_oEO5iyE.

57   Consequently, labor's share of GDP declined since 1980. St. Louis Fed, series LABSHPUSA156NRUG.

58   *Bill Moyers Journal*, "Simon Johnson and Marcy Kaptur, Interview," October 9, 2009.

59   Sewell Chan, "Financial Crisis Was Avoidable, Inquiry Finds," *The New York Times*, January 25, 2011.

60   Rick Claypool, "Pharmaceutical Industry Profits Exceed Industry's Self-Reported R&D Costs," *Public Citizen*, March 31, 2017.

61   "They [lobbyists working for major corporations] killed a major labor law reform, rolled back regulation, lowered their taxes, and helped to move public opinion in favor of less government intervention in the economy." Lee Drutman, "How Corporate Lobbyists Conquered American Democracy," *The Atlantic*, April 20, 2015.

62   https://www.statista.com/statistics/207579/public-approval-rating-of-the-us-congress/.

63   John Kenneth Galbraith, *American Capitalism: The Concept of Countervailing Power* (Houghton Mifflin, 1952).

64   In a Freudian slip, Representative Spencer Bachus of Alabama, chairman of the House Financial Services Committee, told *The Birmingham News* that "Washington and the regulators are there to serve the banks," revealing that high finance has captured Washington. Editorial, "How to Derail Financial Reform," *The New York Times*, December 26, 2010.

65   David Cay Johnston, "How Corporate Socialism Destroys," Reuters, June 1, 2012.

7 Returns to the Factors of Production

No society can surely be flourishing and happy, of which the far greater part of the members are poor and miserable.

–Adam Smith[1]

Payments to the factors of production include the compensation to labor, the payment to the owners of capital and of natural resources, and the rent on land. Labor compensation includes wages, salary, bonuses, health insurance premiums, and social security contributions of employers. In perfectly competitive markets, labor, capital, and CEOs receive their just rewards: their *opportunity cost* or the value of their contribution to the firm. Since the rewards are appropriate, there is no need to think seriously about inequality. There is hardly any role for government in this fantasy economy as everything runs smoothly. The residual between revenue and payments to factors and the cost of raw materials is profit, but in a perfectly competitive market there are no profits to wrangle over since all problems are solved conveniently by the market (see Figure 6.2). This is the conventional view, but it is an unreasonable description of the real-existing economy made up of powerful oligopolies and monopolies instead of perfectly competitive firms.

Corporations combine factors of production to produce goods and services. Infrastructure, entrepreneurship, social capital, legal and other institutions, knowledge, human capital, culture, social capital, and natural resources are additional important factors of production often disregarded. In today's *knowledge economy*, in which production is based mainly on information-technology-intensive activities, the role of *intangible factors* like *human capital* and information (including big data) gain in significance.[2] In addition, firms use resources provided by the community, including *public goods* and the legal system without which they could not function.

7.1 Marginal Theory of Everything

Marginal utility (MU), marginal cost (MC), *marginal product of labor* (MP_L), and marginal revenue (MR)–let's just call these abstractions *marginal everything* (ME)–are key variables in economics. MU is the change in utility due to an increase in consumption by one unit. The marginal values of the other variables are defined similarly: the change induced by an additional unit.

Mankiw's insidious ten principles of economics include the misleading assertion that "Rational people think at the margin."[3] Students are unlikely to understand that this obscure language refers to *homo oeconomicus* and does not mean that people are actually rational or that people

DOI: 10.4324/9781003174356-7

do think at the margin. Instead, the statement implies that if people were rational, they would think in marginal terms. However, this is a null set since *homo sapiens* are not rational. So, it does not imply that anyone is really thinking about the margin (the last unit being considered), although a cursory reading would suggest it.

If people were rational and if ME were easily ascertainable, then it would make sense that these variables would hold the key to determining output, wages, and consumption. Then the optimal conditions derived on blackboards would be applicable to the real world: output would be constrained by MC, the value of MP_L would equal wages, and MR would equal MC. Yet, this theory lacks coherence in the real world where all these variables are impossible to ascertain and everyone is *satisficing*, basing many of their decisions on judgment or intuition with great uncertainty (see Section 4.5).

The reason is that these hypothetical variables are not observable in the same way temperature is measurable by a thermometer. They are abstractions without a gage to measure them. However, for piece-rate workers like coal miners, the MP_L is measurable because the amount of coal produced can be weighed. Yet, this is impossible in most cases as in doctors in a hospital since output is heterogeneous and the hospital does not hire one doctor at a time until it determines how much revenue increased thereafter, especially since revenue fluctuates. Hence, the concept was more applicable in the nineteenth century when production was simpler but in today's complex economy, MP_L is impossible to measure.

Thus, there are many professions—teachers, policemen, doctors, firemen, soldiers, CEOs, civil servants, and many others—whose MP_L is unknowable in principle because it is not measurable. Their contribution to the economy is a matter of judgment. One-fifth of the labor force works for the government—federal, state, and local—in the US with no measurable MP_L. This distorts the rest of the labor market. So, even if we could measure MP_L in the rest of the economy, the measurement would still be inaccurate.

What about MU? I do not have a clear sense of what the marginal utility of my consuming a piece of cake is. It is a surge of fleeting pleasure that is soon forgotten and turns into remorse. Besides, the waiter would not bring out half a slice as I really wanted. Behavioral economists have shown how many cognitive errors people make about their own utility (see Section 4.3); it would be far-fetched to think that people can even approximate the MU of consuming anything. Given the impossibility of calculating ME, we generally substitute a rule of thumb, a heuristic, a convention, or follow habit to reach a good-enough solution. That is the essence of satisficing for both consumers and producers (see Section 4.5). We make decisions without knowing ME. Otherwise, we would become catatonic.

There is an additional problem of aggregating the factors of production. How do we add computers, automobiles, and buildings to calculate the total capital stock (Section 7.3)? And how should we aggregate janitors with computer programmers and CEOs to obtain the total labor force? If we are unable to compute these aggregates, we are unable to compute the output of the last worker or that of the last capital stock added to the firm's operation. And what is the contribution to output of public goods like the internet? There are too many controversial questions for the theory to hold any credibility.

Another contentious issue is that often there are fixed proportions in production. The corporation has one CEO and the output is a joint product between the CEO and the rest of the employees. The marginal principle is not applicable in case of *joint production* because we do not know how much of the output to attribute to the CEO or the other employees.

The theory also assumes that everything is continuously divisible, so that the ME functions are differentiable. The calculation of MP_L would require hiring one additional worker to ascertain her contribution to output. But that is impossible in real-world situations. Firms cannot hire managers by the hour or the day to ascertain what their contribution to total product is. Capital is similarly lumpy, not divisible either.

7.2 Labor Compensation Lags Far Behind Productivity: The Steady Ascent of the Ominous Wage Gap

According to traditional theory, wages equal the dollar value of labor's marginal product. This implies that *real wages and labor productivity should grow at the same rate*. However, this theory is conceived for a fictitious perfect labor market without search or transaction costs and without considering the role of power in real markets. It also overlooks the difficulties employers have in ascertaining the applicants' productivity and disregards the importance of government's role in devising the framework within which bargaining occurs between employers and employees in a situation of asymmetric power relations. So, the conventional theory is incomplete.

Nonetheless, the theory did work well as predicted, as long as labor unions were sufficiently powerful to ensure that compensation was commensurate with productivity (Figure 7.1). Both wages and productivity almost doubled, growing at an impressive rate of 2.7 percent per annum in the 1950s and 1960s (Table 7.1, row 1). At the beginning of Richard Nixon's presidency (1969), the gap was still inconsequential: the growth in wages since 1947 was practically identical to the growth in productivity (97.3 percent) (Figure 7.2).

However, this post-World War II golden age of labor ended in the 1970s: the growth in their inflation-adjusted compensation (wages, bonuses, and benefits) began to lag slightly the growth in productivity. The 1970s experienced two major oil shocks and double-digit inflation and growth in productivity was cut in half to 1.4 percent per annum and growth of real compensation declined to 1.1 percent. Nonetheless, they were still linked: the difference was merely 0.3 percent per annum (Table 7.1, row 2). By 1976, the end of the Nixon-Ford era, the gap reached 9.3

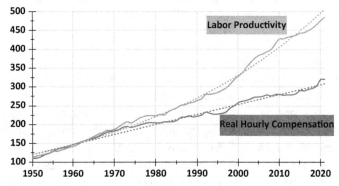

Figure 7.1 Index of the productivity-wage gap in the US

Note: 1947 = 100.

Source: Susan Fleck, John Glaser, and Shawn Sprague, "The Compensation-Productivity Gap: A Visual Essay," *Monthly Labor Review*, January 2011: 57–69. Data for 2012–2021 was kindly provided by Shawn Sprague of the BLS.

Table 7.1 Growth in productivity and real compensation, US, 1947–2021 (%)

	Years	Number of years	Productivity	Compensation	Ratio	Difference
1	1947–1970	23	2.7	2.7	1.0	0.0
2	1970–1982	12	1.4	1.1	1.4	−0.3
3	1982–2021	39	2.0	1.1	1.8	−0.9
3a	1982–1999	17	2.1	1.1	1.9	−0.9
3b	1999–2010	11	2.7	1.1	2.5	−1.6
3c	2010–2021	11	1.2	1.2	1.0	0.0

Note: Annual compounded growth rate is reported. Ratio is the ratio of productivity growth rates divided by the compensation growth rates. 2021 refers to the first half of the year. Wages refers to total compensation including wages, salaries, benefits, and bonuses.
Source: Susan Fleck, John Glaser, and Shawn Sprague, "The Compensation-Productivity Gap: A Visual Essay," *Monthly Labor Review*, January 2011: 57–69.

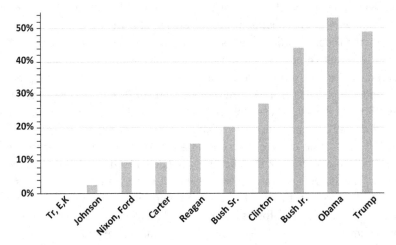

Figure 7.2 Cumulative gap between productivity and wages
Source: Susan Fleck, John Glaser, and Shawn Sprague, "The Compensation-Productivity Gap: A Visual Essay," *Monthly Labor Review*, January 2011: 57–69. Data for 2012–2021 was kindly provided by Shawn Sprague of the BLS.

percentage points (ppts), i.e., wages growth was 90.7 percent of productivity growth (Figure 7.2). Much to Carter's credit, his administration was able to prevent the gap from increasing!

However, the permanent structural break in the relationship began with *Reaganomics* as labor's political and economic power waned and a gaping wedge emerged thereafter and increased continuously until the present: productivity growth rebounded to 2.0 percent per annum, 1.8 times as fast as the growth in compensation, at 1.1 percent per annum (Table 7.1, row 3). By the end of the Reagan-Bush Sr. presidencies, the gap had reached 20 percent, i.e., productivity grew 20 percent faster than compensation (Figure 7.1),[4] revealing Reagan's anti-labor policies, such as allowing the minimum wage to decline by 25 percent.

Clinton was unmoved by the plight of labor, in stark contrast to traditional Democratic Party ideology, and permitted the gap to continue to widen to 27 percent. Under Bush Jr.'s presidency, the gap jumped by a record 17 ppts and reached 44 percent. By the end of the period under consideration, the gap was at 50 percent (Figure 7.2).

Consequently, during these four decades (1981-2021) the theoretical prediction that wages would keep up with productivity in a competitive labor market was undeniably falsified: productivity more than doubled, increasing by 115 percent, while compensation increased by 55 percent, just half as much. The difference accrued to profits. In many sectors, the gap is even wider: in manufacturing the productivity grew 4 times as fast as wages, in the IT sector by 3.6 times as fast, and in the retail trade by 14 times as fast.[5] This extraordinary disparity blatantly contradicts the theory of wage determination (Table 7.1). Yet, the theory continues to be taught, which confirms the unscientific nature of the economics discipline. Economists avoid the refutation of their theories by ignoring contradictory evidence.

That is not all. The official statistics consider the remuneration of CEOs as labor income! Hence, their compensation is conflated with the wages of typical workers (Table 7.1 and Figure 7.1). Yet only a tiny fraction of CEO salaries is labor income because they really *share in profits*. Hence, actually, most of CEO compensation is *economic rent* and humanistic economists would not consider it labor income.[6] So, the labor compensation data is biased upward (Table 7.1) The wages of typical workers fell even further behind than indicated (Figure 7.1).[7]

The abrupt divergence between wages and productivity in the 1980s was brought about by the changing *balance of power* in favor of big business and the concomitant decline of the countervailing power of organized labor (see Section 15.3). Reagan dealt a summary blow to the unions by squelching the strike of air-traffic controllers. Union membership declined subsequently from 30 percent of the labor force to 12 percent, and half of those remaining were in the public sector.[8] The increased power of corporations enabled it to depress wages and further game the system (see Sections 9.3 and 9.4).[9] For instance, franchises are prohibited from hiring workers from other franchises. So, one Burger King may not hire workers from another Burger King.[10] Since switching jobs is an important strategy for advancement, this restriction puts a damper on mobility and wage growth. This practice affects 3.5 million workers in the fast-food industry whose average wage is $11.50/hour or $24,000 per annum, below the poverty line for a family of four.[11]

Additionally, mega-corporations took advantage of *the increasing labor-force participation of women* to compress wages as their share of the labor force increased from 28 percent to 47 percent. In the 1960s and 1970s, their numbers swelled by 22.3 million, whereas the number of men increased by 15.0 million.[12] Since the Equal Rights Amendment failed and since women had been underpaid historically—earning around 60 percent of that of men—women were willing to accept lower wages than men, especially in low- and mid-skilled occupations.[13] A 10 percent increase in the number of women in the labor force lowered the wages of high school graduates by 3 percent. Thus, the 100 percent increase in the number of women in the labor force between 1960 and 1980, probably depressed men's wages by 30 percent in those sectors in which they competed.[14] Over time the gender wage gap declined but it still persists: in 2020, it was still 18 percent.[15] Part of the gap is due to education and experience, but educational outcomes are also part of the discriminatory process, as it is with ethnic minorities. Women produced as much as men but at lower wages, contributing to the productivity-wage gap (Figure 7.3).

Globalization also contributed to the wage gap. In the 1950s and 1960s, the US enjoyed a slight trade surplus which supported a strong job market (Table 7.2). In the 1970s, this advantage evaporated, although the deficits were still tiny. However, as with many other variables, developments turned sour with Reaganomics and the trade deficits became not only endemic but were increasing substantially, reaching $300 billion (2021 dollars), as exports floundered throughout the 1980s (see Figure 13.2). Then Clinton inaugurated the North American Free

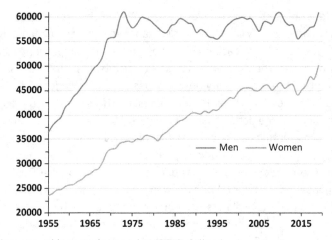

Figure 7.3 Median annual income by gender (2019 dollars)
Source: US Census, Historical Income Table P36. Full-Time, Year-Round Workers by Median Income and Sex.

Table 7.2 Foreign trade surplus or deficit as a percent of GDP

	Imports	Exports	Difference
1947–1959	4.0	4.8	0.9
1960s	4.4	5.0	0.6
1970s	7.4	7.2	-0.2
1980–1994	10.1	8.2	-1.8
1995–2001	12.7	10.5	-2.2
2002–2007	13.2	10.3	-4.2
2008	17.4	12.4	-5.0
2009–2016	15.9	12.8	-3.1
2017–2021	14.6	11.5	-3.1

Source: St. Louis Fed series GDP, IMPGS, EXPGS.

Trade Agreement (NAFTA) in 1993 and imports shot up from 10.5 percent (1993) to 14.4 percent of GDP (2000), dealing a crushing blow to low-skilled labor. Soon thereafter Clinton approved China's joining the World Trade Organization (2001) and imports jumped to 17.4 percent of GDP by 2008 (Table 7.2). So, the trade deficits associated with globalization exported jobs by the millions causing immense dislocation within the US labor force.[16]

It is well known that trade deficits export jobs. However, it is less well-known that *imports have an independent impact in a dual economy* because the workers displaced in the low-wage sector are unemployable in the expending IT sector. Hence, the magnitude of imports is a better indication of the pressure on low-skilled labor than the trade deficit. So, the increased penetration of imports produced by cheap labor—reaching an average of 14.7 percent of GDP in the twenty-first century—put enormous pressure on low-skilled US wages (see Section 13.5) and was a major factor in all the vicissitudes of the new century (see Figure 13.5).

Technological unemployment associated with the IT revolution also began to be felt by the 1990s. Given the persistent productivity-wage gap, it is hardly surprising that adjusted for inflation the annual median earnings of men have floundered for half a century since 1973 (see Figure 7.3).[17] Low-skilled men struggled the most. The wages of men with a high-school diploma (without college) declined by 18 percent from $23.80 to $19.60 (1973–1996) and then drifted sideways for two decades (Figure 7.4). Similarly, the wages of men without a high school diploma declined by 27 percent by 1996.[18] In 2020, the earnings of those without a college degree were still below their 1973 level. Such adverse developments have not been experienced since the Great Depression of the 1930s!

There was yet another aspect to the downward social mobility of low-skilled men, namely that the wages of women *without* a college degree held steady (Figure 7.5). So, low-skilled men's wages also declined relative to that of women. In 1973, men *without* a high-school diploma earned $4/hour more than women *with* a high-school diploma (no college). However, by 2016, they were earning $1.20/hour less, a decline of $5.20/hour in their relative incomes. That also mattered to their psychological well-being.

Moreover, the 4.4 million people who worked part-time in 2019 for lack of a full-time job also fared poorly. Their wages fluctuated around $280/week between 2000 to 2015 and then rose by $32 until 2021, hardly enough to keep body and soul together (see Figure 18.2).[19]

Understandably, these limitations in earnings among low-skilled men had major repercussions on the social and political systems (see Chapters 15 and 17). Their impact even on demographic aspects of living standards was appreciable: the difference in life expectancy at age 25 between those with and without a college degree more than doubled between 1992 and 2019 from 2.6 years to 6.3 years. This is astonishing evidence of the pummeling of their quality of life.[20] Men without a college degree still composed 37 percent of the labor force in 2020, down

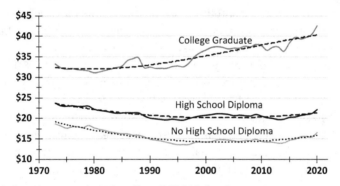

Figure 7.4 Men's hourly wages by education (2020 dollars)
Source: Economic Policy Institute, https://www.epi.org/data/#/?subject=wage-education&g=*.

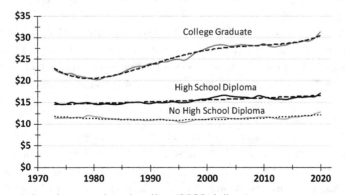

Figure 7.5 Women's hourly wages by education (2020 dollars)
Source: Economic Policy Institute, https://www.epi.org/data/#/?subject=wage-education&g=*.

from 66 percent in 1973. They found it challenging to accept their fate since not only did their income decline but did so while college graduates' earnings increased by $9/hour.

The implication is that the increase in wages in Table 7.1 and Figure 7.1 was limited mainly to college graduates. Consequently, millions of men dropped out of the labor force completely as the prospect of finding suitable jobs evaporated. In 1960, 97 percent of men at the peak of their productivity (between the ages of 25 and 54) were in the labor force. By 2020, that share was down to 88 percent, a decline of 9 percentage points.[21]

However, women's salaries increased substantially from $23,000 to $50,000 per annum, although their income was still $10,000 below those of men (Figure 7.3). While low-skilled women continued to be at a disadvantage, at least their wages did not decline as did those of men (see Figure 7.5). That the productivity of men without a college education would have declined while those of women with the same education would have remained unchanged is implausible. Hence, the productivity hypothesis of wage determination is also refuted by this evidence.

How are wages determined if not by the value of MP_L? Given the difficulty of ascertaining MP_L because of imperfect information, firms satisfice by using heuristics and signals to find viable remunerations through bargaining (see Section 4.5). The signals they use as approximate gages of expected productivity include education, diplomas, work experience, age, gender, ethnicity, and physical appearance. (Better-looking people earn more while women and minorities earn less than average.)[22] In addition, the degree of unionization, concentration within the industry, the profit of the firm, and the institutional structures also matter.

Evidence of the importance of institutional setting comes from the oligopolistic financial sector in which 40 percent of earnings is actually economic rent, so much above the wage of comparable employees in other sectors, i.e., "financiers are overpaid."[23] The extra earnings began when the institutional framework changed because of deregulation in the 1980s. The employees in those sectors continue to capture a share of the extraordinary profits of these oligopolists.

The regional concentration of firms increases their bargaining power in the labor market and enables them to keep wages below the value of marginal product.[24] There is overwhelming evidence that firms' bargaining power has increased since Reaganomics, thereby putting downward pressure on wages.[25] Arthur Pigou, a famous Cambridge economist of the early twentieth century, recognized that wages are "unfair" if workers were not paid the value of their marginal product.[26]

Custom and the history of wages also have a role to play, for example, in the male-female wage gap and the lower salaries of minorities.[27] Part-time employees also earn less per hour than full-time workers even at the same firm in the same occupation and have the same education and other characteristics.[28] Such wage gaps have historical roots: it has been customary to pay part-time workers less because students and housewives were willing to work part-time at a lower wage than the main breadwinner, because their income used to be supplementary to household income. This is no longer true; in July 2021, 4.5 million people had no choice but to work part-time because full-time employment was unavailable.[29] They are part of the labor force known as the *working poor*.

It is worth reiterating that part of the wage is a return on the employees' natural intelligence, physical features, and inborn talent. While these attributes might enhance productivity, the difference between these and the conventional determinates of wages is that employees did not do anything to acquire those characteristics. Instead, it was a matter of the "genetic lottery" that they were born with those characteristics. According to Rawls, employees do not deserve to receive compensation for those traits since those payments are pure rent, that is, they did nothing to acquire them (see Section 5.7). Hence, paying for those attributes is not an incentive to supply them since their supply is fixed at birth.

7.3 Earnings of Physical Capital

The financial returns on physical capital (investments) are the earnings of capital. The rate of return is the net income (after-tax profits) divided by the book value of the capital stock (its purchase price less depreciation). Theoretically, if this return is greater than the interest rate, firms should borrow to invest in more capital.[30] In the long run, the return on capital should decline until the rate of return on the last capital good purchased (MP_K) equals the rate of interest. This equality does not hold in the real world, just like MP_L = wage does not hold (see Figure 7.1).

The rate of return on equity in US banking in 2017 was 8.5 percent, at a time when the corporate bond yield was 3.7 percent. Obviously, there were barriers to entry into the banking sector which increased the return on capital.[31] Other iconic oligopolists achieved much higher returns on capital (in 12 months ending in June 2021):

Apple:	*40 percent*
Mastercard:	34 percent
Facebook:	27 percent
Microsoft:	28 percent
Google:	22 percent
Walmart:	19 percent
Netflix:	18 percent
Visa:	19 percent
Amazon:	12 percent
General Motors:	9 percent.

Yet the federal funds rate was near zero.[32]

However, mainstream economists argue that the book value of capital is not the best measure of the capital stock's value. Instead, they prefer its market value, which is the discounted expected future profits created by the invested capital. However, to calculate it, we need to know the future interest rate, otherwise we are unable to discount future profits produced by the capital stock. Since we have only guesstimates of both future profits and future interest rate, this is not a realistic procedure to determine the true value of the capital stock.

For example: suppose a firm pays $1 wages annually and buys a machine for $1 that lasts one period. So, the rate of depreciation is 100 percent. Suppose the rate of interest is 5 percent and that the machine and worker produce goods worth $3.05. In order to determine profits, we have to subtract all expenses: $1 for the used-up capital, 5 cents for the opportunity cost of capital invested in the machine, plus $1 for wages. This leaves $1 for profit (profit = revenue − expenses). This implies that the rate of return on investment was ($3.05 − $2.05)/$1 = 100 percent. Yet, mainstream economists might argue that the value of the machine was really $2, and profit was actually zero, because the historic cost of capital is immaterial to them: what counts is the value produced by the machine; the owner of the firm should have been able to sell the machine for $2, so that determines its market value. However, why would anyone pay $2 for a machine that could be purchased for $1? So, the real value of the machine at the beginning of the period was the historic price; the value could not be a function of an unknown entity—future net income. In any case, there is no reason why the $1 profit should be attributed to capital rather than to labor. The $1 profit was produced jointly. The issue of how to calculate profits and the value of capital is a major conundrum known as the Cambridge capital controversy.[33]

7.4 Human Capital in the Information Revolution

The extraordinary rates of return on capital reported in Section 7.3 is because those mega-corporations need small amounts of physical capital but use large amounts of *intangible capital*, not included in the rate of return calculations although it is also a factor of production. Knowledge embodied in people is *human capital*. It includes skills, education, training, talent, creativity, and even health since health also increases productivity. Knowledge is a *public good (non-rival)* since it is available to anyone, but what individuals learn becomes their private human capital. *Human capital differs from physical capital because it does not depreciate through use.* On the contrary, its productivity increases with use, through *learning-by-doing*, although it can become obsolete through the discovery of new knowledge.[34] Although measuring human capital is challenging, it is obvious that its contribution to economic growth has been substantial in tandem with the advances in science and the widespread use of complex technology. In today's knowledge economy, human capital has become of paramount importance. In the *post-industrial economy*, re-skilling and mid-career training became essential aspects of good economic policy.

Expenditure on education is an investment in human capital. In 1900, less than 10 percent of the US youth had a high school diploma. In 1960, 70 percent did.[35] That provided a solid basis for economic growth in the twentieth century. However, during the transition from an industrial to a knowledge economy, high-school education became inadequate to meet the skills required in a knowledge economy. The mediocre educational system, coupled with the expenses of a college education, meant that the supply of human capital became inadequate to meet the demand by Big Tech. This led to an import of talent which contributed to the anti-immigrant political movement. It also led to the *skill-mismatch*, implying that many open positions were left unfilled even though many people were looking for jobs. In other words, the supply of human capital was insufficient for the human capital demanded in the labor market. This also signifies a substantial *waste of human resources* because children are deprived of an adequate education. "A child born in the United States today will be 70 percent as productive when she grows up as she could be if she enjoyed complete education and full health."[36] The US is placed 35th in the World Bank's Human Development Index. Singapore, Hong Kong, Japan, and South Korea top the list.[37]

7.5 Other Forms of Intangible Capital

Other forms of intangible capital—social, cultural, and institutional—all differ from the common factors of production since they are public goods like knowledge. They are not rivalrous, meaning that there is no rivalry in their use. Public goods are not private property since no one can be excluded from their use. Just because someone learns computer programming does not prevent anyone else from using that knowledge. Similarly, the law is available to all. Everyone gains from having a functioning legal system that defines rights and obligations unambiguously, without having to pay for benefiting from it. The economy would become catatonic if each generation had to create the legal system anew. Hence, adequate laws and their enforcement mechanisms are priceless gifts from prior generations. While we are unable to repay it, we can honor their legacy by passing it on to subsequent generations.

Similarly, cultural attitudes are important in economic performance.[38] These include soft skills and habits of thought formed by the culture, including the propensity to trust counterparties. Trust fosters cooperation among strangers, thereby lowering transaction and enforcement costs. Trust promotes "spontaneous sociability," priceless for a well-functioning economy.[39] "Virtually every commercial transaction has within itself an element of trust … much of the economic backwardness in the world can be explained by the lack of mutual confidence."[40] We realized its importance in September 2008, when trust suddenly evaporated from financial markets and major banks were not willing to lend money to another bank even overnight. They were not sure if the other bank would reopen in the morning. It is much more efficient to instill in everyone the inclination to honor their obligation.

The feeling of community, collective identity, and the network of friends, colleagues, and acquaintances with a shared identity that bond people together are considered *social capital*. These connections enhance our ability to understand the society around us, lower information costs because credible advice conveniently accessible improves our ability to make reasonable decisions in a complex and uncertain marketplace, thereby contributing to economic success.[41] Children of well-connected families inherit the network of their parents, contributing substantially to their economic mobility. That is one reason why there is a positive correlation in income across generations.

Bill Gates provides an example of how networks contribute to economic success. The key to his becoming a billionaire was the fact that his mother and the president of IBM served on the same board of directors of a bank. She told him to call her son about an operating system IBM needed. That casual suggestion to someone in her network was worth billions of dollars and Gates would not now be among the richest persons in the world without it. In contrast, poor people bear the burden of navigating the complex economy without such networks.

The declining social capital and civic engagement in the US is one of the many sources of the economic malaise.[42] For instance, the culture of greed within the financial sector was instrumental in bringing about the disaster of 2008. The financiers had no moral stake in the interest of the community. Social capital based on mutual sympathy, social cohesion, and shared cultural norms and values had evaporated and was overtaken by an all-encompassing greed unimaginable to an earlier generation of bankers. Thus, intangibles also have an enormous effect on economic processes.

7.6 Institutions as Capital

Institutions are political, social, and economic structures or organizations that constrain or incentivize human behavior. They can be formal (laws) or informal rules (traditions), mechanisms which govern (influence/control) human action. They constitute the rules, norms, and framework within which the economy operates and, thus, are a crucial factor in determining transaction costs, production costs, profits, and economic outcomes. *Institutions are intangible capital* because they also enhance production as physical capital does. Markets would not work effectively without institutions that provide a well-functioning legal system to reduce uncertainty in business affairs, and to guarantee property rights.[43] The legal system provides mechanisms for the enforcement of contracts, laws, and regulations, without which the incentive structure of the society would be inefficient.

Institutions are unique in that they are not created by markets but develop through social, political, and cultural processes. These evolve slowly out of historical experience and the value system of the society.[44] The economy is embedded in its institutional framework and depends on it in crucial ways and cannot exist without it. Successful economies need inclusive institutions which can prevent the formation of an oligarchy, avoid unfair regulations, and eliminate barriers to entry into markets.[45] The set of institutions of the economy determines its effectiveness. They differ from physical capital in that sub-optimal institutions can also hinder the production process (see Figure 10.7).

7.7 Profit Rules

Profits are the residual from revenues minus the cost of production. In markets with perfect competition, there are zero profits (see Figure 6.2), but that is irrelevant to today's economy as most production is concentrated in oligopolies. Humongous profits in the iconic mega-corporations have persisted as competition is limited through high cost of entry into the sectors, potential competitors have been gobbled up by big tech, government anti-trust enforcement has been lenient, and unions have been vanquished, enabling squeezing labor costs to a minimum. Thus, corporate profits were light years from the perfectly competitive model (Table 7.3).

Obviously, these employees were not compensated adequately for their contribution to profits. The profitless long run of mainstream economics has never arrived for these multinationals. Corporate profit was the sole economic variable that was unambiguously robust in the twenty-first century.

After lingering around 6.2 percent of GDP in the twentieth century US *post-tax* corporate profits increased to 9.4 percent before the financial crisis (2007).[46] As labor's share in GDP was squeezed, profits' share increased continuously and with the tax windfalls of 2017 reached $2.6 trillion, or 11.4 percent of GDP (in 2021). So, profits almost doubled relative to GDP.

Another anomaly is that the share of finance in corporate profits was 23 percent (in 2021).[47] An intermediary sector is not expected to capture such a large chunk of profits. The US commercial banking sector earned 14 percent return on equity between 1994 and 2007 and 11 percent

Table 7.3 Corporate profits in 2021 and selected profit per employee

Company	Billion dollars	Company	Billion dollars
Apple	57	Intel	21
Microsoft	44	Bank of America	18
Berkshire Hathaway	42	Verizon	18
Google	40	United Health	15
Facebook	29	Johnson & Johnson	15
JPMorgan Chase	29	Walmart	13
Amazon	21	Proctor & Gamble	13
Profit per employee (dollars)			
Johnson & Johnson	411000	Google	288000
Apple	403000	Microsoft	272000

Source: *Fortune* "Global 500," https://fortune.com/global500/2021/search/?fg500_profits=desc; Wikipedia, "List of Largest Corporate Profits and Losses;" https://www.statista.com/statistics/267728/apples-net-income-since-2005/; https://www.statista.com/statistics/267728/apples-net-income-since-2005/.

in 2019.[48] Even during the Great Recession (in 2009), the financial sector generated profits of $330 billion (32 percent of all profits), thanks to the taxpayer bailout.[49] No wonder many are frustrated by the system that works impressively for Wall Street financiers but less impressively for those on Main Street.

7.8 The Troubling Decline in Labor's Share of GDP

Because of stagnating or declining wages, the spread of the gig economy, the skills mismatch, and the inferior bargaining position of labor, their share of GDP has declined by 4.3 percentage points since the 1970s (Figure 7.6).[50] In a $23 trillion economy (in 2021) that decline is worth $950 billion, implying that $5,900 will be missing annually in perpetuity from every employee's paycheck.[51] This loss is the reverse side of profit hoarding by corporations. Labor's ability to share in corporate profits declined because their bargaining position weakened in the wake of the decline in union power and changes in industrial structure, forced by technological change, and import penetration. This implies that "the American economy has become more ruthless, as declining unionization, increasingly demanding and empowered shareholders, decreasing real minimum wages, reduced worker protections, and the increases in outsourcing … have disempowered workers."[52] In contrast, Canada and Germany were able to maintain labor's share at 65 percent and 63 percent respectively.[53]

The above measure of labor's share is upwardly biased because it includes proprietor's income (unincorporated owner-operated businesses, including farms and partnerships). Labor's share would be significantly smaller without it: 45 percent (2014) instead of 60 percent.[54] Another reason why this is the case is because it includes compensation to management which includes substantial *economic rents* that they capture from profits. So, the decline in the true labor's share is considerably larger.

Labor's share in finance is just 23 percent. The largest *decrease* in labor's share was in nondurable goods production (food, clothing): a loss of 15 percentage points, in contrast to the −4.3 percentage points documented in Figure 7.6. (Nondurables make up 20 percent of GDP.) Clearly, globalization and the IT revolution put pressure on labor's share, but if the countervailing power of labor had been maintained, unions would have mitigated the harm caused by these impersonal economic forces.[55]

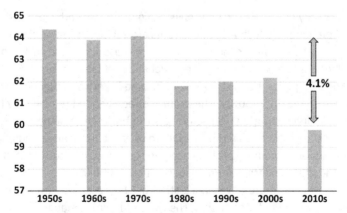

Figure 7.6 Share of labor income in GDP (%)
Source: St. Louis Fed, series LABSHPUSA156NRUG.

Human beings differ from capital because they are sentient—they have feelings and a sense of fairness. Treating labor and capital symmetrically is unethical. Labor has basic needs, machines do not. Hence, humanistic economists would not treat workers as objects. In order to improve social welfare, it is crucial to treat workers with the dignity appropriate for human beings and not dehumanize work by treating it as just another factor of production.

7.9 Natural Resources Are Finite and Important

Natural resources are also important inputs into the production process. Some are reproducible, like trees and fisheries, while others are not, like land and minerals. While the total amount of minerals available is unknown, it is clear that the supply is finite. The atmosphere and oceans are also valuable resources because they support life and because they absorb carbon dioxide and carbon monoxide and have a major impact on the economy through changes in the climate.

Some natural resources are essential for life (water, air) while others are found in nature and needed for production (land, iron, crude oil). Many of them are being depleted at an accelerating rate. Moreover, there are many ominous developments in climate change, water and air quality, biodiversity loss, loss of ecosystems, fires and floods associated with global warming (see Section 11.9). This is a portentous challenge to humanity since they threaten the very foundations of the economic system.[56] Moreover, the depletion of natural resources and global warming are not accounted for properly in GDP accounts (see Section 10.10). This is a potential high-intensity time-bomb.

Minerals and land also differ from other forms of capital because they are not man-made. In Norway, the oil resources of the country are not privatized but are owned by the people. The Norwegian oil fund with assets of $1.3 trillion belongs to the people.[57] It is based on the responsible principle that the oil extracted from its territory is a natural treasure and that the windfall should build financial wealth for the benefit of "both current and future generations" instead of enriching only corporations.[58] Many countries like China, Australia, and in the Middle East also have such funds.[59] The Alaska Permanent Fund is also financed by oil revenue and pays $1,600 annual dividend to Alaskans as basic income.

7.10 Poverty vs Affluence: The Stupendous Rise in Inequality

The conventional theory of income distribution is straightforward: both labor and capital receive the value of their marginal product, and since profits are zero, distributing the rewards is child's play. Consequently, mainstream economists do not discuss income distribution extensively. However, labor does not receive its marginal product and profits are enormous. In today's economy dominated by oligopolies, the distribution of income is derived essentially from the distribution of economic and political power. The profit that accrues to the residual claimant is also a matter of the legal and institutional structure; distribution cannot be derived from economic theory alone. For instance, monopoly rights awarded to sports franchises and pharmaceuticals obviously grant them extraordinary profits based on the law. In our current system, corporate profits accrue to the shareholders, after management claims their share. Their ability to dip into profits depends on the corporate governance structure based on the law. Output is produced jointly by workers, management, and capital. The value of their individual contribution is impossible to disentangle in practice since it is a joint product. How much of the profits is contributed by management and how much by workers is indeterminate.

It is common knowledge that inequality in the US has increased enormously since 1980.[60] Actually, it has become so intolerable that it causes numerous social, political, and economic problems. It was brought about by the productivity gap (see Figure 7.1), the fall in labor's share (see Figure 7.6), low tax rate on billionaires, humongous corporate profits, and exorbitant CEO salaries. So, being flippant about this development by emphasizing that "policies that penalize the successful and reward the unsuccessful reduce the incentive to succeed" is extremely short-sighted and even irresponsible.[61] The "equality-equity tradeoff" is propaganda because there is scant evidence to support the assertion that "the more equally the pie is divided, the smaller the pie becomes."[62] The US economy actually performed better when the society was more equal and the Western European economies are doing just fine with a much lower level of inequality and a lower level of internal conflict. In reality, the rise in inequality gave an impetus to the rise in populism (see Chapter 15).

In a dual economy, there are billionaires but there are also millions of families living precarious lives near the edge of subsistence: 34 million people, 10 percent of the US population lived below the poverty line in 2019, which, for a family of four (including two children), was $26,000.[63] This amount was deemed sufficient to meet basic needs and minimum social needs. The average poor family's income was $10,700 below the poverty threshold.[64] Poverty rates were much higher among Blacks (18.8 percent), Hispanics (15.7 percent), children and youth (14.4 percent), those without a high-school diploma (24 percent); unemployed all year (26 percent), single females (22 percent), and highest among children living in single female households (46 percent).

There were additionally 12 million people (4 percent) living near poverty, defined as within 25 percent of poverty income, i.e., between $26,000 and $31,000 for a family of four. The changes in the composition of those living just above poverty provides some insights into the process of pauperization during the era of neoliberal dominance. In 1966, most of those living just above poverty were children and youth (43 percent). By 2012, most were working age (55 percent). In 1966, most did not have a high school diploma, by 2012, most did. In 1966, most were either working or looking for work (65 percent); in 2012, most had dropped out of the labor force and were not looking for work (59 percent).[65]

In contrast, 199,000 taxpayers (0.13 percent) earned an average $6.6 million pre-tax (Table 7.4, rows 1–3). And the top 1.1 percent of taxpayers earned 21.7 percent of the total income of the US, that is, one out of every five dollars generated in the economy went to the richest 1.1 percent. That is the *one-percent problem*. In fact, the bottom 56 percent of taxpayers–numbering 87,000,000 earned practically as much as the top 0.356 percent–numbering 539,000 taxpayers (Table 7.4, rows 1–4 and row 6). Yet, the bottom 56 percent of taxpayers earned an average taxable income of $22,600 (around the poverty line) while the people on Park Avenue averaged $3,300,000. This enormous cleavage between the ultra-rich and the rest is at the root of the widespread discontent, the political dysfunction, the rise of populism, and the rise of an oligarchy (see Chapter 15).[66]

There is also a spatial aspect to income inequality because the ultra-poor are not distributed uniformly across the country. Poverty is concentrated in enclaves or slums–often in close proximity to pockets of wealth–upscale neighborhoods.[67] Some neighborhoods have median annual household income of $14,000, far below the poverty line (see Table 16.3). An economy with such discrepancies is usually headed for rockier times.

In addition to tax records, we also have data collected by the Census on household income. These are analyzed by arranging the 128.6 million households by quintiles from poorest

Table 7.4 Tax returns of the super-rich (2018 dollars)

		% of All Returns	Number of Returns	Total Income (billions)	Average Income	% of Total Income	Taxes as % of income
1)	Top 0.015	22,000	659	29,803,000	5.7	24.8
2)	Next 0.023	35,000	238	6,850,000	2.0	27.3
3)	Next 0.094	142,000	422	2,970,000	3.6	27.5
1-3)	Top 0.132	199,000	1,319	6,600,000	11.3	26.1
4)	Next 0.224	340,000	461	1,356,000	4.0	26.5
1-4)	Top 0.356	539,000	1,780	3,302,412	15.3	26.1
5)	Next 0.730	1,110,000	747	674,000	6.4	26.0
1-5)	Top 1.1	1,649,000	2,527	1,500,000	21.7	25.3
6)	Bottom 56%	87,000,000	1,962	22,600	16.7	3.3

Source: "IRS SOI Tax Stats–Individual Statistical Tables by Size of Adjusted Gross Income," www.irs.gov/statistics/soi-tax-stats-individual-statistical-tables-by-size-of-adjusted-gross-income.

Illustration 7.1 Life would just not be the same if I had to travel on a commercial airline
Credit: iStock.com/Extreme-Photographer.

to richest and dividing them into five groups. Each of the five quintiles includes 25.7 million households–20 percent of the total–roughly 67 million people. We calculate the share of total US income earned by each of the five groups to find that the poorest group earned just 3.1 percent of the total income, while the top quintile received 51 percent (Figure 7.7a). Moreover, the top 5 percent of households received 22.6 percent of total income (Figure 7.7b), i.e., the *top* 6.4 million households received a bit less than the bottom 77 million households. No matter how the income distribution is considered, the data reveal a disturbing and unsustainable level of inequality.

It is also disconcerting that today's low-skilled wages do not compare well to the $5-a-day paid by the Ford Motor Company in 1914 (see Figure 7.6) which is worth $139/day today ($17.40 per hour).[68] Among the 147 million workers, 40 percent earn less than the Ford workers did a century ago (Figure 7.8). Actually, 85 percent of the 13.5 million employees in the "Food Preparation and Serving Related" occupation and of the 8.6 million "Retail Sales Workers"

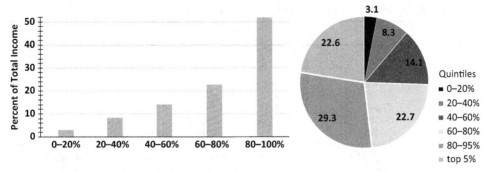

Figure 7.7 (a) and (b) Distribution of household income by quintiles, US, 2019
Source: Department of Commerce, US Census Bureau, table H-2. Share of Aggregate Income Received by Each Fifth and Top 5 percent of Households. www.census.gov/data/tables/time-series/demo/income-poverty/historical-income-households.html.

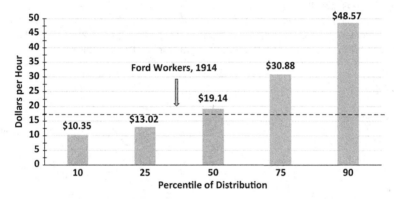

Figure 7.8 Distribution of earnings in 2019 compared to Ford workers of 1914
Source: Bureau of Labor Statistics, "Occupational Employment Statistics," www.bls.gov/oes/2019/may/oes_nat.htm#00-0000.

earn less than Ford workers did in 1914.[69] This does not point to great progress for millions of working poor.[70]

Differences in median household incomes by ethnicity are substantial (Table 7.5). Asian households fared best, earning $7,000 more than whites. African-American households earn $30,600 less than whites and the gap has widened since 2000 (see Chapter 16). Black incomes are consistently the lowest while Hispanic incomes have been also consistently below those of whites although their gap decreased by $8,000 (Figure 7.9). American Natives' incomes are the lowest, and the rate of poverty the highest (not shown in Figure 7.9).

7.11 The Second Gilded Age of High Tech, High Finance, and Celebrities

The stupendous redistribution of income shares toward the super-rich characterized the *Second Gilded Age*. Instead of Carnegie, Ford, Mellon, J.P. Morgan, Rockefeller, and Vanderbilt, we have Ballmer, Bezos, Bloomberg, Brin, Buffett, Dell, Ellison, Gates, Koch, Musk, Page, Walton, and Zuckerberg.[71] The trends reveal that the transition to a new global knowledge economy benefited exclusively the super-rich, the top 5 percent of the income distribution, the rich (80–95

Table 7.5 Real household median income by ethnicity (2019 dollars)

Ethnicity	Income		Relative to whites		
	2000	2019	2000	2019	Change
Whites	70320	76057			
Blacks	45093	45438	−25227	−30619	5392
Hispanics	47840	56113	−22480	−19944	−2536
Asians	89589	98174	+19269	+22177	2,908
All	64493	68703	−5827	−7354	−1,527

Note: Changes made in 2014 by the Census in the questionnaire used for the survey increased median household income by 3.17 percent but could be as high as 6 percent if the margin of error is taken into consideration. The biases by ethnicity are: whites: 3.53 percent, Blacks 2.10 percent, Asians: 7.93 percent, Hispanics −3.115 percent. The estimates prior to 2014 were adjusted by these amounts in the above data.
Sources: US Census Bureau Table H-5. Race and Hispanic Origin of Householder–Households by Median and Mean Income: 1967 to 2019, https://www.census.gov/data/tables/time-series/demo/income-poverty/historical-income-households.html; Kayla Fontenot et al., Current Population Reports P60-263, 2018, https://www.census.gov/content/dam/Census/library/publications/2018/demo/p60-263.pdf, p. 4; Appendix D, https://www.census.gov/content/dam/Census/library/publications/2015/demo/p60-252.pdf; Jonathan Rothbaum, "Processing Changes to Income in the CPS ASEC," SEHSD Working Paper #2019-18.

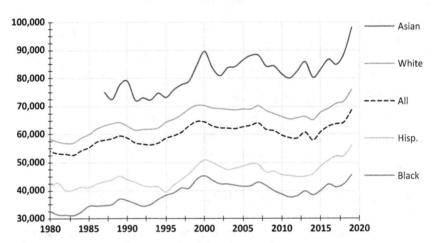

Figure 7.9 Median household income by ethnicity (2019 dollars)
Source: US Census Bureau Table H-5. Race and Hispanic Origin of Householder–Households by Median and Mean Income: 1967 to 2019, https://www.census.gov/data/tables/time-series/demo/income-poverty/historical-income-households.html.

percent) made slight gains, while everyone else lost income shares (Figure 7.10 and Table 7.6, Column 5).

In the 1970s, the distribution changed minimally. Note that until 1981 the ultra-rich (5 percent) and the middle class (40–60 percent) had equal shares: 17 percent. However, By the end of the Reagan-Bush presidencies, the ultra-rich had increased their share by 4.5 percent and then added another 1.3 percent by 2019 (Figure 7.11). Thus, the *hollowing out of the middle class* started in 1981 with an obvious kink in the trend that meant an ominous loss of middle-class income share, and with it, political clout (see Chapter 15).[72] By 2019, the top 5 percent had 23 percent of total income, while that of the middle class declined to 14 percent (Figure 7.10 and

Table 7.6 Distribution of income in the US, 1967 and 2019

	1	*2*	*3*	*4*	*5*	*6*	*7*	*8*	*9*
						Income			
		Percentile of	Percent of total Income			Hypoth.	Actual	Loss/Gain (52 years)	
Quintile		*population*	*1967*	*2019*	*change*	*2019*		*dollars*	*(%)*
Poor	1	0–20	4.0	3.1	–0.9	19,700	15,000	–4,400	–29.3
Lower-Middle Class	2	20–40	10.8	8.3	–2.5	53,000	41,000	–12,500	–30.5
Middle Class	3	40–60	17.3	14.1	–3.2	85,000	69,000	–16,300	–23.6
Upper-Middle Class	4	60–80	24.2	22.7	–1.5	119,000	111,000	–8,000	–7.2
Rich	5	80–95	26.4	28.9	+2.5	173,000	189,000	+16,000	+8.2
Ultra Rich	5	Top 5%	17.2	23.0	+5.8	339,000	451,000	+112,000	+24.9

Note: Hypothetical income in column 6 is calculated by assuming that the respective group's share was the same as in 1967. It is the hypothetical value that would have obtained if shares had remained unchanged since 1967. Column 9: percent Loss/Gain relative to Actual income in 2019

Source: US Census Bureau Table H-5. Race and Hispanic Origin of Householder-Households by Median and Mean Income: 1967 to 2019, https://www.census.gov/data/tables/time-series/demo/income-poverty/historical-income-households.html.

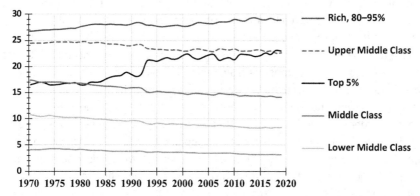

Figure 7.10 Trends in the share of total household income (%)
Note: the first four quintiles are referred to as the Poor, Lower Middle Class, Middle Class, Upper Middle Class and fifth quintile is divided into the Rich, the 80-95 percentile, and the ultra-rich, the top 5 percent.

Table 7.6, column 4). This implies that the income of a typical household in the top 5 percent increased from 4 times the income of a middle-class households to 6.6 times as much (Table 7.6, column 7).

The middle class experienced the largest decline in income share (3.2 percentage points) (Table 7.6, Column 5). The actual average household incomes earned is reported in column 7. The hypothetical income is the income that would have obtained in 2019, had the 1967 income share remained unchanged (Table 7.6, Column 6). So, the poor's income in 2019 would have been $19,700 instead of $15,000 if their share of total income remained at 4.0 percent instead of decreasing to 3.1 percent (Table 7.6, columns 6 and 7).[73] The first four quintiles—80 percent of households—lost on average $10,000 (column 8). In contrast, the income of the top quintile was $1.0 trillion more than it would have been had incomes been distributed as in 1967.[74]

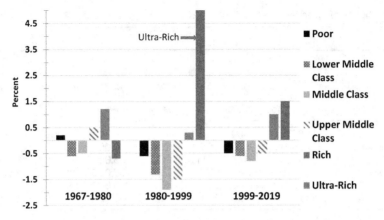

Figure 7.11 Changes in the share of total household income in three epochs
Note: The fifth quintile is divided into the Rich (80–95th percentile) and the Ultra-rich (top 5 percent).
Source: Department of Commerce, US Census Bureau, Table H-2. Share of Aggregate Income Received
by Each Fifth and Top 5 percent of Households. www.census.gov/data/tables/time-series/demo/income-
poverty/historical-income-households.html.

By the twenty-first century the top quintile were receiving half of total income. The rest of the
80 percent of the society (260 million people) shared the other half. There is no economic or
ethical justification for such a reallocation of riches in favor of the rich and ultra-rich. This is
grim evidence of the failure of neoliberal policies to create an inclusive economy.[75]

The above data pertain to market incomes. Post-tax, post-transfer incomes subtracts taxes
from market incomes and adds transfers from government to individuals, such as food stamps,
Medicaid assistance, housing vouchers, and unemployment benefits.[76] A shortcoming of this
approach is that, given the endemic government budget deficits, the transfers are at the
expense of future generations. That implies that an increase in government debt adds to the net
disposable income of current recipients, but this appears to be a free lunch, since the debt will
burden generations yet unborn, whose welfare is disregarded. While this is not great accounting
practice, this income measure does afford another perspective on the current purchasing power
and welfare of the various social classes.

This disposable income measure corroborates that income inequality increased substantially
between Reagan and Trump.[77] The growth of disposable income of the three middle-class quintiles was far below that of the top quintile, further evidence of the "hollowing out of the middle
class" (Figure 7.12).[78] The top 1 percent stood out as the true beneficiaries of this epoch since
their income growth reached an unimaginable $1,384,000, having grown at 3.3 percent per
annum. That meant that by *2018 their after-tax income increased by nearly $1 million* in the
intervening 39 years (Table 7.7). So, every year their disposable income is $1 million more than
it was in 1979, after adjusting for inflation. The next group from the top (96–99 percent) gained
$162,900. The amount that trickled down past the top quintile was a tiny fraction (1–4 percent)
of the amount that accrued to the top 1 percent. Put another way, poor households' annual disposable income was less than private college tuition (excluding board) in 1979 and still less in
2018. College would be unaffordable even if they did not spend on anything else.

We compare the ratio of each group's income to that of the 1st quintile (Figure 7.13). This
indicates that, in 1979, the ratio of the income of the top 1 percent was 20 times as large as that
of the 1st quintile, but, by 2018, it had reached a multiple of 73. The relative income of the other

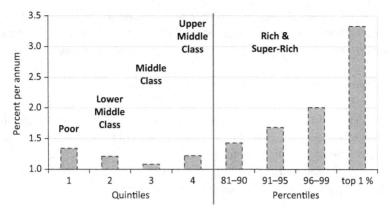

Figure 7.12 Growth of real after-tax household income, 1979-2018

Source: Congressional Budget Office, "The Distribution of Household Income, 2018," August 4, 2021; https://www.cbo.gov/publication/57061#data; data was extracted from "Additional Data for Researchers," Table 3.

Table 7.7 Real disposable household income in the US, 1979 and 2018

| | (%) | | | | | | | |
	0-20	21-40	41-60	61-80	81-90	91-95	96-99	Top 1
1979	18.9	34.2	48.0	63.0	80.4	98.6	138.9	385.8
2018	32.8	54.7	73.1	101.2	139.6	189.2	301.8	1,384.2
Increase	13.9	20.5	25.1	38.2	59.2	90.6	162.9	998.4
% of top 1%'s gain	1	2	3	4	6	9	16	100

Note: Thousands of 2018 dollars unless otherwise noted.

Source: Congressional Budget Office, "The Distribution of Household Income, 2018," August 4, 2021; https://www.cbo.gov/publication/57061#data; data was extracted from "Additional Data for Researchers," Table 3.

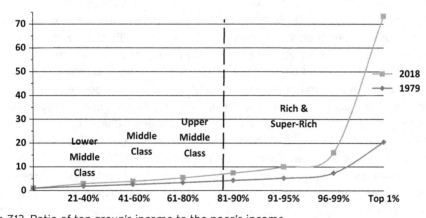

Figure 7.13 Ratio of top group's income to the poor's income

Source: Congressional Budget Office, "The Distribution of Household Income, 2018," August 4, 2021; https://www.cbo.gov/publication/57061#data; data was extracted from "Additional Data for Researchers," Table 3.

groups in the top quintile also increased somewhat but none of the three middle classes did. This is yet another indication of the huge inequality but also how little of the income growth trickled down beyond the top 1 percent.[79] The super-rich managed to keep practically all of it to themselves.

There are several reasons for this stupendous increase in inequality. Among these are the Reagan tax cuts that gave the super-rich a windfall that boosted its wealth and set the stage for the accumulation of more wealth and political power (see Table 12.2 and Chapter 15).[80] In addition, globalization also benefited primarily those who were rich to begin with and could take advantage of the opportunities of doing business in low-wage countries (see Section 13.5). These included those who had access to good education and benefited from the expanding knowledge economy and could take advantage of the internet.

7.12 Exorbitant Incomes Exacerbate Inequality

In 1980, major league baseball players earned ten times as much as K-12 teachers. However, by 2000, their salary reached 45 times teachers' salaries, because the internet enabled a much larger audience to view their games.[81] This is a distortion of the free market, since the contribution of teachers to social welfare is considerably larger than that of baseball players. So, it would be justified to put a surtax on those occupations that benefited from the internet, since the basic research that made it possible was funded by taxpayers. Hence, taxpayers should earn a return on their investment.

Another reason that sportsman earn humongous salaries is that sport franchises are privileged by being exempt from antitrust laws. This institutional structure protects the teams from competition. Consequently, they are monopolies and hence earn monopoly profits. That is why ten players in the NBA earned more than $39 million in salary alone in 2021-2022. They reap the benefits of laws that grant the franchise privileged status.[82] They would not be earning such astronomical salaries without this legislation. Hence, their salaries are not solely the product of free-market supply-and-demand forces but also of the laws that allow sport associations to be legal cartels. Of course, they can earn extraordinary salaries from these monopoly rights.

Even if this might be a reasonable way to organize sports, there is no reason why the players or the franchises should profit from the legislation. This illustrates the extent to which the income distribution depends on institutional structure and prevailing laws. Hence, the salaries of baseball players—and this is true for CEOs and other celebrities—is not determined solely by their own efforts or by market forces but are also influenced by laws and regulation. The astronomical salaries are out of proportion to the players' contribution to social welfare.

The argument also applies to the high and mighty of finance. In 2018, the annual compensation of James Gorman (Morgan Stanley), Jamie Dimon (J.P.Morgan Chase), Charles Scharf (Wells Fargo) were around ($31-$36 million), and of Michael Corbat (Citigroup), Brian Moynihan (Bank of America), and Lloyd Blankfein (Goldman Sachs) were close ($25 million).[83] None of them would have earned $9,000+ per hour without the generous bailouts at taxpayers' expense. They would also not earn such exorbitant salaries if the market for CEOs were open to competition. They are paid far above their opportunity cost. I think there are thousands of executives who could run these institutions as effectively for a fraction of the above amounts if the positions had been advertised in open competition.[84]

Moreover, the CEOs are not producing by themselves but jointly with their employees, using the social and institutional capital of society. How that joint product is apportioned is based on the political power structure, the prevailing institutions, the legal system, and their ability to influence politicians.[85] Everyone benefits from using public goods. There is no ethical justification for CEOs getting paid for the portion of their productivity derived from public goods such as the satellites used for internet communication created at taxpayers' expense. The basic research for the internet and the whole IT revolution was financed in the 1960s by the taxpayers; so a substantial portion of the benefits derived from these innovations should have accrued to taxpayers rather than to private firms. CEOs should not profit from the internet more than average workers. They are lucky that their occupation benefited from the internet, but in a fair society earnings would not be a function of luck (see Section 5.7).

The infrastructure was created by prior generations. We are beneficiaries of the sacrifices they made in blood and treasure, for example, on the beaches of Normandy. How much should celebrities compensate the descendants of those who fought in such places for not having had to fight there?

Since Reagan, enormous salaries for CEOs became the norm and deviation from that norm becomes difficult due to expectations and peer pressure. The reason for the astronomical CEO salaries is that they were able to capture a share of the increasing oligopolistic profits because of the decline in the unions' countervailing power. Moreover, they have inside information and can appoint their friends to the board of directors, thereby gaining assurance that they will have the "power to extract concessions."[86] The board of directors has no incentive to strike a hard bargain since they are not spending their own money but that of the shareholders. The board members would not retain any of the potential savings for themselves.[87] In other words, the exorbitant CEO salaries are due to "deficiencies of corporate governance."[88] Besides, there is no market for CEOs of the iconic firms. The positions are not advertised and there is no transparency on how they are chosen. Firms are not finding the lowest bidder for the job.

Illustration 7.2 You did not bleed on Omaha Beach (Normandy) on June 6, 1944. The least you owe to the memory of those who did is to leave the Earth as nice as you found it
Credit: In the public domain.

Furthermore, the CEOs know what the firm's profits are; they are close to the cash registers and are essentially writing their own checks to themselves, as though they were the owners of the firms.[89] Warren Buffett has been on the board of 19 corporations; he describes boardroom dynamics vividly:

> Accountability and stewardship withered in the last decade, becoming qualities deemed of little importance ... Too many ... have in recent years behaved badly at the office, fudging numbers and drawing obscene pay for mediocre business achievements ... If able but greedy managers over-reach and try to dip too deeply into the shareholders' pockets, directors must slap their hands. Over-reaching has become common but few hands have been slapped. Why have intelligent and decent directors failed so miserably? The answer lies ... in what I'd call "boardroom atmosphere" ... When the compensation committee—armed, as always, with support from a high-paid consultant—reports on a mega-grant of options to the CEO, it would be like belching at the dinner table for a director to suggest that the committee reconsider ... My own behavior frequently fell short as well: Too often I was silent when management made proposals that I judged to be counter to the interests of shareholders. In those cases, collegiality trumped independence ... In recent years compensation committees too often have been tail-wagging puppy dogs meekly following recommendations by consultants, a breed not known for allegiance to the faceless shareholders who pay their fees ... This costly charade should cease.[90]

This is not the cogitations of a blackboard economist, or an anti-globalization radical, but a renowned investor, with a successful career in the corporate world, who is a supporter of free markets. But he was an eyewitness to the dynamics in many boardrooms and has sufficient common sense to recognize a holdup when he sees one. Overpayment has become the accepted and expected norm.

In such an institutional structure, the average compensation of CEOs rose to $20 million in 2019 at the top 350 US corporations.[91] The ratio of CEO pay to that of typical workers increased enormously just as the compensation-productivity gap widened. In 1978, the ratio was "merely" 31:1, but by 1989 it had risen to 61:1 and accelerated thereafter, reaching 307:1 by 2019. The productivity of CEOs could not have increased ten times more than that of workers.[92] In short, the CEOs captured a part of the productivity gains of their employees.[93]

> Exorbitant CEO pay is a major contributor to rising inequality ... CEOs are getting more because of their power to set pay and because so much of their pay (more than 80 percent) is stock-related, not because they are increasing their productivity or possess specific, high-demand skills.[94]

CEOs also benefited enormously from the Federal Reserve's asset purchases which inflated stock prices since CEO bonuses were linked to stock prices (see Figures 10.5 and 17.8).[95]

The customary argument that capping salaries would be inefficient is invalid in these cases because these *salaries are rents*, i.e., "income not related to a corresponding growth in productivity."[96] So the supposed incentives do not bring forth more talent, intelligence, or effort and capping CEO pay "would ... [have] no adverse impact on the economy's output or on employment."[97] The firms would still need a CEO and they would work as hard at a fraction of their current salary, provided the cap were economy-wide. What else would they do? It would still be the most they could earn. The marginal tax rate in the top income bracket under the Eisenhower

Table 7.8 International comparison of CEO compensation

	Compensation	% of US(2)	CEO-worker	
	$ millions		ratio	year
US(1)	24.2		351	2021
US(2)	17.0		300	2015
Switzerland	10.6	62	180	2015
UK	9.6	56	230	2015
Canada	9.3	55	200	2015
Germany	8.4	49	175	2015
The Netherlands	8.2	48	171	2018
France	2.8	17	70	2015
Japan	2.4	14	60	2015

Note: US (1) refers to the top 350 firms.
Sources: Lawrence Mishel and Jori Kandra, "CEO Pay Has Skyrocketed 1,322 Percent Since 1978," Economic Policy Institute, August 10, 2021; Wei Lu and Anders Melin, "The Best and Worst Countries to Be a Rich CEO," *Bloomberg News*, November 16, 2016; https://www.statista.com/statistics/424159/pay-gap-between-ceos-and-average-workers-in-world-by-country/.

administration was 88 percent, and under President Nixon it was still 70 percent, and yet there was no shortage of CEOs or of celebrities or football players.

Smaller salaries have not harmed German, Swiss, French, or Japanese firms although their CEOs earn a fraction of their US counterparts (Table 7.8). For instance, the head of the Norway's energy company, Equinor, earns less than $2 million. In contrast, the CEO of ConocoPhillips, a comparable-sized American company, receives more than ten times as much. Their productivity does not differ appreciably.[98]

Corporate governance makes a difference. In Germany, representatives of unions and of the local government have a seat on the board of directors since they also have a stake in the future of the enterprise.[99] They also participate in the discussion of CEO salaries. In the Netherlands, Sweden, Norway, and Switzerland, shareholders have a binding vote on CEO compensation.[100] This legal framework provides countervailing power to keep CEO greed within bounds.[101] Capping US executive salaries at European levels throughout the US would be a reasonable start to turn the tide.

Furthermore, many CEOs endured the Covid-19 crisis with their millions intact. T-Mobile's Mike Sievert received $55 million in 2020. Hilton Hotels lost $700 million, laid off a quarter of its workforce, yet its CEO, Chris Nassetta, took home $56 million. Boeing had a bad year with a loss of $12 billion and furloughed 30,000 workers. Yet, its CEO, David Calhoun, still received $21 million.[102] This is mindboggling.

7.13 Welfare Does Not Grow at the Same Rate as the Economy

Mainstream economists think that *real* income (*I*) is identical to living standards, welfare (*W*), well-being, or life satisfaction. In other words, they assume implicitly that *W equals I*. This neglects that income is an intermediate product of economic activity and *welfare is actually the final outcome* of that activity. It also overlooks the economic principle that *marginal utility diminishes with income*: $10,000 gain for Jeff Bezos with a net worth of $185,000 million would be meaningless, whereas the same increment to someone in the South Bronx would be a heaven-sent game changer. Hence, humanistic economists do not equate income with welfare since the welfare generated depends on who receives the increment of income.

Income should be transformed into welfare using one of the plausible mathematical functions that has the property of diminishing marginal utility of income. We chose a simple standard function: welfare as the square root of income:

$$W = \sqrt{I}$$

That implies that if income increased from 1 to 4, welfare would increase from 1 to 2. With such a function, the growth rates of welfare averaged across the five quintiles becomes 0.7 percent per annum (1979-2018).

$$W = log(I)$$

is another possible function. In that case, the growth of welfare would become 0.1 percent per annum. Although median household income has been growing at a rate of 1.5 percent per annum (1979-2018), it has been in the range of 0.1 to 0.7 percent per annum, i.e., much slower. The slower welfare growth is a consequence of the diminishing marginal utility of income and of the fact that most of the income accrued to the superwealthy households.

7.14 Relative Incomes Matter Most in Developed Societies

Regrettably, the real world is even more complicated than described above, because

$$W = \sqrt{I}$$

assumes that one's welfare depends exclusively on one's own income. However, that is unrealistic: humanistic economists stress that *relative incomes matter* a lot (see Section 5.1).[103] One's contentment is a function not only of own income but also of the income of reference groups, the social norm, or relative income. In other words, an increase in income does not necessarily generate an increase in well-being if the increment to income was smaller than that of the reference group. Well-being can decrease even if income increases.

Thus, if some people are buying the newest iPhone, those who cannot afford it, will covet it, and feel frustrated. With fewer super-wealthy consumers Apple would produce fewer new iPhones. Since utility functions are reference-dependent or interdependent, the super-wealthy generate a negative externality.

A reasonable way to define such a welfare function is to use the 5th quintile as the reference group:

$$W_{(i)} = \sqrt{\frac{I(i)}{I(5) - I(i)}}$$

where $I(i = 1, \ldots 4)$ represents one of the first four quintiles. The intuition behind this formula is that welfare is determined by the square root of relative income, where the relative income is the ratio of one's own income $I(i)$ divided by the difference between the 5th quintile's income $I(5)$ and one's own income $I(i)$. The larger is the denominator—the difference between $I(5)$ and

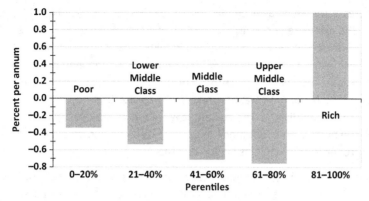

Figure 7.14 Growth of welfare with relative incomes, 1979-2018
Source: Congressional Budget Office, "The Distribution of Household Income, 2018," August 4, 2021; https://www.cbo.gov/publication/57061#data; data was extracted from "Additional Data for Researchers," Table 3.

I(i)–the smaller is the ratio, and smaller is the relative income of that quintile, and the smaller is the welfare generated by one's absolute income.

This calculation is done four times, i.e., for each of the first four quintiles separately. The formula is not used for the 5th quintile, because it is its own reference group. The calculation is done for 1979 and again for 2018. Next, we calculate the growth rates of W between the two values obtained 39 years apart for each of the four quintiles. The results yield that the *first four quintiles' welfare declined*, because the 5th quintile's income grew faster than that of all other quintiles (Figure 7.14).

This result is crucial because it helps us understand the widespread discontent in the US population (see Chapter 15). Otherwise, it would make little sense since incomes grew in all quintiles (see Figure 7.12). Positive income growth would not induce discontent unless *relative* incomes were a significant determinant of one's subjective well-being. Repeated surveys prove that, despite substantial economic growth, life satisfaction or happiness has not increased at all since 1946 (see Figures 2.1 and 11.3).[104] This is explained by the negative growth in relative incomes for most of the population. Humanistic economists suggest that we should pay much more attention to the distribution of income and not focus solely on economic growth.

7.15 Ethics and the Skewed Distribution of Income

John Rawls argued that the current distribution of income is unjust, because "no one deserves his place in the distribution of talents, nor his starting place in society." Rewarding talent is rewarding our random genetic configuration or the luck of having been born into a well-endowed family (see Section 5.7). He continued, "In the light of what principle can free and equal moral persons permit their relations to be affected by social fortune and the natural lottery?"[105] By "natural lottery" he meant that we did not earn our initial endowment. We do not deserve our skin color, ethnicity, or to be born into a rich or a poor family, or to be smarter or better-looking than average. All this was a matter of luck.

Thus, the substantial advantages or disadvantages those provide were not earned through our own effort, hence are not deserved, and there is no reason to be compensated for them. Nonetheless, these talents, wealth, and other attributes obtained at birth, or the lack thereof, play an immense role in one's economic prospects throughout the life course.[106] The return to these random attributes is, therefore, an economic rent, or a privilege. It is based on birth rather than on merit. In short, the extensive economic inequality has no moral basis, as people's "life prospects are significantly affected by their family and class origins," that is, through no action of their own.

Hence, these considerations suggest that the immense income inequality is not justified by a meritocracy. Stiglitz argues that while those at the top in the US enjoy the best health care, education, and other benefits of wealth, they fail to realize that "their fate is bound up with how the other 99 percent live."[107] The current level of inequality does not reflect the society's values, even if the myth of the "self-made man" is widespread and embedded in the folklore of the American Dream. Buffett explains his fortune this way:

> I've worked in an economy that rewards someone who saves the lives of others on a battle-field with a medal, rewards a great teacher with thank-you notes from parents, but rewards those who can detect the mispricing of securities with sums reaching into the billions. In short, fate's distribution of long straws is wildly capricious.[108]

The new privileged class is no longer the owners of capital (the shareholders), as in the nineteenth century, but the executives who control the capital and the corporate bank account. Even prominent conservative commentator William Buckley, Jr. referred to CEO pay as "plunder": "Because extortions of that size tell us, really, that the market system is not working—in respect of executive remuneration. What is going on is phony. It is shoddy, it is contemptible, and it is philosophically blasphemous."[109]

Moreover, because of its institutional, legal, and tax structures, the US is the most unequal society among developed countries.[110] Figure 7.15 shows the ratio of the income of a person in the 90th percentile of the income distribution to that of someone in the 10th percentile. This P90/P10 ratio is a measure of the range of the income distribution. Evidently, the ratio in the US is the largest in the developed world and closer to that of Latin American countries than to European ones. This ratio in the Scandinavian countries is half as large as in the US. The Gini coefficients show essentially the same pattern (see Figure 2.4).[111]

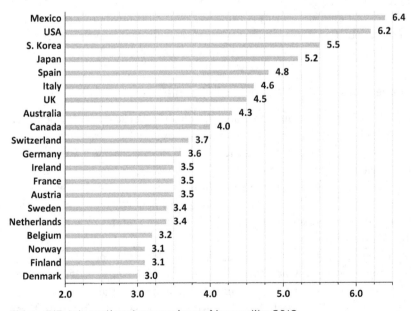

Figure 7.15 International comparison of inequality, 2018
Source: OECD Data. "Income Inequality," https://data.oecd.org/inequality/income-inequality.htm.

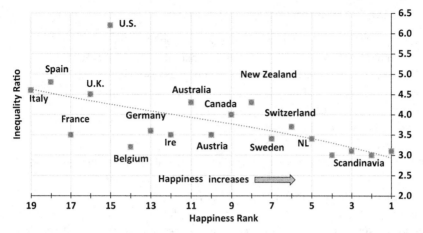

Figure 7.16 Inequality is inversely related to happiness
Source: OECD Data. "Income Inequality," https://data.oecd.org/inequality/income-inequality.htm; https://worldhappiness.report/ed/2019/changing-world-happiness/, Chapter 2, Figure 2.7.

Moreover, the more equal a society is, the happier is its population; this is another indication that relative incomes matter to subjective well-being (Figure 7.16). Year after year, the happiest people are in Scandinavia, and they also have the lowest inequality ratio (and Switzerland is not far behind) (see Figure 7.15). While some argue that all we need for a just society is equality of opportunity, the evidence on happiness contradicts this notion. There should be *de facto* equal opportunity for everyone, even those who were born on the wrong side of the tracks.

In short, the current economic system is not a *meritocracy*.[112] It is extremely difficult for those who did not choose their parents well to advance up the social ladder since education is so important to advancement and educational opportunities are so limited in poor neighborhoods (see Table 7.5). Consequently, the opportunity for social mobility is limited for those who were born in poor neighborhoods (see Section 11.6). Consequently, there are few self-made men and women among the elite as their career paths were determined mainly by circumstances of birth and innate talent.[113] This is not the system we would have devised behind a veil of ignorance had we started from scratch.

7.16 Takeaways

In contrast to mainstream theorizing, workers do not receive their just rewards in the real-existing economy. The inconvenient truth is that since 1980 productivity had increased by 50 percent more than wages; so the gains in productivity did not accrue to workers but to owners of capital, and CEOs who write their own checks because of the lax oversight by the board of directors. The average income of the top 22,000 taxpayers was $30 million and they paid taxes of only 25 percent. Hence, their after-tax income of $22.5 million left plenty of cash for conspicuous consumption, to influence the political process, and to hire economists to sing their praises. In contrast, the unemployed, the homeless, and the minimum wage workers, have no lobbyists in Washington.

This is hardly the kind of economy we would construct from scratch behind a "veil of ignorance," i.e., if we did not know in which part of the income distribution we would land. It would be too risky, unless we created an inclusive economy in which everyone had a decent job appropriate to their talents, in which wages kept pace with productivity, and the benefits of growth were not monopolized by a privileged few.

Questions for Discussion

1   What do you think is the value of the US Constitution?
2   Do you think trust is increasing/decreasing/constant in the economy?
3   Explain why trust is important from an economic perspective.
4   Do you think that labor should be treated by firms like they treat other factors of production such as physical capital?
5   How does knowledge capital differ from physical capital?
6   Why is social capital important for the economy?
7   Should we be more careful about how we use natural resources in the process of production?
8   Do you think we do enough to protect the environment?
9   What is the value of the marginal product of a professor? Of a policeman? Of a nurse?
10 Why do you suppose that wages have not kept pace with the productivity of labor?
11 Who benefited from the increased productivity if not the workers?
12 Why do you suppose women's wages have increased while those of men have stagnated?
13 Do you think CEOs receive competitive wages? Do they receive their just rewards?
14 How much of the income of superstars such as LeBron James or Beyoncé is due to the internet that was created at taxpayers' expense?
15 Should celebrities pay a special internet tax for the benefits they reap through its use?
16 Should we care about the welfare of future generations yet unborn?
17 Do you accept Rawls' conception of a "just" society?
18 Should CEOs' salaries be determined by the owners of the firm, namely the shareholders, rather than the board of directors?
19 Should firms be forced to pay the same salaries for men and women for the same work?
20 Is it just that those who contribute most to social welfare, like scientists who develop new vaccines to fight diseases, earn very little in comparison to celebrities?
21 Should luck play a role in determining salaries in a just society?
22 Should people be paid for having been born smart, beautiful, talented, or tall?
23 Do you think football players should earn more than primary school teachers? Which job is more important?
24 Do you think it is warranted to grant monopoly rights to sports teams?
25 Are we living in a "just" society? Why or why not?
26 "No man is an island." Discuss.

Notes

1   Adam Smith, *An Inquiry into the Nature and Causes of the Wealth of Nations* (Strahan and Cadell, 1776), Book 1, Chapter 8.
2   Fritz Machlup, *The Production and Distribution of Knowledge in the United States* (Princeton University Press, 1962).
3   Gregory Mankiw, *Principles of Economics*, 8th edn. (Cengage, 2018), p. 8.
4   B. Ravikumar and Lin Shao, "Labor Compensation and Labor Productivity: Recent Recoveries and the Long-Term Trend," *Economic Synopses*, The St. Louis Fed, No. 16, 2016.
5   (This is not a typo.) Michael Brill, et al., "Understanding the Labor Productivity and Compensation Gap," Bureau of Labor Statistics, *Productivity*, 6 (2017), Chart 1.

6 Lawrence Mishel and Josh Bivens, "The Pay of Corporate Executives and Financial Professionals as Evidence of Rents in Top 1 Percent Incomes," Economic Policy Institute Working Paper no. 296, June 20, 2013.

7 Nikolaos Balafas and Chris Florackis, "CEO Compensation and Future Shareholder Returns: Evidence for the London Stock Exchange," *Journal of Empirical Finance* 27 (2014): 97–115.

8 Susan Carter et al. (eds.), *Historical Statistics of the United States, Earliest Times to the Present: Millennial Edition* (Cambridge University Press, 2006), Tables Ba4783 and Ba4788.

9 Economic Policy Institute, "Worker Rights Preemption in the US."

10 Rachel Abrams, "Why Aren't Paychecks Growing? A Burger-Joint Clause Offers a Clue," *The New York Times*, September 27, 2017.

11 BLS, "Occupational Employment and Wages, May 2020, 35-3023 Fast Food and Counter Workers," https://www.bls.gov/oes/current/oes353023.htm#(3).

12 Francine Blau and Lawrence Kahn, "The US Gender Pay Gap in the 1990s: Slowing Convergence," *Industrial & Labor Relations Review* 60 (2006): 45–66.

13 The Council of Economic Advisers, "Explaining Trends in the Gender Wage Gap," June 1998.

14 Daron Acemoglu et al., "Women, War, and Wages: The Effect of Female Labor Supply on the Wage Structure at Midcentury," *Journal of Political Economy* 112 (2004), 3: 497–551; here p. 544.

15 Full-time workers. Jessica Semega et al., "Income and Poverty in the United States: 2019," US Census Bureau, Report Number P60-270, September 15, 2020.

16 St. Louis Fed, series BPBLTT01USA637S.

17 Weekly earnings of men in the first quarter of 2020 were the same as in 1979. St. Louis Fed, series LES1252881900Q. The difference between weekly wages and year-round workers is that the former includes those who worked part of the year.

18 In 2015 prices. Economic Policy Institute, "Data Library. Wages by Education." www.epi.org/data/#?subject=wage-education.

19 Adjusted for inflation. St. Louis Fed, series LEU0262881500Q; Cindy Brown Barnes, "Low-Income Workers. Millions of Full-Time Workers in the Private Sector Rely on Federal Health Care and Food Assistance Programs," Testimony Before the Committee on the Budget, US Senate, February 25, 2021; https://www.gao.gov/assets/720/712589.pdf.

20 Anne Case and Angus Deaton, "Mortality Rates by College Degree Before and During Covid-19," NBER Working Paper no. 29318.

21 St. Louis Fed, series LRAC25MAUSM156S.

22 Daniel Hamermesh, *Beauty Pays: Why Attractive People Are More Successful* (Princeton University Press, 2011).

23 Thomas Philippon and Ariell Reshef, "Wages and Human Capital in the US Financial Industry: 1909–2006," *Quarterly Journal of Economics* 127 (2012), 4: 1551–1609.

24 Ioana Marinescu et al., "Wages, Hires, and Labor Market Concentration," *Journal of Economic Behavior & Organization* 184 (2021), C: 506–605.

25 Matias Covarrubias et al., "From Good to Bad Concentration? US Industries over the Past 30 years," *NBER Macroeconomics Annual* 34 (2019): 1–34.

26 Arthur Pigou, *The Economics of Welfare*, 4th edn. (Macmillan, 1932), p. 20.

27 Among men, the white–Black wage gap in the same occupation after accounting for the usual determinants of wages like education is about 16 percent while the gap among women is smaller and statistically less significant. William Rodgers and John Holmes, "New Estimates of Within Occupation African American-White Wage Gaps," *The Review of Black Political Economy* 31 (2004), 4: 69–88.

28 Michael Lettau, "Compensation in Part-Time Jobs Versus Full-Time Jobs: What If the Job Is the Same?" Bureau of Labor Statistics (BLS) Working Paper no. 260, December 1994.

29 St. Louis Fed, series LNS12032194.

30 Since the interest rate, r, is linked to the funds rate set by the Federal Reserve, the cost of capital is not determined by the market alone.

31 St. Louis Fed, series AAA and DDEI06USA156NWDB.

32 Finbox, The Complete Toolbox for Investors, Data Explorer for Apple: https://finbox.com/NASDAQGS: AAPL/explorer/roic#:~:text=Apple'spercent20returnpercent20onpercent20investedpercent20capital, in percent20June percent202021 percent20at percent2040.6 percent25.

33 Piero Sraffa, *Production of Commodities by Means of Commodities: Prelude to a Critique of Economic Theory* (Cambridge University Press, 1960); Avi Cohen and Geoffrey Harcourt, "Whatever Happened to the Cambridge Capital Theory Controversies?" *Journal of Economic Perspectives* 17 (2003), 1: 199-214.

34 This generalization may not hold for professional athletes, who can be injured or whose capabilities decline with age.

35 Claudia Goldin and Lawrence Katz, *The Race between Education and Technology* (Harvard University Press, 2008).

36 The World Bank, "Human Capital Project – September 2020, United States, Human Capital Index 2020," https://databank.worldbank.org/data/download/hci/HCI_1pager_USA.pdf?cid=GGH_e_hcpexternal_en_ext.

37 The World Bank, *The Human Capital Index, 2020 Update: Human Capital in the Time of Covid-19*, p. 41; https://openknowledge.worldbank.org/handle/10986/34432.

38 Francis Fukuyama, *Trust: The Social Virtues and the Creation of Prosperity* (Free Press, 1995); Robert Putnam, *Making Democracy Work* (Princeton University Press, 1993).

39 David Brooks, "America Is Having a Moral Convulsion," *The Atlantic*, October 5, 2020.

40 Kenneth Arrow, "Gifts and Exchanges," *Philosophy & Public Affairs* (1972), 1: 343-362.

41 James Coleman, "Social Capital in the Creation of Human Capital," *American Journal of Sociology* 94 (1988): S95-S120. https://www.socialcapitalresearch.com/social-capitalism/.

42 Robert Putnam, *Bowling Alone: The Collapse and Revival of American Community* (Simon & Schuster, 2000); Michael Sandel, *Democracy's Discontent: America in Search of a Public Philosophy* (Belknap Press, 1996); Theda Skocpol, *Diminished Democracy: From Membership to Management in American Civic Life* (University of Oklahoma Press, 2003).

43 Douglass North, "Institutions," *Journal of Economic Perspectives* 5 (1991), 1: 97-112.

44 Douglass North, "Economic Performance Through Time," *American Economic Review* 84 (1994), 3: 359-368.

45 Daron Acemoglu and James Robinson, *Why Nations Fail* (Crown Business, 2012).

46 St. Louis Fed, series CP and GDP.

47 Does not include profits made abroad. Bureau of Economic Analysis, "Table 6.16D Corporate Profits by Industry."

48 Morten Bech and Tara Rice, "Profits and Balance Sheet Developments at US Commercial Banks in 2008," Federal Reserve Bulletin, June 2009; https://www.statista.com/statistics/211988/return-on-average-equity-for-all-us-banks/.

49 Bureau of Economic Analysis, "Table 6.16D Corporate Profits by Industry."

50 Lawrence Mishel et al., "Wage Stagnation in Nine Charts," Economic Policy Institute Report, January 6, 2015.

51 Simcha Barkai, "Declining Labor and Capital Shares," *The Journal of Finance* 75 (2020), 5: 2421-2463.

52 Anna Stansbury and Lawrence Summers, "The Declining Worker Power Hypothesis: An Explanation for the Recent Evolution of the American Economy," *Brookings Papers on Economic Activity* (Spring 2020): 1-77; here p. 63.

53 St. Louis Fed, series LABSHPCAA156NRUG and LABSHPDEA156NRUG.

54 Michael Giandrea and Shawn Sprague, "Estimating the US Labor Share," *Monthly Labor Review*, February 2017.

55 David Autor et al., "Concentrating on the Fall of the Labor Share," *American Economic Review* 107 (2017), 5: 180-185.

56 Edward Fullbrook and Jamie Morgan (eds.), *Economics and the Ecosystem* (World Economics Association, 2019).

57 Wikipedia, "Government Pension Fund of Norway."

58 https://www.nbim.no/.

59 Wikipedia, "List of Countries by Sovereign Wealth Funds."

60 Thomas Piketty and Emmanuel Saez, "How Progressive Is the US Federal Tax System? A Historical and International Perspective," *Journal of Economic Perspectives* 21 (2007), 1: 3-24; Frank Stilwell, *The Political Economy of Inequality* (Polity, 2019).

61 Mankiw, *Principles of Economics*, op. cit., p. 457.

62 Ibid.

63 US Census Bureau, "Poverty Thresholds," https://www.census.gov/data/tables/time-series/demo/income-poverty/historical-poverty-thresholds.html.

64 Jessica Semega et al., "Income and Poverty in the United States: 2019," *Current Population Reports*, US Census Bureau, 2020, P60-270, p. 19.

65 Charles Hokayem and Misty Heggeness, "Living in Near Poverty in the United States: 1966-2012," *Current Population Reports*, P60-248, May 2014.

66 Ganesh Sitaraman, *The Crisis of the Middle-Class Constitution: Why Economic Inequality Threatens Our Republic* (Knopf, 2017).

67 In 2016, the income of the top 5 percent was more than 14 times as much as that of the bottom 20 percent in Atlanta, Washington, Providence, New Orleans, Miami, San Francisco, Boston, and New York. Alan Berube, "City and Metropolitan Income Inequality Data Reveal Ups and Downs through 2016," *Brookings Reports*, February 5, 2013.

68 The price index increased by a factor of 27.8 between 1914 and 2019. The $5/hour meant $0.625 per hour. So 27.8×0.625=$17.4 per hour. St. Louis Fed, series CUUR0000SA0R.

69 Bureau of Labor Statistics, "Occupational Employment Statistics," www.bls.gov/oes/2019/may/oes_nat.htm#00-0000.

70 Barbara Ehrenreich, *Bait and Switch: The (Futile) Pursuit of the American Dream* (Metropolitan Books, 2005).

71 Anand Giridharadas, *Winner Take All: The Elite Charade of Changing the World* (Knopf, 2018).

72 Elizabeth Warren, "The Coming Collapse of the Middle Class: Higher Risks, Lower Rewards, and a Shrinking Safety Net," YouTube video, "UCTV," 2007; Elizabeth Warren, "The Vanishing Middle Class," in John Edwards et al. (eds.), *Ending Poverty in America: How to Restore the American Dream* (New Press, 2007).

73 Aggregate personal income was $12.7 trillion in 2019.

74 There are 25.7 million households per quintile. ($16,415 × 19.3 million)+($114,250 × 6.4 million) = $1tr.

75 Drew Desilver, "America's Middle Class Is Shrinking. So Who's Leaving It?" Pew Research Center, December 14, 2015.

76 John Komlos, "Growth of Income and Welfare in the US, 1979-2011," NBER Working Paper no. 22211, 2016.

77 Pew Research Center, "America's Shrinking Middle Class: A Close Look at Changes Within Metropolitan Areas," May 11, 2016.

78 Rana Foroohar, *Makers and Takers: How Wall Street Destroyed Main Street* (Crown Business, 2016).

79 William Lazonick, "Labor in the Twenty-First Century: The Top 0.1 percent and the Disappearing Middle-Class," in Christian Weller (ed.), *Inequality, Uncertainty and Opportunity: The Varied and Growing Role of Finance in Labor Relations* (Cornell University Press, 2015), pp. 143-192.

80 Andrew Van Dam, "Is the GOP Tax Plan an Unprecedented Windfall for the Wealthy? We Look at 50 Years of Data to Find Out," *The Washington Post*, December 4, 2017.

81 John Siegfried and Wendy Stock, "The Labor Market for New Ph.D. Economists in 2002," *American Economic Review* 94 (May 2004) 94: 272-285.

82 Wikipedia, "Highest-Paid NBA Players by Season." There were eleven baseball players who earned more than $28 million. Wikipedia, "List of Highest-Paid Major League Baseball Players."

83 Marissa Mayer is said to have received a golden parachute of $186 million. Berkeley Lovelace, "Ex-Yahoo President Sue Decker Rips Marissa Mayer's $186 Million Exit Package," *CNBC*, May 5, 2017.

84 Even college presidents have joined the millionaires' club. Stephanie Saul, "Big Jump in Million-Dollar Pay Packages for Private College Leaders," *The New York Times*, December 10, 2017.

85 Katharina Pistor, *The Code of Capital: How the Law Creates Wealth and Inequality* (Princeton University Press, 2019).

86 Lawrence Mishel and Jori Kandra, "CEO Pay Has Skyrocketed 1,322 Percent since 1978," Economic Policy Institute, August 10, 2021.

87 Steven Clifford, *The CEO Pay Machine: How It Trashes America and How to Stop It* (Penguin Random House, 2017).

88 A bizarre example of the brazen misuse of power is the use of a back-up airplane to follow the travels of Jeff Immelt, then CEO of General Electric, just in case the airplane in which he was flying broke down. James Stewart, "Metaphor for G.E.'s Ills: A Corporate Jet with No Passengers," *The New York Times*, November 2, 2017.

89 William Lazonick, "Profits Without Prosperity: How Stock Buybacks Manipulate the Market, and Leaves Most Americans Worse off," *Harvard Business Review*, September 2014; John Alexander Burton and Christian Weller, "Supersize This: How CEO Pay Took Off While America's Middle Class Struggled," Center for American Progress, May 2005.

90 "Berkshire's Corporate Performance vs. the S&P 500," Berkshire Hathaway, Inc., February 21, 2003.

91 These millions are included in labor compensation of Table 7.1. Hence, the productivity-compensation gap is even larger for typical employees than Figure 7.1 implies.

92 Randall Thomas and Jennifer Hill (eds.), *Research Handbook on Executive Pay* (Edward Elgar, 2012); Franz Christian Ebert et al., "Executive Compensation: Trends and Policy Issues," International Institute for Labour Studies, Geneva, Discussion Paper 190, 2008, p. 6.

93 Julian Bebchuk and Jesse Fried, *Pay Without Performance: The Unfulfilled Promise of Executive Compensation* (Harvard University Press, 2004); Carola Frydman and Raven Saks, "Executive Compensation: A New View from a Long-Term Perspective, 1936-2005," *Review of Financial Studies* 23 (2010), 5: 2099-2138.

94 Mishel and Kandra, "CEO Pay," op. cit.

95 Marianne Bertrand and Sendhil Mullainathan, "Are CEOs Rewarded for Luck? The Ones Without Principals Are," *The Quarterly Journal of Economics*, 116 (2001), 3: 901-932; Eric Ohrn, "Corporate Tax Breaks and Executive Compensation," unpublished manuscript, Grinnell College, 2021; Sarah Anderson et al., "Executive Excess 2008: How Average Taxpayers Subsidize Runaway Pay," Institute for Policy Studies, 2008.

96 Mishel and Kandra, "CEO Pay," op. cit.

97 Ibid

98 Lance Taylor with Özlem Ömer, *Macroeconomic Inequality from Reagan to Trump: Market Power, Wage Repression, Asset Price Inflation, and Industrial Decline* (Cambridge University Press, 2020), p. 86.

99 Peter Goodman, "The Robots Are Coming, and Sweden Is Fine," *The New York Times*, December 27, 2017.

100 Raghavendra Rau, "Transparency and Executive Compensation," in Jens Forssbaeck and Lars Oxelheim (eds.), *The Oxford Handbook of Economic and Institutional Transparency* (Oxford University Press, 2015), pp. 413-433; here p. 419.

101 C-Span, "A Conversation on the State of the Economy with Paul Krugman and Joseph E. Stiglitz," October 23, 2012. www.c-span.org/video/?309551-1/conversation-state-economy.

102 David Gelles, "C.E.O. Pay Remains Stratospheric, Even at Companies Battered by Pandemic," *The New York Times*, April 21, 2021.

103 Robert Frank, "Positional Externalities Cause Large and Preventable Welfare Losses," *American Economic Review* 95 (2005), 2: 137-141.

104 Richard Easterlin, "Does Economic Growth Improve the Human Lot?" in *Nations and Households in Economic Growth: Essays in Honor of Moses Abramovitz*, ed. Paul David and Melvin Reder (Academic Press, 1974); Robert Frank, "How Not to Buy Happiness," *Dœdalus* 133 (2004), 2: 69-79.

105 By "social fortune" he means the family into which one is born. John Rawls, "Some Reasons for the Maximin Criterion," *American Economic Review* 64 (1974), 2: 141-146.

106 John Rawls, *A Theory of Justice* (Harvard University Press, 1971).

107 Joseph Stiglitz, *The Price of Inequality: How Today's Divided Society Endangers Our Future* (Norton, 2012).

108 Wikipedia, "Warren Buffett."

109 William Buckley, "Capitalism's Boil," *National Review Online*, April 20, 2005.

110 OECD, "Income Inequality Update," November 2016; www.oecd.org/social/OECD2016-Income-Inequality-Update.pdf. Jon Clifton, "The Happiest and Unhappiest Countries in the World," Gallup News, March 20, 2017; October 3, 2017; http://news.gallup.com/opinion/gallup/206468/happiest-unhappiest-countries-world.aspx.

111 The correlation between the P90/P10 ratios and the Gini coefficients is +0.85.

112 Robert Frank, *Success and Luck: Good Fortune and the Myth of Meritocracy* (Princeton University Press, 2016).

113 Malcolm Gladwell, *Outliers: The Story of Success* (Little Brown, 2008).

8 The Case for Oversight, Regulation, and Management of Markets

> If the state is strong, it crushes us.
> If it is weak, we perish.
> —Paul Valéry[1]

Many aspects of markets are hidden from students in introductory textbooks. These deviations from ideal markets are obliquely called *imperfections*. Actually, these are the "Achilles' heels" of markets because they are ubiquitous powerful shortcomings that render a goodly share of the population vulnerable. In order to overcome the challenges posed by these Achilles' heels, markets have to be managed through oversight, regulation, and enforcement mechanisms in order to increase the welfare of the population and avoid pain and insecurity. This chapter explores these issues further.

8.1 Market Failure Is Ubiquitous and Ominous

Whenever markets deviate from ideal perfect markets, they are imperfect and inefficient. *Market failure exists if markets are inefficient*, i.e., do not achieve optimal production or optimal consumption. In such cases markets are not Pareto optimal because someone could be made better off without making anyone else worse off. Market failure exists in the case of capital market imperfections (insufficient collateral, human capital cannot be used as collateral), in the case of collusion, common property (atmosphere, ocean), corruption (insider trading), externalities (pollution), discrimination, expensive enforcement of contracts, illicit activity (fraud), imperfect information (quality), imperfect foresight, market power (monopolies), missing markets (future generations), moral hazard, non-insurable risks (flooding, war, rise in sea levels), opportunistic behavior (deception), radical uncertainty, regulatory capture, or transaction costs. Since such imperfections are ubiquitous, real-world markets are always inefficient without adequate oversight. This should be the default model instead of the perfect competition model in complete markets.[2]

Competition is a necessary but insufficient condition for market efficiency. Heightened competition can also lead to a race to the bottom: a business might undercut prices at the expense of an intangible aspect of its product like worker safety, thereby gaining a competitive edge and obtaining an increased market share. This can have a negative impact on other firms.

Markets cannot overcome their own limitations by themselves. It requires concerted community effort. There is no guarantee that such cooperation between business and government will occur, but many countries (Sweden, Switzerland, Singapore) have been able to accomplish it,

DOI: 10.4324/9781003174356-8

and these can serve as the guideposts. Humanistic economists advocate overcoming the limitations of market failure through economic policy to increase life satisfaction.

Market failure also afflicts the US educational system because so many students attend mediocre schools where they are unable to reach their potential. The students are helpless because they do not have the money or collateral and are therefore credit constrained. They are unable to choose which school to attend although that will influence the rest of their lives. That depends on the income of their parents. That is inefficient and an enormous waste of human resources since their lifetime earnings will be substantially less than they could have been.

8.2 The Principal-Agent Quandary

When people work for themselves, they are considered self-employed. They receive all the value they produce. There are no intermediaries. However, they are merely 10 percent of the US labor force.[3] So, 90 percent of the labor force works for someone else; they are "agents" of the principal (the owners), usually the shareholders of the corporation. These workers do not receive all the value they produce. So, their incentives to exert themselves are not identical to those of the self-employed.

This *"principal-agent" problem* is a subset of the *information asymmetry problem*, because the principals (the owners of the firm) do not have credible information on all the attributes of their agents (employees) that are important for the firm's success, like their honesty, knowledge of the firm's operation, commonsense judgment under pressure, emotional maturity, resilience in unexpected circumstances, or the amount of effort they are willing to expand on the job. Fundamental to the principal-agent problem is the impossibility of writing a perfect contract to align the incentives between the principals and their agents so that it is mutually advantageous in all unforeseen situations. The world is far too complex to specify every eventuality in a contract since the future is unpredictable and we do not know what we do not know. Providing adequate oversight is a parallel problem since the principals are far from the day-to-day decisions.

Although agents' decisions might damage the company, they often do not have to bear responsibility for the consequences of those actions as was demonstrated during the Meltdown of 2008. This occurs if: (1) there is a conflict between short-term gains of the firm at the expense of long-term losses; (2) in the presence of moral hazard, agents can benefit from risky decisions if they can reap short-term profits but can transfer eventual losses to others; (3) the losses can be hidden for a while; and (4) the responsibility is diffused in a group. The challenge within an organization at every level is to supervise the subordinates effectively to ensure the timely flow of information up the chain of authority.

Given the lax corporate governance structure, agents can often manipulate outcomes to advance their own short-term financial advantages even at the principals' long-term detriment without being held accountable. Scores of CEOs have walked away from their firms with "golden parachutes" after bringing their firms to the brink of calamity. For example, Maurice Greenberg retired from AIG with a preposterous $4.3 billion before it became insolvent and had to be bailed out at taxpayers' largesse.[4] Stanley O'Neal brought Merrill Lynch close to ruin, yet received a $160 million compensation package plus a salary of $91 million (2006). James Cayne, CEO of Bear Stearns, was named one of the "Worst American CEOs of All Time," but retained $61 million while the firm was falling on hard times.[5] The list of modern-day Robber Barons and their chicanery could be extended ad infinitum.[6]

It is not as though these captains of finance were the brightest in the room. Rather, they had the character to elbow their way into the corner office. For instance, Dick Fuld, the CEO of Lehman Brothers, was arrogant and displayed excessive "misguided bravado," and a "pathetic display of macho arrogance."[7] Nicknamed the gorilla, he revealed his true character by saying that he would like "to rip out the hearts of short sellers and eat them" when short sellers were depressing the price of Lehman's shares.[8] He also hid $50 billion in "balance sheet manipulation."[9] His wealth is still $250 million and he remained one of the superrich 1 percent-ers, while his shareholders walked away with a pittance and the collateral damage to the economy was immeasurable.[10] Ernst & Young, Lehman's accounting firm was fined $10 million for helping to "deceive investors" and paid $99 million damages to investors. Of course, this was a trifle for a firm whose revenue was $28,000 million.[11] Hubris, egoism, greed, and dishonesty were pervasive. Obviously, this is inefficient from the point of view of the firms' owners. If the risks pay off, the agent gains; if not, the principal and/or taxpayer lose. "Heads I win, tails you lose" does not lead to a stable economy.

With lackadaisical supervision from boards of directors, and ineffective *clawback* provisions that would enable the principals to regain some benefits granted to CEOs if in subsequent years their actions culminated in calamity, US CEOs can focus on immediate rewards without consideration of how those decisions affect future profits. If we presume that people are selfish, then why would we suppose that CEOs have the shareholders' best interest in mind rather than their own? The two assumptions are inconsistent.

Consequently, lenient oversight by the board of directors exacerbates the principal-agent dilemma.[12] For example, John Thain, CEO of Merrill Lynch, spent $1.2 million renovating his office a few months before the firm was bailed out at taxpayers' expense. He also paid $4 billion in bonuses a few days before the US government forced a shotgun wedding between Merrill Lynch and Bank of America. Of course, the $4 billion was not his money, and it made no difference to him whatsoever. He was not penalized for his bad judgment.[13] Another example: AIG spent some $86,000 on partridge hunting while the government was injecting $186 billion into the company to keep it afloat. Clawback clauses in executive compensation would lessen the principal-agent problem, but the SEC has not followed up on this problem forcefully.[14]

The research on *contract theory* concludes that profit maximization is essentially unattainable under real-world circumstances. As in consumption, the principals can satisfice, that is, search for a satisfactory solution to their problem but it does not always yield satisfactory results. Alan Greenspan, in charge of the stability of the financial system for 19 years, was negligent in thinking that the bankers could be trusted to look out for the interests of their shareholders. Nobelist Daniel Kahneman criticized Greenspan for being careless about the inherent conflict of interest in the principal-agent problem during the run-up to the financial crisis:

> [Greenspan's] assumption [is] that agents are fully rational, and there is a lot of evidence clearly that they're not. The other is the idea that firms are actors; that firms are rational agents. But firms are really not actors ... there are executives making decisions; the interest of those executives and the interest of that abstract idea that we call the firm are clearly not aligned and if we want to understand why firms are suicidal it is in part because the agents are ... quite frequently not committing suicide. So, there is a mismatch between firms and the actors who act in their behalf.[15]

Disregarding the principal-agent problem proved catastrophic, because management maximized their own bonuses, which did appear to align with the shareholders' interest in the short run but indefinitely. Their immediate bonuses conflicted with the firm's long-run viability because agents hid the accumulated risks from the principals. The profits of the banks appeared as though they were pure profits. Instead, they were returns on risks they were accumulating. So, the blackboard conceptualization of the modern firm makes little sense without incorporating the principal-agent problem and its inherent conflict of interest.

This issue is not new to the modern world. Adam Smith was well aware of it:

> The directors of such companies ... being the managers ... of other peoples' money than of their own, it cannot well be expected, that they should watch over it with the same anxious vigilance with which the partners in a private copartnery [partnership] frequently watch over their own ... Negligence and profusion, therefore, must always prevail more or less, in the management of the affairs of such a company.[16]

8.3 Moral Hazard Disrupts the Efficient Market Hypothesis

Moral hazard is another subset of the imperfect information problem. It occurs when the two sides to a contract do not have the identical information (asymmetric information) and the existence of the contract might alter the behavior of one of the contracting parties. For example, an insurance company does not know as much about the insured persons' driving habits as the persons themselves. If they price the contract for the average driver, the more careful drivers would be less likely to buy insurance while accident-prone people are more likely to purchase them. This is challenging for insurance companies because they have to offer a price without knowing much about the insured. Furthermore, once people buy insurance, they might be less careful, because they can pass the adverse consequences of their actions onto others (see Section 6.6). Hence, insurance contracts include co-payments to reduce moral hazard. And car insurance is mandated by government in order to avoid the moral hazard problem.

8.4 Transaction Costs Increase the True Price of a Product

Transaction costs are an important hindrance to efficient choice because every important decision involves significant *search costs* to find the available alternatives. Searching for a job, a college, an apartment to rent, a house to buy, a cellphone contract are all complicated, challenging, and involve asymmetric information. Consequently, consumers have to expand considerable amounts of time, energy, and money to find satisfactory solutions to complex problems. Intuitive judgment, experience, and intelligence are all important in finding reasonable solutions to the economic problems at hand and the results are uncertain. Important (non-reversible) decisions have to be made with incomplete information. The solution does not drop out of a mathematical formula.

Thus, the true price of a complex product includes not only the ticket price but also additional transaction costs of acquiring it. Increasing the transaction costs of acquiring information about the attributes of a product or making it difficult to do comparison shopping is a tactic retailers use sell their products.[17] Automobile prices are never advertised on TV, the monthly payments are. This is a selection device to separate those seriously interested in the product from those who are less so, and once the serious consumers invest in finding out the price, they are less likely to switch to a competitor, because that would take additional investment of time and effort with an uncertain payoff. According to this *search theory*, "seemingly small frictions can have large effects on outcomes."[18] Transaction costs are considered *"frictions"* because the economy does not run as smoothly as generally assumed.

Even small transaction costs can limit competition, leading to a pricing strategy that resembles monopoly prices.[19] Obviously, searching is a dynamic process that requires the expenditure of effort and money in real time, creating obstacles to attaining an efficient outcome. The process can best be described as satisficing (see Section 4.5).

Health insurance companies make their contracts so complicated that searching is extremely confusing and time-consuming so that consumers too often give up and buy products without being adequately informed about alternatives (see Figure 4.1). There is a lot of uncertainty how much longer one should search for additional information and how much success one would have finding a superior alternative. Only in the process of searching does one begin to ascertain incrementally the costs involved.[20]

Transaction costs are most onerous for those who can least afford them. Hence, poor consumers have the most difficulty making good decisions and consume effectively (see Section 16.4.2). Clearly those who cannot afford to search, or do not have the patience to wait until a better alternative is reached, are much more likely to end up with inferior outcomes.

8.5 Opportunistic Behavior Leads to Suboptimal Allocation

Opportunistic behavior means deception or manipulation of counterparties in order to increase profits at another's expense. It is prevalent in the context of *incomplete contracts*, asymmetric information, gullibility, cognitive biases, fraud, bribery, or the inferior mental ability of counterparties. Free markets open up a myriad of possibilities for opportunistic behavior, i.e., for people to take advantage of others in a cunning, crafty, dishonest, deceitful, fraudulent, immoral, misleading, unethical, or unlawful manner and lead to misallocation of resources and inefficient outcomes.[21] Since contracts are generally incomplete, many opportunities arise to take advantage of ambiguities and manipulate contingencies that were unforeseen when the contract was written.[22] Moreover, unscrupulous people can benefit from legal loopholes, enabling them to profit by disregarding ethical norms.[23] Opportunism is another reason why *maximization of utility is impossible* in the real world.

The inherent propensity of greedy people to overreach or deceive without scruples implies that markets need effective oversight and sanctions: people's actions must be constrained so that they will refrain from taking advantage of the weaknesses or lack of information of others, for instance, by selling contaminated drugs or food. (There are 3,000 deaths from food poisoning annually in the US.)[24] In sum, freedom is a two-edged sword: it also begets opportunistic behavior.[25]

The increase in opportunistic behavior necessitated the increase in government oversight and regulation. A generation ago, old-fashioned bankers would have been much less willing to entice people to sign up for variable-rate mortgages that they knew would increase unreasonably the risk exposure of their customers. However, with the current sensibilities there was plenty of "irresponsible lending," fraud, and opportunistic behavior in the run-up to the Great Meltdown.[26] Hence, culture matters.

A culture that tolerates fraud will experience a decline in trust and an increase in the costs of doing business that include enforcing contracts. The contemporary world is witnessing an epidemic of fraud: executives are being jailed and companies are fined practically daily. In 2012,

GlaxoSmithKline was fined $3 billion,[27] a Citibank executive received an eight-year sentence for embezzling $22 million,[28] and 324 people were convicted of fraud since the Meltdown, all of them low-level employees. The Lords of Wall Street were too big to jail! No executive was prosecuted in connection with the Meltdown.[29] However, some were jailed for insider trading, including hedge-fund billionaire Raj Rajaratnam, sentenced to 11 years in prison (released in 2019), and Rajat Gupta, jailed for two years.[30] Elizabeth Holmes, CEO of Theranos, was found guilty of defrauding investors and patients. Many banks have been fined also. The government collected some $150 billion in fines and consumer relief. Barclays Bank was fined $450 million for rigging interest rates (Libor scandal). United Bank of Switzerland paid $1.5 billion for the same crime. Cybercrime is on an industrial scale.

Allen Stanford was sentenced to a 110-year term in a $7 billion Ponzi scheme. Dennis Kozlowski, former CEO of Tyco International, 6.5 years. He was released in 2014. Jeff Skilling, former president of Enron, served 12 years in jail; Bernard Ebbers of WorldCom, served 13 years of a 25-year sentence. Oliver Schmidt, a Volkswagen executive is serving seven years in prison for his role in the company's violation of the Clean Air Act. The fraud cost the company $20 billion in fines and settlements.[31] And these are only the people who were caught—the tip of the iceberg. Fraud complaints including scams and identity theft have been growing by 165,000 a year to reach 3 million in 2019 with damages of $1.9 billion.[32] The FBI made 241 convictions in 2011 for corporate fraud.[33] This is not the characteristic of an efficient market.

Between 1991 and 2015, pharmaceuticals paid $36 billion in fines for illegal activities like off-label marketing or for overcharging Medicare.[34] Household names like Enron, Arthur Andersen, WorldCom, Adelphia Communications, and Purdue Pharma have disappeared in the wake of fraud, embezzlement, insider trading, or obstruction of justice.[35] Johnson & Johnson and other pharmaceuticals were fined $26 billion for their contribution to the opioid epidemic and the Sackler family, makers of OxyContin, paid $4.5 billion for their role in it. Probably 11 percent of US large corporations engage in some corporate fraud.[36] A survey of MBA students with two-years' work experience revealed that 15 percent had been asked to do something illegal.[37]

Fraud decreases efficiency because it destroys trust and cooperation and increases the enforcement costs of contracts. It also induces people to be more cautious and that also increases transaction costs, lowering living standards and contributing to the accumulation of frustration. For instance, worry about carrying cash induces people to pay with credit cards, but they pay an inordinate amount of $150 billion annually for that service (2019).[38]

 Excessive freedom increases opportunistic behavior. Welfare and efficiency increase as freedom increases until the optimal level. However, beyond the optimum level as freedom continues to increase, welfare and efficiency decrease, because of the damages caused by increasing opportunistic behavior. Beyond that point the harm of opportunistic behavior outweighs the benefits of increased freedom (Figure 8.1).

Economists have been complacent about the costs of opportunistic behavior: "The capitalist economy lives in an institutional-less vacuum where markets miraculously monitor opportunistic behavior."[39] This is an enormous problem in the real economy because the temptation of extra profits is high so that deceptive practices are rampant; 49 percent of the US population thinks that morals are "poor."[40] Opportunistic behavior adds an additional layer of inefficiency to the economy.

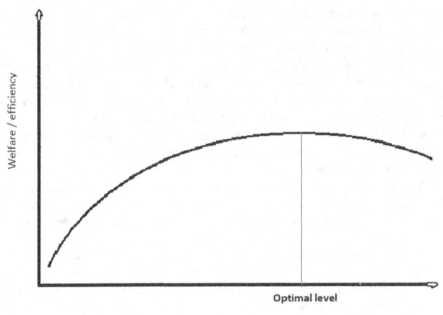

Figure 8.1 The optimum level of freedom in an economy

8.6 Regulatory Capture Is a Consequence of Rampant Inequality

The advancement of private interest instead of public interest by government agencies is called *regulatory capture*; it has taken on immense proportions.[41] Legislation, regulation, administration in the common interest is confronted by the immense concentration of income and wealth, because lobbies spend $3 billion annually to influence politicians to serve their parochial interests.[42] Consequently, the lobbies extract benefits (rents) for their members at society's expense.[43] Moreover, the wealthy invest millions in political campaigns to influence the political process, while ordinary citizens have a disproportionately smaller impact relative to their far greater number. This unbalanced incentive structure led to corporate dominance (Figure 8.2). Regulatory capture betrays the public trust, leads to suboptimal outcomes, and leads to the distrust of political institutions.

Mega-corporations provide regulators with another motivation to cooperate with them—high-paying future employment. People shuttling back and forth between government and the corporate sector is the *"revolving door,"* a subtle form of regulatory capture. One of the thousands of examples is Wendy Gramm, who granted Enron an exemption from regulation in trading of energy derivatives while she headed the Commodity Futures Trading Commission. After she left the commission, she was appointed to Enron's board of directors and received between $1 and $2 million in compensation before the firm went bankrupt. Her husband, Phil Gramm, was also rewarded by Enron. This is legal corruption.[44] Timothy Geithner is another example. As Treasury Secretary, he fought tooth and nail to bail out the financial sector on terms favorable to the bankers with unconscionable disregard of Everyman on Main Street.[45] He was amply rewarded thereafter by becoming president of a hedge fund with millions of dollars in salary. Moreover, JPMorgan Chase, a bank he previously regulated, extended a line of credit to him also

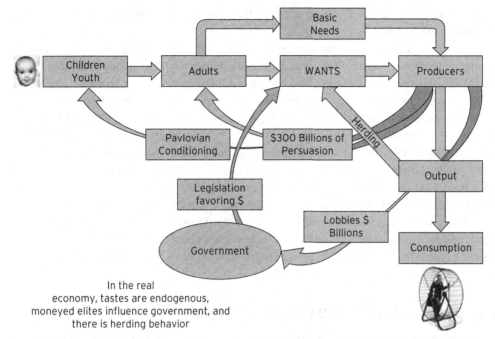

Figure 8.2 Corporations invest heavily in order to tilt the playing field in their direction

in the millions, to help increase his personal investments.[46] In sum, one hand washes the other. It is nothing less than a legal form of bribery. It is plausible that his policies at Treasury were influenced by the anticipation that he would be rewarded magnificently subsequently, provided he conducted himself appropriately. Everyman on Main Street had nothing to offer. Of course, economists can be captured as well.[47] Those who support policies advocated by politicians and businessmen are rewarded generously.[48]

8.7 Regulation in the Public Interest Is Essential

Government regulation increases exponentially with the size and complexity of markets in order to provide oversight and maintain institutions that work in the public interest; otherwise, markets would implode. There is a large scope for government regulation in areas in which markets are not aligned with society's interest, as discussed above in cases of market failure. This is especially the case if intangibles are involved in market exchange like safety, risk, uncertainty, or if decisions pertain to the distant future. The invisible hand does not work well with intangibles without ample regulation and enforcement because of imperfect information.

There are also transactions that are prohibited because they are considered repugnant by the culture; these include selling organs, selling oneself into slavery (even for a limited time), or selling babies.[49]

Lenient regulation and government oversight can lead to disaster, as in 2008 (see Chapter 14).[50] Similarly, the deregulation of the electricity market in the 1990s led to the Enron scandal and its bankruptcy. Such problems are ubiquitous from bus companies, blood supplies,[51] fashion models,[52] or overcharging students by for-profit colleges.[53] Chinese imported drywall contaminated 100,000 homes with noxious gases.[54] Legal remedies seldom bring satisfaction in such cases because the cost of litigation is prohibitive and because it is easy for "unscrupulous" businesses to disappear.[55]

Instead of regulation, governments can also *nudge* people into doing the right thing thereby improving their lives.[56] People can be guided to follow commonsense behavior without compulsion if they do not have sufficient self-control, knowledge, insight, or foresight to recognize by themselves the right choice. For example, some employers help their employees save for retirement by having a default option that serves the employee's interest. If the default option is zero (unless the employee checks one of the other boxes) people save much less than if the default option is 5 percent (unless the employee chooses zero). Thus, setting the default option strategically nudges employees to save for a rainy day. People make predictable mistakes that a thoughtful expert can help them avoid. Because saving for retirement is a smart thing to do, a nudge to make the right choice makes sense from the society's viewpoint. Putting healthy foods in easy-to-reach places while making junk food harder to reach in school cafeterias is another example of how authorities can intervene to help students improve their diet. It is ethical to help people increase their living standards by avoiding inadequate choices in health, finance, and the environment.[57]

8.8 Morality Should Not Be Delegated to Markets

Free markets do not function well without moral constraints because laws are costly to enforce if they are not adequately supported voluntarily and if they are not considered just.[58] Without widespread trust the transaction and enforcement costs for orderly exchange increase rapidly. Hence, capitalism was well served by the Judeo-Christian ethic, which kept opportunistic behavior low. People internalized the belief that dishonesty was immoral, thereby fostering trust and lowering transaction costs. The vanishing of such moral constraint brought about the diminution in trust, and increased opportunism, thereby increasing the cost of doing business.

Examples of the proliferation of unsavory business practices abound. Wachovia bank's CEO, Kennedy Thompson, received $15 million before the bank's bankruptcy.[59] The bank was fined $160 million for laundering Mexican drug money and another $144 million for being negligent about cashing checks stolen through identity theft. Thomas Hayes, the culprit in the LIBOR interest-rate fixing scandal, received an 11-year sentence and is still in jail (2021).[60] Verizon Communications overcharged customers;[61] foreclosures were carried out illegally; banks broke rules without scruples.[62] Banks around the globe were fined a staggering $700 million in just the second quarter of 2021 for money laundering.[63] "GlaxoSmithKline agreed to pay $750 million to settle criminal and civil complaints that the company for years knowingly sold contaminated baby ointment and an ineffective antidepressant."[64]

Bank of America was fined $16.6 billion for fraud.[65] Wells Fargo Bank created millions of fake accounts to bolster the executives' bonuses.[66] Then it defrauded customers by failing to refund insurance money, and then it was found manipulating foreign exchange.[67] These were not run-of-the-mill finagling. They were brazen violations of the law with a low probability of success for an extended period of time. Yet, these executives were willing to take risks associated with illegal activity and had thousands of collaborators willing to execute their directives.[68] The list could continue ad infinitum. Such blatant deceit of millions of customers would not have been possible in an age when moral restraint was still effective.

Illustration 8.1 Doctors for Camel exploit consumers' gullibility
Credit: From the collection of Stanford Research into the Impact of Tobacco Advertising (tobacco.stanford.edu).

8.9 Exploitation Is Detrimental to the Social Fabric

The notion of exploitation does not exist in today's conventional economics, although Stiglitz recognizes its significance in today's economy, for instance, the extent to which monopoly drug prices hurt people.[69] Furthermore, a famous economist of an earlier era also recognized that an "element of exploitation" was involved if workers were not paid the value of their marginal product.[70] And that is precisely how subordinate classes feel when they are taken advantage of, for example, by bankers who "exploited the financially unsophisticated."[71] If a firm knowingly deceives or misleads a customer or employee in order to profit at the other's expense, the exchange is abusive. The one who takes advantage of a counterparty in an unfair manner is exploiting their vulnerabilities. The weakness can stem from asymmetric information, from asymmetric cognitive ability or from asymmetric power relations as in monopoly or monopsony. "Market power also allows firms to exploit workers directly by paying lower wages than they would otherwise ..."[72]

Such lopsided power relationships form the basis of predatory capitalism.[73] People with more reliable information, more extensive social networks, more power, and who are smarter have an advantage in free markets and can exploit that advantage to their benefit.[74] Such unequal exchanges were rampant during the run-up to the crisis of 2008 since the mortgage originators talked unaware consumers into risky mortgages they did not understand. During the Covid-19 pandemic low-skilled workers were forced to endanger their lives by continuing to work, because they had no other means of support. That is another way of being taken advantage of.

8.10 Time and Space

The significance of time and space is not sufficiently acknowledged in mainstream economics. Yet, they are essential to understanding why real markets are generally inefficient because they impose transaction costs and make it more difficult to acquire information. The recent development of the new economic geography, which emphasizes the clustering of economic activity and consequent regional disparities, is important.[75]

Time is a unique resource with six features: (1) it is distributed equally throughout the population; (2) it is an essential element in every economic transaction; (3) it has no substitutes; (4) it cannot be borrowed; (5) it cannot be accumulated; and (6) it moves only in one direction. These unique attributes pose formidable obstacles to the smooth and efficient functioning of markets: they lead to inefficiencies, to regrets, and to path dependence.

8.11 Path Dependence or Sequential Decisions

Path dependence means that today's decisions are influenced not only by the objective conditions today but also by irreversible decisions that were made yesterday without knowing what today would be like.[76] Consequently, our investment, production, and consumption decisions may not be efficient because of limitations imposed by earlier decisions. Prior decisions act as a constraint on decisions today. The implementation of new technologies, the creation of institutions, and the adoption of laws or new social norms are generally not a single event. Rather, they evolve through a series of sequential decisions over time.

Everyone faces an uncertain future since nobody possesses perfect foresight about how technologies, institutions, laws, regulations, prices, political developments, or other features of the economy will evolve. They therefore base their decisions on current knowledge, and these initial choices might lock them into an inferior developmental path such that the optimal technology, the optimal institutions, or optimal investments are unattainable.

According to the orthodoxy, competition ensures that the best firms will prevail and therefore the economic system will reach an optimum. Inferior technologies are supposed to become unprofitable and be displaced by the competition. However, this theory overlooks the complex, uncertain, and sequential nature of development in real time with imperfect information and without perfect foresight. Technological change—all change—is an evolutionary process; hence, a static single-decision model is unrealistic; the future offshoots of the initial technology are not yet evident when initial crucial decisions are made. Time only moves in one direction and many processes are practically irreversible. Once investments are made in large infrastructure projects like highways, railroads, or dams, it is unfeasible to change them.

The usual assumption is that firms decide to invest at time T and expect a payoff in the future, say, at time T+2, two years later (Figure 8.3). With such perfect foresight, the optimal choice is a "no brainer:" firms will choose technology A, the one with the largest payoff. Most Econ-101 problems are structured in this simple way.

However, the outcome is different if at time T, the technologies that will exist at T+2 are unknown. Suppose at time T only the options at T+1 are known, and one has perfect foresight only until T+1 (Figure 8.4). Firms must choose between investments E and F without knowing their technological offshoots. In this case, the optimal choice is F. The difference between the perfect foresight model and the path-dependent process becomes evident at time T+1, because at T+1 the two technologies E and F have offshoots A, B, C, and D, which were unknown at time T (Figure 8.5). Having chosen F, the firm is unable to adopt the optimal technology A and is thus

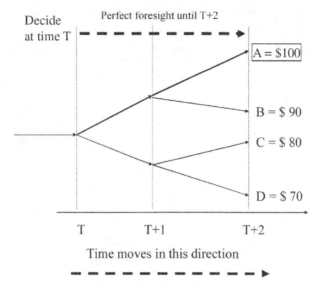

Figure 8.3 Investment decision with perfect foresight two periods ahead is easy

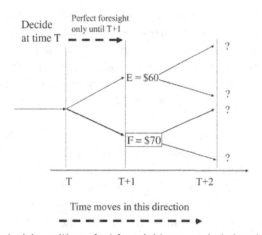

Figure 8.4 Investment decision with perfect foresight one period ahead is also easy

"locked" into a choice between C and D. In this case, the rational choice becomes C because A is unachievable (Figure 8.5). In short, although one chooses the optimum in each period, with only one-period-ahead foresight one is locked into an inferior technology, C, with sequential choice.[77] This is quite different from the neoclassical assumption that optimizing rational investors will achieve an optimum outcome. In the path-dependent framework, the equilibrium reached might be inefficient. For instance, arguably the Windows operating system is not the best possible operating system. Yet, it won the competition because of chance and an early-mover advantage that was irreversible.

To be sure, there might be cases in which the decision to choose F is reversible and the firm could switch to technology E and then A at time T+2, provided it bears the costs of accomplishing this. But the switching is frequently not cost effective. Furthermore, vested interests might be able to prevent the switch to the social optimum through political lobbying, regardless of the switching costs. Hence, there is no guarantee that people will be able to make optimal investment decisions in a sequential-choice framework without perfect foresight.

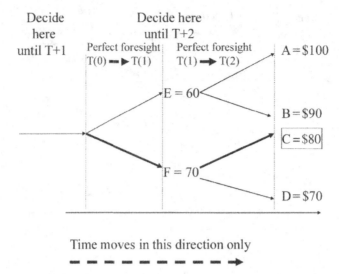

Figure 8.5 With sequential decision, optimum technology "A" is no longer feasible

This path-dependent model is applicable to other kinds of sequential decisions, including institutional change, infrastructure, or investment in education. Suppose 30 years ago high school graduates decided not to go to college because decent-paying jobs were available without a college degree. However, they would realize 30 years later that the decision was suboptimal because technological change devalued their high school diploma. At the age of 50 it is not easy to reverse such a decision and acquire new skills. Millions of people experienced this kind of disappointment.

Early adoption of an inferior technology might provide sufficient benefits because of *network externalities* that it can outcompete a latecomer even if the latecomer is a superior technology. A network externality lowers information and transaction costs. It means that a product is easier to use as more people are using it. Thus, subsequent consumers will choose it because they gain the benefit of many users. This might be advantageous in the case of a game, for example, since there are more people with whom to play the game. It is also true for the Windows operating system. The more people adopted it, the easier it was to obtain help with the program, thereby lowering transaction costs.

Suppose a technology is introduced in year 1 and some people begin to adopt it. If a competing technology is introduced subsequently, it will face an uphill battle, because the first technology has adherents already that will provide benefits to new users even if the latecomer were superior from a technical standpoint. Furthermore, because the first mover's output is larger in year 2, its production costs are lower due to *economies of scale in production*, providing another advantage over the latecomer. So, the latecomer is not likely to be successful because the *first-mover advantage* is like a barrier to entry even for superior technologies.

Learning to plan sequentially is an important part of succeeding in life. Choosing a job, for instance, starts many years earlier in high school when one selects courses that will be needed subsequently. Students must work appropriately so that the grades suffice for the level of aspirations. The decision to become a doctor is not made on the spot. Its realization takes years of planning and making appropriate choices. Investment strategies like buying a house require planning years in advance for a down payment and imply making many sacrifices along the way. The strategic planning and perseverance needed to reach these goals must be learned and practiced over an extended period of time. Such decisions are much more complex than a typical one-period optimization problem with perfect foresight. The poor are trapped in a culture of poverty partly because they do not have the opportunity to learn these skills early in life, particularly those who grow up in dysfunctional neighborhoods with mediocre school systems.

8.12 Limits and Standards

Generally setting limits and standards by decentralized markets is difficult. Consequently, the portions at restaurants are too big and contribute to the obesity epidemic. There are too many retail stores, most of which are often practically empty leading to the underutilization of resources. Moreover, the common wisdom is that increased choice increases utility. However, good things in excess can become undesirable. For example, the availability of dozens of salad dressings is excessive choice and detracts from our ability to make wise decisions and thus decreases welfare.[78] There are times when "more is less," as the conventional canon disregards the increased transaction costs, i.e., the time and effort needed to learn about the products offered.

The Aristotelian golden mean (between the two extremes of excess and deficiency) is unattainable as a competitive equilibrium in real markets. That is why we have too many products, too many choices, and too much debt on our credit cards.

8.13 Takeaways

If markets deviate from ideal perfect markets, they are inefficient. Inefficient markets do not achieve optimal production or optimal consumption. In such cases, markets are not Pareto optimal as someone could be made better off without making anyone else worse off. Market failure exists in the case of capital market imperfections (insufficient collateral, human capital is not accepted as collateral), in the case of collusion, common property (atmosphere, ocean), corruption (insider trading), externalities (pollution), discrimination, expensive enforcement of contracts, illicit activity (fraud), imperfect information (quality), imperfect foresight, market power (monopolies), missing markets (future generations), moral hazard, non-insurable risks (flooding, war, rise in sea levels), opportunistic behavior (deception), radical uncertainty (unknown probability distribution), regulatory capture, and transaction costs. Since such imperfections are ubiquitous, real-world markets are always inefficient without adequate regulation.

Markets function well only within the appropriate framework that only governments can provide. Markets have many Achilles' heels that prevent them from leading to a flourishing society. Moreover, markets have difficulty executing long-range plans as they are focused on immediate gratification and disregard the needs of future generations. Because markets are myopic, global warming is a major threat to the long-run survival of human civilization.

Questions for Discussion

1   What do you think could be done to raise ethical standards in the marketplace?
2   Do you know people who acted opportunistically to advance their own cause at others' expense?
3   Are there some markets that should be more tightly regulated than others?
4   Have you ever bought an unsafe product?

5   Do you think that predatory lending should have been prohibited?
6   Do you think that there is too much freedom in the financial markets?
7   Do we need government meat inspectors, or could the meat industry regulate itself?
8   Are markets good at providing safe products? Why or why not? Give examples.
9   Markets are democratic as you vote with your dollars instead of the ballot box. Discuss.
10 Do you think that lobbying is part of the democratic process?
11 Do you think that corporations should be allowed to contribute to political campaigns?
12 Do you think that Wall Street has too much influence in Washington?
13 Have you ever been outsmarted by a company?
14 Have you ever paid more for a product than you should have?
15 Do you think that corporations can devise contracts so as to exploit the weaknesses of some people?
16 Has the cost of searching ever made it difficult for you to buy the product best suited for you?
17 Have you ever been trapped by choices you made earlier?
18 Have you regretted purchasing a product?
19 Have you ever found that your choices were limited by decisions you made at an earlier period without full knowledge of their hidden consequences?
20 Did you ever make hasty choices because of the lack of time?
21 Can you give an example of path dependence?
22 Do you think it would be useful to adopt an energy policy based on renewable energy?
23 Do you think the government should invest heavily into solar energy?
24 Are markets patient, or do they emphasize immediate gratification?
25 Did you ever have to make sequential choices in the presence of uncertainty?
26 Do you think that global warming will be a threat in your lifetime?
27 Should we preserve the ecosystem (endangered species) for your grandchildren?
28 Do you think trading pollutants is a good idea?
29 Are you sometimes overwhelmed by the number of choices available to you?

Notes

1   Paul Valéry (1871–1945), French poet.
2   "People of the same trade seldom meet together, even for merriment and diversion, but the conversation ends in a conspiracy against the public, or in some contrivance to raise prices." Adam Smith, *An Inquiry into the Nature and Causes of the Wealth of Nations* (Strahan and Cadell, 1776), Book I, Chapter X, Section 82.
3   Steven Hipple and Laurer Hammond, "Self-Employment in the United States," US Bureau of Labor Statistics, March 2016.
4   Mary Williams Walsh, "Insurance Giant A.I.G. Takes Ex-Chief to Court," *The New York Times*, June 14, 2009.
5   "Portfolio's Worst American CEOs of All Time," *CNBC*.
6   "The 15 Worst CEOs in American History," *Business Insider*, May 4, 2010.
7   William Cohan, "Lehman E-Mails Show Arrogance Led to the Fall," *Bloomberg View*, May 6, 2012. www.bloomberg.com/view/articles/2012-05-06/lehman-e-mails-show-wall-street-arrogance-led-to-the-fall.
8   "Dick Fuld Rip Out Your Heart," https://www.youtube.com/watch?v=GZCmWkQuyPc.
9   Michael de la Merced and Andres Ross Sorkin, "Report Details How Lehman Hid Its Woes," *The New York Times*, March 11, 2020.

10   About $50 billion worth of value was destroyed by the bankruptcy. Editor, "How Much Value Was Destroyed by the Lehman Bankruptcy?" *Harvard Law School Bankruptcy Roundtable*, February 2019.

11   Karen Freifeld, "Ernst & Young Settles with N.Y. for $10 Million over Lehman Auditing," *Reuters*, April 15, 2015.

12   Richard Arnott and Joseph Stiglitz, "Labor Turnover, Wage Structures, and Moral Hazard: The Inefficiency of Competitive Markets," *Journal of Labor Economics* 3 (1985), 4: 434–462.

13   His current annual salary is still around $6 million although he did repay the million dollars he spent renovating the office he soon vacated.

14   Wayne Carnall and Veronica Uwumarogie, "Dodd-Frank Clawback Rule: Recovery of Erroneously Awarded Compensation," PwC, July 8, 2015.

15   "Reflection on a Crisis," @ 18 minutes. https://www.youtube.com/watch?v=LjGI6bZF6zs.

16   Smith, *Wealth of Nations*, op. cit., Book V, Chapter I, Section 107.

17   Sharon Begley, "Looking for a Good Doctor? Good Luck," *Reuters*, September 27, 2012.

18   Peter Diamond, "Unemployment, Vacancies, Wages," *American Economic Review*, 101 (2011), 4: 1045–1072.

19   Joseph Stiglitz, "Information and the Change in the Paradigm in Economics," *American Economic Review* 92 (2002), 3: 460–501; here p. 477.

20   Oliver Williamson, *Markets and Hierarchies: Analysis and Antitrust Implications* (The Free Press, 1975).

21   Wikipedia, "Opportunism."

22   Oliver Hart, *Firms, Contracts, and Financial Structure* (Oxford University Press, 1995).

23   Liz Hoffman and Dave Michaels, "Goldman Pays Billions," *The Wall Street Journal*, October 23, 2020.

24   There are 48 million cases of food poisoning and 128,000 hospitalizations annually. Center for Disease Control and Prevention, "Food Safety," https://www.cdc.gov/foodsafety/foodborne-germs.html.

25   Jan Hoffman and Katie Benner, "Purdue Pharma Pleads Guilty to Criminal Charges for Opioid Sales," *The New York Times*, August 17, 2021.

26   Paul Krugman, "Wall Street Whitewash," *The New York Times*, December 16, 2010.

27   The company discovered that its diabetes drug Avandia posed risks to the heart. "But instead of publishing the results, the company spent the next 11 years trying to cover them up." Gardiner Harris, "Diabetes Drug Maker Hid Test Data, Files Indicate," *The New York Times*, July 13, 2010; Peter Landers and Jeanne Whalen, "Glaxo to Plead Guilty, Pay $3bil to US to Resolve Fraud Allegations," *The Wall Street Journal*, July 2, 2012.

28   "Gary Foster, Ex-Citigroup Exec, Headed to the Slammer," *Huffington Post*, June 29, 2012.

29   Kara Scannell and Richard Milne, "Who Was Convicted Because of the Global Financial Crisis?" *Financial Times*, August 9, 2017.

30   Michael Rothfeld, "In Gupta Sentencing, a Judgment Call," *The Wall Street Journal*, October 10, 2012.

31   Bill Vlasic, "Volkswagen Official Gets 7-Year Term in Diesel Emissions Cheating," *The New York Times*, December 6, 2017.

32   Federal Trade Commission, "Consumer Sentinel Network, Data Book 2019," January 2020.

33   https://www.fbi.gov/stats-services/publications/financial-crimes-report-2010-2011.

34   Sammy Almashat et al., "Twenty-Five Years of Pharmaceutical Industry Criminal and Civil Penalties: 1991 Through 2015," *Public Citizen*, March 31, 2016.

35   Wikipedia, "List of Corporate Collapses and Scandals."

36   Alexander Dyck et al., "How Pervasive Is Corporate Fraud?" http://faculty.haas.berkeley.edu/morse/research/papers/DyckMorseZingalesPervasive.pdf.

37   Ibid.

38   https://fred.stlouisfed.org/series/REVEF52221ALLEST#; https://www.census.gov/newsroom/archives/2014-pr/cb14-tps73.html.

39   Daron Acemoglu, "The Crisis of 2008: Structural Lessons for and from Economics," January 11, 2009. https://economics.mit.edu/files/3722.

40   Justin McCarthy, "About Half of Americans Say US Moral Values Are 'Poor,'" *Gallup News*, June 1, 2018.

41   Neil Barofsky, *Bailout: An Inside Account of How Washington Abandoned Main Street While Rescuing Wall Street* (Free Press, 2012).

42   William Novak, "A Revisionist History of Regulatory Capture," in Daniel Carpenter and David Moss (eds.), *Preventing Regulatory Capture: Special Interest Influence and How to Limit it* (Cambridge University Press, 2014), pp. 25–48.

43   Mancur Olson, *The Rise and Decline of Nations: Economic Growth, Stagflation, and Social Rigidities* (Yale University Press, 1982).

44   Wikipedia, "Wendy Lee Gramm"; Bob Herbert, "Enron and the Gramms," *The New York Times*, January 17, 2002.

45   John Komlos, "The Banality of a Bureaucrat, Timothy Geithner and the Sinking of the US Economy," *Challenge: The Magazine of Economic Affairs* 57 (2014), 5: 87–99.

46   Lucinda Shea, "Timothy Geithner Got a J.P.Morgan Credit Line for His Investments," *Fortune*, February 8, 2016.

47   Luigi Zingales, "Preventing Economists' Capture," in Daniel Carpenter and David Moss (eds.), *Preventing Regulatory Capture: Special Interest Influence and How to Limit It* (Cambridge University Press, 2014), pp. 124–151.

48   Norbert Häring and Niall Douglas, *Economists and the Powerful: Convenient Theories, Distorted Facts, Ample Rewards* (Anthem Press, 2012).

49   Alvin Roth, "Repugnance as a Constraint on Markets," *Journal of Economic Perspectives* 21 (2007), 3: 37–58.

50   Hyman Minsky, *Stabilizing an Unstable Economy* (McGraw-Hill, 1986).

51   Contaminated supplies of Chinese Heparin, an anticoagulant, killed 81. Gardiner Harris, "US Identifies Tainted Heparin in 11 Countries," *The New York Times*, April 22, 2008.

52   Laura Stampler, "France Just Banned Ultra-Thin Models," *Time*, April 3, 2015. Many models died after dieting excessively. Eric Wilson, "Health Guidelines Suggested for Models," *The New York Times*, January 6, 2007.

53   Editorial, "Let the Students Profit," *The New York Times*, September 11, 2010.

54   Years of litigation followed contaminated Chinese drywall. Andrew Martin, "Drywall Flaws: Owners Gain Limited Relief," *The New York Times*, September 17, 2010.

55   Patrick McGeehan, "Federal Officials Shut Down 26 Bus Operators," *The New York Times*, May 31, 2012.

56   Cass Sunstein, *Why Nudge? The Politics of Libertarian Paternalism* (Yale University Press, 2015).

57   Cass Sunstein, *The Ethics of Influence: Government in the Age of Behavioral Science* (Cambridge University Press, 2016).

58   Jean Tirole, *Economics for the Common Good* (Princeton University Press, 2017).

59   Wikipedia, "G. Kennedy Thompson"; Ed Vulliamy, "How a Big US Bank Laundered Billions from Mexico's Murderous Drug Gangs," *The Observer*, April 2, 2011.

60   Jill Treanor, "Libor Interest Rate to Be Phased Out After String of Scandals," *The Guardian*, July 28, 2017.

61   Editorial, "Verizon Wireless Says Oops," *The New York Times*, October 5, 2010.

62   David Streitfeld and Gretchen Morgenson, "Foreclosure Furor Rises; Many Call for a Freeze," *The New York Times*, October 5, 2010.

63   https://www.kyckr.com/aml-bank-fines-q2-2021/?utm_source=WN; https://www.idmerit.com/blog/7-anti-money-laundering-fines-you-may-have-missed-multinational-banks-held-accountable-by-regulators-for-compliance-missteps/.

64   "The latest in a growing number of whistle-blower lawsuits that drug makers have settled with multi-million dollar fines," Gardiner Harris and Duff Wilson, "Glaxo to Pay $750 Million for Sale of Bad Products," *The New York Times*, October 26, 2010.

65   US Department of Justice, "Bank of America to Pay $16.65 Billion in Historic Justice Department Settlement for Financial Fraud," August 21, 2014; https://www.justice.gov/opa/pr/bank-america-pay-1665-billion-historic-justice-department-settlement-financial-fraud-leading.

66 Gillian White, "One Year After Its Fake-Accounts Scandal, Wells Fargo Isn't a Better Bank," *The Atlantic*, October 3, 2017; The bank was punished by not allowing it to grow beyond its size at the end of 2017. Emily Flitter et al., "Federal Reserve Shackles Wells Fargo After Fraud Scandal," *The New York Times*, February 2, 2018.

67 Gretchen Morgenson, "Wells Fargo, Awash in Scandal, Faces Violations Over Car Insurance Refunds," *The New York Times*, August 7, 2017; David Z. Morris, "Wells Fargo Scandals Expand with Firing of Foreign Exchange Bankers," *Fortune*, October 21, 2017.

68 Emily Glazer, "Wells Fargo's Sales-Scandal Tally Grows to Around 3.5 Million Accounts," *Wall Street Journal*, August 31, 2017.

69 Joseph Stiglitz, *People, Power and Profits: Progressive Capitalism for the Age of Discontent* (Norton, 2019), pp. 23, 26.

70 Arthur Pigou, *The Economics of Welfare*, 4th edn. (Macmillan, 1932), p. 20.

71 Stiglitz, *People, Power*, op. cit., p. 113.

72 Ibid., p. 49.

73 Matthew Desmond, "In order to understand the brutality of America capitalism, you have to start on the plantation," *The New York Times*, August 14, 2019.

74 "Today, we understand that the market is rife with imperfections—including imperfections of information and competition—that provide ample opportunity for discrimination and exploitation," Joseph Stiglitz, "When Shall We Overcome?" *Project Syndicate*, March 12, 2018.

75 Anthony Venables, "New Economic Geography," in Steven Durlauf and Lawrence Blume (eds.), *The New Palgrave Dictionary of Economics*, 2nd edn. (Palgrave Macmillan, 2008).

76 Brian Arthur, *Increasing Returns and Path Dependence in the Economy* (University of Michigan Press, 1994).

77 Brian Arthur, "Competing Technologies, Increasing Returns, and Lock-In by Historical Events," *Economic Journal* 99 (1989), 394: 116-131; Paul David, "Clio and the Economics of QWERTY," *American Economic Review* 75 (1985), 2: 332-337; Paul David, "Path Dependence, its Critics and the Quest for 'Historical Economics'," in Pierre Garrouste and Stavros Ioannides (eds.), *Evolution and Path Dependence in Economic Ideas: Past and Present* (Edward Elgar, 2001), pp. 15-40.

78 Barry Schwartz, *The Paradox of Choice: Why More Is Less* (Ecco, 2003). "The Paradox of Choice: Why More Is Less," YouTube video, 1:04:08, posted by "GoogleTalksArchive," April 27, 2006.

9 Microeconomic Applications On and Off the Blackboard

There shall be no poor among you.
−Deuteronomy, 15:4[1]

We next analyze a number of critical issues in real-world economics. Standard textbook analysis of these problems applies the perfectly competitive model, whereas we consider such models irrelevant in today's economy dominated by oligopolies. Hence, we use models characterized by imperfect competition. The conclusions differ substantially.

9.1 Minimum Wage Is Good for Workers and Good for the Economy

According to the received dogma, a government-imposed minimum wage interferes with free markets and is therefore inefficient and creates unemployment. It raises the price of unskilled labor; therefore, firms will demand fewer workers, leading to unemployment among low-wage workers. Some 79 percent of economists believe that a minimum wage increases unemployment among young and unskilled workers, as a simple application of supply and demand analysis indicates.[2] This conclusion is correct in perfectly competitive markets in which there are no profits and no unemployment. This is the model Mankiw uses: "if the government doesn't intervene, the wage normally adjusts to balance labor supply and labor demand."[3] He is a Pinocchio for that statement because normally labor markets are not balanced at all. Unemployment is persistent and there are millions of unemployed who are not even counted as such (see Table 11.1). The last time demand and supply intersected at full employment was in 1944! Yet, Mankiw claims−without any evidence whatsoever− that "the result [of a minimum wage] is unemployment."[4] The reason he does not provide evidence is that there isn't any.[5] His thinking is confined to hypotheticals in Alice-in-Wonderland markets.

Actually, the federal minimum wage peaked at $11.90 in 1968 (2020 dollars) but is $7.25 in 2022. It is so low, that numerous localities, including Seattle, set the minimum wage higher. It phased in a minimum wage of $15 that became fully effective in 2017 (and was indexed to inflation thereafter). It had absolutely no impact on the unemployment rate (Figure 9.1). This is the case although the increase was huge: $5.50 or nearly 60 percent. Not only did unemployment *not* increase, but it actually declined and reached a pre-Covid low of 2.8 percent. Obviously, the unemployment rate was driven by general economic conditions and not by the minimum wage. The correlation coefficient of Seattle's unemployment rate with that of surrounding King County and of the State of Washington, with a lower minimum wage, was +0.99 and +0.93 respectively between 2014 and 2019.[6] The correlation with the US rate was +0.90.

DOI: 10.4324/9781003174356-9

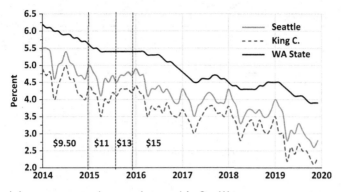

Figure 9.1 The minimum wage and unemployment in Seattle
Source: FRED Graph Observations, Federal Reserve Economic Data, Economic Research Division, Federal Reserve Bank of St. Louis Link: https://fred.stlouisfed.org.

The Seattle experience adds to a large body of empirical evidence *refuting* mainstream theorizing in hypothetical markets.[7] The minimum wage does not cause unemployment if the increase in wage can come out of profits and if the prevailing wage is below the marginal product of labor, or when there is unemployment.[8] Because today's economy is dominated by oligopolies, many of which also have substantial power in the local labor market, they use that power to depress wages.[9]

So, the perfectly competitive labor market Mankiw has in mind is nowhere in sight. In markets dominated by oligopolies, increases in the minimum wage transfer money from profits to workers *without* creating unemployment.[10] Consider the case of McDonald's. While it competes with other fast-food chains, its profits were $6 billion (2019) because of its well-chosen locations, brand recognition, advertisement campaigns, consumer loyalty, and unique menu. The Big Mac price index does not indicate any increase in prices, adjusted for inflation after the federal minimum wage increased by $0.70 in July 2007 and again by $1.40 by July 2009 to reach $7.25 (Table 9.1). Between May 2006 and June 2007–before the increase in the minimum wage–the price of a Big Mac increased by 23 cents but in the subsequent 12 months, after the increase in the minimum wage by a substantial $2.10 (40 percent), its price remained essentially unchanged for more than 2 years, rising by only 15 cents at the end of the third year (Table 9.1). Evidently, the profits sufficed to absorb the wage increases without adjusting Big Mac's price. Since the price of Big Macs remained unchanged, the demand for Big Macs also remained unchanged and therefore the company needed the same number of employees to produce the same number of Big Macs. No reason to lay anyone off.

Another quantitative analysis of 10,000 McDonald's franchises' reaction to minimum wage increases concludes that a $1 increase in the minimum wage increased the price of Big Macs by 7 cents between 2016 and 2020.[11] That is not substantial enough to have a measurable impact on demand for Big Macs. Hence, the demand for labor would not have been affected appreciably.

To understand why this is the case, consider the demand for Big Macs at the neighborhood McDonald's. Suppose it sells 500 Big Macs a day and needs 5 workers to make them (Figure 9.2). The franchise is earning a profit of $1 on each Big Mac. The manager knows that if he/she wants to continue to meet the demand for 500 Big Macs, it still needs 5 workers even after the minimum wage is raised. Hence, with such an inelastic demand for labor, it would not decrease its labor force (Figure 9.3). To be sure, profits decline after an increase in the minimum wage. This is a transfer of $2.10 per hour per worker from profits to wages. Hence, in profitable oligopolies and

Table 9.1 Big Mac price index (2010 dollars)

	Nominal	CPI	Real price	Minimum
	dollars	index		wage
May 2006	3.10	92.5	3.35	5.15
January 2007	3.22	93.5	3.44	5.15
June 2007	3.41	95.2	3.58	5.15
	Minimum wage increase +$0.70			
June 2008	3.57	99.9	3.57	5.85
	Minimum wage increase +$1.40			
July 2009	3.57	98.7	3.57	7.25
January 2010	3.58	99.9	3.58	7.25
July 2010	3.73	100.0	3.73	7.25

Note: Minimum wage was raised, effective July 2007, July 2008, and July 2009, each by $0.70. Real prices are in July 2010 dollars.
Sources: St. Louis Fed series CPIAUCSL; *The Economist*, https://github.com/TheEconomist/big-mac-data/blob/master/output-data/big-mac-2019-01-01.xls.

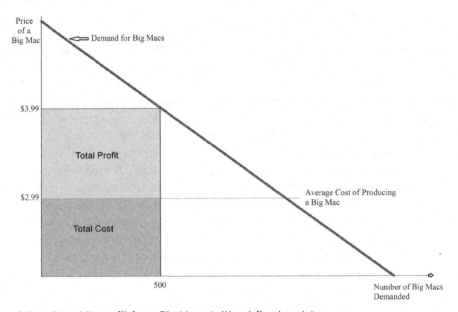

Figure 9.2 McDonald's profit from Big Macs (without fixed costs)

quasi-monopolies an increase in the minimum wage does not cause unemployment but leads to a redistribution of income from profits to wages. So, a model with imperfect competition provides more insight into the working of today's low-wage sector than the perfectly competitive model does.

Adam Smith recognized that businessmen complain about the effect of wages on sales but not about the effect of profits on raising prices and impeding sales:

> Our merchants and masters complain much of the bad effects of high wages in raising the price and lessening the sale of goods. They say nothing concerning the bad effects of high profits. They are silent with regard to the pernicious effects of their own gains. They complain only of those of other people.[12]

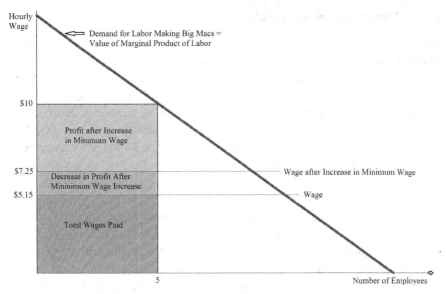

Figure 9.3 An increase in the minimum wage transfers some profits to workers

Similarly, those who complain about the minimum wage are silent about the exorbitant earnings of CEOs. McDonald's CEO, Steve Easterbrook, received $15 million in 2016 while his successor, Chris Kempczinski received $18 million in 2019, and $11 million in 2020.[13] The lower 2020 pay was still 1,200 times as much as that of the median employee working for him at $9,100 per annum.[14] The CEO pay was not considered excessive for the mainstream, but a raise above the current pittance for his employees would be considered extravagant. Note, furthermore, that McDonald's workers earn $20 an hour in Denmark with paid vacation and the fast-food market does not collapse as a consequence.[15]

Anyhow, the working poor live a miserable life of bare subsistence. A full-time annual income at minimum wage is $12,500, below the poverty level for a single individual ($13,171).[16] It is illuminating, however, to consider that about 25 million workers in 2019 earned less than the minimum wage of 1968.[17] Many low-wage workers are being supported by food stamps so they can meet their basic needs, a form of subsidy to their employers paid by the taxpayers. FDR recognized that people need and deserve a living wage:

> It seems … equally plain that no business which depends for existence on paying less than living wages to its workers has any right to continue in this country … By living wages I mean more than a bare subsistence level – I mean the wages of decent living.[18]

In addition to raising some households above destitution, the minimum wage has other positive feedback effects on the labor market because other wages are pegged to it. An increase in the minimum wage therefore leads also to a rise in the wage of other workers near the poverty line. Furthermore, it also increases purchasing power and thereby aggregate demand. In addition, an increase in the minimum wage motivates workers to exert more effort, thereby increasing productivity. It also lowers worker turnover that increases productivity. Higher wages also have positive health effects that increase productivity. Thus, there are many reasons to support an increase in the federal minimum wage.

9.2 Price Controls Can Also Help

Price controls are similarly harmful in the view of mainstream economists because supposedly they create shortages. Yet, meeting the basic needs of everyone is a legitimate social and political concern that markets alone cannot guarantee (see Section 3.3). Moreover, the public does not like price gouging during emergencies, like airplane tickets during evacuations related to Hurricane Irma or increases in gasoline prices following Russia's invasion of Ukraine. So, governments have a legitimate role to prevent firms from making a profit from such crisis. Additionally, it would be unfair if only wealthy people could afford gasoline during an oil embargo, as happened in 1973. The increase in the price of basic necessities, like food or gasoline, affects the welfare of the poor far more than that of the rich. Moreover, some market outcomes are morally repugnant.[19]

Additionally, the unequitable distribution of basic goods can be socially destabilizing. In the case of a gasoline shortage, using the queuing mechanism for rationing is fairer because time is equally distributed, whereas money is not. Using time as a rationing device is fairer in such cases. Competition for gasoline would then be on a more level playing field. Although the wealthy would be inconvenienced, the working poor would experience greater frustration if they were unable to drive to work because they could not afford to buy gasoline at exorbitant prices. In sum, in the case of supply shortages, it is harmful to let markets allocate basic needs and allow war profiteering. This is also the case with health care.[20]

Price ceilings can also induce monopolists and oligopolists to lower their price, increase output, and produce closer to the socially optimum output, thereby increasing social welfare (Figure 9.4). For instance, the pharmaceutical industry is exploiting its monopoly power and causing untold harm to those who need the drugs but cannot afford them. Martin Shkreli infamously increased the price of a malaria drug overnight from $13.50 to $750. (He is now facing seven years in prison for an unrelated crime of defrauding investors.) Heather Bresch similarly raised

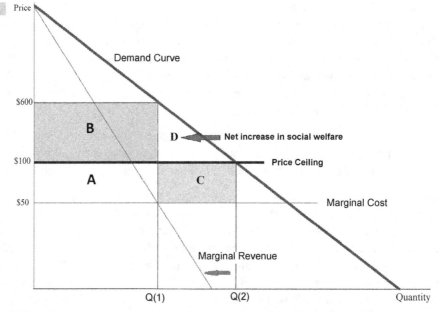

Figure 9.4 The effect of a price ceiling on a monopolist (without fixed costs)

the price of an anti-allergy EpiPen injection, from $100 to $600 for no apparent reason.[21] Such scandalous exploitation of people's critical needs was called "sickening" by a lawmaker.[22]

Such exploitation of monopoly power can be mitigated with a price ceiling. A pharmaceutical monopolist's initial profit-maximizing output is Q(1) at the monopoly price of $600. Its revenue is $600 × Q(1) and its total cost is $50 × Q(1), assuming no fixed costs. Profit is equal to the area of the rectangles A + B = $550 × Q(1). If the government were to impose a price ceiling of $100, profits would decrease by the area of rectangle B. However, at the lower price, demand would increase and production would increase to Q(2). Since the price is still above marginal cost, the area of rectangle C represents additional profits. However, C is smaller than B. So, profits decline by (B – C). However, consumers gain because they benefit from the medicine's lower price. They gain area B, which is a transfer of money from producers to consumers, and they also gain the triangle D (because they valued the drug more than the $100 ceiling price they paid for it. Consequently, a price ceiling: (1) decreases the profits of pharmaceutical firms by (B – C); (2) transfers B dollars from pharmaceuticals to consumers; (3) increases consumer satisfaction by (B + D); and (4) increases social welfare by (B + D – B = D). This is the net gain due to the price ceiling. Thus, a price ceiling can increase social welfare in the case of monopoly pricing.

9.3 Monopsony: Bargaining Power of Firms in the Labor Market

"The time has come to recognize that many–or even most–firms have some wage-setting power."[23] Firms that employ a significant share of the local labor force use their power *to depress wages*.[24] In the presence of search costs many teenagers, poor people without transportation, and part-time workers are often unable to commute long distances and generally look for work near home, leading to imperfect competition.[25] Consequently, local businesses hiring those workers have a captive market and use their market power to set wages below the perfectly competitive level.[26] This is *monopsony power*, analogous to monopoly power, except that firm's power is not used to increase prices but to depress wages.[27] Monopsonists pay wages below the free-market rate because they take advantage of the lack of options available to local low-skilled workers to work outside of their immediate vicinity.[28] The concentration of firms means that production is concentrated in a handful of firms and these firms dominate local hiring. Concentration has increased substantially, particularly in rural areas, where there are few employers, leading to limited competition (monopsony power) in the labor market and depressed wages by as much as 25 percent.[29] In sum, the wage stagnation is caused not only by globalization and by technological unemployment but also by the "high degree of employer power in labor markets."[30] Monopsony wages are abusive.[31]

An increase in the minimum wage would provide workers some relief in those concentrated markets. Reasons for the high concentration is the large number of mergers, slack anti-trust enforcement, and inter-firm agreements limiting labor market competition.[32] In Silicon Valley, firms like Adobe, Apple, Google, and Intel paid $415 million settlement for conspiring to suppress the competition for high tech employees and thereby limit their salaries.[33]

9.4 Unions and Countervailing Power

Unions are the boogeyman in Econ-101. Like the minimum wage, they are considered an unwarranted *interference* in labor markets. Allegedly, raising the wages of union members above the equilibrium wage determined by supply and demand is inefficient, bad for business, and bad for non-union workers because it increases unemployment.[34] As is the case with the minimum wage, such logic is pertinent only in markets where firms are not earning a profit; however, unions never thrived in such markets. Rather, they flourished solely in sectors in which *power* was exercised to depress wages.[35] This occurred either in industries dominated by oligopolies in which considerable profits were generated, or in the public sector—where there are no profits, but wages are determined administratively.[36]

Unions provide *countervailing power* to powerless workers.[37] Without that leverage, workers are divided and unable to obtain a share of the rents they generate for oligopolies.[38] In oligopolistic sectors unions forced firms into a profit-sharing arrangement, thereby converting some profits into labor rents, especially for the lower-middle class, by as much as 15-20 percent.[39] Moreover, unions also protect workers from the power of monopsonists to depress wages and exploit workers.[40] Labor rents were the basis on which the gains of labor in the post-World War II heady days were predicated (see Figure 7.1).[41] In 2020, union workers earned $10,000 more per annum than non-union workers (+23 percent).[42]

A decisive moment in the decline in union power was the 1981 strike of the Professional Air Traffic Controllers Organization (PATCO), squashed by President Reagan. 11,000 employees were fired, signaling the end of the union and the end of the influence of big labor.[43] Intimidated, the number of strikes involving at least 1,000 workers declined thereafter precipitously from 235 in 1979 to 17 by 1999.[44] The share of the labor force in unions under Reagan diminished from 26 percent to 17 percent, a decline of 30 percent.[45] In contrast, union membership held steady at 26 percent *throughout* the Carter administration.

Unions were also important because of the existence of asymmetric information: unions hired economists who knew how much labor productivity had grown, they knew how much profit

Illustration 9.1 United in unions, labor would have countervailing power and obtain a share of profits. Divided, it has none
Credit: Harris & Ewing collection, Library of Congress.

the firm earned, they could argue with management at the bargaining table, and could threaten to strike, their ultimate weapon. Individual workers had no such knowledge and had no such leverage to sway management. They could easily be replaced.

Today's economy is dominated by oligopolies that earn profits. The profit of such firms is illustrated in Figure 9.5. The demand for the firm's product can be produced by N number of employers. Because the firm has market power, its output is less than that of a perfectly competitive firm. Supply of labor intersects the demand for labor at E, which would be the perfectly competitive equilibrium. However, the oligopolist hires fewer workers because it only needs N workers in order to produce as much as it needs to satisfy demand. Workers receive a wage W although the value of their marginal product (MP_L) is larger. The area of the rectangle is profit = $N*(\$MP_L - W)$. Note that for Apple the area of the rectangle was $95 billion (2021) and MP_L - W = $619,000 per employee (see Section 7.6). Obviously, its employees were not earning the value of their marginal product.

The union uses its countervailing power to extract some of the profit at the bargaining table by increasing the wage above W. Note that for this oligopolist, the demand for labor is inelastic because it is derived from the amount of output demanded, and that would not change. The price is not a function of the wage. A steel manufacturer has to deliver a certain tonnage of steel demanded by bridge builders, car manufacturers, and firms building skyscrapers so that the number of workers it employs would remain at N. Thus, the increase in the wage would only decrease the firm's profit, thereby securing a more equitable distribution of income. In other words, the union's bargaining power is used to share in some of the profits.

There is no evidence at all that unions cause unemployment. The fluctuations in the unemployment rate depend on macroeconomic conditions and not on unions. Note that the decline of

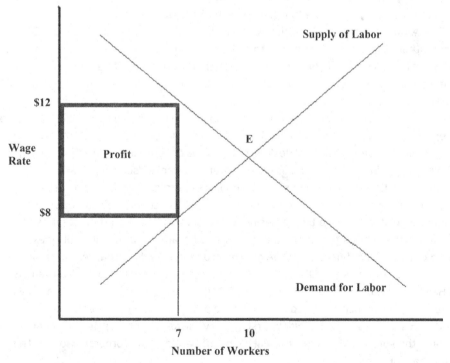

Figure 9.5 Profit of an oligopolist

unions since 1981 redistributed power and profits to the corporate world.[46] The decline in union bargaining power contributed to (1) the steep rise in inequality (see Figure 7.10); (2) the decline in wages relative to productivity, beginning in 1980 (see Figure 7.1); (3) the stagnation in median income of men since 1973 (see Figure 7.3); (4) the absolute decline in the wages of low-skilled men (see Figure 7.4); (5) the decline in labor's share in GDP (see Figure 7.6); (6) the sluggish growth of real household income since 2000 (0.3 percent per annum) (see Figure 7.9); and (7) the steep rise in CEO pay. The reason is that "unions traditionally helped bolster the wages of lower- and middle-wage workers, thereby reducing inequality. The correlation between unionization and inequality is clear ... the decline in the number of unionized workers has coincided with overall rising inequality."[47]

Consider Apple's lopsided wage structure.[48] Its CEO, Tim Cook, received a salary of $15 million in 2020. Additionally, he received a bonus of $300 million for his efforts of the last nine years or $33 million per annum. He has a net worth of $1.4 billion. Four other members of senior management received $26 million each. Contrast this vast largesse to the wages of Apple's sales associates, who sold $274 billion worth of its products and earned $19 per hour (2021), received no incentive pay, bonuses, or stock options. According to common sense, neither Cook's nor the salesforce's wages equals the value of their marginal product because their output is joint: Apple could not exist without a CEO or without salespeople. The latter's salary is low because monopsony power keeps a ceiling on their wages, while Cook's salary is protected from competition, although I presume that thousands of qualified people would be willing to do the job for a few millions less. When it was time to fill Cook's job, it was not advertised. There was no search for a competition to find the lowest-bid qualified applicant. Moreover, neither salary is fair. If there were a union at Apple, it would strive to increase the salary of salespeople to that paid for Tiffany's salespeople, for instance, at $28 an hour.[49]

Suppose the union were able to increase each of 100,000 salesperson's salary by $9.00 an hour. That would reduce Apple's profits by $1.5 billion (2.6 percent) to $55.5 billion (2020). Conclusion: without the help of a union, the salesforce is unable to gain a middle-class income. This is not a fair outcome for one of the iconic multinationals of today. If Rawls were to design the system behind a veil of ignorance, he certainly would not design one with a range from $19 to $7,500 per hour, differing by a factor of 400.

Mainstream economists argue that by increasing the wages of union members, unions actually depress the wages of the non-union low-skilled labor force. That conjecture is refuted, however, by the steady and substantial decline in the wages of non-union men without a high school degree beginning in the 1980s, just as union power was waning (see Figure 7.4).

Another significant role of unions was to support government vis-à-vis big business and help maintain the balance of political and economic power. The countervailing power of Big Labor prevented regulatory capture by Big Business (see Section 8.7). Government on its own could not continue to maintain that balance of power and became subservient to business interests because of its massive financial resources. The drug industry, for instance, spent $106 million lobbying Congress between 2014 and 2016. Congressman Tom Marino (R-Utah) and Senator Orin Hatch (R-Utah) received $100,000 and $177,000 respectively in order to advance a bill through Congress to increase the profits of opioid producers despite the epidemic that claimed 200,000 lives by 2016.[50] By the twenty-first century, lawmakers could safely disregard the general will of the voters and cater to the will of the affluent and the corporate world.[51] This is the making of a plutocracy.[52]

9.5 The American Medical Association Is a Harmful Cartel

A *cartel* is an organization that fosters the competitive economic advantage of its members. The influential American Medical Association (AMA) is such a cartel since it restricts competition, allegedly to foster excellence in medical care but by restricting the number of doctors, it increases their salaries far above competitive levels (Figure 9.6).[53] Despite the shortage of doctors, only half of those applying to medical school are accepted although only the most qualified apply.[54] Consequently, they earn between two and five times as much as doctors in other rich countries.

To increase the number of physicians per capita to Norway's level, the number of doctors in the US would have to be increased by 764,000 (Figure 9.6)! Compared to the 866,000 physicians active in the US (2019), this would be a 88 percent increase. The US position relative to Norway worsened since 2004 when the US lagged behind Norway by only 1.0 physician per 1,000 population. By 2019, the gap was 2.3 physicians. No doubt catching up to Norway would put a downward pressure on US medical costs and improve the health of the US population closer to European levels.

The AMA constrains the number of medical schools and the number of students they can admit, thereby constraining the number of doctors (Figure 9.7). In competitive equilibrium *N′*

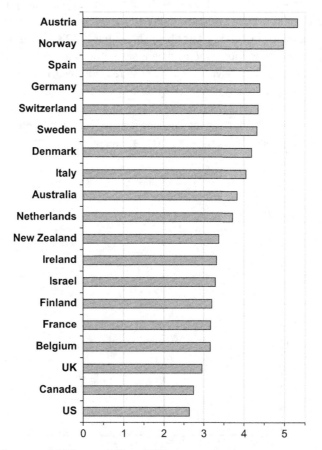

Figure 9.6 Physicians per 1,000 population, 2019
Source: OECD Health Data 2016. www.stats.oecd.org/Index.aspx?DataSetCode=HEALTH_REAC.

would be 1.6 million, closer to the Norwegian level. Consequently, the income of physicians is far above the competitive level: $200,000 vs $100,000 in Germany and Canada.[55] The salary of medical school deans is $400,000.[56] Cardiologists earn $386,000.[57] Some argue that the reason doctors' salaries are so high is that medical school is so expensive although the causation is the reverse: medical schools increased their tuition to capture a share of the rents earned by doctors, known as *rent seeking*.

While the number of law schools has been increasing, the number of medical schools has not. There are just 141 medical schools in the US, and the number of students admitted annually is limited to 20,000.[58] In contrast, there are 205 law schools, and the salaries of lawyers are half of those of doctors.[59] The AMA has been able to achieve this by restricting supply.[60]

The reason the US medical system is in such disarray is because it is based on free-market principles, but it is a market full of imperfections.[61] For instance, one finds such gobbledygook in a leading textbook as: "Health care is an economic commodity like shoes and gasoline."[62] This is a Pinocchio untruth because it disregards the *essential* differences between an extremely complex basic need and a simpler product like shoes. Obviously, perfect competition does not apply to health markets.[63] Health care is unique because there is asymmetric information between the counterparties: patients have to rely on the doctors' good will. Moreover, there is a conflict of interest in which complex decisions are made with considerable uncertainty and hospitals profit from additional procedures while patients' ability to ascertain the best treatment is limited. I personally have experienced doctors prescribing superfluous MRIs, X-rays, and more. Another difference is that price competition is non-existent since prices are not easily available. Try to find out the price of an x-ray before you go to the hospital. Moreover, health expenses can cause bankruptcy, whereas buying shoes cannot. Furthermore, a shoe is a tangible good. Hence, its quality is readily ascertained whereas the true quality of a doctor, a hospital, or a health insurance contract might take years to discover. Gasoline is also entirely different. It is produced from an exhaustible resource, pollutes, and therefore has major environmental effects. Thus, the

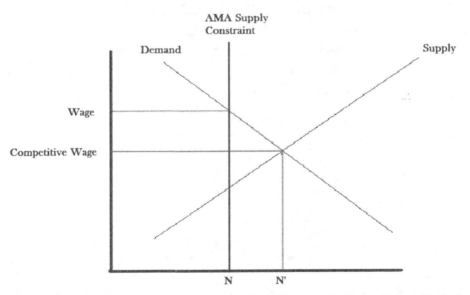

Figure 9.7 The market for doctors with supply constraint imposed by the American Medical Association

essence of the three markets could not differ more. To conflate them willfully defies common sense and confuses the reader.

9.6 Redistribution Would Help

Poverty can be both absolute and relative. It is absolute if a household is unable to meet its basic needs (see Section 3.4). Additionally, one can feel disadvantaged relative to the consumption of a reference group even if one's basic needs are met (see Section 7.10). This is *relative depriva-tion* and is a comparable threat to social order as absolute poverty.

Redistribution from billionaires to the poor is justified out of a feeling of moral obligation, a sense of fairness, empathy for the plight of the poor, or because of concern for social disintegra-tion.[64] The feeling of discomfort among third parties created by the suffering of the poor is a *negative externality*. One need not be a purist and strive for perfect equality but merely create a fairer distribution of income that at least eliminates deprivation and ensures that at least basic needs—including health and education—are adequately met for everyone, especially for children, who are not accountable for the circumstances into which they were born. This is fundamentally the Scandinavian model and the capitalism with a human face.

It is unethical to allow 38 percent of the 17 million single mothers to be poor,[65] while the top 25 hedge fund managers have a combined income of $32 billion, an astronomical $1,300 million each. Such enormous incomes are, in reality, economic rents, far beyond the value of their contribution to society. They are undeserved windfall. They would have done their job at a small fraction of that salary. The top 400 wealthiest families enjoy the additional privilege of paying merely 8 percent of their income in taxes.[66] To neglect squalor amidst such plenty, while children grow up deprived of a decent education and consequently are deprived of equal opportunity, has an ominous impact not only on their lives but also on the whole society. Such misallocation leads to a tremendous waste of human resources, increases crime, adds to the prison population, and those living on welfare, and, therefore, the social cost of such neglect is unacceptable public policy.

Because of the decreasing marginal utility of income, social welfare would be increased considerably if we redistributed income from the wealthy to the poor (Figure 9.8). The length of the X-axis (OC = OA + AC) represents the total income in this two-person economy. For Per-son 1, the origin is at O, while, for Person 2, the origin is a C. Initially, poor Person 1 receives the segment OA while rich Person 2 receives the segment AC. The marginal utility curve for Person 1 is DC and for Person 2 it is HO. These two curves translate the dollars into utility. The initial distribution implies that Person 1 enjoys total utility represented by the trapezoid OAED while that of Person 2 is ACHF. Total utility is made up of these two trapezoids. However, total utility could be increased if income represented by the segment AB were transferred from Person 2 to Person 1. Then the total utility of Person 1 would increase to OBGD and that of Person 2 would decrease to BCHG. So, the total utility of Person 1 would increase by ABGE and that of Person 2 would decrease by ABGF. The gain of Person 1 is greater than the loss of Person 2 by the triangle FEG. The net gain of total utility is analogous to the *increase in social welfare*.

An argument against redistribution is that we are unable to compare utility levels across indi-viduals. While it is true that some people might like oranges while others might prefer apples, we are not discussing such minor issues of taste. Rather, we are comparing humongous differences

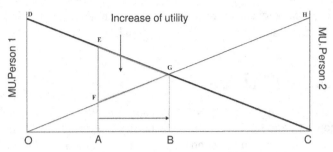

Figure 9.8 Redistribution of income increases total utility of the society

in basic needs like education and health care available to people because it is safe to assume that people do not differ substantially in their basic needs. The pangs of hunger of one person cannot be much different from those of another. A toothache for one is much like that of anyone else. Every parent wants a decent education for their children.[67] Humanistic economists advocate a distribution of income such that all members of society can meet their basic needs while increasing their self-esteem.

In reality, interpersonal comparisons of utility are not at all impossible. Here is a Nobelist's view:

> It seems to me that economists and philosophers influenced by logical positivism have greatly exaggerated the difficulties we face in making interpersonal utility comparison with respect to the utilities and disutilities that people derive from ordinary commodities and, more generally, from the ordinary pleasures and calamities of human life.[68]

Yet mainstream economists resist making such comparisons, although they have no qualms assuming that a single agent can represent everyone in macroeconomic models, an assumption that implies a homogeneous society (see Section 10.6).

Another argument against income redistribution is that it generates inefficiencies. This efficiency-equity trade-off supposedly reduces the incentive of high-productivity workers to work, thereby decreasing total income. However, this claim assumes, without evidence, that everyone works less if tax rates increase in the upper income brackets. However, there is no evidence supporting this claim.[69] Would the 724 US billionaires work less if their tax rate were doubled? Would lawyers work less if their after-tax salary is reduced from $1,200 to $800 per hour? Would Beyoncé sing fewer songs? Would LeBron James shoot fewer baskets? Would Tim Cook introduce fewer iPhone models? Not likely. Instead, the only effect would be to reduce the intensity of conspicuous consumption and the negative externalities it creates.

Properly conceived, redistribution would increase efficiency, rather than decrease, if it was used to improve educational achievement because that would significantly increase the productivity of subsequent generations. Consequently, productivity and economic growth would increase through redistribution if all children had access to excellent schools. Currently, an immense amount of human capital is wasted in the US by depriving children and youth of an optimal education.[70] A transfer of funds from the owners of $300 million yachts to underprivileged school systems would increase enormously the efficiency of the educational system without straining the lifestyle of the wealthy.[71] This would lead to a huge increase in productivity, efficiency, and economic growth.

9.7 Takeaways

In the theoretical world of blackboard economics with Mom-and-Pop firms in perfectly competitive markets, a minimum wage is superfluous, even counterproductive. The same is true for labor unions. However, in the real-world, existing economy dominated by multinational oligopolies, unions and the minimum wage are needed to redress the imbalance of power between mega-corporations and their employees. Once we abandon the price-taking model and include the concept of power to set wages and prices, we can understand why the middle class has been hollowed out since the 1980s and why labor's share of GDP has declined by nearly a $1 trillion per annum. Hence, a middle-class family's income would have been $16,000 more in 2019 if its share of GDP had remained at its 1967 level. In the real world the minimum wage and unions do not cause unemployment; instead, they increase the living standards of workers at the expense of corporate profits, making the income distribution more reasonable. With the decline of unions and the diminution of the real value of the federal minimum wage, so the income of the middle class also declined. Thus, economic policy has ethical facets as well. Earning a living wage and an equitable distribution of income is a prerequisite of a just economy.

Questions for Discussion

1   Do you think that minimum wage should have kept up with inflation?
2   Have you ever worked for the minimum wage? How did you feel about it?
3   Do you think gas stations should be allowed to raise the price of gasoline during an oil embargo or war?
4   How should scarce drinking water be rationed during a hurricane?
5   Do you think unions empower workers to obtain a living wage?
6   Why don't CEOs need unions?
7   With so many poor people not voting, it is little wonder that their interests are not represented in government. Discuss.
8   Do you think there should be equal pay for equal work for women? For African Americans?
9   Do you think that part-time workers should receive the same hourly wage as full-time workers doing the same work?
10 Would basketball players play fewer games if their tax rate were higher? Would they change occupations?
11 How much utility would a gift of $1,000 give you? How much would it give to Oprah Winfrey?
12 Are you better off than your father or mother was at your age? Would they want to change places with you?
13 Do you think that the distribution of income in the United States is acceptable/reasonable/fair?
14 Should we be concerned with justice in economics, or should it be left to philosophers to ponder?
15 How do unions serve their members?
16 Should everyone have health insurance? Is health care a human right?
17 Are doctors overpaid?
18 Do you know anyone without health insurance?
19 Should robots be taxed?

Notes

1   From the Fifth book of the Torah of Judaism or the Old Testament of Christianity. All religions express similar concern for the poor and disadvantaged. For example, Muhammed said, "He is not a believer whose stomach is filled while the neighbor to his side goes hungry" (al-Sunan al-Kubrá, 19049).

2   Gregory Mankiw, *Principles of Economics*, 8th edn. (Cengage, 2018), p. 33.

3   Ibid., p. 126.

4   Although Mankiw says that "the minimum wage has its greatest impact on the market for teenage labor," merely 17 percent of the 1.6 million people who worked at or below the minimum wage, were teenagers, ibid., p. 127; Bureau of Labor Statistics, "Characteristics of Minimum Wage Workers, 2019," *BLS Reports*, April 2020.

5   Alan Krueger, "Teaching the Minimum Wage in Econ 101 in Light of the New Economics of the Minimum Wage," *The Journal of Economic Education* 32 (2001), 3: 243–258; Michael Reich et al., "The Effects of a $15 Minimum Wage in New York State," *Policy Brief*, Center on Wage and Employment Dynamics, March 2016; David Card and Alan Krueger, *Myth and Measurement: The New Economics of the Minimum Wage* (Princeton University Press, 1995); Paul Sonn and Yannet Lathrop, "Raise Wages, Kill Jobs? Seven Decades of Historical Data Find No Correlation Between Minimum Wage Increases and Employment Levels," *Data Brief*, National Employment Law Project, May 2016.

6   St. Louis Fed, series SEAT653URN, WAKING5URN, UNRATE. Washington State's minimum wage is binding in King County, which has a special minimum wage on companies selling to the county in excess of $100,000, https://lni.wa.gov/workers-rights/wages/minimum-wage/; https://kingcounty.gov/depts/finance-business-operations/procurement/about-us/Living-Wage.aspx.

7   John Schmitt, "Why Does the Minimum Wage Have No Discernible Effect on Employment?" Center for Economic and Policy Research, February 2013.

8   José Azar et al., "Minimum Wage Employment Effects and Labor Market Concentration," NBER Working Paper 26101, July 2019.

9   Yue Qiu and Aaron Sojourner, "Labor-Market Concentration and Labor Compensation," IZA Discussion Papers no. 12089, 2019.

10 Card and Krueger, *Myth and Measurement*, op. cit.

11 Orley Ashenfelter and Štěpán Jurajda, "Wages, Minimum Wages, and Price Pass-Through: The Case of McDonald's Restaurants," NBER Working Paper no. 28506.

12 Adam Smith, *An Inquiry into the Nature and Causes of the Wealth of Nations* (W. Strahan and T. Cadell, 1776), Book I, Chapter VIII, Section 24.

13 Samantha Bomkamp, "McDonald's CEO Easterbook Sees Pay Package Nearly Double to $15.4 Million," *Chicago Tribune*, April 13, 2017.

14 https://www.cnbc.com/2021/04/08/mcdonalds-ceo-chris-kempczinski-made-more-than-10point8-million-in-2020.html.

15 Paul Krugman, "What Europe Can Teach Us About Jobs," *The New York Times*, November 29, 2021.

16 US Department of Commerce, United States Census Bureau, "Poverty Thresholds, 2016."

17 https://www.bls.gov/oes/2019/may/oes_nat.htm#00-0000; https://www.census.gov/data/tables/time-series/demo/income-poverty/historical-poverty-thresholds.html.

18 "Franklin Roosevelt's Statement on the National Industrial Recovery Act," June 16, 1933.

19 Alvin Roth, "Repugnance as a Constraint on Markets," *Journal of Economic Perspectives*, 21 (2007), 3: 37–58.

20 A monopolist drug maker charged $28,000 for a vial of medication that cost $1,650 in 2007 and costs just $300 to produce. Andrew Pollock, "Questcor Finds Profits, at $28,000 a Vial," *The New York Times*, December 29, 2012.

21 Ben Popken, "Martin Shkreli Weighs in on EpiPen Scandal, Calls Drug Makers 'Vultures,'" *NBC News*, August 19, 2016.

22   Jill Disis, "Lawmakers Say EpiPen Hikes Made Mylan Executives 'Filthy Rich,'" *CNN*, September 22, 2016.

23   David Card, "Who Set Your Wage?" *American Economic Review* 112 (2022), 4: 1075-1090; David Berger et al., "Labor Market Power," *American Economic Review* 112 (2022), 4: 1147-1193.

24   Council of Economic Advisers, "Labor Market Monopsony: Trends, Consequences, and Policy Responses," *Issue Brief*, October 2016; https://obamawhitehouse.archives.gov/sites/default/files/page/files/20161025_monopsony_labor_mrkt_cea.pdf.

25   Orley Ashenfelter et al., "Monopsony in the Labor Market: New Empirical Results and New Public Policies," *Journal of Human Resources*, forthcoming; Kahn, Matthew and Joseph Tracy. 2019. "Monopsony in Spatial Equilibrium, NBER Working Paper no. 26295, September; https://www.nber.org/papers/w26295.

26   Alan Manning, "Monopsony in Labor Markets: A Review," *ILR Review* 74 (2021), 1: 3-26.

27   Joan Robinson, *The Economics of Imperfect Competition* (Macmillan, 1933).

28   Efraim Benmelech et al., "Strong Employers and Weak Employees: How Does Employer Concentration Affect Wages?" *The Journal of Human Resources* doi: 10.3368/jhr.monopsony.0119-10007R1.

29   José Azar et al., "Labor Market Concentration," *The Journal of Human Resources*, forthcoming, doi: 10.3368/jhr.monopsony.1218-9914R1; Noam Scheiber and Ben Casselman, "Why Is Pay Lagging? Maybe Too Many Mergers in the Heartland," *The New York Times*, January 25, 2018.

30   José Azar et al., "Concentration in US Labor Markets: Evidence from Online Vacancy Data," *Labour Economics* 66 (2020), no page number; Matias Covarrubias et al., "From Good to Bad Concentration? US Industries over the Past 30 Years," *NBER Macroeconomics Annual* 34 (2019): 1-46.

31   Joseph Stiglitz, *People, Power and Profits: Progressive Capitalism for the Age of Discontent* (Norton, 2019), p. 47.

32   Thomas Philippon, *The Great Reversal: How America Gave Up on Free Markets* (Harvard University Press, 2019); Jonathan Baker, *The Antitrust Paradigm: Restoring a Competitive Economy* (Harvard University Press, 2019).

33   Wikepedia, "High-Tech Employee Antitrust Litigation."

34   Paul Samuelson and William Nordhaus, *Economics*, 19th edn. (McGraw-Hill, 2009), p. 260.

35   Larry Cohen and Steve Early, *Globalization and De-Unionization in Telecommunications: Three Case Studies in Resistance* (Cornell University Press, 2018).

36   Jeffrey Rothstein, *When Good Jobs Go Bad: Globalization, De-unionization, and Declining Job Quality in the North American Auto Industry* (Rutgers University Press, 2016).

37   John Kenneth Galbraith, *American Capitalism* (Routledge, 1993).

38   Josh Bivens, et al., "Raising America's Pay: Why It's Our Central Economic Policy Challenge," Economic Policy Institute, June 4, 2014.

39   Henry Farber et al., "Unions and Inequality over the Twentieth Century: New Evidence from Survey Data," *The Quarterly Journal of Economics* 136 (2021), 3: 1325-1385.

40   Stiglitz, *People, Power*, op. cit., p. 49.

41   Jake Rosenfeld, *What Unions No Longer Do* (Harvard University Press, 2014); Juliet Schor, *After the Gig: How the Sharing Economy Got Hijacked and How to Win It Back* (University of California Press, 2019).

42   BLS News Release, "Union Members,-2020," January 22, 2021.

43   Joseph McCartin, "Professional Air Traffic Controllers Strike (1981)," in Eric Arnesen, *Encyclopedia of US Labor and Working-class History*, Vol. 1 (Taylor and Francis, 2007), p. 1126.

44   Ibid.

45   Bureau of Labor Statistics, "Table 1. Union Affiliation of Employed Wage and Salary Workers." www.bls.gov/webapps/legacy/cpslutab1.htm.

46   Nicholas Kristof, "The Cost of Decline in Unions," *The New York Times*, February 9, 2015; Richard Trumka, "Preserving the American Dream in the Face of Change," *Monthly Labor Review*, US Bureau of Labor Statistics, August 2015.

47   Council of Economic Advisers Issue Brief, "Worker Voice in a Time of Rising Inequality," October 2015.

48   Apple's 2021 proxy statement to the Securities and Exchange Commission, p. 46.

49   Includes bonuses, according to the website Glassdoor.

50   Scott Higham and Lenny Bernstein, "The Drug Industry's Triumph over the DEA," *The Washington Post*, October 15, 2017.

51   Larry Bartels, *Unequal Democracy: The Political Economy of the New Gilded Age*, 2nd edn. (Russell Sage Foundation, 2016).

52   Martin Gilens and Benjamin Page, *Democracy in America? What Has Gone Wrong and What We Can Do About It* (University of Chicago Press, 2017).

53   Milton Friedman called the AMA the strongest trade union in the country. The AMA is for doctors what OPEC is to the gasoline market. For the blood-bank cartel, see George Baxter, *Every Last Drop: How the Blood Industry Betrayed the Public Trust* (Trafford, 2013).

54   The AMA also opposes the internships of foreign doctors. Anemona Hartocollis, "Medical Schools in Region Fight Caribbean Flow," *The New York Times*, December 22, 2010.

55   Mark Perry, "The Medical Cartel: Why Are MD Salaries So High?" *Wall Street Pit*, June 24, 2009. James Hamblin, "What Doctors Make," *The Atlantic*, January 27, 2015.

56   www1.salary.com/Dean-of-Medicine-salaries.html.

57   https://www.glassdoor.com/Salaries/us-medical-doctor-salary-SRCH_IL.0,2_IN1_KO3,17.htm.

58   Joanna Broder, "Record Number of Med Students, but More Needed to Help Physician Shortage," *Medscape*, October 29, 2013. List of Medical Schools and the number of students enrolled can be found on the website of the Association of American Medical Colleges, Table B-1: Total Enrollment by US Medical School.

59   American Bar Association, "ABA-Approved Law Schools."

60   Other countries have been able to cap costs by adopting a more efficient system because administrative costs are much less, and costs are kept down by the bargaining power of government so that excessive profits are not generated in medicine. Hence, a single payer not-for-profit system is much more efficient than a free-market for-profit system.

61   Christine Corlet Walker et al., "A Critique of the Marketisation of Long-Term Residential and Nursing Home Care," March 21, 2022, doi: https://doi.org/10.1016/S2666-7568(22)00040-X.

62   Samuelson and Nordhaus, *Economics*, op. cit., p. 221.

63   Kenneth Arrow, "Uncertainty and the Welfare Economics of Medical Care," *American Economic Review* 53 (1963), 5: 141–149.

64   Amartya Sen, *Poverty and Famines: An Essay on Entitlement and Deprivation* (Oxford University Press, 1981).

65   US Census, Poverty Table B-2. "Families and People in Poverty by Type of Family; 2019 and 2020."

66   Andrew Ross Sorkin et al., "Billion-Dollar Paydays in a Pandemic," *The New York Times*, February 22, 2021; Greg Leiserson and Danny Yagan, "What Is the Average Federal Individual Income Tax Rate on the Wealthiest Americans?" September 23, 2021; https://www.whitehouse.gov/cea/blog/2021/09/23/what-is-the-average-federal-individual-income-tax-rate-on-the-wealthiest-americans/.

67   Christina Gibson-Davis and Heather Hill, "Childhood Wealth Inequality in the United States: Implications for Social Stratification and Well-Being," *The Russell Sage Foundation Journal of the Social Sciences* 7 (2021), 3: 1–26.

68   John Harsanyi, "Interpersonal Utility Comparisons," in Steven Durlauf and Lawrence Blume (eds.), *The New Palgrave Dictionary of Economics*, 2nd edn. (Palgrave Macmillan, 2008), pp. 3247–3250.

69   "Empirical evidence … suggests that the damage of taxes on work effort is limited … Most studies find that taxes have only a small impact on labor effort for middle-income and high-income workers," Samuelson and Nordhaus, *Economics*, op. cit., p. 333.

70   James Heckman, "Skill Formation and the Economics of Investing in Disadvantaged Children." *Science* 312 (2006) 5782: 1900–1902.

71   There are 140,000 people worldwide with assets of $50 million or more, half of them in the US. Scott Shane et al., "How Business Titans, Pop Stars and Royals Hide Their Wealth," *The New York Times*, November 7, 2017.

10 What Is Macroeconomics?

In the long run we are all dead.
–John Maynard Keynes[1]

Until now, we have focused on microeconomics–the economy's atomic units: the individual consumers and producers. We also considered sectors of the economy like health care or the market for doctors, and now we turn to macroeconomics, a bird's-eye view of the economy, considering aggregate aspects of economic activity: total output or the *gross domestic product* (GDP), the money supply, and *aggregate demand*–the value of all goods and services produced in the economy.

10.1 Keynes, the Savior of Capitalism

John Maynard Keynes is the father of macroeconomics. The revolution his genius sparked in the 1930s saved the intellectual foundations of capitalism from the then competing totalitarian ideologies of Nazism, Fascism, and Communism by turning squarely against his neoclassical forerunners. He was revolutionary because he advocated a *paradigm shift* while maintaining the basic liberal democratic principles. He upheld two essential pillars of the established order: private property rights and the free market system with its price mechanism. However, he was justifiably concerned that 25 percent unemployment in the UK and the US could destabilize the political system. After all, hunger had brought Hitler to power in 1933. Keynes understood that the labor market was not self-regulating, and it would be ludicrous to continue to wait for the economy's self-correcting mechanism to eliminate unemployment, as the classical economists unrelentingly maintained.

The labor market differs from markets for inanimate objects. It has many impediments that prevent the simple feedback mechanism of supply and demand–which supposedly reinstates equilibrium–from eliminating the "general glut," and the immense suffering it caused (see Figure 4.11). The mainstream economists never predicted how long the elimination of the crisis would take. Consequently, Keynes, quipped, "in the long run we are all dead," that is to say that the long run is completely irrelevant. After all, machines can be idle indefinitely, but workers have to eat today.

There were many obstacles to the establishment of a new macroeconomic equilibrium. Prices, wages, and profit were all diminishing because of falling aggregate demand. *Deflation*–a decline in the general price level–meant that *nominal debt became a greater burden* for both

DOI: 10.4324/9781003174356-10

firms and households. Debt remained unchanged, regardless of the price level and regardless of wages. As prices declined, the profits of firms declined as well and they could not make their debt payments, so bankruptcies cascaded. Farmers were also in this predicament as prices of their produce declined and they also could not meet their obligations and many lost their farms as a consequence. Furthermore, those workers whose wages declined also could not pay their mortgages, apartment rents, or car payments which bound them to a series of *nominal* payments. With a fall in wages, it was not sufficient if the price of bread declined in tandem, since their debt payments remained at the pre-Depression level. Hence, deflation was a drag on the economy as those who were indebted had less purchasing power for consumer goods, thereby exacerbating the Depression and inhibiting the return to equilibrium.

While some wages were diminishing, other *wages were sticky*, as some workers defended—sometimes violently—their pre-Depression nominal income for psychological reasons of loss aversion, but also because otherwise they could not make their obligatory payments. Yet, constant nominal wages [*w*] and a decline in prices meant that *real* wages $\left[\dfrac{W}{P}\right]$ for a part of the labor force actually increased at a time when they should have been declining, making it more difficult for businesses to keep them on the payroll, thereby exacerbating unemployment.

That is why *deflation is a threat to the macroeconomy* and why the Federal Reserve has been adamant about preventing it. In short, Keynes argued that the economic system was not as flexible as neoclassical economists claimed, and a new full-employment equilibrium could not be attained within the relevant time frame. Thus, aggregate demand could persist below full-employment level indefinitely.

The diminution in aggregate demand meant that prices would decline further, thereby creating a vicious circle that prevented recovery and exacerbating unemployment and prolonging the slump. In short, frustration was accumulating while conventional economists lacked credible recommendations besides waiting for the markets to adjust. Yet, years passed without improvement, thereby threatening the whole capitalist architecture.

Additionally, Keynes rejected the *homo oeconomicus* model. Rather, he recognized that both investors and consumers were subject to bouts of optimism and pessimism he called "animal spirits." Keynes understood that with years of Depression a general gloom permeated the country's mood:

> Even apart from the instability due to speculation, there is the instability due to the characteristic of human nature that a large proportion of our ... activities depend on spontaneous optimism ... Most, probably .... our decisions to do something ... [are] the result of animal spirits—a spontaneous urge to action rather than inaction.[2]

Herding behavior meant that these mood swings were contagious. Therefore, it was fallacious to consider aggregate demand to be a stable function of prices. Rather, aggregate demand fluctuated markedly with psychological swings in consumer confidence, causing analogous fluctuations in GDP and unemployment (Figure 10.1).

While the demand for necessities does not vary substantially because of animal spirits, the demand for business investments, consumer durables, and luxuries does fluctuate appreciably (Figure 10.2). For instance, the demand for automobiles declined from 7.9 million in 1955 to 4.5 million in 1958 (Figure 10.3). Expectations also play a role in demand: if prices are expected to decrease, consumers will postpone purchasing pricey durables and wait until

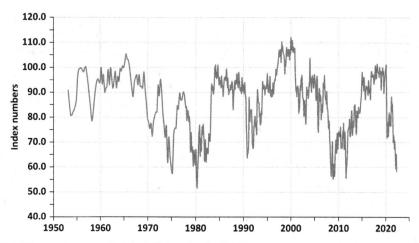

Figure 10.1 US consumer confidence index, 1950-2020
Note: 1996 = 100.
Source: St. Louis Fed, series UMCSENT.

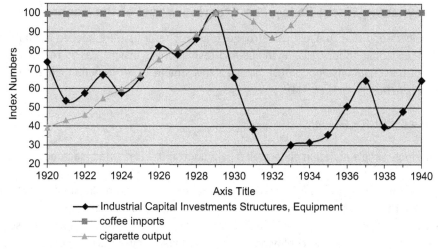

Figure 10.2 Fluctuating demand during the Great Depression
Source: Susan Carter et al., *Historical Statistics of the Unites States: Millennial Edition* (Cambridge University Press, 2006), Tables Dd347, Dd377, Dd843, Table Df343.

prices stabilize.[3] Why buy it this year if next year it might be cheaper? This is another setback of deflation.

Furthermore, Keynes realized that these problems would not remain confined to the economy; they might infect the political arena. The hungry and destitute threatened the stability of democracy and might even turn against it, as in Germany. The legitimate fear was that the social order would unravel faster than the economic system would repair itself.[4] Politics and economics are inexorably intertwined as became also evident with the triumph of Trumpism in 2016 (see Chapter 15).[5]

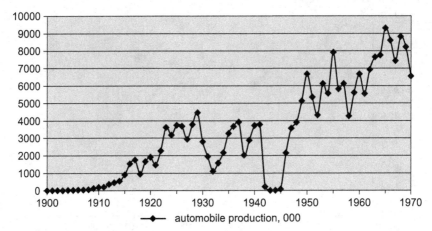

Figure 10.3 Automobile production in the US, 1900–1970 (thousands)
Source: Susan Carter et al., *Historical Statistics of the Unites States: Millennial Edition* (Cambridge University Press, 2006), Tables Dd347, Dd377, Dd843, Table Df343.

10.2 Keynesian Fiscal Policy, the Steering Wheel of the Economy

Keynes understood that to avoid catastrophe, dramatic reforms were needed in public policy guided by economic theory. His ingenious and revolutionary insight was to realize that GDP consists of personal consumption (C), business investment (I), government expenditures (G), and exports minus imports (X – M):

GDP = C + I + G + (X – M)

This amazingly simple equation generated a paradigm shift and created macroeconomics. Economics would never be the same.

Keynes argued that in order to stabilize the political system, employment would have to increase. For that to occur, GDP would have to increase but which of the four terms on the right side of the equation could increase? Consumption would not increase by itself because unemployment remained high, and confidence was low. Similarly, businesses had excess capacity: they lacked enough demand for their products. So, why would they increase investments? The whole world was suffering in the Depression, so exports would not increase either. Hence, only G remained still capable of independent action to increase GDP. Hence, government expenditures must be increased through borrowing to establish a new equilibrium. It would be foolish to let the economy continue to flounder. When private demand falters and a gap exists between actual and potential output, the public sector should make up the difference through *deficit spending*. This key insight gave birth to fiscal policy.

Fiscal policy abandoned the classical framework by not relying on the private sector to realign through price and wage adjustments. The system was so much out of kilter that markets, by themselves, would be unable to establish a new equilibrium, or at least not quickly enough to be meaningful for the people who had been suffering since 1930. Moreover, public spending–particularly on infrastructure–would have a magnified impact through the *multiplier*: the initial beneficiaries of government expenditure would spend their income, thereby increasing the income of others. The spending of one becomes the income of another and the benefits would cascade.

This was another brilliant innovation: the multiplier is crucial in breaking out of the down-ward spiral of unemployment, deflation, and more unemployment, thereby re-establishing a new full-employment equilibrium. The multiplier became a crucial policy parameter. It works only if there is *a gap between actual GDP and potential GDP*, i.e., if the economy is in recession or Depression.[6] If the economy is already producing as much as possible, then the multiplier cannot work. Estimates of the multiplier in recessions are 2.5 but can be as high as 2.9 if spent on infrastructure, and 3.6 if spent on defense.[7] This means that $1 spent by government in a recession would increase GDP by around $2.5.

The economic system created by this new activist government would be a more humane form of capitalism, which–unlike socialism or Communism–retained private property rights and the social pecking order but would crucially alleviate the scourge of unemployment and the misery and political instability associated with it. These brilliant insights made Keynes one of the greatest economists of all time.

10.3 Monetary Policy Is Also Essential

Monetary policy was another major Keynesian innovation. It is an important instrument by which a central bank influences output and employment. By setting the *discount rate*–the interest rate it charges for loans to member banks–it can increase or decrease the amount of money in circulation. By lending money to banks, the Federal Reserve (the Fed Reserve) increases the money supply. By buying Treasury securities, it puts more money into circulation, while if it sells securities, it is decreasing the quantity of money in circulation (known as open-market operations).[8] Additionally, the Fed can influence the money supply indirectly by setting reserve requirements: lowering them enables banks to lend more. While the Fed controls the monetary base (currency and banks' reserves), commercial banks influence the money supply by lending.

In normal circumstances, a decrease in the discount rate when the economy is decelerating has a stimulating effect on the economy, because banks will also decrease the interest rate they charge borrowers. This incentivizes consumers to purchase more durable goods on credit like cars and houses. Simultaneously, at the lower interest rate, businesses will also borrow more to invest in new equipment, thereby also spurring economic activity and employment. Thus, the interest rate is like an accelerator of economic activity. By lowering it, the Fed basically steps on the accelerator. This was exactly the playbook during the 2001 recession, for example: between December 2000 and January 2002 the Fed lowered the discount rate from 6 percent to 1.25 percent. Consequently, the recession lasted only two quarters.[9] However, in another part of the business cycle, if inflation is above the Fed's 2 percent benchmark, it takes its foot off the accelerator and steps on the brakes instead by increasing the interest rate to reduce economic activity.

This is the monetary mechanism in normal times. However, *this mechanism does not work in a financial panic* when firms and consumers are unwilling to borrow, and instead, hoard cash, so that the decrease in interest rate is neutralized by the lack of confidence. If consumers and investors are overextended and have too much debt relative to income and want to deleverage to lower their debt burden, then lowering interest rates is inconsequential. Similarly, if busi-nesses have excess capacity and experience sluggish demand for their products, they will not risk new investments despite lower interest rates. Everyone strives to improve their balance sheet and cash is at a premium. That is the case of the *liquidity trap*.

10.4 The Liquidity Trap Renders Monetary Policy Ineffective

Keynes realized that, in a crisis, monetary policy becomes ineffective. So much uncertainty accumulates in the population that even at a near-zero interest rate people prefer to hoard cash rather than spend or invest. Interest rate was near zero for seven years between January 2009 and 2016 and then again beginning in March 2020 until January 2022. The near-zero-interest-rate policy of the Fed also exacerbates inequality because it privileges financial institutions by giving them easy access to funds and penalizes savers who receive meagre compensation.[10]

Zero is the theoretical lower bound for interest rates, although the European Central Bank, and the Bank of Japan, anxious to incentivize banks to make loans instead of depositing their cash with them, began experimenting with negative interest rates on deposits. Negative interest rate is like a fee for safekeeping, a safe deposit fee. Defying the unthinkable, by May 2019, $10 trillion worth of bonds traded globally at negative interest rates.[11]

The US Fed has avoided negative interest rates. It determines two rates that are very close to one another (Figure 10.4): (1) the discount rate is the interest rate it charges for loans to its member banks who borrow from it on collateral, and (2) the funds rate, which is the interest rate it mandates member banks must charge one another on overnight loans. Until March 2020, commercial banks were obligated to deposit their required reserves with the Fed. If one bank had less deposits than was mandatory, it could borrow at the funds rate (without collateral) from a bank that had excess reserves on deposit with the Fed. However, as of March 2020, the reserve requirements of banks on many type of deposits have been eliminated. So, the excess reserves at the Fed have been discontinued.[12]

Although monetary policy becomes ineffective in the liquidity trap near the *zero lower bound*, fiscal policy can still increase aggregate demand and raise the economy out of a recession because it does not work indirectly through the interest rate but directly through spending. However, fiscal policy requires congressional approval which was not forthcoming in the US in adequate amounts during the 2008 crisis. To overcome this impasse, the Fed started printing money rebranded as *"quantitative easing"* (QE) to stimulate the economy in an attempt to overcome the limitation of the zero lower bound on nominal interest rates. QE is

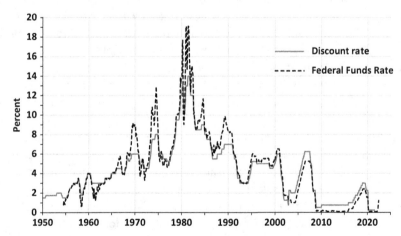

Figure 10.4 The discount rate and the federal funds rate
Source: St. Louis Fed, series FEDFUNDS and INTDSRUSM193N.

a euphemism for buying financial assets, thereby injecting liquidity into the financial sector by creating money on an astronomical scale. It sounds neutral and less worrisome to the public than printing money.

With QE the Fed injected trillions of dollars into the financial sector by purchasing bonds and mortgage-backed securities, hoping to induce banks to lend more freely. Within two weeks of Lehman Brothers' collapse on September 15, 2008, Bernanke minted $500 billion, and by end of October doubled the bank's balance sheet from thin air, initiating an era of *bailout capitalism* (see Sections 10.8 and 17.3). Its assets rose from less than $1 trillion to $2 trillion within a few weeks. Until September the Fed bought only Treasury securities, but Bernanke broke with tradition and purchased practically worthless mortgage-backed securities *on par* thereby rewarding the banks for all their negligence. Altogether Bernanke injected a hitherto unimaginable $3.6 trillion ($3.6 million millions or $3.6 with 12 zeros) into the economy between 2008 and 2014, in three waves (QE1, QE2, QE3), increasing the bank's assets by a multiple of five from $900 billion to $4.5 trillion (Figure 10.5).

While QE1 was necessary to stabilize the imploding financial system, QE2 and QE3 led primarily to *asset-price inflation* as money was chasing assets and investors bought stocks instead of lending to the public (Figure 10.5). Greenspan was of the same opinion: "the expansion of assets has had very little impact on the economy."[13] Investment in the real economy continued to flounder because of the weakness in aggregate demand and GDP growth remained sluggish (Figure 10.5). Bernanke's leaning against the Keynesian liquidity trap did not bear fruit after 2009. An essential aspect of monetary policy that Bernanke overlooked was that low interest rates and accommodating liquidity were necessary but not sufficient for economic growth. Other factors also played a role, including opportunities for investment in the real economy and purchasing power of consumers. Supporting consumers at the lower end of the income distribution would have increased aggregate demand since they had a backlog of demand for goods and services. Instead, the bailouts supported the rich who used that money to buy financial assets rather than goods that would increase employment. These were the missing factors that neutralized the expansionary monetary policy. Consequently, the recovery was the most tepid on record since the Great Depression (see Figure 17.5).

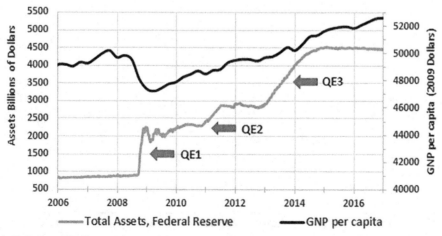

Figure 10.5 Quantitative easing and GNP per capita
Source: St. Louis Fed, series WALCL and A791RX0Q048SBEA.

Another justification of QE was that asset inflation would increase consumers' wealth, thereby increasing optimism and through that channel increase aggregate demand. However, the increase in wealth was limited to a small segment of the population whose propensity to consume was limited and therefore they saved most of their new-found wealth (see Section 7.15). So, the newly created wealth stayed within the financial sector and its impact on the real economy was tepid. So, GDP continued to flounder about $1 trillion below potential (see Figure 14.4). Moreover, this is unchartered territory since it makes the Fed into an alchemist, creating wealth out of thin air by printing money, but this wealth is really pseudo-wealth untethered from fundamental values.[14]

Contrary to Keynes' views, an older theory maintained by Milton Friedman and the Monetarist School alleged that money was "neutral" and did not affect GDP. They contended that the quantity of money only determined the price level. They would be correct if the economy was already producing as much as it could. If the economy was at full employment, then obviously injecting more money into the economy could not increase output so the quantity of money in circulation, M1, would be directly proportional to nominal GDP:

$$M1*V = pY, \text{ or } V1 = \frac{pY}{M1}$$

where *M1* is the stock of money (physical currency in circulation + demand deposits), *p* is price level, *Y* is real GDP, *pY* is nominal GDP, and *V* is the velocity of circulation.[15] The velocity, *V1*, is the number of times a dollar changes hands annually. The faster money circulates, the larger is *V*, and the more income is generated because every time a dollar changes hands it becomes someone's income. Contrary to the *quantity theory*, V1 is extremely unstable, increasing from 4 to 14 just before the 2008 Meltdown; this meant that a dollar changed hands 14 times annually, but *V1* declined to 7 in 2020, and reached an all-time low of 3.8 during the Covid-19 recession. So, *V1* fluctuated markedly (Figure 10.6).[16]

One reason velocity is unstable is that consumers can purchase goods and services on credit cards and therefore are not constrained by their money income. Moreover, how much money individuals hold in their checking or savings account depends on the uncertainties in

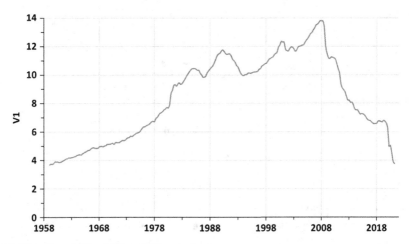

Figure 10.6 Velocity of circulation of M1
Source: St. Louis Fed, series CURRDD and GDP.

the economy—how likely it is that they will lose their job, for instance. That is why Bernanke's QE2 and QE3 programs did not impact the real economy. Instead, it merely lowered the velocity of circulation. People were not spending their money as quickly as before; they were holding it longer because of all the uncertainty in the economy. In addition, the Fed has found it impossible to get back to normal monetary policy and continued to subsidize the financial sector with near-zero interest rates. Whether the Fed will ever be able to get back to normal interest rate of 5 percent remains to be seen.

10.5 Neoclassical Synthesis Was an Uneasy Compromise with Keynesianism

After World War II, Keynesian economics became dominant through the neoclassical synthesis popularized by Paul Samuelson.[17] The synthesis, merging Keynesian macroeconomics with neoclassical microeconomics, was the basis of mainstream economics between 1950 and 1980. However, this combination lacked coherence since it assumed the existence of *homo oeconomicus* in microeconomics but disregarded rationality in the macroeconomics. It was inconsistent to assume that individuals were rational and maximized utility as consumers but not as workers.

Instead of being rational, workers were assumed to be subject to the *"money illusion."*[18] They were not well informed about price level. After all, it is difficult to calculate, and many of their obligations were in nominal terms and were unaffected by inflation. Therefore, workers insisted on retaining their nominal wages even if prices were falling, and their real wage was actually increasing as far as their employers were concerned. These *sticky wages* lead to involuntary unemployment because the fall in product prices and constant wages squeezed profits. Money illusion, based on asymmetric information, prevents wages from adjusting in Keynesian models, contrary to standard demand and supply models. So, nominal wages can be above equilibrium perpetually.

The *"Phillips curve,"* another key Keynesian concept, postulated a trade-off between unemployment and inflation.[19] *When inflation increased, unemployment decreased and when inflation decreased, unemployment increased.* Accordingly, as prices rose, the *real* wages of workers declined, but they were willing to continue to work for the same *nominal* wage because they were not well informed about the price level. Firms benefited because they knew that the price of their products increased but their wage bill remained constant. So, their profits rose, inducing them to expand production and hire more workers at the same nominal wage. Thus, the mechanism for the Phillips curve is based on workers' money illusion coupled with asymmetric information.

However, money illusion would not last forever. Eventually workers signed new rent contracts for their apartments or bought a new car, so they realized that their nominal wages had eroded. So, the Phillips curve was valid only in the short run and—as Milton Friedman argued—eventually employees would demand higher wages, thereby erasing firms' profits. Inflation cannot create jobs permanently.

This is what happened in the 1970s after the US left the gold standard and two oil shocks caused both inflation and unemployment, dubbed *"stagflation."* The price level doubled between 1973 and 1981 and so did unemployment from 5 percent to 10 percent, the opposite of the Phillips curve's prediction. This contradiction was used by the opponents of Keynesian economics to discredit his framework altogether. Of course, the Phillips curve was conceived for low-level inflation that could stay under the radar of employees. It was hardly surprising that it did not work with double-digit inflation. When prices were increasing so rapidly for so long, workers would not be subject to money illusion. In addition, the boycott of the US by OPEC oil producers in 1973 and 1979 created bottlenecks that generated unemployment independent of inflation. Nonetheless, Keynesian policies lost popularity after this episode of stagflation and the dominance of neoclassical macroeconomics began.

10.6 The Monetarist Counterrevolution

There were five elements in Keynesianism that were anathema to the orthodox dogma:

1. Keynesian macroeconomics was independent of and inconsistent with neoclassical microeconomics, i.e., the neoclassical synthesis did not assume rational economic agents; *homo oeconomicus* would not be subject to money illusion and sticky wages (see Section 10.5).
2. Keynes assumed that consumption was influenced by emotions and confidence, i.e., "animal spirits"–bouts of optimism or pessimism; that also contradicted the rational-agent model.
3. Keynesianism suggested that money mattered to aggregate output whereas the classical school contended that money played merely a passive role by determining only the price level and not output, aggregate demand, or unemployment.
4. The government played a central role in Keynesian macroeconomics with fiscal and monetary policy, thereby limiting free markets and individual freedoms.
5. Keynesian macroeconomics was not a perfectly-competitive equilibrium model: the labor market failed to adjust instantaneously to demand and supply.

These five points provoked a monetarist backlash in the wake of the episode of stagflation.

In contrast to Keynes's top-down approach, the neoclassical economists insisted that individuals are the essential unit of analysis and wanted to build macroeconomic models starting with rational utility-maximizing individuals called *representative agents*. Thus, macroeconomics was given *microeconomic foundations* (also called microfoundations) by assuming that "macroeconomic theory ... can be derived from microeconomic theory."[20] Their models summed up individual-level variables to obtain the total values of macroeconomic variables.[21] This strategy–based on the ideology of *methodological individualism*–gave rise to the *real-business-cycle* school.[22]

They assumed (incomprehensibly) that the economic activities of hundreds of millions of people can be characterized by a *single individual*, a representative agent.[23] This was inconsistent with assertions in other sections of their canon that utility functions are not comparable since everyone is different.[24] Yet, in these models, everyone is supposedly the same.[25] The assumption is also inconsistent with Arrow's impossibility theorem which proved that preferences cannot be aggregated in a consistent manner.[26] Hence, in collective decision-making, a representative agent's utility function cannot possibly represent everyone's preferences.

Despite its implausible philosophical foundations, neoclassical macroeconomics has been dominated by this framework since the 1980s. Although they appear sophisticated, they are based on fairy-tale assumptions. They assume that the economy is inhabited by *homo oeconomicus*, although the species never existed; they use exponential discounting for intertemporal decisions, although *we know* that hyperbolic discounting is valid; they disregard the soft budget constraint offered by credit cards; they assume that agents have rational expectations, i.e., they do not make systematic errors predicting future developments, although that overlooks behavioral economics (see Section 4.10); they ignored complications associated with animal spirits and financial panics until reality struck in 2008;[27] they assume that real wages matter to employment since they reject money illusion; money plays no role in these models; instead, they focus on a barter economy; they assume that the distribution of income does not impact macroeconomic outcomes, although *we know* how important it is for all aggregate macroeconomic variables.[28]

That is not all. They also assume that the economy is a stable system in long-run equilibrium and is occasionally perturbed by random unanticipated technological shocks that surprises people in the short run.[29] In the long run, aggregate demand equals aggregate supply, and prices adjust instantaneously to equate the two.[30] There is no involuntary unemployment and no involuntary part-time workers, although there were 4.5 million of them in July 2021.[31] In contrast, complexity theory assumes that the economy is never in equilibrium but is in a constant state of flux, which is more realistic (see Section 11.7).

Another reason the real-business-cycle models are implausible is that their models are not holistic: methodological individualism disregards that obviously the whole is greater than the sum of its component parts.[32] Assuming that the society is a collection of identical individuals *without interaction effects* is known as the *fallacy of composition*, or the aggregation problem.[33] What is true for one individual multiplied by a million is not necessarily true for the million people in the society.[34] Larry Summers makes this clear: "real business cycle models … have nothing to do with the business cycle phenomena observed in the United States or other capitalist economies."[35] No wonder such Alice-in-Wonderland models were irrelevant for economic policy.[36] Their proponents failed even to suspect that the 2008 financial crisis was approaching.[37] Moreover, they had no advice either on how to overcome the anemic aftermath of the crisis or how to combat the Covid-19 pandemic. They suffered from paradigm paralysis because they assumed that such crisis was "virtually impossible" in an advanced developed economy.[38] These blackboard models do not include bubbles, bankruptcies, forecast errors, or incomplete contracts that are breached when economic reality turns out to be inconsistent with expectations. They truly belong in "the Museum of Implausible Economic Models."[39]

10.7 "Poor, Poor, Pitiful Macroeconomists"[40]

Because of the above ideological schism, macroeconomics is in intellectual disarray and leads to much confusion in academic journals and in public discourse.[41] Its inadequacy is illustrated by the news conference to honor Christopher Sims's and Thomas Sargent's Nobel Prizes in 2011.[42] A reporter asked their "opinion about what the government has done so far in the United States to support the economy. If you think it has been appropriate. How can we actually support the economy, create jobs? You know those questions everybody [is] asking themselves." Their response to this perfectly appropriate question, was followed by prolonged laughter during which the two macroeconomists looked at each other seemingly amused, indicating that they were clueless about the application of economic policy off the blackboard. Sims finally said:

> I think part of the point of this prize and the area that we work in is that answers to questions like that require careful thinking, a lot of data analysis, and that the answers are not likely to be simple. So that asking Tom and me for answers off the top of our heads to these questions is … You shouldn't expect much from us. [Laughter][43]

Sargent added: "I don't have much to add to that … I was hoping you'd ask me about Europe." [Laughter]

Great fun! Three years after the start of the most destructive economic crisis in 80 years, two influential macroeconomists (and Nobel Prize-winners in Economics!) did not find suffi-cient time to think about the real-world problems confronting the nation and were unable to respond coherently "from the top of their heads." Outside of the classroom they were like fish out of water and trivialized a serious question. This illustrates the current muddled state of macroeconomics.

Stiglitz laments the staggering deficiencies of this research agenda: "the heart of the failure [of macroeconomics] were the wrong microfoundations, which failed to incorporate key aspects of economic behaviour."[44] Moreover, they disregarded:

> [i]nsights from information economics and behavioural economics. Inadequate modelling of the financial sector meant they [the models] were ill-suited for predicting or respond-ing to a financial crisis; and a reliance on representative agent models meant they were ill-suited for analysing either the role of distribution in fluctuations and crises or the conse-quences of fluctuations on inequality.[45]

Another critic points out that:

> [i]t is as if the information economics revolution … had not occurred. The combination of assumptions, when coupled with the trivialization of risk and uncertainty … render money, credit and asset prices largely irrelevant … [they] typically ignore inconvenient truths.[46]

Consequently, these models "may have set back by decades serious investigations of aggregate economic behaviour and economic policy-relevant understanding. It was a costly waste of time and resources."[47] In short, the neoclassical macroeconomists were merely playing intellectual computer games which bore no relevance to the actual economy. In such a contentious intel-lectual environment, politicians could pick the economist suitable for their ideology, thereby fueling political controversies and contributing to the population's confusion. For instance, dur-ing the debate over the tax bill of 2017, conservative economists supported the bill while pro-gressives strictly opposed it.[48]

While Keynesian policies made a brief comeback during the 2008 crisis, they turned out to be politically unsustainable and fell out of favor yet again until the next crisis made Keynesian policies indispensable again.[49] The real-business-cycle school is silent during a crisis. So, we are left with short-term palliatives like Bernanke's digital printing press, Trump's lower taxes, government-sponsored capitalism, and a lot of wishful thinking that the life supports will work, and the patient will recover. Not likely, since *bailout capitalism* cannot work indefinitely.[50]

Consequently, we need to explore new perspectives. The German, Scandinavian, or Swiss models of capitalism might well be a good place to start thinking about a new macroeconomics for our era, as their economies are still characterized by the virtues of discipline, thrift, concern for the environment and for society, free college education, a solid safety net, universal health care, less inequality, a more vibrant democracy, with a sprinkling of the old-fashioned work ethic.[51] Underemployment in these countries is not a problem, people are less anxious and are able to lead a more dignified life. Instant gratification, greed, debt, and lower taxes, as in the US, will not provide the political, social, and economic stability that we crave. The US needs to learn from these successful societies and adopt universal health care and universal college educa-tion because educated and healthy people are more productive, cause fewer social problems, and lead a more satisfied life. By depriving millions of people of adequate education, the US is wasting an incredible amount of human resources. Such waste is a blatant inconsistency for a society that has a very high regard for efficiency. The 2017 US tax cuts, costing $1.5 trillion, would have had an order-of-magnitude larger impact on economic growth if it had been spent on education instead.

10.8 Bailout Capitalism's Modern Monetary Theory

Some theoreticians argue that the US government can print money unconstrained.[52] If it leads to inflation, it can always reverse it by increasing taxes.[53] However, this is counterintuitive because increasing taxes is hardly a breeze. If it were so easy to prevent hyperinflation, German shoppers in 1923 would not have needed a wheelbarrow full of banknotes to buy a loaf of bread. The largest denomination bill ever issued was a Hungarian 100 quintillion note in 1946.

However, the infusion of money into the economy during the crisis of 2008 and again during the Covid-19 pandemic is interpreted to imply that there is no limit to money creation since the dollar is a reserve currency and there is infinite demand for it. Admittedly, the stupendous increase in the money stock has not led to the kind of inflation that one would have expected on the basis of the quantity equation (see Section 10.6).[54] However, it did lead immediately to sizeable asset inflation: for every trillion dollars of assets purchased by the Fed in 2020 the S&P 500 rose by 500 points (see Figure 17.8). However, that was considered a positive development as people felt wealthier. This has become the Fed's clandestine third mandate orchestrated through Wall Street.[55] However, the Fed has entered unchartered territory by conditioning finance to rely on its virtual printing press. Inflation also started with some delay as prices rose faster than the Fed's 2 percent annual target rate since March 2021 and reached 8.7 percent in June 2022.[56] Yet, tax increases are nowhere in sight. We'll see if the Fed can easily reverse this trend.

10.9 The Production Possibilities Frontier

The production possibilities frontier (PPF) describes the maximum quantity of goods and services that can be produced in an economy with the given amount of resources, know-how, technology, labor, effort, and human and physical capital (Figure 10.7). It is analogous to the concept of *potential GDP*. However, the concept is ambiguous because the maximum depends on fluid factors—effort, labor force participation rate, and cultural norms. For example, during World War II, the PPF expanded because patriotism induced women to enter the labor force. Similarly, the cultural change that increased women's labor-force participation rate after the 1970s shifted the PPF outward substantially.

The economy is supposedly producing efficiently if it is producing as much as the PPF allows—then there is no unemployment. However, that is hardly ever obtained except in times of war because there are *always* unemployed resources in a modern economy. With chronic unemployment of both labor and capital, the concept of PPF loses its significance. In August 2021, the true unemployment rate was around 8.8 percent, while factories were producing at 76 percent of capacity (Figure 10.8).[57] That implies that 24 percent of the capital stock was idle. In the automobile industry, utilization was at 62 percent.[58] Thus, the US is producing less than its resources would allow—as at point P(1) (see Figure 10.7). At P(1), production is inefficient since it is inside the PPF, indicating that there are unemployed resources in the economy.

The PPF also depends on public goods like laws, institutions, and cultural factors. For instance, prohibition of child labor shifts the PPF inward in the short run but increases it eventually because human capital increases productivity. Moreover, laws might impose inefficient

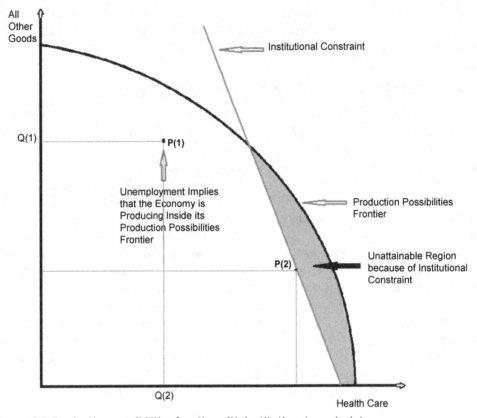

Figure 10.7 Production possibilities frontier with institutional constraint

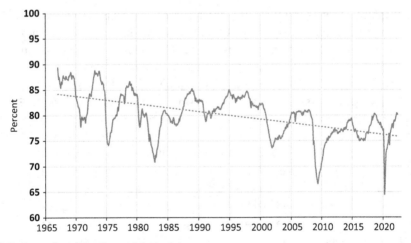

Figure 10.8 Capacity utilization, all industries
Source: St. Louis Fed, series TCU.

modes of production. The fear of litigation, for instance, means that doctors prescribe excessive procedures to guard against malpractice suits. This implies that a segment of the PPF curve is unattainable because of institutional constraints like at P(2) (see Figure 10.7). At P(1), the institutional constraint is not binding: the constraint does not affect production; other reasons prevent the economy from producing closer to its PPF. However, at P(2), the institutional constraint is binding and prevents efficient production. Examples of institutional constraints include the organization of the medical system and big Pharma's monopoly pricing strategy (see Section 9.5). Breaking their stranglehold would enable the economy to expand toward its PPF.

10.10 GDP Is a Misleading Measure of Welfare

GDP is designed to measure the total amount of goods and services produced in the economy. However, it is imprecise, because it excludes output not purchased in markets, like childcare and other housework (see Section 11.10). Moreover, its frequent use as a bellwether living-standard indicator is inappropriate because it fails to exclude negative externalities like pollution. So, the value of the electricity generated by a power plant is part of the GDP, but its CO_2 emissions are ignored, although the damage it causes to health and the environment is a cost to society and should be subtracted from GDP. For example, the asthma caused by pollution increases GDP, since the drugs and doctor bills are part of GDP, although the harm is an externality that should be subtracted from GDP.[59] This is not good accounting practice.

Similarly, the Gulf of Mexico oil spill (2010), the largest marine oil spill in history, increased GDP rather than diminished it. A correct accounting of GDP would deduct the value of environmental degradation. Consequently, products that pollute are mispriced, implying that all products are mispriced, and consequently GDP is a flawed measure of welfare. Humanistic economists do not use GDP as a measure of living standards.

The amount of well-being a given amount of output generates also depends on its distribution. Other factors also lead to errors like health care, which was 18 percent of US GDP pre-Covid. Consider that pre-term births cost ten times more than full-term infants; they added $26 billion to US GDP and have increased by one-third since 1980. Yet, it is absurd that a phenomenon associated with harm makes it appear as though welfare has increased because GDP has increased.[60]

The US medical system is inefficient compared to Western Europe because its administration is so much more convoluted and because of monopoly pricing (see Section 9.5). So, immense amounts of money are spent inefficiently, do not increase welfare, but they nonetheless contribute to GDP. The relationship between sickness and welfare is depicted in Figure 10.9. The person is healthy at time T(1) and has welfare of W(1). At T(1) a malady decreases his/her welfare to W(2). The patient takes medication until T(2) and his/her health improves and his/her welfare

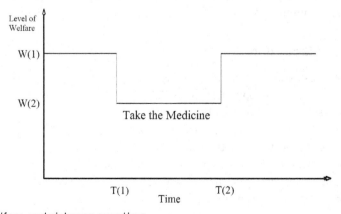

Figure 10.9 Welfare and sickness over time

returns to the initial level W(1). Their spending on the doctor and medication increased GDP and welfare relative to T(2) but welfare did not increase relative to the initial level T(1). Rather, the medical expenditure restored the level of welfare to its pre-malady level. This is yet another reason why GDP is a misleading indicator of welfare.

The fashion industry has similar properties. A new fashion reduces the value of old clothing. GDP increases if consumers buy the new style, but their welfare is merely restored to the level that prevailed before the new style became fashionable. Again, GDP increases but welfare does not.

In addition, average growth rates obscure the damages caused by the steep rise in inequality (see Chapter 15). Considered per household, the top 1 percent captured an astonishing 71 percent of the gains between 1979 and 2018. A household in the next 9 percent gained 18 percent of the benefits. Hence, the remaining 90 percent of households received an insignificant 11 percent of total benefits of growth (see Table 7.7). The decline in relative incomes exacerbate the feeling of being left behind and is an urgent problem in US's dual economy (see Figure 7.14). The proximate goal should be to reach a level of contentment of the population prevailing in Scandinavian societies. Unfortunately, life satisfaction and the quality of life are not even discussed in mainstream textbooks, although it is among the more important concepts in economics.

10.11 Takeaways

Keynesian macroeconomics was conceived as an antidote to the misery of the 1930s. Its prescription was straightforward: if aggregate demand is insufficient to provide work for all because private consumption and business investment are weak, then government is the only institution left to overcome the doldrums of a Depression. It can borrow and spend, thereby increasing aggregate demand, putting people back to work, and eliminating the gap between actual and potential GDP. But Keynesianism was abhorred by those who advocated small government out of fear of a dictatorship. They preferred unfettered capitalism because they were insensitive to evidence contradicting their ideology: they were unwilling to admit that, without an adequate safety net, decent jobs for everyone, and an equitable distribution of income, the glue that holds society together might come unstuck. They were blind to the examples of the European welfare states which remained democratic, yet created institutions that guided the markets in such a way as to provide a higher quality of life to their citizens than is the case in the US. Because of the ideological divide between Keynesians and neoliberals we are unable to solve the considerable challenges posed by the IT revolution, robotics, globalization, and the concomitant rise in inequality of the twenty-first century.

Questions for Discussion

1   What was Keynes's contribution to economics?
2   Did Keynes believe that people were rational?
3   What was his solution to the Great Depression?
4   Why does deflation pose difficulties for the economy?
5   Who is threatened most by deflation?
6   What is the implication of Keynes's notion of "animal spirits"?
7   What is the role of expectations in the formation of aggregate demand?
8   What is the multiplier and how does it work?

9   What is the neoclassical synthesis?

10 What is the Phillips curve and what explains it?

11 What are the assumptions of the real-business-cycle school of macroeconomics?

12 Which school of macroeconomics has better policy recommendations, in your opinion?

13 If you were a politician, do you think you would advocate Keynesian countercyclical fiscal policy?

14 Do you think it is reasonable to represent the whole economy by a single individual?

15 What is your opinion of the bailouts?

16 What do you think influences the consumer confidence index?

17 What makes aggregate demand fluctuate?

18 Do you think quantitative easing was successful?

19 Why is the velocity of circulation (V1) so volatile?

20 Do you think it was a good idea for the Fed to buy so many assets?

21 Do you think it was a good idea to keep the Federal Funds rate near zero for so long?

22 What is the liquidity trap and why is it important in a crisis?

Notes

1   John Maynard Keynes, *A Tract on Monetary Reform* (Macmillan, 1923), p. 80.

2   John Maynard Keynes, *The General Theory of Employment, Interest and Money* (Macmillan, 1936), pp. 161–162.

3   John Komlos and Larry Allen, "Expectations-Augmented Demand Curve for Teaching How Bubbles Form," *Australasian Journal of Economics Education* 17 (2020), 1: 56–66.

4   Dan Fastenberg, "Workplace Violence: Is the Recession Inspiring Worker Rage?" *AOL Jobs*, August 3, 2012.

5   John Komlos, "The Triumph of Trumpism," *Journal of Contextual Economics, Schmollers Jahrbuch* 137 (2017), 4: 421–440.

6   St. Louis Fed FRED, series GDPC1, GDPPOT.

7   Alan Auerbach and Yuriy Gorodnichenko, "Measuring the Output Responses to Fiscal Policy," *American Economic Journal: Economic Policy* 4 (2012), 2: 1–27; here p. 9; Lawrence Christiano et al., "When Is the Government Spending Multiplier Large?" *Journal of Political Economy* 119 (2011), 1: 78–121; Daniel Shoag, "The Impact of Government Spending Shocks: Evidence on the Multiplier from State Pension Plan Returns," Working Paper, Harvard University, 2010.

8   "The Fed Explained," https://www.federalreserve.gov/aboutthefed/files/the-fed-explained.pdf.

9   St. Louis Fed FRED, series GDPC1.

10 Pablo Duarte and Gunther Schnabl, "Monetary Policy, Inequality and Political Instability," *The World Economy* 42 (2019), 2: 614–634.

11 Andrew Lilley and Kenneth Rogoff, "The Case for Implementing Effective Negative Interest Rate Policy," in John Cochrane and John Taylor (eds.), *Strategies for Monetary Policy* (Hoover Institution Press, 2020).

12 St. Louis Fed, series EXCSRESNS and REQRESNS.

13 Bruno Navarro, "Alan Greenspan Sees 'Two Separate Economies'," *CNBC*, July 12, 2012, https://web.archive.org/web/20120718001743; https://finance.yahoo.com/news/alan-greenspan-sees-two-separate-161122638.html.

14 Martin Guzman and Joseph Stiglitz, "A Theory of Pseudo-Wealth," in Joseph Stiglitz and Martin Guzman (eds.), *Contemporary Issues in Macroeconomics* (Palgrave Macmillan, 2016), pp. 21–33.

15 The Fed changed the definition of M1, the money stock, on May 4, 2020, to include savings deposits including money market deposits; https://fred.stlouisfed.org/series/M1. Consequently, M1 increased

from $4.8 trillion to $16.3 trillion; Money Stock Measures – H.6 Release, https://www.federalreserve.gov/releases/h6/current/default.htm. The velocity here is calculated using the previous definition of currency plus demand deposits.

16   M2, another measure of the money supply, adds savings deposits and money market deposits to M1. *V2*, the velocity of circulation of M2, was more stable until 1993. The correlation between *V1* and *V2* was 0.7 until 2003 and then increased to 0.97, near perfect correlation.

17   Neva Goodwin et al., *Macroeconomics in Context*, 3rd edn. (Routledge, 2020).

18   Eldar Shafir et al., "On Money Illusion," *Quarterly Journal of Economics* 112 (1997), 2: 341–374.

19   Irving Fisher, "A Statistical Relation Between Unemployment and Price Changes," *Journal of Political Economy* 81 (1973), 2: 496–502.

20   Kevin Hoover, "Idealizing Reduction: The Microfoundations of Macroeconomics," *Erkenntnis* 73 (2010): 329–347.

21   Simon Wren-Lewis, "Ending the Microfoundations Hegemony," *Oxford Review of Economic Policy* 34 (2018), 1–2: 55–69.

22   These models are also called dynamic stochastic general equilibrium models.

23   "Larry Summers's remark (quoted by Robert Waldmann) that the day when economists first started to think that asset prices should be explained by the characteristics of a representative agent's utility function was not a particularly good day for economic science," Christopher Carroll, "Punter of Last Resort," VoxEu, March 13, 2009.

24   Alan Kirman, "Whom or What Does the Representative Individual Represent?" *Journal of Economic Perspectives* 6 (1992), 2: 117–136.

25   George Akerlof, "Behavioral Macroeconomics and Macroeconomic Behavior," *American Economic Review* 92 (2002), 3: 411–433.

26   Kenneth Arrow, *Social Choice and Individual Values* (John Wiley & Sons, 1951).

27   George Akerlof and Robert Shiller, *Animal Spirits: How Human Psychology Drives the Economy, and Why It Matters for Global Capitalism* (Princeton University Press, 2009).

28   Andrew Haldane and Arthur Turrell, "An Interdisciplinary Model for Macroeconomics," *Oxford Review of Economic Policy* 34 (2018), 1–2: 219–251.

29   This is misleading because there are many more surprises than technological change: "there are always unanticipated events" and there are always incomplete markets. Joseph Stiglitz, "Economic Fluctuations and Pseudo-Wealth," NBER Working Paper no. 28415, January 2021, p. 29.

30   In some "New-Keynesian" real-business-cycle models, prices adjust slower.

31   St. Louis Fed, series LNS12032194#0.

32   Brian Epstein, "Why Macroeconomics Does Not Supervene on Microeconomics," *Journal of Economic Methodology* 21 (2014), 1: 3–18.

33   Kenneth Arrow, "Rationality of Self and Others in an Economic System," *The Journal of Business* 59 (1986), S4: S385–S399.

34   Lawrence Summers, "Some Skeptical Observations on Real Business Cycle Theory," Federal Reserve Bank of Minneapolis, *Quarterly Review* 10 (1986), 4: 23–27.

35   Ibid.

36   David Hendry and John Muellbauer, "The Future of Macroeconomics: Macro Theory and Models at the Bank of England," *Oxford Review of Economic Policy* 34 (2018), 1–2: 287–328.

37   The Nobelist Christopher Sims admits it: "The recent financial crash and recession [were] not predicted by the DSGE models." "A Statistical Modeling of Monetary Policy and its Effects," December 8, 2011, www.nobelprize.org/nobel_prizes/economic-sciences/laureates/2011/sims_lecture.pdf.

38   Stiglitz, "Economic Fluctuations and Pseudo-Wealth," op. cit., p. 11.

39   Servaas Storm, "Cordon of Conformity: Why DSGE Models Are Not the Future of Macroeconomics," *International Journal of Political Economy* 50 (2021), 2: 77–98; Mario Seccareccia, "The Desperate Need for a Paradigm Shift in Establishment Macroeconomics," https://www.policyalternatives.ca/sites/default/files/

uploads/publications/National percent20Office/2021/08/Galbraith percent20lecture_FINAL_August percent206 percent202021.pdf.

40 Paul Romer, "Trouble with Macroeconomics, Update," September 21, 2016; Louis-Philippe Rochon and Sergio Rossi, *An Introduction to Macroeconomics: A Heterodox Approach*, 2nd edn. (Edward Elgar, 2021).

41 Paul Romer, "The Trouble with Macroeconomics," September 14, 2016; https://paulromer.net/trouble-with-macroeconomics-update/WP-Trouble.pdf; Editors, "Economists Still Lack a Proper Understanding of Business Cycles," *The Economist*, April 19, 2018.

42 Princeton University, "Princeton News Conference with Nobel Prize in Economics Winners Sims, Sargent," YouTube @ 14:11 minutes. www.youtube.com/watch?v=bVIOCIT4Rws.

43 To which he added the mundane observation:

> My own view is that what we ought to do is the kind of thing that Chairman Ben Bernanke urged the US government to do: make good long-run plans for resolving our budget difficulties without imposing severe fiscal stringency in the short run and accommodating monetary policy is a good idea. But these are not very original ideas.

44 Joseph Stiglitz, "Where Modern Macroeconomics Went Wrong," *Oxford Review of Economic Policy* 34 (2018), 1-2: 70-106.

45 Ibid.

46 John Muellbauer, "Household Decisions, Credit Markets and the Macroeconomy: Implications for the Design of Central Bank Models," Bank for International Settlements Discussion Paper 306, March 2010.

47 Willem Buiter, "The Unfortunate Uselessness of Most 'State of the Art' Academic Monetary Economics," Vox, CEPR's Policy Portal, March 6, 2009.

48 "An Open Letter to Congress Signed by 137 Economists Supporting GOP Tax Reform Bill," *CNBC*, November 29, 2017.

49 Robert Skidelsky, *Keynes: The Return of the Master* (Allen Lane, 2009).

50 Thomas Philippon, *The Great Reversal: How America Gave Up on Free Markets* (Harvard University Press, 2019).

51 Only 7.4 percent of transactions in Germany are paid by credit cards and two-thirds of Germans do not have a credit card. Tom Fairless, "Germans Warm to Credit Cards–Slowly," *The Wall Street Journal*, October 17, 2012.

52 William Mitchell et al., *Macroeconomics* (Red Globe Press, 2019); Edward Fullbrook and Jamie Morgan (eds.), *Modern Monetary Theory and Its Critics* (World Economics Association, 2020).

53 Stephanie Kelton, *The Deficit Myth: Modern Monetary Theory and the Birth of the People's Economy* (Public Affairs, 2020); Randall Wray, *Modern Money Theory*, 2nd edn. (Palgrave Macmillan, 2015).

54 Reserve currency means that foreigners hoard dollars for business transactions, for safety in case their currency depreciates, plus they can purchase US real estate, businesses, or other equity with it.

55 Jeanna Smialek, "Top US Officials Consulted with BlackRock as Markets Melted Down," *The New York Times*, June 24, 2021.

56 St. Louis Fed, series CPALTT01USM657N.

57 St. Louis Fed, series U6RATE.

58 St. Louis Fed, series CAPUTLG3361SQ.

59 Moses Abramovitz, *The Allocation of Economic Resources* (Stanford University Press, 1959).

60 Christopher Howson et al. (eds.), *Born Too Soon: The Global Action Report on Preterm Birth* (WHO, 2012).

11 Macroeconomics Part II

Markets can remain irrational longer than you can remain solvent.
–Attributed to John Maynard Keynes

We next discuss the labor market's paramount importance in the economy. We learn that the organization of the labor market is unfair because the available work is distributed unevenly: many work 70 hours per week, while others are excluded completely because they are unable to master the high barriers to entry.

11.1 Finagling with the Unemployment Numbers

The *official* unemployment rate, called *U-3* by the Bureau of Labor Statistics (BLS), is woefully biased because: (1) it conflates full-time with part-time workers; U-3 includes even those part-time workers who would like to work full-time but cannot find full-time employment; and (2) its definition of unemployment is excessively stringent: jobless persons are *officially* unemployed only if they have looked for work during the prior four weeks; this arbitrary rule excludes millions of jobless people who do want to work.[1] This is unreasonable because searching for work should not be a prerequisite of being considered unemployed. *Wanting* to work should be a sufficient criterion. Mainstream economists refer to them as nonemployed or underemployed. Hence, U-3 is biased downward by as much as 100 percent. (The BLS has a more realistic and more inclusive measure of the unemployment called *U-6*, but it is seldom mentioned in the media and hardly ever used in research.)[2]

We redress these shortcomings of the official unemployment rate: (1) by calculating the unemployment rate standardized on a full-time-equivalent workweek of 39 hours, and (2) by considering all those without a job who affirm that they would like to work as *de facto* unemployed, whether they have looked for work or not.[3] The hours worked by part-time workers is 62.7 percent of the hours worked by full time workers.[4] Note that there are two kinds of part-time workers: (1) those who are content working part-time (voluntary, μ), and (2) those who would like to work full-time (involuntary, *i*).[5] The voluntary are considered the equivalent to 0.627 full-time workers and are not counted as unemployed (Table 11.1, row 2). The involuntary (*i*) are considered full members of the labor force. Thus, they are considered 62.7 percent employed (Table 11.1, row 2) and 37.3 percent unemployed in terms of full-time equivalents (Table 11.1, rows 7).

DOI: 10.4324/9781003174356-11

Table 11.1 The *real* US unemployment rate, 2019

	Labor force	Millions	(%)
1	Civilian labor force full-time (*ft*)	130.6	
2	Part-time (0.627*26.9 million) (*v+i*)	16.9	
3	Military (*m*)	1.3	
4	Really unemployed (*ru*) from row 9	12.7	
5	Total actual labor force (*lf*)	161.4	
	Unemployed		
6	Official unemployed (*ou*)	6.0	3.7
7	Part-time involuntary (0.373* 4.4 million) (*i*)	1.6	1.0
8	Want job, did not look (*ww*)	5.0	3.1
9	Total *really* unemployed (*ru*)	12.7	7.8
10	Hidden unemployment (*hu*)	6.7	4.1

Sources: All data except the military data are from the St. Louis Fed. The various series are: Line (1) full-time workers: LNS12500000; line (2) part-time workers: LNS12600000, worked only 62.7 percent as many hours as full-time workers in 2019; line (4) from line 9; line (5) sum of rows 1–4; line (6) UNEMPLOY; line (7) LNS12032194; line (8) NILFWJN; line (9) sum of lines 6, 7, and 8. The Military data on line (3) is from: US Department of Defense, "Number of Military and DoD Appropriated Fund (APF) Civilian Personnel Permanently Assigned," 31 December 2017, and David Coleman, "US Military Personnel 1954–2014," https://historyinpieces.com/research/us-military-personnel-1954-2014. See also: Bureau of Labor Statistics, Table A-1. "Employment status of the civilian population by sex and age, Table A-8. Employed persons by class of worker and part-time status," Table A-15. "Alternative measures of labor underutilization," series LNS15026639.

Furthermore, soldiers are considered full-time workers since they receive a salary just like other government workers (*m*) (Table 11.1, row 3). This yields a total *effective* labor force of 161.4 million (*lf*):

$$lf = ft+0.627*(v +i)+m + ru$$

where ru is the number of unemployed. This estimate is lower than the official estimate, because the voluntary part-time workers are counted as 0.627 full-time workers instead as 1.0 as in the official statistics (Table 11.1, row 8).[6]

The *actual* unemployed consists of those who are officially unemployed (*ou* = 6 million) (Table 11.1, row 6), plus 37.3 percent of the involuntary part-time workers (*i* =1.6 million) (Table 11.1, row 7). We add the number of those who declare that they want to work but have not looked for work within the previous month (*ww* = 5 million) (Table 11.1, row 8). Hence, *ru* = 12.7 million (Table 11.1, row 9), and the real unemployment rate becomes *ru/lf* = 7.8 percent (Table 11.1, row 9) and the hidden unemployment rate is: *hu = ru - ou* = 4.1 percent (Table 11.1, row 10).[7] The estimated number of unemployed in 2019 becomes 12.7 million and the *true* unemployment (7.8 percent) is more than twice the *official* unemployment rate (3.7 percent) and 0.7 percent higher than the U-6 rate.[8] Yet even Table 11.1 leaves out 2.2 million incarcerated persons, although they were not working.[9]

Thus, the claim of mainstream economists that the US economy reached full employment in 2019 is mistaken (Figure 11.1).[10] These considerations reveal why wages were stagnating in a supposedly full-employment economy: hidden unemployment kept wages low. Moreover, the situation is worse among minorities, the official unemployment rate among Blacks is usually

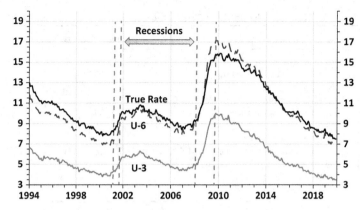

Figure 11.1 U-3, U-6, and the true unemployment rate (%)
Source: St. Louis Fed, series UNRATE, U6RATE, and see Table 11.1.

twice that of whites and the pre-Covid U-6 rate was at 11.5 percent, which reflects the true pain among African Americans (see Figure 16.3).[11]

In 2019, 21 percent of the official unemployed were unemployed for more than half a year. The median duration of unemployment was 9 weeks, and the average was 22 weeks.[12] Yet, those who did have full-time jobs work an average of 46.7 hours weekly and 39 percent work more than 50 hours.[13] In contrast to the unemployed, in 2019, there were 8.1 million people who held two jobs.[14]

Furthermore, Americans work 400 hours more annually than Western Europeans, although US incomes are higher and they could afford more leisure.[15] It is baffling that, given endemic unemployment, many US workers are overworked, working nearly as much as in 1960 and struggling with work-life balance.[16] Keynes was mistaken in predicting that his grandchildren's generation would work 15 hours per week.[17] With more income one would expect people to enjoy more leisure, since leisure is a normal good. The main reason for this conundrum is that people work hard in spite of higher income to "keep up with the Joneses" in competition for status.[18] This is like an "arms race," in which everyone works harder just to stay in place without providing a lasting advantage for individuals.[19]

Therefore, the available work is also unevenly distributed—like wealth and income.[20] A problem lies in the way the labor market is organized: firms adjust to fluctuations in the demand for labor by dismissing employees, causing their labor time to fall precipitously to zero. This is a *binary labor market*: one either has a job or does not have a job. Does a rigid system with such extremes—with working times ranging from 0 to 70 hours per week make sense? Would one design such a system from scratch, "behind a veil of ignorance" not knowing if they would end up among the ranks of the overworked or those of the underemployed? Risk-averse people would be too apprehensive about ending up among the losers to design such a system (see Section 5.7).

Instead of accepting unemployment as normal, we need institutional innovation to establish a system of perpetual full employment. For instance, it would be more equitable to adjust the number of hours worked instead of laying off employees. Then the available work would be divided among the labor force. A work-sharing program would be a more flexible shock absorber of fluctuations in the demand for labor.[21] This would eliminate unemployment completely.[22] Such a program worked in Germany where unemployment did not increase during the Meltdown and Iceland experimented with a four-day (36-hour) workweek successfully.[23]

Furthermore, a shorter workday by 40 minutes would distribute the available work more evenly.[24] Such a system would increase the quality of life, because it would reduce the psychological and financial burden of unemployment, increase leisure time, and reduce envy by reducing conspicuous consumption. Additionally, it would be a fairer method of distributing the pain of the economic rollercoaster than the prevailing binary system, especially since it is unevenly distributed both spatially and across ethnic groups.

Profit-sharing wages would also reduce unemployment.[25] Wages would increase in upswings and decrease in downturns, so that workers would not have to be fired, keeping the share of total wages in revenue unchanged.[26] *Cooperatives* are also less likely to fire members. Instead, they adjust compensation to fluctuations in demand.[27]

The government could also become the *employer of last resort*, just as central banks are the lenders of last resort.[28] A job guarantee would maintain labor market stability and *real* full employment, just as it is responsible for the stability of the financial sector.[29] In sum, one could introduce several shock absorbers into the labor market to replace the current crude binary one. It would be more humane to distribute the burden of cyclical economic downturns more equitably than concentrating it among 12.7 million people, disproportionally minorities. Full employment might also gain wider support among the electorate than a basic income policy.[30] Of course, full employment policy could be combined with a basic income policy. They are not mutually exclusive.

Work is also important from a psychological perspective: the unemployed are excluded from the labor market and are disparaged as unproductive members of society and lose self-esteem. Their skills depreciate over time, so they become unemployable. Unemployment has adverse side effects like increases in criminality and stress. It has a destabilizing effect on society both politically and socially. The unemployed are twice as likely to be sad or depressed as the employed and 50 percent more likely to be angry.[31] They are also more likely to be struggling financially (54 percent) than the employed (38 percent). The shortage of middle-class jobs will increase with the spread of artificial intelligence and robotization. The developed world is threatened by technological unemployment unless far-reaching policies are enacted.[32] Nearly half of all US employees are at risk of being displaced.[33] Humanistic economists recommend institutional innovation to avoid social conflict stemming from unemployment.

11.2 The Natural Rate of Unemployment Is Not Natural at All

Another mistake of mainstream theory is that it accepts 5 percent unemployment as *natural* and equates it with full employment. This verbal contortion comes about because mainstream economists consider the *non-accelerating inflation rate of unemployment* (NAIRU) or *natural rate of unemployment* for short, as the minimum level of unemployment attainable without accelerating inflation, given the labor market's institutional structure. The institutional structure includes search costs, and the time needed to find a matching job. Theoretically, an unemployment rate below the NAIRU would be possible but only temporarily at a cost of increasing inflation, and in the long run, unemployment would return to its "natural" level at a higher inflation rate.

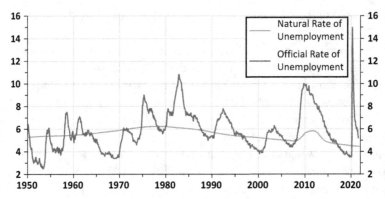

Figure 11.2 The official unemployment rate and the natural rate (%)
Source: St. Louis Fed, series NROUST, UNRATE.

Thus, it would be futile to use monetary or fiscal policy to force the unemployment rate below its natural rate. It would only lead to inflation. Hence, conservative economists, like Ben Bernanke of Princeton University and Martin Feldstein of Harvard University, confidently refer to 5 percent level of unemployment as "full employment."[34] Feldstein declared in 2016 that "We are *essentially* at full employment with the overall unemployment rate at 5 percent."[35] Ten months before Trump's triumph, he neglected the frustration in the labor market (see Table 11.1).

Thus, 5 percent unemployment must be tolerated, according to mainstream ideologues, because it is inherent in the nature of the economy. However, that dogma merely rationalizes the inability of the labor market to provide employment for all and does not allow for institutional innovation to achieve *real* full employment.[36] That makes the natural rate of unemployment a disingenuous concept, "an idea past its sell-by date."[37] Way past ...

Moreover, the Federal Reserve arbitrarily increases the natural rate in times of high unemployment and lowers it when times improve (Figure 11.2). So, it fluctuates subjectively between 6.2 percent and 4.5 percent.[38] Moreover, the *official* unemployment rate is often below the natural rate including between March 2017 and March 2020 *without* accelerating inflation.[39] Since the official unemployment rate was below the "full employment" level as indicated by the natural rate of unemployment and there was no inflation, the theory of NAIRU is not useful. It also shows the extent to which the official unemployment rate is inaccurate.

Institutional innovation to eliminate unemployment should include using the internet at the national level to match vacancies with unemployed workers instantaneously, thereby eliminating frictional unemployment. Moreover, the government could subsidize the cost of searching for employment, relocating expenses, and also provide reskilling opportunities as necessary. In combination with work-sharing, profit-sharing, and the government becoming the employer of last resort, we could achieve *real* full employment. Humanistic economists do not accept 5 percent unemployment as natural. After all, the UN's Universal Declaration of Human Rights states, "Everyone has the right to work ... and to protection against unemployment."[40] It is high time to implement that right.

11.3 Economic Growth: When Is Enough Enough?

Economic growth is a cherished goal of macroeconomic policy. Because growth has been practically continuous in the West for 250 years, with the exception of the Great Depression–it is natural to assume that it is inherent in the nature of capitalism and should continue indefinitely. However, such an economic law does not exist. As part of the twenty-first-century's new normal we should realize that our civilization has reached a new stage of development when further growth is superfluous.[41]

What do we need more of? Erich Fromm realized that "production and consumption have become ends in themselves. We produce and consume more and more, and if we ask "why," "what for" we don't quite know the answer."[42] Actually, the rich countries produce so much that they should be content with what they have and not crave for more.[43] The main goal should be to improve the quality of life by working less and enjoying it more, to save the planet, to redistribute wealth so that frustration is reduced, thereby rejuvenating our political institutions, and help developing nations so that international conflicts can be avoided. This implies that we must overcome our insatiability, discard growth fetishism—and strive to grow mentally and spiritually rather than materialistically.[44] New institutions and a new mindset to adapt to the new circumstances of the twenty-first century are crucial. Improvement of education is essential. Technology harnessed in the service of these goals is essential. These are the recommendations of humanistic economics for a brighter future instead of economic growth. The superabundance of the developed world suffices to satisfy the needs of the population if we would only distribute output more equitably.

Yet, "the relentless pursuit of economic growth" is *still* a central tenet of our culture and our policies, although we have experienced a quarter millennium of unprecedented economic growth without the anticipated increase in life satisfaction.[45] This realization, coupled with the frustration with environmental degradation, led to the *degrowth* movement "to purposefully slow things down in order to minimize harm to humans and earth systems."[46] Consequently, the purpose of the economy should be to increase life satisfaction and ensure our survival by stabilizing environmental imbalances, rather than unrelenting growth.[47]

11.4 Growth Has Not Increased Life Satisfaction

Growth has not created the expected Nirvana. Amount of life satisfaction has languished since the 1970s despite steady economic growth. The evidence comes from Gallup surveys that revealed pre-Covid that only 55 percent of the US population were thriving, while 42 percent were struggling and 3 percent were suffering, not a reassuring achievement for a $23 trillion economy.[48]

> It is the paradox of modernity that as choice and material prosperity increase ... personal satisfaction decline[s] ... it is the rare American who manages to step back from the hedonic treadmill long enough to savor his or her good fortune.[49]

The reason for the stagnation of life satisfaction in rich countries in spite of increases in income is the crucial role played by relative income in life satisfaction. A decrease in relative incomes will be frustrating even if nominal income increases (see Section 7.13, Figures 2.1 and 7.16). Despite the doubling of GDP per capita in the US, the share of "very happy" people in the population has declined by 6 percent and the share of those "not too happy" has increased by (7 percent) (Figure 11.3).

The United States has achieved striking economic and technological progress over the past half-century without gains in the self-reported happiness of the citizenry. Instead, uncertainties and anxieties are high, social and economic inequalities have widened considerably, social trust

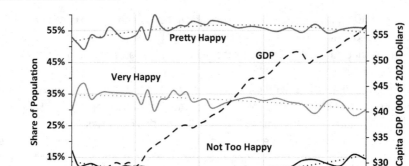

Figure 11.3 Real GDP per capita and the population's happiness
Sources: Tom Smith et al., "General Social Survey Final Report: Trends in Psychological Well-Being, 1972-2014," NORC, University of Chicago, 2015; St. Louis Fed, series A939RX0Q048SBEA; data for 2016 and 2018 extracted from https://gss.norc.org/.

has evaporated, and failure to redress genuine grievances has led to the frustration with the political system. Perhaps for these reasons, life satisfaction has remained nearly constant during decades of rising Gross National Product (GNP) per capita.[50]

Moreover, the ratio of female to male life satisfaction has declined in the US since the 1970s, despite the Women's Liberation Movement and rise in women's income.[51] In the 1970s, 4.3 percent more women than men were "very happy" but by the twenty-first century that advantage had shrunk to 1.2 percent.[52] Alcoholic liver disease is also rising faster among women than among men.[53] If absolute income were decisive, why would women be so stressed?[54]

In sum, growth will not solve our fundamental problems. More goods touted by Madison Avenue are short-term palliatives. Instead, we need to feel good about ourselves and about our place in society, which is achievable only if we are healthy (physically and mentally), financially secure, and can live with dignity and nourishing personal relationships. Humanistic economists suggest that we need to learn how to obtain more happiness from current GDP and catch up with the Scandinavian countries in life satisfaction (see Figure 2.1).

11.5 Technological Change Is a Double-Edged Sword

Economic growth is fueled by technological change, but innovation also harbors destructive elements that detract from its benefits.[55] For instance, the recent wave of innovation in financial technology posed dangerous systemic risks (negative externalities) that were disregarded. Aldous Huxley's *Brave New World* (1931) and George Orwell's *1984* (1948) were early warnings of the dangers of technological change, its dehumanizing effects, and unintended consequences.

Innovation entails *"creative destruction"*–the new brings about the obsolescence of old technologies.[56] Innovation creates both winners and losers and is therefore *never "Pareto optimal."* Furthermore, it often leads to *social dislocation*.[57] While mainstream economists argue against redistribution of wealth because it is not Pareto optimal, even if it would increase productivity, they nonetheless venerate technological change, although it is also not Pareto optimal. This is another blatant inconsistency in the mainstream canon.

Economists argue that the losers do not have to be compensated actually; the mere possibility of compensation suffices to make an innovation or policy initiative advantageous. If gainers gain more than losers lose, the policy is said to be efficient (according to the *Kaldor-Hicks criterion*), but, of course, such hypothetical compensation is useless for the losers and is therefore not a humanistic approach to economic policy.[58] A major shortcoming of the economic system is that the losers are never compensated by the winners and therefore innovation also creates much frustration. Until we create institutions that compensate the losers, economic growth will not improve life satisfaction, as technical progress is obtained at the cost of inflicting pain.

The destructive element in innovation is a *negative externality*. If an innovation creates a new consumer product valued at $10, but destroys an old one valued at $5, its contribution to welfare is not $10 but $5. While GDP increases by $10, the innovation appears to create more utility than it actually does. This is a (hidden) negative externality. For instance, a new generation of iPhone renders the previous version unfashionable and makes consumers covet the new. Buying the new brings them back to their old level of welfare (see Figure 10.9). We alleviated the discomfort created by the new, but by buying the new we did not achieve a higher level of welfare than we had enjoyed before it came onto the market.

Furthermore, not all new products are actual improvements. Windows operating system was a substantial achievement, but several subsequent versions (Vista, Windows 8) were not real improvements and were released because of Microsoft's profit-increasing strategy. Moreover, the strategy of *planned obsolescence* is profitable for the firm because of consumers' status-consciousness and because the new product's quality is not immediately obvious.[59] Aspects can be hidden initially. For example, years went by before the financial innovations became toxic (see Chapter 14). They were profitable until their dangerous characteristics emerged.

Ex-Federal Reserve Chairman, Paul Volcker thought that financial innovations' primary aim was *rent seeking* and failed to raise productivity. The automated teller machine is an exception, but it was designed by mechanical engineers and not by financial engineers.[60]

Consider, furthermore, that tablet computers expanded to the detriment of laptop computers; Amazon replaced countless local bookstores including Borders, which had 1,200 stores in 2003. Digital replaced print advertisement dollar for dollar.[61] The smartphone replaced traditional cameras. The "selfie" replaced the "Kodak moment," but Kodak employed 145,000 people at its peak (and paid mostly middle-class wages), while in 2020, after emerging from bankruptcy, it had a skeleton workforce of 4,500.[62]

Western culture venerates disruptive innovation but overlooks its destructive components and the pain it inflicts through *technological unemployment*.[63] The displaced workers are often unemployable in the expanding sectors, or receive lower salaries or join the gig economy.[64] For instance, Uber's market capitalization of $88 billion (October 2021), is greater than that of Ford Motor ($56 billion).[65] The success of this mobile ride-request company, founded in 2009, is based largely on extracting economic rents from the taxi business. The gains in productivity associated with the firm are small, but it reduced taxi drivers' incomes substantially. Net financial gains are slight and spread out over many consumers while the pain is great and concentrated among a few drivers. A driver earns around $9.20 per hour. Uber accounts for merely 91,000 full-time equivalent workers.[66] Yet, it was a disruptive innovation. In New York City, a taxi medallion was worth $1 million in 2014 but merely $137,000 in 2019.[67]

Pharma companies also extend their monopoly rents on their patented drugs in the guise of innovation by patenting new ways to administer a known compound.[68] Minor changes in formulations can also extend a drug's patent as can new uses different from the one originally patented. Another creative defense of monopoly rents is to combine two drugs into one tablet and apply for a new patent. Such strategies of rent seeking disguised as innovation do not improve living standards.[69]

A downside of Big Tech is that it is not as labor-intensive as the iconic firms in the past; it is human capital-intensive. Apple employs 147,000; eBay 130,000; Google 100,000; Microsoft 100,000; Facebook 59,000.[70] Altogether they do not employ as many as the US automobile industry did by itself in the 1970s (1 million) without even the 300,000 jobs in related industries.[71] Amazon is the only exception with one million workers, but it pays mostly sub-middle-class wages for warehouse workers at $15 an hour.[72] Ford Motor Company was paying as much in 1914 (see Figure 7.8).

Technological change also creates negative externalities called "bite-backs": "most technologies developed in the 20th century had unanticipated side effects, most of them negative."[73] Innovations like DDT, chlorofluorocarbons, leaded gasoline, fast food, asbestos, opioid drugs, and lead-based paint are all examples of technological regress.[74] They all generated negative externalities whose true impact was discovered long after they were implemented and created an illusion of productivity increases. Furthermore, the long-praised financial innovations also culminated in an immense "bite-back" which threatened the global economy and had to be propped up with trillions of dollars worth of taxpayers support in the US alone (see Chapter 14).[75]

The misuse of social media platforms by Russian infiltrators that manipulated the 2016 US presidential election is a menacing example of a humongous "bite-back" of internet-based technology.[76] Facebook and Twitter undermined democratic political institutions and therefore their contribution to GNP is illusory.[77] Not only have these tech companies uprooted, redistributed, and destroyed much but with "Surveillance Capitalism" it brought us closer to Orwell's dystopian vision.[78] These social media powerhouses were unwilling to devise adequate safeguards that would reduce their profits and defend democracy.[79] This is the kind of technological threat that Huxley and Orwell warned us about.[80]

11.6 Social and Economic Mobility

The origin of *social status* is the level of respect or deference people enjoy in their society, while *social mobility* is the movement up or down the social scale. Similarly, *economic mobility* is movement along the distribution of income within one's lifetime or across generations. The higher the correlation of social status across generations, the smaller is mobility. Higher status individuals are healthier, live longer, are better educated, with a more stable family structure, live in upscale neighborhoods with higher incomes, and have social networks conducive to maintaining or advancing social status. Their children attend better schools and therefore have more opportunities open to them. Income inequality, discrimination, and access to education impact mobility. Concentration of wealth is passed down through many generations, dubbed "The Great Gatsby Curve."[81]

That the children of oil-magnate John D. Rockefeller would be wealthy is obvious but that one of his grandsons would become Governor of New York and Vice President of the US, another the Governor of Arkansas, and a great-grandson would become Governor of and Senator from West Virginia are less obvious but illustrate the extent to which wealth, status, and political influence persist across many generations. Numerous of his great grandchildren are still philanthropists.[82]

In contrast, one-third of children in the US have experienced a decline in family income between 1975 and 2011.[83]

America has become a low-mobility country because of lax inheritance taxation and because of bottlenecks in access to excellent educational opportunities. The poor are confined to areas with mediocre school systems that prevents them from obtaining a college diploma, a prerequisite for advancement in today's knowledge economy. Only 18 percent of children whose parents did not attend college were able to obtain a college degree. Furthermore, 44 percent of Americans believe that they are not better off than their parents were at the same age.[84]

Societies with high income inequality have low social mobility because the wealthy create hurdles within the economic system so as to maintain their status by influencing public policy. Only the UK and Italy have lower levels of income mobility than the US. The Scandinavian countries are again at the top of the pack.[85] In the US, sons born to rich parents have a 50 percent chance of landing above the 70 percent percentile in the income distribution and merely 3 percent will land in the bottom decile. In contrast, those who are born to poor parents have a high probability of remaining poor. Only 7 percent will make it to the top decile.

The gap between rich and poor parents' annual expenditures on their children's enrichment—on books, computers, childcare, summer camps, private schooling—has increased by $4,800 between 1972 and 2006.[86] Consequently, by age 4, children of rich parents score in the 69th percentile on tests of literacy while those of poor parents score in the 34th percentile.[87] They have already fallen behind. Children of poor parents are rare in the most competitive colleges. Moreover, if wealthy families had difficulty getting their children into elite institutions, the parents resorted to bribes in an illegal effort to pass on their privilege.[88] Thirty-five parents spent $35 million to gain access to "social-status-granting institutions" in "the worst scandal involving elite universities in the history of the United States."[89] The scandal reflects the increased angst of failing to obtain a competitive diploma to fulfill upwardly mobile aspirations (see Section 5.12). The minimal opportunity for upward mobility and exclusive college admissions contributes to the grievances of those left behind and fuels populism that is at the basis of the dysfunctional political system.

11.7 Complex Economies Evolve in Perpetual Disequilibrium

Mainstream economics assumes that the economy evolves in perpetual equilibrium or if it experiences deviations because of unanticipated developments like a disruptive technology referred to as a "shock," it will return to equilibrium in short order.[90] In stark contrast,

> complexity economics sees the economy … as not necessarily in equilibrium, its decision makers … as not super-rational, the problems they face as not necessarily well-defined and the economy not as a perfectly humming machine but as an ever-changing ecology of beliefs, organizing principles and behaviours.[91]

The essential difference between complexity economics and the mainstream macroeconomic models is that the latter assume the existence of a solitary perfectly rational "agent" who supposedly represents everyone in the economy, while complexity economics assumes that *millions* of economic agents—firms, consumers, and investors—interact in strategic ways at the microeconomic level and those interactions result in patterns of behaviors, actions, and choices that should be analyzed. In turn, people adapt to those outcomes and react to them in turn, resulting in rearranged networks and incessantly forming new patterns. These interactions give rise to an emerging and evolving macroeconomic system yielding variables of interest, such as GDP, inflation, and unemployment in a non-linear dynamic system.

The rules of the participants' interaction are designed to model realistic social and economic behavior, including incentives, motives, and information flows, instead of the optimal behavior of neoclassical economic agents. These agent-based computer simulation models assume bounded rationality; participants learn from their frequent interactions and the emerging patterns. Hence, this non-equilibrium economy is in a constant state of flux. Complex dynamic systems stress the interaction effects among agents that adapt to the continually changing economic environment and through that create new economic outcomes that can give rise to non-linear dynamics, including chaotic ones.[92]

11.8 Missing Markets Are an Existential Threat

That economic systems are incomplete, is another one of the Achilles' heels of markets. They are incomplete because there are crucial *missing markets*. Their absence poses a substantial threat to the welfare of future generations who are unable to influence today's decision-makers.[93] No one owns the Earth's public goods like the atmosphere, the oceans, the ecosystems, and, consequently, pollution and global warming have become an immense threat to the globe (see Figure 11.4).[94]

Another way missing markets affect the lives of generations yet unborn is through the growing national debt (see Figure 12.1).[95] Future generations cannot influence us to live within our means, so they will have to pay for the debt we accumulate. Those who advocate that "greed is good" fail to understand that it also leads to disregard for the welfare of future generations.[96]

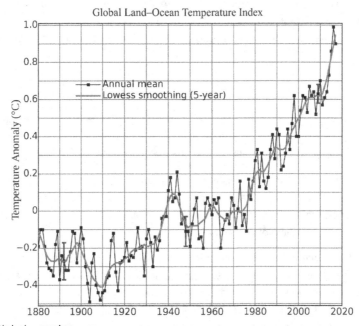

Figure 11.4 Global warming
Source: NASA Goddard Institute for Space Studies. http://data.giss.nasa.gov/gistemp/graphs/, Public Domain, https://commons.wikimedia.org/w/index.php?curid=24363898.

Standard textbooks do not consider this problem seriously enough. For instance, diagrams of the circular flow of macroeconomic activity ignore the crucial role played by resources and by the environment in macroeconomic activity.[97] This is foolhardy, because the contribution of the world's ecosystem and of natural resources to the economy is both substantial and essential.[98] An additional problem is that with a low birth rate in the developed world, fewer people care deeply about the plight of future generations since many people are not concerned about passing on their genes anyhow. So, protecting the environment is challenging, although the developed world could afford to do a lot more in the defense of the environment.

11.9 "There Is No Planet B"[99]

Two hundred and fifty years of economic growth have brought us to a watershed moment.[100] It does not take much imagination to suppose that the consequences can be ominous.[101] The Earth's temperature has risen 1.0° Centigrade since 1978, raising the sea level by 7 inches (Figure 11.4). Coastal regions, river deltas, small islands, and much of Florida are likely to be inundated.[102] Ecological problems can also lead to political and social tensions of tectonic proportions.[103]

Although it is difficult to create incentives to mitigate the myopic nature of decision-making, some countries have been adopting policies to curb CO_2 pollutants. They have either started taxing greenhouse gases or adopted a cap-and-trade system which sets limits on the total amount of carbon allowed to be discharged into the atmosphere and grant allowances by industries. The allowances can be traded, enabling the cost of pollution to be incorporated into the price system. Canada introduced a price for carbon emissions that will reach \$170/ton by 2030 but CO_2 emission is still free in the US.[104] That leads to inefficient production and uneconomic growth.[105] So, markets, by themselves, produce excessive amounts of pollution without adequate regulation and jeopardize the Earth's ecosystem.[106]

"Climate change and increasing income inequality have emerged as twin threats to contemporary standards of living, peace and democracy."[107] Extreme weather events have become more frequent, more disruptive, and costlier in lives and destruction.[108] In 2017, three hurricanes, Irma, Harvey, and Maria, caused \$366 billion in damages and killed 300 people, making the year the most expensive disaster year until then on record.[109] There were 16 disasters causing more than \$1 billion in damages each. In 1980, there were only three disasters of comparable size. Superstorm Sandy—the largest Atlantic hurricane on record—killed 147 people and caused \$75 billion in damages; Hurricane Katrina killed 1,836 and caused \$108 billion in damages.[110] The damages were not subtracted from GDP. On the contrary, the expenditures to rebuild increased GDP. Estimates of environmental damage amount to 11 percent of global GDP.[111]

Other types of disasters caused by climate change include tornadoes, heat waves, floods, mud slides, wildfires, and blizzards.[112] Between 2000 and 2017, 3,631 people were killed by natural disasters in the US.[113] The Fukushima nuclear disaster displaced 160,000 persons and will take 40 years to clean up. The Chernobyl nuclear disaster killed 4,000. The BP oil spill in the Gulf of Mexico in 2010 polluted 68,000 square miles of ocean with 175 million gallons of oil.[114] The damage was not confined to the environment: 11 people perished, and the psychological toll was also evident: the number of people with a clinical diagnosis of depression increased from a pre-spill level of 5.6 percent to 20.4 percent among coastal residents.[115] We ignore these threats at our peril.[116] The mainstream does not treat the problem with the urgency it requires.[117]

Illustration 11.1 Global warming is causing unconscionable damage to the environment
Credit: Shutterstock, 1609549078.

In order to save the planet, humanistic economists advocate "greening" the economy with renewable energy and quickly phasing out the use of fossil fuels. The developed West should be satisfied with its current level of output and should abandon the mantra of growing the economy. The rich countries consume far too much already. Moreover, we should avoid the mental trap of techno-optimism—the risky idea that technological innovation will somehow save us from global warming.[118] Saving the planet will require "restructuring the current economic system," as advocated in this volume.[119]

11.10 Feminist Economics: If Women Counted

Feminists stress that traditional economics is not objective because it is culturally predominantly masculine, focusing on concepts like competition, selfishness, and rationality, and disregards traditional feminine values like cooperation, altruism, and emotional intelligence.[120] They also reject as biased major assumptions of neoclassical economics since it wrongly "presumes that humans are autonomous, impervious to social influences and lack sufficient emotional connection to each other to make empathy possible."[121] Another blatant inconsistency in the conventional canon is that "empathic emotional connections between individuals are emphasized in the family whereas they are denied in analyzing markets."[122]

Furthermore, feminists criticize the flaws in GDP estimates because they ignore unpaid work, traditionally the responsibility of women, such as childcare, shopping, housecleaning, cooking, nurturing, and chauffeuring children to activities. Actually, these kinds of care work without remuneration are a sizeable share of the economy.[123] Their imputed value is likely to be around one-third of GDP.[124] In the US, that could amount to $7 trillion (annually). That is an incredible amount of economic value to overlook and undervalues the contribution of females to the economy. The value of unpaid work could be imputed in national accounts because GDP does include the imputed value of owner-occupied housing. Thus, omitting care work from GDP is inconsistent.

Since home-produced goods are omitted from GDP, as women transitioned from home production to market production, much of economic growth was caused by the substitution of goods produced in the market for home-produced goods. A crucial implication is that the inclusion of unpaid work would reduce GDP growth rates considerably in the US by possibly as much as 0.65 percent per annum (1975–2016).[125] Consequently, the inclusion of unpaid work would reduce the real growth of per capita GDP from 1.4 percent per annum in the twenty-first century to 0.75 percent per annum (see Figure 12.3). This is also crucial to the understanding of the rise of discontent.

11.11 Takeaways

Despite being a bellwether statistic, GDP is a misleading indicator of living standards because it does not take pollution into consideration, it excludes unpaid work—a big part of the economy—completely disregards the distribution of income, overlooks the depletion of non-renewable resources, uses prices that do not reflect fundamental values during bubbles, and omits unpaid work. If the GNP estimates were to take these factors into consideration, they would be more accurate and most likely reveal that in reality the US economy is not growing at all.

The official unemployment rate is also misleading because it does not count discouraged workers, those who have given up looking for work because finding work seems hopeless to them. Moreover, it counts those part-time workers who are unable to find full-time employment as though they were fully employed, a major error. Hence, in 2019, the official unemployment rate was 3.7 percent, but the real rate was 7.8 percent since there was 4.1 percent hidden unemployment, as 6.7 million unemployed workers were omitted from the statistics. Thus, even in what was dubbed a "roaring economy," 12.7 million people were without work, an unacceptable level. We should strive for real full employment and not accept 5 percent unemployment as full employment. The U-6 unemployment rate is close to the true value and is a better gage of the slack in the labor market than the official unemployment rate.

Questions for Discussion

1   Why is GDP a misleading measure of welfare of the people living and working in an economy?
2   What do you think is the living standard of those in the bottom 20 percent of the income distribution?
3   Do you think that the damage caused by pollution should be subtracted from GNP?
4   Will growing the economy solve our problems?
5   Are we addicted to economic growth?
6   What is most important: economic growth, the environment, or the quality of life?
7   Should we leave the environment as good as we found it for future generations?
8   Should the benefits of economic growth be shared widely?
9   Do you think everyone has a right to a job?
10 Would you say that the official unemployment rate is a good estimate of the idle human resources in the economy?
11 Do you think that we should strive for *real* full employment? Do you think it is attainable, and, if so, how?
12 Do you think the economy is efficient, given the huge numbers of underemployed people?

13   Do you think that work sharing instead of laying people off is a good idea?

14   Do you think that those incarcerated should be counted as unemployed? Now they are not.

15   Do you think that it is unfair that the available work is distributed so unevenly?

16   Would you say that the "binary" labor market is efficient or just?

17   How would you organize the labor market if you were to create it from scratch behind a "veil of ignorance"?

18   Would you be willing to participate voluntarily in a work-sharing program as an insurance against unemployment?

19   Do you think that the right to a job should be guaranteed in the Bill of Rights?

20   How could we induce people to be more content with what they have?

21   How important is the government to economic growth?

22   Do you think that environmental protection is as important as economic growth or more important?

23   Have we become insatiable so that contentment will always elude us?

24   Do you think sustainable growth is a worthy goal?

25   Do you think it is great that we have robots working instead of people in factories?

26   How could economic growth become more inclusive?

27   Should the government become the employer of last resort just as it has become the lender of last resort?

28   Do you think technology will improve the quality of our lives?

29   Do you think that economic slowdown has become the new normal?

30   Do you think that a guaranteed basic income is a good idea?

Notes

1   David Blanchflower, *Not Working: Where Have All the Good Jobs Gone?* (Princeton University Press, 2019).

2   The U-6 rate includes all part-time workers and those "marginally attached" who looked for work or did work within the past 12 months, are jobless, but have not looked for work within the past month. US Department of Labor, "Glossary," www.bls.gov/bls/glossary.htm#M.

3   Joan Robinson, "Disguised Unemployment." *Economic Journal* 46, (1936), 182: 225-237.

4   Bureau of Labor Statistics, "Labor Force Statistics from the Current Population Survey," Table 19. https://www.bls.gov/cps/lfcharacteristics.htm#fullpart.

5   https://data.bls.gov/timeseries/LNS12032194.

6   St Louis Fed, series CLF16OV. Bureau of Labor Statistics, "Persons Not in the Labor Force by Desire and Availability for Work, Age, and Sex," Table 35. www.bls.gov/web/empsit/cpseea38.pdf.

7   Rows 6-10 use the actual labor force (row 5) to calculate the percentages.

8   Even this might be biased downward since 18 percent of the 250 million adults "wanted more work in late 2019." That makes 45 million people. That means that the unemployment in Table 11.1 is a lower bound. To be sure, we do not know how much more those workers would like to work. It could be just a few hours more per week. Board of Governors of the Federal Reserve System, "Report on the Economic Well-Being of US Households in 2019," May 2020, pp. 2, 15; https://www.federalreserve.gov/publications/files/2019-report-economic-well-being-us-households-202005.pdf.

9   Their inclusion would raise the unemployment rate to 9.0 percent.

10   "The US Economy Is in Good Shape," *Wall Street Journal*, February 21, 2016; https://www.wsj.com/articles/the-u-s-economy-is-in-good-shape-1456097121.

11 Economic Policy Institute, "Underemployment by Race." www.epi.org/data/#?subject=underemp&r=*; The BLS does not publish U-6 by race, probably because of the unwelcome mirror it holds up to the labor market.

12 Bureau of Labor Statistics, https://www.bls.gov/webapps/legacy/cpsatab12.htm/Table-A-12-Unemployed-persons-by-duration-of-unemployment.

13 Lydia Saad, "The 40-Hour Workweek Is Actually Longer–by Seven Hours," *Gallup*, August 29, 2014. Managers and professionals worked an average 45 hours per week in the 1990s, and their share of working more than 49 hours was 38 percent. US Department of Labor, Bureau of Labor Statistics, "Are Managers and Professionals Really Working More?" *Issues in Labor Statistics*, May 12, 2000.

14 Some 4.5 million held a part-time job in addition to their full-time employment, 2.1 million work two part-time jobs, 0.3 million hold two full-time jobs, and 1.1 million have variable hours on both jobs. Bureau of Labor Statistics, "36. Multiple Jobholders by Selected Characteristics." www.bls.gov/cps/cpsaat36.pdf.

15 Organization for Economic Cooperation and Development (OECD), "OECD Statistical Extracts." The time worked by married couples combined increased by 11 hours within a generation at the end of the twentieth century from 56 to 67 hours per week. Bureau of Labor Statistics, "Working in the 21st Century." www.bls.gov/opub/working/page17b.htm.

16 Juliet Schor, *The Overworked American: The Unexpected Decline of Leisure* (Basic Books, 1993). OECD, "Average Usual Hours Worked on the Main Job." https://stats.oecd.org/Index. aspx?DataSetCode=ANHRS#. In 1961, they worked 40.5 hours per week. St. Louis Fed, series M08354USM310NNBR; US Department of Labor, Bureau of Labor Statistics, "Current Employment Statistics-CES (National): Technical Notes to Establishment Survey Data," May 8, 2012.

17 John Maynard Keynes, *Economic Possibilities for Our Grandchildren* (Entropy, 1930).

18 "People are happier when they spend money on experiences instead of material objects, when they relish what they plan to buy long before they buy it, and when they stop trying to outdo the Joneses," Stephanie Rosenbloom, "But Will It Make You Happy?" *The New York Times*, August 7, 2010.

19 Robert Frank, *The Darwin Economy: Liberty, Competition, and the Common Good* (Princeton University Press, 2011).

20 John Maynard Keynes, *The General Theory of Employment, Interest and Money* (Macmillan, 1936), Chapter 24, p. 372.

21 Dean Baker, *Work Sharing: The Quick Route Back to Full Employment* (Center for Economic and Policy Research), June 2011.

22 Some steps were taken in the 2012 "Job Creation Act."

23 Paul Krugman, "Kurzarbeit," *The New York Times*, September 2, 2010; BBC NEWS, "Four-Day Week 'An Overwhelming Success' in Iceland," July 6, 2021.

24 The reduction of the workweek in France from 39 to 35 hours in large firms in the year 2000 is estimated to have reduced the unemployment rate by 1.6 percent by 2002. Zaichao Du, Hua Yin, and Lin Zhang, "The Macroeconomic Effects of the 35-Hr Workweek Regulation in France," *B.E. Journal of Macroeconomics* 13 (2013), 1: 881–901.

25 John Restakis, *Humanizing the Economy: Cooperatives in the Age of Capital* (New Society Publishers, 2010).

26 Martin Weitzman, *The Share Economy* (Harvard University Press, 1984); David Ellerman, *The Democratic Worker-Owned Firm* (Routledge, 1990).

27 John Pencavel, *Worker Participation. Lessons from the Worker Co-ops of the Pacific Northwest* (Russell Sage Foundation, 2002).

28 Pavlina Tcherneva, "The Federal Job Guarantee: Prevention, Not Just a Cure," *Challenge, The Magazine of Economic Affairs*, 62 (2019), 4: 253–272; Sakia Klosse and Joan Muysken, "Curbing the Labour Market Divide by Fostering Inclusive Labour Markets Through a Job Guarantee Scheme," *Psychosociological Issues in Human Resource Management* 4 (2016), 2: 185–219.

29   Pavlina Tcherneva, *The Case for a Job Guarantee* (Polity, 2020); Sean Patrick Farrell, "The Robot Factory Future," *The New York Times*, video, 3:58, August 18, 2012; David Colander, "A Guaranteed Jobs Proposal," in David Colander (ed.), *Solutions to Unemployment* (Harcourt Brace Jovanovich, 1981), pp. 204–208.

30   Peter Goodman, "Finland Has Second Thoughts About Giving Free Money to Jobless People," *The New York Times*, April 24, 2018.

31   Jenny Marlar, "The Emotional Cost of Underemployment," *Gallup*, March 9, 2010; Anna Manchin, "Depression Hits Jobless in UK, US More than in Germany," *Gallup*, November 21, 2012.

32   Erik Brynjolfsson and Andrew McAfee, *Race Against the Machine: How the Digital Revolution Is Accelerating Innovation, Driving Productivity, and Irreversibly Transforming Employment and the Economy* (Digital Frontier Press, 2012); Robert Skidelsky, "Racing the Machine," *Project Syndicate*, December 22, 2017; "Jobless Future." www.amazon.com/Rise-Robots-Technology-Threat-Jobless/dp/0465097537.

33   Carl Benedikt Frey and Michael Osborne, "The Future of Employment: How Susceptible Are Jobs to Computerisation?" *Technological Forecasting and Social Change* 114 (2017): 254–280.

34   Martin Feldstein, "Dealing with Long-Term Deficits," *American Economic Review: Papers & Proceedings* 106 (2016), 5: 35–38.

35   Martin Feldstein, "United States Economy: Where To from Here?" Paper presented at the American Economic Association's meeting in San Francisco, January 3, 2016; https://www.aeaweb.org/webcasts/2016/Economy.php @ 19minutes.

36   William Mitchell and Joan Muysken, *Full Employment Abandoned: Shifting Sands and Policy Failures* (Edward Elgar, 2008).

37   Roger Farmer, "The Natural Rate Hypothesis: An Idea Past Its Sell-By-Date," *Bank of England Quarterly Bulletin* 3 (2013): 244–256.

38   Theoretically, the natural rate is not a function of the interest rate.

39   The average inflation rate 2017–2020 was 2.1 percent, the Fed's target rate. St. Louis Fed, series CPI-AUCSL, CPALTT01USM657N

40   United Nations, "The Universal Declaration of Human Rights," adopted in 1948.

41   Yuval Rosenberg, "Forget GDP: The Radical Plans to Go Beyond Growth," *Fiscal Times*, April 5, 2012. This is also the message of the steady-state-economy movement. Herman Daly, *Steady-State Economics: The Economics of Biophysical Equilibrium and Moral Growth* (W.H. Freeman, 1978).

42   Mike Wallace interview: Erich Fromm, May 25, 1958.

43   Robert Skidelsky and Edward Skidelsky, *How Much Is Enough? Money and the Good Life* (Other Press, 2012).

44   Joseph Stiglitz, "GDP Fetishism," *Project Syndicate*, September 7, 2009. A fetish is an irrational reverence or obsessive devotion—a fixation—an almost superstitious belief in something like a totem pole, or in this case, the free market.

45   Gallup, "What Happiness Today Tells Us About the World Tomorrow," 2017.

46   Jason Hickel, *Less Is More: How Degrowth Will Save the World* (William Heinemann, 2020); Serge Latouche, *Farewell to Growth* (Polity Press, 2009); Lorenz Keyßer and Manfred Lenzen, "1.5 °C Degrowth Scenarios Suggest the Need for New Mitigation Pathways," *Nature Communications* 12 (2021), 2676.

47   Dietrich Vollrath, *Fully Grown: Why a Stagnant Economy Is a Sign of Success* (University of Chicago Press, 2019); Tim Jackson, *Prosperity without Growth: Foundations for the Economy of Tomorrow*, 2nd edn. (Routledge, 2016).

48   Dan Witters and Jim Harter, "Worry and Stress Fuel Record Drop in US Life Satisfaction," Gallup, May 8, 2020.

49   Peter Whybrow, "Dangerously Addictive: Why We Are Biologically Ill-Suited to the Riches of Modern America," *The Chronicle of Higher Education*, March 13, 2009.

50   John Helliwell et al., "World Happiness Report, 2012," p. 3. World Happiness Report.pdf (columbia.edu).

51 Betsey Stevenson and Justin Wolfers, "The Paradox of Declining Female Happiness," *American Economic Journal: Economic Policy* 1 (2009), 2: 190-225.

52 Tom Smith et al., "General Social Survey Final Report: Trends in Psychological Well-Being, 1972-2014," NORC, University of Chicago, 2015, Table 6.

53 Young-Hee Yoon et al., "Alcoholic Liver Disease in the US, 1999-2018," *American Journal of Preventive Medicine* 59 (2020), 4: 469-480.

54 Rosenbloom, "But Will It Make You Happy?" op. cit.

55 John Komlos, "Has Creative Destruction Become More Destructive?" *B.E. Journal of Economic Analysis and Policy* 16 (2016), 4: 1-12.

56 Joseph Schumpeter, *Capitalism, Socialism and Democracy* (Harper, 1942).

57 Fabio D'Orlando et al., *Economic Change and Wellbeing: The True Cost of Creative Destruction and Globalization* (Routledge, 2021).

58 Nicholas Kaldor, "Welfare Propositions in Economics and Interpersonal Comparisons of Utility," *The Economic Journal* 49 (1939), 195: 549-552; John Hicks, "The Foundations of Welfare Economics," *The Economic Journal* 49 (1939), 196: 696-712.

59 Vance Packard, *The Waste Makers* (David McKay, 1960).

60 "Paul Volcker: Think More Boldly," *The Wall Street Journal*, December 14, 2009; Thomas Philippon, "Has the US Finance Industry Become Less Efficient? On the Theory and Measurement of Financial Intermediation," *American Economic Review* 105 (2015), 4: 1408-1438.

61 Shane Greenstein, "The Economics of Digitization," NBER *Reporter* 2, July 2020.

62 David Teather, "Kodak Pulls Shutter Down on Its Past," *The Guardian*, January 22, 2014; Steven Pearlstein, "Review: 'The Second Machine Age,' by Erik Brynjolfsson and Anderew McAfee," *The Washington Post*, January 17, 2014.

63 Carl Frey, *The Technology Trap: Capital Labor, and Power in the Age of Automation* (Princeton University Press, 2019).

64 Patrick McGeehan, "They Risked Their Lives During Covid. They Still Don't Earn Minimum Wage," *The New York Times*, July 15, 2021.

65 Natalie Walters, "How Much Uber Is Worth after its Rough Year," *Business Insider*, December 13, 2017. www.businessinsider.com/how-much-uber-is-worth-after-its-rough-year-2017-12.

66 Lawrence Mishel, "Uber and the Labor Market," Economic Policy Institute, May 15, 2018.

67 Wikipedia, "Taxi Medallion."

68 Himanshu Gupta et al., "Patent Protection Strategies," *Journal of Pharmacy and Bioallied Sciences* 2 (2010), 1: 2-7.

69 Paul Heidhues et al., "Exploitative Innovation," *American Economic Journal: Microeconomics* 8 (2016), 1: 1-25.

70 The Statistics Portal. www.statista.com/.

71 Christopher Singleton, "Auto Industry Jobs in the 1980s: A Decade of Transition." www.bls.gov/opub/mlr/1992/02/art2full.pdf.

72 Glassdoor, www.glassdoor.com/Hourly-Pay/Amazon-Hourly-Pay-E6036.htm.

73 Joel Mokyr, "Riding the Technology Dragon," *Milken Institute Review* 2 (2014): 87-94.

74 David Cutler and Edward Glaeser, "When Innovation Goes Wrong: Technological Regress and the Opioid Epidemic," *Journal of Economic Perspectives* 35 (2021), 4: 171-196.

75 Moreover, the rise in the financial sector can hinder productivity growth in other sectors by attracting highly skilled employees at the expense of the other sectors. Stephen Cecchetti and Enisse Kharroubi, "Why Does Financial Sector Growth Crowd Out Real Economic Growth?" Bank of International Settlement, Working Papers no. 490, February 2015.

76 Kathleen Jamieson, *Cyberwar: How Russian Hackers and Trolls Helped Elect a President–What We Don't, Can't, and Do Know* (Oxford University Press, 2018).

77   Roger McNamee, *Zucked: Waking up to the Facebook Catastrophe* (Penguin Press, 2019); Rana Foroohar, *Don't Be Evil: How Big Tech Betrayed Its Founding Principles – and All of Us* (Currency, 2019).

78   Shoshana Zuboff, *The Age of Surveillance Capitalism: The Fight for a Human Future at the New Frontier of Power* (Public Affairs, 2019).

79   Matthew Rosenberg et al., "How Trump Consultants Exploited the Facebook Data of Millions," *The New York Times*, March 17, 2018.

80   Natalia Osipova and Aaron Byrd, "Inside Russia's Network of Bots and Trolls," *The New York Times*, November 1, 2017.

81   Alan Krueger, "The Rise and Consequences of Inequality in the United States," January 12, 2012; https://obamawhitehouse.archives.gov/sites/default/files/krueger_cap_speech_final_remarks.pdf.

82   Wikipedia, "The Rockefeller Family."

83   Michael Greenstone et al., "Thirteen Economic Facts about Social Mobility and the Role of Education," *Brookings Report*, June 26, 2013.

84   Board of Governors of the Federal Reserve System, "Report on the Economic Well-Being of US Households in 2019," May 2020, Table 2 and Figure 30; https://www.federalreserve.gov/publications/files/2019-report-economic-well-being-us-households-202005.pdf.

85   Miles Corak, "Income Inequality, Equality of Opportunity, and Intergenerational Mobility," *Journal of Economic Perspectives* 27 (2013), 3: 79-102.

86   Ibid., p. 91.

87   Greenstone et al., "Thirteen Economic Facts."

88   Wikipedia, "2019 College Admissions Bribery Scandal."

89   Adam Harris, "One Way to Stop College-Admissions Insanity: Admit More Students," *The Atlantic*, March 13, 2019; https://insider.foxnews.com/2019/03/12/alan-dershowitz-college-admissions-scam-involving-felicity-huffman-lori-loughlin.

90   Brian Arthur, *Complexity and the Economy* (Oxford University Press, 2014); John Blatt, *Dynamic Economic Systems* (Routledge, 1983); Ping Chen, *Economic Complexity and Equilibrium Illusion: Essays on Market Instability and Macro Vitality* (Routledge, 2010).

91   Brian Arthur, "Foundations of Complexity Economics," *Nature Reviews Physics* 3 (2021): 136-145; http://tuvalu.santafe.edu/~wbarthur/; Eric Beinhocker, *The Origin of Wealth: Evolution, Complexity, and the Radical Remaking of Economics* (Harvard Business School Press, 2006).

92   Arthur, "Foundations of Complexity Economics," op. cit.

93   Herman Daly, "Economics in a Full World," *Scientific American* 293 (2005), 3: 100-107. Wikipedia, "Global Warming."

94   Intergovernmental Panel on Climate Change, "IPCC Fourth Assessment Report: Climate Change 2007." IPCC – Intergovernmental Panel on Climate Change.

95   Laurence Kotlikoff, *Generational Accounting: Knowing Who Pays, and When, for What We Spend* (Free Press, 1992).

96   Paul Krugman, "Greed Is Bad," *The New York Times*, June 4, 2002.

97   Nicholas Georgescu-Roegen, *The Entropy Law and the Economic Process* (Harvard University Press, 1971); Barry Commoner, *Making Peace with the Planet* (Pantheon, 1990); Herman Daly, *Ecological Economics and Sustainable Development* (Edward Elgar, 2007); Jeffrey Sachs, *The Age of Sustainable Development* (Columbia University Press, 2015).

98   By some estimates, it is as high as $50 trillion a year. This is roughly the value of the world's total gross domestic product at the beginning of the twenty-first century. Paul Sutton et al., "The Real Wealth of Nations: Mapping and Monetizing the Human Ecological Footprint," *Ecological Indicators* 16 (2012): 11-22.

99   French President Emmanuel Macron in a speech to US Congress, April 25, 2018.

100 Diane Coyle, *The Economics of Enough: How to Run the Economy as if the Future Matters* (Princeton University Press, 2011).

101 Christopher Flavelle, "Climate Change Could Cut World Economy by $23tr in 2050, Insurance Giant Warns," *The New York Times*, April 22, 2021.

102 Benjamin Strauss et al., "Can You Guess What America Will Look Like in 10,000 Years?" *The New York Times*, April 20, 2018.

103 Emilio Moran, *People and Nature: An Introduction to Human Ecological Relations* (Blackwell, 2006).

104 However, Montgomery County, Maryland, Boulder, Colorado, and the San Francisco Bay Area have adopted tiny carbon taxes.

105 Martin Weitzman, "On Modeling and Interpreting the Economics of Catastrophic Climate Change," *Review of Economics and Statistics* 91 (2009), 1: 1-19.

106 Joseph Stiglitz, *Making Globalization Work* (Norton, 2006).

107 Simone D'Alessandro et al., "Feasible Alternatives to Green Growth," *Nature Sustainability* 3 (2020): 329-335.

108 Brad Plumer and Nadja Popovich, "How Global Warming Fueled Five Extreme Weather Events," *The New York Times*, December 14, 2017.

109 Kendra Pierre-Louis, "These Billion-Dollar Natural Disasters Set a US Record in 2017," *The New York Times*, January 8, 2018. National Oceanic and Atmospheric Administration; https://www.ncdc.noaa.gov/billions/summary-stats. Stiglitz said about Harvey's devastation of Houston: "It is ironic, of course, that an event so related to climate change would occur in a state that is home to so many climate-change deniers—and where the economy depends so heavily on the fossil fuels that drive global warming." Joseph Stiglitz, "Learning from Harvey," *Project Syndicate*, September 8, 2017.

110 Sandy had a diameter of 1,100 miles and devastated the US mid-Atlantic region. Wikipedia, "List of Natural Disasters in the United States."

111 Kenneth Boulding, "The Economics of the Coming Spaceship Earth," in Henry Jarrett (ed.), *Environmental Quality in a Growing Economy* (Resources for the Future, 1966); Philip O'Hara, "Political Economy of Climate Change, Ecological Destruction and Uneven Development," *Ecological Economics*, 69 (2009), 2: 223-234; Nicholas Stern, *Why Are We Waiting?: The Logic, Urgency, and Promise of Tackling Climate Change* (MIT Press, 2015).

112 Jennifer Medina et al., "Mudslides Strike Southern California, Leaving at Least 13 Dead," *The New York Times*, January 9, 2018.

113 Tornadoes alone in 2011 claimed the lives of 500. The Chicago heat wave of 1995 killed an amazing 739 people. Wikipedia, "List of Natural Disasters in the United States."

114 Wikipedia, "Deepwater Horizon Oil Spill," "List of Oil Spills."

115 Dan Witters, "Gulf Coast Residents Remain Worse Off Emotionally Post-Spill," *Gallup*, May 7, 2012.

116 Martin Weitzman, "On Modeling and Interpreting the Economics of Catastrophic Climate Change," *Review of Economics and Statistics* 91 (2009), 1: 1-19.

117 Petter Naess and Leigh Price (eds.), *Crisis System: A Critical Realist and Environmental Critique of Economics and the Economy* (Routledge, 2016).

118 Naomi Klein, *On Fire: The (Burning) Case for a Green New Deal* (Simon & Schuster, 2019); Jeremy Rifkin, *The Green New Deal: Why the Fossil Fuel Civilization Will Collapse by 2028, and the Bold Economic Plan to Save Life on Earth* (St. Martin's Press, 2019).

119 Miriam Aczel, "Confronting Climate Change," *Science* 366 (2019), 6462: 191.

120 Marilyn Waring, *If Women Counted: A New Feminist Economics* (Harper & Row, 1988); Drucilla Berker, et al., *Liberating Economics: Feminist Perspectives on Families, Work, and Globalization*, 2nd edn (University of Michigan Press, 2021).

121 Paula England, "The Separative Self: Androcentric Bias in Neoclassical Assumption," in Marianne Ferber and Julie Nelson (eds.), *Beyond Economic Man: Feminist Theory and Economics* (University of Chicago Press, 1993), pp. 37-53; here p. 37.

122 Ibid.

123   Nancy Folbre (ed.), *For Love Or Money: Care Provision in the United States* (Russell Sage Foundation, 2012).

124   Ian Macredie and Dale Sewell, "Statistics Canada's Measurement and Valuation of Unpaid Work," October 28, 1998.

125   Peter van de Ven et al., "Including Unpaid Household Activities: An Estimate of Its Impact on Macro-Economic Indicators in the G7 Economies and the Way Forward," OECD Working Paper no. 91, July 25, 2018 https://www.oecd.org/officialdocuments/publicdisplaydocumentpdf/?cote=SDD/DOC (2018)4&docLanguage=En.

12 Macroeconomics Part III

> When my information changes, I alter my conclusions. What do you do, sir?
> —John Maynard Keynes[1]

We continue the bird's-eye view of the economy by examining other macroeconomic variables such as taxes, national debt, and savings. We argue that taxes are essential, because they pay for public goods and basic research that the private sector does not supply. The government's role in the economy is further enhanced by its use of fiscal and monetary policy to influence aggregate demand and thus reduce the volatility of the business cycle and overcome crisis.

12.1 The Government Is an Integral Part of the Economy

The government ought not be expunged from economic theory because the economy does not function well without effective cooperation between government and the private sector. In Western Europe, with the highest standard of living, and in those economies that caught up with the West, i.e., South Korea, Taiwan, Hong Kong, Japan, and Singapore, the government has played a major role in their success. Governments not only spend and provide a safety net, but they also invest in infrastructure, education, basic research, limit opportunism, and build the institutional structure for the economy, which are all extremely important because they are the lifeblood of the economy.

In 2019, state, local, and federal governments in the US invested $740 billion; that is 17 percent of all investments.[2] US government expenditure was about 17 percent of GDP in 2019, the lowest share since 1950.[3] In developed economies it is as high as 40 percent to 50 percent. This explains why the US social and physical infrastructure has deteriorated. Of government expenditure of $3.7 trillion in 2019, $848 billion (23 percent) was for the military.

12.2 The Challenges of Keynesian Fiscal Policy

Keynesian *fiscal policy* is the "steering wheel" of the economy. Fiscal policy refers to changes in government expenditures and revenues designed to improve and stabilize economic performance and increase employment. However, fiscal policy should be *countercyclical*: expansionary in downturns and contractionary in upswings, i.e., the steering should be against the wind, implying that the goal is to smooth out the extreme ups and downs of the business cycle.

DOI: 10.4324/9781003174356-12

That way, government budgets could be balanced over the business cycle. Keynes did not want government debt to accumulate. It should borrow and spend during recessions or lower taxes, but it should reverse that policy by increasing taxes or by cutting government expenditures in good times. Alas, countercyclical fiscal policy to "fine tune" the economy proved impractical in practice, and US budget deficits became endemic beginning with the Reagan administration (Figure 12.1).

Deficit spending or cutting taxes during a recession is straightforward but reversing the policy to limit *aggregate demand* toward the peak of the business cycle turned out to be politically unmanageable at least in the US. Politicians would lose popularity and campaign contributions if they were increasing taxes or reducing expenditures to cool the economy. Yet, a handful of countries, including Germany, Italy, Sweden, Switzerland, and Spain bound themselves by enacting balanced-budget laws so that deficits would not accumulate.[4] (The 50 US states also cannot run deficits.)

Once Reagan and the Republican Party abandoned any semblance of balancing the budget, the deficits became endemic: in only three years under Clinton's Democratic administration did the budget see positive territory during the subsequent four decades. Total government debt at the beginning of Reagan's term was $965 billion; by the time he left, it had increased by $1,775 billion to reach $2,740 billion, tripling the debt; half of the increase went to the military. Public debt as a percentage of GDP doubled from 30 percent to 60 percent by the middle of Bush Sr.'s term (see Figure 12.1).

The flow of red ink became the new normal, regardless of the business cycle. That was definitely not what Keynes had in mind. This was one of the reasons why Friedrich Hayek and Milton Friedman were critical of Keynesian macroeconomics. They did not think that the political system was agile enough to fine tune the economy. Another challenge was that many mistook Keynesian theory as a prescription for economic growth. It wasn't. Keynes' theory was to overcome the glut of the Depression and thereby alleviate the worst shortcomings of capitalism. His prescription would make the economy overcome the doldrums, but budget deficits would not bring about long-run economic growth after the Depression was over. Rather, that would come from the usual sources: innovation, education, technical change, investments, capital

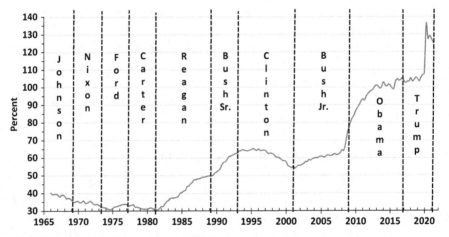

Figure 12.1 US national debt as percent of GDP
Source: St. Louis Fed, series GFDEGDQ188S.

accumulation, and public goods like basic research and infrastructure. Growth in the long run was not his immediate concern, as captured by his famous saying, "in the long run, we are all dead."[5] His focus was on shortening the breadlines; economic growth would come later.

12.3 Crowding Out Private Investment

Prior generations of economists believed that public borrowing increases the interest rate and thereby discourages—crowds out—private investment to some degree and is therefore counterproductive. However, this logic no longer holds in the twenty-first century with near-zero interest rates for extended periods. Government borrowing has had no effect on interest rates and thus does not impact private business investment. Moreover, the supply of savings available globally has been elastic due to the Asian *savings glut*. Hence, crowding out is no longer a serious threat.

The significant increase in the supply of global savings is due to the high savings rate in China, based on their large trade surpluses. Because their domestic economy is unable to absorb these savings immediately, a significant share of the funds flow back into the US financial sector, thereby increasing liquidity. Moreover, corporations, which used to borrow from banks in order to invest, no longer need to do so because they are flush with profits and have difficulty finding lucrative investments. That also adds to the savings glut. In 2021, Apple was sitting on $200 billion, Google on $137 billion, Microsoft on $132 billion, Amazon on $84 billion, and Facebook on $62 billion. Even a traditional company, like Ford Motors had $50 billion in the bank.[6] These funds are not reinvested into businesses that could provide decent jobs. That is how the US morphed into a dual economy.[7] So the concept of crowding out is no longer meaningful.

12.4 The Ominous US National Debt

The near-zero interest rates and strong liquidity do not mean that accumulating national debt is benign. At the end of 2021, the debt reached $29 trillion (123 percent of GDP) and 1/5 of all tax receipts was earmarked for interest payments on the debt: $504 billion, although interest rates were near historic lows (1.8 percent). Combined with military expenditures, interest payments made up more than half of total tax revenues.[8]

There are hidden dangers in this development because it is uncertain how long interest rates will remain low. If they were to increase substantially to historical norms, servicing the debt could become challenging. The US could always print dollars, so there is no danger of bankruptcy, but the question is how long can the government rely on the printing press before the threat of hyperinflation appears on the horizon?

Moreover, foreign holdings of the debt increased from $1 trillion in 2001 to $7.2 trillion, of which China holds $1.3 trillion.[9] The question arises, how long will it continue to lend the US money on favorable terms and finance our living beyond our means, especially since they are a rising power and want to expand their global influence? There is no way to know. However, dependence on an adversary is imprudent.[10] The deficit was $2.7 trillion in 2021 or 12 percent of GDP, down from a record high of $3.1 trillion in 2020.[11] The deficit for the next ten years is optimistically projected to be a cumulative $17 trillion.[12] Thus, balancing the budget or reducing the debt is illusory. Future generations will feel betrayed by the burdens they inherited and will likely want to pass them on to their descendants.

These factors call into question the sustainability of the current course of economic policy. How different would our situation be if we had invested the $1.5 trillion Trump tax cuts into education, infrastructure, renewable energy, or other public goods that foster economic growth and bear dividends? Or the Bush Jr. tax cuts of $1.8 trillion?[13] Then we would have more productive and a healthier labor force, more income and less debt and our response to the pandemic would have been more robust. Only Dr. Pangloss would think that the US can maintain the current lifestyle indefinitely.

Other countries are more prudent. Government debt as a percentage of GDP is smaller in Denmark (33 percent), Sweden (37 percent), New Zealand (38 percent), Australia (34 percent), Norway (37 percent), Switzerland (39 percent), and South Korea (41 percent).

12.5 Taxes Are Good for Us

Taxes are viewed with apprehension in mainstream economic canon. They supposedly "burden" the economy and create *"dead weight losses,"* that is, they are inefficient. Allegedly "taxing the rich is bad for economic growth." Textbooks reinforce this dogma by insisting that "Taxes adversely affect the allocation of resources: Taxes distort prices and thus the decisions of households and firms."[14] "Taxation subtracts from incomes, reduces private spending, and affects private saving. In addition, it affects investment and potential output."[15] In popular imagination taxes are seen as a diminution of freedom, a threat to "rugged individualism" that keeps people from reaching the "American Dream."

The advocates of the orthodoxy neglect that many countries manage to invest just fine without having a US-like abyss between rich and poor and, like Denmark, Finland, and Switzerland, have the happiest people in the world (see Figures 2.1, 7.16, and 11.3).[16] Moreover, they also ignore the inconvenient truth that "the most rapid gross-domestic-product growth achieved in the United States took place in the 1950s, 1960s and 1970s, when top tax rates were nearly twice as high as now" (Table 12.1).[17] And the effective corporate tax rate was 40 percent instead of the 12.7 percent in 2021.[18]

Politicians have to solve four conundrums about taxes: (1) how many government services to provide; the rich want less because they can afford to provide everything for themselves, while the poor rely on government services and transfer payment; (2) free riding is attractive as people justify their benefiting from government services without paying their fair share of

Table 12.1 There is no relationship between economic growth and the top tax rate

Years	Top marginal tax rates		GDP growth (%)
	On income (%)	On capital gains (%)	
1950s	90	25	2.50
1960s	80	25	3.10
1970s	70	35	2.20
1980s	48	24	2.20
1990s	37	28	2.00
21st Century	37	15	1.30

Note: The twenty-first century is 2000–2019; GDP growth is per capita.
Source: Thomas Hungerford, "Taxes and the Economy: An Economic Analysis of the Top Tax Rates Since 1945," Congressional Research Service, no. 7-5700, December 12, 2012; St. Louis Fed, series A939RX0Q048SBEA. Years 2013–2019: St. Louis Fed, series A053RC1Q027SBEA.

taxes; this is what Warren Buffett meant by saying "there's been class warfare going on for the last 20 years, and my class has won;"[19] (3) it becomes tempting to pay for government services by borrowing against the earnings of generations yet unborn (see Section 11.8); since they are unable to protect themselves, there is political pressure for government debt to grow; and (4) the distribution of the tax burden depends on political power (see Section 6.8).

Since income is distributed unequally, taxes should be progressive so that the utility of after-tax income across households is ethically acceptable. The declining marginal utility of income implies that tax rates should increase with income, a formidable task if the upper crust has more political clout. US tax-rates cease to be progressive near the top of the income distribution. Those who earn $674,000 per annum pay a higher rate (26.0 percent) than those who earn $29.8 million (24.8 percent) (see Table 7.4). Social security taxes are also not progressive because incomes above $142,800 are exempt.

The combined income of 1.1 percent of US taxpayers, 1.6 million households, was $2.5 trillion in 2018 (see Table 7.4). They paid 25.3 percent in taxes, leaving them a disposable income of $1.2 million per taxpayer. Krugman suggested: "It wouldn't be hard to devise taxes that would raise a significant amount of revenue from those super-high-income individuals."[20] The government could easily collect an additional few hundred billion dollars from this privileged group without excessively pinching their ostentatious habits.

Furthermore, pre-tax corporate profits reached $3.0 trillion, on which they paid $272 billion in taxes (in 2021).[21] So their effective tax rate was merely 9.1 percent, near an all-time low, and a substantial decline from the 40 percent rate in the 1950s (see Figure 6.5). The last thing the economy needed was to lower corporate taxes, increase inequality, and burden the budget deficit further.

The tax cuts of 2017 were projected to increase the national debt to 150 percent of GDP by 2047.[22] The debt will be much larger than that. The actual deficits caused by the Reagan tax cuts of 1981 were 29 percent greater than projections, and those caused by the Bush Jr. tax cuts were 8.8 percent higher.[23] In sum, the mainstream's treatment of taxes as burdensome destabilized the US economy and society.

12.6 Trickle-Down Economics Is Bogus

Depriving the government of revenue by slashing taxes is an extremist strategy known as "starving the beast"; it came into vogue under Reagan.[24] He set the tone of his administration by infamously declaring in his inaugural address that "government is not the solution to our problem; government is the problem." The ideology was to give money to the ultra-rich, who will invest it, create jobs, raise wages, and the benefits will trickle down to the rest of the society.[25]

Trickle-down economics or supply-side economics is not based on formal economic theory or on empirical evidence. No wonder it didn't work. Investments as a share of GDP were 13.6 percent under Carter and remained at exactly that level under Reagan despite two tax cuts (1981 and 1986) and despite giving millionaires an immense annual windfall of $404,000 (by 1985) (Figure 12.2 and Table 12.2).[26] And the benefits to the rest of the society trickled like molasses: actually, the rich kept it all (see Figures 7.10–7.13, 12.6).

The tax cuts failed to stimulate investments because the rich spent the windfall on ostentatious consumption, on overseas investments, or on political campaigns instead of creating US jobs.[27] Besides, Warren Buffett, the legendary investor with assets worth $100 billion, concurred: he knows no one who makes investment decisions on the basis of the tax rate.[28] Conventional

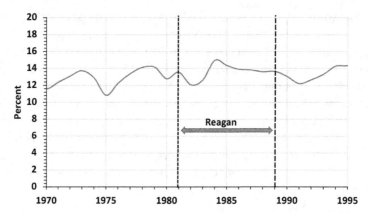

Figure 12.2 Investments as a percent of GDP and the Reagan tax cuts
Source: St. Louis Fed, series GPDICA, GDPC1.

Table 12.2 Tax savings in 1985 compared to 1980

Income bracket (thousands of 1985 dollars)	Average gross income	Tax rate (%)			Percent of 1980 tax rate	Tax savings in dollars	
		1980	1985	Difference		1980	1985
9-10	9	7.0	5.0	-2.1	-29.6	-187	-431
20-25	22	17.3	10.2	-7.2	-41.5	-1611	-3700
200-500	290	39.2	31.9	-7.3	-18.7	-21276	-49000
500-1000	670	43.4	36.0	-7.4	-17.0	-49456	-114000
>1 million	2316	46.7	39.2	-7.6	-16.2	-175861	-404000

Note: Thousands of dollars unless otherwise noted; CPI-U-RS is used for the final column; only a few tax brackets are shown for clarity.
Sources: https://www.irs.gov/statistics/soi-tax-stats-archive-1954-to-1999-individual-income-tax-return-reports; https://www.bls.gov/cpi/research-series/r-cpi-u-rs-home.htm.

theories overlooked that investments depended not only on the available funds, but also on *available domestic opportunities* offering decent profits; in the absence of such opportunities, the money would go abroad instead of trickling down in the US. So, Reaganomics failed to produce an economic miracle as hyped. Instead, GDP growth was unspectacular compared to the 1970s or the 1990s (Figure 12.3). After the recovery from the recession, GDP returned to potential GDP, but did not outperform prior recessions and failed to meet expectations (Figure 12.4). Stiglitz noted: "Lower [tax] rates have done nothing for growth."[29] Lack of evidence notwithstanding, the theory is still stuck in textbooks, the media, and in public consciousness that lower tax rates promote economic growth.[30]

Another misconception of supply-side theory is that lowering tax rates increases government revenue. Krugman calls it "old voodoo economics—the belief, refuted by study after study, that tax cuts pay for themselves."[31] This is the infamous Laffer curve.[32] Even Feldstein, a conservative supporter of tax cuts, was skeptical.[33] In reality, the income tax rate could be as high as 70 percent without having a negative effect on either revenue or output. In addition, the consumption tax-revenue curve does not have a peak at all.[34] That means that reducing tax rates increases government deficits. After Reagan decreased taxes, government revenue declined from 12 percent of GDP to 10 percent and deficits skyrocketed to $1 trillion per annum in 2020 dollars (Figure 12.5). Inequality also rose substantially: "The share of income accruing to the top

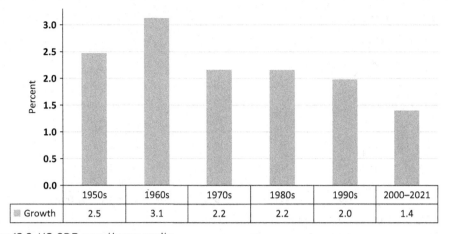

Figure 12.3 US GDP growth per capita
Note: Growth rates are the averages of annual growth rates.

	1950s	1960s	1970s	1980s	1990s	2000–2021
▨ Growth	2.5	3.1	2.2	2.2	2.0	1.4

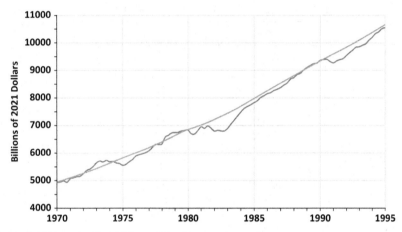

Figure 12.4 US GDP: potential GDP, and the Reagan tax cuts
Source: St. Louis Fed, series GDPC1, GDPPOT.

0.1 percent of US families increased from 4.2 percent in 1945 to 12.3 percent by 2007."[35] No won-der: with an annual windfall of $400,000, it was child's play to increase wealth with compound interest (see Table 12.2).

The textbook treatment of taxes is hopelessly biased because it fails to acknowledge that taxes finance productive investments on health, human capital, basic research, and infrastruc-ture that promote economic growth. It fails to acknowledge that higher tax rate on millionaires lowers the pursuit of rent seeking and improves efficiency through that pathway also.[36]

Hence, people in high-tax countries with a robust safety net are the happiest in the world (see Figure 7.16).[37] The reason is that they have less anguish about their future, they do not worry about paying for their children's schooling, or their medical bills, crime, unemployment, retire-ment, or other unpredictable events in their lives. In short, they live in a low-pressure economy (see Section 2.2). In fact, those nations whose populations are happier than those of the US all have higher tax rates, all have universal health coverage, and free college education, thereby shielding their citizens from many unnecessary stresses (Table 12.3).[38]

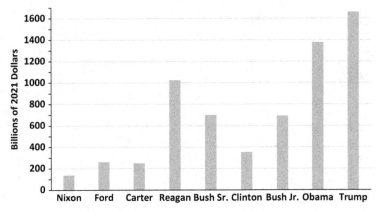

Figure 12.5 Average annual US federal government budget deficits
Note: The deficits are in 2020 prices.
Source: St. Louis Fed, series GFDEBTN and CPIAUCSL.

Table 12.3 Happiness rank and average tax rates

Rank	Country	Tax rate (%)
1	Norway	38.0
2	Denmark	45.9
3	Iceland	36.4
4	Switzerland	27.8
5	Finland	44.1
6	The Netherlands	38.8
7	Canada	31.7
8	New Zealand	32.1
9	Australia	28.2
10	Sweden	44.1
11	Israel	31.2
12	Costa Rica	n.a.
13	Austria	42.7
14	US	26.0

Note: Tax rates are federal government revenue as a percentage of GDP.
Sources: United Nations, *World Happiness Report*, 2017, p. 20; OECD Revenue Statistics; http://stats.oecd.org/Index.aspx?DataSetCode=REV.

Today's knowledge economy owes its very existence to investments that were initially financed by taxes. Taxes paid for the basic research for the internet, for rocket science—making satellite communication possible, and for biotechnology that revolutionized medicine—including the Covid vaccine based on messenger RNA technology. Some 4.2 billion people use the internet.[39] This would have been impossible without government investments. So, taxes do not subtract from income, as claimed by the mainstream. Instead, they contributed an immense amount to technological change and laid the foundations of long-run economic growth. So, taxes grow the economy through investment, support domestic tranquility, and lower the anxiety level of the population. These are crucial roles of taxes that are missing from blackboard economics.

Low tax rates are one reason for the anemic growth of the US economy, because "starving the beast" led to the neglect of education, basic research, and the health of the workforce.

Low taxes also meant the neglect of infrastructure the economy desperately needed. A collapsing bridge in Minneapolis killed 13 and injured 145 (2007).[40] Some 200,000 people were evacuated when the Oroville Dam, California, failed (2017). Texas power grid failure left millions without electricity. The Society of Civil Engineers gives the US infrastructure a grade of C-.[41] Transit was rated the lowest with a grade of D-; dams, levees, roads, stormwater D; aviation, hazardous waste, inland waterways, public parks, schools, wastewater D+; drinking water, energy, C-; bridges C; solid waste C+; ports B-, and rail B. None was rated A. They all need upgrading, maintenance, and expansion. In 2021, $1.2 trillion was allocated to infrastructure although the backlog is valued at $3 trillion.[42] This decades-long neglect will continue to be a major drag on the economy and on the welfare of future generations.

The inadequate investments in human capital and social safety net leads to high crime rates and fosters the school-to-prison pipeline (see Section 2.3). This leads to a staggeringly inefficient waste of human resources. Higher taxes would lower income redistribution through crime (and lower insurance costs), thereby enhancing social capital, trust, and cooperation, all of which lower transaction costs and increase life satisfaction.[43] The net burden of crime in the US exceeds $1 trillion, $4,000 per capita.[44]

Higher tax rates have not hurt the European economies.[45] The reason is that the super-rich's labor supply is inelastic and do not respond to higher taxes, while the social spending supported by high taxes increases the productivity of lower income groups by providing universal education, and universal health care that lowers stress. Europeans work less, live longer, have longer vacations, and live less harried lives; they are subject to less uncertainty and less criminality; they have fewer slums and fewer dysfunctional schools and eliminate the need for high levels of indebtedness among college graduates. European students enter the labor force with zero debt, while recent US graduates have $30,000 outstanding when they receive their diploma. Total student debt reached an unprecedented $1.7 trillion in 2021.[46] This is not only immoral, but also poses problems for the economy since the indebtedness lowers aggregate demand. Thus, high taxes in Europe are efficient at improving the quality of life of its citizens.

12.7 The Scarcity of Savings

Savings are important for economic development and for stability as they provide a cushion for the need for unexpected expenditures of households, firms, and governments. Economic life becomes more volatile without that cushion. Yet, their importance is inadequately appreciated because it is inimical to corporate interests. Businesses want people to spend now, thereby increasing sales and profits. No wonder there are few advertisements promoting frugality. "A penny saved is a penny earned" is no longer a US cultural norm. According to standard theory, savings is a normal good that should increase with income.[47] However, the facts contradict this proposition: the savings rate declined from 13.5 percent of disposable personal income in 1971 to a low of 3.4 percent in 2007, despite substantial increases in income (Table 12.4).[48] It also contradicts the tenets of Reaganomics, according to which the decline in the tax rate should have encouraged savings. Yet, the precipitous decline in savings began right after Reagan's tax cuts and continued unabated until the financial crisis. Thus, it coincided with the tax cuts-induced rise in inequality and a long period of stagnating wages (see Figures 7.3-7.5, 7.10-7.13). While this is an anomaly in conventional economics, it is understood easily in terms of the trends in relative incomes, as the middle class tried to keep up with the consumption habits of the affluent, whose income was rapidly increasing, while those of the rest of the society was lagging behind

Table 12.4 Personal savings as a percentage of disposable income

Date	(%)
1950s	10.6
1960s	11.2
1970s	12.2
1980s	9.9
1990s	7.3
2000s	4.6
2010s	7.2
2020	16.6
2021	12.3

Source: St. Louis Fed, series A072RC1A156NBEA.

Table 12.5 Financial insecurity in the US, 2019

Inability to pay for	Percent	Millions
Unexpected expense of $400	37	94
Current month's bills	16	41
Medical care, doctor or dentist during year	25	64
Medical debt in household	18	46
Other indicators		
No retirement savings (non-retirees)	25	50
Do not have 3-month savings cushion	47	120

Note: Percent refers to the share of the adult population of 255 million except for non-retirees whose number is 200 million.
Source: Board of Governors of the Federal Reserve System, "Report on the Economic Well-Being of US Households in 2019," May 2020; https://www.federalreserve.gov/publications/files/2019-report-economic-well-being-us-households-202005.pdf.

(see Section 7.14). The only way to keep up with the social norms was to decrease savings and reach for a credit card. The mainstream disregards that savings is a non-positional good—savings account balances are not common knowledge in the way status goods are.

Self-control—the ability to delay gratification—is a crucial precondition for saving and for a successful life. It was confirmed by the "Marshmallow Experiment": toddlers had a marshmallow placed in front of them and were told that they could eat it but if they waited 15 minutes, they could eat two marshmallows. The startling finding was that those children who resisted the temptation of immediate gratification grew up to have significantly higher SAT scores, educational attainment, and income.[49] Persons not in control of their passions lose control of their destiny. People who do not save have to face the challenges of the business cycle unprepared.

However, throughout their life, consumers are inundated with advertisements that hype the wonders of consumption. Thus, the puritan ethic of frugality morphed into the post-modern consumer society.[50] Instant gratification became part of the dominant culture but not by popular choice. Instead, this world-view was imposed upon the society by Madison Avenue, Wall Street, Hollywood, and Silicon Valley (see Section 3.2). That is how the US became an indebted nation, both private and public; that is how the obesity epidemic spread, and why the savings rate declined. All point to the diminution of the ability to control our appetite and greed, leading to precarious lives with financial insecurity. Consequently, 94 million people would not be able to pay out of pocket for an unexpected expense of $400 (Table 12.5).

Extremists argue that the decline in the saving rate was caused by the introduction of Social Security in 1935 which provided a small amount of financial security for retired people. However, the trend in savings does not support this claim since the saving rate rose from 10.6 percent to 12.2 percent well after the enactment of this social safety net (see Table 12.4). The rate began to decrease only in 1985. Reaganomics had many unforeseen and unintended negative consequences: the decline in the saving rate was one of them.

Saving is disparaged also because of the paradox of thrift. In the standard Keynesian short-run models, an increase in savings implies that consumers spend less, thereby lowering aggregate demand, GDP, and increasing unemployment. Thus, politicians and corporations are wary of increased savings as a damper on growth, government revenue, and corporate profits. Obviously, this is a short-run view. Nevertheless, over time, savings are a crucial shock absorber against unanticipated downturns. But the anti-saving narrative fits well with the focus on the short run in an instant-gratification society.

12.8 Wealth: the "Poor Ain't Got None"

Wealth is the accumulation of savings net of debt. Understandably, wealth is far more unevenly distributed than income, because the poor are unable to save from their meagre income while the savings of the rich accumulate and grow exponentially over time and are inherited by subsequent generations (see Table 12.5).[51] The poor have negative wealth, i.e., their debt exceeds the value of their assets and belongings, including their furniture and other durables. The lowest 10 percent of households in the wealth distribution has an average net wealth of -$5,700 while the top 10 percent has $1,200,000.[52] Single females under the age of 35 are among the poorest, having net wealth of $1,300 and that includes their refrigerator and car.[53] Those who rent their dwelling, instead of owning it, have a net wealth of $3,000. They do not have much skin in the game either. Half of the US population has negligible wealth that actually declined by $4,000 to $29,000 by 2019 (see Figure 12.6 and Table 12.6, row 1, column 3). The reason for this value's relative constancy is that household durables are included in wealth, and the infrastructure of a typical household did not change substantially during this time span. All households in the US need some furniture, car(s), refrigerator, cell phone, and so forth. So, the data imply that half the population owns nothing beyond the basics necessities of life in a modern economy. The 50-90

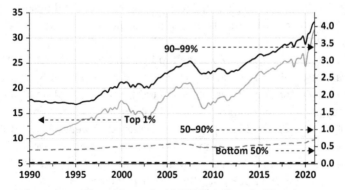

Figure 12.6 Trends in real wealth per household, 2020 dollars (millions)
Source: https://www.federalreserve.gov/releases/z1/dataviz/dfa/distribute/table/; St. Louis Fed, series CPIAUCSL.
Source: St. Louis Fed, series A939RX0Q048SBEA.

Table 12.6 Wealth distribution in the US, 1990 and 2019

Stratum (%)	Per household within the respective group					Group's share in total		
	1	2	3	4	5	6	7	8
	2020 dollars (millions)			%	Annual		%	
	1990	2019	Gain	Gain	growth %	1990	2019	Change
Bottom 50	0.033	0.029	-0.004	-11.9	-0.44	3.7	1.7	-1.9
50-90	0.4	0.61	0.21	51.7	1.45	35.9	28.9	-7.1
90-99	1.82	3.63	1.81	99.3	2.41	37.0	38.6	1.6
Top 1	10.6	26.11	15.51	146.3	3.16	23.4	30.8	7.5

Source: https://www.federalreserve.gov/releases/z1/dataviz/dfa/distribute/table/; St. Louis Fed, series CPIAUCSL.

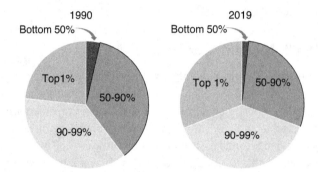

Figure 12.7 Wealth distribution in the US, 1990 and 2019.
Source: https://www.federalreserve.gov/releases/z1/dataviz/dfa/distribute/table/; St. Louis Fed, series CPIAUCSL.

percentile fared better, reaching a peak wealth of $570,000 in 2006 and took this 40 percent of the population ten years to recover their losses from the financial crisis (Figure 12.6). However, the group's share of wealth declined by 7.1 percentage points during this period as a concomitant of the hollowing out of the middle class (Figure 12.7).[54]

In contrast, those in the 90-99 percent doubled their wealth at an annual rate of 2.4 percent (see Table 12.6, columns 4 and 5). The top 1 percent did astoundingly well. Their wealth grew at an annual rate of 3.2 percent to reach $26.1 million per household by 2019 (see Table 12.6, columns 2 and 5). Also notable is that their wealth accumulation accelerated during the Covid pandemic (Figure 12.7).

It is breathtaking to think that in 2019 the top 1 percent (or 1.3 million) of households own more wealth than the combined wealth of 90 percent (115.2 million) of US households. The data also expose how much the top 10 percent benefited from the Covid pandemic bailouts. The wealth of the top 1 percent households rose by $5 million and the next 9 percent by $430,000, whereas the bottom 50 percent of the population increased its wealth by $8,700.

Given asset inflation caused by the Fed's asset purchases, the perceived wealth of individuals exceeded the actual wealth of the economy. This is pseudo-wealth. The Fed injected $3.6 trillion into the economy between 2008 and 2015 and then another $3 trillion in just three months between March and May 2020.[55] During the following year it injected $17 billion weekly for another trillion dollars. During that year, the S&P 500 stock price index doubled from 2,200 to 4,300, creating an immense amount of pseudo-wealth (see Figure 17.8).[56] This is the essence of asset inflation.

12.9 Inflation and Deflation

Inflation is harmful because it devalues savings and incomes and is therefore an invisible tax. By reducing the incentive to save, it also lowers the savings rate. In addition, it makes it difficult to keep track of all the changes in relative prices, because not all prices increase at the same rate. Deflation is the opposite of inflation and is also bad for the economy (see Section 10.1). The control of the price level is one of the two mandates of the Federal Reserve (the other is to reduce unemployment).

The Fed has an *arbitrary* target inflation rate of 2 percent. In their judgment that is the "most consistent with their mandate for price stability and maximum employment."[57] It is clear why the Fed would want to avoid deflation, but that does not explain why the 2 percent rate is better than a 0.5 percent or 1 percent rate. The Fed struggled to reach the 2 percent target after the financial crisis although it squeezed $3.6 trillion into the economy, more than it had done during the previous 94 years of its existence.[58] The stock of money (M1) took 20 years to double, reaching $1.4 trillion in 2008, but then it doubled again in six years.

Reasons for the low inflation during the financial crisis bailouts despite the unprecedented money creation were:

1. Most of the money stayed in Wall Street, creating asset inflation, which is not part of the consumer price index.
2. The money did not reach Main Street, so it did not increase aggregate demand.
3. The banks found it lucrative to deposit their money with the Fed in reserves, because they received risk-free interest on their deposits. Until 2015, the interest rate was a meagre 0.25 percent, but by 2018 the rate had increased to 1.5 percent. Given that in early 2018 the commercial banks still had $2.2 trillion on deposit with the Fed, they gained $33 billion of easy profits without having to do anything for it.[59] That was certainly easier than financing factories. During Covid the Fed lowered the required reserves to zero, thereby ending the distinction between excess and required reserves.
4. Hyperglobalization implied that many products were supplied perfectly elastically pre-Covid. If demand rose for a product before hyperglobalization became paramount in the twenty-first century, firms experienced labor-supply and raw material constraints if they wanted to expand production substantially. They had to raise wages and prices in order to find more workers. This was no longer the case pre-Covid. With the integration of global markets, billions of workers could produce to satisfy US consumers' demand. Consequently, the supply of goods could be increased without increasing the retail price (see Section 6.4). Nonetheless, the Fed was finally able to reach its inflation target in 2017: prices rose by 2.1 percent.

A caveat is in order since during the Covid-19 bailouts inflation rate began to accelerate from an annual rate of 1.7 percent in February 2021 and reached 7.9 percent in February 2022.[60] This is due to the fact that, in contrast to the 2008 crisis, some bailout money actually reached individuals. While money supply increased by 19 percent between the end of 2019 to 2020 (Q2), production was down by 10.3 percent (see Figure 17.6).[61] By January 2022, the money supply had more than doubled while output was up by merely 2.1 percent! So, it became a classic case of far too much money chasing too few goods especially since the pandemic led to substantial bottlenecks in production. Furthermore, once inflation began, it gained its own momentum, because expectations play the role of a self-fulfilling prophecy (see Figure 4.12). Expectations finally gave producers a window of opportunity to raise prices. Russia's invasion of Ukraine interrupted the flow of international trade fueling inflation further.

12.10 The New Wave of Industrial Policy

The essence of humanistic economics is that markets are a necessary but by themselves insufficient instrument to achieve a thriving society. In contrast, market fundamentalism or neoliberalism, advocated by Milton Friedman and Friedrich Hayek, and put into practice by Reaganomics and Thatcherism, as embodied in the "Washington Consensus," has been soundly rejected throughout the world, because it fostered immense social, economic, political, and environmental instability.[62] In contrast, the "Beijing Consensus" is based on the Chinese economic miracle of gradual structural change and cautious, experimental industrial policy coupled with protectionism in defense of national interests.[63] Its eightfold increase in GDP forged the world's largest manufacturing sector and has led to renewed interest in proactive industrial policy.[64]

In 2004, China's industrial production was just 40 percent of that of the US and 60 percent of that of Japan.[65] By 2010, it had caught up to the US and was 60 percent ahead of Japan. Such spectacular catch-up growth, following a disciplined strategy of export-led industrial development obviously called into question the market-friendly policies of the IMF and the World Bank. Technology transfer to the geopolitical rival is also concerning, as is the fear of falling behind technologically.[66]

The German version of capitalism, the social-market economy, is a less extreme form of capitalism than the one formulated in the Washington Consensus. German economists realized after World War II that the market's coordination mechanism needed to be supplanted by administrative oversight, because government institutions are better capable of seeing the interlinkages among the subordinate segments of the economy than the individual participants.[67] Moreover, they are able to formulate longer-term policies considering the needs of future generations in mind and better able to keep the common weal in mind than decentralized markets that tend to be myopic and disregard many important aspects of production, including the environment and generations yet unborn. German economists did believe in the invisible hand, but not unconditionally. They saw the need to confirm that it was serving also the public interest, not only private ones.

So, the German government adopted smart industrial policy to maintain its manufacturing base without being overbearing. It exports half of GDP and has a positive trade balance of 7.5 percent of GDP.[68] The fact that local stakeholders sit on the board of major corporations reflects the philosophy of its version of capitalism called the *social-market economy*. Thus, the Minister-President of the State of Lower Saxony has a seat on the board of directors, as does a representative of the state's Ministry of Economic Affairs (with a doctorate in economics and social sciences), and *seven* union representatives sit on Volkswagen's supervisory board. That means that the wider implications of the firm's decisions are considered at crucial junctures. Germany has the largest manufacturing output after China and the United States, on a par with all of Latin America.[69] Its industrial output was still 22 percent of GDP in 2019, while in the US it has declined to 11 percent.[70]

Germany's comparative advantage is based entirely on the close cooperation between government and industry in funding an apprenticeship program without which the specialization on high-quality products like machinery and automobiles would be untenable. As an automotive executive put it: "Training costs money; not to train costs a great deal more money." Because of such an attitude, Germany probably has the best-educated industrial workforce in the world and many "regard themselves as serious professionals with a stake in their company and are usually treated as such."[71]

Stiglitz recognizes that governments have played a crucial role in economic development.[72] Clearly, new industrial policy will continue to be on the agenda. It should be formulated to overcome market failure with society's welfare in mind. These include forging long-range plans, educating the workforce, easing the transition to a renewable-energy economy, reducing the pains of globalization and of disruptive technologies, subsidizing industries to foster increasing returns to scale and to take advantage of learning-by-doing, overseeing markets so that competition is maintained and startups are not gobbled up by big tech, and national security is taken into consideration. Spatially concentrated policies are also needed for regions hurt by globalization: "subsidizing employment in such places could reduce the rate of not working ... plausibly reduce suffering and materially improve economic performance."[73] Such policies would generate *network externalities* whereby the benefits depend on the number of firms already in existence at a location. This can lower transaction and information costs and thereby induce positive externalities that lead to conglomeration of new firms. Such policies would become a *magnification mechanism* leading to renewed prosperity. These policies should not be used for political purposes or for protectionist strategies to prop up antiquated sectors. However, antiquated sectors should be phased out at such a rate that the workers released can find employment in other sectors of the economy.

12.11 Takeaways

Ever since the influence of Keynesian ideas, governments have used fiscal and monetary policy to smooth out aggregate demand over the business cycle. However, Keynesian policies were too difficult to formulate because it was easy to spend during recessions but politically nearly impossible to cut back on spending at the peaks of business cycles. In the US, it became easier to finance current expenditures by passing the burden of debt on to future generations. Thus, fiscal policy was not practiced countercyclically as Keynes suggested and led to endemic government deficits.

Larry Summers dubbed the slowdown in economic growth as secular stagnation. In the first 21 years of the twenty-first century real per-capita growth has been 1/3 slower than during the final decades of the twentieth century. The US economy faces the headwinds of a slow-down in innovation, slower productivity growth, deteriorating infrastructure, global warming, mediocre educational attainment, student debt, financial instability, income concentration, and a large trade deficit that exports jobs. Summers concludes that "the economy as currently structured is not capable of achieving satisfactory growth and stable financial conditions simultaneously."

Questions for Discussion

1. How efficient would the economy be without government regulation and oversight?
2. Imagine the economy today without the internet.
3. Has your family benefited from government transfers/subsidies/expenditures?
4. Why are both inflation and deflation bad for the economy?
5. Was the Federal Reserve's Quantitative Easing program successful?
6. Why have foreigners continued to buy US government securities despite the low interest rate?
7. What are some differences between Keynesians and their opponents, the real business-cycle school of macroeconomists?

8. Do you think workers are interested mostly in their nominal or real income?
9. Do you think that lowering taxes increases the quality of life?
10. Do you think that subsidizing savings would be desirable?
11. Do you think that "keeping up with the Joneses" was mainly responsible for the increase in indebtedness of US consumers?
12. Has anyone suggested that you save for a rainy day?
13. Have you seen any advertisements urging people to save? Why do you suppose?
14. Discuss: saving is no longer important because so much money is available for the US from China and Japan. They can do our saving for us.
15. How much debt do you or your family have? Savings?
16. Can you think of advertisements that encourage instant gratification?
17. How could one incentivize Americans to save more and spend less?
18. Are taxes bad for the economy?
19. Do you agree with Warren Buffett that millionaires should pay higher taxes?
20. Name some important items you use that were subsidized by taxes.
21. Do you think it is fair that a few people are able to capture a large portion of the income generated by the economy?
22. Do you think that millionaires are job creators?
23. Do you think that "starving the beast" is an unethical goal?
24. Do you think that we should adopt a balanced budget amendment?

Notes

1 Reply to a criticism that he changed his position on monetary policy, as quoted in Paul Samuelson, "The Keynes Centenary," *The Economist* 287 (1983): 19.
2 St. Louis Fed, Table 1.1.5, "Gross Domestic Product." https://fred.stlouisfed.org/release/tables?rid=53&eid=41047; Table 3.1 Government Current Receipts and Expenditures, line 39; www.bea.gov/iTable/iTable.cfm?reqid=19&step=2#reqid=19&step=3&isuri=1&1921=survey&1903=86.
3 St. Louis Fed, series A822RE1A156NBEA.
4 In those countries the budget must be balanced over the business cycle. Wikipedia, "Balanced Budget Amendment."
5 Robert Skidelsky, *Keynes: The Return of the Master* (Allen Lane, 2009), p. 79.
6 Laurie Meisler, "The 50 Largest Stashes of Cash Companies Keep Overseas," *Bloomberg*, June 13, 2017; https://www.yahoo.com/now/15-companies-most-cash-reserves-182708211.html.
7 Peter Temin, *The Vanishing Middle Class: Prejudice and Power in a Dual Economy* (MIT Press, 2017).
8 Drew Desilver, "5 Facts About the National Debt," Pew Research Center, August 17, 2017.
9 St. Louis Fed, series FDHBFIN, GFDEBTN.
10 Congressional Budget Office, "Federal Debt and the Risk of Fiscal Crisis," July 27, 2010.
11 St. Louis Fed, series FYFSD.
12 Congressional Budget Office, "An Update to the Budget and Economic Outlook: 2021 to 2031," July 2021; https://www.cbo.gov/publication/57339.
13 How much have we benefited from the 47,000 mile-long Eisenhower Interstate Highway System that cost $425 billion (2006 dollars)? Wikipedia, "Interstate Highway System."
14 Gregory Mankiw, *Principles of Economics*, 8th edn. (Cengage, 2018), p. 9.
15 Paul Samuelson and William Nordhaus, *Economics*, 19th edn. (McGraw-Hill/Irwin, 2009), p. 376.
16 Patrick Kingsley, "It's Cold, Dark, and Lacks Parking. But Is This Finnish Town The World's Happiest?" *The New York Times*, December 24, 2018.

17   Lawrence Summers, "The Trump Administration's Tax Plan Is an Atrocity," *The Washington Post*, October 8, 2017.

18   St. Louis Fed, series series/A053RC1Q027SBEA#0 and CP.

19   Greg Sargent, "There's Been Class Warfare for the Last 20 years, and My Class Has Won," *The Washington Post*, September 30, 2011; Warren Buffett, "Stop Coddling the Super-Rich," *The New York Times*, August 14, 2011; Emmanuel Saez and Gabriel Zucman, *The Triumph of Injustice: How the Rich Dodge Taxes and How to Make Them Pay* (W.W. Norton, 2019); Bill Gates supported a Washington State measure to "create a 5 percent tax rate on annual income exceeding $200,000." Some 130 millionaires signed a petition asking Congress to raise their taxes including Nouriel Roubini; "Patriotic Millionaires for Fiscal Strength," https://patrioticmillionaires.org/.

20   Paul Krugman, "Things to Tax," *The New York Times*, November 27, 2011.

21   St. Louis Fed, series A053RC1Q027SBEA; FCTAX.

22   Congressional Budget Office, "The 2017 Long-Term Budget Outlook," March 2017. www.cbo.gov/system/files/115th-congress-2017-2018/reports/52480-ltbo.pdf.

23   Nick Timiraos and Youjin Shin, "How Tax Cuts Affect Revenue," *The Wall Street Journal*, December 21, 2017.

24   "Beast" refers pejoratively to the US government. The strategy assumes that the increased deficits will put downward pressure on expenditures; it was first articulated by Alan Greenspan but the name originated in the Reagan administration. The strategy was pernicious because it ignored that vested interests would resist lowering expenditures, thereby leading to persistent government deficits as the road of least resistance. Bruce Bartlett, "Tax Cuts and 'Starving the Beast': The Most Pernicious Fiscal Doctrine in History," *Forbes*, May 7, 2012.

25   Also dubbed the horse-and-swallow theory: "If you feed the horse enough oats, some will pass through to the road for the sparrows." John Galbraith, "Recession Economics," *The New York Review of Books*, February 4, 1982.

26   The top tax rate was lowered in 1981 to 50 percent and in 1986 to 38.5 percent.

27   Danny Yagan, "Capital Tax Reform and the Real Economy: The Effects of the 2003 Dividend Tax Cut," *American Economic Review* 105 (2015), 12: 3531-3563.

28   Laura Saunders and Siobhan Hughes, "Buffett Builds His Tax-the-Rich Case," *The Wall Street Journal*, October 13, 2011.

29   Joseph Stiglitz, *Rewriting the Rules of the American Economy: An Agenda for Growth and Shared Prosperity* (Norton, 2015).

30   One could tax factors in inelastic supply like land. Henry George, *Progress and Poverty* (Appleton and Company, 1879).

31   Paul Krugman, "The New Voodoo," *The New York Times*, December 30, 2010.

32   Arthur Laffer, "Government Exactions and Revenue Deficiencies," *Cato Journal* 1 (1981), 1: 1-21.

33   Martin Feldstein, "Supply Side Economics: Old Truths and New Claims," *American Economic Review* 76 (1986), 2: 26-30.

34   Mathias Trabandt and Harald Uhlig, "The Laffer Curve Revisited," *Journal of Monetary Economics* 58 (2011), 4: 305-327, p. 314.

35   Thomas Hungerford, "Taxes and the Economy: An Economic Analysis of the Top Tax Rates Since 1945," Congressional Research Service, Report 7-5700, September 14, 2012.

36   "A Conversation on the State of the Economy with Paul Krugman and Joseph E. Stiglitz," Institute for New Economic Thinking, October 23, 2012.

37   Gunnar Svendsen and Gert Svendsen, *Trust, Social Capital and the Scandinavian Welfare State: Explaining the Flight of the Bumblebee* (Edward Elgar, 2016).

38   United Nations, *World Happiness Report*, 2017; Tax Policy Center Briefing Book, www.taxpolicycenter.org/briefing-book/how-do-us-taxes-compare-internationally.

39   "Internet Usage Statistics." www.internetworldstats.com/stats.htm.

40 Wikipedia, "I-35W Mississippi River Bridge."

41 ASCE, "Infrastructure Report Card," 2021; https://infrastructurereportcard.org/.

42 The National Academy of Sciences estimates that in 2015, 21 million people were exposed to unsafe drinking water. Brad Plumer and Nadja Popovich, "Here Are the Places That Struggle to Meet the Rules on Safe Drinking Water," *The New York Times*, February 12, 2018.

43 David Blankenhorn and Jean Bethke Elshtain, *A Call to Civil Society: Why Democracy Needs Moral Truths* (Institute for American Values, 1998),

44 This does not include $600 million transferred from the victims to criminals. David A. Anderson, "The Aggregate Burden of Crime," *Journal of Law and Economics* 42 (1999), 2: 611–642; Neil Schoenherr, "Cost of Incarceration in the US More Than $1tr," *The Source*, September 7, 2016.

45 Peter Lindert, *Growing Public, vol. 1, Social Spending and Economic Growth Since the Eighteenth Century* (Cambridge University Press, 2004).

46 St. Louis Fed, series SLOAS.

47 A normal good is one whose consumption increases with rising income, if its relative price remains unchanged.

48 St. Louis Fed, series BOGZ1FA156007016Q, A072RC1A156NBEA, PSAVERT.

49 Walter Mischel et al., "Delay of Gratification in Children," *Science* 244 (1989), 4907: 933–938.

50 Paul Roberts, *The Impulse Society: America in the Age of Instant Gratification* (Bloomsbury, 2014).

51 Edward Wolff, *A Century of Wealth in America* (Harvard University Press, 2017).

52 Jonathan Eggleston et al., "The Wealth of Households: 2017," *Current Population Reports*, August 2020; https://www.census.gov/content/dam/Census/library/publications/2020/demo/p70br-170.pdf.

53 Including: motor vehicles, furniture, rugs, light fixtures, household appliances, audio/video/photo equipment, computers, boats, books, jewelry, watches, health and therapeutic equipment, and luggage. Michael Batty et al., "Introducing the Distributional Financial Accounts of the United States," Finance and Economics Discussion Series 2019-017, 2019; https://www.federalreserve.gov/econres/feds/files/2019017pap.pdf.

54 Edward Wolff, "Recent Trends in Household Wealth in the United States: Rising Debt and the Middle-Class Squeeze—an Update to 2007," Levy Economics Institute of Bard College Working Paper 589, March 2010.

55 https://fred.stlouisfed.org/series/WALCL.

56 https://fred.stlouisfed.org/series/SP500. The Case-Shiller national home price index increased from 213 to 249 in 14 months at an annual rate of 14 percent. https://fred.stlouisfed.org/series/CSUSHPINSA.

57 Board of Governors of the Federal Reserve System, "Why Does the Federal Reserve Aim for 2 Percent Inflation Over Time?"

58 St. Louis Fed, series CPALTT01USM659N, BOGMBASE, M1SL.

59 St. Louis Fed, series WRESBAL and IOER.

60 St. Louis Fed, series CPIAUCSL.

61 St. Louis Fed, series CURRDD, A939RX0Q048SBEA.

62 Dani Rodrik, "Premature Deindustrialization." *Journal of Economic Growth* 21 (2016), 1: 1-33; Ha-Joon Chang, *Kicking Away the Ladder: Development Strategy in Historical Perspective* (Anthem Press, 2002); Robin Hahnel, *Democratic Economic Planning* (Routledge, 2022).

63 Joshua Cooper Ramo, *The Beijing Consensus* (Foreign Policy Centre, 2004).

64 Karl Aiginger and Dani Rodrik, "Rebirth of Industrial Policy and an Agenda for the Twenty-first Century," *Journal of Industry, Competition and Trade* 20 (2020): 189-207; David Bailey et al., "Industrial Policy Back on the Agenda: Putting Industrial Policy in Its place?," *Cambridge Journal of Regions, Economy and Society* 12 (2019), 3: 319-326.

65 World Bank, "Manufacturing, Value Added," https://data.worldbank.org/indicator/NV.IND.MANF.CD.

66 David Barboza, "Clyde Prestowitz on the China Fallacy," *The Wire*, June 12, 2021; https://www.thewirechina.com/2021/06/13/clyde-prestowitz-on-the-china-fallacy/.

67   Alan Peacock and Hans Willgerodt (eds.), *Neo-Liberals and the Social Market Economy* (Palgrave, 1989).

68   St. Louis Fed, series DEUB6BLTTO2STSAQ, BPBLTD01DEQ637S.

69   World Bank, "Manufacturing, Value Added," op. cit.

70   St. Louis Fed, series VAPGDPMA; also BEA, https://www.bea.gov/sites/default/files/2021-12/gdp3q21_3rd.pdf; Statistische Bundesamt, "Volkswirtschaftliche Gesamtrechnungen, Inlandsprodukt-berechnung – Detaillierte Jahresergebnisse," February 2022, Tables 2.1.1 and 3.2.1; https://www.destatis.de/SiteGlobals/Forms/Suche/Expertensuche_Formular.html?resourceId=2402&input_=2408&pageLocale=de&templateQueryString=gdp+deutschland&submit.x=0&submit.y=0.

71   US Department of the Army, country studies, http://countrystudies.us/germany/143.htm.

72   Joseph Stiglitz, *The Price of Inequality* (Norton, 2012).

73   Benjamin Austin et al., "Jobs for the Heartland: Place-Based Policies in the 21st-Century America," *Brookings Papers on Economic Activity*, Spring (2018): 151–255.

13 The Tsunami of Globalization

> We can have democracy in this country, or we can have great wealth concentrated in the hands of a few, but we can't have both.
>
> —Attributed to Chief Justice Louis Brandeis

Globalization is a double-edged sword. It brings new opportunities to those who can take advantage of them while creating obstacles for those whose skills are devalued and are unable to compete in the international labor market. Hence, the smart way to transition to globalization is to make sure that the losers are compensated sufficiently so that they are not demoralized and turn against the socio-economic and political system. The silly way is the high-pressure way: to let the losers fend for themselves. The US chose the high-stress way and is paying a very heavy price for it in terms of its devastating social, political, and demographic consequences. Michael Sandel of Harvard University is not alone in thinking that "the election of Trump was an angry verdict on decades of rising inequality and a version of globalization that benefits those at the top but leaves ordinary people feeling disempowered."[1]

Globalization is qualitatively more than international trade. By the twenty-first century it also encompassed the movement of capital and information with lightning speed across the globe and a much slower movement of people.[2] International trade is a critical aspect of the macroeconomy:

$$GDP = C+I+G+(X - M)$$

where X stands for exports and M for imports. (X - M) is the international trade surplus or deficit, an important determinant of GDP and therefore of employment. We analyze its impact on the economy, especially in the presence of unemployment and endemic trade deficits.

The mainstream made two devastating mistakes in thinking about globalization: (1) they completely disregarded that the *size* of the trade deficit matters: a small adjustment relative to GDP in response to a change in tariffs differs qualitatively from a tsunami of hyperglobalization;[3] (2) they completely ignored the well-known fact that *trade is never Pareto optimal*. There are winners and losers. The mainstream disregarded the plight of the losers, whose pain instigated the rise of populism, thereby damaging the foundations of democracy. As Krugman admitted belatedly: "The models that scholars used to measure the impact of exports from developing countries in the 1990s underestimated the effect on jobs and inequality."[4]

DOI: 10.4324/9781003174356-13

13.1 The Theory of Comparative Advantage

No concept is as firmly engrained in mainstream economics as the theory of comparative advantage. For some, it is not a theorem but a "truth," carved into the firmament of knowledge.[5] Both countries benefit from trade if they each specialize in the production of goods which they can produce more efficiently, and therefore cheaper.[6] Mankiw is a Pinocchio for stating that "Trade can make everyone better off."[7] This is a clever but unconscionable sleight-of-hand, because students will undoubtedly get the impression that *everyone does benefit*. However, this is blatantly false since it is well known that in practice trade never ever does make everyone better off. By ignoring the losers—a familiar principle of international trade, he duped tens of millions of students.[8]

Moreover, the theorem is misleading because it has many limitations that are concealed from students with profound consequences to their understanding. The secret assumptions include that:

1. The theorem is actually about barter and not trade in the modern sense of using money. The introduction of money is a complicating factor because of the possibility of trade deficits, credit, and exchange rate manipulation.

2. The theorem does not consider the possibility that trade deficits cause unemployment if the exchange rate does not respond to bring the trade account into balance. The hidden assumption is that those who lose their jobs in the shrinking sector will find employment in the expanding sector. However, if trade does cause unemployment, the country might not benefit at all from trade and might actually be worse off.

3. The decline in the relative price of unskilled-labor-intensive goods will depress the wages of unskilled labor, as it did in the US, because of the cheap import of manufactured goods (see Figure 7.4).[9] In the US, *globalization redistributes income from unskilled to skilled workers* and the ethical aspect of this redistribution is disregarded. The question is framed in terms of increases in total income within a country, and that trade is not Pareto optimal is forgotten. This is inconsistent, since in other sections of the same textbooks some welfare-enhancing policies are prohibited because they are not Pareto optimal, while in this case, policies are advocated although they are also not Pareto optimal. Mankiw meant that theoretically the gainers could compensate the losers. However, this is no consolation to the losers since they are not made whole. The covert redistribution of income from the unskilled to the skilled is without moral foundation since it is unethical to enact a policy that hurts some even if others benefit.

4. The political and social implications of the income redistribution are ignored. This is a serious flaw because the losers are susceptible to manipulation and can bring about massive social and political realignments like Trumpism (see Section 15.4).

5. The theorem is derived for two countries trading two goods being produced by two factors. However, the theorem no longer holds with many countries, many goods, and many factors, conditions that are more realistic in the real world. Hence, the theorem is not applicable to the real world.

6. The theorem assumes that traded goods are produced by perfectly competitive firms and neglects that they are produced mostly by oligopolies. That implies that profits are also transferred to other countries (see Section 13.7).

7. Free trade is not a prescription for economic growth for developed countries. The

theorem considers the gains from trade from a static framework from the point of view of consumer benefits and is unrelated to the theory of economic growth. The evidence indicates that developing nations benefit from free access to developed markets if they can at the same time protect their own markets. *Export-led growth* was important in the development of South Korea, Japan, Taiwan, Singapore, and China.[10]

In sum, the theory has numerous limitations which may eliminate the alleged gains. Yet, economists and policy-makers pretend that it can be applied mechanically in the real world without thinking hard about its ramifications. However, the theory is repeated so frequently that it is subject to the *illusory-truth effect,* a tendency to believe misleading information after hearing it often enough.

13.2 The Effects of Tariffs on Welfare Are Complicated by Unemployment

Samuelson and Nordhaus offer a typical example of the consequences of a tariff: suppose the initial price of clothing is $4 per unit, domestic output is 100 units, consumption is 300 units, so imports are 200 units (Figure 13.1). After a $2.00 per unit tariff is imposed, the domestic price increases to $6, domestic production increases to 150 units, and domestic consumption declines to 250 units so imports decline to 100 units. They conclude that "the overall social impact [of the tariff] is …. a gain to producers of $250, a gain to the government of $200, and a loss to consumers of $550. The net social cost (counting each of these dollars equally) is therefore $100."[11]

These amounts are calculated as follows: the area of the trapezoid A equals the gain to producers since they are selling their products at a higher price:

($2 × 100) + ½($2 × 50) = $250

The first term is the area of the rectangle (the increase in price times the amount produced initially). The second term is the area of the triangle. Its area is the increase in production (50 units) times the increase in domestic price, i.e., the tariff ($2) divided by 2. However, the producers' gain is at the expense of consumers who buy the product at the higher price. Hence, $250 is

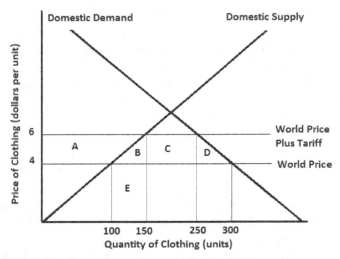

Figure 13.1 The effect of tariffs on domestic production and consumption

a transfer from consumers to producers and not a net gain to the country. Area C is government tariff revenue, which is assumed to be given back to the consumers, so it is neither a loss nor a gain. The area of triangle B is:

$$\frac{1}{2}*(\$2 \times 50) = \$50$$

It is the value of labor and other resources competed away from other sectors of the economy in order to induce them to produce clothing instead of something else, although the economy was better suited to the production of that something else. The production of something else declines consequently. The diversion of resources into the production of clothing is inefficient since the economy could have obtained this quantity of clothing from abroad cheaper. Therefore, B is a net loss to consumers. Furthermore,

$$D = \frac{1}{2}*(\$2 \times 50) = \$50$$

Thus, the area D is also a loss to consumers because they consume less clothing than before. So, the tariff introduces a distortion between world price and domestic price and induces a net loss (*dead-weight loss*) of ($50 + $50) = $100, equal to the areas B + D.

However, there are hidden assumptions in this standard model. For instance, in the microeconomics section of the mainstream textbooks, economists argue that the utility of one individual is not comparable to someone else's. Yet, in the macroeconomics section they stealthily do exactly that: they compare the income gained by producers to that lost by consumers. But incomes are not the relevant unit of comparison unless they are converted into utility, since a dollar produces more utility for a poor person than for a rich one. However, here economists find it convenient to "count each dollar equally."[12] To overcome this inconsistency one should consider how much utility is being produced by these dollars going to different people. Thus, who gets the gains and who gets the losses should be considered.

Additionally, the assumption of full employment in this model is never ever mentioned. However, with unemployment, B would not be a loss but a gain of $50 to workers who have a job after the tariffs are imposed. In addition, area E would also be a gain because these dollars would then accrue to workers who were previously idle, so they would not have to be diverted from other sectors of the economy. That would be a gain of:

$$\$4 \times 50 = \$200$$

This is a transfer from foreign workers to domestic workers. Hence, the total gain to domestic workers is:

$$E + B = \$50 + 200 = \$250$$

of which, $50 is a transfer from consumers to workers. So, the existence of unemployment converts an alleged social loss of $100 to an actual gain for the society of

$$B + E - B - D \text{ or } \$250 - \$100 = \$150[13]$$

The increase of $150 in the domestic economy would also have multiplier effects in the presence of unemployment, so the actual gain is greater.[14]

Another issue overlooked is that the losses are spread among many consumers, but the gains are concentrated among a few workers. Assume that each dollar in this example represents $1,000. Then if the $100,000 loss due to the tariffs were divided among a million consumers, then the 10-cent loss per person would have a trivial impact on their utility. In contrast, if the gain to workers of $250,000 were divided among five workers, then the gain per worker of $50,000 would mean their livelihood and a substantial increase in their welfare. Thus, measured in terms of utility, the cost-benefit calculation is even more in favor of a tariff in the presence of unemployment.

The aficionados of globalization failed to consider the implications of the factor-price equalization theorem, which implies that wages in the two trading countries will tend to become equal.[15] Hence, the wages of unskilled labor will rise in China but will stagnate or decline in the US. Indeed, this is precisely the reason why unskilled wages have fallen among men in the US (see Figure 7.4). Most affected were men living in areas in which the penetration of imports from China were the largest.[16] Obviously, this development had major ethical and political implications even if the men did not become unemployed because their lower incomes meant that they would experience downward social mobility.

If the tariffs are lowered instead of increased, the results are symmetric. In the presence of unemployment, lowering tariffs induces a net loss to society of (B + E − B − D), which amounts to $150. B + E represent the jobs exported worth $250. Consumers' gain from B + D is worth $100; so the net loss of the reduction of tariffs is $250 − $100 = $150. Admittedly, economists *assume* that workers who lose their jobs because of the elimination of tariff will find other employment. In that case the net gain would remain $100 since the areas B and E would not be considered losses. That might have been true in the 1950s when jobs were plentiful but not anymore in the dual economy in the United States.[17] That workers with a high-school education, displaced from low-skilled occupations could find jobs in the expanding IT sector is illusory. The best they can hope for is to trade their lower-middle-class income for Walmart wages and join the ranks of the working poor on food stamps. The loss of the wages of those who were displaced by the influx of foreign products should be subtracted from the gains from trade.

In short, the simplifications of the theorem of comparative advantage overlook the main socioeconomic, political, and ethical challenges of coping with the effects of factory shutdowns and declining wages as a consequence of hyperglobalization. Humanistic economics would prescribe not only that "the US as a whole" benefits from trade but that no one is hurt by it. Hence, the losers should be fully compensated by the gainers. Then trade would become Pareto optimal. Hypothetical compensation is illusory.

13.3 Free Trade Is Not an Engine of Growth

For developing economies, export-led growth is a winning strategy but free trade is not a prescription for growth for developed economies. Comparative advantage and gains from trade pertain mainly to consumer welfare in the static sense and are irrelevant to economic growth. Increases in consumer welfare is not the foundation of economic growth (see Figure 13.1). Consumers can buy shirts cheaper, and the domestic production of shirts decreases, there is no guarantee that another sector will expand. Long-term growth depends on other factors (see Section 11.3). No developing country—neither Germany nor the US in the nineteenth century, nor the Asian Tigers in the twentieth—was able to catch up with developed countries without protecting its own industry from competition from the most advanced country.[18] Without substantial protection of its own market, China would not have been able to compete with the technologically advanced nations and its growth would have been stifled. The historical record indicates that free trade is not a winning strategy for catching-up with developed economies.

The impulse for growth for economies on the technological frontier must come from elsewhere: innovation, education, and public investments in infrastructure and basic research (see Section 12.10). The Chinese were able to translate their gains into growth because they reinvested their profits, whereas the US bought consumer goods that had no growth effects. The cheaper shirts bought decades ago are no longer being used, whereas the Chinese capital investments are still generating returns.

Note that Chinese labor is not more productive than American workers in terms of labor hours. Instead, China can produce labor-intensive goods cheaper because wages are lower since the standard of living is lower and because of the seemingly unlimited supply of inexpensive labor. This implies that firms produce at the location where labor earns less.[19]

13.4 Protection of Infant Industries

Being first to produce a product or to be the first region to develop an industry confers advantages that pose an obstacle to other firms or other regions to develop. These first-mover advantages accrue because firms gain experience in producing a new product and because network externalities make it difficult for others to catch up. *Learning-by-doing* lowers the production cost of firms who produced a product first so that latecomers can never catch up. They retain their competitive edge for no other reason than having had the good fortune of being the first to have produced the product.

In the early stages of economic development industrial growth can be fostered by subsidizing *infant industries* or by protecting them with tariffs from foreign competition so producers learn how to lower their cost of production and catch up with more advanced producers.[20] For example, suppose computers were invented in country A and a firm can produce them for $100. While manufacturing them it accumulates knowledge about how to build them better and cheaper—learning by doing—and subsequently can build them for $95. If firms in country B want to produce computers without knowing the best practice, they must begin as a higher-cost producer at $100. So, producers in country A enjoy a first-mover advantage and producers in country B will only produce computers if the government provides a $5 subsidy or levies a tariff of $5 on computers. First-mover advantage means that follower countries play catch-up and free trade would stifle their infant industry. That is why the US government has been subsidizing wind-turbine production, for instance.[21]

13.5 Unbalanced Trade Generates the Anguish of Unemployment

In the real world, exports might not equal imports: the deficits can be paid by money and IOUs. US international trade was balanced practically continuously until Reagan opened the floodgates with endemic deficits (see Figures 12.1, 13.2, Table 7.2). Trade deficits and government budget deficits are so closely linked that they are called *twin deficits*.[22] Hence, Reagan's budget deficits became trade deficits as well, and the trade deficit jumped from 0.2 percent to 1.8 percent of GDP. The kink in the graphs signal a genuine turning point, as with Reagan's other policies. Then came two other turning points: The North American Free Trade Agreement (NAFTA)[23] in 1994 and China's entry into the World Trade Organization (WTO) in 2001. In their wake, the

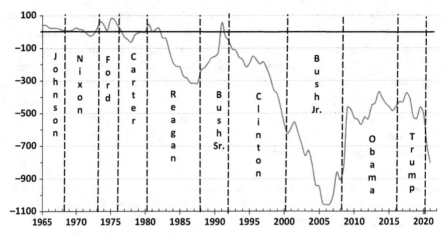

Figure 13.2 US trade balance in goods and services, 2021 dollars (billions)
Source: St. Louis Fed, Series NETFI, USAGDPDEFQISMEI.

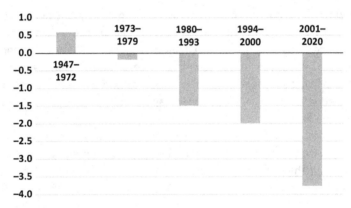

Figure 13.3 US trade balance as a percent of GDP
Source: St. Louis Fed, Series NETFI, USAGDPDEFQISMEI.

trade deficits reached hitherto unfathomable proportions (Figure 13.2). By 2005-2007, they were nearing $1 trillion before settling to a pre-Covid average of $500 billion or 3.8 percent of GDP (Figure 13.3).[24]

This immense transfer of wealth has been a low-skilled job destroyer in manufacturing, causing social dislocation and political conflict (see Chapter 15) and implies, furthermore, a reduction in future generations' living standards.[25] Since the country imports products it previously produced, jobs are exported, and US workers become unemployed, retire on social security disability benefits, work in the drug trade, go to jail, or accept lower wages, but many also turn to opioids or commit suicide.[26] A million-dollar deficit exports about five jobs; consequently, $500 billion deficit exports 2.5 million jobs and contributes to the hollowing out of the middle class. So, its elimination would reduce unemployment rate by 20 percent (see Table 11.1).

The accumulated trade deficits amount to a gigantic $33 trillion stimulus to the rest of the world's economy and drained an immense amount of purchasing power from the US (Figure 13.4).[27] No wonder the Chinese economy has been booming and no wonder the US economy has been in low gear in the twenty-first century. That the benefits of lower-priced imported

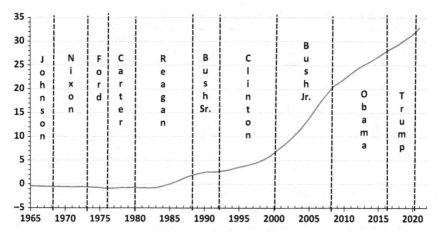

Figure 13.4 US accumulated trade deficits, 2021 dollars (trillions)
Source: St. Louis Fed, Series NETFI, USAGDPDEFQISMEI.

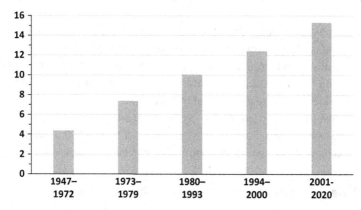

Figure 13.5 US imports as a percent of GDP
Source: St. Louis Fed, Series NETFI, USAGDPDEFQISMEI.

consumer goods outweigh the immense costs of social dislocation is unlikely, given the political turbulence it engendered (see Chapter 15).

Deficits are not the only variable that matter in a dual economy. The amount of imports matters by itself because low-skilled workers displaced in the import-competing sectors were unemployable in the expanding IT and finance sectors. So, the 15.6 percent of GDP imported annually in the 2010s dealt a major blow to domestic low-skilled workers (see Table 7.2 and Figure 13.5). They remained trapped, unemployable, and became discontented due to downward social mobility.[28]

Theoretically, financial markets should resolve such balance of payments deficits by devaluing the dollar. However, since the dollar is a reserve currency foreigners demand dollar-denominated assets as safe investments in a volatile world. Hence, the dollar has not depreciated despite the endemic trade deficits. This imbalance has led to a massive export of IOUs on which interest will accrue indefinitely.[29] While this lifts current US living standards, it does so at the expense of future generations (see Section 11.8).

The takeaway is that the destructive forces of globalization should have been mitigated by a government safety net that helped those who were adversely affected by foreign competition.

Table 13.1 US trade with China (billions of dollars)

	US exports	US imports	Deficits
2021	151	506	-355
2020	124	434	-310
2019	106	450	-344
2018	120	538	-418
2017	130	505	-375
2016	115	462	-347

Source: https://www.census.gov/foreign-trade/balance/c5700.html#2021.

This could have been done by controlling the speed at which tariffs were lowered and imports were allowed to penetrate and demolish old industries so that the displaced workers could find their footing in the economy. Those workers who were unable to find ready employment could have been retrained at taxpayers' expense so that they could remain productive members of the society. Hence, humanistic economics advocates that there should not be any losers of globalization.

Since globalization is path-dependent, the above processes are irreversible (see Section 8.11). The imposition of import tariffs would not succeed now because it is well known that the counterparties will retaliate, thereby reducing US exports. The trade war with China, initiated by the Trump administration in July 2018, failed utterly, and was doomed to fail.[30] The deficits with China actually increased after the initiation of the trade war from $190 billion in the first half of 2018 to $247 billion in the second half (Table 13.1) to reach $437 billion for the year. In 2019, they continued to increase to $472 billion and reached $616 billion in 2020. However, there exists a policy that could achieve balanced trade without the possibility of punitive counter-measures.

13.6 Import Certificates Could Eliminate the Trade Deficits

Warren Buffett implored policy-makers to use import certificates to "halt this trading of assets for consumables."[31] This would fix the problem of deficits without attacking any nation or putting tariffs on any single good. He warned that:

> The U.S. trade deficit is a bigger threat to the domestic economy than either the federal budget deficit or consumer debt and could lead to political turmoil … Right now, the rest of the world owns $3tr more of us than we own of them.[32]

Meanwhile, the net international investment position of the United States has ballooned to –$15.4 trillion (2021), half of which were Treasury securities, and the interest on those assets obligates future generations.[33] To counter this trend, Buffett's suggestion was that the US government should issue import certificates to exporting firms in amounts equal to the value of their exports. In turn, the exporters would sell the certificates to US importers. The importers would have to buy the certificates in the appropriate amounts in order to bring goods into the country. That would be a subsidy to exporters paid by importers. The price for the certificates would rise until trade would be balanced.[34] If the US is unable to devalue its currency to rebalance trade, it can raise the price of all foreign products in this manner.

The sale of import certificates would lower the price of US exports, thereby increasing demand for them and lowering unemployment. The 2.5 million US jobs thus created would also generate additional tax revenues, thereby easing the budget deficit. Although the price of imports would increase, its impact would be diffused while the job creation would be concentrated among the unemployed who need their fortunes lifted. While increasing tariffs affords other nations the opportunity to retaliate, the certificates does not. Just the opposite, it would induce foreigners to buy US products because the more they buy, the more they can sell. This makes import certificates preferable to tariffs as a means of bringing foreign trade into balance.

In the first quarter of 2022, US imports peaked at (an annual rate of) $3.9 trillion, $1.2 trillion or 44 percent above $2.7 trillion exports.[35] The balanced trade policy could be phased in over several years by initially granting, say, $1.25 worth of certificates for every $1.00 worth of exports. Such a policy would eliminate all the deficits in a matter of years with a substantial boost to the economy without costing the government anything.

Moreover, the foreign debt is concentrated: Japan and China each owns US Treasury securities worth $1.3 trillion each.[36] The interest on them will be due in perpetuity. The savings glut also enables Chinese companies to buy US businesses, including iconic firms like GE Appliances, Smithfield Foods, Waldorf Astoria, Motorola Mobility, Hoover, and high-tech companies like Complete Genomics, a California DNA sequencing company, although the Chinese limit foreign direct investments to joint ventures in their country.[37] This implies that the US is exchanging ownership rights to firms for Chinese consumer goods, and the profits of those firms will no longer accrue to future generations of US citizens.[38]

13.7 New Trade Theory

Paul Krugman received the Nobel Prize for refuting the old trade theory.[39] Modern trade patterns differ from those of the past. Instead of trading Portuguese wine for British textiles based on factor endowment advantages, as in Ricardo's famous example, today most advanced industrialized countries trade comparable products: Volkswagens are sold in France while Citroens are sold in Germany. The motivation behind such trade is not comparative advantage but the existence of economies of scale, differentiated products, imperfect competition, quality, style, branding, patent rights, transaction costs, advertisements, and diversity in consumption. If it makes little difference which car one drives, then both cars will find markets in both countries. These goods are not produced in perfectly competitive markets as supposed in textbooks, but by profitable oligopolies. Volkswagen has a monopoly on making cars with the VW logo, so the perfectly competitive model does not apply to such branded products (see Sections 6.3 and 7.7). Yet, these oligopolistic profits are not included in the old trade theory but are crucial for the economy, for they are the source of taxes, future innovation, investments, growth, and income for the middle class.[40]

Furthermore, there are first-mover advantages (see Section 13.4). Once these brands are established, they become quasi-monopolies and the profits they generate are not easily competed away. The size of the domestic market matters. "Countries will tend to export those goods for which they have relatively large domestic markets."[41] A larger domestic market offers the opportunity to produce greater quantities at a lower unit cost because economies of scale. For instance, the large domestic market in Germany for high-quality automobiles provides comparative advantages to BMW, Mercedes, Porsche, and Audi to compete successfully in the high-quality niche of the international automobile market.

Increasing-returns technology also changes substantially the static analysis of tariffs (see Section 13.2). In conventional analysis, increasing tariffs induces domestic firms to increase production and supposedly welfare decreases because the utility of consumers decreases. However, if the good is produced using increasing returns to scale technology, the larger domestic production could reduce the unit cost of production, thereby changing the math. In short, new trade theory implies that governmental trade policy through subsidies, tariffs, or import cer-tificates can improve welfare, productivity, and long-run growth (see Section 12.10). Free trade is no longer necessarily the optimum policy.[42] Rather, new trade theory suggests that context matters. The question remains: can the US transition to a set of institutions that foster real full employment industrial policy, which would have to include a trade policy that is much nimbler than currently practiced? These issues must be put on the agenda if we want to alleviate the endemic structural imbalances plaguing the US economy since Reaganomics.

13.8 Takeaways

Globalization has been mismanaged in the US where it became a chaotic retreat from manufac-turing, causing much anxiety among low-skilled, less-educated men, many of whom were losing well-paying union jobs before becoming unemployable. The inflation-adjusted hourly wage of those who did find employment declined between 1973 and 2019 by $3 per hour or by 17 percent in the interim 46 years.

The theorem of comparative advantage, the principle upon which free-trade aficionados based their support for globalization, is invalid in the real world if it causes large-scale unem-ployment, as it did in the US, because the displaced workers were not qualified to find employ-ment in the expanding knowledge economy. For the have-nots in distress anti-social behavior became manifestations of a deep malaise signifying an unprecedented emotional emptiness brought about by downward social mobility.

Globalization should have been carried out in a Pareto-optimal way so that there would not be any losers. The tariffs should have been lowered, and old industries phased out, at such a rate that the displaced workers could have been absorbed by the expanding industries, or could have been retrained, or that the unemployed were actually fully compensated for their losses by the gainers. Allowing the benefits of globalization to be captured by the wealthy was a mistake of historical proportions.

Questions for Discussion

1. What should be done about the endemic trade deficits in the US?
2. Do you think American industry should have been protected by tariffs?
3. Do you know anyone who has become unemployed or underemployed because of competi-tion by foreign producers?
4. Do you think it is fair to introduce economic policies that help the economy grow but hurt some individuals?
5. Do you think that those workers who lost their jobs because of NAFTA should have been fully compensated for their losses and guaranteed a job with as high a wage as they had prior to the change in tariffs?
6. Do you think that an industrial policy would be useful?
7. What are some major challenges we face in today's globalized world?
8. Do you think that free trade is beneficial to the US economy?
9. Do you like the idea of eliminating the endemic trade deficits using import certificates?
10. Do you think it is fair to burden future generations with so much debt?
11. Do you think the government should subsidize green industries like solar and wind power to help their development?

12. Who benefits from a tariff?
13. Who benefits from a reduction of tariffs?
14. What is a dead-weight loss?
15. Has the US exported jobs because of globalization?
16. Would you advocate for a Pareto-optimal trade policy?

Notes

1   Michael Sandel, "Populism, Trump, and the Future of Democracy," Institute for New Economic Thinking, March 15, 2019.
2   Dani Rodrik, *Straight Talk on Trade: Ideas for a Sane World* (Princeton University Press, 2018).
3   Lawrence Mishel, "Tired of Economists' Misdirection on Globalization," Economic Policy Institute, April 26, 2016; https://www.epi.org/blog/tired-of-economists-misdirection-on-globalization/.
4   Paul Krugman, "What Economists (Including Me) Got Wrong About Globalization," *Bloomberg Opinion*, October 10, 2019.
5   "one of the deepest truths in all of economics." Paul Samuelson and William Nordhaus, *Economics*, 19th edn. (McGraw-Hill/Irwin, 2009), p. 349.
6   Gregory Mankiw and Phillip Swagel, "The Politics and Economics of Offshore Outsourcing," *Journal of Monetary Economics* 53 (2006), 5: 1027-1056.
7   Gregory Mankiw, *Principles of Economics*, 8th edn. (Cengage, 2018), p. 8; Stephen Marglin, "Heterodox Economics: Alternatives to Mankiw's Ideology," Occupy Harvard Teach-In on Heterodox Economics. December 7, 2011; https://www.youtube.com/watch?v=Pf0-E8X-GHo&feature=player_embedded.
8   Wolfgang Stolper and Paul Samuelson, "Protection and Real Wages," *Review of Economic Studies* 9 (1941), 1: 58-73.
9   Paul Samuelson, "International Trade and the Equalisation of Factor Prices," *Economic Journal* 58 (1948), 230: 163-184.
10 Isabella Weber, *How China Escaped Shock Therapy: The Market Reform Debate* (Routledge, 2021).
11 Samuelson and Nordhaus, *Economics*, op. cit., p. 353.
12 Ibid., p. 353.
13 Another way of seeing this is to subtract the $550 loss of consumers from the total amounts gained by producers, workers, and government:
    $250 + $250 + $200 = $700 and 700 - 550 = 150.
14 John Culbertson, "The Folly of Free Trade," *Harvard Business Review* 64 (1986), 5: 122-128.
15 Paul Samuelson, "International Trade and the Equalisation of Factor Prices," *Economic Journal* 58 (1948): 163-184.
16 Justin Pierce and Peter Schott. "Trade Liberalization and Mortality: Evidence from U.S. Counties," *American Economic Review: Insights* 2 (2020), 1: 47-64.
17 St. Louis Fed, series UEMPMEAN.
18 Ha-Joon Chang, *Bad Samaritans: The Myth of Free Trade and the Secret History of Capitalism* (Bloomsbury Press, 2008).
19 Michael Lind, "The Strange Career of Paul Krugman," *Tablet*, November 22, 2021.
20 Friedrich List, *The National System of Political Economy* (Longmans, Green, and Co. 1885).
21 Congressional Research Service, "Reports, January 16, 2013." https://www.everycrsreport.com/reports/R42023.html.
22 Douglas Bernheim, "Budget Deficits and the Balance of Trade," in Lawrence Summers (ed.), *Tax Policy and the Economy*, Vol. 2 (MIT Press, 1988), pp. 1-32.
23 Includes Mexico, Canada, and the US, but superseded as the United States-Mexico-Canada Agreement in 2020.
24 President Trump claimed that the US trade deficit was $800 billion. This was the deficit in trade in goods and neglects trade in services. In 2016, the US had a $257 billion surplus in trade in services.

Bureau of Economic Analysis, "2017 NIPA Annual Update Results Table," www.bea.gov/national/pdf/NIPA-Revision-Table-9-11-17.pdf.

25   Justin Pierce and Peter Schott, "The Surprisingly Swift Decline of US Manufacturing Employment," *American Economic Review*, 106 (2016), 7: 1632-1662.

26   Byron Dorgan, *Take This Job and Ship It: How Corporate Greed and Brain-Dead Politics Are Selling Out America* (Thomas Dunne Books/St. Martin's Press, 2006).

27   Board of Governors of the Federal Reserve System, "Industrial Production and Capacity Utilization–G.17," January 16, 2013.

28   Demos, "Stacked Deck: How the Dominance of Politics by the Affluent & Business Undermines Economic Mobility in America." February 13, 2013.

29   U.S. Department of Commerce, Bureau of Economic Analysis, "U.S. International Transactions Accounts Data," various dates.

30   Wikipedia, "China–United States Trade War."

31   Warren Buffett, "America's Growing Trade Deficit Is Selling the Nation Out from Under Us. Here's a Way to Fix the Problem—and We Need to Do It Now," *Fortune*, November 10, 2003.

32   Ibid. He reaffirmed his earlier position in Warren Buffett, "Here's How I Would Solve the Trade Problem," *Fortune*, April 29, 2016.

33   www.bea.gov/newsreleases/international/intinv/intinvnewsrelease.htm; U.S. Treasury, "Major Foreign Holders of Treasury Securities," http://ticdata.treasury.gov/Publish/mfh.txt.

34   There could be exemptions for strategic products and "threshold values" so small importers could be exempted.

35   Bureau of Economic Analysis, "Table 4.1. Foreign Transactions in the National Income and Product Accounts," https://apps.bea.gov/iTable/index_nipa.cfm.

36   U.S. Treasury, "Major Foreign Holders of Treasury Securities," https://ticdata.treasury.gov/Publish/mfh.txt; see also https://www.bea.gov/sites/default/files/2021-08/effects-of-selected-federal-pandemic-response-programs-on-federal-government-receipts-expenditures-and-saving-2021q2-2nd.pdf; and https://www.treasurydirect.gov/govt/reports/pd/mspd/2021/opds112021.pdf.

37   "When the U.S. allowed China to join the World Trade Organization in 2001 and gain much less restricted access to our markets, we gave China the right to keep protecting parts of its market—because it was a 'developing economy.'" Thomas Friedman, "Trump Lies. China Thrives," *The New York Times*, June 7, 2017. It also used intellectual property theft to its advantage. That includes "counterfeiting American fashion designs, pirating movies and video games, patent infringement and stealing proprietary technology and software." Dennis Blair and Keith Alexander, "China's Intellectual Property Theft Must Stop," *The New York Times*, August 15, 2017.

38   Michele Nash-Hoff, "Should We Allow the Chinese to Buy Any US Company They Want?" *Industry Week*, January 9, 2018, https://www.industryweek.com/the-economy/article/22024894/should-we-allow-the-chinese-to-buy-any-us-company-they-want; Andrew Pollack, "U.S. Clears DNA Firm's Acquisition by Chinese," *The New York Times*, December 30, 2012.

39   Elhanan Helpman and Paul Krugman, *Market Structure and Foreign Trade* (MIT Press, 1989); Paul Krugman, *Geography and Trade* (MIT Press, 2000). Paul Krugman, "Increasing Returns, Monopolistic Competition, and International Trade," *Journal of International Economics* 9 (1979), 4: 469-480.

40   John Komlos, "Is Free Trade Passé? A Comment," *Journal of Economic Perspectives* 2 (1988), 4: 207-209.

41   Paul Krugman, "Scale Economies, Product Differentiation and the Pattern of Trade," *American Economic Review* 70 (1980), 5: 950-959; here p. 950.

42   Ralph Gomory and William Baumol, *Global Trade and Conflicting National Interests* (MIT Press, 2000); Paul Samuelson, "Where Ricardo and Mill Rebut and Confirm Arguments of Mainstream Economists Supporting Globalization," *Journal of Economic Perspectives* 18 (2004), 3: 135-146.

14 The Financial Crisis of 2008

> Today we have involved ourselves in a colossal muddle, having blundered in the control of a delicate machine, the working of which we do not understand. The result is that our possibilities of wealth may run to waste for a time—perhaps for a long time.
>
> —John Maynard Keynes[1]

The start of the new millennium witnessed the worst economic crisis since the 1930s.[2] The Meltdown of 2008 was a decisive watershed in world history that shook the very foundations of Western liberal political order with aftershocks that still are reverberating. The collapse of the house of cards built on the erroneous neoclassical dogma of laissez-faire finance with lax regulation and substandard oversight culminated in the subprime mortgage crisis and the demise of Lehmann Brothers, the fourth largest investment bank in the US, threatening the whole capitalistic system with disaster. The impact of the crisis was exacerbated by the tsunami of hyperglobalization and the absurd levels of inequality. Keynes' words ring true for our time: we, too, have blundered and become immersed in a "colossal muddle," and we, too, still do not understand the economy of our time. And, yes, we have been wasting much of our productive energies and will continue to do so for an extended period of time.

The shockwaves of financial crises of the magnitude of 1929 or of 2008 are so powerful, because they hurt so many people: millions lose their job, are ruined financially, were evicted from their homes, thereby shattering dreams through financial losses. Wealth is destroyed, pensions lost, and savings accounts depleted. And even those who did retain their job are, nonetheless, anxious. The rise of Trumpism is hard to fathom without the dislocations of 2008. Similarly, the devastations of 1929 brought about the New Deal: a revolutionary set of policies. Hence, such financial crises are catalysts that create watershed political moments in which history suddenly, violently, and unexpectedly, takes a ninety-degree turn.

Ironically, to big-league observers, all seemed fine. Nobel Prize-winning macroeconomist Robert Lucas, for instance, boasted in his 2003 presidential address to the American Economic Association that the "central problem of depression-prevention has been solved, for all practical purposes."[3] Why worry? Economists know it all. Shortly thereafter, prominent Princeton macroeconomist Ben Bernanke, then member of the Federal Reserve's Board of Governors and Chair of Bush Jr.'s Council of Economic Advisors, and soon-to-be Greenspan's successor as Chairman of the Federal Reserve, declared with identical hubris, that the era of "Great Moderation," had arrived with "a substantial decline in macroeconomic volatility."[4] These pronouncements suggested that recessions were no longer a credible threat due to improved demand management and monetary policy.[5]

DOI: 10.4324/9781003174356-14

Similarly, the chief economist at the International Monetary Fund suggested literally minutes before the Meltdown that "The state of macroeconomics is good."[6] They were all dead wrong.[7] Four years later the world was confronted with a catastrophic financial crisis.[8] The problem was not merely the failure to predict the crisis. "More important was the profession's blindness to the very possibility of catastrophic failures in a market economy."[9] The Bible warns us that, "Pride comes before destruction, and an arrogant spirit before a fall."[10]

14.1 Preliminaries

To his credit, Federal Reserve Chairman Alan Greenspan successfully overcame several crises during his 19-year tenure, beginning in 1987. For the peso crisis of 1994 he coordinated a $50 billion bailout for Mexico. Then came the Asian crisis of 1997 and devaluation of currencies, including those of Thailand and South Korea, also based on a shortage of dollars. As the recession engulfed many of the Asian countries, the price of oil declined so much that it forced the Russian government into bankruptcy. This, in turn, bankrupted Long-Term Capital Management (LTCM), a major US hedge fund, heavily invested there. Again, Greenspan came to the rescue by organizing a $3.6 billion bailout by the private sector. All these successes made him into a "rock star" of finance; Wall Street called it the *"Greenspan put,"* i.e., no need to worry: Greenspan will rescue us in a crunch.[11]

In the wake of these accomplishments, *Time* magazine reflected the market's view by idolizing Greenspan and his two allies, Robert Rubin,[12] and Larry Summers,[13] on its cover in 1999 as "The Committee to Save the World," making the "three marketeers" appear invincible.[14] In addition to the expected adulation, it stealthy expressed some misgivings: "By fighting off one collapse after another—and defending their economic policy from political meddling—the three men have so far protected American growth, making investors deliriously, perhaps delusionally, happy in the process."[15] "Delusional" did not auger well for the crises ahead. Summers' conceited statement follows: "we start with the idea that you can't repeal the laws of economics. Even if they are inconvenient." Sure, but he carelessly neglected two crucial aspects of economics, namely the role of *asymmetric information* and systemic risk in finance. Stiglitz and Akerlof proved decades earlier that in the presence of asymmetric information—which is obviously pervasive in finance—*markets are inefficient*. That, too, is an integral part of the "laws of economics" which the triumvirate inexcusably ignored; yet asymmetric information turned out to be at the heart of the crisis.

The takeaway from LTCM's bankruptcy should have been that the *quants of finance* and their computer programs were fallible, i.e., that the assumed sophistication of the money managers was deceptive. After all, the two Nobelists who derived the Black-Scholes-Merton model for *derivative* pricing sat on LTCM's board of directors. The model worked perfectly on the blackboard but not in the real world, and the hedge fund's exposure to the Asian and Russian financial crises generated losses of $3.6 billion. However, Greenspan organized a bailout by private banks, so, the fallout of the bankruptcy was minimal. Consequently, the episode bolstered the market's faith in the Greenspan put, instead of generating some skepticism about the mathematical models used in finance.

The Dot-Com bubble came next. The fundamental value of equity is the discounted value of future dividends. However, investors do not know future dividends or future interest rates. So, they use past earnings as a guide to gage future dividends. The price/earnings ratio is an indicator of the fundamental value of the stock. Robert Shiller, a guru of finance, advocates using the

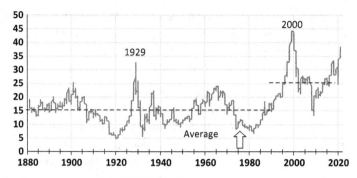

Figure 14.1 Price-to-earnings ratio of S&P 500 stocks
Source: Stock market data used in Robert J. Shiller, *Irrational Exuberance*. Princeton University Press,
2000, 2005, 2015, updated. www.econ.yale.edu/~shiller/data.htm.

average earnings of the past ten years in the denominator to calculate the ratio. Its inverse is
the rate of return.

However, this concept was inappropriate for internet companies, because they had zero profits, only expected ones. Nonetheless, the disruptive technology of the "new economy" and eventual superprofits were enticing to many investors. Consequently, speculative bets dominated.
Keynesian "animal spirits," the ebb and flow of optimism and pessimism fueled the frenzy leading to a positive feedback loop (see Figure 4.12) and skyrocketing prices beginning in 1995.[16] In
1996, Greenspan did mention "irrational exuberance" once and never again and did nothing to
mitigate the frenzy. The 115-year average price/earnings ratio (1880–1995) is 14.8 (Figure 14.1).
Its inverse is the rate of return on those investments:

$$\frac{1}{14.8} = 6.75\%^{[17]}$$

At the peak of the Dot-Com bubble, the ratio reached 43, three times the average of the previous century, implying a return of merely 2.3 percent, a clear signal of a bubble. Only once previously had the P/E ratio risen above 32: in 1929. That should have signaled to Greenspan and
investors that the market was in tenuous territory.

When the Dot-Com bubble burst, countless firms failed and a shallow recession followed that
lasted but eight months.[18] However, Greenspan lived up to his reputation, followed the usual scenario, lowered interest rates that accelerated economic activity (see Section 10.3). The economy
recovered unscathed. Yet, all was not well. Greenspan was navigating the US into a doom loop:
from one bubble into another.[19]

14.2 The End of Boring Banking

The 45 years between 1935 and 1980 were an era of "boring banking."[20] Franklin Roosevelt's
new regulations of the financial sector inaugurated an unprecedented era of stability. He created the Securities and Exchange Commission to prevent manipulation of the stock market in
order to protect investors, and created the Federal Deposit Insurance Corporations to safeguard
deposits. Moreover, the *Glass-Steagall Act* (1933) prohibited commercial banks from investing in
stocks, so banks could not speculate with other people's money. This was reasonable because
it would have been imprudent to allow banks to assume excessive risks by speculating with

deposits backed by the government. However, the success of the New Deal legislation and the consequent stability of the financial system harbored some hidden perils, as pointed out by the guru of instability, Hyman Minsky.

Minsky had warned that stability breeds instability for two reasons:

1. On the one hand, the long period of stability deceives regulators into complacency; as the experience of prior crises recedes in memory, and since everything is running smoothly, those in authority become overconfident and become convinced that they can reduce financial regulation and relax enforcement of regulations still in effect. And that was precisely the attitude of the US government beginning with the Reagan administration and Alan Greenspan's 19-year reign as financial czar.
2. However, the private sector does not remain complacent at all. Pursuing superprofits, financiers seize the opportunity afforded by minimal oversight and circumvent even those regulations that remain in place and take advantage of lax oversight to innovate continuously. Staying under the radar of regulators makes it easier for them to undermine the institutions that were responsible for financial stability in the first place, thereby enabling them to engage in increasingly risky behavior.

Thus, Minsky warned in vain that the complacency of regulators and new business models in finance reinforce each other in transforming a stable system into an unstable one. This describes precisely what happened on Greenspan's watch and Minsky's prognosis became a reality. The only way the crisis could have been avoided was for the regulatory authorities to overcome their complacency and remain vigilant. However, that was not to be.

Financial innovations afforded exciting and irresistible investment opportunities. Since Western culture is fascinated by innovation, economists and regulators followed strictly the neoliberal doctrine to cheer both deregulation and financial innovation.[21] Yet, in bouts of irrational exuberance, it is easy for investors to neglect the dangers of downside risk and that made for a toxic market environment.

Mortgage securitization by private banks was a significant innovation. In the old model of lending, a local bank provided the mortgage for the purchase of a home. Since it relied on the repayment for 30 years, the bank had the incentive to scrutinize borrowers thoroughly. Did the person have a good credit rating, a permanent job, adequate income, assets, and stable family life? This model worked perfectly well, with one caveat: it had the drawback that the amount of funds available to local banks was limited by local savings. Hence, the mortgage market was ripe for innovation that would solve this credit constraint.

Beginning in 1968, the Government National Mortgage Association (GNMA), sponsored by the Department of Housing and Urban Development, started pooling thousands of mortgages into a new type of investment bond called a *mortgage-backed security* (MBS). Thus, *securitization* began. These are also called *collateralized debt obligations* since the underlying real estate is the collateral. They are *derivatives* because their value is *derived* from the fundamental value of another asset, in this case, mortgages. Soon Fannie Mae and Freddie Mac, two other government-sponsored agencies, adopted this innovation.[22] These agencies held the local banks to stringent underwriting standards, i.e., the buyer's income had to be strictly documented. So, a national mortgage market was born. It is also known as financial deepening. This was great, because the new model provided safe opportunities for investors with excess cash and enabled money to flow to local communities throughout the US, thereby eliminating the scarcity of local credit.

However, private banks wanted to obtain some of the profits and successfully lobbied the Reagan administration to eliminate regulations prohibiting them from securitizing mortgages in 1984.[23] The Securities and Exchange Commission (SEC) would regulate mortgaged-backed securities so there was no need to worry.[24] So, 45 years of boring banking ended as investments were becoming more exciting. The path-dependent process to the financial crisis had begun.

However, the private banks were unable to compete with Fannie and Freddie backed by the full credit of the US government in the *prime mortgage* market. Fannie and Freddie accepted only those mortgages for securitization in which the borrower had a strong credit rating. However, the private banks found their niche in the *subprime mortgage* market where the borrowers' credit rating was blemished. That turned out to be toxic.

The next innovation in *financial engineering* was to lower the risk of subprime mortgages by dividing the bonds into two or more parts (tranches/slices). Suppose an MBS security was composed of 1,000 individual mortgages, each of which made monthly payments into the MBS pool. The incoming payments of all the mortgages included in the MBS were pooled, and the owners of the top slice received priority for getting paid. Whatever money remained after the owners of the top slice were paid would go to the investors of the second slice and then the third slice. So, the top tranche became an AAA investment since all borrowers would not stop paying simultaneously. The top tranche also paid the lowest interest. The lower tranches received progressively higher interest rates because they were riskier.

For instance, an MBS, created by Citicorp and purchased by Chinese, German, French, and Italian investors, incorporated 4,500 mortgages worth $950 million.[25] The senior tranche was worth $700 million. The credit agencies rated this part "AAA." It paid the lowest interest because even if 1,000 mortgagors defaulted (out of the 4,500) the investors in the top tranche would still be paid in full. It was inconceivable that more than 1,000 mortgages would default simultaneously. Hence, the top portion of an MBS was considered a prime investment although the MBS itself included *some* subprime mortgages. Thus, the financial engineers were like alchemists: they created "AAA" bonds out of subprime mortgages and investors from around the globe eagerly purchased these MBSs.

This was a useful model, but without adequate regulation and oversight had one toxic flaw that Summers, Greenspan, Bernanke, and all their sidekicks overlooked: the powerful deleterious effect of asymmetric information. The local banks realized that they no longer needed to scrutinize the borrowers meticulously because they could sell the mortgages immediately to investment banks like Lehman Brothers for securitization. So, the creditworthiness of the borrower became immaterial since Lehman was not concerned either. They could sell the MBSs to foreign investors who might not even know where Akron was, let alone if the house values in the mortgage pool were properly assessed or if the borrower really had an income. So, the financial engineers had injected a humongous amount of asymmetric information into the system and created concomitant risks that no *due diligence* could solve. That meant that the investors in Singapore did not know what they were buying and obviously the sellers of the securities took advantage of that. Asymmetric information enabled fraud to become widespread. This became the Achilles' heel of financial engineering.

An additional innovation was born in 1994: *credit default swaps* (CDS). It was an insurance contract that insured the owner of a security against default. Suppose Goldman Sachs invested $1 million in an MBS from Lehman Brothers. Goldman could buy insurance on that bond from American International Group (AIG). If Lehman were to default, AIG would *swap* the MBS for $1 million cash.

Swap is a euphemism in order to circumvent the State Insurance Departments that regulate insurance contracts. After all, an insurance contract is like a swap. In case you destroy your car, you'll swap the wreck for money with the insurance company. However, the state regulators make sure that the insurance companies have enough money to make payment on their contractual obligations.

Hence, a CDS is a fancy name for an insurance contract. Its invention was good because insurance is useful in general. However, insurance markets do not work without oversight; consequently, without such oversight the CDS market became toxic. Clinton and Congress even *prohibited* their regulation with The Commodity Futures Modernization Act in 2000. CDSs also fueled the subprime mortgage pipeline because now they could be insured. Boring banking was long gone: finance had become really exciting.

14.3 Double Trouble: Greenspan's Bubble

Bubbles are not part of conventional economics because the efficient-market theory dogmatically rules them out: since investors are rational, bubbles cannot develop, and markets cannot crash (see Section 10.6). There is no speculation, bandwagon effect, herding, contagion, information cascades, fraud, finagling underwriting standards, animal spirits, asymmetric information, opportunistic behavior, or positive feedback loops in the canon. Markets are running harmoniously. Thus, financial instability was excluded from mainstream macroeconomic models that central banks and academics were using to forecast (see Section 10.7). The use of these (real-business-cycle) blackboard models meant that those in charge of the economy failed utterly to understand finance in real time. The fact that Wall Street crashed in 1929 and in 1987 was ignored since investors were supposedly much more sophisticated.

A bubble occurs when an asset's prices drift far above their *fundamental value*. It often involves a novel asset with which investors have not had much experience and which excites the emotions because their future appears lucrative. It is hard to motivate investors about older

Illustration 14.1 Blowing bubbles can be fun, but it's not good for financial stability
Credit: Shutterstock 1290049264

assets, but new investment opportunities in vogue like the internet stocks in the 1990s, MBSs, and CDSs in the 2000s energize the fantasy and greed of investors.

The concept of "fundamental value" is also absent in orthodox finance. Value is defined by what people are willing to pay: the market price. The market cannot err in blackboard economics. Then, in 2005, as house prices *doubled* (1998-2005), even Greenspan noticed some "froth" in the market and "pointed to an increase in speculation in homes." As a result, he said, there are "a lot of local bubbles" around the country.[26] Nonetheless, he dismissed the threat of a national bubble and consequently did absolutely nothing about it.

However, in *behavioral finance* markets do make mistakes. Robert Shiller received a Nobel Prize for his pioneering contributions.[27] In 2009, he acknowledged that the 55 percent decline in the S&P stock prices was due to a "speculative boom," adding:

> [p]sychology really matters ... you can't ignore the psychology, which unfortunately the economics profession has tended to do with recent theorizing; the so-called efficient market hypothesis which says that markets efficiently incorporate all information and work with precision which I think is one of the most remarkable errors in the history of economic thought. This is not efficient markets.[28]

"The most remarkable error" was to believe in efficient markets during the formation of the housing bubble.[29] Conservative economists supported Greenspan's view that piercing bubbles was not his job. The Fed has a dual mandate: to "promote maximum employment, stable prices, and moderate long-term interest rates." Yet, maintaining the stability of the financial system is indirectly an integral part of the mandate, because if finance implodes, unemployment would skyrocket, and price stability would become untenable. So, piercing bubbles should be an integral part of its agenda. And, of course, Greenspan and Bernanke had the means to stop the housing market from overheating. They could have prevented underwriting standards from deteriorating, stopped predatory loans, and prosecuted fraudulent mortgage brokers.[30] And if they thought that they needed more policy instruments, they should have gone to Congress to obtain them.

Admittedly, some bubbles are challenging to identify. The fundamental value of Bitcoin is ambiguous, for instance. However, bubbles in houses are easily recognized because they

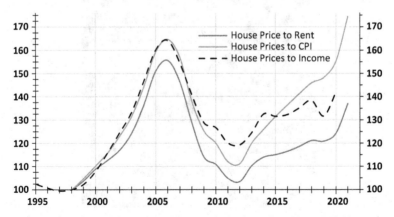

Figure 14.2 Ratio of US house prices to rents, to nominal median household income, and to the consumer price index, Index 1998 = 100

Source: St. Louis Fed, series CSUSHPISA, CUSR0000SEHA, CPIAUCSL.

provide real services whose value is the rent to live in them. Hence, the house price to rent ratio is an easy indicator of fundamental values. Obviously, the bubble began in 1998 since the ratio increased by 20 percent in the subsequent four years, by 40 percent through 2004 and peaked at 59 percent in 2006 (Figure 14.2). Moreover, house prices increased even faster relative to median household income: 65 percent. So, a bubble at the national level should have been evident to Greenspan and Bernanke: house prices increased far above their fundamental value. The quants on Wall Street and the thousand PhDs at the Fed should have taken notice.

14.4 Greenspan Saw Nothing, Bernanke Heard Nothing, and the Fed Said Nothing

The bubble was not on the Fed's radar screen. However, people who saw "the writing on the wall," included Brooksley Born, Edward Gramlich, Steven Keen, Paul Krugman, Raghuram Rajan, Nouriel Roubini, Peter Schiff, Robert Shiller, Joseph Stiglitz, Nassim Taleb, and John Taylor.[31] They were not strangers to Greenspan, Bernanke, or to the establishment. They were not outsiders. They were mostly distinguished scholars at major universities. However, Greenspan and Bernanke wore ideological blinders; their minds were closed and cavalierly they dismissed the warnings.

Greenspan cold-bloodedly thwarted Brooksley Born's valiant efforts to regulate derivative financial instruments in 1998.[32] When Born became Chair of the Commodity Futures Trading Commission, CDSs were new but growing and she was the only one clever enough to recognize that they were futures contracts, so her agency should regulate them. However, she ran into a

Illustration 14.2 Brooksley Born was a hero, the Joan of Arc of US finance. Her attempt to save the system was torpedoed by Alan Greenspan, Robert Rubin, and Larry Summers
Credit: Larry Levanti.

whirlwind of opposition. Her congressional interrogators asked, "What are you trying to protect?" She answered: "We're trying to protect the money of the American public."[33] Greenspan became "livid" and supposedly spread rumors that she was "irascible, stubborn, and unreasonable."[34] The establishment ganged up and ran her out of town. To his discredit, Clinton did nothing to support her. Instead, he signed the law that *prohibited* the regulation of derivatives, inching closer toward the Meltdown. No wonder the *Time* article referred to Greenspan, Rubin, and Summers as a "free-market Politburo on economic matters."[35] They won that fight but lost control of the financial markets.

Amazingly, Born, along with Sheila Bair, Chair of the FDIC between 2006–2011, were the only two heroes of the financial crisis. Financial commonsense spanning three administrations was limited to these two women. In 2009, they both received the "John F. Kennedy Profiles in Courage Award" in recognition of the "political courage each demonstrated in sounding early warnings about conditions that contributed to the current global financial crisis." According to Caroline Kennedy, "Brooksley Born recognized that the financial security of all Americans was being put at risk by the greed, negligence and opposition of powerful and well-connected interests."[36]

Warren Buffett sounded the next significant warning in his 2002 annual report to shareholders. He pointed out that "derivatives are financial weapons of mass destruction, carrying dangers that, while now latent, are potentially lethal."[37] Among economists, Dean Baker recognized the housing bubble also in 2002.[38] Were incomes increasing, one could understand the rising demand for houses, but they were not increasing at all. Instead, real median household incomes were falling, while the median price of single-family houses increased from $152,000 to $245,000.[39] This made little economic sense.

By 2004, the worrying intensified. The portentous article, "Blowing Bubbles" appeared in *The New Yorker*, with a circulation of 1 million, reporting that "even some of Greenspan's colleagues are concerned that one bubble has given way to another ... [Yet] Greenspan refuses to contemplate such a catastrophe. On Capitol Hill recently, he insisted that the economy 'seems to be on track.'"[40]

Then, in 2005, a critical warning came from inside the finance establishment from Raghuram Rajan of the University of Chicago Business School, who later became the Governor of the Reserve Bank of India. At a symposium of the Federal Reserve at Jackson Hole, Wyoming, to celebrate Greenspan's retirement, Rajan warned about the accumulation of risk and cautioned about the deceptive nature of financial innovation.[41] He spoke of perverse developments so that managers have:

> the incentive to take risk that is concealed from investors—since risk and return are related, the manager then looks as if he outperforms peers given the risk he takes. Typically, the kinds of risks that can most easily be concealed, ... are risks that generate severe adverse consequences with small probability but, in return, offer generous compensation the rest of the time. These risks are known as tail risks.

A second form of perverse behavior is the incentive to herd with other investment managers on investment choices because herding provides insurance that the manager will not underperform his peers. Herd behavior can move asset prices away from fundamentals.[42]

In short, asymmetric information was leading to the mispricing of assets while *groupthink* intensified the bubble. Rajan continued:

> In fact, the data suggest that despite a deepening of financial markets, banks may not be any safer than in the past. Moreover, the risk they now bear is a small ... tip of an iceberg

of risk they have created ... They [banks] also may create a greater (albeit still small) probability of a catastrophic meltdown.[43]

Besides Greenspan, Bernanke, and Timothy Geithner, then President of the New York Fed and subsequently Obama's bailout chief, were in the audience. So were correspondents of major financial media including *The Financial Times* and *The Wall Street Journal*, governors of foreign central banks, chief economists of major banks, and luminaries from academia.[44] Yet, Rajan's powerful warning fell on deaf ears.

Interviews with Bernanke are indicative of the dominant mind-set. Queried about a possible housing-market bubble in 2005, he responded:

> Unquestionably housing prices are up quite a bit. I think it's important to note that fundamentals are also very strong: we've *got* a growing economy, jobs, incomes; we've got very low mortgage rates; we've got demographics supporting housing growth; we've got restricted supply in some places; so, it's certainly understandable that prices would go up some. I don't know whether prices are exactly where they should be, but I think it's fair to say that what's happened is supported by the strength of the economy.[45]

That was newspeak 21 years after *1984*. The doubling of house prices is much more than "*some*" increase. Have we really "*got*" incomes when real incomes were falling? Have we really "got" jobs when millions have dropped out of the labor force and were killing themselves by the thousands?[46] And there was no demographics that fueled the bubble. But he had to avoid committing a "thoughtcrime" in order to become Greenspan's successor. Consequently, he misled the public.

When another reporter asked him in July 2005 for his worst-case scenario, he responded disingenuously:

> I guess I don't buy your premise; it's a pretty unlikely possibility. We've never had a decline in house prices on a nationwide basis. [He knew that we *did* have such a decline during the Great Depression!] So what I think is more likely is that house prices will slow, maybe stabilize, might slow consumption spending a bit; I don't think it will drive the economy too far from its full employment path though.[47]

Note that he was wrong about the economic situation and spoke of full employment at a time when there were 7.6 million people officially unemployed and another 9 million unemployed without being counted as such.[48] His misleading statement caused many people to feel safe about continuing to invest in property in 2005-2007 and lose their money in the Meltdown. Nonetheless, Bernanke did become Greenspan's successor.

Then, in 2006, Nouriel Roubini suggested that the housing market is going "through an ugly and nasty bust," and a recession was around the corner.[49] But none of these early warnings was taken seriously. Finance had a momentum of its own as Charles Prince—CEO of Citigroup—quipped in July 2007, "as long as the music is playing, you've got to get up and dance."[50] The music was playing for him for another three months. Then he resigned.

14.5 The Minsky Moment: The Meltdown of 2008

The Meltdown was straight out of Minsky's playbook.[51] Minsky had warned in vain that the financial system was inherently unstable, that debt accumulation was dangerous, and that financial crises were endogenous.[52] Similar to Keynes' notion of animal spirits, Minsky was keenly aware that loan contracts committed firms to payments from expected future profits and if business-men were overly optimistic about their ability to repay those debt and if the business cycle turned against them, a cascade of bankruptcies could ensue. The question is: to what extent were the future profits correctly anticipated, and what happens if those expectations are not realized? In his prescient words:

> The first theorem of the financial instability hypothesis is that the economy has financ-ing regimes under which it is stable and financing regimes under which it is unstable. The second theorem ... is that over periods of prolonged prosperity, the economy transits from financial relations that make for a stable system to financial relations that make for an unstable system.[53]

After a bubble bursts, asset prices decline and the net worth of firms "will quickly evaporate. Consequently, businesses with cash flow shortfalls will be forced to try to make position by sell-ing out position. This is likely to lead to a collapse of asset values."[54] *Systemic risk* implies that one bankruptcy triggers the insolvency of other firms so that a domino effect threatens the whole economy. This is the exact scenario of the Meltdown.

Of course, remaining vigilant is not easy for regulators since there is a lot of pressure put on them. *Regulation always costs money in the short run because of foregone profits.* Its beneficial effects are uncertain and realized in the distant future. This provides a powerful incentive for myopic bankers to advocate deregulation. What have you got against profits? So, beginning with the Reagan administration and continuing through Clinton's presidency, they succeeded in undoing regulations that provided the guardrails of stability. Clinton even repealed the Glass-Steagall Act and replaced it with the Financial Services Modernization Act of 1999. He signed another "modernization" Act the following year. So Clinton succumbed to the dominant dogma of the time that financial markets could regulate themselves and oversight was superfluous. Anyone who dared to question the received wisdom was vilified.[55]

While government oversight relaxed, the financial sector innovated, with derivatives, mort-gage-backed securities, credit default swaps, collateralized debt obligations, securitization, interstate banking, and variable rate mortgages.

Moreover, the *shadow banking system* blossomed, outsmarting the regulations in place. The shadow banks were investment banks like Lehman, Bear Stearns, Goldman Sachs, Morgan Stan-ley, and Merrill Lynch. Greenspan and Bernanke made the naïve mistake of thinking that the shadow banks were isolated from the commercial banking sector because their deposits were not guaranteed by the FDIC.[56] They were also not eligible to borrow from the Fed like commer-cial banks were. So, the Fed was not responsible for them, and they remained under the Fed's radar. However, the reality was that the two parts of the financial world were interlinked in numerous ways through investments in each other's bonds and through the insurance policies written on those bonds. However, as the systems were running smoothly, naysayers—including Brooksley Born—were silenced mercilessly.

Minsky also emphasized the role of "*euphoric*" booms in financial instability.[57] During euphoric manias both lenders and borrowers made systematic errors of judgment about the loans they contracted by undervaluing the probability of default. Expectations were hopelessly biased. Minsky's models—derived from the historical record rather than from *a priori* theorizing about idealized markets—did not fit well into the popular rational-agent framework. To apply the perfectly competitive model to the financial sector, as Greenspan and Bernanke did, was negligent.

Consequently, Minsky's ideas were cavalierly dismissed by narrow-minded policy makers like Bernanke.[58] Stability was deceiving, as the financial sector evolved and bypassed regulations. The innovations were not designed to improve the productivity of the real economy, i.e., to increase the efficiency of investments, productivity, and GDP; instead, they were designed for *rent seeking* (obtaining a bigger share of profits generated by the real sector of the economy). These innovations injected immense amounts of asymmetric information and systemic risk into the macroeconomy.

Another major problem was that the investors buying these new financial instruments had no experience pricing the risks associated with them: being new, historical evidence of their volatility during a recession was not available. Therefore, during the euphoric episodes of easy money, the risks were woefully mispriced. The overall financial architecture was not designed to accommodate such innovations without enhanced oversight.

Thus, the extraordinary profits of the financial sector were deceptive since they were immediate and obvious, whereas the risks associated with them were intangible, opaque, uncertain, and well into the future. The extraordinary profits enriched executives and everyone involved in the chain of command. To remain prudent under such conditions was practically impossible because their returns would be below industry norms due to the smaller risks they were taking. However, the risks were invisible to investors; hence, the investors would have attributed the lower returns not to lower risks but to the money managers' incompetence. They would not have remained in business for long as investors would have withdrawn their funds and transferred them to the higher-return, higher-risk money managers.

Moreover, the investment banks were highly leveraged and relied on billions of dollars' worth of new loans *daily* to remain in business. When it became apparent that they had made systematic errors in pricing risks, the flow of credit froze, and they were all threatened with insolvency. So, it was a risky business model with many hidden dangerous tipping points, based on mispricing of risk, and being exposed to the shocks of negative externalities, i.e., systemic effects.

Speculation was not confined to investment banks. Consumers were also caught up in the euphoria and were exposed to excessive risks or fell prey to predatory lenders.[59] Dubious practices included low teaser rates sometimes for as short as three months, false advertising, misinformation about adjustable-rate mortgages, interest-only loans, payment option loans, and no-documentation loans.[60] In sum, finagling and fraud were ubiquitous and risk was ill understood, and underpriced. Instead of diversifying risk, the shadow banking system amplified it while Greenspan and Bernanke fell asleep at the wheel.

14.6 Thirty-Two Causes of the Meltdown

The Meltdown was a complex event that marked the confluence of developments decades in the making. The causes include:

1   *Greenspan's free-market ideology* was the main culprit. For 19 years he was the most powerful economic authority in the world. He could have reined in the runaway financiers, but he was fundamentally skeptical of regulating. He had excessive faith in the efficient-market hypothesis and in the self-regulating mechanism of markets. He overlooked the principal-agent problem, moral hazard, systemic risks, asymmetric information, fraud in

underwriting, predatory loans, and the mispricing of risk. This was negligence, not mere miscalculation. That liberal-Democrat Clinton reappointed Greenspan, an arch-conservative Republican, in 1996 is yet another evidence of bad judgment.

2   *The financial innovations* (MBSs and CDSs) introduced financial instruments with which investors were unfamiliar. Minsky called such innovations "displacements," i.e., they were new, exciting, and captured investors' imagination. Based on the historical record, he warned that bubbles start with such displacements. These derivatives were not well understood, and finance was overwhelmed by asymmetric information. Although investors did not know the risks involved, in a euphoria these investments became popular and widespread.

3   *The rise of the shadow banking system,* largely outside the purview of regulators, grew immensely, relative to the commercial banks which were under the Fed's protective umbrella. In 1990, the assets of the shadow banking system amounted to half of the assets of commercial banks, but by 2000 the two systems were on par, and, on the eve of the crisis, shadow banks were $3 trillion ahead of commercial banks ($13 vs $10 trillion).[61] These financial institutions (hedge funds, investment banks, money market mutual funds, and mortgage lenders) functioned like banks but the loophole was that they were not regulated as banks.

The Meltdown swept away all five giant investment banks. Their business model was faulty because they required the inflow of billions every day to sustain their day-to-day operations. At the end of 2007, for instance, Bear Stearns needed $70 billion daily to remain in business.[62] Because of a crisis of confidence the inflow of credit suddenly stopped, and these banks were threatened with insolvency. This was similar to a traditional bank run but the customers did not queue up at the teller windows; instead, depositors clicked on the "refund" button in cyberspace.

4   *Greenspan's and Bernanke's neglect of systemic risk,* as an amplification mechanism, was inexcusable. Systemic risk is like a negative externality because one bank's mistake can lead to a liquidity crisis of other banks and through contagion can affect the whole system. One firm's failure causes losses of asset values of other firms, causing panic, bank runs, and a cascade of insolvencies. History is replete with such episodes. Yet, the Fed was impervious to that threat. Bernanke claimed naïvely as late as May 2007 that:

> Importantly, we see no serious broader spillover to banks or thrift institutions from problems in the subprime market; the troubled lenders, for the most part, have not been institutions with federally insured deposits . . . we do not expect significant spillovers from the subprime market to the rest of the economy or to the financial system.[63]

Spillover effect is another term for systemic effect. In Bernanke's simplistic view, the failure of a bank like Lehman Brothers would not affect other banks. It is incomprehensible that he completely disregarded the interlinked obligations between the shadow banking system and conventional commercial banks like the credit default swaps that created systemic risks.

However, these became evident with Lehman's bankruptcy, because the insurer of its bonds, AIG, was unable to honor its obligations and swap the worthless bonds for billions of dollars. The whole financial architecture was tottering.[64] In order to avoid the implosion of the system, Bernanke bailed out AIG with $186 billion at the taxpayers' expense.[65] The full $86 billion of it was paid the day after Lehman's bankruptcy. He did not bargain for a discount but paid dollar for dollar, after all, it was not his money. And the economy entered a new phase of *bailout capitalism* in which the economy is so far out of equilibrium that the only way to stabilize the system is through government support to businesses and households.[66]

5   *Credit rating agencies* were useless because they had perverse incentives to commit financial alchemy. Their seal of approval turned subprime mortgages into triple-A-rated mortgage-backed securities. Since they were paid by the banks, these could threaten to turn to the competition if the rating agencies did not give them high ratings. There was no reason for the agencies to resist since they were not guaranteeing their ratings. So, Lehman's ratings were not downgraded until its collapse was imminent.[67] From 2000 to 2007, Moody's rated nearly 45,000 mortgage-related securities as triple A. In 2006 alone, Moody's put its triple-A stamp of approval on 30 mortgage-related securities every day. The results were disastrous: 83 percent of the mortgage securities rated AAA that year were ultimately downgraded.[68] No one was watching the watchers.

6   *The Dot-Com bubble* was linked to the subprime mortgage bubble. The recession that followed the Dot-Com bubble prompted Greenspan to lower the interest rate from 6.5 percent in summer 2000 to 1.25 percent by the end of 2002.[69] That worked, and the recession was over in eight months despite 9/11, reinforcing the Greenspan put. The drawback was that Greenspan and Bernanke both believed that the subprime crisis could be managed as easily as the Dot-Com bubble. This inference was flawed because the two bubbles were completely different. The ownership of internet stocks was limited to relatively few speculators. In contrast, 73 million households held mortgages and a decline in home prices impacted them powerfully. That made an order of magnitude difference. Moreover, the Dot-Com IPOs amounted to $27 billion in 1997–1999 whereas subprime mortgages totaled $3.5 trillion.[70] That also differed by an order of magnitude. Additionally, Dot-Com stocks were not insured by CDSs, as were the mortgage-backed securities, which meant that Dot-Com bubble had negligible systemic effects. Greenspan and Bernanke were myopic to ignore these salient differences.

7   For once in his life Greenspan blundered by *lowering interest rates* in 2003, because by the summer real GDP was growing at a good clip of 3.2 percent (Figure 14.3).[71] There was no reason to lower the Federal Funds rate further to 1 percent. Moreover, he kept them low for another year! That added oil to the fire. Consequently, the economy overheated and grew in excess of 4.2 percent for six quarters.[72] Thus, Greenspan contributed to the ballooning of the subprime mortgage crisis by creating too much liquidity for too long after the Dot-Com bubble. After 16 years of being the world's financial wizard, he committed a single tragic mistake.

8   *According to Minsky's model, liquidity is necessary for the formation of a bubble.* The fact that easy money was chasing assets drives asset prices higher. This is exactly what happened not only because of the low interest rates set by Greenspan but also because the Asian *savings glut* channeled a lot of money back into the US banking system, adding to the excess supply of credit. The *easy credit* led to asset inflation.

9   *The savings glut was based on the US endemic trade deficits* (see Figure 13.3) which gave the rest of the world a lot of dollars that were saved and funneled back into the US financial system adding to the easy-money policy of the Fed.

10 Flush with funds, *banks lowered underwriting standards* on a wide scale to attract new customers. There was no other way they could profit from the excess supply of funds. So, mortgage originators misreported incomes, appraisers inflated home values, and the supply of *fraudulent credit proliferated*.[73]

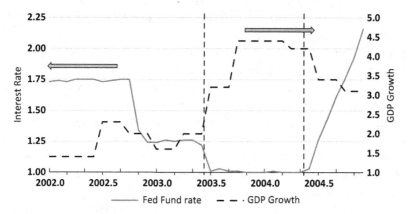

Figure 14.3 The Fed's interest rate and GDP growth
Source: Federal Reserve Bank of St. Louis, series FEDFUNDS and A191RO1Q156NBEA.

"NINJA loans" ("no income, no job, no assets") signaled the decline in underwriting standards. These were no documentation loans, implying that income was fictitious, and its repayment implausible. Although fraudulent, Greenspan remained unfazed, since he believed that the market would price those risks into its models. Underwriting standards deteriorated further with pay-option adjustable-rate mortgages which allowed debtors to pay lower monthly amounts. The balance would be added to the outstanding loan.

11 *By lowering underwriting standards, subprime lending expanded* in 2004 in tandem with Greenspan's easy-money policy. Subprime mortgages had been 6 percent of total mortgage originations in 2001-2003 but in 2004 they surged to almost 20 percent and stayed there for two more years. In 2004–2006, subprime mortgage originations totaled $1.7 trillion– half of all subprime–and the Rubicon was crossed.[74]

12 *Predatory lending* made matters worse. The gimmicks included "balloon payments with unrealistic repayment terms," "excessive fees not justified by the costs of services provided and the credit and interest rate risks involved," "abusive collection practices," "excessive interest rates," "teaser interest rates," "fraud," "lending without regard to ability to repay," "no documentation loans," and "equity stripping."[75] Ameriquest Mortgage, the largest subprime mortgage lender, was accused of having broken the law, "deceiving borrowers about the terms of their loans, forging documents, falsifying appraisals and fabricating borrowers' income to qualify them for loans they couldn't afford."[76] It was fined $325 million. Yet, nobody was charged with fraud.

Consumers were manipulated by enticing them with deceptive promises. Countrywide was fishing for gullible people by signaling that they were open to commit fraud. The announcer in one of their advertisements said, "I got them all approved," even for a "business owner whose income was hard to document," after no less than three banks had turned him down.[77] Washington Mutual also boasted that their lenders "write their own approval rules,"[78] or that they had "flexible lending rules" while the lending officer was breaking the rules symbolically with his hands.[79]

Greenspan was a veritable cheerleader of subprime: "American consumers might benefit if lenders provided greater mortgage product alternatives to the traditional fixed-rate mortgage."[80] He put a Panglossian spin on dubious lending by contending in 2005: "With these advances in technology, lenders have taken advantage of credit-scoring models and other techniques for efficiently extending credit to a broader spectrum of consumers."[81] History proved him wrong.

13   *Fraudulent mortgages were thus obtained by those who had no means to repay them.* These developments created fertile ground for a humongous bubble in home prices. Bernanke should have known that house prices were far above their fundamental value (see Figure 14.2). After all, between 1997 and 2005 house prices doubled although real median household income declined by $1,847 from their peak value (in 2019 prices) (see Figure 7.9).[82] It was obviously a bubble based on irrational exuberance, on the deterioration in underwriting standards, and on the low interest rates, while Greenspan and Bernanke looked the other way. House prices peaked in June 2006 and wavered until February 2007 and then collapsed precipitously, falling by 26 percent until February 2012.

14   As Minsky warned, *the illusion of tranquility was deceptive,* and stability bred instability. While the Fed relaxed its oversight, finance innovated, thereby increasing the fragility in the system. This was a major cause of the crisis, according to the IMF.[83]

15   The spirit of the times supported Greenspan's ideology of *deregulation and lax enforcement of regulations* that were still on the books. It started under the Reagan administration. He allowed private banks to securitize mortgages and to grant variable rate mortgages. He deregulated savings banks and allowed them to expand into the commercial banking business. Clinton was no more prudent. In 1994, he lifted the ban on interstate banking that led to the too-big-to-fail banks.

16   *Groupthink* meant that Greenspan's views were sacrosanct within the Fed. Dissent from the party line was taboo and the culprit faced ostracism. Such intolerance frequently leads to dysfunctional group dynamics and that pertained also to the pre-crisis Fed. Greenspan continued to repeat that "no one saw the crisis coming," which is obviously nonsense.[84] He was simply not open to alternative perspectives. He ran Brooksley Born out of town and when Fed colleague Ed Gramlich proposed cracking down on predatory lending, Greenspan shooed him away.[85] Greenspan heard Rajan's lecture at Jackson Hole since he was in the audience, yet still he did nothing. He did not care about Shiller's warning (2005) that "the [housing] market is in the throes of a bubble of unprecedented proportions that probably will end ugly."[86] Bernanke also failed to listen to Roubini's warning that the recession will be "ugly." Their minds were simply made up and they *chose* not to listen while the storm was brewing.

17   *Excessive faith in quantitative finance* was pervasive, although it had not been tested in a crisis and although their data did not extend back far enough, so, number crunching that included the 1930s was impossible.[87] The bankruptcy of LTCM was forgotten. The Dot-Com bubble was a breeze. The Wall Street engineers had impressive PhDs from MIT and built complex computer models that worked perfectly on blackboards. Surely, the sophisticated "quants" could calculate probabilities and manage risk with high-speed computers. However, they lacked experience, were insensitive to the fragility of the system, and ignored 1929. Hence, they neglected the possibility of a panic and the "odds of catastrophic price changes."[88] One would have had to use common sense, which was not so common among the quants.

18   *An indebtedness was disadvantageous* because it limited the government's response to the crisis. How much more effective Obama's response could have been if the debt to GDP ratio was still 30 percent as at Reagan's inauguration instead of 64 percent (see Figure 12.1). If Bush Jr. had only not added 10 percent to the debt ratio before the crisis, Obama's response

could have been more vigorous. By mid-2012, the ratio exceeded 100 percent, not comfortably situated for the next crisis to come in 2020!

Similarly, households without adequate savings were unable to meet commitments in a downturn leading to bankruptcies, foreclosures, and evictions. The increase in the mortgage debt from $92,000 to $150,000 per household between 2001 and 2007 burdened their balance sheet, especially when real incomes were declining.[89] Households were not well prepared for a recession. Such an unbalanced economy is more susceptible to gyrations.

19 *Financialization* is the growing importance of finance in the economy at the expense of manufacturing.[90] It implies that the economy lacks diversification and is tantamount to putting too many eggs into one basket. Finance accounted for 4 percent of GDP and 17 percent of corporate profits in 1980, but its importance doubled by the early twenty-first century to 8 percent and its share in corporate profits reached 27 percent between 2001 and 2007.[91] This was problematic because finance is not a job creator that could absorb the millions displaced from manufacturing: finance employed just 5.7 percent of the labor force in 2020 and is projected to decline by 0.2 percentage points by 2030.[92] This development fostered the dual economy.

20 *Herd mentality* meant that investors followed their peers in underpricing risk. Competition meant a race to the bottom. Keynes recognized that "it is better to fail conventionally than succeed unconventionally." Roubini echoes Keynes in explaining:

> Who wants to stick their neck out and call for a recession when your entire colleagues on Wall Street claim otherwise? If you follow the herd and you are wrong you can hide in the herd and everyone was wrong ... There is a meaningful conflict of interest considering the costs and benefits of sticking one's head out of the herd.[93]

Money managers taking excessive risks were earning extraordinary returns without their clients knowing that those were not pure returns but payments for being exposed to tail risks.[94] Competitors taking less risk could not stay in business because it appeared like they were underperforming rather than being prudent. Herding behavior also meant that the speculative fever was contagious as people assumed that home prices would increase indefinitely.

21 *Mispricing of risk* was ubiquitous.[95] Risk is intangible and therefore difficult to price for improbable events. The left tail of the probability distribution of Lehman defaulting was an order-of-magnitude bigger than the quants guesstimated. This is called *"fat tails."* Based on the price of CDS (insurance), the market's estimate in 2005 of the probability of Lehman defaulting was

$$\frac{1}{500} = (0.2\%)$$

i.e., would occur twice in a millennium. Three years later Lehman was bankrupt. In March 2008, just prior to Bear Stearns' demise, the market was still estimating Lehman's probability of bankruptcy as between $\frac{1}{200}$ (0.5 percent) and 1.0 percent.[96] Immediately after the Bear Stearns crisis, the probability reached 9 percent and then climbed to 19 percent on September 11, although the Meltdown was imminent.[97] These were ostrich-like estimates—light-years away from an efficient market.

22 *The Securities and Exchange Commission (SEC) was also negligent.* The audio recording of a meeting provides evidence of the irresponsible exercise of oversight. In 2004, the

SEC made a fateful change to the rules governing the risk management of the five biggest investment banks. They petitioned to increase their leverage by using their own computer models to assess risks instead of the SEC's existing objective rules.

Chairman William Donaldson pontificated:

> If we do this wisely, and we and our fellow regulators listen to and learn from each other, we will help the investing public by using the best available tools to manage risk to the health of our markets ... by allowing the market for financial services to continue to evolve.

Commissioner Harvey Goldschmid was the only one who expressed some reservations:

> [W]e said these are the big guys ... but that means if anything goes wrong, it's going to be an awfully big mess [laughter] and do we feel secure if there are these drops in capital and other things, we really will have investor protection?

Annette Nazareth, the director of market regulation answered, "We are going to be meeting with these firms on a monthly basis ... we'll have, you know, hopefully a lot of early warnings, and the ability to constrict activity that we think is problematic."

Harvey Goldschmid still had some doubts: "This is going to be much more complicated compliance inspection, understanding of risk than we've ever had to do. Mike, I trust you to no end, but I take it you think we can do this." [More laughter]

A staff member responded:

> We're going to depend on the firms obviously. They're in the front line. They're going to have to develop their entire risk framework. We'll be reading that first and they'll have to explain that to us in a way that makes sense and then we'll do the examination process in addition to approving their models and their risk control systems. So, I mean but it's a large undertaking. I'm not going to try to do it alone. [laughter again]

"I..I..I'm very happy to support it," added Commissioner Roel Campos, adding "And I keep my fingers crossed for the future."[98]

The committee's approval was unanimous, an example of groupthink in action. "With that, the five big independent investment firms were unleashed."[99] The meeting was a travesty: it is a bad idea to support such momentous decision while keeping one's fingers crossed. Thereafter the SEC relied on the firms to police themselves.

23   Thereafter, *leverage got out of control*: Morgan Stanley's rose from 22 to 33, Bear Stearns' from 27 to 33, Lehman's from 22 to 32, Merrill Lynch's from 16 to 32, and Goldman Sachs' from 18 to 24. Thus, their own capital made up a tiny share (3 percent) of their investments. If the value of their assets dropped by just 3 percent, their capital would evaporate, and they would become insolvent. Obviously, this was an extremely risky business model and one vulnerable to bank runs. When their balance sheet deteriorated, i.e., the value of their stock prices plummeted, investors were unwilling to lend them the billions they required daily to stay in business.

Only the Fed's printing presses saved them. That SEC meeting with all its levity and cavalier handling of the serious issue of risk management contributed to the destabilization of the shadow banking system. That was a watershed moment and soon all five investment banks were history. Lehman was bankrupt, Bear Stearns was taken over by JPMorgan Chase with $29 billion subsidy from the Fed, Hank Paulson blackmailed Bank of America

CEO Ken Lewis to take over Merrill Lynch and sweetened the deal with a $20 billion super-secret "exceptional" loan,[100] while Goldman Sachs and Morgan Stanley sought the Fed's protection acquiring commercial bank charters so they could borrow from the Fed and receive billions of taxpayer dollars.[101] Their risky business models brought an end to these behemoth investment banks.

24 *Globalization magnified the bubble* in three ways: (a) through the Asian savings glut that injected much liquidity into the US financial system that ended up in the subprime mortgage market; (b) by amplifying the US trade deficit which was the source of the savings glut; and (c) by providing a global market for the MBS securities created by Wall Street. By the time those securities reached faraway places information about them had evaporated. For instance, eight tiny municipalities near the Arctic Circle in Norway lost $75 million—by buying from a Norwegian broker highly leveraged and extremely risky Citibank bonds. The investors were clueless: their downside was enormous and completely disproportional to their possible gains. Risk was obviously mispriced, the investors gullible, the documents mistranslated, and the opportunist broker took advantage of asymmetric information.[102]

25 *Moral hazard had accumulated.* The market's trust in the "Greenspan put" was unrealistic. As John Cassidy noted: "Given Greenspan's role in promoting and prolonging the stock-market bubble that burst in 2000, the deference that surrounds him seems a little over-done."[103] This perception was reinforced when in March 2008 the Fed, by then under Bernanke's leadership, subsidized Bear Stearns's takeover by JPMorgan Chase with $29 billion. Consequently, Lehman's bankruptcy six months later caught the markets off-guard, creating turmoil. Financiers panicked when they realized that they had put too much faith in the Fed.

26 *Lack of historical perspective was a shortcoming*, because it contributed to the sense of infallibility. Wall Street forgot the past and was therefore condemned to repeat its mistakes. With a few exceptions, most CEOs like Dick Fuld (Lehman Brothers), Jamie Dimon (JPMorgan Chase), Ken Lewis (Bank of America), John Thain (Merrill Lynch), or Lloyd Blankfein (Goldman Sachs) were all baby boomers whose character was formed during the post-World War II heady days. Of course, the traders and money managers were much younger; for them the Great Depression might as well have happened on another planet. History was irrelevant for them.

27 *Hubris was ubiquitous.* Being conceited is a mental bias that becomes toxic if it infects people in positions of authority. It manifested itself in Bernanke's pronouncement of the "Great Moderation." It was demonstrated in daily exaltations of the sophistication of the financial engineers. It was revealed in Fuld's rage about short sellers depressing share prices in 2007. He fulminated that he wanted to:

> [s]queeze some of those shorts ... squeeze them hard ... Not that I want to hurt them. Don't get that please. That's just not who I am. I'm soft, I'm lovable, but what I really want to do ... is I want to reach in, rip out their heart, and eat it before they die.[104]

The financial sector was full of people with such abnormal egos.

28 *A culture that considers greed normal* is prone to generate instability. Greed is bad because it blinds and magnifies the effect of irrational exuberance.[105] Greed goes beyond the normal limits of profit seeking. It is egocentricity taken to an extreme: insatiable selfishness. Because it knows no moral limits and because it usually hurts others, it is destabilizing and harmful. No wonder that avarice was considered a mortal sin for millennia.

29   *Inequality of income also contributed to the crisis.* The predatory-mortgage model was based on tempting consumers with poor credit ratings. The middle class already had mortgages. They could not absorb the excess liquidity caused by the savings glut and by Greenspan's easy-money policy. Having been shut out of the "American Dream," the poor were easily manipulated into believing that this was their once-in-a-lifetime opportunity to reach it.

30   *Corporate governance was also a factor* because the board of directors' supervision of the banks' CEOs was lax; they disregarded the principal-agent problem. The remuneration structure incentivized the CEOs, the brokers, and the mortgage originators to reach for high yields in pursuit of bonuses but the accumulating risk was not their concern. The CEOs did well financially even as they bankrupted their firms. They gained from the upside, but shareholders and taxpayers were left with the downside. That's the basics of moral hazard. None of them slipped out of the 1 percent into the middle class. Angelo Mozilo (Countrywide Financial) still has $600 million; Dick Fuld (Lehman Brothers) has $250 million; John Thain (Merrill Lynch) has $100 million.[106] Charles Prince received $40 million for bringing Citigroup to the brink. Kenneth Lewis (Bank of America) (2001-2009) received an average salary of $30 million per annum while he was guiding the bank to the brink, saved only by the generous taxpayer-financed bailouts.[107]

Even those CEOs who bankrupted their companies received astronomical compensation. John Thain received $83 million just before Merrill Lynch became insolvent.[108] His predecessor left the firm with a golden parachute of $159 million although the firm lost $8 billion.[109] G. Kennedy Thompson received $15.7 million before Wachovia became history. This evidence contradicts the idea that CEO compensation is based on the value of their marginal product.

Even during the Great Recession when the banks were being propped up by Uncle Sam, the CEOs were getting away with millions: Lloyd Blankfein (Goldman Sachs) $25.8 million; John Stumpf (Wells Fargo) 13.8; Ken Lewis (Bank of America) $9 million; Jamie Dimon (JPMorgan Chase) $8.5 million; Vikram Pandit (Citigroup) $2.9 million.[110] Even the CEO of General Motors received $2.3 million while in bankruptcy court. "The fact that these high earners failed so miserably should add to the evidence against a direct link between higher rewards and better performance."[111]

31   *The revolving door* is a metaphor describing the movement of executives into government and subsequently returning to the private sector. This is unhealthy for democracy because it limits the perspectives of government officials. An independent view of finance and its social implications eludes them. Instead, they have more concern for Wall Street than for Main Street, like the millionaires Hank Paulson and Robert Rubin, both Treasury Secretaries from Goldman Sachs. The revolving door leads to *cognitive capture* because the corporate mentality dominates in government. This contributes to *regulatory capture* (see Section 8.7). The revolving door also provides powerful incentives for government officials to anticipate their prospects after they leave government and support policy on behalf of corporations that might hire them.

This was Timothy Geithner's strategy, Obama's first Treasury Secretary. He was amply rewarded for this tenacious support of Wall Street without any consideration for Main Street. After he quit the Treasury, he went directly to a private equity firm and became a proud member of the 1 percent-ers. After leaving the Fed, Ben Bernanke is also amply re-warded, earning millions from the largesse of the financial sector for his speeches.

32   *The media was not informing the population of the bubble.* It was not presenting the facts that housing prices had doubled, that incomes were not increasing, that this could not last forever, and perhaps a bit more caution is warranted.

In sum, a confluence of powerful impersonal economic forces coupled with ideological myopia and greed led to the Meltdown. No wonder that the crisis was so devastating. Monocausal explanations are inadequate. The crisis was brought about and magnified by the above 32 factors; they were intertwined into one convoluted "Gordian knot."

Some conservative commentators attempted to pin the crisis on Fannie Mae and Freddie Mac,[112] two government-sponsored mortgage agencies. This is unfounded. They were not the driving force in the crisis. They were not among the largest players in the subprime market. Countrywide Financial, Washington Mutual, or Ameriquest were the largest originators of subprime and they "forged documents, hyped customers' creditworthiness, and 'juiced' mortgages with hidden rates and fees."[113] And they were not responsible for the spread of CDSs either.[114] Subprime lending peaked 2004-2006, when Fannie and Freddie's share of that segment of the market fell relative to the private firms.[115] In 2006, 84 percent of subprime mortgages were issued by the private sector.

Some also cite the Community Reinvestment Act of 1977 as a cause of the crisis.[116] But the Act only specified that banks should invest also in the communities in which they operate branch offices "so long as these activities didn't impair their own financial safety and soundness."[117] Congress was concerned that the banks also serve underprivileged neighborhoods instead of syphoning off capital from them.[118] The Act did not induce them to commit fraud or to grant subprime mortgages, and securitize them. Moreover, the main culprits like Countrywide were not affected by the Act anyhow. These are silly arguments by ideologues who have no respect for the evidence. The roots of the crisis can be found in the Reagan administration's "Secondary Mortgage Market Enhancement Act of 1984," which allowed private banks to securitize mortgages.

The Financial Crisis Inquiry Commission rightly blamed Greenspan and Bernanke the most: "the Federal Reserve's pivotal failure to stem the flow of toxic mortgages, which it could have done by setting prudent mortgage-lending standards. The Federal Reserve was the one entity empowered to do so and it did not." However, others blundered as well:

> Financial institutions made, bought, and sold mortgage securities they never examined, did not care to examine, or knew to be defective; firms depended on tens of billions of dollars of borrowing that had to be renewed each and every night, secured by subprime mortgage securities; and major firms and investors blindly relied on credit rating agencies as their arbiters of risk.[119]

The commission concluded that:

> The captains of finance and the public stewards of our financial system ignored warnings and failed to question, understand, and manage evolving risks within a system essential to the well-being of the American public. Theirs was a big miss, not a stumble... To paraphrase Shakespeare, the fault lies not in the stars, but in us.[120]

14.7 Bailout Capitalism: The Crisis Obama Wasted

The Great Recession followed the subprime mortgage crisis. The economy tanked: GDP per capita declined by 5 percent (see Figure 17.5), the *real* unemployment rate (U-6) reached 17 percent, foreclosures rose steeply (9 million), with widespread pain and untold suffering. The investment in residential housing was cut in half between 2006 and 2009, which put a $400 billion hole in aggregate demand. Net investment in tangible assets (including housing) declined by 78 percent, or by $614 billion.[121] This was the most severe and longest calamity in the US since the Great Depression. Yet, nobody was held accountable.

At the first sign of the Meltdown, arch-conservative Hank Paulson, the Treasury Secretary, immediately scrapped the laissez-faire principles he had advocated as CEO of Goldman Sachs and invoked the power of the state in the service of his and his friends' interests by bailing out Wall Street.[122] His $700 million wealth was also at stake. To paraphrase Joseph Stiglitz, capitalism was reserved for Main Street, while socialism was reserved for Wall Street.[123] In other words, Everyman on Main Street was shown no mercy; they had to fend for themselves, while the Lords of finance could enjoy corporate welfarism.[124] Its profits had been privatized but its losses were socialized. Its future profits, generated by the bailouts, were also theirs to keep. Although the bank repaid the loans, the taxpayers received nothing from the upside.

By purchasing $3.6 trillion's worth of toxic assets, Bernanke resuscitated Wall Street, brought it back from the brink, but the structural problems facing the US economy were neglected.[125] Even more moral hazard was introduced into the system and the too-big-to-fail banks became even bigger to fail. The Fed's policies destroyed the logic of Schumpeterian "creative destruction," which should cleanse the economy of inefficient and imprudent firms. The Fed also generated much animosity with its no-strings-attached bailouts and especially for allowing bonus payments from the bailout money, which led to the greatest redistribution of wealth from taxpayers to the top 1 percent in the history of mankind.

In the first edition of this book, I wrote: "It is questionable that such a system is sustainable in the long run with as much moral hazard as exists today."[126] In the second edition I changed the last phrase to "with as much distrust, polarization, and anger as exists today."[127] These were prescient thoughts. With the rise of Trumpism and the January 6th insurrection, we witnessed the neoliberal edifice tottering (see Chapter 15). In other words, the failures and frustrations associated with the wasted crisis were evident early in the Obama administration. With large hidden and endemic unemployment and the eviction of nine million families, it was clear that the Obama administration, the Congress, the Fed, and the Treasury had failed miserably to help ordinary people. It was an unconscionable failure of policy, and it should have been evident that it would have political repercussions. And so it did. The lopsided bailouts was not going to be cheered by the electorate.

Although the bailouts did save the financial system from collapse and although another Great Depression was avoided, the economy's performance continued to be underwhelming. The banks were deleveraging, i.e., they were reluctant to lend and accumulated excess reserves instead. This was the reason for the sluggish lending after the Meltdown despite the Fed's easy-money policy.

The major shortcoming of the bailouts was that nothing was done to rebalance the economy. The structural problems of the economy persisted: immense trade imbalances (see Figure 13.3), endemic budget deficits (see Figure 12.1), skill mismatch because of the mediocre educational system,[128] exorbitant health-care costs, deteriorating infrastructure, falling or stagnating low-skilled wages (see Figure 7.4), growing student debt, obscene levels of inequality (see Figure 12.7), and global warming (Figure 11.4).[129] These weighed heavily on future growth, living standards, and promoted political discontent. Hence, the economic growth between the Dot-Com bubble and the 2008 Meltdown was a mirage underwritten by easy credit and the savings glut.

So, the Obama administration neglected these structural imbalances and focused on overcoming the crisis quickly. They forgot Machiavelli's lesson that only in a crisis can the political inertia be mastered in such a complex economy with innumerable powerful vested interests, and once Wall Street was resuscitated, the government would no longer be able to reform the structural problems and rebalance the economy. While the bankers were on their knees, the Obama administration held all the cards, thereafter the balance of power tilted in the other direction.

In normal times economic reforms are easily stymied by vested interests. Yet, Obama failed to grasp the opportunity and did nothing for education, infrastructure, inequality, and protected the bankers, declaring that he alone stood between them and the "pitchforks."[130] That is how 2008 became a wasted crisis.[131] The crisis was a missed opportunity that appears once in a lifetime:

> The American purveyors of the ancient régime hope that a few superficial fixes will get us back on our way. This is not to be. Sustained and widespread future prosperity will require basic reforms in global macroeconomic governance and in macroeconomic science ... [requiring] new ways of thinking. Yet business as usual could prove calamitous.[132]

The missed opportunity for reform increased the already growing level of frustration in the population. But it did not have to be that way.

The strategy of the Geithner-Bernanke-Summers triumvirate did stop the economy's collapse, but at the cost of genuine reforms of the structural problems and the prospect of a solid recovery. GDP grew at a tepid rate, and the impact of the recession lingered for 5.75 years; that is how long it took for output to exceed the pre-crisis peak.[133] Moreover, real median household income in 2016 was still at the level of 1999 (see Figure 7.9).[134] No wonder the recovery did not feel like one. Krugman dubbed it a "sour economy."[135]

Illustration 14.3 Wasted crisis, a mistake of historical proportions
Credit: Shutterstock 21240175.

14.8 Obama's Tepid Stimulus

Liberal economists supported the $800 billion stimulus of February 2009, although they considered it too little, given the urgency of the calamity. According to Krugman: "It helped end the economy's plunge; it created or saved millions of jobs; it left behind an important legacy of public and private investment."[136] The Congressional Budget Office—an independent governmental agency—estimated that GDP in 2009 increased by 1.4-3.8 percent on account of the stimulus.[137] Moody's Analytics, a forecasting firm, estimated that it saved 2.5 million jobs.[138] Nonetheless conservatives opposed the legislation and only three Republicans voted for it.

Trend in unemployment also supports the beneficial impact of this Keynesian policy. The official unemployment rate had been increasing at 0.5 percent per month during the three preceding months. In February, the economy was shedding 800,000 jobs monthly, pushing the number officially unemployed to 14 million.[139] However, *immediately* after the bill's adoption the rate of increase of the official unemployment rate decelerated: from 0.5 percent to 0.4 percent and in April to 0.3 percent. By the summer it was increasing at only 0.1-0.2 percent per month, and by November 2009 it reached bottom. This was not a mere coincidence. The skeptics argued that job losses could not possibly continue indefinitely at the 800,000 monthly rate. However, it defies commonsense to think that the shedding of jobs would have started to decelerate immediately after the stimulus by coincidence.

Despite the stimulus, plenty of economic pain remained. In January 2010, 15.3 million people were still officially unemployed as the rate peaked at 10 percent. However, the real unemployment rate was closer to 16.5 percent, and the Black and Hispanic rate reached 23 percent. That implied that 25 million adults were without a job and, counting dependents, around 50 million people were leading precarious lives.

Because of the numerous structural problems and because of the timid response to the financial crisis, the US economy entered a phase of slower growth. The dotted line in Figure 14.4 is the extrapolation of the growth trend during the eight years prior to the Meltdown. It is an estimate of the potential output of the economy (see Section 10.9). The post-recession growth of GDP was parallel to this dashed line. It shows that GDP was $1 trillion less than the economy was capable of producing (Figure 14.4). That is an annual loss of nearly $4,000 for every US man, woman, and child.

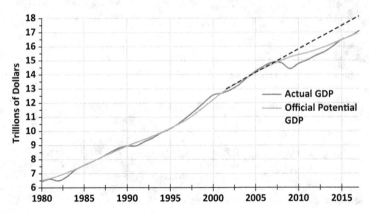

Figure 14.4 Real GDP and potential GDP, 2009 prices
Source: Federal Reserve Bank of St. Louis, series GDPCA and GDPPOT.

The official potential GDP was initially close to the extrapolated line, but over time the official statisticians *bent* the potential to approach the actual GDP. Hence, the inefficiency disappeared. It did not do so because GDP accelerated but because the statisticians finagled the potential GDP until the gap disappeared artificially. Their rationalization was that the people who lost their job dropped out of the labor force and were no longer capable of working. Supposedly, their skills have depreciated, or they are receiving disability benefits, or are accustomed to watching television.

These rationalizations are invalid, because 5 million people who were disregarded in the official labor force statistics *did want to work* and 4.4 million part-time workers wanted to work full-time but could not find full-time jobs (see Table 11.1 and Figure 18.1).[140] Note also that after previous recessions (1982, 1991, 2001), actual GDP snapped back to potential GDP without the statisticians having to bend the potential (Figure 14.4). This time was different: this is the new normal.[141]

14.9 Nationalization of the Too-Big-To-Fail Banks as Pre-Privatization

Admittedly, bailing out the financial system was essential to avoid chaos, but *no one ever said* that the Bush Jr.-Paulson-Obama-Geithner-Bernanke way was the only means to do it. Geithner kept parroting that we had to "put out the fire" but behind that metaphor was a firm conviction that the Everyman on Main Street did not matter. In his mind, the fire was on Wall Street.[142] However, to avoid the revolt of the masses, it would have been crucial to avoid bailing out the wealthy financiers who speculated during the boom and were responsible for the crisis in the first place. Main Street should have been included in the bailouts, and the bailout of AIG and the banks should have had enough strings attached so that taxpayers also owned the upside and not only the downside. It was possible to assist homeowners to refinance their mortgages and save nine million families from losing their homes.

The Boston Fed sent exactly such a proposal to Larry Summers.[143] It read, "We propose a government payment-sharing arrangement that would work with the home-owner's existing mortgage and significantly reduce monthly payments while the homeowner is unemployed."[144] The government would have taken a stake in the equity, offer to homeowners zero-percent refinancing of mortgages, and cut their payments in half until the economy recovered. Thus, the government would have recouped fully its investment in due course. The program would have cost merely $25 billion annually. That would have been a pittance compared to the trillions of dollars funneled to the Lords of Wall Street. Yet, the proposal went nowhere. It was a missed opportunity to devise a fairer program to stabilize the economy.

Helping distressed homeowners was a prerequisite of gaining popular support for the bailouts and fending off the groundswell of populism and *the Fed had the emergency powers to bail out Main Street*: Section 13(3) of the Federal Reserve Act stated: "Discounts for individuals, partnerships, and corporations. In unusual and exigent circumstances, the Board of Governors… may authorize to discount notes, drafts, and bills of exchange."[145] After all, homeowners are "individuals." While the Fed abandoned homeowners, they acted creatively and unconventionally when it came to helping their friends on Wall Street or foreign central banks. Only through the Freedom of Information Act lawsuit did the public learn that Lehman received billions *in secret loans* from the Fed months before its collapse.[146] They *secretly* supported banks with $1.2 trillion *in addition to* the $700 billion funneled through the Congressional Troubled Asset Relief Program (TARP), dubbed "Cash for Trash."[147] They could use strongarm tactics when it came to forcing Bank of America to proceed with its purchase of Merrill Lynch or when they forced Wells Fargo to accept a $25 billion loan from TARP. Yet, when it came to helping ordinary folks, they ran out of ideas.

Moreover, the Obama administration's relegating responsibility to the bankers to "help the American people" by refinancing their mortgages was negligent. If he wanted to bail out the underwater homeowners, he should have done it himself rather than delegating it to third parties. Even arch-conservative Greenspan contemplated nationalization of the insolvent banks: Stiglitz, Krugman, and Roubini also supported the idea:[148]

> It may be necessary to temporarily nationalize some banks in order to facilitate a swift and orderly restructuring ... You take banks over, you clean them up, and you sell them in rapid order to the private sector—it's clear that it's temporary ... The idea that government will fork out trillions of dollars to try to rescue financial institutions, and throw more money after bad dollars, is not appealing because then the fiscal cost is much larger. So rather than being seen as something Bolshevik, nationalization is seen as pragmatic ... The proposal is more market-friendly than the alternative of zombie banks.[149]

On the heels of the Meltdown, banks and households were deleveraging, decreasing their debt burden. Everyone wanted to improve their balance sheet.[150] Deleveraging amplified the recession, because instead of lending, the banks were using the government largesse to improve their portfolios. The outcome was a credit crunch, slower economic growth, and the accumulation of political discontent.

Instead, Obama could have ended no-strings-attached bailouts. Nationalization of insolvent banks would have had immense advantages: the government could have broken them up, ending the tyranny of too-big-to-fail banks; without robust lobbies it could have enacted effective regulation, thereby eliminating systemic risk; it could have ensured that underwater mortgages were refinanced with zero percent interest rates, thereby eliminating toxic assets and gaining the political support of the middle class; it could have eliminated the million-dollar bonuses to irresponsible executives, thus eliminating moral hazard; it could have stopped foreclosures, thereby preventing the rise in populism.[151] Taking over the big banks temporarily would have been a win-win strategy.

With near-zero interest rate financing available to homeowners, the population would have been grateful to Obama. The recession would have been much milder and shorter, and stability would have returned. If the Fed had lent 9 million homeowners $10,000 (per annum) to support their mortgage payments, the total bailout would have been $180 billion for two years, a tiny amount relative to the $3.6 trillion "printed" by the Fed. The homeowner bailout would have been paid back when the homeowners regained their job or sold their homes. This would have had far greater beneficial impact for Everyman and on the economy than the bailout of Wall Street alone. That would have put the economy back on the right track.[152]

Moreover, the profits of the financial sector, hundreds of billions of dollars annually, would have accrued to Uncle Sam, and not to the one-percenters. Add a substantial tax on financial transactions and the "starving beast" would have been starving no more. Instead of becoming subservient to the banks, Everyman would have tried on the shoes of the Lords of Finance and would have found the fit very comfortable, indeed. In turn, Obama would have been hailed by the masses as a knight in shining armor serving capitalism with a human face, and willing to wield his lance as well. The Democrats would have avoided the thrashing of 2010, a dysfunctional Congress, and Obama's legacy would not have been the triumph of Trumpism.

Bernanke knew that such a scenario was feasible. An internal Fed memo concluded that help-ing homeowners would be a viable option: "The costs of the plan are moderate, and the benefits should help not only the participating homeowners but also the housing industry, the financial markets, and the economy more broadly."[153] But he found it easier to transfer the trillions to the same financiers whose greed had brought the nation to the edge of the precipice. Thus, bailing out Main Street would have been feasible and much better both politically and economically.

In sum, to implement the fundamental structural reforms that were urgently required, the country needed a leader with unflinching self-confidence backed by a creative team of experts. The deep structural imbalances of the US economy could not be mended by band aid. The econ-omy is path-dependent: its institutions, and the momentum of the social, cultural, and political processes in which it is embedded were created in the prior 28 years of neoliberal dominance. It could not be transformed as a gentlemanly sport. But with the strategy outlined above, the US could have transitioned from turbo-capitalism to a capitalism with a human face, but only if a leader combining the tensile strength of Lincoln with the self-confidence of FDR, and the political acumen of LBJ was in the Oval Office. Instead, Obama was a novice who dreamed about bipartisanship, reconciliation, and compromise, that was unrealistic from the get-go, and to top it off diligently protected the privileged from the pitchforks.[154] That strengthened the forces of populism. That is how Trump became his legacy.

14.10 Takeaways

The financial Meltdown of 2008 was a watershed moment in the history of mankind. It unfolded according to Minsky's playbook. The stability of the prior half-century misled Fed chairman Alan Greenspan and his successor, Ben Bernanke, into disregarding all the warnings. The crisis was caused by a confluence of developments including deregulation, the introduction of new deriva-tives that spread an immense amount of asymmetric information through the system, animal spirits craving for euphoric profits, predatory mortgages, low interest rates, mispricing of tail risk, and plenty of money chasing assets that induced investors around the globe to buy tril-lions of dollars' worth of risky assets whose complexity was not well understood. Moreover, the shadow banking system increased the leverage of their investments well beyond prudent limits until excessive debt and excessive systemic risk in the form of credit default swaps accumu-lated. Thus, precisely as Minsky had predicted in his "financial instability hypothesis," a robust finance morphed into a fragile one as speculation led to a humongous bubble. There was an ideological background to the crisis as well since the dogmatic belief that "free" markets were self-regulating provided intellectual succour for the lax regulation. The neoliberal dogma that assumed that such a financial crisis could not possibly occur in the sophisticated financial world of the twenty-first century was a mistake of historic proportions.

Questions for Discussion

1 Why do you suppose Alan Greenspan did not heed the warnings voiced during the run-up to the financial crisis?
2 Why is the financial sector so fragile?
3 Why do you suppose the ideas of Hyman Minsky were banned from mainstream economics?
4 Do you think that the financial sector should be allowed to have such a large weight in the economy?

5   Do you think that "too-big-to-fail" banks should be broken up like AT&T in 1982 and Stand-ard Oil in 1911?

6   Why does the accumulation of debt lead to economic instability?

7   Explain how stability bred instability in the financial sector.

8   What was boring banking? Would you advocate bringing it back?

9   Did financial innovations have a positive impact on the real economy?

10   What was the shadow banking system?

11   What kind of insurance is a credit default swap?

12   Is a credit default swap a futures contract?

13   Do you think we should have bailed out Goldman Sachs, JPMorgan Chase, Citigroup, Mor-gan Stanley, and Bank of America?

14   Do you think that Dick Fuld should be allowed to keep the $250 million wealth he accumu-lated while bankrupting Lehman Brothers?

15   Do you think that Main Street should have been bailed out also?

16   Discuss Stiglitz's quip that capitalism is for Main Street and socialism is for Wall Street.

17   Why do you think that Main Street was not bailed out?

18   Do you think that Obama's stimulus package was effective?

19   What are the major challenges faced in today's globalized world?

20   Do you think that the "American Dream" will be within your reach in your lifetime or that of your children and grandchildren?

21   Why do you think that Ben Bernanke misled the public during the run-up to the financial crisis?

22   Do you think that the financial sector has become too powerful?

23   What is your opinion of President Obama's economic team: Geithner, Bernanke, and Sum-mers?

24   What is your opinion of President Obama's handling of the financial crisis?

25   Do you think that the Meltdown of 2008 was a crisis wasted?

26   Do you think Donald Trump would have been elected had Main Street been bailed out?

27   Do you think it was a mistake to repeal the Glass-Steagall Act? Do you think it should be reinstituted?

28   Do you know anyone who suffered losses during the financial crisis?

Notes

1   "The Great Slump of 1930," *The Nation and Athenaeum*, December 20, 1930, p. 126.

2   William Quinn and John Turner, *Boom and Bust: A Global History of Financial Bubbles* (Cambridge University Press, 2020).

3   Robert Lucas, "Macroeconomic Priorities," *American Economic Review* 93 (2003), 1: 1-14.

4   "The Great Moderation," remarks by Governor Ben S. Bernanke at the meetings of the Eastern Economic Association, Washington, February 20, 2004, https://www.federalreserve.gov/boarddocs/speeches/2004/20040220/.

5   The standard deviation of real GDP growth in the US declined from 2.7 percent between 1960 and 1983 to 1.6 percent thereafter.

6   Olivier Blanchard, "The State of Macro," NBER Working Paper no. 14259, August 2008. Inexplicably, he retained this opinion in the published version after the failure of macroeconomic policies became evident: *Annual Review of Economics* 1 (2009): 209-228.

7   Anya Schiffrin, *Bad News: How America's Business Press Missed the Story of the Century* (The New Press, 2011).

8   Adam Tooze, *Crashed: How a Decade of Financial Crises Changed the World* (Viking, 2018); Giancarlo Bertocco, *Crisis and the Failure of Economic Theory: The Responsibility of Economists* (Edward Edgar, 2017).

9   Paul Krugman, "How Did Economists Get It So Wrong?," *The New York Times*, September 2, 2009.

10 Proverbs, 16:18.

11 In 2001, 74 percent of the population trusted Greenspan. No one has come close. Bernanke's highest rating was 50 percent just before the crisis and sank to 39 percent by 2012. Lydia Saad, "Americans Lack Confidence in Key Economic Leaders," *Gallup Politics*, April 20, 2018.

12 Ex-Goldman Sachs Co-Chairman and Treasury Secretary.

13 Became Treasury Secretary six months later.

14 Joshua Cooper Ramo, "The Three Marketeers," *Time*, February 15, 1999.

15 Ibid.

16 "It is obvious that animal spirits ... can give rise to marked changes in aggregate demand—irrational optimism to a boom and irrational pessimism to a bust." Joseph Stiglitz, "Economic Fluctuations and Pseudo-Wealth," NBER Working Paper no. 28415, January 2021, p. 31.

17 For instance, Coca-Cola Co.'s stock price rose from $7.2 in 1994 to $26 in 2000 without substantial change in dividends. So, its price/earnings ratio rose from 9 to 37 and the return on a share declined from 11 percent to 2.7 percent. http://www.econ.yale.edu/~shiller/data.htm.

18 Some firms survived and became iconic: Amazon (1994), Yahoo (1994), eBay (1995), PayPal (1998), and Google (1998).

19 Andrew Haldane "The Doom Loop," *London Review of Books*, February 23, 2012; Andrew Haldane, "Banking on the State," *BIS Review*, November 11, 2009, https://www.bis.org/review/r091111e.pdf?frames=0; Simon Johnson, "America's Economic 'Doom Loop,'" *The New Republic*, November 17, 2009.

20 Paul Krugman, "Making Banking Boring," *The New York Times*, April 9, 2009.

21 Robert Shiller, *Irrational Exuberance and the New Financial Order* (Princeton University Press, 2000).

22 Federal National Mortgage Association and Federal Home Loan Mortgage Corporation.

23 The Secondary Mortgage Market Enhancement Act of 1984.

24 These were called "private label" mortgage-backed securities while Fannie and Freddie's were called "agency" MBSs.

25 The Financial Crisis Inquiry Commission, *The Financial Crisis Inquiry Report* (Government Printing Office, 2011), p. 116.

26 Edmund Andrews, "Greenspan Is Concerned About 'Froth' in Housing," *The New York Times*, May 21, 2005.

27 Robert Shiller, "Do Stock Prices Move Too Much to be Justified by Subsequent Changes in Dividends?," *American Economic Review* 71 (1981), 3: 421–436; www.econ.yale.edu/~shiller/publications.htm#1978.

28 YouTube, "Robert Shiller on How Human Psychology Drives the Economy, the New School," July 16, 2009; @ 11.20 minutes; https://www.youtube.com/watch?v=8RrKScRg5KM.

29 "Markets can remain irrational longer than you and I can remain solvent," John M. Keynes, as quoted in Roger Lowenstein, *When Genius Failed: The Rise and Fall of Long-Term Capital Management* (Random House, 2000), p. 123.

30 According to the Financial Crisis Inquiry Commission:

> More than 30 years of deregulation and reliance on self-regulation by financial institutions, championed by former Federal Reserve chairman Alan Greenspan and others, supported by successive administrations and Congresses, and actively pushed by the powerful financial industry at every turn, had stripped away key safeguards, which could have helped avoid catastrophe.
>
> (*The Financial Crisis Inquiry Report*, Government Printing Office, 2011, p. xviii)

31   Micheline Maynard, "Being Right Is Bittersweet for a Critic of Lenders," *The New York Times*, August 18, 2007.

32   PBS, *Frontline*, "The Warning." www.pbs.org/wgbh/frontline/film/warning/; https://www.youtube.com/watch?v=S_EVqOJhmvQ.

33   PBS, *Frontline*, "The Warning," trailer. YouTube. https://www.youtube.com/watch?v=kXgkUPOxLGA.

34   According to SEC Chairman Arthur Levitt Jr. in "The Warning."

35   Ramo, "The Three Marketeers," op. cit.; "Politburo" intimates that they aggressively enforced the orthodoxy of laissez-faire economics. The politburo is the executive organ of a Communist Party, a totalitarian, institution. In the Soviet Union it was responsible for the concentration camps in the Siberian Gulag where upwards of a million people perished.

36   John F. Kennedy, Presidential Library and Museum, Profile in Courage Award, Award Announcement, Brooksley Born.

37   Warren Buffett, *Berkshire Hathaway Inc. 2002 Annual Report*; www.berkshirehathaway.com.

38   Dean Baker, "The Run-up in Home Prices: A Bubble," *Challenge* 45 (2002), 6: 93–119. For earlier warnings of the skyrocketing debt to GDP ratio, see Steve Keen, *Debunking Economics: The Naked Emperor of the Social Sciences* (Zed Books, 2001).

39   St. Louis Fed, series MSPUS, MEHOINUSA672N.

40   John Cassidy, "Blowing Bubbles," *The New Yorker*, July 14, 2004.

41   Raghuram Rajan, *The Third Pillar: How Markets and the State Leave the Community Behind* (Penguin, 2019).

42   Raghuram Rajan, "Has Financial Development Made the World Riskier?" NBER Working Paper no. 11728, November 2005.

43   Ibid.

44   Federal Reserve Bank of Kansas City, "The Participants," https://www.kansascityfed.org/research/jackson-hole-economic-symposium/the-greenspan-era-lessons-for-the-future/; https://www.kansascityfed.org/documents/3338/PDF-participants2005.pdf.

45   YouTube Video, "Ben Bernanke Was Wrong." www.youtube.com/watch?v=INmqvibv4UU&t=2s.

46   The increase in opioid prescriptions can account for about 43 percent of the decline in men's labor force participation. Alan Krueger, "Where Have All the Workers Gone?" *Brookings Papers on Economic Activity*, Fall 2017.

47   "Ben Bernanke Was Wrong," op. cit.

48   Some 5 million wanted a job but were too discouraged to look for one and 4 million were working part-time although they wanted full-time work. Bureau of Labor Statistics, *Labor Force Statistics from the Current Population Survey. Characteristics of the Unemployed*, Tables 1, 20, and 35; www.bls.gov/cps/cps_aa2005.htm.

49   Nouriel Roubini, "How Much Will Home Prices Fall During This Housing Bust? At Least 20 percent to 30 percent!" *EconoMonitor*, September 10, 2006.

50   Prince got $38 million reward in 2007 for making irresponsible decisions.

51   Steve Keen, "Finance and Economic Breakdown: Modeling Minsky's Financial Instability Hypothesis," *Journal of Post Keynesian Economics* 17 (1995), 4: 607–635.

52   Hyman Minsky, *Can "It" Happen Again?* (M.E. Sharpe, 1982); Charles Kindleberger, *Manias, Panics, and Crashes* (Wiley, 1978).

53   Hyman Minsky, "The Financial Instability Hypothesis," The Jerome Levy Economics Institute of Bard College, Working Paper 74, May 1992.

54   Ibid.

55   PBS, *Frontline*, "The Warning," op. cit.

56   Francisco Louçã and Michael Ash, *Shadow Networks: Financial Disorder and the System that Caused Crisis* (Oxford University Press, 2018).

57   Hyman Minsky, "Financial Instability Revisited: The Economics of Disaster," unpublished manuscript (1966).

58 Bernanke made a dismissive reference to Minsky: "Hyman Minsky (1977) and Charles Kindleberger (1978) have ... argued for the inherent instability of the financial system, but in doing so have had to depart from the assumption of rational economic behavior." "Nonmonetary Effects of the Financial Crisis in the Propagation of the Great Depression," *American Economic Review* (1983), 3: 257–276, at p. 258. He added in a footnote: "I do not deny the possible importance of irrationality in economic life; however, it seems that the best research strategy is to push the rationality postulate as far as it will go." He failed to specify on what basis he determined what the best strategy was. It "seemed" to him that the best strategy was to disregard Minsky.

59 George Akerlof and Robert Shiller, *Phishing for Phools: The Economics of Manipulation and Deception* (Princeton University Press, 2015).

60 Ruth Simon, "Teaser Rates on Mortgages Approach 0 percent," *The Wall Street Journal*, February 15, 2005.

61 The Financial Crisis Inquiry Commission, *Report*, op. cit., p. 32.

62 Ibid., p. xx.

63 Ben Bernanke, "The Subprime Mortgage Market," Board of Governors of the Federal Reserve System, May 17, 2007.

64 The Financial Crisis Inquiry Commission, *Report*, op. cit., p. xxiv.

65 William Greider, "The AIG Bailout Scandal," *The Nation*, August 6, 2010.

66 Bernanke funneled $3.6 trillion into the financial market, thereby leading to asset inflation. Then Jay Powell, the current president injected another $4 trillion. The ratio in October 2021 was 38.3; hence the return on stocks was 2.6 percent, 1 percent above the yield on 10-year (risk-free) government bonds, not an extravagant amount for holding risky assets; https://www.treasury.gov/resource-center/data-chart-center/interest-rates/pages/TextView.aspx?data=yield.

67 Reuters Staff, "Moody's, Fitch Slash Lehman Ratings on Bankruptcy," *Reuters*, September 15, 2008; Roman Frydman and Michael Goldberg, "Lehman Brothers Collapse: Was Capitalism to Blame?" *The Guardian*, September 13, 2013.

68 The Financial Crisis Inquiry Commission, *Report*, p. xxv.

69 St. Louis Fed, series FEDFUNDS.

70 "The $1.7 trillion Dot.Com Lesson," *CNN Money*, November 9, 2000.

71 St. Louis Fed, series A191RO1Q156NBEA.

72 John Taylor, "The Financial Crisis and the Policy Responses: An Empirical Analysis of What Went Wrong," *Critical Review: A Journal of Politics and Society* 21 (2009), 2–3: 341–364.

73 John Griffin, "Ten Years of Evidence: Was Fraud a Force in the Financial Crisis?" *Journal of Economic Literature* 59 (2021), 4: 1293–1321.

74 Federal Reserve Bank of San Francisco, "The Subprime Mortgage Market," 2007 Annual Report; The Financial Crisis Inquiry Commission, *Report*, op. cit., p. 70.

75 FDIC, Office of Inspector General, "Challenges and FDIC Efforts Related to Predatory Lending," Report No. 06–11, June 2006.

76 Mike Hudson and Scott Reckard, "Workers Say Lender Ran 'Boiler Rooms,'" *Los Angeles Times*, February 4, 2005.

77 YouTube, "Countrywide Commercial 3," https://www.youtbe.com/watch?v=Ei5OrV-CmHg.

78 YouTube, "WAMU–'Roy'" https://www.youtube.com/watch?v=EkOHWxeD9sE.

79 YouTube, "WAMU–'Paul'" https://www.youtube.com/watch?v=-wAGi8PT-qg.

80 Sue Kirchhoff and Barbara Hagenbaugh, "Greenspan Says ARMS Might Be Better Deal," *USA TODAY*, February 23, 2004.

81 Adding:

   Where once more-marginal applicants would simply have been denied credit, lenders are now able to quite efficiently judge the risk posed by individual applicants and to price that risk appropriately. These improvements have led to rapid growth in subprime mortgage lending; indeed, today subprime mortgages account for roughly 10 percent of the number of all mortgages outstanding, up from just 1 or 2 percent in the early 1990s.

The Federal Reserve Board, "Remarks by Chairman Alan Greenspan at the Federal Reserve System's Fourth Annual Community Affairs Research Conference," Washington. April 8, 2005.

82   St. Louis Fed, series CSUSHPISA and MEHOINUSA672N.

83   "What Went Wrong," *The Economist*, March 6, 2009.

84   Michael Burry, "I Saw the Crisis Coming. Why Didn't the Fed?" *The New York Times*, April 3, 2010.

85   Greg Ip, "Did Greenspan Add to Subprime Woes?" *The Wall Street Journal*, June 9, 2007.

86   "The Bubble's New Home," *Barron's*, June 20, 2005; David Leonhardt, "Be Warned: Mr. Bubble's Worried Again," *The New York Times*, August 21, 2005; Paul Krugman, "That Hissing Sound," *The New York Times*, August 8, 2015; "Peter Schiff was right," November 13, 2006, https://www.youtube.com/watch?v=h2Gj5snyn_M.

87   Jean-Philippe Bouchaud, "Economics Needs a Scientific Revolution," *Nature* 455 (2008), 1181.

88   Benoit Mandelbrot and Richard Hudson, *The (Mis)Behavior of Markets* (Basic Books, 2004).

89   The Financial Crisis Inquiry Commission, *Report*, op. cit., p. xx.

90   In Minsky's view, financialization reflected "money manager capitalism," in which financial leverage gained paramount importance with debt financing at center stage.

91   The Financial Crisis Inquiry Commission, *Report*, op. cit., p. xvii. Thomas Philippon, "Has the US Finance Industry Become Less Efficient? On the Theory and Measurement of Financial Intermediation," *American Economic Review* 105 (2015), 4: 1408-1438. These data omit profits generated abroad because those are not reported by sector. Bureau of Economic Analysis, Interactive Data, GDP & Personal Income, Section 6-Income and Employment by Industry, "Table 6.16D Corporate Profits by Industry."

92   Bureau of Labor Statistics, Table 2.1, "Employment by Major Industry Sector." https://www.bls.gov/emp/tables/employment-by-major-industry-sector.htm.

93   Nouriel Roubini, "March 2001: 95 percent of Forecasters Predicted No Recession … Too Bad the Recession Had Already Started Then," *EconoMonitor*, September 8, 2006.

94   This is different than pricing life, health, or car insurance since those prices are based on known probability distributions.

95   Sheila Dow, "Addressing Uncertainty in Economics and the Economy," *Cambridge Journal of Economics* 39 (2015), 1: 33-47.

96   Chenyu Zhang, "Empirical Essays on Inferring Information from Options and Other Financial Derivatives," unpublished PhD dissertation, Lancaster University, UK, April 2017, pp. 23, 42; the month before Bear Stearns and Merrill Lynch became insolvent, their bankruptcy probabilities were just 3.1 percent and 2.3 percent.

97   Stephen Taylor et al., "Bankruptcy Probabilities Inferred from Option Prices," *Journal of Derivatives* 22 (2014), 2: 8-31, here pp. 13, 25.

98   "The Day the S.E.C. Changed the Game," *The New York Times*, September 27, 2009; https://www.youtube.com/watch?v=ADVoEO_dAcA. The agenda and synopsis of the meeting are found at: www.sec.gov/news/openmeetings/agenda042804.htm.

99   Stephen Labaton, "Agency's '04 Rule Let Banks Pile Up New Debt," *The New York Times*, October 2, 2008.

100 Anne Flaherty, "Lawmakers: Bank of America, Merill (*sic*) Lynch Deal Was 'Shotgun Wedding'," *The Seattle Times*, June 12, 2009; "Moynihands Full," *The Economist*, April 15, 2010.

101 Simon Johnson and James Kwak, *13 Bankers: The Wall Street Takeover and the Next Financial Meltdown* (Pantheon, 2010); Robert Shiller, *The Subprime Solution: How Today's Global Financial Crisis Happened, and What to Do About It* (Princeton University Press, 2008); Paul Krugman, *The Return of Depression Economics and the Crisis of 2008* (Norton, 2009).

102 Wikipedia, "Terra Securities Scandal."

103 John Cassidy, "Blowing Bubbles," *The New Yorker*, July 12, 2004.

104 His facial contortions while speaking revealed his sociopathic nature. His nickname was "gorilla." YouTube, "Dick Fuld Rip Out Your Heart," October 28, 2011. During his congressional testimony, he denied his mistakes: "I believed these decisions and actions were both prudent and appropriate." "Lehman Brothers CEO Testifies on Capitol Hill," Associated Press, www.youtube.com/watch?v=ZkEkxGsXmPI.

105 William Bernstein, *The Delusions of Crowds: Why People Go Mad in Groups* (Atlantic Monthly Press, 2021).

106 According to the website "Celebrity Net Worth."

107 Forbes Staff, "By the Numbers: Overpaid Bosses," *Forbes*, April 22, 2009.

108 "25 Highest-Paid Men, 8. John Thain," *Fortune*, 2008.

109 Andrew Clark, "Merrill Lynch, the Firm Lost $8bn and the Chief Executive Had to Go—With $159m," *The Guardian*, October 30, 2007.

110 Forbes Staff, "By the Numbers: Bailout Bosses," *Forbes*, April 22, 2009. www.forbes.com/2009/04/22/tarp-bailout-companies-leadership-compensation-best-boss-09-tarp_slide_2.html.

111 Dan Ariely, "Mo' Money, Mo' Problems," *Forbes*, February 20, 2009.

112 Federal National Mortgage Association and Federal Home Loan Mortgage Corp.

113 Braden Goyette, "Cheat Sheet: What's Happened to the Big Players in the Financial Crisis," *ProPublica*, October 26, 2011.

114 Joe Nocera, "The Big Lie," *The New York Times*, December 23, 2011; Paul Krugman, "Joe Nocera Gets Mad," *The New York Times*, December 24, 2011.

115 David Goldstein and Kevin G. Hall, "Private Sector Loans, Not Fannie or Freddie, Triggered Crisis," *McClatchy Newspapers*, October 12, 2008.

116 Political Correction, "Private Wall Street Companies Caused the Financial Crisis—Not Fannie Mae, Freddie Mac Or the Community Reinvestment Act," October 14, 2011.

117 The Financial Crisis Inquiry Commission, *Report*, op. cit., p. 72.

118 Jill Littrell and Fred Brooks, "In Defense of the Community Reinvestment Act," *Journal of Community Practice* 18 (2010), 4: 417–439.

119 Ibid.

120 The Financial Crisis Inquiry Commission, *Report*, p. xvii.

121 Board of Governors of the Federal Reserve System, "Flow of Funds Accounts of the United States. Flows and Outstandings, Fourth Quarter 2010."

122 Paul Krugman on *Real Time with Bill Maher*, Season 7, episode 28, September 25, 2009; https://trakt.tv/shows/real-time-with-bill-maher/seasons/7/episodes/28#overview.

123 Joseph Stiglitz, "America's Socialism for the Rich," *The Guardian*, June 12, 2009; Joseph Stiglitz, *Freefall: America, Free Markets, and the Sinking of the World Economy* (Norton, 2010).

124 James Galbraith calls this the "corporate republic," *The Predator State: How Conservatives Abandoned the Free Market and Why Liberals Should Too* (The Free Press, 2008).

125 Peter Boone and Simon Johnson, "The Doomsday Cycle," *CentrePiece* (Winter 2009/10): 2–6.

126 John Komlos, *The Foundations of Real-World Economics* (Routledge, 2014), p. 232.

127 John Komlos, *The Foundations of Real-World Economics*, 2nd edn. (Routledge, 2019), p. 253.

128 Skill mismatch means that the vacancies in the labor market cannot be filled because the available labor does not have the required skills. Narayana Kocherlakota, "Inside the FOMC." President's Speech, Marquette, MI, August 17, 2010. http://www.minneapolisfed.org/news_events/pres/speech_display.cfm?id=4525.

129 Emma Kerr and Sarah Wood, "10 Years of Average Total Student Loan Debt," *US News*, September 14, 2021.

130 Lindsey Ellerson, "Obama to Bankers: I'm Standing 'Between You and the Pitchforks,'" *ABC News*, April 3, 2009.

131 Paul Starr, "A Wasted Crisis?" *The New Republic*, July 12, 2013; Philip Mirowski, *Never Let a Serious Crisis Go to Waste: How Neoliberalism Survived the Financial Meltdown* (Verso, 2013); Nolan McCarty et al.,

"How to Waste a Crisis," in *Political Bubbles*: *Financial Crises and the Failure of American Democracy* (Princeton University Press, 2013), pp. 251–274.

132   Jeffrey Sachs, "Rethinking Macroeconomics," *Capitalism and Society* 4 (2009), 3: 1–9; Bill McGuire, "Fed Loaned Bankers Trillions in Bailout, Bloomberg Reports," *ABC News*, November 28, 2011.

133   St. Louis Fed, series A939RX0Q048SBEA.

134   In 2019 dollars, 2016 is reported to have been $257 greater than it was in 1999. However, income reporting changed in 2014 which increased reported incomes by 3.5 percent. Accounting for this change in statistical procedure, incomes were still $1,728 below the level of 1999. See note to Table 7.5.

135   Paul Krugman, *End This Depression Now!* (Norton, 2012).

136   Paul Krugman, "The Stimulus Tragedy," *The New York Times*, February 20, 2014.

137   Congressional Budget Office, "Estimated Macroeconomic Impacts of HR 1 as Passed by the House and by the Senate."

138   Christina Romer and Jared Bernstein, "The Job Impact of the American Recovery and Reinvestment Plan," January 9, 2009; https://www.ampo.org/assets/library/184_obama.pdf. David Leonhardt, "Economic Scene: Judging Stimulus by Job Data Reveals Success," *The New York Times*, February 16, 2010.

139   St. Louis Fed, series CLF16OV and UNRATE.

140   Bureau of Labor Statistics, "Labor Force Statistics from the Current Population Survey," Series LNU05026639.

141   James Galbraith, *The End of Normal: The Great Crisis and the Future of Growth* (Simon & Schuster, 2015).

142   For a whitewashed and self-promoting biased version of the bailouts, see Ben Bernanke et al., *Firefighting: The Financial Crisis and Its Lessons* (Profile Books, 2019); Timothy Geithner, *Stress Test: Reflections on Financial Crises* (Crown, 2014); Ben Bernanke, *The Courage to Act: A Memoir of a Crisis and its Aftermath* (Norton, 2015).

143   Years later, in a personal communication, Larry Summers did not recall this proposal.

144   Chris Foote et al., "A Proposal to Help Distressed Homeowners: A Government Payment-Sharing Plan," Federal Reserve Bank of Boston, *Public Policy Brief* No. 2009-1.

145   Board of Governors of the Federal Reserve System, "Federal Reserve Act," www.federalreserve.gov/aboutthefed/section13.htm.

146   Bloomberg News sued the Fed which fought releasing the information to the Supreme Court but lost. Richard Blackden, "Lehman Brothers Secretly Borrowed from the Fed Before Collapse," *The Telegraph*, July 8, 2011. Wikipedia, "Bloomberg L.P. v. Board of Governors of the Federal Reserve System."

147   Paul Krugman, "Cash for Trash," *The New York Times*, September 21, 2008.

148   Paul Krugman, "Banking on the Brink," *The New York Times*, February 22, 2009; YouTube, "Stiglitz: Temporary Nationalization Necessary to Save Troubled Banks," posted by ColumbiaBusiness, February 19, 2009.

149   Tunku Varadaraja, "'Nationalize' the Banks: Dr. Doom Says a Takeover and Resale Is the Market-Friendly Solution," *The Wall Street Journal*, February 21, 2009.

150   Richard Koo, *The Escape from Balance Sheet Recession and the QE Trap: A Hazardous Road for the World Economy* (Blackwell, 2014).

151   "Stiglitz Says US Is Paying for Failure to Nationalize Banks," *Bloomberg News*, November 1, 2009.

152   Allen Barton also advocated subsidies to homeowners, "Letter: Another Take on 'Why Paulson is Wrong,'" *The Economists' Voice* 5 (2008), 5: Article 9.

153   Foote et al., "A Proposal," op. cit.

154   Ryan Lizza, "The Obama Memos: The Making of a Post-Partisan Presidency," *The New Yorker*, January 22, 2012.

15 Economists' Mistakes Lead to Right-Wing Populism Plus an Insurrection

> Obviously, the passion for power is one of the most moving passions that exists in Man; … all democracies are based on the proposition that power is very dangerous and that it is extremely important not to let any one man or any one small group have too much power for too long a time.
>
> −Aldous Huxley[1]

15.1 Four Tsunamis Pave the Path to Populism

The impact of flawed economic theories did not remain confined to academia.[2] They also formed the basis of economic policies that disadvantaged millions who eventually lost faith in the political establishment.[3] Three-quarters of the population were dissatisfied with developments in the US, and one-third thought that violence against the government can be justified, a stark reflection of the elite's fall from grace.[4] The misguided ivory-tower theories also penetrated popular culture sufficiently to gain political support at the polls because complex issues were distorted until the citizenry became incapable of making sense of them, as "the fabric of American democracy has been stretched thin."[5]

An important Achilles' heel of mainstream economics is its callous indifference to the social and political implications of its blackboard policy recommendations.[6] This resulted in the severely flawed policies that culminated in political dysfunction, a polarized society, and the January 6th insurrection by a ferocious mob intent on lynching and destruction.[7] Consequently, the US has been classified as a "Backsliding Democracy."[8] Neoliberal blunders included the adoption of a super-individualistic ideology that demeaned the welfare state and advocated instead for a lax safety net that left too many low-skilled, less-educated people earning meager wages that contributed to their loss of self-esteem and left them without a lifeline to grasp onto in time of need.[9]

The orthodox canon neglected that an equitable distribution of income is a prerequisite of social and political stability. Hence, mainstream economists had no qualms about supporting across-the-board tax cuts which magnified inequality and insecurity, and gnawed away at social cohesion, because practically all of their benefits accrued to the wealthy.[10] That made it impossible for millions to keep up with the social norms and fostered a "whitelash" among less-skilled and less-educated white men who were lost in the new economy and experienced their "race and gender privilege" erosion.[11] They turned against the establishment with a vengeance.[12]

DOI: 10.4324/9781003174356-15

Illustration 15.1 The storming of the Capitol was an inexcusable blot on American democracy
Credit: Shutterstock, 1913474197.

This chapter summarizes the political and social ramifications of these deficient economic policies and the accumulation of frustration they caused among those white men without a college degree who lost all hope in the political system and rebelled.[13] Only 25 percent of them voted for Hillary Clinton.[14] They were left far behind and, while they were mostly unable to understand the complex interlinkages of the economic disruptions that ruined their lives, they were right to blame the elites who were responsible for those policies without regard to their welfare.[15] So, their frustration accumulated until they were willing to support even a "narcissistic sexual harasser and a routine liar" in order to topple the powers that be.[16]

In normal times, Trump would have been considered a "carnival barker,"[17] although he bragged about his "genius."[18] To understand the path-dependent processes that culminated in the rise of Trumpism—as a form of right-wing populism—one must examine the economic history of the previous four decades during which three powerful economic developments, Reaganomics, globalization, and the financial crisis, guided by false economic theories, plus the IT revolution in the post-industrial knowledge economy added up to four powerful impersonal forces that inflicted irreparable damage to the social contract, the glue that binds the society, the economy, and the political system together.[19]

15.2 "It's the Economy, Stupid"[20]

The rise of populism in the US was supported by the economic policies of five administrations that failed miserably to provide inclusive prosperity and led to the accumulation of an animosity within the American underclass, the ones Hillary unkindly christened a "basket of deplorables."[21] The venom was directed at the political system that allowed their lives to be shattered in the name of nebulous laissez-faire principles like comparative advantage (see Section 13.1).[22] The vulnerable groups were rife for Trump's slogan—borrowed from Reagan—to "Make America Great Again," to bring back jobs, and to blame immigrants, Moslems, and Washington politicians for their ills.[23] Scapegoating is a typical practice among authoritarian personalities leading populist movements.[24] Hopelessness, frustration, and inequality are mighty political forces and Trump harvested the anger of the have-nots, who reached for the American Dream but found a nightmare instead.[25] These grievances generated enough frustration, among the underclass, the less educated, the evicted, and those who were excluded from the dual economy's prosperous half and lost social status, that they were finally willing to overthrow the establishment by sending Donald Trump into the White House, come what may.[26] After all, he alone was willing to "drain the swamp."[27] No wonder that Trump loved the poorly educated who no longer recognized their self-interest and put their faith in the billionaire class:[28]

Trump exploited low and middle-income white people's anger over their deteriorating life prospects to mobilise racial animus and xenophobia and enlist their support for policies that benefit high-income people and corporations and threaten health. His signature legislative achievement, a trillion-dollar tax cut for corporations and high-income individuals, opened a budget hole that he used to justify cutting food subsidies and health care. His appeals to racism, nativism, and religious bigotry have emboldened white nationalists and vigilantes, and encouraged police violence and, at the end of his term in office, insurrection ... Trump's actions ... represent an aggressive acceleration of neoliberal policies that date back 40 years. These policies reversed New Deal and civil rights-era advances in economic and racial equality. Subsequently, inequality widened, with many people in the USA being denied the benefits of economic growth.[29]

The evidence for the primacy of economics in the rise of populism comes from the miniscule margins in three Rust Belt states, Pennsylvania, Michigan, and Wisconsin, that put Trump over the top.[30] This region had suffered devastation by the unrelenting decline of manufacturing and the callous neglect by the political elite.[31] No wonder that the losers in this social Darwinist economy were keen to overthrow the establishment.[32] A change of a miniscule 39,000 votes from Trump to Clinton in these states would have clinched her victory (Table 15.1). They have not voted for a Republican president since 1988. That they all supported Barack Obama in 2008 and 2012 implies that their 2016 vote was not because of Trump's racism.

The Rust Belt's abandoned factories and its consequences, the dilapidated homes, dysfunctional families, and neighborhoods were real enough to affect the anxiety-ridden underclass stuck at the bottom of the social hierarchy, who saw no way out of their predicament. They became convinced that the elites had rigged the system and consequently the economy allocates rewards so unfairly that it became unbearable. Real incomes were down, workers lost hope by the droves as they dropped out of the labor force, manufacturing employment was down by nearly a third, and food-stamp recipients had increased (Table 15.2). Loss of livelihood and self-esteem led to desperation, opioid addiction and to high overdose deaths.[33] Economic distress of the working class was the salient vote-generator for Trump: "In the Industrial Midwest, Trump out-performed Romney by an average of 16.3 percent in the most economically distressed counties compared to 6.2 percent in the least economically distressed counties."[34]

Lower life expectancy was a marker for marginalization, a sense of disenfranchisement, and a willingness to support Trump: "Resident of counties left out from broader life expectancy gains abandoned the Democratic Party in the 2016 presidential election."[35]

Table 15.1 Trump's plurality in three Rust-Belt states in the 2016 election

	Trump's plurality	*Electoral votes*
Pennsylvania	44,292	20
Michigan	10,704	16
Wisconsin	22,748	10
Total	77,744	46

Source: National Archives, "2016 Electoral College Results."

Table 15.2 Economic indicators for the Rust Belt, 2016

		Michigan	Wisconsin	Pennsylvania
	Change 1999-2016			
(1)	Real Household Income ($)	-6648	-10246	unchanged
(2)	Labor Force Participation Rate (%)	-7.6	-6.0	-1.8
(3)	Manufacturing Employment (%)	-30	-22	-35
(4)	Food Stamp Recipients	+800000	+534000	+1040000
(5)	Food Stamp Recipients % of pop	+7.9	+8.9	+7.7
	In 2016			
(6)	U-6 Unemployment Rate (%)	11.2	8.1	10.6
(7)	Children in Poverty (%)	20.7	15.7	18.5
(8)	Food Stamp Recipients % of pop	14.6	12.4	14.5

Note: (1) Real income in 2021 dollars; In making these comparisons, one has to keep in mind that income reporting changed in 2014, see Table 7.6.
Sources: St. Louis Fed, series: (1) MEHOINUSWIA672N, MEHOINUSMIA672N, MEHOINUSPAA672N; (2) LBSSA26, LBSSA55, LBSSA42; (3) MIMFG, WIMFG, PAMFG; (4) BRWI55M647NCEN, BRMI26M647NCEN, BR-PA42M647NCEN; (5) MIPOP, WIPOP, PAPOP; (6) U6UNEM6MI, U6UNEM6WI, U6UNEM6PA, https://nwlc.org/wp-content/uploads/2017/09/Poverty-Rates-State-by-State-2016.pdf.

15.3 Reaganomics Was the Gamechanger

Four decades of grave policy mistakes began in 1981 because Reagan reversed many of the accomplishments of the New Deal and replaced them with policies based on an ideology seeped in social Darwinism that privileged the powerful, the well-heeled, and well-connected.[36] The socio-economic and political impact of his two major tax cuts (1981 and 1986) was a turning point since it put the country on a trajectory of inequality that transformed it into a lopsided economy, placing the working class at a distinct disadvantage (see Figure 7.4).[37]

The seismic effect was immediate because the $400,000 windfall for the top 1 percent, that accrued annually thereafter and grew with compound interest, was a stupendous blow to the political balance of power. The superrich "usually spend most of their resources in order to purchase influence, prestige, and power."[38] So, it was with the Reagan windfall. Instead of building factories, they bought political influence and lobbied relentlessly for more deregulation; they also supported think tanks with tax-deductible contributions and subsidized academic economists who championed the corporate world's free-market ideology. These flooded the media with so much propaganda that it led to *cognitive capture*.

After all, it is nearly impossible for typical citizens to realize how an "across-the-board" tax cut will affect them throughout lives. How low taxes will come back to haunt them in mediocre schools for their children, lower unemployment insurance, and a lower safety net. So, the tax cuts and the consequent cognitive capture were detrimental for the long-run stability of the system. The ratchet effect meant that the tax cuts were irreversible: taxes can be lowered but next-to-impossible to raise; so, slowly a dual economy emerged, and a "patrimonial capitalism" became Reagan's true legacy.[39] It was not coincidental that "Greed is good" became the preferred slogan of the nouveau riche in the 1980s.[40] America had crossed the Rubicon in the moral realm as well.

Kinks sprang up in every set of statistics, evidence of the new era. The kinks are significant because they signal a fundamental turning point in the underlying economic processes, reversing the decline inequality since 1930 (see Figures 7.1, 7.2, 7.4, 7.6, 7.10, 7.11, 12.5).[41] A kink appeared

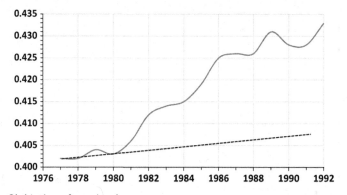

Figure 15.1 The Gini Index of pre-tax income
Source: Income Gini Ratio for Households by Race of Householder, All Races, Ratio, Annual, Not Seasonally Adjusted. FRED Graph Observations, Federal Reserve Economic Data, Economic Research Division, Federal Reserve Bank of St. Louis. https://fred.stlouisfed.org.

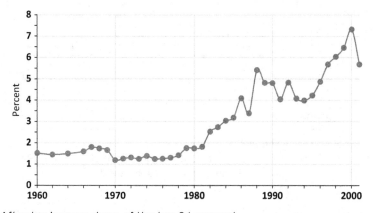

Figure 15.2 After-tax income share of the top 0.1 percent
Note: Computations by authors on tax return statistics. Taxpayers are ranked by gross income (excluding capital gains and government transfers). Income of non-filers is imputed as 20 percent of average income. Groups defined relative to all tax units (filers and non-filers). Income includes employer payroll taxes, realized capital gains, and imputed corporate taxes. Taxes include federal individual, payroll, corporate, and estate and gift taxes.
Source: Thomas Piketty and Emmanuel Saez, "How Progressive is the US Federal Tax System? A Historical and International Perspective," *Journal of Economic Perspectives* 21 (2007), 1: 3-24.

in all indicators of inequality in 1981, soon erasing the gains of the previous half-century (Figure 15.1). The share of post-tax income of the top 0.1 percent of taxpayers jumped from 1.8 percent of total income in 1981, where it had been for two decades, to 2.5 percent in a single year and then rose relentlessly (Figure 15.2). By 2000, it had reached 7 percent, increasing by a factor of four! By 2020, the top 1.5 million taxpayers earned as much as the bottom 65 million, a reflection of a lopsided economy (see Table 7.4). This had adverse effects on the rest of the population because those incomes became their reference values for their relative income and gave them the feeling of progressively falling behind.

Yet another kink appeared immediately after the 1981 tax cut in the number of taxpayers earning more than $200,000 (1976 dollars, worth $950,000 adjusted for inflation in 2021) (Figure 15.3). The rate at which their numbers increased doubled after the tax cut. An additional

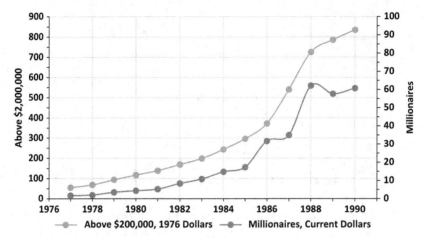

Figure 15.3 Number of high-income tax returns
Source: IRS Staff, "High-Income Tax Returns for 1990," Winter, 1994: 104--132; https://www.irs.gov/pub/irs-soi/90hiintr.pdf.

Table 15.3 The annual rate of increase in the number of millionaires

Date	Number
1978-1981	21000
1982-1986	47000
1987-1990	116000

Note: Millionaires in 2021 dollars.
Source: IRS Staff, "High-Income Tax Returns for 1990," Winter, 1994: 104-132; https://www.irs.gov/pub/irs-soi/90hiintr.pdf.

kink appeared after the 1986 tax cut. At the beginning of Reagan's tenure there were 138,000 millionaires; by its end, there were 725,000. Obviously, such a humongous redistribution of wealth had massive consequences everywhere.[42]

The millionaires took their inspiration from the infamous "Powell Memorandum" of 1971 written by the future Justice of the Supreme Court and helped cement the grip of corporations on the political system:

> The memo called for corporate America to become more aggressive in molding society's thinking about business, government, politics, and law in the US. It inspired wealthy heirs ... to use their private charitable foundations (which did not have to report their political activities) to fund Powell's vision of a pro-business, anti-socialist, minimally government regulated America based on what he thought America had been in the heyday of early American industrialism ... The Powell Memorandum thus became a blueprint for the rise of the American Conservative movement and the formation of a network of influential right-wing think tanks and lobbying organizations ... Following the memo's directives, conservative foundations greatly increased, pouring money into think tanks. The rise of conservative philanthropy led to the conservative intellectual movement and its increasing influence over mainstream political discourse, starting in the 1970s and '80s, and due chiefly to the works of the American Enterprise Institute and the Heritage Foundation.[43]

Reaganomics effectively put into practice the aim of the memorandum. The impact was not confined to tax policy. Reagan let the *real* federal minimum wage decline by 25 percent.[44] He allowed stock buybacks (1982) which increased their price. He allowed private banks to securitize mortgages.[45]

His hostility toward labor is revealed by the appointment of the first businessman as Secretary of Labor who began a long process of advocating anti-labor and pro-business laws, regulations, and practices also at the state level.[46] These included right-to-work laws which have a positive ring to it, but which really meant that employers had the right to hire non-union workers. Under the guise of "freedom," these laws incentivized workers to become free riders, thereby weakening unions because workers could benefit from union representation without paying union dues. These developments changed entirely the balance of power in favor of corporations thereby contributing to the rise of the *precariat* (those without secure employment in the gig economy), and the concomitant hollowing out of the middle class.[47]

He attacked unions vehemently.[48] Hence, another kink appeared in union membership: by the time Reagan left office, union membership had fallen by 30 percent.[49] The countervailing power of unions had been the backbone of the lower-middle class, extricating some wage rents for their members from the profits of oligopolies and protecting them from being exploited by monopsonists (see Sections 8.9, 9.3, and 9.4). Their demise was followed by the decimation of the lower-middle class which three decades later supported the populist movement.

These economic policies also impacted the health of the population *immediately* through several pathways that included increased stress, unaffordable drug prices, less money in the budget for health care, and fewer union jobs. There was even a *kink* in life expectancy. Its rate of increase suddenly decelerated in 1981 (Figure 15.4). Until 1980, life expectancy at birth in the US was ahead of several rich countries but by 2000 Ireland was the single West-European country behind the US. By 2018, the US was behind even Costa Rica, Chile, and the Czech Republic.[50]

The *sudden* and *simultaneous* reversal of so many important empirical indicators, in wages, in income share, in life expectancy, is uncanny evidence that Reaganomics was detrimental to the well-being of the working class. Stiglitz recognized it as such: "Reagan began hollowing out the middle class and skewing the benefits of growth to those at the top ...."[51] The powerful economic processes unleashed inequality, low taxes, twin deficits, coupled with an anti-government ideology that would have been extremely difficult to reverse and consequently were not reversed. That is the essence of path dependence (see Section 8.11).

15.4 The Destructive Forces of Globalization Amplified Reagan's Mistakes

The tsunami of hyperglobalization made it even more difficult for those with low qualifications to live a dignified life (see Section 13.5).[52] By the 1990s, the free-market ideology had become so dominant that Democrat Bill Clinton moved to the right and coopted the Reagan-Bush agenda since it took much less effort to continue to rely on the market to distribute income and wealth than to try to reverse the path-dependence of economic development. Thus, Clinton did as much damage as Reagan by continuing to deregulate the financial sector (see Section 14.2), and by unleashing the mighty forces of globalization which exacerbated the trends in inequality since in a winner-takes-all economy millions of losers lose all.

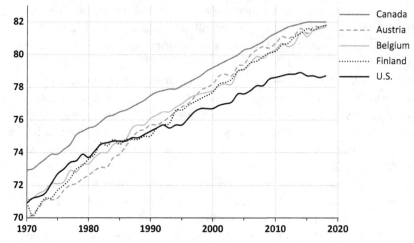

Figure 15.4 Life expectancy trends in the OECD
Source: OECD; https://stats.oecd.org/.

Economists fixated on the theorem of comparative advantage willfully overlooked the well-known predictions that the lives of millions of low-skilled and mid-skilled workers would be shattered as they slipped out of the middle class since there was no way they could compete with their Chinese counterparts.[53] Yet, in signing NAFTA, Clinton predicted pompously that it will "promote more growth, more equality ... and create 200,000 jobs in this country by 1995 alone."[54] He neglected to mention how many low-wage jobs would be destroyed by imports—one estimate put it at 880,000 by 2002. Although exports did well in the 1990s and manufacturing employment even increased (Table 15.4), the unfortunate reality in a dual economy is that the jobs created were not open to the low-skilled workers displaced by imports.

In concluding the ceremony, Clinton nonchalantly remarked: "I call on all of us ... to join with me to urge the Congress to create the world's best worker training and retraining system."[55] He should have been ashamed of himself, for anyone even with superficial knowledge of politics should have known that retraining workers should have been a prerequisite of signing NAFTA and not a lame afterthought.[56] Of course, practically nothing of significance was done to diminish the blow to those hammered by the deep penetration of imports into America's heartland (see Figures 13.3 and 13.5).

Globalization morphed into hyperglobalization after Clinton signed the Bill granting China Permanent Normal Trade Relations with the World Trade Organization (in 2000) (see Table 7.2). He put the identical enthusiastic spin on it: "We'll be able to export products without exporting jobs."[57] He was delusional for disregarding that "in the absence of a more concerted government response, too much globalization would deepen societal cleavages, exacerbate distributional problems, [and] undermine domestic social bargains."[58] Instead, Clinton sounded the death knell for labor-intensive manufacturing.[59] Within one year, 800,000 jobs disappeared and by year two 2 million jobs had vanished. By 2007, 3.3 million jobs were gone (Table 15.4). Globalization was said to be good for America, but no one *ever* said that it would be good for *everyone* in America, and it wasn't. "Roughly 40 percent of the aggregate increase in non-employment during 2000-2011 can be attributed to manufacturing decline."[60] By the 2016 election, 28 percent of the manufacturing jobs had vanished, adding fuel to the populist movement. Yet, economists sang the praises of free trade in unison, irresponsibly ignoring its impact on the lives of those who were devastated, a clear misapplication of blackboard economics (see Section 13.2).

Those who were hurt in the Rust Belt were hapless, helpless, and hopeless. The expanding IT sector was closed to them. Although the demand for labor increased rapidly in IT from 450,000 employees in 1970 to 4.6 million in 2014, 22 percent of them had a master's degree or beyond.[61] The skills of the displaced workers in the Rust Belt did not match the requirements of the IT sector. That is the idea of the *skill mismatch*.

Few reprimanded their colleagues for the obvious failure of neoliberal economic theories as succinctly as Dani Rodrik, an economist in Harvard's Kennedy School. He answered his rhetorical question, "Are economists partly responsible for Donald Trump's shocking victory in the US Presidential election?" in the affirmative and continued:

> It has long been an unspoken rule of public engagement for economists that they should champion trade and not dwell too much on the fine print … The standard models of trade… typically yield sharp distributional effects: income losses by certain groups are the flip side of the gains from trade … And economists have long known that … poorly functioning labor markets, credit market imperfections, - can interfere with reaping those gains … Nonetheless, economists can be counted on to parrot the wonders of comparative advantage and free trade whenever trade agreements come up. They have consistently minimized distributional concerns, even though it is now clear that the distributional impact of NAFTA or China's entry into the World Trade Organization were significant for the most directly affected communities in the United States … They have overstated the magnitude of gains from trade deals, though such gains have been relatively small since at least the 1990s.[62]

That is a strong indictment of the mainstream canon. But there is more, because it is clear that Trump benefited greatly from Bill Clinton's mistakes:

> Michigan, Wisconsin, Pennsylvania, and North Carolina would have elected the Democrat instead of the Republican candidate if, ceteris paribus, the growth in Chinese import penetration had been 50 percent lower than the actual growth during the period of analysis. The Democrat candidate would also have obtained a majority in the electoral college in this counterfactual scenario.[63]

Table 15.4 Number of employees in US manufacturing

Date	Millions	Change (%)
1960s	16.6	
1970s	18.1	1.4
1980s	17.9	-0.2
1993	16.8	-1.1
2000	17.2	0.4
2007	13.9	-3.3
2016	12.4	-1.5
2021	12.3	-0.1

Source: St. Louis Fed, series MANEMP.

15.5 After Reagan, Bush Sr., Clinton, and Bush Jr., Obama Adds Fuel to the Fire

The impersonal powerful forces of ever rising inequality, hyperglobalization, and technological disruptions would have sufficed to disorient the underclass, but more challenges lay ahead: the financial crisis. Bush Jr. remained on the path forged by Reagan by lowering taxes twice that continued to aggravate inequality and continued to add to the national deficit. The instability of the financial sector due to decades of deregulation and lax oversight finally culminated under his watch in the devastating financial crisis of 2008. In response, his administration adopted the neoliberal blueprint by rescuing Wall Street while ignoring Main Street (see Chapter 14). But he was in charge of the panic for only four months and then passed the torch onto Barack Obama.

Elected on a platform of reform and change, Obama disappointed his followers by supporting the status quo and following in Bush Jr.'s footsteps. He did not have the experience to forge a new vision for the nation and instead appointed members of the old guard, Larry Summers from the Clinton administration and Timothy Geithner from the Bush Jr. administration. So, he continued to bail out the banks while ignoring the fate of the homeowners and even made Bush Jr.'s tax cuts permanent in 2013 (otherwise they would have expired) (see Section 14.7).[64] He solidified the power of the financial sector and added nine million evicted families to the discontented. The crisis magnified the economic distortions of the previous decades. "The painful consequences of financial crisis are a function of both the conditions that precede the crisis and the amplification effect of the crisis itself."[65]

> The crash demonstrated the emptiness of the claim that markets could regulate themselves. It should have led to the disgrace of neoliberalism—the belief that unregulated markets produce and distribute goods and services more efficiently than regulated ones. Instead, the old order reasserted itself, and with calamitous consequences. Gross economic imbalances of power and wealth persisted.[66]

Illustration 15.2 Millions of families lost their homes because of the financial crisis, but the financiers who caused the crisis were not among them. Allowing this to happen is a severe blot on the Obama administration
Credit: iStock.com/fstop123.

The asymmetric bailout that fostered the *unprecedented* upward redistribution of wealth was not the way capitalism was supposed to work.[67] So, the US mutated into an "ersatz capitalism," or "lemon capitalism," no longer the real thing.[68] Sheila Bair, Chairwoman of the Federal Deposit Insurance Corporation during the crisis, noted, "You don't need to protect the jobs and bonuses of dunderheads at places like AIG and Citi who got their institutions into trouble."[69]

But Obama did defend them unabashedly, betraying his mandate for change and alienating additional millions. He chose the easy way out of the crisis: "In the early days of his presidency, Barack Obama had the power to overhaul the economy, but instead he focused on smaller, less effective fixes."[70] He failed to recognize the significance of the structural imbalances. So, inequality persisted, downward social mobility persisted, and despair continued to accumulate. He wasted a crisis that provided a once-in-a-lifetime opportunity to rebuke Reagan's legacy. His failure left the door open to Trump's brand of populism.[71]

> We were naive about what the globalized economy would do to the working class, naive to think the internet would bring us together, naive to think the global mixing of people would breed harmony, ... We didn't predict that ... demagogues ... [in] the US would ignite ethnic hatreds.[72]

15.6 From Reagan to Trump in One Generation

Of the OECD countries, the US experienced the most polarization,[73] because it also experienced the steepest upsurge in inequality. The reason is that an oligarchy and democracy are incompatible.[74] The January 6th storming of the Capitol was the culmination of a path-dependent socio-economic process beginning in 1981 through which the US became a dual economy that failed those without a college degree.[75] An obvious indicator of the pain inflicted on them is that their life expectancy was way below that of those in the other half of the dual economy. In fact, the ratio of their mortality rate to those with a college degree was an astonishing 3.4 even before Covid-19.[76] That means that a BA amazingly provides 70 percent protection against death. The mortality ratio was highest among whites: 3.6, higher than for Blacks: 2.9 and for Hispanics: 2.6. Hard to avoid connecting these dots to the rise of white nationalism.

Clearly, the elites had rigged the economic system so that it choked off opportunity for low-skilled men.[77] The modern-day proletarians felt powerless, alienated, insecure, angry, and estranged from the system tilted against them.[78] Panicked by an existential threat, the pre-frontal cortex loses control.[79] It is circumvented by the primordial survival instinct that makes it easier for demagogues to manipulate emotions so much so that people no longer recognize their self-interest, let alone their enlightened self-interest.[80]

Status anxiety generated resentment toward the political establishment that morphed into a desire to exact vengeance.[81] This was an additional motivator for the downtrodden to support anyone who would cause trepidation in Washington.[82] Their exasperation was based on "more than just economic insecurity but [also on] a deep-seated feeling of precarity about their personal situation ... And that precarity – combined with a sense of betrayal or anger ... – mobilized a lot of people that day."[83] Being snubbed by the political establishment felt oppressive: the political elite allowed their skills to be degraded and made it impossible for them to compete in a social Darwinist global economy.[84] They were the losers but they felt that it was not their fault: the rules of the game were unfairly tilted against them.[85] They became "emotionally sick,"[86] and felt, like the Patriots of 1776, that they had the right to overthrow a tyrannical system to make America great again.

Illustration 15.3 Hillary's deplorables, disadvantaged in a hot economy, break into Congress to redress their grievances
Credit: Shutterstock, 1889190715.

The dispersion of power is the foundation of democracy. The gradual emergence of a greedy "overclass" and a political elite no longer focused on the commonweal undermined the stability of the US socio-economic system in the course of five administrations and inaugurated an era of political dysfunction and instability.[87] Even neoliberal Alan Greenspan recognized presciently that inequality was a serious threat: He said that if we don't reverse "a quarter century of increases in income inequality, the cultural ties that bind our society could become undone. Disaffection, breakdowns of authority, even large-scale violence could ensue, jeopardizing the civility on which growing economies depend."[88]

He was not alone. Zbigniew Brzezinski, also a staunch anti-socialist, expressed very similar concerns years before Trump's election.[89] Nobel Prize-winning Princeton economist, Angus Deaton, did so as well:

> If we can only generate good lives for an elite that's about a third of the population, then we have a real problem ... if we can't fix this, it really is a crisis of capitalism ... it doesn't seem to be working for the people who are not very well educated.[90]

Thus, the conclusion emerges that neoliberal economic polices had corrosive consequences on the very foundations of the political order and created an economy that has "fallen short of any conception of a 'good economy'—an economy offering a 'good life'."[91]

Reaganomics did not cause Trumpism, but it did unleash the "darkest spirits of capitalists."[92] And the path-dependent process he initiated, once it had gathered momentum, could have been reversed, especially in 2009 when its proponents were at their weakest, but Obama squandered that opportunity, and the process entered a new phase with the triumph of Trumpism in 2016.[93]

Western civilization once again finds itself in the middle of a major socio-economic transformation, this time from an economy producing goods and services to a post-industrial knowledge economy. According to the historical record, such economic realignments are always complicated, never linear, and seldom free of conflict. The transition from feudalism to capitalism had its own birth pangs. England had two major upheavals in the seventeenth century during which one king was beheaded and another deposed through machinations that resembled a modern *coup d'état*. Insofar as such transformations reshuffle the political, social, and economic hierarchy, they are invariably accompanied by conflict. After all, France had four revolutions during the transition. It is difficult to give up power and privilege. We should have known that entering the Information Age was not going to be easy sailing for mankind.

15.7 Takeaways

America's troubles began with Reaganomics because it put the US economy on a path that was hard to reverse thereafter. It made unsubstantiated claims that the humongous tax windfall granted to millionaires would eventually trickle down to the masses, but the dollars failed to trickle as the top 1 percent figured out how to keep practically all of it. The wealthy also invested heavily in the political process to profit further from deregulation. They also supported think tanks that hired economists to sing the praises of free markets until laissez-faire principles became the dominant ideology of the land. Next came globalization and the less skilled, less educated workers suddenly faced competition from an army of workers willing to work for a pittance in less developed nations. They too became disgruntled when they lost their job and were unable to find decent employment in the new economy. The neoliberal blunders included the deregulation of the financial sector that led to a crisis of historical proportions with millions evicted from their homes, further fueling the discontent. The impact of four decades of flawed economic policies was a loss of faith in the political establishment that culminated in political dysfunction, a polarized society, and the January 6th insurrection by a ferocious mob intent on destruction.

Questions for Discussion

1 Do you know anyone who supported the populist insurrection?
2 Which economic factors do you think were most important in destabilizing the political system?
3 Do you think that low-skilled workers were treated fairly by the economic system?
4 Do you think that it was fair to give millionaires a $400,000 windfall in the 1980s while giving poor people $400?
5 How could white nationalists be persuaded to give up their ideology?
6 Is an equitable income distribution a prerequisite of social stability?
7 Do you know anyone who is struggling to pay their bills? What are their political views?
8 Do you know anyone who is indebted? What are their political views?
9 Why do you think Hillary Clinton lost the election to Donald Trump?
10 Do you think that globalization could have been managed without creating havoc among low-skilled men?
11 Which false economic theories are most responsible for the rise of populism?
12 Do you think that the rise of populism was avoidable?
13 Discuss: globalization was responsible for the destruction of American industry.
14 What industrial policy would help the Rust Belt?
15 Do you think it is easy to go to college for someone born into a dysfunctional neighborhood? Dysfunctional family? Slum?
16 What caused the opioid epidemic? The rise of extremism?
17 Discuss the strong correlation at the county level between economic distress and the support for Donald Trump.

18   Discuss the correlation at the county level between lower life expectancy and the support for Donald Trump.
19   What is marginalization? Downward social mobility?
20   Do you agree that Reaganomics was a gamechanger?
21   Do you think that Trumpism became the legacy of Obama's economic policies?
22   Do you think it would be good to raise taxes on the superrich?
23   Do you think that greed is good?
24   Why do you think there is so much hostility toward organized labor among conservative politicians?
25   What do you think is needed for a dignified life?
26   Why do you think that downward social mobility is so difficult to bear?

Notes

1   Interview by Mike Wallace, May 18, 1958, by permission of the Harry Ransom Center, the University of Texas at Austin.
2   James Kwak, *Economism: Bad Economics and the Rise of Inequality* (Pantheon Books, 2017); Robert Kuttner, *Everything for Sale: The Virtues and Limits of Markets* (Alfred Arnold, 1997).
3   Binyamin Appelbaum, *The Economists' Hour: False Prophets, Free Markets, and the Fracture of Society* (Little, Brown, and Company, 2019); David Harvey, *Anti-Capitalist Chronicles* (Pluto Press, 2020); Charles Wilber and Kenneth Jameson, *Beyond Reaganomics: A Further Inquiry into the Poverty of Economics* (University of Notre Dame Press, 1990).
4   Gallup Poll, June 10, 2020; https://news.gallup.com/poll/312575/satisfaction-direction-lowest-four-years.aspx; Anonymous, "Dec.17-19, 2021, Washington Post University of Maryland poll," *The Washington Post*, January 1, 2022.
5   The Editorial Board, "The America We Need," *The New York Times*, April 9, 2020.
6   Jeffrey Madrick, *Seven Bad Ideas: How Mainstream Economists Have Damaged America and the World* (Knopf, 2014).
7   Ronald Formisano, *Plutocracy in America: How Increasing Inequality Destroys the Middle Class and Exploits the Poor* (Johns Hopkins University Press, 2015).
8   International Institute for Democracy and Electoral Assistance, "The Global State of Democracy 2021," p. 8; https://www.idea.int/gsod/sites/default/files/2021-11/the-global-state-of-democracy-2021_1.pdf.
9   David Harvey, *A Brief History of Neoliberalism* (Oxford University Press, 2007).
10   Joseph Stiglitz, "Of the 1 Percent, by the 1 Percent, for the 1 Percent," *Vanity Fair*, May 2011.
11   John Miller, "The Economics of Whitelash," *Dollars&Sense*, March/April 2017.
12   Barbara Walter, *How Civil Wars Start: And How to Stop Them* (Crown, 2022).
13   "Donald Trump's astonishing victory … has made one thing abundantly clear: too many Americans—particularly white male Americans—feel left behind." Joseph Stiglitz, "What America's Economy Needs from Trump," *Project Syndicate*, November 13, 2016.
14   Wikipedia Contributors, "United States Presidential Election, 2016."
15   Jeff Faux, *The Servant Economy: Where America's Elite Is Sending the Middle Class* (Wiley, 2012).
16   David Brooks, "The G.O.P. Is Rotting," *The New York Times*, December 7, 2017.
17   Russell Berman, "The 'Carnival Barker' Joins the 2016 Circus," *The Atlantic*, June 16, 2015.
18   "15 Times Trump Bragged about His Intelligence," CNN, http://www.cnn.com/videos/politics/2017/10/10/times-trump-bragged-about-intelligence-orig-alee.cnn.
19   Bruce Bartlett, *The New American Economy: The Failure of Reaganomics and a New Way Forward* (St. Martin's Press, 2009); Benjamin Friedman, *Day of Reckoning: The Consequences of American Economic Policy* (Random House, 1988); Jean-Michel Paul, *The Economics of Discontent: From Failing Elites to the Rise of Populism* (Tomson, 2019).

20   A slogan during Bill Clinton's election campaign.

21   Martin Gilens, *Affluence and Influence: Economic Inequality and Political Power in America* (Princeton University Press, 2012).

22   Michiko Kakutani, *The Death of Truth: Notes on Falsehood in the Age of Trump* (Tim Duggan Books, 2018).

23   Jonathan Rothwell and Pablo Diego-Rosell, "Explaining Nationalist Political Views: The Case of Donald Trump," https://papers.ssrn.com/sol3/Papers.cfm?abstract_id=2822059 (November 2, 2016).

24   Robert Paxton, *The Anatomy of Fascism* (Vintage Books, 2004); Umberto Eco, "Ur-Fascism", *The New York Review of Books*, June 22, 1995.

25   Hedrick Smith, *Who Stole the American Dream?* (Random House, 2012); Thomas Palley, *Plenty of Nothing: The Downsizing of the American Dream and the Case For Structural Keynesianism* (Princeton University Press, 1998).

26   Walter Scheidel, *The Great Leveler: Violence and the History of Inequality from the Stone Age to the Twenty-First Century* (Princeton University Press, 2017).

27   Richard Wolffe, "Donald Trump's Victory Is Nothing Short of a Revolution," *The Guardian*, November 9, 2016. Conor Friedersdorf, "Trump Has Filled, Not Drained, the Swamp," *The Atlantic*, September 21, 2017.

28   Josh Hafner, "Donald Trump Loves the 'Poorly Educated' and They Love Him," *USA Today*, February 24, 2016.

29   Steffie Wolhandler et al., "Public Policy and Health in the Trump Era," *Lancet* 397 (2021), 397: 705-753; here p. 705.

30   Brian Alexander, *Glass House: The 1 Percent Economy and the Shattering of an All-American Town* (St. Martin's Press, 2017).

31   Suggestions to rescue it through a Reconstruction Finance Corporation were ignored. Felix Rohatyn, "Reconstructing America," *The New York Review of Books*, March 5, 1981. Instead, Gregory Mankiw, as chairmen of the president's Council of Economic Advisers, justified outsourcing jobs, saying it is "probably a plus for the economy in the long run." CNN, "Bush Adviser Backs Off Pro-Outsourcing Comment," February 12, 2004.

32   Editorial Board, "Donald Trump's Revolution: Voters Rebuke America's Political Establishment," *Chicago Tribune*, November 9, 2016.

33   James Goodwin et al., "Association of Chronic Opioid Use with Presidential Voting Patterns in US Counties in 2016," *JAMA Network Open* (2018), 1(2): e180450; Dan Keating and Lenny Bernstein, "100,000 American Died of Drug Overdoses in 12 Months During the Pandemic," *The Washington Post*, November 17, 2021.

34   Shannon Monnat, "Deaths of Despair and Support for Trump in the 2016 Presidential Election," Pennsylvania State University Research Brief, December 4, 2016.

35   Jacob Bor, "Diverging Life Expectancies and Voting Patterns in the 2016 US Presidential Election," *American Journal of Public Health* 107 (2017), 10: 1560-1562; Jason Wasfy et al., "County Community Health Associations of Net Voting Shift in the 2016 US Presidential Election," *PLOS ONE*, October 2017; https://doi.org/10.1371/journal.pone.0185051; Howard Koh et al., "Confronting the Rise and Fall of US Life Expectancy," *Journal of the American Medical Association* 322 (2019), 20: 1963-1965.

36   Kim Phillips-Fein, *Invisible Hands: The Businessmen's Crusade Against the New Deal* (Norton, 2010); William Greider, "The Education of David Stockman," *The Atlantic*, December 1981. https://www.theatlantic.com/magazine/archive/1981/12/the-education-of-david-stockman/305760/.

37   Christopher Lasch, "Reagan's Victims," *The New York Review of Books*, July 21, 1988.

38   Thomas Piketty, "About *Capital in the Twenty-First Century*," *American Economic Review* 105 (2015), 5: 48-53, here p. 52.

39   Thomas Piketty, *Capital in the Twenty-First Century* (Harvard University Press, 2014); Jacob Hacker and Paul Pierson, *Winner-Take-All Politics: How Washington Made the Rich Richer-and Turned Its Back on the Middle Class* (Simon & Schuster, 2010).

40   John Dickerson, "Battling Boeskys," *Time*, May 3, 1993. An episode of a CNN miniseries on the "Eight-ies" aired in 2016, was titled "Greed is Good."

41   Peter Lindert and Jeffrey Williamson, *Unequal Gains: American Growth and Inequality since 1700* (Princeton University Press, 2016); Thomas Piketty and Emmanuel Saez, "Inequality in the Long Run," *Science* 344 (May 23, 2014), issue 6186, pp. 838–843; supplement 1–8.

42   Philip Burch, *Reagan, Bush, and Right-Wing Politics: Elites, Think Tanks, Power and Policy* (Jai Press, 1997); Diane Ravitch, "Big Money Rules," *The New York Review of Books*, December 7, 2017.

43   Wikipedia, "Lewis F. Powell Jr."

44   St. Louis Fed, series STTMINWGFG and CPI.

45   Frank Ackerman, *Hazardous to Our Wealth: Economic Policies in the 1980s* (South End Press, 1984).

46   Wikipedia, "Raymond J. Donovan."

47   Lawrence Mishel, "Unions, Inequality, and Faltering Middle-Class Wages," Economic Policy Institute Report, August 29, 2012; Louis Uchitelle, "How the Loss of Union Power Has Hurt American Manu-facturing," *The New York Times*, April 20, 2018; Alexandrea Ravenelle, *Hustle and Gig: Struggling and Surviving in the Sharing Economy* (University of California Press, 2019); Guy Standing, "Understanding the Precariat through Labour and Work," *Development and Change* 45 (2014), 5: 963–980.

48   Jacob Hacker and Paul Pierson, *American Amnesia: How the War on Government Led US to Forget What Made America Prosper* (Simon & Schuster, 2016).

49   Economic Policy Institute, "Union Coverage," https://www.epi.org/data/#?subject=unioncov.

50   David Leonhardt and Stuart Thompson, "How Working-Class Life Is Killing Americans," *The New York Times*, March 6, 2020.

51   Nathan Kelly, *The Politics of Income Inequality in the United States* (Cambridge University Press, 2009).

52   Andrew Cherlin, *Labor's Love Lost: The Rise and Fall of the Working-Class Family in America* (Russell Sage Foundation, 2014).

53   Joseph Stiglitz, *Globalization and Its Discontents Revisited: Anti-Globalization in the Era of Trump* (Nor-ton & Co., 2017).

54   William Clinton, "Remarks on Signing the North American Free Trade Agreement Implementation Act," December 8, 1993.

55   Ibid.

56   Thomas Frank, *Listen, Liberal: Or, What Ever Happened to the Party of the People?* (Metropolitan Books, 2016).

57   "Full Text of Clinton's Speech on China Trade Bill," March 9, 2000, https://www.iatp.org/sites/default/files/Full_Text_of_Clintons_Speech_on_China_Trade_Bi.htm.

58   Dani Rodrik, "Straight Talk on Trade," Project Syndicate, November 15, 2016. www.project-syndicate.org/commentary/trump-win-economists-responsible-by-dani-rodrik-2016-11?barrier=accessreg, citing his earlier work: *Has Globalization Gone Too Far?* (Institute for International Economics, 1997).

59   Daron Acemoglu et al., "Import Competition and the Great US Employment Sag of the 2000s," *Journal of Labor Economics* 34 (2016), S1: S141–198.

60   Kerwin Kofi Charles et al., "Housing Booms, Manufacturing Decline and Labour Market Outcomes," *Economic Journal* 129 (2019), 617: 209–248.

61   Julia Beckhusen, "American Community Survey Reports. Occupations in Information Technology," no. 3, August 2016.

62   Rodrik, "Straight Talk," op. cit.

63   David Autor et al., "Importing Political Polarization? The Electoral Consequences of Rising Trade Expo-sure," *American Economic Review* 110 (2020), 10: 3139–3183.

64   Noam Scheiber, *The Escape Artists: How Obama's Team Fumbled the Recovery* (Simon & Schuster, 2011).

65   Amir Sufi and Alan Taylor, "Financial Crises: A Survey," NBER Working Paper 28155, August 2021.

66   Robert Kuttner, "The Crash That Failed," *The New York Review of Books*, November 22, 2018.

67   Yves Smith, *ECONned: How Unenlightened Self Interest Undermined Democracy and Corrupted Capitalism* (Palgrave Macmillan, 2010).

68   Joseph Stiglitz, "America's Socialism for the Rich," *The Economists' Voice*, 6: 5, June 2009.

69   Sheila Bair, "Why I Recommend Tim Geithner's Book," *Fortune*, May 19, 2014. http://finance.fortune.cnn.com/2014/05/19/sheila-bair-tim-geithner/.

70   Farhad Manjoo, "Barack Obama's Biggest Mistake," *The New York Times*, September 18, 2019.

71   Reed Hundt, *A Crisis Wasted: Barack Obama's Defining Decisions* (Rosetta Books, 2019).

72   David Brooks, "America Is Having a Moral Convulsion," *The Atlantic*, October 5, 2020.

73   Levi Boxell et al., "Cross-Country Trends in Affective Polarization," Unpublished manuscript, August 2021; https://www.brown.edu/Research/Shapiro/pdfs/cross-polar.pdf.

74   Thom Hartmann Program, "President Jimmy Carter: The United States Is an Oligarchy," https://www.youtube.com/watch?v=hDsPWmioSHg.

75   Thomas Mann and Norman Ornstein, *It's Even Worse Than it Looks: How the American Constitutional System Collided with the New Politics of Extremism* (Basic Books, 2012); Jane Mayer, *Dark Money: The Hidden History of the Billionaires Behind the Rise of The Radical Right* (Doubleday, 2016).

76   Anne Case and Angus Deaton, "Mortality Rates by College Degree Before and During Covid-19," NBER Working Paper no 29318, Figure 3.

77   Joseph Stiglitz, "How Trump Happened," *Project Syndicate*, October 14, 2016.

78   Michael Graetz and Ian Shapiro, *The Wolf at the Door: The Menace of Economic Insecurity and How to Fight It* (Harvard University Press, 2020); Paul Krugman, "Trump's Potemkin Economy," *The New York Times*, June 30, 2018.

79   Ronald Inglehart and Pippa Norris, "Trump and the Populist Authoritarian Parties: The Silent Revolution in Reverse," *Perspectives on Politics* 15 (2017), 2: 443-454.

80   Arlie Hochschild, *Strangers in Their Own Land: Anger and Mourning on the American Right* (The New Press, 2016); Jason Stanley, *How Propaganda Works* (Princeton University Press, 2015); Thomas Frank, *What's the Matter with Kansas? How Conservatives Won the Heart of America* (Metropolitan Books, 2004).

81   Thomas Edsall, "The Resentment That Never Sleeps," *The New York Times*, December 9, 2020; Elaine Tyler May, *Fortress America: How We Embraced Fear and Abandoned Democracy* (Basic Books, 2017).

82   The journal *Social Neuroscience* has some pertinent articles on radicalization, as does https://cpost.uchicago.edu/publications/a_multilevel_social_neuroscience_perspective_on_radicalization_and_terroris/.

83   Todd Frankel, "A Majority of the People Arrested for Capitol Riot Had a History of Financial Trouble," *The Washington Post*, February 10, 2021.

84   Kay Lehman Schlozman et al., *The Unheavenly Chorus: Unequal Political Voice and the Broken Promise of American Democracy* (Princeton University Press, 2012); Dani Rodrik, "Populism and the Economics of Globalization," *Journal of International Business Policy* 1 (2018), 1-2: 12-33.

85   Jean-Michel Paul, *The Economics of Discontent: From Failing Elites to the Rise of Populism* (Tomson, 2019).

86   David Brooks, "The Virtue of Radical Honesty," *The New York Times*, February 22, 2018.

87   Michael Lind, *The New Class War: Saving Democracy from the Managerial Elite* (Penguin, 2020); Steven Levitsky and Daniel Ziblatt, *How Democracies Die* (Crown Publishing, 2018); David Cay Johnston, *It's Even Worse Than You Think: What the Trump Administration Is Doing to America* (Simon & Schuster, 2018); Wikipedia, "Power Elite"; Charles Wright Mills, *The Power Elite* (Oxford University Press, 1956).

88   Alan Greenspan, *The Age of Turbulence: Adventures in a New World* (Penguin Press, 2007), p. 468.

89   "The Great US Wealth Gap Could Cause a Social Conflict: Zbigniew Brzezinski—Fast Forward," Reuters TV video, 4:12, July 18, 2012.

90   Jason Belline, "Why 'Deaths of Despair' May Be a Warning Sign for America-Moving Upstream," *The Wall Street Journal*, February 27, 2018; the quote is @5.54.

91   Edmund Phelps, "What Is Wrong with the West's Economies?" *The New York Review of Books*, August 13, 2015.

92   Emma Rothschild, "The Philosophy of Reaganism," *The New York Review of Books*, April 15, 1982.

93   Benjamin Friedman, "Reagan Lives!" *The New York Review of Books*, December 20, 1990; Michael Gilbert, *Reaganomics vs. the Modern Economy: The Conflict that Divides America* (North Loop Book, 2016).

16 Hidden Racist Elements in Blackboard Economics

> We shall overcome because the arc of the moral universe is long,
> But it bends toward justice.
>
> –Martin Luther King, Jr[1]

16.1 Introduction to Covert Racism

In Chapter 15, we elaborated how false economic theories led to false policies that fostered the rise of populism. This chapter discusses how false economic theories feed into *covert* racism.[2] That does not imply that economists or their theories are themselves *overtly* racist.[3] Rather, the market fundamentalism they promulgate is intent on preserving the status quo which privileges the well-to-do but massively disadvantages the have-nots who are disproportionately marginalized members of minority groups.[4]

Overt racism is deliberate while covert racism might be unintended. Mainstream economics is *covertly racist* because it provides theoretical support for an economic system that contributes to keeping disadvantaged groups at the bottom of the socio-economic hierarchy.[5] Color-blind, covert, implicit, institutional, laissez-faire, structural, or systemic racism is

> a system in which public policies, institutional policies … and other norms work … to perpetuate racial group inequity. It identifies … [aspects] that have allowed … disadvantages associated with 'color' to endure … Structural racism … has been a feature of the social, economic, and political systems in which we all exist.[6]

Covert racism can also be considered "as individual- and group-level processes and structures that are implicated in the reproduction of racial inequality in diffuse and often subtle ways."[7] The flip side of Black disadvantage is white privilege.[8] Similar issues appear in legal studies, sociology, and other disciplines.[9]

16.2 The Descendants of Slaves Are Still at the Bottom of the Totem Pole

While mainstream economists emphasize that "the US economy is in good shape,"[10] the living standards of the descendants of slaves more than a century and a half after emancipation are hardly within their purview. They ignore that the plight of minorities is dismal by all indicators. African American households' real median household income in 2019 was $30,600 less than that of whites, and the gap had increased by $5,400 since 2000 (see Table 7.5).

DOI: 10.4324/9781003174356-16

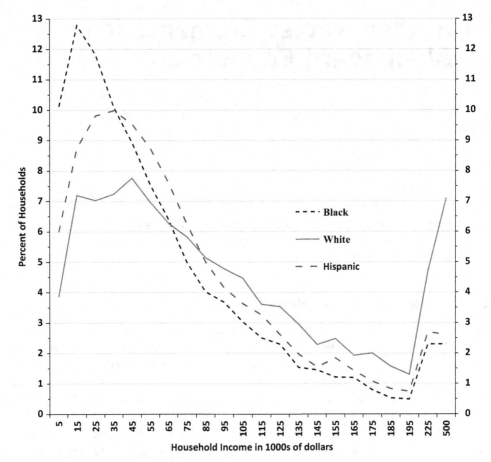

Figure 16.1 Distribution of household income by ethnicity, US, 2019
Note: Last category is incomes over $250,000 assumed to be $500,000 on average.
Source: US Census, HINC-06. "Income Distribution to $250,000 or More for Households: 2019"; https://
www.census.gov/data/tables/time-series/demo/income-poverty/cps-hinc/hinc-06.2019.html.

Table 16.1 Distribution of household income by ethnicity, US, 2020 (%)

	<15K	15-25K	25-50K	50-100K	100-150K	150-200K	>200K
White	7.6	8.0	18.4	28.8	16.6	9.0	11.7
Black	18.0	11.7	23.6	27.0	10.7	4.1	4.8
Hispanic	10.6	9.8	25	30.7	10.7	4.1	4.8

Note: Last category is open-ended.
Source: Emily Shrider et al., "Income and Poverty in the United States: 2020," *Current Population Reports*,
September 2021. https://www.census.gov/content/dam/Census/library/publications/2021/demo/p60-273.pdf.

They are the only ethnic group whose real median household income has been stagnating for two decades, as a lingering legacy of the evils of slavery and subsequent legal discrimination (see Figure 7.9).[11] The mean income of the bottom fifth of African American households was a meager $8,300.[12] The real median weekly earnings of full-time Black wage and salary workers were 80 percent of white earnings during the first two decades of the twenty-first century.[13] Blacks are highly concentrated in the left tail of the income distribution (Figure 16.1).

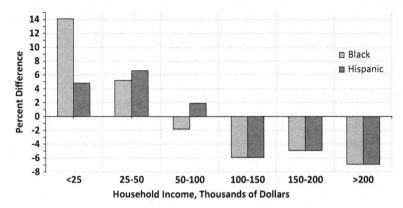

Figure 16.2 Differences in income distribution relative to whites, US, 2020
Note: Percent difference is the share of the population of minorities in the relevant income category minus the share of whites in that income category.
Source: Emily Shrider et al., "Income and Poverty in the United States: 2020," *Current Population Reports*, September 2021. https://www.census.gov/content/dam/Census/library/publications/2021/demo/p60-273.pdf.

The income of 30 percent of African American households and 20 percent of Hispanic households was less than $25,000 in 2020, implying that they are barely eking out a living (Table 16.1). Minorities are significantly overrepresented in every income bracket below $50,000 and underrepresented above $100,000 (Figure 16.2). While 20 percent of Black households, and 24 percent of Hispanic households have an annual income over $100,000, 37 percent of white households do.

The distribution of wealth shows an even greater disparity because wealth represents past accumulation that was hindered during years of overt racial discrimination.[14] This is how past injustices are transmitted through generations to the present.[15] No wonder that nearly one-fifth of the 101 million African Americans and Hispanics in the US in 2021, were poor.[16] That is more than twice the rate for whites. The racial bias of poverty is disconcerting: US Blacks are 1.8 times and Hispanics 1.5 times as likely to be poor than their share of the population.[17] Furthermore, 38 percent of Blacks with some college education were unable to meet their current bills compared to 18 percent of whites.[18]

Moreover, their imprisonment rate, unemployment rate, life expectancy, schooling, wealth, financial security, upward mobility, and every single other indicator of well-being are inferior to that of whites and usually by substantial margins.[19] Pre-Covid life expectancy among Black men in the US, at 72.2 years was 4.4 years behind that of whites and below that of Algeria and China.[20]

Despite the Civil Rights movement, disadvantages persist and has even widened: the white-Black wage gap is 22 percent among men and 12 percent among women (controlling for education).[21] This is a lower-bound estimate considering that differences in educational attainment are also due to discrimination and poverty.[22] When the media boasted that the *official* unemployment rate was 4.6 percent in October 2021, the *true* unemployment rate (U-6) was about 16.0 percent among minorities (Figure 16.3).[23] This reflects more accurately than the official figures the real pain in a dual labor market. It was still worse stratified by educational attainment since the true unemployment rate reached 29.9 percent among African Americans without a high school degree (Table 16.2).

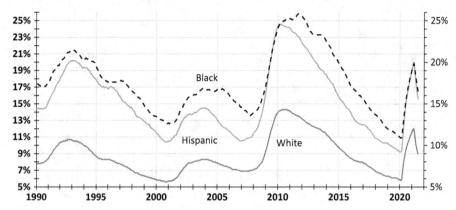

Figure 16.3 The U-6 unemployment rate by ethnicity
Source: Economic Policy Institute, State of Working America Data Library, "Underemployment," 2021;
https://www.epi.org/data/#/?subject=underemp&r=*.

Table 16.2 The U-6 unemployment rate by ethnicity and education, 2021

	All	High school diploma		College diploma		Advanced degree
		No	Yes	No	Yes	
Black	16.5	29.9	21.5	15.7	10.5	7.8
Hispanic	15.6	20.3	17.3	14.3	11.1	6.8
White	9.0	16.3	11.6	9.9	7.1	5.0
All	11.4	19.8	14.8	11.8	8.2	5.5

Source: Economic Policy Institute, State of Working America Data Library, "Underemployment," 2021;
https://www.epi.org/data/#/?subject=underemp&r=*.

16.3 Alice-in-Wonderland Discrimination in Economic Theory

Blackboard economists argue that discrimination is benign because competition will ultimately overcome its deleterious effects. Ever since Gary Becker's 1955 dissertation, the economic theories of discrimination have failed woefully to appreciate the deep ethical nature of the problem and skirt its devastating impact on minorities. Becker's callous reference to discrimination as a "non-pecuniary element" in transactions or as a "disutility caused by contact with some individuals" is an insidious pretense at objectivity.[24] His framing of the issue nonchalantly as a case of "personal preferences" makes segregation appear legitimate: essentially equating it with our taste for any consumption good.[25] The "taste for discrimination" thereby became a component of the benign theory of free choice and part of the liberal democratic tradition of market exchange between equals.[26]

The theory also presumes that discriminating firms will pay higher wages to whites which will lower their profits. Consequently, the discrimination also hurts those who discriminate: "the discriminating employer incurs greater expense to obtain the same productivity."[27] Moreover, the Blacks will be hired by non-discriminating firms which can, therefore, provide the product or service at a lower price. Supposedly, the higher profits of non-discriminating firms will attract other non-discriminating firms. Hence, the discriminating firm will be at a further disadvantage; so, the logic of Becker's analysis suggests that the discriminating firm will be outcompeted, mitigating the impact of discrimination.[28]

In this "Alice-in-Wonderland" economy, there is no peer pressure to maintain a united front against the oppressed, no lynchings, and no KKK to enforce and perpetuate subjugation. Such theories should have been discarded ages ago, as it was obviously falsified by overwhelming evidence (including experimental evidence) that markets fail to alleviate discrimination and the victims pay dearly for it.[29]

One reason for the persistence of discrimination is that it begins early within the educational system so that minorities enter the labor force at a distinct disadvantage. Moreover, social pressure to enforce the norm of discrimination are often so overwhelming that non-discriminating firms do not come into existence to compete with discriminating ones. There were no bus companies that competed with the one in Montgomery, Alabama, that made Rosa Parks sit in the back of the bus. There were no firms competing with Woolworth that would serve both whites and blacks in Greensboro, North Carolina.[30] It is very strange that free markets were organized in such a way that the ability to buy a cup of coffee depended on the consumer's skin color. It took the Civil Rights Act of 1964 to end such overt segregation. These rights were not obtained through competition from non-discriminating entrepreneurs who wanted to profit from the victimization of Blacks. It is ridiculous to perpetuate a theory that suggests otherwise.

Becker's cavalier treatment of discrimination was complemented by a theory in which discrimination became a rational response to

> [the] scarcity of information about the ... characteristics of workers ... If the cost of gaining information about the individual applicants is excessive, skin color or sex is taken as a proxy for relevant data not sampled. The a priori belief in the probable preferability of a white or a male over a black or female candidate ... might stem from the employer's previous statistical experience ....[31]

Put another way: "skin color is a cheap source of information and therefore may be used by an employer in discriminating against what he believes to be inferior workers."[32] This kind of signaling in the presence of asymmetric information is known as "statistical discrimination" (see Section 5.12).

This line of overtly racist reasoning not only has survived but still dominates the discussion of discrimination in most popular textbooks *without* caveats and not only at the introductory or intermediate levels but also in labor economics and in graduate lectures.[33] None discuss the pernicious nature and injustice of discrimination and the social ills (like extensive imprisonment) that stem from it. None emphasize its illegal character, the urgency of ending it, or that laissez-faire market processes have failed to end it.

Instead, most economists unabashedly reiterate Becker's argument that discrimination is self-correcting, because

> Nondiscriminating firms could enter the market, undercut the costs and prices of the discriminating firms by hiring mainly brown-eyed workers, and drive the discriminating firms out of business. Thus, even if some employers are biased against a group of workers, their bias should not be sufficient to reduce that group's income.[34]

Note the phrasing: they "could" enter, but did they? No, they did not. Then there is "their bias should not be sufficient to reduce that groups income." It is common knowledge that it was sufficient but apparently the evidence does not matter to them. Note also that they frame the issue in terms of "blue-eyed" versus "brown-eyed workers," which skirts the issue of the deeply corrosive nature of real-world discrimination as it pertains to skin color of the descendants of American slaves.

Mainstream textbooks also overlook the many hidden unjustified assumptions in Becker's theory, including that productivity is easily ascertainable prior to hiring someone. However, if that is not the case, then the mechanism Becker invoked would not work because the non-discriminating manager might conclude that people are willing to work for less because they are less productive. Becker's theory is also misleading, because it assumes that those who discriminate are making conscious decisions to do so based on a cost-benefit analysis, whereas they are often conformists, afraid to break the social norm.[35] So, there are many reasons for refuting the theory rather than repeating it.

Subsequently, Samuelson and Nordhaus discuss statistical discrimination by asserting that "[o]ne of the most interesting variants of discrimination occurs because of the interplay between incomplete information and perverse incentives."[36] Wow! There is nothing at all interesting about discrimination, and it is illegal to boot. Similarly, Mankiw dances around the seriousness of the issue:

> at least some of the difference between the wages of whites and the wages of blacks can be traced to differences in educational attainment ... In the end, the study of wage differences among groups does not establish any clear conclusion about the prevalence of discrimination in US labor markets. Most economists believe that some of the observed wage differentials are attributable to discrimination, but there is no consensus about how much.[37]

Yet, of the circa 21 percent differences in wages, about half is due to education (11 percent) and half to outright discrimination (10 percent).[38] Of course, the difference in educational attainment is also due to discrimination in housing and educational opportunities. Mankiw continues with Becker's argument that "the profit motive is a strong force acting to eliminate discriminatory wage differentials, but there are limits to its corrective abilities. Two important limiting factors are customer preferences and government policies."[39] Note that in this version, the government becomes part of the problem that limits the market's ability to shed itself of discrimination. That, in the main, is the tenor of the canon on discrimination.[40]

Another overlooked factor in the above assertions is the use of violence in enforcing the norm of discrimination and suppressing upward mobility of minorities. It does not need to be practiced on a daily basis to be effective. One lynching can stifle ambitions for generations. The destruction of "Black Wall Street" in Tulsa in 1921 sent a signal that still resonates. The unmistakable message, that it is useless for Blacks to attempt to accumulate wealth, does not fit well into the above narratives.

In contrast, the tone of progressive economists are more generous to minorities.[41] They point out that discrimination "was based on racist beliefs that certain groups were innately inferior" and that it has been against the law since 1964. They also refer to a case study of FedEx which was fined $3 million for violating that law.[42] Nonetheless the dominance of orthodox theory means that millions of students study economics without appreciating the true significance of discrimination.

16.4 The Achilles' Heels of Real-Existing Markets Disadvantage Minorities

The status quo-preserving nature of neoclassical economic theory disadvantages poor people who are disproportionally minorities. This is because the canon is based on incorrect assumptions which have an asymmetric impact on different segments of the population. The effect of the 16 mistakes described below are not uniformly distributed: they hurt poor people the most.[43]

16.4.1 Ignoring the Significance of Power

The concentration of power forces those with less financial resources to participate in markets on unequal terms. Insofar as wealth and income translate directly into economic as well as political power, the disregard of their distribution leaves a gaping hiatus between real markets and imaginary ones.[44] As the Nobelist Kenneth Arrow observed, "economic power can be translated into political power by channels too obvious for mention. In a capitalist society, economic power is very unequally distributed ...."[45]

This disadvantages poor people because the concentration of political power shapes institutions, influences legislation, sways cultural norms, and reinforces a dominant ideology so as to maintain the status quo social hierarchy. Insofar as minorities are a disproportionate share of the poor, the imbalance of power implies that their needs are not adequately represented in the political arena. Under such circumstances the market's playing field is tilted in favor of the wealthy, structuring obstacles so as to hinder the advancement of poor people. "We were ... naive to think the privileged wouldn't pull up the ladders of opportunity behind them."[46] For example, the minimum wage is not indexed to inflation in order to increase the profits of the firms. There is no racist motive behind it, but it does hurt minorities the most because they are the most affected by the legislation. Note that tax brackets are indexed to inflation which helps those with higher incomes pay less taxes. Medicare drug pricing is another example. The government is not allowed to bargain over drug prices. The motivation presumably is to increase the profits of pharmaceuticals. Nonetheless, the law burdens minorities the most because the monopoly drug prices are a bigger share of their income. Hence, disregarding the crucial role of the distribution of wealth and power overlooks an important reason why real free markets deprive minorities of *de facto* equal opportunity and how economic theory feeds into institutional racism with intergenerational effects.

16.4.2 Belittling the Significance of Information

Information in mainstream theory is not given the central importance it deserves. Yet, the acquisition of credible information is crucial in making satisfactory economic decisions. This poses a formidable obstacle for minorities, since obtaining reliable information is a much larger share of their income than for those with ample resources. Consequently, disregarding the cost of acquiring information makes it appear as though the poor are better off than they really are, because they have to spend part of their income (and time) on something that is assumed to be free. (Their budget constraint is closer to the origin than it seems from their disposable income.)

Moreover, some information is not only costly, but is simply out of reach for minorities, because they often lack the social network that facilitates the acquisition of information necessary to made a reasoned decision about a complex product.[47] Therefore, they have a daunting task of navigating an incredibly complicated economy, full of uncertainty,[48] and full of tricks and traps set for them by powerful interests and unscrupulous firms. Avoiding those pitfalls is a prerequisite to successfully mastering the art of living in a convoluted labyrinth that is today's economy. Therefore, minorities are at an extraordinary disadvantage in free markets in the Information Age since access to credible information is a prerequisite of success. Without adequate information, their actions appear perplexing to those who possess those information. Consequently, the disregard of the crucial role of information in the economy opens up the possibility of patronizing poor people for making seemingly uninformed decisions. So, trivializing the role of information in economics by mainstream economists feeds into systemic racism.

16.4.3 Neglecting Children

Mainstream economists disregard the formative years of human development since they begin their analysis with adults. This oversight has huge implications for the discipline because it ignores completely a critical stage of life during which market processes have an immense influence on the development of their character, world-view, aspirations, educational attainment, soft skills, and every other human attribute important to flourishing. Since everyone enters the market economy early in life, markets have two decades to influence the formation of their taste and character so that they conform to corporate interests.

Hence, a seemingly harmless assumption that tastes are exogenous actually gives corporations an opening to propagate cultural characteristics which disregard unprofitable human attributes including frugality, safety, circumspection, education, morality, and being far-sighted. Thus, during the growing years, children can become fixated on material aspects of life and the population's psychological and moral development is stymied.[49] This is obviously crucial for children because they do not have agency to shape their future and therefore depend on their parents and the community to provide for them:

> [I]t is important to recognize three distinct credit constraints operating on the family and its children. First, the inability of a child to choose its parents. This is the fundamental constraint imposed by the accident of birth. Second, the inability of parents to borrow against their children's future income to finance investments in their education. Third, the inability of parents to borrow against their own income to finance investments in their children.[50]

This has an especially harsh impact on poor children, because they are more likely to be living in low-income single-mother households, and less likely to be supervised for much of the day, exposing them longer to advertisements that hype the wonders of consumption and influence their desires for years.[51] Quality child-care is normally unavailable for poor families and their children are frequently glued to their monitors but "television often promotes lifestyles not conducive to prosperity."[52] They are also vulnerable to junk food advertisements, increasing childhood obesity among poor families.[53] The prevalence of obesity among Black and Hispanic children and youth is 22 percent and 26 percent respectively while it is 14 percent among their white counterparts. This is a symptom of the damaging impact of poverty on minority children.[54] *Thus, neglecting the influence of markets on children's character is an unforgiving deficiency of mainstream theorizing.*[55] This oversight is particularly deleterious for minorities.

In addition, this lack of understanding provides an opportunity for elites to look down on minorities for having the wrong cultural values to succeed in the market. It makes it appear as though it was their own fault if they lack the "Protestant work ethic." As a blatant example of this inclination, Nobelist George Stigler expressed this kind of bias by claiming that the "negros" are "inferior workers" and "[the] problem is that on average he lacks a desire to improve himself, and lacks a willingness to discipline himself to this end."[56]

16.4.4 Assuming that People Are Superhuman

The challenges associated with acquiring information, the inferior schooling opportunities available to them, and experiencing suboptimal Pavlovian conditioning in their formative years, far too often pose nearly insurmountable burdens on the poor.[57] These early life circumstances make it extremely difficult to acquire soft skills like self-control, ability to delay gratification, develop a healthy work ethic, punctuality—that are crucial attributes for success in a highly competitive labor market.[58] Their subconscious is inundated with commercial messaging through the media. Hence, the poor are more vulnerable than average to the myriad problems associated with bounded rationality that puts them at a significant disadvantage in the marketplace. Thus, minorities are susceptible to being manipulated and exploited by those in power: by the advertisement giants on Madison Avenue, finance on Wall Street, the Washington political elite, those who dominate the culture industry in Hollywood, as well as the tech titans of Silicon Valley.

However, the assumption that the economy is populated by a superhuman species of *homo oeconomicus* enables those responsible for policy to argue that market outcomes are preferable since they are the result of free will by rational adults. Since the lifestyle of minorities is based on their rational choices and since they are optimizing their utility function, government should not intervene on their behalf; it would deprive them of agency over their own lives. Consumer protection is disrespectful, superfluous, and deprives people of their autonomy.

Hence, the seemingly innocuous assumption that people are rational has profound deleterious impact on minorities, even if unintended. It is an essential mechanism in keeping them subordinate and preventing them from taking advantage of opportunities afforded to those higher up the social hierarchy. By ignoring these formidable challenges facing minorities in the real-existing economy, economic theory supports the fiction that minorities are in control of their own destiny and therefore deserve their place in society. In this way, the rationality assumption provides succor for the maintenance of the status quo socio-economic order.

16.4.5 Discounting the Challenges Posed by Opportunists

Neoliberal economists praise the freedom afforded by laissez-faire markets, regardless of opportunists who exploit the vulnerabilities of those unable to defend themselves. Because of less schooling and less reliable information available to them, the poor are more exposed to the vagaries of scams, predatory advertisements, and dubious business practices of opportunists. Lack of money also limits their recourse to the legal system when deceived. The freedom afforded to one group becomes the unfreedom of their weaker compatriots.

The purchase of most durables in today's economy is complicated and the long-run implications of decisions are ambiguous and uncertain. Cell phone contracts, mortgage contracts, education, leases, insurance, and credit card rules often contain hidden elements, and are nearly impossible to understand in most cases by untrained consumers.[59] Hence, free markets allow unprincipled actors to entice and exploit poor people's lack of information and schooling.[60] Disregard of this issue enables policy-makers to argue that oversight of markets is superfluous, thereby creating an institutional structure that disadvantages minorities the most.

16.4.6 Disregarding Society

When Margaret Thatcher famously quipped that "there's no such thing as society," she was echoing the philosophy of mainstream economics: methodological individualism.[61] By ignoring social interactions and cultural norms, mainstream economics overlooks a crucial determinant of market outcomes. Society's value system influences people's aspirations, constrains choices, and channels actions throughout the life course.[62] Moreover, society contributes greatly to defining the terms under which we can become full-fledged esteemed members of the society.[63] Methodological individualism hides "the role of discriminatory institutions and other political and social structures that ... perpetuate ... discrimination."[64]

The social realities in underprivileged neighborhoods characterized by mediocre schools, high crime rates, unstable families, limited social services, and meager employment opportunities are not conducive to healthy development, putting poor children at an obvious disadvantage. Conforming to the prevailing attitudes, mores, peer pressure, and accepted behavior prevalent in such a social environment is a formidable obstacle to escaping poverty.[65] Children learn from role models how they should behave, what they should consider important in their lives, and what will gain them social acceptance. Far too frequently underprivileged children learn the art of living in environments that will not launch them out of poverty.[66] Idolizing professional athletes, movie stars, or local influencers is not exactly the type of socialization process that prepares poor children for mobility into the middle class.

In brief, it is through the social environment that the burdens associated with the culture of poverty are propagated across generations. Most importantly, by ignoring these crucial issues in their canon, mainstream economists provide another convenient way for the privileged groups to feel superior and justified in their moral resentment toward those who are less successful and disparage the "subordinated racial groups" as irresponsible free riders and undeserving of society's compassion, lacking the work ethic, and who thereby "justify existing racial inequalities."[67] This kind of stereotyping has been described as "laissez-faire racism."[68]

By disregarding the crucial role of social expectations in economic interactions, mainstream economists also overlook that many of society's most pressing challenges cannot be solved by individuals acting alone but require collective action.[69] Methodological individualism will not enable poor people to support excellent public schools and thereby eliminate a humongous amount of waste in human resources.[70] Yet, economists are silent on this important source of inefficiency, thereby covertly supporting the status quo that limits the advancement of minorities.

16.4.7 Disdain for Basic Needs

Since mainstream economics does not acknowledge the existence of "basic needs" to sustain life, it casually tolerates the reality that scores of millions are deprived of adequate food, shelter, clothing, clean water, or health care.[71] Yet, it became more obvious than ever during the Covid-19 pandemic that survival needs should be prioritized over other kinds of discretionary wants. Because the invisible hand does not alleviate deprivation among the impoverished, safety-net programs are essential for maintaining life.[72] About one-fifth of Americans receive welfare transfers, of which 42 million people received food stamps in 2019, about half of them minority.[73]

Therefore, twenty-first-century economic theory should incorporate the concept of basic needs into its canon and prioritize its provisioning through universal health care, basic income, free college education, and job guarantee, especially since robotization, globalization, artificial intelligence, and technological unemployment will continue to challenge not only the underprivileged but the social peace more broadly.[74] The concept of full employment should be reformulated so that it pertains also to the full employment of minorities and is linked to institutional innovation that can realize racial equality.[75]

16.4.8 Banning Morals

While mainstream economists extoll the virtues of efficiency and of economic growth that are hardly value-neutral, they ban morality when it comes to distributional issues or the plight of descendants of injustice.[76] Instead, they leave markets to adjudicate such issues, disregarding that markets are not designed to provide moral oversight: "markets are not morally neutral instruments for defining the common good" since they advantage those already privileged.[77] Ethical considerations must come from outside of the market system. This is crucial: a basic principle of humanistic economics is that we should first decide the outlines of a morally acceptable society and then provide railguards to ensure that we are moving toward that ideal.

As the Nobelist Amartya Sen put it, "there is a critical need for paying special attention to the underdogs of society ...."[78] To this end, the Rawlsian conception of justice suggests that our aim should be to create a society in which all subpopulations enjoy the same living standard. That does not necessarily imply that everyone should have the same income. It means that the average Black income should not differ from the average white income. *Legal equality of opportunity is insufficient for a moral society. De facto* equality is necessary to eliminate racial disparities.[79] This coincides with Immanuel Kant's concept of a categorical imperative because it implies that the economic system should be such that people's chances to succeed are not conditional on their skin color.[80] The mainstream's disregard of the moral dimension of economics stealthily supports the status quo disparities.[81]

16.4.9 Trusting Perfect Competition

Mainstream economics has excessive confidence in the perfectly competitive model although such markets are a rarity in today's real-existing economy dominated by gigantic multinational oligopolies, monopolies, and monopsonists wielding enormous market and political power to their advantage.[82] These firms use their power to lower wages and increase prices. They target minorities with influencers and advertising campaigns, they discriminate in business loans, auto insurance rates, mortgages, and credit cards.[83] Moreover, they oppose unions, lobby against increasing the minimum wage, and advocate a culture of instant gratification and a spendthrift lifestyle.[84] *The high prices charged by firms with market power hurt poor people the most* because the excess burden is a large share of their income.[85]

Furthermore, the superprofits earned by mega-corporations are used to propagate the ideology that supports a technocratic meritocracy that justifies the distribution of income by arguing that people deserve what they earn:

> This emphasis has a corrosive effect on the way we interpret our success or the lack of it. The notion that the system rewards talent and hard work encourages the winners to consider their success their own doing, a measure of their virtue and to look down upon those less fortunate than themselves. Now those who lose out may complain that the system is rigged that the winners have cheated and manipulated their way to the top ....[86]

But that will not be much of a consolation. By trivializing the role of oligopolies and concentrating on perfect competition, mainstream economists provide an additional justification for the social status of minorities.[87]

16.4.10 Overlooking Exploitation

In the absence of countervailing power, discrimination leads to oppression.[88] "Today, we understand that the market is rife with imperfections—including imperfections of information and competition—that provide ample opportunity for discrimination and exploitation."[89] The economically weak are more susceptible to being abused by predatory loans, by little-understood variable-rate mortgages, by check-cashing sharks, late-fee penalties, and notorious payday loans. Minorities have fewer defenses against such schemes and traps. That is why minorities are callously harmed by the economists' argument that consumer protection is superfluous. This hurts minorities the most because they are the most exposed to opportunists. The lack of consumer protection is an important element in the perpetuation of the poverty trap.

Exploitation also occurs when workers are compelled to work by force of circumstances. The threat of hunger forced workers to accept dangerous assignments during the Covid-19 pandemic, for instance, that is so coercive that it becomes exploitative. That is one of the reasons why Blacks perished at twice the rate of whites during the pandemic and Hispanics were three times as likely to be infected:[90]

> They make up a disproportionate share of the low-paid "essential workers" who were expected to staff grocery stores and warehouses, clean buildings, and deliver mail while the pandemic raged around them. Earning hourly wages without paid sick leave, they couldn't afford to miss shifts even when symptomatic. They faced risky commutes on crowded public transportation while more privileged people teleworked from the safety of isolation.[91]

16.4.11 Omitting Space

There are no neighborhoods in mainstream economics; yet poverty is not evenly distributed across the landscape. Rather, *poverty is spatially concentrated*. This hurts minorities, because it makes it easier to discriminate in granting mortgages, and other zip-code-based contracts. Thus, too many poor children live in slums—concentrated areas of poverty, ethnically segregated, with limited tax base, inferior housing, substandard infrastructure, high crime rates, mediocre schools, endemic unemployment—that are generally not conducive places for children's healthy development and deprive them of an adequate start in life, particularly in education, socialization, and role models that would be so important for their future development.[92]

Every major American city has such neighborhoods.[93] For instance, in Cleveland's zip code 44115 neighborhood, one of the poorest in the country, with a median household income of $15,034, 85 percent of the children are minority, mostly Black (Table 16.3).[94] The average minority share in the 16 poorest zip code areas is 73 percent with a median household income of $15,634.[95] Because in the US primary and secondary schools are financed mainly locally, the high concentration of poverty means that poor children attend mediocre schools which stymies their development and restricts severely their advancement in society for the rest of their lives. Note that out of the 16 neighborhoods six are represented in Congress by Republicans, a party which is inimical to the interests of poor people. This is indicative of the extent to which the US political system is incapable of representing the interests of the disadvantaged.

Growing up in slums has long-term adverse (path-dependent) consequences on everything that pertains to a successful life. The adult is the result of the habits acquired in childhood. So, for poor children, being confined to a substandard educational system is an insurmountable hurdle to their labor market chances. It becomes an impediment to accumulating soft skills,

Table 16.3 The Poorest Neighborhoods in U.S., 2016-2021

			Percent minority		Median	Congressional
		Zip code	Zip code	Schools	Income	Representative
Youngstown	OH	44503	66	86	$9,015	Democrat
Erie	PA	16501	37	n.a.	$11,516	Republican
Waterbury	CT	06702	74	56	$11,663	Democrat
El Paso	TX	79901	99	98	$12,025	Democrat
Memphis	TN	38126	96	100	$12,200	Democrat
Toledo	OH	43604	70	83	$15,029	Democrat
Cleveland	OH	44115	70	85	$15,034	Republican
Livingston	AL	35470	69	97	$16,233	Republican
Cleveland	OH	44104	98	99	$16,650	Democrat
Cincinnati	OH	45225	84	95	$16,672	Democrat
Stockton	CA	95202	81	93	$17,260	Republican
Chattanooga	TN	37402	64	66	$18,319	Republican
Johnstown	PA	15901	30	n.a.	$19,022	Democrat
Cincinnati	OH	45203	85	99	$21,169	Republican
Average			73	88	$15,129	
Median			72	94	$15,634	

Source: ZipData Maps, https://www.zipdatamaps.com/44115; https://www.incomebyzipcode.com/search.

emotional intelligence, as well as attaining further education desperately needed in today's knowledge economy short of skilled workers. Subsequently, they are handicapped from the get-go. Moreover, mediocre education provides the privileged another opportunity to rationalize the inferior social status of minorities. In this way, markets magnify initial disadvantages and erect a daunting invisible barrier around those born into poverty that preserves the status quo. This is the essence of the poverty trap.

Hence, living in slums with inferior schools is a significant factor in perpetuating poverty across generations.[96] No wonder that those trapped by such circumstances are unable to escape their predicament, and far too often turn to acts of desperation out of sheer frustration that often brings them into confrontation with the legal system. Consequently, "though African Americans and Hispanics make up approximately 32 percent of the US population, they comprised 56 percent of all incarcerated people."[97] They also face difficulties upon gaining their freedom since felons face an uphill battle in the labor market. The disregard of this spatial aspect of the real-existing economy makes the mainstream canon support status quo institutional racism.

16.4.12 Ignoring Time

Although mostly disregarded in the mainstream canon, time is an essential element in all economic activity.[98] Furthermore, the most important economic decisions are sequential and long-term, which require foresight, moderation, self-control, planning, and judgment, another issue ignored by the mainstream. That *developmental processes are irreversible* is crucial for poor children, because inadequate schooling opportunities lock them into an inferior developmental path that leads to lower social status. Path-dependence implies that those born in slums are confined to poverty indefinitely.

Moreover, learning to plan sequentially is another important part of growing up to succeed. The strategic planning, perseverance, and self-control needed to reach these goals must be learned and nurtured, starting early in life and practiced over an extended period.[99] Life-course decisions require not only planning but also judgment and are much more complex than a typical one-period optimization problem discussed in typical classrooms. The poor who grow up in dysfunctional neighborhoods are trapped partly because they lack the opportunity to acquire these skills through school and role models.

Additionally, perseverance requires the reasonable likelihood of success. The frustration of prior generations poses an obstacle for youngsters to forego immediate gratification and to strive over an extended period of time for the kind of success that eluded their parents. This can easily induce them to look for role-models which often become permanent roadblocks out of poverty. This is another reason why economists should not begin their analysis with adults. By belittling the significance of path-dependence, mainstream economics supports the status quo economy.

16.4.13 Downplaying the Role of Government

As far as neoliberal economists are concerned, the government needs only to enforce contracts, define property rights, correct externalities, and protect us from outside foes. We need not worry about discrimination, sustainability, volatility, scams, social stability, education, inequality, and health care, food security, or other basic needs. The government need not support unions or a minimum wage, because they only create unemployment while taxes lead to dead-weight losses and disturb the efficiency achieved by optimizing rational economic agents. In this intellectual framework markets can do all the heavy lifting; there is no need for a social safety net.

However, minorities lack any substantial institutional support other than the government. Lacking adequate schooling and minimal access to the capital market, they are unable to pull themselves up by their bootstraps. Social Security and the minimum wage lifted millions out of poverty, and its expansion in 1966 reduced "racial economic disparities."[100] The government-sponsored Civil Rights Acts of the 1960s, Medicare, Medicaid, and unemployment insurance also helped the poor.[101] Hence, as far as minorities are concerned, government support is indispensable. After all, it was not until the federal government intervened that Rosa Parks could sit anywhere she liked on a bus and colored people could be served coffee at Woolworth's soda counter in Greensboro. Many had to sacrifice their lives before markets ceased to overtly support segregation.

16.4.14 Trivializing Relative Incomes

The mainstream's claim that utility functions are independent of one another is unjustifiable because it is common knowledge that consumption is influenced by social norms. Consequently,

> what matters [for an individual's sense of well-being] is not just an individual's absolute income, but his income relative to that of others ... the problem of 'keeping up with the Joneses'—helps explain why so many Americans live beyond their means.[102]

This puts poor people under double psychological pressure: not only do they have to struggle to meet basic needs, but they have to cope with falling further behind social norms influenced by the rich and famous. Being at a disadvantage in the legal labor market and being excluded from middle-class jobs because of their mediocre educational opportunities, a substantial number of those who are unable to cope gamble by engaging in illegal activity and end up in jail.[103]

16.4.15 Disparaging Taxes

The mainstream emphasizes the dead-weight loss of taxes, the negative welfare effects of taxes, and advocate for minimizing them. However, they never mention that taxes are also welfare-enhancing insofar as they support education, health care, basic needs, basic research, infrastructure, environment, and safety net programs. The neglect of the positive effect of taxes disadvantages minorities because they rely on government services the most. Low taxes leave schools underfunded in poor neighborhoods, which is not an impediment for the wealthy since they can afford private schools. The poor need public transport, the affluent do not. Disparaging taxes is an important way in which the mainstream covertly supports policies that disadvantages poor people, and especially minorities.

16.4.16 Excluding Pain

Mainstream economics does not acknowledge the existence of pain, frustration, or anxiety. Nonetheless, these are important human emotions and their infliction through discrimination, prejudicial treatment, humiliation, or being ostracized the way minorities have been treated unfairly in the economy creates emotional harm that persists throughout life and are passed on to subsequent generations. Feeling degraded, excluded, socially inferior, wrongfully disadvantaged, snubbed, victimized, stigmatized, harmed, or treated inhumanly creates emotional distress that influences aspiration levels, self-esteem, physical and mental health, and performance at work and in school, and forms a mental barrier for pulling oneself up by the bootstraps. It still persists: half of Blacks believe that being Black has hurt their ability to get ahead for various reasons, including discrimination or having less access to high-paying jobs or to good schools.[104] The cumulative disadvantages are substantial and include intergenerational effects: "minor forms of everyday discrimination people may experience ... can matter cumulatively, not just episodically."[105] By disregarding the impact of such painful episodes on the life of minorities, economists contribute to the lack of understanding of their economic predicament.

16.5 Time to Purge the Curse of Systemic Racism from Economics

In the era of renewed racial tensions, it is crucial to recognize that the unrealistic assumptions of mainstream economists contain numerous hidden elements that disadvantage poor people and, since minorities are disproportionally poor, the burden of inappropriate economic theory falls disproportionally on minorities, which in the US are Hispanics, Indigenous people, and the descendants of slaves. The deductive theories at the core of the canon provide succor for the persistence of an economic system that burdens underprivileged groups the most, and essentially vindicates the system for their disadvantages. By remaining neutral about the distribution of benefits, economists support the established power structure and privilege that constrains the opportunities and capabilities of those born at the bottom of the socio-economic hierarchy. This, nuanced conceptualization of covert racism focuses on the outcomes generated by the system that needs to be reformed for our turbulent times.

Illustration 16.1 Black Lives Matter Movement in the wake of the cold-blooded killing of George Floyd
Credit: Shutterstock 1794791068.

Despite a substantial body of research on racism *in the economy*–although not in the top ten journals, in which a negligible 0.2 percent of the articles has been devoted to the topic–racism in *economic theory itself* is at its inception.[106] To be sure, some do recognize that "economics has a diversity problem,"[107] but they fail to recognize that a discipline that trivializes discrimination and dubs prejudice a "taste" will be naturally shunned by minority students. Moreover, a canon that adulates unfettered markets will likely appear objectionable to the descendants of slaves since the market mechanism was obviously incapable of reducing, let alone eradicating, the evils of discrimination.[108] Thus, to continue to teach models of discrimination, conceived in the twilight of the Jim Crow era, that belittle the injustices associated with prejudice is worse than anachronistic. In the era of the Black Lives Matter movement, it is in bad taste and should be seen as providing scholarly support for systemic racism.[109]

Hence, covert racism will not be purged from the economic canon–and the bias against the disadvantaged disappear–until these 16 Achilles' heels are addressed appropriately in all textbooks and classrooms from the very beginning of the educational experience. There has to be a widespread understanding that laissez-faire economics has a status-quo bias which magnifies the privileges of those already privileged, i.e., that the economy's playing field is tilted in favor of the wealthy. In turn, the implication is that the consequences of racism of the distant past are propagated from generation to generation, putting obstacles in the way of disadvantaged groups and preventing their flourishing and socio-economic advancement. After all, the rules of the system were written by those in power, and they devised ways to perpetuate that power.

The Aspen Institute defines a racially equitable society as one in which

> the distribution of society's benefits and burdens would not be skewed by race ... Racial equity would be a reality in which a person is no more or less likely to experience society's benefits or burdens just because of the color of their skin.[110]

In short, in a post-racist society, economic outcomes would be comparable along racial lines including incomes, wealth, educational attainment, health, life expectancy, or unemployment.

Righteousness will not flow like a mighty stream[111] as long as our minds are trapped in the Arrow-Debreu world of general equilibrium, which is eloquent on academic blackboards but is harmful in the slums, especially for groups disadvantaged from birth because of their race by the real-existing economy.[112] Humanistic economists advocate a post-racist economic theory for a post-racist society.

16.6 Takeaways

An economic system that favors some segment of the population over another segment is considered unjust, according to Rawlsian or Kantian ethical principles. Theoretical equal opportunity is insufficient for a just economy. There must be *de facto* equal opportunity for an economy to be considered fair. Insofar as capitalism, as currently constituted in the US, disadvantages the poor from birth, it is unjust. The disadvantages arise because the poor are confined to neighborhoods with poor schools, thereby depriving them of access to an excellent education they need in order to enter the labor market on equal footing with those born into wealthy families. Those disadvantaged are disproportionately marginalized members of minority groups. That makes the economy covertly racist.

Racism does not have to be intentional. Mainstream economics is covertly racist because it preserves the status quo, thereby providing theoretical support for an economic system that contributes to keeping disadvantaged groups at the bottom of the socio-economic hierarchy. In such cases we speak of institutional, structural, or systemic racism. The institutions and legal structures of the US economy are such that the descendants of slaves, Hispanics, and Indigenous groups are trapped in poverty.

Questions for Discussion

1   Have you ever experienced discrimination or known someone to have been subject to discrimination?
2   Can someone be racist without intending to be racist?
3   Do you think that income should depend on skin color?
4   How much income differences would there be in a just society?
5   What is the difference between overt and covert racism?
6   Do you think American Indians have an equal opportunity in today's knowledge economy?
7   How does the economic system disadvantage poor people?
8   Why does the wealth distribution show even more disparity than the income distribution?
9   How are past injustices transmitted across the generations?
10   Why is the correlation between parents' income and children's income so high?
11   How much poverty should a rich country tolerate?
12   Do you think it is still appropriate to teach Gary Becker's theory of discrimination?
13   Do you think that discrimination is a personal preference like any other?
14   What is wrong with Becker's theory of discrimination?
15   What is the difference between Becker's theory of discrimination and the so-called statistical discrimination?
16   Is the market fair to all participants?
17   Why is the minimum wage not indexed to inflation?
18   Why is Medicare not allowed by law to negotiate drug prices with pharmaceuticals?
19   Have you had difficulties searching for information about a product or contract and made decisions based on limited information?
20   Do you think minorities living in slums have difficulties obtaining the right information about products?
21   Do you know anyone who is a racist/white supremacist?

Notes

1   Inscribed on the south wall of his statue in Washington, DC.
2   Eduardo Bonilla-Silva, *Racism Without Racists: Color-Blind Racism and the Persistence of Racial Inequality in the United States*, 4th edn. (Rowman & Littlefield, 2014); Joe Feagin, *Systemic Racism: A Theory of Oppression* (Routledge, 2006); Ibram Kendi, *How to Be an Antiracist* (One World, 2019); Tim Koechlin, "Whitewashing Capitalism: Mainstream Economics' Resounding Silence on Race and Racism," *Review of Radical Political Economics* 51 (2019), 4: 562–571.
3   Nonetheless, at times they were willing to espouse policies—like the school voucher program—that overlapped with those of outright segregationists. Nancy MacLean, "How Milton Friedman Exploited White Supremacy to Privatize Education," Institute for New Economic Thinking, September, 2021; https://www.ineteconomics.org/perspectives/blog/how-milton-friedman-aided-and-abetted-segregationists-in-his-quest-to-privatize-public-education.
4   Matthew Watson, "Crusoe, Friday and the Raced Market Frame of Orthodox Economics Textbooks," *New Political Economy* 23 (2018), 5: 544–559.
5   Patrick Mason et al., "Is There Racism in Economic Research?" *European Journal of Political Economy* 21 (2005), 3: 755–761.
6   Aspen Institute Staff, "11 Terms You Should Know to Better Understand Structural Racism," Aspen Institute, July 11, 2020; https://www.aspeninstitute.org/blog-posts/structural-racism-definition/. See also Wikipedia Contributors, "Institutional Racism."
7   Matthew Clair and Jeffrey Denis, "Racism, Sociology of," in *International Encyclopedia of the Social & Behavioral Sciences*, 2nd edn, Vol. 19 (Pergamon, 2015), pp. 857–863; here p. 857.
8   Paula Rothenberg, *White Privilege: Essential Readings on the Other Side of Racism* (Worth Publishers, 2002).
9   Roberto Unger, *The Critical Legal Studies Movement* (Verso, 2015); Alan Hunt, "The Theory of Critical Legal Studies," *Oxford Journal of Legal Studies* 6 (1986), 1: 1–45; Kimberlé Williams Crenshaw et al. (eds.), *Seeing Race Again: Countering Colorblindness across the Disciplines* (University of California Press, 2019).
10 Martin Feldstein, "The US Economy Is in Good Shape," *Wall Street Journal*, February 21, 2016.
11 William Darity and Patrick Mason, "Evidence on Discrimination in Employment: Codes of Color, Codes of Gender," *Journal of Economic Perspectives* 12 (1998), 2: 63–90.
12 U.S. Census Bureau, Table H-3; https://www.census.gov/data/tables/time-series/demo/income-poverty/historical-income-households.html; Emily Shrider et al., "Income and Poverty in the United States: 2020," *Current Population Reports*, September 2021. https://www.census.gov/content/dam/Census/library/publications/2021/demo/p60-273.pdf.
13 St. Louis Fed, series LES1252881600Q, LEU0252884600Q.
14 Lisa Dettling et al., "Recent Trends in Wealth-Holding by Race and Ethnicity: Evidence from the Survey of Consumer Finances," *FEDS Notes*, September 27, 2017.
15 Robert Williams, "Wealth, Privilege and the Racial Wealth Gap: A Case Study in Economic Stratification," *The Review of Black Political Economy* 44 (2017), 3: 303–325.
16 Shrider et al., "Income and Poverty in the United States: 2020," op. cit.
17 POV-04. "Primary Families by Age of Householder"; https://www.census.gov/data/tables/time-series/demo/income-poverty/cps-pov/pov-04.html.
18 Board of Governors of the Federal Reserve System, "Report on the Economic Well-Being of US Households in 2017," 2018.
19 Raj Chetty et al., "Race and Economic Opportunity in the United States: An Intergenerational Perspective," *The Quarterly Journal of Economics* 135 (2020), 2: 711–783.
20 Statista, "Average Life Expectancy in North America for Those Born in 2017, by Gender and Region (in Years)"; WHO, World Health Organization, "World Health Statistics 2016, Annex B"; http://www.who.int/gho/publications/world_health_statistics/2016/Annex_B/en/; CDC, Centers for Disease Control and Prevention, National Center for Health Statistics, Table 015. "Life Expectancy at Birth, ... by Sex, Race,

Hidden Racist Elements in Blackboard Economics 335

and Hispanic Origin: United States, Selected Years 1900-2016," 2017; https://www.cdc.gov/nchs/hus/contents2017.htm#015.

21 Valerie Wilson and William Rodgers, "Black-White Wage Gaps Expand with Rising Wage Inequality," Economic Policy Institute, September 20, 2016.

22 Mary Daly et al., "Disappointing Facts about the Black-White Wage Gap," *Economic Letters*, Federal Reserve Bank of San Francisco, September 5, 2017; Mary Waters and Karl Eschbach, "Immigration and Ethnic and Racial Inequality in the United States," *Annual Review of Sociology* 21 (1995): 419-446; William Darity (ed.), *Economics and Discrimination* (Edward Elgar, 1995); Darrick Hamilton and William Darity, "The Political Economy of Education, Financial Literacy, and the Racial Wealth Gap," *Review*, Federal Reserve Bank of St. Louis, 99 (2017), 1: 59-76.

23 St. Louis Fed, series UNRATE; Economic Policy Institute, State of Working America Data Library, "[Underemployment]," 2021.

24 Gary Becker, *The Economics of Discrimination*, 2nd edn. (University of Chicago Press, 1971), p. 13.

25 Kerwin Kofi Charles and Jonathan Guryan, "Taste-Based Discrimination," in Macmillan Publishers Ltd. (eds.), *The New Palgrave Dictionary of Economics* (Palgrave Macmillan, 2009).

26 This was discussed at a meeting of the American Economic Association. "Annual Business Meeting," *American Economic Review* 60 (1970), 2: 487-489.

27 Kevin Murphy, "How Gary Becker Saw the Scourge of Discrimination," *Chicago Booth Review*, Winter 2015; https://review.chicagobooth.edu/magazine/winter-2014/how-gary-becker-saw-the-scourge-of-discrimination.

28 Kevin Lang and Ariella Kahn-Lang Spitzer, "Race Discrimination: An Economic Perspective," *Journal of Economic Perspectives* 34 (2020), 2: 68-89.

29 Kenneth Arrow, "What Has Economics to Say About Racial Discrimination?" *Journal of Economic Perspectives* 12 (1998), 2: 91-100; Kevin Lang and Jee-Yeon Lehmann, "Racial Discrimination in the Labor Market: Theory and Empirics," *Journal of Economic Literature* 50 (2012), 4: 959-1006; David Neumark, "Experimental Research on Labor Market Discrimination," *Journal of Economic Literature* 56 (2018), 3: 799-866.

30 Wikipedia, "Greensboro Sit-Ins."

31 "Discrimination is no less damaging to its victims for being statistical." Edmund Phelps, "The Statistical Theory of Racism and Sexism," *The American Economic Review* 62 (1972), 4: 659-661; here p. 659.

32 Kenneth Arrow, "Some Models of Racial Discrimination in the Labor Market," Santa Monica: The Rand Corporation, Research Memorandum 6253, February 1971, p. 27; published as "Some Mathematical Models of Race in the Labor Market," in A.H. Pascal (ed.), *Racial Discrimination in Economic Life* (Lexington Books, 1972), pp. 187-204.

33 George Borjas, *Labor Economics*, 3rd edn. (McGraw-Hill, 2005), Chapter 10; David Autor, "Lecture Note: The Economics of Discrimination – Theory," November 24, 2003; https://economics.mit.edu/files/553.

34 Paul Samuelson and William Nordhaus, *Economics*, 19th edn. (McGraw-Hill, 2009), p. 261.

35 Marianne Bertrand et al., "Implicit Discrimination," *American Economic Review* 95 (2005), 2: 94-98.

36 Samuelson and Nordhaus, op cit., p. 262.

37 Gregory Mankiw, *Principles of Economics*, 8th edn. (Cengage, 2018), p. 392.

38 Joseph Altonji and Rebecca Blank, "Race and Gender in the Labor Market," in Orley Ashenfelter and David Card (eds.), *Handbook of Labor Economics*, Vol. 3, part C (Elsevier, 1999), Table 5.

39 Mankiw, op. cit., p. 395.

40 Other examples: "employers who discriminate pay an economic penalty." Glenn Hubbard et al., *Microeconomics*, 4th edn. (Pearson Australia, 2013), p. 388. According to Paul Krugman et al.:

> Market forces tend to work against discrimination ... Discrimination has sometimes been institutionalized in government policy. This institutionalization of discrimination has made it easier to maintain it against market pressure ... Companies that engage in workplace discrimination but whose competitors do not are likely to have lower profits as a result of their actions.
>
> (*Essentials of Economics*, Worth Publishers, 2007, pp. 229-230)

41   Irene Bruegel, "Labour Market Discrimination," in Macmillan Publishers Ltd (eds.), *The New Palgrave Dictionary of Economics* (Palgrave Macmillan, 2018).

42   Neva Goodwin et al., *Principles of Economics in Context* (Taylor and Francis, 2015), pp. 238–240.

43   Michelle Holder, *African American Men and the Labor Market during the Great Recession* (Palgrave Macmillan, 2017).

44   Joseph Stiglitz, *People, Power and Profits: Progressive Capitalism for the Age of Discontent* (Norton, 2019), p. 46.

45   Kenneth Arrow, "A Cautious Case for Socialism," *Dissent Magazine*, Fall 1978: 472–480; here p. 479; https://www.dissentmagazine.org/wp-content/files_mf/1426269747ACautiousCaseforSocialism.pdf.

46   David Brooks, "America Is Having a Moral Convulsion," *The Atlantic*, October 5, 2020; Keith Payne, *The Broken Ladder: How Inequality Affects the Way We Think, Live, and Die* (Viking, 2012).

47   Ngina Chiteji and Darrick Hamilton, "Family Connections and the Black-White Wealth Gap Among Middle-Class Families," *The Review of Black Political Economy* 30 (2002), 1: 9–28.

48   Frank Knight, *Risk, Uncertainty, and Profit* (Houghton Mifflin, 1921).

49   Douglas Almond et al., "Childhood Circumstances and Adult Outcomes: Act II." *Journal of Economic Literature* 56 (2018), 4: 1360–1446.

50   Flavio Cunha and James Heckman, "The Technology of Skill Formation," *American Economic Review* 97 (2007), 2: 31–47.

51   Andrew Ribner et al., "Family Socioeconomic Status Moderates Associations Between Television Viewing and School Readiness Skills," *Journal of Developmental & Behavioral Pediatrics* 38 (2017), 3: 233–239.

52   Josh Bivens et al., "It's Time for an Ambitious National Investment in America's Children," Economic Policy Institute, April 6, 2016.

53   Matthew Hutson, "Lust Now, Pay Later: Keeping Up with Your Joneses," *Psychology Today*, May 1, 2008; Gang Zhang et al., "Television Watching and Risk of Childhood Obesity: A Meta-Analysis," *European Journal of Public Health* 26 (2015), 1: 13–18.

54   Craig Hales et al., "Prevalence of Obesity Among Adults and Youth: United States, 2015–2016," *NCHS Data Brief*, No. 288, October 2017.

55   Jorge Luis Garcia et al., "The Lasting Effects of Early Childhood Education on Promoting the Skills and Social Mobility of Disadvantaged African Americans," NBER Working Paper no. 29057.

56   George Stigler, "The Problem of the Negro," *New Guard*, 5 (December, 1965): 11–12.

57   Peter Streufert, "The Effect of Underclass Social Isolation on Schooling Choice," *Journal of Public Economic Theory* 2 (2000), 4: 461–482.

58   James Heckman and Tim Kautz, "Hard Evidence on Soft Skills," *Labour Economics* 19 (2012), 4: 451–464.

59   The Editorial Board, "Predatory Colleges, Freed to Fleece Students," *The New York Times*, May 28, 2018.

60   David Cay Johnston, *The Fine Print: How Big Companies Use "Plain English" to Rob You Blind* (Portfolio Books, 2012).

61   Douglas Keay, "AIDS, Education, and the Year 2000: An Interview with Margaret Thatcher," *Woman's Own*, October 31, 1987, pp. 8–10.

62   Streufert, "The Effect of Underclass Social Isolation," op. cit.

63   David Myers, *Social Psychology*, 10th edn. (McGraw-Hill, 2010).

64   Ingrid Kvangraven and Surbhi Kesar, "Why Do Economists Have Trouble Understanding Racialized Inequalities?" Institute of New Economic Thinking, August 3, 2020; https://www.ineteconomics.org/perspectives/blog/why-do-economists-have-trouble-understanding-racialized-inequalities.

65   George Akerlof and Rachel Kranton, *Identity Economics: How Our Identities Shape Our Work, Wages, and Well-Being* (Princeton University Press, 2010).

66   Robert Merton and Alice Kitt, "Contributions to the Theory of Reference Group Behavior," in Robert Merton and Paul Lazarsfeld (eds.), *Continuities in Social Research: Studies in the Scope and Method of the American Soldier* (The Free Press, 1950), pp. 40–105.

67 Matthew Clair and Jeffrey Denis, "Racism," in James Wright (ed.), *International Encyclopedia of the Social and Behavioral Sciences* 19 (2015): 857-863; here p. 859.

68 Lawrence Bobo et al., "Laissez-Faire Racism: The Crystallization of a 'Kinder, Gentler' Anti-black Ideology," in Jack Martin, and Steven Tuch (eds.), *Racial Attitudes in the 1990s* (Praeger, 1997), pp. 15-44.

69 The word "culture" does not even appear in Mankiw's *Principles*.

70 James Heckman, "Skill Formation and the Economics of Investing in Disadvantaged Children," *Science* 312 (2006), 5782: 1900-1902.

71 James Banks et al., "Disease and Disadvantage in the United States and in England," *Journal of the American Medical Association* 295 (2006), 17: 2037-2045; William Darity and Darrick Hamilton, "Bold Policies for Economic Justice," *The Review of Black Political Economy* 39 (2012), 1: 79-85.

72 Feeding America, "The Impact of the Coronavirus on Food Insecurity in 2020 and 2021," March 2021, https://www.feedingamerica.org/sites/default/files/2021-03/Nationalpercent20Projectionsperc ent20Brief_3.9.2021_0.pdf; "Feeding America, Hunger in America 2014," August 2014; https://www. secondharvestmidtn.org/wp-content/uploads/2019/09/National-Hunger-In-America-2014.pdf.

73 USDA, Food and Nutrition Service, "Characteristics of SNAP Households: FY 2019," March 29, 2021.

74 William Darity, "A Direct Route to Full Employment," *The Review of Black Political Economy* 37 (2010), 3: 179-181; William Darity and Darrick Hamilton, "The Federal Job Guarantee," *Intereconomics: Review of European Economic Policy* 53 (2018), 3: 179-180.

75 Dean Baker et al., "The Full Employment Mandate of the Federal Reserve: Its Origins and Importance," Center for Economic and Policy Research, July 2017; http://cepr.net/images/stories/reports/full-employment-mandate-2017-07.pdf; Mark Paul et al., "A Path to Ending Poverty by Way of Ending Unemployment: A Federal Job Guarantee," *RSF: The Russell Sage Foundation Journal of the Social Sciences* 4 (2018), 3: 44-63; Heather Long, "Democrats Introduce Bill to Give the Federal Reserve a New Mission: Ending Racial Inequality," *The Washington Post*, August 5, 2020; Roberto Unger, "Conclusion: The Task of the Social Innovation Movement," in Alex Nicholls et al. (eds.), *New Frontiers in Social Innovation Research* (Palgrave Macmillan, 2015).

76 Hendrik van Dalen, "Values of Economists Matter in the Art and Science of Economics," *Kyklos* 72 (2019), 3: 472-499.

77 Michael Sandel, "The Moral Limits of Markets," YouTube video, New Economic Thinking, 2013, https://www.youtube.com/watch?v=UbBv2ZGC2VI.

78 Amartya Sen, "Capitalism Beyond the Crisis," *New York Review of Books*, March 28, 2009.

79 Darrick Hamilton, "The Moral Burden on Economists," *The Review of Black Political Economy* 47 (2020), 4: 331-342; Samuel Bowles, *The Moral Economy: Why Good Incentives Are No Substitute for Good Citizens* (Yale University Press, 2016).

80 Amartya Sen, "Equality of What?" in Sterling McMurrin, *The Tanner Lecture on Human Values* (Cambridge University Press, 1980), Vol. I, pp. 197-220.

81 Jonathan Rothwell, *A Republic of Equals: A Manifesto for a Just Society* (Princeton University Press, 2019).

82 William Lazonick, "Innovative Enterprise or Sweatshop Economics? In Search of Foundations of Economic Analysis," *Challenge: The Magazine of Economic Affairs* 59 (2016), 2: 65-114.

83 Ian Ayres and Peter Siegelman, "Race and Gender Discrimination in Bargaining for a New Car," *American Economic Review* 85 (1995), 3: 304-321.

84 Lee Drutman, *The Business of America Is Lobbying: How Corporations Became Politicized and Politics Became More Corporate* (Oxford University Press, 2015).

85 Jan Eeckhout, *The Profit Paradox: How Thriving Firms Threaten the Future of Work* (Princeton University Press, 2021).

86 Michael Sandel, "Is Democracy in Peril? Politics in the Age of Trump," YouTube video, 2018, @18:20 minutes, https://www.youtube.com/watch?v=GGslRc9WIeA&t=3840s.

87 Nancy MacLean, "How Milton Friedman Aided and Abetted Segregationists in His Quest to Privatize Public Education," Institute for New Economic Thinking, September 27, 2021.

88   Steven Shulman and William Darity (eds.), *The Question of Discrimination: Racial Inequality in the US Labor Market* (Wesleyan University Press, 1989).

89   Joseph Stiglitz, "When Shall We Overcome?" *Project Syndicate*, March 12, 2018.

90   Steven Greenhouse, "The Coronavirus Pandemic Has Intensified Systemic Economic Racism Against Black Americans," *The New Yorker*, July 30, 2020.

91   Ed Yong, "How the Pandemic Defeated America," *The Atlantic*, September 2020.

92   Raj Chetty and Nathaniel Hendren, "The Effects of Neighborhoods on Intergenerational Mobility I: Childhood Exposure Effects," *The Quarterly Journal of Economics* 133 (2018), 3: 1107-1162; Prottoy Akbar et al., "Racial Segregation in Housing Markets and the Erosion of Black Wealth," NBER Working Paper no. 25805, May 2019.

93   Nancy McArdle et al., "Disparities in Neighborhood Poverty of Poor Black and White Children," *Diversity Data Briefs* 1 (2007); http://diversitydata.org/Publications/brief7.pdf.

94   Irma Wallace, "The Poorest ZIP Codes in America," *Infographics*, February 20, 2019; https://infographicjournal.com/the-poorest-zip-codes-in-america/.

95   ZipData Maps; https://www.zipdatamaps.com/44115.

96   William Julius Wilson, *The Truly Disadvantaged: The Inner City, the Underclass, and Public Policy* (University of Chicago Press, 1987).

97   NAACP, "Criminal Justice Fact Sheet." https://www.naacp.org/criminal-justice-fact-sheet/.

98   Staffan Linder, *The Harried Leisure Class* (Columbia University Press, 1970).

99   Avner Offer, *The Challenge of Affluence: Self-Control and Well-Being in the United States and Britain Since 1950* (Oxford University Press, 2006).

100   Ellora Derenoncourt and Claire Montialoux, "Minimum Wages and Racial Inequality," *Quarterly Journal of Economics* 135 (2021), 169-228.

101   The "Federal Jobs Guarantee Development Act of 2018," was introduced in the Senate of the 115th Congress by Senator Cory Booker in April 2018.

102   Joseph Stiglitz, *The Price of Inequality* (Norton, 2012), p. 131.

103   Bureau of Justice Statistics, "Correctional Populations in the United States," https://www.bjs.gov/content/pub/pdf/cpus1718.pdf; Ann Carson, "Prisoners in 2014," *Bulletin*, Bureau of Justice Statistics, September 2015, https://www.bjs.gov/content/pub/pdf/p14.pdf, p. 15.

104   Juliana Menasce Horowitz et al., "Race in America 2019," Pew Research Center, April 2019, pp. 5, 10.

105   Mario Small and Devah Pager, "Sociological Perspectives on Racial Discrimination," *Journal of Economic Perspectives* 34 (2020), 2: 49-67; here p. 64.

106   Martin Čihák et al., "Race in Economics," *Finance and Development* (September 2020): 36-38.

107   Amanda Bayer, "How You Can Work to Increase the Presence and Improve the Experience of Black, Latinx, and Native American People in the Economics Profession," *Journal of Economic Perspectives* 34 (2020), 3: 193-219.

108   Michael Reich, *Racial Inequality: A Political-Economic Analysis* (Princeton University Press, 1981).

109   Sandra Peart and David Levy, "Economists, Race, and Racism: The Long View," Paper presented at the AEA Annual Meeting, January 2021.

110   https://www.aspeninstitute.org/blog-posts/structural-racism-definition/; this follows the Rawlsian conception of justice.

111   Paraphrasing Martin Luther King Jr.'s words from his letter from the Birmingham Jail.

112   Kenneth Arrow, "General Economic Equilibrium: Purpose, Analytical Techniques, Collective Choice," *American Economic Review* 64 (1974), 3: 253-272.

17 The Covid-19 Pandemic Exposed the Need for a Black-Swan-Robust Economy

> These are times that try men's souls.
> —Thomas Paine[1]

Warren Buffett's idiom, "It's only when the tide goes out that you learn who's been swimming naked," is a vivid portrayal of the vicissitudes faced by humanity during the Covid-19 pandemic that struck in early 2020. Much of the world was, swimming naked, i.e., they were tragically unprepared for meeting the challenges posed by the virus. The twenty-first-century normal business cycles have been transformed into *black-swan shocks*: ordinary inventory cycles, trade cycles, or demographic cycles have waned in significance and have been overtaken by low-probability extremely high-impact events that are described using the metaphor of a "black swan."[2]

Yet, the twenty-first century has become an "era of predictable unpredictability,"[3] since such low-probability disasters have been appearing with uncanny frequency: the Dot-Com bubble, 9/11, the financial Meltdown, the pandemic, and the Ukraine war.[4] Hence, economists should take these threats to the stability of the system far more seriously. In 2018, the risk of an infectious disease was rated among the least likely of all the risks faced by humanity.[5] We must explore ways to create a black-swan-robust economy that would be less vulnerable to the impact of high-cost low-probability events.[6]

Of course, politicians, the media, and academic economists would not concede that we were "swimming naked." The pandemic had already begun its destruction when President Trump boasted that "our economy is the best it has ever been," we have a "roaring economy," emphasizing that the "stock markets have soared."[7] This assessments reverberated throughout the media with celebratory headlines like "Job growth smashes expectations."[8] However, they failed to add that many were precarious jobs with low and insecure incomes or were part-time.[9] Six million such "contingent workers" in 2017 were in the *gig economy*, like "independent contractors," "on-call workers," "temporary help," who worked mostly without unemployment insurance or health insurance benefits or pension plans.[10] The spread of the gig economy is hardly a sign of a thriving and robust labor force capable of living a dignified life and able to withstand adversity.[11] Yet, just days before the pandemic Jerome Powell, Chair of the Federal Reserve, said that the "economy was in a very good place."[12] Academic economists agreed.

17.1 An Economy in Disequilibrium Is Vulnerable

The headlines were woefully misleading and one million deaths later the pandemic is still claiming hundreds of victims daily in the US alone. These observers mistook a Potemkin village for

DOI: 10.4324/9781003174356-17

Illustration 17.1 One flag, one life. A small virus showed what a big mistake economists made by disregarding basic needs
Credit: Shutterstock 2044543556.

reality.[13] They were mesmerized by the official statistics, but failed to recognize the significance of the economy's deep structural weaknesses, its fragility, and endemic imbalances including the twin deficits, the uncanny inequality, as well as the widespread disaffection among the citizens.[14] As the editors of *The New York Times* reflected: "This nation was ailing long before the coronavirus reached its shores."[15] At least four fundamental problems plagued the American system that weakened its ability to fight the pandemic.

Methodological individualism is the wrong ideology to cope with a pandemic that has a high transmission rate, i.e., a powerful negative externality. "[T]he pandemic demonstrates ... the limits of individualism. Everyone is vulnerable. Everyone's health depends on the health of others. No one is safe unless everyone takes responsibility for the welfare of others."[16] The dominant culture that emphasizes laissez-faire and minimizes government interference in personal decisions will not be successful in fighting an onslaught of the invisible deadly invaders.

Second, large segments of the US population had pre-existing conditions like obesity. The population was not as healthy and its health-care system not as good as it should have been, given its wealth.[17] Life expectancy had been declining or floundering since 2014 and has not been keeping up with trends in the rich countries since 1984 (see Figures 15.4 and 17.1).[18] The pandemic unmasked the drawback of running the economy at full throttle assuming the system was invulnerable to low-probability high-impact events (see Section 2.2). Life expectancy in 2020 and 2021 declined by 2.7 years, reversing the improvements of the previous 26 years. This is in contrast to peer countries whose life expectancy declined by just 0.3 years, i.e., 1/10 of that of the US.[19]

Third, there was a deep-rooted bias against creating a robust *social safety net*; this came back to haunt American society in 2020.[20] The gig economy did not provide sick leave or health insurance and most households had virtually no savings for any emergency.[21] The threat of hunger forced poor essential workers to accept dangerous assignments during the pandemic that had a coercive aspect to it, since they had to work to survive but many of them did not survive because they had to work. These essential workers included 32 million workers in the service sector such as in grocery and drug stores, public transit, warehousing, trucking, cleaning, and health care, making up about 20 percent of the labor force.[22] Minorities were overrepresented among the menial, front-line, low-wage workers; most of them required face-to-face contact such as cashiers,

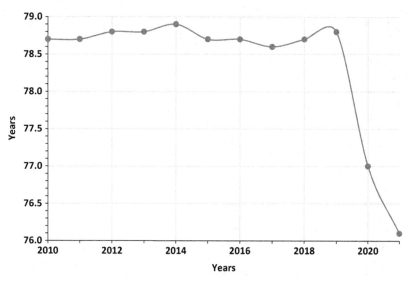

Figure 17.1 Life expectancy at birth in the US
Source: National Center for Health Statistics, "Health, United States, Table 15. Life Expectancy at Birth," https://www.cdc.gov/nchs/hus/contents2017.htm#015; Elizabeth Arias and Jiaquan Xu, "United States Life Tables, 2020," *National Vital Statistics Reports* 71, August 8, 2022, no. 1; Elizabeth Arias, et al., "Provisional Life Expectancy Estimates for 2021," *Vital Statistics Rapid Release*, August 2022, No. 23.

work that could not be done over the internet. Consequently, minorities were much more exposed to the ravages of the infection. That is why Blacks perished at twice the rate of whites during the pandemic. Another reason was that their health status was inferior to that of whites and pre-existing conditions increased the risk of Covid-19 mortality. Compared to the average decline in life expectancy of 1.8 years in 2020, that of Black males declined by an incredible 3.5 years, that of Black females by 2.7 years, that of Hispanic men by 4.5 years and that of Hispanic women by 3.1 years.[23] The difference between white and Black male life expectancy at birth in 2020 was 7 years and between white men and American Indian men 11 years! In short, inequities were piled upon inequities and continued to deteriorate in 2021 according to the provisional estimates (Figure 17.1).

Fourth, running the economy at full throttle meant that the system had multiple vulnerabilities. There was no slack in the system that would have been useful in the lockdown. With schools closed, parents had to scramble for childcare, accentuating the vulnerabilities of single-parent households and even two-parent households that depended on both parents working.[24] Additionally, running the economy at full throttle also meant keeping the government as small as possible which in turn meant that public health was neglected before the crisis. Therefore, funds supporting local health departments were reduced and supply stockpiles depleted.[25] Short of N95 masks, testing equipment, ventilators, nurses used garbage bags for protection. The system was caught swimming naked.

Moreover, the leadership to fight the epidemic was bungling from the start.[26] In contrast, by December 31, 2019, Taiwan responded to reports about an unusual disease in Wuhan and people coming from there were quarantined.[27] China had published the genetic code of the virus by January 11, yet the US still did absolutely nothing.[28] President Trump was mentally unfit to lead a life-and-death struggle against an invisible enemy and offered Alice-in-Wonderland panacea until the virus became uncontrollable.[29] His incompetence, including inducing a free-for-all bidding for equipment and masks, insufficient testing, and inadequate guidelines for social

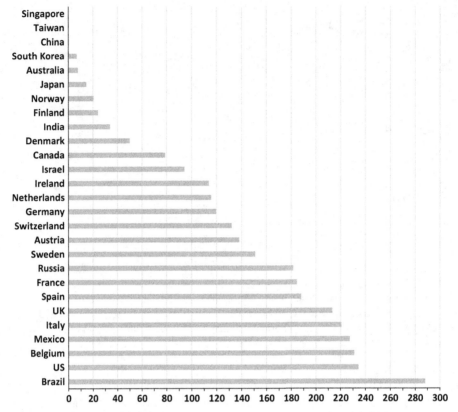

Figure 17.2 Covid-19 mortality rate per 100,000 population, November 26, 2021
Note: Deaths per 100,000.
Source: https://coronavirus.jhu.edu/map.html.

distancing, was outdone only by the Brazilian President Bolsonaro. That is why the US experienced the highest death rate in the world after Brazil (Figure 17.2).[30]

17.2 The Economic Crisis

The economy contracted instantaneously like never before.[31] By May 2020, nearly a quarter of the labor force was really unemployed. During the Great Depression, the economy contracted as much, but it took four years to do so! As usual, the U-6 rate at 23 percent was close to the true unemployment rate while the official rate was woefully biased downward at 15 percent because it ignored 4.5 million people who did not look for a job within the prior month but did not have a job (Figure 17.3).[32] The weaker elements of the society bore the brunt of the misery brought on by the pandemic. These were the young, less skilled, and less educated segment of the working class. The number of actually unemployed during the pandemic fluctuated between 21 and 41 million people, a disproportionate share of whom were minorities. That African Americans without a high-school degree had a *real* unemployment rate of 31 percent, a remarkable 12 percentage points (ppts) above those of whites with the same education, is indicative of the plight of the minorities during the pandemic.

There was a monotonic decrease in the U6 rate by educational attainment (Table 17.1). The difference between high school dropouts and those who have an advanced degree was a huge 15 ppts but is even greater among African Americans (23.7 ppts). The unemployment rate, at 22.7 percent, was high among youth between the ages of 16 and 24 and highest among African American youth at 31.1 percent (Table 17.2).

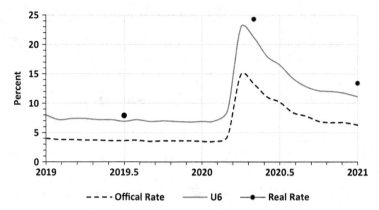

Figure 17.3 The *real* unemployment rate, U-6, and U-3 during Covid-19
Source: "The Actual US Unemployment Rate was 24.4 percent in May 2020," CESifo Working Paper no. 8383. Bureau of Labor Statistics, "Update on the Misclassification that Affected the Unemployment Rate," June 29, 2020; https://blogs.bls.gov/blog/2020/06/29/update-on-the-misclassification-that-affected-theunemployment-rate/.

The labor market experience of developed nations during the pandemic falls into three groups: (1) those whose unemployment rate remained essentially unchanged during the pandemic;[33] this group included most of the developed countries sandwiched between Japan at the low end and Sweden at the top; (2) the US and Canada with a large spike in unemployment in April that subsequently dissipated, gradually converging to the levels of those in the first category by Autumn 2020; and (3) Spain and Greece which started the year with a very high unemployment rate that persisted throughout 2020 (Figure 17.4).

Table 17.1 The U-6 unemployment rate by education and ethnicity, September 2020 (%)

Education	All	White	Black	Hispanic
All	12.5	10.3	16.9	16.6
Less than HS	21.5	18.9	30.9	21.1
High school	15.8	12.9	22.1	18.0
Some college	13.1	11.2	16.3	16.2
Bachelor's degree	9.0	8.1	10.3	12.1
Advanced degree	6.5	6.2	7.2	8.0
Range	15.0	12.7	23.7	13.1

Note: The data are averages for the previous 12 months.
Source: Economic Policy Institute, State of Working America Data Library, "Underemployment."

Table 17.2 The U-6 unemployment rate by age and ethnicity, September 2020 (%)

Age	All	White	Black	Hispanic
All	12.5	10.3	16.9	16.6
16–24	22.7	19.0	31.1	26.1
25–54	11.1	9.0	14.9	14.7
55–64	10.3	9.0	12.3	15.1
65+	11.8	10.6	15.5	16.6

Source: Economic Policy Institute, State of Working America Data Library, "Underemployment."

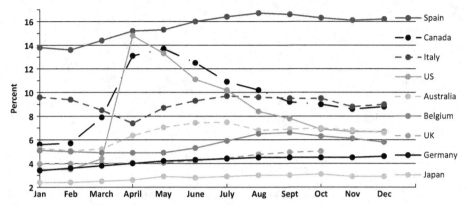

Figure 17.4 The official unemployment rate in selected countries, 2020 (%)
Source: OECD Data "Unemployment \rate"; https://data.oecd.org/unemp/unemploymentrate.htm.

17.3 Bailout Capitalism to the Rescue

The recession measured by real GDP per capita indicates the unprecedented intensity of the downturn (Figure 17.5). Never before has output declined so precipitously only to snap back to pre-Covid levels within 6 quarters. In contrast, the 2008 recession was shallower but far longer (21 quarters). Admittedly, the quick rebound of 2020 is somewhat misleading because it was accomplished by shifting the burden onto future generations.

The economy was put on life support by the Fed's asset purchases of $4 trillion (Figure 17.6). Within one week after March 11, it bought assets worth $500 billion and in the following week as well. By May, it had purchased $2 trillions' worth of assets. GDP rebounded with a two-month lag. GDP is estimated quarterly so that the unemployment rate, estimated monthly, provides a better indication of the speed of response to the asset purchases. The lag in response of the

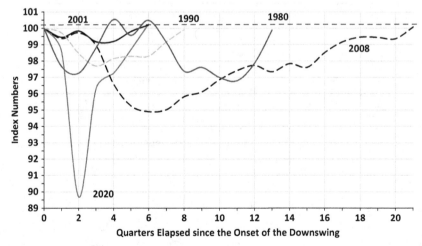

Figure 17.5 GDP per capita in five recessions
Note: Index numbers; peak prior to the recession = 100.
Source: St. Louis Fed, series A939RX0Q048SBEA.

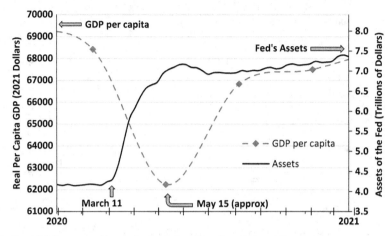

Figure 17.6 Real GDP per capita and assets held by the Federal Reserve
Source: St. Louis Fed, series WALCL, A939RX0Q048SBEA, CPIAUCSL.

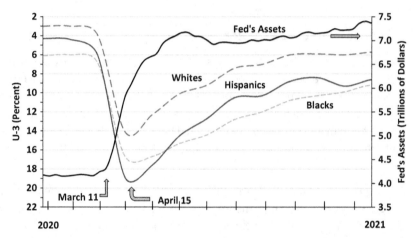

Figure 17.7 The Fed's assets and the official unemployment rate during Covid-19 by ethnicity
Source: St. Louis Fed, series WALCL, LNS14000003, LNS14000006, LNS14000009.

unemployment rate was shorter. The Fed started purchasing assets after March 11 and unemployment began to rebound within the next month (Figure 17.7). The rebound among minorities was considerably slower than that of whites. The rebound of the stock market started even earlier. The S&P 500 reached rock bottom on March 23, in response to the $1 trillion the Fed injected into the financial markets. Within four days the Index had jumped 400 points or 18 percent (Figure 17.8).[34]

Government expenditure was supported by the Treasury, which pays the bills of the United States, selling bonds to the Fed whose holdings of assets rose to $9 trillion, an eleven-fold increase since the start of the 2008 Meltdown (see Figure 10.6). The deficit in the final year of the Trump administration reached $3.6 trillion and $2.6 trillion in 2021, the first year of the Biden administration.[35] The national debt increased stupendously to 125 percent of GDP to reach $30 trillion by the end of 2021 (see Figure 12.1).

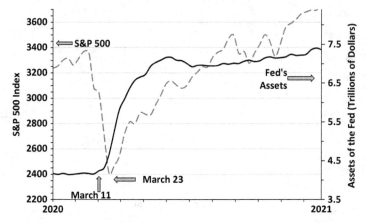

Figure 17.8 The S&P 500 Index and the assets held by the Federal Reserve
Note: The correlation coefficient between the two series is 0.81.
Source: St. Louis Fed, series WALCL, and SP500.

17.4 The Goal of a Black-Swan-Robust Economy

A shaken US government spent $5.3 trillion to subsidize the economy. Nearly a quarter of GDP or 29 percent of disposable personal income was spent on the nation's credit card to keep the economy afloat. Instead of acting in such an ad hoc manner, it would be much better to make long-range plans to counter such emergencies.[36] Nassim Taleb has ten suggestions to improve the ability of the economy to withstand unanticipated high-impact shocks. Many of these relate to finance but others are common-sensical enough to be generalizable to other types of shocks also:[37]

1. "What is fragile should break early while it is still small." Identify and nip in the bud a bubble early before it expands to unmanageable scale. If a firm is too big to fail, it is too big to exist. Society cannot afford to be beholden to the vagaries of humongous firms.
2. "No socialisation of losses and privatisation of gains." To avoid the accumulation of moral hazard, firms that are so vital to the national economy that they cannot be allowed to become bankrupt should be nationalized in a crisis. A system that allows gains to be privatized and losses socialized is not going to be stable in the long term.
3. Experts who were responsible for making mistakes in the past should not be given another chance by being appointed again to positions of authority, like Obama appointed Summers and Geithner and reappointed Bernanke (2010), who all shared responsibility for the 2008 crisis. They have lost legitimacy. "Instead, find the smart people whose hands are clean."
4. "No incentives without disincentives: capitalism is about rewards and punishments, not just rewards." Be careful with incentive bonuses because it is easy to hide risks in finance and incentives can induce money managers to take on excessive risks to increase returns, such as during the financial crisis.
5. Beware of complexity. Complex systems are sensitive even to small perturbations and can easily become erratic. Leverage should be mitigated. Slack, redundancy, inefficiency must be part of macroprudential architecture as shock absorbers of unanticipated events. That also implies that rethinking the concept of efficiency is necessary to accommodate such unanticipated shocks.

6. "Citizens must be protected from themselves." That means that complex derivatives should be banned because they are dangerous and "nobody understands them" and they do not increase the efficiency of the system. Government should incentivize consumers to save more and spend less on credit cards to have a cushion in case of an economic downturn (see Section 12.7).

7. Governments should not be in the position of having to support confidence in the system. If the system needs government cheerleaders, there must be something wrong.

8. "The debt crisis is not a temporary problem, it is a structural problem." We should be more prudent with debt and not continue to increase it indefinitely just because we can.

9. Retirement should be safe from financial vicissitudes. Citizens should not have to live in constant anxiety about their future security.

10. "Makeshift repairs" of the economic system should be avoided. "Let us move voluntarily into Capitalism 2.0" by making the necessary structural changes for a robust economic system.

Additionally, much more attention must be paid to social welfare policies, basic needs, and strategies to end the structural imbalances: (1) institutional innovation to nudge households to save more; (2) decrease advertisements so that people are not tempted to consume more; (3) eliminate the twin deficits so the structural imbalances are mitigated; (4) improve the safety net; (5) introduce universal health care; (6) force mega-corporations and the billionaires to pay their fair share of taxes so that public health can be improved; (7) learn to run the economy at less than full throttle, i.e., transition to a lower-pressure economy by decreasing competition and create a more harmonious economy; (8) improve education; and (9) all this also requires cultural changes so that the goal becomes the enhancement of human flourishing instead of the current focus on growth.

17.5 Covid-19 Exposed the Deep Fissures, Endemic Imbalances, and Precarious Nature of the US Economy

The pandemic struck the underbelly of a vulnerable high-pressure economy. A system in endemic disequilibrium is vulnerable and can easily be destabilized. Its fragility magnified the impact of an invisible enemy. It had not been an inclusive economy in which all who wanted to work had found decent stable full-time jobs. It was not an economy with ample savings and with deep safety nets in case of an improbable calamity.[38] The government faced endemic deficits of $1 trillion even before the epidemic and too many households were maxed out on their credit cards. International trade was unbalanced. Hubris was so widespread that preparing for the remote possibility of a major pandemic appeared unreasonably cautious. The prevalence of hyperbolic discounting made it even more unlikely that planning would be adequate (see Section 5.12).

The goal of policy-makers and economists to "reboot the US economy," or to focus on "economic recovery," is therefore short-sighted. Instead of aspiring to return to a frail economy, policy-makers should strengthen the social contract and insist on creating a black-swan-robust economy. They should prioritize institutional innovation and far-sighted policies, including the introduction of *"failure-mode analysis"* (fail-safe strategies) as occurs in structural engineering.[39] We need a new Keynes for our time.[40] Capitalism with a human face, advocated in this book, would be such an economy.[41]

Each epoch puts its stamp on the economic canon, and this life-threatening epidemic will do so also. It would be a folly to continue casual theorizing as usual. The experience of the pandemic must motivate economists to rethink seriously many fundamental concepts and policy recommendations and pay more attention to resilience, to cooperative solutions instead of competition, and to basic needs, a concept that has been conspicuously purged from their canon. They will have to rethink the need for safety nets and the role of government in the proper functioning of an economy. The conceptualization of efficiency must be reformulated, so that maximization includes the threat of tail events; this will increase the urgency of industrial policy (see Section 12.10).[42] "Post Covid-19, our priority should be to build resilient systems explicitly designed to withstand worst-case scenarios."[43]

17.6 Takeaways

Large-impact improbable events, dubbed black-swan events, have been occurring frequently in the twenty-first century. The Dot-Com bubble, 9/11, the Meltdown of 2008, the coronavirus pandemic, and the Russian invasion of Ukraine mean that these threats occur with sufficient regularity that we should build a black-swan-robust economy so that we are less vulnerable to their impact. Such crises reveal the fragility of the neoliberal economic system. The markets work until they don't and then the economy needs government bailouts of trillions of dollars. The Federal Reserve gave birth to bailout capitalism by injecting $8 trillion dollars into the financial system between 2008 and 2022.

The problems that plagued the American system led to the highest death rate from the pandemic after Brazil. The dominant culture that emphasizes laissez-faire and minimizes government interference in personal decisions cannot be successful in fighting an invisible deadly invader like the virus. Moreover, large segments of the US population had pre-existing health conditions such as being overweight. Life expectancy has been falling behind those in rich countries since 1984, another legacy of Reaganomics. In addition, there has been a deep-rooted bias against creating a robust social safety net; this came back to haunt American society in 2020. The gig economy did not provide sick leave or health insurance and most households had virtually no savings for an emergency. Life expectancy declined by 2.7 years during the pandemic.

Questions for Discussion

1   How do you think the response to the Covid pandemic could have been improved?
2   What was your experience during the Covid pandemic?
3   Do you think that the twenty-first century has become an era of instability?
4   Why is the US more vulnerable to a black-swan events than peer countries?
5   What would a black-swan-robust economy look like?
6   Discuss: the high rate of pre-existing health conditions is one of the reasons for the high US mortality rate during the pandemic.
7   Do you think that the economy should be run at full throttle?
8   What is the meaning of an efficient economy, considering the experience with the pandemic?
9   Do you think that a tight social safety net is superfluous in a modern economy?
10   Do you think it was fair to force essential workers to expose themselves to the dangers of the virus during the pandemic?

11   According to neoliberal dogma, that government is best that governs the least. Discuss.

12   Do you think that bailout capitalism is sustainable?

13   Do you think that the higher-than-average death rate among African American men during the pandemic is indicative of systemic racism?

14   Do you think government support of households and businesses was necessary?

15   Do you think the federal government deficit is sustainable?

Notes

1   "The Crisis," December 23, 1776.

2   The metaphor arose when black swans, unknown in Europe, were discovered in Australia. Nassim Taleb, *The Black Swan: The Impact of the Highly Improbable* (Random House, 2007).

3   Anon., "The New Normal Is Already Here. Get Used to It," *The Economist*, December 18, 2021.

4   In addition, in the last two decades these regional catastrophes claimed upwards of 6,000 lives and caused damages of $600 billion. Wikipedia contributors, "List of Disasters in the United States by Death Toll."

5   It was rated 26th of 30 risks on a par with weapons of mass destruction. World Economic Forum, "The Global Risks, Report 2018," Insight Report, 13th edn. (Geneva: WEF); http://wef.ch/risks2018.

6   Threats in the foreseeable future include global environmental degradation, hostile artificial intelligence, the endemic US national debt, domestic terrorism, and the possibility of untoward acts of adversaries around the globe.

7   Donald Trump, "Full Transcript: Trump's 2020 State of the Union Address," *The New York Times*, February 5, 2020. Earlier he boasted about "an unprecedented economic boom," adding that we have "the hottest economy anywhere" and that "our economy is the envy of the world" because "an economic miracle is taking place in the United States." Donald Trump, "Remarks by President Trump in State of the Union Address," February 6, 2019; https://www.whitehouse.gov/briefings-statements/remarks-president-trump-state-union-address-2/.

8   Jeff Cox, "Job Growth Smashes Expectations for February as Unemployment Falls Back to 3.5 Percent," *CNBC*, March 6, 2020.

9   Albena Azmanova, *Capitalism on Edge: How Fighting Precarity Can Achieve Radical Change Without Crisis or Utopia* (Columbia University Press, 2020).

10   Karen Kosanovich, "A Look at Contingent Workers," *Spotlight on Statistics*, US Bureau of Labor Statistics, September 2018; https://www.bls.gov/spotlight/2018/contingent-workers/home.htm; Gerald Friedman, "Workers Without Employers: Shadow Corporations and the Rise of the Gig Economy," *Review of Keynesian Economics* 2 (2014), 171-188.

11   Alex Rosenblat, *Uberland: How Algorithms Are Rewriting the Rules of Work* (University of California Press, 2019).

12   Heather Long, "Fed Chair Powell Warns Congress that $1 Trillion Budget Deficits Are Unsustainable," *The Washington Post*, February 11, 2020. Some of the news clips were collected and reposted: "America's Economy Is Roaring," White House, "Shifting Into High Gear: America's Economy Is Roaring," July 27, 2018; https://www.presidency.ucsb.edu/documents/press-release-shifting-into-high-gear-americas-economy-roaring.

13   Joseph Stiglitz, "The Economy We Need," *Project Syndicate*, May 3, 2019; Jochen Hartwig, "On Spurious Differences in Growth Performance and on the Misuse of National Accounts Data for Governance Purposes," *Review of International Political Economy* 13 (2006): 535-558.

14   Jacob Hacker, "The Economy Is Strong. So Why Do So Many Americans Still Feel at Risk?" *The New York Times*, May 21, 2019.

15   The Editorial Board, "The America We Need," *The New York Times*, April 9, 2020.

16   George Packer, "America's Plastic Hour Is Upon Us," *The Atlantic*, October 2020.

17   Eric Schneider et al., "Mirror, Mirror 2021: Reflecting Poorly. Heath Care in the US Compared to Other High-Income Countries," *Commonwealth Fund Reports*, August 4, 2021.

18   Steven Woolf and Heidi Schoomaker, "Life Expectancy and Mortality Rates in the United States, 1959-2017," *Journal of the American Medical Association* 322 (2019), 20: 1996-2016.

19   Ryan Masters et al., "Changes in Life Expectancy between 2019 and 2021 in the United States and 21 Peer Countries," medRxiv, June 1, 2022; https://www.medrxiv.org/content/10.1101/2022.04.05.22273393v4.

20   *The Economist*, "How to Make a Social Safety-Net for the Post-Covid World," March 6, 2021; Joseph Stiglitz, "Solidarity Now," *Project Syndicate*, February 28, 2020.

21   Dan Murphy, "Economic Impact Payments: Uses, Payment Methods, and Costs to Recipients," Economic Studies, Brookings, February 2021.

22   Hye Jin Rho et al., "A Basic Demographic Profile of Workers in Frontline Industries," CEPR Publications, April 7, 2020; Theresa Andrasfay and Noreen Goldman, "Reductions in 2020 US Life Expectancy Due to Covid-19 and the Disproportionate Impact on the Black and Latino Populations," *Proceedings of the National Academy of Sciences of the United States of America* 118 (2021), 5: n.p.

23   Elizabeth Arias and Jiaquan Xu, "United States Life Tables, 2020," *National Vital Statistics Reports* 71, August 8, 2022, no. 1.

24   Elizabeth Warren and Amelia Tyagi, *The Two Income Trap: Why Middle-Class Parents Are Going Broke* (Basic Books, 2003).

25   Donald Cohen and Allen Mikaelian, *The Privatization of Everything: How the Plunder of Public Goods Transformed America and How We Can Fight Back* (The New Press, 2021).

26   Adam Tooze, *Shutdown: How Covid Shook the World's Economy* (Viking, 2021).

27   Shih-Chung Chen, "Taiwan's Experience in Fighting Covid-19," *Nature Immunology* 22 (2021): 293-394.

28   Michael Osterholm and Mark Olshaker, "Chronicle of a Pandemic Foretold," *Foreign Affairs* 99 (2020), 4: 10-24.

29   Philipp Carlsson-Szlezak et al., "Understanding the Economic Shock of Coronavirus," *Harvard Business Review*, March 27, 2020.

30   Covid-19 National Preparedness Collaborators, "Pandemic Preparedness and Covid-19: An Exploratory Analysis of Infection and Fatality Rates, and Contextual Factors Associated with Preparedness in 177 Countries, from Jan 1, 2020, to Sept 30, 2021," *The Lancet*, February 1, 2022.

31   Tomaz Cajner et al., "The US Labor Market during the Beginning of the Pandemic Recession," National Bureau of Economic Research, Working Paper no. 27159, May 2020.

32   St. Louis Fed, series CLF16OV.

33   Jorge Luis Garcia et al., "The Lasting Effects of Early Childhood Education on Promoting the Skills and Social Mobility of Disadvantaged African Americans," NBER Working Paper no. 29057.

34   These are daily values. The values in the graph are weekly averages.

35   St. Louis Fed, series GFDEBTN.

36   Steve Keen, *Can We Avoid Another Financial Crisis?* (Polity, 2017).

37   Nassim Taleb, "Ten Principles for a Black Swan-Proof World," *Financial Times*, April 7, 2009.

38   Editors, "How to Make a Social Safety-Net ," op. cit.

39   Brian Arthur, "All Systems Will Be Gamed: Exploitive Behavior in Economic and Social Systems," SFI Working Paper, 6-16-2014; https://www.santafe.edu/research/results/working-papers/all-systems-will-be-gamed-exploitive-behavior-in-e.

40   Stephen Marglin, *Raising Keynes: A Twenty-First-Century General Theory* (Harvard University Press, 2021).

41   Michal Lewis, *The Premonition: A Pandemic Story* (Norton: 2021).

42   "Coronavirus," https://americanprogress.org/topic/coronavirus/

43   Jonathan Aldred, "This Pandemic Has Exposed the Uselessness of Orthodox Economics," *The Guardian*, July 5, 2020.

18 Conclusion

Toward a Capitalism with a Human Face

> It always seems impossible until it's done.
> —Nelson Mandela

18.1 Summing Up: Imaginary vs. Real Markets

This volume examines the salient differences between imaginary and real markets.[1] While mainstream textbooks sing hymns to the invisible hand, we followed an empirical approach to examine the actual workings of markets with real human beings in the real world, rather than analyzing fictional economic agents, *homo oeconomicus*, in hypothetical markets.[2] We thereby take economic principles beyond the basics by emphasizing how the really existing economy deviates from blackboard models discussed in classrooms around the globe. This discrepancy is most severe for most of the population in the lower half of the income distribution.[3] We conclude that markets are *necessary* but *insufficient* to a *good* economy, one that provides a fulfilled life for the whole population.[4] We find that without well-designed institutions, rigorous oversight, and a political system capable of interpreting and implementing the *general will* of society, real markets become inefficient, unstable, accumulate inequities, fail miserably to distribute the fruits of the economy ethically or equitably, and lead to an unstable democracy.[5] The winner-take-all (losers-lose-all) design of markets magnifies initial inequities, which leads to a dual economy, social instability, and the rise of an oligarchy that culminates in political dysfunction and the rise of right-wing populism.[6] These magnification mechanisms are crucial in understanding how the system works for the benefit of the few and the detriment of the many. The have-nots, those who are squeezed by monopoly drug prices and hospital costs, who could not afford a college education, who experienced downward social mobility because of globalization, and eviction and unemployment during the financial crisis, will not be happy citizens supportive of the political elite, no matter what the *average* income is.[7] "These are dangerous times for democracy" because of the "failure of technocratic liberalism."[8]

This is obvious in today's global economy, in which the degree of complexity poses a major challenge to navigate through the system from birth to adulthood in the absence of adequate guidance, education, and good will emanating from the establishment. As emphasized throughout the text, there are innumerable formidable obstacles to the adequate functioning of markets: the presence of imperfect information, opportunistic behavior, heterogeneous cognitive ability, opportunism, externalities, pollution, safety, nonexistent markets, transaction costs, uncertainty, sustainability, too-big-to-fail oligopolies, monopolies, and monopsonies, protection

DOI: 10.4324/9781003174356-18

of children, power imbalances, nonrationality, and the unequal distribution of opportunity, work, wealth, and income. These are exactly the topics introductory mainstream textbooks bypass but are imperative for understanding the actual functioning of the real-existing economy without which millions of students leave their economics courses hopelessly misinformed.

Most mainstream textbooks ignore crucial concepts analyzed by Nobelists such as Herbert Simon (1978, satisficing), Amartya Sen (1998, capabilities, positive freedom), George Akerlof (2001, asymmetric information), Michael Spence (2001, signaling), Joseph Stiglitz (2001, information economics), Daniel Kahneman (2002, behavioral economics), Paul Krugman (2008, new trade theory), Oliver Williamson (2009, transaction costs), Robert Shiller (2013, behavioral finance), and Richard Thaler (2017, behavioral economics). Without these ideas, textbooks delude students into thinking that markets work flawlessly without government meddling.

The claim that these topics cannot be studied in Econ-101 because of their complexity or because of insufficient time is preposterous. Without this knowledge students are indoctrinated into a fundamentalist ideology. In contrast, this volume focuses on the working of actual markets in real time and demonstrates that without this elaboration standard economics fails Feynman's test of "utter honesty."[9] Wrong economic theories have led to defective economic policies which in turn led to blunders of historic proportions:[10]

1. Economists' refrain that cutting taxes is good for the economy and that the benefits will trickle down to the masses failed miserably.[11] The theorists depended on increased incentives to save, invest, and work but none of that materialized.[12] Instead, the tax policy under Reagan led to immense endemic deficits of half a trillion dollars (in 2021 prices).[13] Reaganomics failed because *they overlooked the powerful impact the windfall had on inequality* since the benefits accrued exclusively to the top 1 percent.[14] They thought the lower classes would be content with a tiny increase in their after-tax income, but they neglected completely that the considerable decline in their income relative to the new social norms set by the superrich would increase their discontent substantially. The theoreticians ignored the powerful destabilizing political and social effects of the immense increase in inequality. Even arch-conservative Alan Greenspan acknowledged in 2007, after he left office, that the increase in inequality might "spark ... an economically destructive backlash," a prediction that came so true in 2016.[15] Thus, the increase in inequality was toxic for social and political harmony.[16] An economy in which a hedge-fund manager can buy a $238 million apartment in Manhattan while half a million Americans are homeless is not likely to be permanently stable.[17]

2. Trade theorists claimed that globalization would improve Americans' lives but instead it has had devastating social, political, and demographic consequences, because *they disregarded the fate of millions of low-skilled workers* whose lives were shattered in the wake of enormous penetration of imports from China.[18]

3. Conventional economists predicted that economic growth would lead to human progress. Yet, it caused an immense amount of discontent because *they ignored the significance of relative incomes* and that falling behind the social norms would incite a groundswell of discontent. In turn, demagogues would take advantage of that discontent to unleash an assault on the establishment. Instead of a rise in the standard of living, economic growth led to deaths of despair, mass murders, and other symptoms of erosion of social cohesion.

4. Deregulation was supposed to increase efficiency and therefore increase living standards. Instead, it led to an immense financial meltdown because *economists ignored Minsky's*

warnings about financial instability and disregarded the role of systemic effects in destabi-lizing the economy.[19]

5.   Technological change was supposedly the mainspring of human progress, but instead it swelled the number of have-nots and created gig work, Facebook, Russian trolls, white nationalist militias, an insurrection, flash-mob robberies, and *contributed mightily to the destabilization of the political system.*

6.   Inequality was supposedly inconsequential but instead the lopsided growth fostered the formation of an oligarchy because *mainstream economists ignored the crucial role of asymmetric power in the economy and political system.*[20]

In fact, there was hardly any *consequential* society-wide predictions by mainstream economists which were near the target. So, the anomalies in the normal science of economics has been accumulating for decades, contradicting essential aspects of the mainstream canon. The real-existing economy bears no resemblance to the Alice-in-Wonderland models sketched on academic blackboards.[21]

18.2 Eight Inconvenient Truths about a Dual Economy

The impression propagated in the media that the US economy was in good shape before Covid is fallacious. Instead, it was a dual economy in which about half of the population was in good-to-excellent shape, but that is inadequate for an economy to be in stable long-run equilibrium. Some of the inconvenient truths that pundits, politicians, and academics overlooked include:

1.   *Anemic GDP growth* is the new normal in the twenty-first-century US. Per capita growth has been 30 percent slower than in the 1990s (see Figure 12.3). After the 2008 financial crisis, GDP has been about $1 trillion below its potential (see Figure 14.4). This is not terrible in itself, since GDP is not correlated with life satisfaction of the population (see Figure 11.3). However, the expectations of the population have not adjusted to this new normal. The slowdown be-comes bad if rising expectations are frustrated. Furthermore, the measurement of GDP needs substantial changes: to account for pollution, i.e., the cost of climate change; to include care work; and to consider the depletion of natural non-renewable resources. Anyway, GDP should no longer be used as a bellwether indicator of well-being.[22] Instead, we should pay more at-tention to the Sustainable Development Index, the Genuine Progress Indicator, the Human Development Index, the Social Progress Index, and the Happiness Index.[23] These take into consideration the health, educational attainment of the population, and the cost of negative externalities like the cost of crime, resource depletion, and environmental damage.[24]

2.   The *productivity slowdown* implies that anemic GDP growth will continue for the foresee-able future (see Section 11.5).[25] Labor productivity growth after 2010 (at 1.1 percent) was half of the prior epoch (see Table 7.1).[26] Average productivity of labor and capital taken together was 0.2 percent after 2010 whereas between 1988 and 2010, it was 1 percent, i.e., five times as high.[27] The low hanging fruit of technological innovation has been reaped: "ideas, and the exponential growth they imply, are getting harder to find."[28] "The cumulative loss in output ... due to the labor productivity slowdown since 2005" has been $11 trillion.[29] The innovations in the pipeline are not likely to improve substantially the quality of life of Every-man on Main Street. That implies that innovation and entrepreneurship can no longer be relied on as the engines of growth. Again, this is a fact of life that the population should understand in order to lower its expectations.

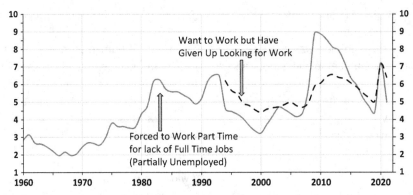

Figure 18.1 Unemployed who are excluded from the official unemployment statistics (millions)
Source: St. Louis Fed, series LNU02032194, NILFWJN.

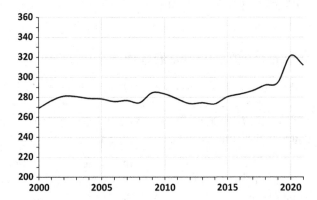

Figure 18.2 Real median weekly earnings of part-time workers (2021 dollars)
Source: St. Louis Fed, series, LEU0262881500Q, CPIAUCSL.

3. The unemployment rate is another bellwether indicator, but its official version is woefully inaccurate, because its definition is far too stringent. The real problem is *endemic under-the-radar unemployment* leading to a divergence between appearance and reality.[30] While the media was proudly proclaiming the virtues of full employment in 2019, still 12.7 million adults (7.8 percent) were without work, although the official numbers were just half as large (see Table 11.1 and Figure 11.1). The discrepancy stems from the fact that not enough full-time jobs were available: in 2021, 5.0 million adults were *forced to work part-time* for the lack of full-time jobs (Figure 18.1).[31] Obviously, available supply of full-time jobs was inadequate to meet demand for such jobs. The salary of part-time workers was $312, hardly enough to keep body and soul together (Figure 18.2). Their weekly salary increased by $31 since 2002, insufficient to improve their living standards markedly.

    Swelling the numbers of unemployed were 6.4 million persons (2021) who gave up searching for employment out of frustration but are ignored by the *official* statistics, although they affirmed that they would have liked to work.[32] Another issue overlooked by the mainstream is that the lack of jobs affects minorities the most. Their unemployment rate is typically twice that of whites (see Figure 16.2).

4. *Technological unemployment* is an increasing threat. The proliferation of robots means that GDP growth is decoupled from well-paying jobs, as firms switch from human labor to

robot labor. People are becoming increasingly redundant through automation and skills mismatch.[33] We need institutional innovation to confront this problem. This includes a combination of reducing the hours worked, as they were reduced in the 1930s, guaranteeing a basic income for all, guaranteeing work for all by the government becoming the employer of last resort, as the Fed is the lender of last resort, and taxing robots to fund the above programs.

5. *Wages of low-skilled workers have been stagnating or declining* for more than a generation, poisoning the political climate and creating distributional conflicts. Those without a college degree have experienced a decline of as much as 10 percent in annual salary (Table 18.1).

The hollowing out of the middle class is evident if one considers how much income it takes to thrive like a middle-class family.[34] The cost of thriving index (COTI) rose much faster than incomes:

> The COTI shows a declining capacity of a male full-time worker to meet the major costs of a typical middle-class household ... The widening gulf ... between what American life costs and what American jobs pay is a central fact of American political economy that the public appears to have understood long before economists.[35]

6 The US economy entered a new era of weak economic performance in the twenty-first century, sometimes dubbed *secular stagnation*.[36] Larry Summers argues that "something is a little bit odd" about the performance of the US economy in the twenty-first century. Before the financial crisis, in spite of the explosion of debt as people withdrew their savings from their home equity, and a "vast amount of imprudent lending" compounded by consumers giddy from their pseudo-wealth "in excess of its reality," the economy was by no means overheating.[37] Summers notes that despite all these factors that should have stimulated aggregate demand, "Capacity utilization wasn't under any great pressure. Unemployment wasn't under any remarkably low level. Inflation was entirely quiescent. So somehow, even a great bubble wasn't enough to produce any excess in aggregate demand." In other words, prices, wages, and output were not growing impressively. Instead, people were dropping out of the labor force by the millions because of limited opportunities or finding a place in the gig economy.

Table 18.1 Real median household income by education (2020 dollars)

Educational attainment	Number (millions)		Income (2020 dollars)		Change in	
	2000	2019	2000	2019	dollars	(%)
No diploma	16.3	10.3	31367	30891	-476	-1.5
High school diploma	31.1	31.1	55056	49316	-5740	-10.4
Some college	18.4	20.4	67261	62684	-4577	-6.8
Associate degree	8.4	13.5	76121	70442	-5679	-7.5
College degree	17.9	29.3	100411	101415	+1004	+1.0
Master's degree	6.6	13.8	118068	118905	+837	+0.7
Professional degree	1.7	1.9	151699	164151	+12452	+8.2
Doctorate	1.4	2.7	143313	144124	+811	+0.6

Note: Professional degree income refers to 1998.
Source: US Census Bureau, Table H-13; www.census.gov/data/tables/time-series/demo/income-poverty/historical-income-households.html.

Krugman considers Summers' thesis to be a "very radical manifesto," since he is suggesting that "we may be an economy that needs bubbles just to achieve something near full employment–that in the absence of bubbles the economy" will continue to falter.[38] Hence, Summers believes that the US economy has shed its dynamic characteristics and morphed into an economy capable only of sluggish performance even if it is supported by easy-money policy and unstable finance. Because of inadequate aggregate demand, the post-industrial service economy will be stuck in low gear for the foreseeable future. Hence, there is no reason to think that an acceleration of economic growth will ease the competition for income share or free up resources for redistribution.

After all, it has been more than *two decades* since the economy grew at a hefty pace supported by sustainable finance. However, the expansion of the 1990s culminated in the Dot.Com bubble. Growth picked up after a short recession, but again was fueled by the Fed's accommodating monetary policy including low interest rates, easy money, lower underwriting standards, and predatory lending, that culminated in the greatest crisis since 1929. Moreover, even in a bubble economy before the crisis of 2008, economic growth was slower than in the last decade of the twentieth century. Summers' thesis is confirmed by the slowdown in GDP growth (see Figure 12.3). This is what the new normal of secular stagnation looks like.

7.   The *level of inequality*, not seen since the Robber Barons reigned in the Gilded Age, is unjust, unsustainable, and corrosive to the social fabric. The appetite of the superrich is insatiable.[39] In 2018, the top 1 percent taxpayers earned an average of $1.1 million per annum after tax and has captured 1/5 of total income (see Table 7.4). In fact, they earned as much as half of the population taken together. The top 20 percent of the income distribution earns one-half of total income (se Figure 7.7b). No wonder despair has been accumulating and the political establishment was routed in 2016 and no wonder the have-nots rose up on January 6th, 2021. Such discrepancies in the distribution of income are not the hallmark of politically stable societies.

8.   The US has a *$23 trillion economy that fails to satisfy*. No matter what metric one chooses, other developed countries do better: in longevity, health, child welfare, poverty, life satisfaction, inequality, happiness, educational attainment, opioid deaths, or incarceration rate; the quality of life is higher in countries in which taxes are higher, but the people have fewer anxieties about their health insurance, college education, and have a secure safety net in case of need (see Figures 2.1-2.7).[40] They respect their government instead of resenting it. The US was doing better in 1990 since the share of those "not too happy" was at a low point of 8 percent (see Figure 11.3). By 2016, that share had doubled to 16 percent. Similarly, the number of happy people was at 36 percent in 1990 while in 2016 it was 28 percent.

Emotional prosperity continues to elude the US because "the American economy has become more ruthless."[41] Running the economy at full throttle leaves the nerves frayed, anxiety high, and leads to a society living on the edge with mental health challenges. The psychological trauma means that a large share of the population is on antidepressants. The 100,000 people who died of opioid overdose during the 12 months ending in April 2021 and the other "deaths of despair" provide ample evidence of the accumulation of anguish at the low end of the income distribution.[42] Such an epidemic of suicide does not occur in a good economy; people do not kill strangers in a good economy; 2.1 million people are not incarcerated in a good economy; 37 million people do not live in poverty in a good economy. Even before Covid, typical Americans were not in good shape: they were overweight, deeply indebted, not in control of their finances or appetite. No wonder the Covid pandemic in the US was among the most devastating in the world (see Figure 17.2).

18.3 The Gordian Knot: The US Economy Is Facing 16 Headwinds, Only One of Them Is Partly Fixable

The above eight challenges facing the US economy are formidable and likely insurmountable. In addition, the US also has to contend with 16 *structural* headwinds in the political, cultural, social, and economic realm which prevent the reestablishment of a stable economy. These impediments are intertwined in a complex network of interrelationships and feedback mechanisms which form a tight Gordian Knot, impossible to disentangle. Only one of these headwinds seems partly rectifiable since the Congress passed a $1tr infrastructure bill in 2021. Consequently, the economic malaise is intractable and most likely will continue. These headwinds are as follows.

1. *The US Constitution is antiquated.*[43] Consequently, the will of the people cannot become reality because (a) votes of the citizens are weighted according to an outmoded scheme; (b) powerful factions with deep pockets impose the will of a minority on the majority; and (c) gerrymandering is an additional obstacle to the realization of the general will.[44] After all, Al Gore won the popular vote, yet Bush Jr. became president and Hillary Clinton received 3 million more votes than Donald Trump and yet she also failed. Hence, the US is no longer a functioning democracy, despite elections, because votes are weighted.

   In 2020, 300,000 California voters sent one elector to the electoral college that chose the president, whereas in the states of Montana, Wyoming, and South and North Dakota, every 140,000 voters sent an elector. Hence, the citizens of those four states were twice as important as those of California. Such weighting schemes also account for the non-representative nature of the Senate. California has two senators whereas the least populated 22 states with the same combined population are represented by 44 senators. No wonder that such a convoluted and anachronistic system became a plutocracy.[45] This is crucial because this is a main reason why the people's general will does not become reality.[46]

2. *The endemic budget deficit* is a sword of Damocles that creates uncertainty about the future and limits the government's ability to solve any of the structural problems faced by the economy even if it could break through the political gridlock (see Figure 12.5). With the moneyed elite unwilling to pay sufficient taxes to balance the budget, the interest payments on the national debt will continue to snowball.[47] The consensus view even before the pandemic was that $1 trillion deficits are unsustainable because of the accumulating interest rate burden.[48] In 2020, the average interest rate on the debt was 2.2 percent, but if it were to increase to historical norms, the burden could become precarious. Interest payments amounted to $562 billion in 2020, or about 1/5th of total government revenue.[49] Endemic government deficits are the sign of an economy living well beyond its means for decades.[50]

   Government deficit, projected to be $1.1 trillion in 2020 before the pandemic, actually reached $3.6 trillion and increased the cumulative federal debt to $30 trillion or 125 percent of GDP (see Figures 12.1 and 18.3).[51] This is in stark contrast to the federal debt in 1981 at 31 percent of GDP. "It would be imprudent to allow the debt-to-GDP ratio to rise forever in an uncertain world."[52] It could become a "recipe for hyperinflation."[53] With bailout capitalism the US has entered unchartered territory: "a range of reasonable estimates implies an unsustainable fiscal path that will generate significant problems if not addressed."[54] It

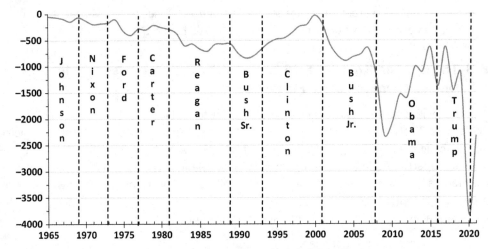

Figure 18.3 US federal deficit (2021 dollars, billions, by administration)
Source: St. Louis Fed, series GFDEBTN, CPIUCSL.

is unlikely that "unconditional liquidity" can become the foundation of a stable economic
model for the twenty-first century.[55]

Another reason this is concerning is that foreigners owned $33 trillion of US securities
of all types (in 2021) on which interest/dividends is owed in perpetuity.[56] Consequently, the
disposable income of future generations will be lower than it would be otherwise.

3. *Private debt* is also a ballast on the economy with credit card debt at $0.8 trillion and stu-
   dent debt at $1.9 trillion (in 2021). Consumer indebtedness implies that aggregate demand
   will be subdued because people in debt will have to curtail their spending.[57] There is "widespread fragility across the entire population – more than one-third of Americans are financially fragile … Financial fragility is not only pervasive, but many middle-income households
   also suffer from the inability to deal with shocks."[58]
4. Most people have *no savings*, which is devastating in a recession and contributes to the
   fragility of the system (see Table 12.5). The dominance of immediate gratification means 74
   percent of people live from paycheck to paycheck unprepared for a recession (see Section
   17.4).[59] This is a sign of a dual economy in which "only 29 percent of Americans are financially healthy" and, even more troublesome, only half of households with income above
   $100,000 were financially healthy. In addition, "54 percent are financially coping … strug-
   gling with some, but not necessarily all, aspects of their financial lives … And 17 percent
   are financially vulnerable." "Women are overwhelmingly bearing the increase in financial
   vulnerability, relative to men."[60]
5. Running an annual *trade deficit* of $800 billion (in 2021) means that the US will continue to
   export jobs that will impede the formation of an inclusive economy (see Figure 13.2).
6. Yet, *costly military commitments* around the globe continue to drain trillions from productive uses.[61] The 2022 military budget is $750 billion, one-third of total government rev-
   enues. It does not take much imagination to think of destabilizing scenarios in which US
   dominance around the globe is challenged and the budget is further strained. The military-
   industrial ecosystem has a powerful influence on the political process and the misallocation
   of resources.

7. The *financial sector is like a cocoon*, decoupled from the real economy engaged primarily in rent seeking. A quarter of all profits stems from finance, but it is not a job creator. In addition, its investment in the real economy is limited:

    > Only about 15 percent of the money coming out of the largest financial institutions goes to new business investment. The rest exists in a closed loop of trading: institutions facilitate and engage in the buying and selling of stocks, bonds, real estate, and other assets that mainly enriches the 20 percent of the population that owns 80 percent of that asset base. This doesn't help growth, but it does fuel the wealth gap ... we [should] start talking about how to create a financial system that really serves society.[62]

8. *GDP growth is decoupled from employment*, especially from full-time middle-class employment. This is partly due to technological unemployment, partly because globalization means that low-skilled workers must compete with their lower-wage counterparts around the globe, partly because the workers lack support either from the government or from unions, and partly because educational opportunities are so limited for a large segment of the population that they lack the skills required in the new economy. This is the making of the skills mismatch: millions of high-tech jobs are unfilled because of lack of a trained workforce; yet, there is extensive unemployment (U-6).

9. The primary and secondary *educational system remains mediocre* overall and does not prepare the next generation for the requirements of the IT revolution. Furthermore, college education is very expensive, pricing a large share of the poor out of the market. Hence, the significant demand for IT professionals is unmet. Money is unavailable to improve the educational system. That implies that the problem will continue to linger. A bill similar to the GI Bill after World War II is not on the political horizon; free community college education is unrealistic, and so is free college education, available in all rich countries.

10. *Infrastructure, the lifeblood of the economy, has been seriously depreciating.* This is the one headwind that is being partly resolved. In 2021, Congress allocated $1 trillion of the $3 trillion needed to fix infrastructure.

11. *Global warming* is a major threat to humanity that will become increasingly costly and politically disorienting. The rate at which we are degrading the ecological environment is widely acknowledged to be unsustainable.[63]

12. *The dominant ideology of neoliberalism* has permeated the popular culture to such an extent that changing it to a more cooperative and inclusive economy would be challenging. After attacking the New Deal principles for decades, it is hard for the citizenry to comprehend that the best government is not one that governs least. It is easy for market aficionados to brand politicians who aspire to improve the condition of the poor through government programs as socialists who would take away their freedoms. Government haters label inheritance taxes "death taxes," and the threat of "death panels" is used as a scare tactic against providing universal health insurance.[64] Thus, politicians who have empathy for the poor are associated with brutal dictatorships and an erosion of personal freedoms. The legitimacy of the government is attacked by the anti-democratic slogan: "stop the steal."

13. That *the economic system is unjust* and not working for half of the population is widely recognized. Moreover, bailout capitalism maintained and exacerbated the inequities. Yet, the political system is nonresponsive because of powerful vested interests. It is not the general will to keep the Federal minimum wage at $7.25. It is not the general will to forbid Medi-

Illustration 18.1 Astronomical inequality generates white supremacist backlash
Source: Shutterstock 1079865011.

care to bargain with pharmaceutical companies over drug prices. It is not the general will to allow hospitals to charge monopoly prices. Such unfair practices led to the widespread perception that the economy allocates rewards unfairly, thereby contributing to the rise of populism and providing fodder for the January 6th insurrection.

14. *Endemic racism* haunts the social fabric and leads to recurring confrontation and consternation that poisons the body politic (see Section 16.4). Programs that would improve the poor's predicament are filibustered because of concern for a racist backlash. The lack of jobs, the mediocre educational system, and the limited safety net available to minorities keep descendants of slaves at the bottom of the totem pole. They are disparaged because of their poverty, but their poverty is due to the way the system deprives them of opportunities available to those who have privileged access to superior schools.

15. The US has entered *a new phase of economic development* in the twenty-first century which would require creative ideas to address the challenges it harbors. However, this remains elusive, because a new historical epoch is difficult to recognize and because the political system is unable to renew itself. Mainstream economists are at a loss to propose a viable policy mix to put the economy back on the road of stability.

16. *Political dysfunction* has become permanent. With the large role of money in politics, and with the average wealth of the top 1 percent of households at $25 million, lobbies and vested interests are so powerful that the political gridlock cannot be broken.

The implication of these 16 gale-force headwinds is that the future economy will not be more inclusive than it has been.[65] Humanistic economists advocate an economy that also works for the 99 percent.[66] The skewed distribution of income is not an epiphenomenon. Rather, it is of paramount importance. Its neglect has had disastrous consequences on the body politic.

The hype of "making the economy grow" is inapt and deceiving, for the average income is not the key determinant of the quality of life: so much of the fruits of economic growth were captured by the top 1 percent, 1.25 million households out of the 124 million![67] These developments do not augur well for the future stability of the country. There is a macroeconomic stalemate about how to end the current malaise and return to normalcy; this implies that high levels of insecurity will continue to haunt the US for the foreseeable future. The prospects of a real inclusive recovery are fading.

Illustration 18.2 A humanistic economy is full of happy people
Source: Shutterstock 144639305.

The tax cut of December 2017 was exactly the wrong medicine for the economic malaise. It will increase the wealth of millionaires significantly, but it will not solve any of the country's problems. On the contrary, it will exacerbate them. The reason is that money begets power and lots of money begets lots more political power, implying that the oligarchy's hold on the body politic will continue. The tax giveaways also mean that the government will not have the funds to address the major headwinds, and sufficient private funds will not be invested in education, renewable energy, and health, the things the economy would need to escape from its malaise.[68]

This textbook accentuates the inconsistencies between mainstream economic theory and reality. It emphasizes the need for a paradigm shift toward a humanistic economics in which the focus is on "increasing people's life satisfaction (or well-being) as opposed to the typical ... focus of economists on growth of output and income."[69] Markets are not intrinsically bad, but they need appropriate institutions, an accommodating culture, adequate regulation, and sufficient oversight to function properly and to create a flourishing economy.[70] A good economy from a humanistic perspective is *not* running "hot" or at full throttle but one in which participants can live carefree, dignified lives, feel good about themselves, and live in harmony with their fellow citizens.[71] It requires an insensitivity to evidence to continue to praise the efficiency and primacy of free markets after the greatest meltdown in the history of mankind followed by the insurrection of January 6, 2021, a symptom of the deep social malaise and disaffection with the way the economy works.[72]

Hence, the reformation of the economics discipline is long overdue.[73] The new paradigm must start with empirical evidence as its foundation rather than deductive theories that appear eloquent in ivory towers but become toxic at street level.[74] People must come before profits.[75] I hope this volume can contribute to creating a new approach to economics that will serve as a foundation for a paradigm shift to Capitalism with a Human Face.[76]

18.4 Takeaways

Each age needs to reform economic theory to meet its needs. The Great Depression of the 1930s showed the errors of neoclassical economics and so Keynesianism was born. However, in the twenty-first century Keynesianism morphed into a bailout capitalism that accentuates the urgent need for a paradigm shift in economic theory because of the US economy's deep structural weaknesses, its fragility, imbalances including the twin endemic deficits in foreign trade and in the federal budget, the uncanny inequality, as well as the widespread disaffection among its citizens. Society needs to recognize that a good economy is not one with a high growth rate because a meaningful life goes well beyond consumption and production. The new paradigm outlined in this book, Capitalism with a Human Face, is an economy which enables people to achieve a satisfactory work-life balance without having to struggle to maintain their basic needs. It must include the ability to live a dignified, less harried, and less precarious life protected by a solid social safety net from the vagaries of the business cycle and one in which the citizenry's need for psychological fulfillment, self-respect, and human contact are satisfied. In short, the goal should be a flourishing society.

Questions for Discussion

1   What is the difference between real and theoretical markets?
2   Can free-market principles create a thriving society?
3   What is more important: growing the economy or saving the environment?
4   Should we leave the environment as good as we found it for future generations?
5   If you were a politician, what policies would you advocate to save the environment?
6   Are you concerned about the welfare of future generations?
7   Do you think that a carbon tax would be useful?
8   Do you think that offshore drilling for oil is a good idea?
9   Do you think that we should set a goal of sustainable development?
10   Do you think that we should be more frugal with natural resources?
11   Do you think we should ban gasoline-powered engines? When?
12   Do you consider global warming a major threat and do you think we will be able to control it?
13   Should we phase out coal mining?
14   What should happen to the coal miners of West Virginia?
15   Have you done something about decreasing your carbon footprint on the environment?
16   Describe some of the major blunders of mainstream economists.
17   Do you agree that economic policy has destabilized the political system?
18   Discuss: technological change has contributed to the destabilization of the political system.
19   Do you know anyone addicted to consumption?
20   Do you expect technological change to improve life for your generation?
21   Do you know anyone who is underemployed?
22   Do you know anyone who has lost his/her job because of technological change? Globalization?
23   Do you know anyone whose salary has been stagnating? Addicted to opioids? Lost social status?
24   Which of the headwinds can be overcome, in your opinion?
25   Do you know anyone who is heavily indebted?
26   Should we decrease our military commitments around the globe?

Notes

1   Tony Lawson, *Economics and Reality* (Routledge, 1997).
2   Editors, "Economists Focus Too Little on What People Really Care About," *The Economist*, May 3, 2018.

3   Steve Keen, *Developing an Economics for the Post-Crisis World* (College Publications, 2016); David Harvey, *Seventeen Contradictions and the End of Capitalism* (Oxford University Press, 2015); Tim Jackson, *Post Growth: Life after Capitalism* (Polity, 2021).

4   Jacob Hacker et al. (eds.), *The American Political Economy: Politics, Markets, and Power* (Cambridge University Press, 2022); Raghuram Rajan and Luigi Zingales, *Saving Capitalism from the Capitalists* (Crown Business, 2003).

5   Anthony Atkinson, *Inequality: What Can Be Done?* (Harvard University Press, 2015).

6   Robert Frank and Philip Cook, *Winner-Take-All Society* (Free Press, 1995).

7   Francis Fukuyama, *Political Order and Political Decay: From the Industrial Revolution to the Globalization of Democracy* (Profile Books, 2014).

8   Michael Sandel, "Populism, Liberalism, and Democracy," *Philosophy & Social Criticism* 44 (2018), 4353-359; here p. 354.

9   Richard Feynman, "Cargo Cult Science," *Engineering and Science* 37 (1974), 7: 10-13.

10 Paul Collier, *The Future of Capitalism: Facing the New Anxieties* (Harper, 2018).

11 Martin Feldstein, "Cutting US Corporate Tax Is Worth the Cost," *Project Syndicate*, November 27, 2017; Martin Feldstein, "Tax Policy in the 1980s: A Personal View," NBER Working Paper no. 4323, 1993; Robert Barro, "How US Corporate-Tax Reform Will Boost Growth," *Project Syndicate*, December 13, 2017; Philip Bump, "How the Republican Tax Bill Benefits the Rich, According to Government Analysis," *Washington Post*, November 30, 2017; Emily Cochrane, "Paul Ryan Deletes Tweet Lauding a $1.50 Benefit from the New Tax Law," *The New York Times*, February 3, 2017.

12 Emma Rothschild, "Reagan and the Real America," *The New York Review of Books*, February 5, 1981; Monica Prasad, "The Popular Origins of Neoliberalism in the Reagan Tax Cut of 1981," *Journal of Policy History* 24 (2012), 3: 351-383.

13 Benjamin Friedman, "Implications of the Government Deficit for US Capital Formation," *The Economics of Large Government Deficits*, Federal Reserve Bank of Boston, *Proceedings of a Conference Held in October 1983*, pp. 73-95.

14 Frank Ackerman, *Reaganomics: Rhetoric vs Reality* (South End Press, 1982); Kim Phillips-Fein, *Invisible Hands: The Making of the Conservative Movement from the New Deal to Reagan* (Norton, 2009).

15 Alan Greenspan, *The Age of Turbulence: Adventures in a New World* (Penguin, 2007), pp. 365, 408.

16 Richard Posner, *The Crisis of Capitalist Democracy* (Harvard University Press, 2011); Lester Thurow, "The Elephant and the Maharajah," *The New York Review of Books*, December 22, 1983; Franco Modigliani, "Reagan's Economic Policies: A Critique," *Oxford Economic Papers* 40 (1988), 3: 397-426; Wallace Peterson, "The Macroeconomic Legacy of Reaganomics," *Journal of Economic Issues* 22 (1988), 1: 1-16.

17 Zach Wichter, "The Hedge Fund Manager Who Just Paid $238 Million for a Manhattan Penthouse," *The New York Times*, January 24, 2019.

18 Dani Rodrik, *The Globalization Paradox: Democracy and the Future of the World Economy* (Norton, 2011).

19 Hyman Minsky, "The Financial Instability Hypothesis: Capitalistic Processes and the Behavior of the Economy," in Charles Kindleberger and Jean-Paul Laffargue (eds.), *Financial Crises: Theory, History, and Policy* (Cambridge University Press, 1982), pp. 12-29.

20 EcoWatch, "Jimmy Carter: The US Is an 'Oligarchy with Unlimited Political Bribery,'" August 3, 2015.

21 Robert Skidelsky, *What's Wrong with Economics: A Primer for the Perplexed* (Yale University Press, 2020); Vernon Smith and Bart Wilson, *Humanomics: Moral Sentiments and the Wealth of Nations for the Twenty-First Century* (Cambridge University Press, 2019).

22 Stephen Macekura, *The Mismeasure of Progress: Economic Growth and Its Critics* (University of Chicago Press, 2020).

23 Bruno Frey and Alois Stutzer, "What Can Economists Learn from Happiness Research?" *Journal of Economic Literature* 40 (2002), 2: 402-435; Marc Fleurbaey, *A Manifesto for Social Progress: Ideas for a Better Society* (Cambridge University Press, 2018).

24   Angus Deaton and Paul Schreyer, "GDP, Wellbeing, and Health: Thoughts on the 2017 Round of the International Comparison Program," *Review of Income and Wealth*, forthcoming.

25   Robert Gordon, *The Rise and Fall of American Growth* (Princeton University Press, 2017); Shawn Sprague, "Below Trend: The US Productivity Slowdown since the Great Recession," *Beyond the Numbers: Productivity*, 6, no. 2, January 2017.

26   St. Louis Fed, series MPU4910063.

27   St. Louis Fed, "Multifactor Productivity," series MPU4900013.

28   Nicholas Bloom et al., "Are Ideas Getting Harder to Find?" *American Economic Review* 110 (2020), 4: 1104-1144.

29   Bureau of Labor Statistics, "The US Productivity Slowdown: An Economy-Wide and Industry-Level Analysis," *Monthly Labor Review*, April 2021.

30   Stijn Baert, "The Iceberg Decomposition: A Parsimonious Way to Map the Health of Labour Markets," IZA Discussion Paper no. 13512, July 2020; David Bell and David Blanchflower, "Underemployment in the US and Europe," *ILR Review* 74 (2019), 1: 56-94.

31   Jeanna Smialek, "Why Top Economists are Citing a Higher-Than-Reported Jobless Rate," *The New York Times*, February 22, 2021.

32   Bureau of Labor Statistics, "Labor Force Statistics from the Current Population Survey," Series LNU05026639; this is the sum of rows 8 and 9 in Table 11.1.

33   Erik Brynjolfsson and Andrew McAfee, *The Second Machine Age: Work, Progress, and Prosperity in a Time of Brilliant Technologies* (Norton, 2014).

34   Tara Siegel Bernard and Karl Russell, "The Middle-Class Crunch: A Look at 4 Family Budgets," *The New York Times*, October 3, 2019.

35   Oren Cass, "The Cost-of-Thriving Index: Reevaluating the Prosperity of the American Family," Manhattan Institute Report, February 2020.

36   Richard Posner, *The Failure of Capitalism: The Crisis of '08 and the Descent into Depression* (Harvard University Press, 2009).

37   Lawrence Summers, "US Economic Prospects: Secular Stagnation, Hysteresis, and the Zero Lower Bound," *Business Economics* 49 (2014): 65-73; Lawrence Summers, "Demand Side Secular Stagnation," *American Economic Review* 105 (2015), 5: 60-65.

38   Paul Krugman, "Secular Stagnation, Coalmines, Bubbles, and Larry Summers," *The New York Times*, November 16, 2013.

39   Emmanuel Saez and Gabriel Zucman, *The Triumph of Injustice: How the Rich Dodge Taxes and How to Make Them Pay* (Norton, 2019).

40   Nicholas Kristof, "We're No. 28! And Dropping!" *The New York Times*, September 9, 2020.

41   Anna Stansbury and Lawrence Summers, "The Declining Worker Power Hypothesis: An Explanation for the Recent Evolution of the American Economy," *Brookings Papers on Economic Activity* (Spring 2020), pp. 1-77; here p. 63.

42   CDC, National Center for Health Statistics, "Provisional Drug Overdose Death Counts," https://www.cdc.gov/nchs/nvss/vsrr/drug-overdose-data.htm.

43   Sanford Levinson, "Our Broken Constitution," *Los Angeles Times*, October 16, 2006 https://web.archive.org/web/20091005132615/http://www.utexas.edu/law/news/2006/101606_latimes.html; Sanford Levinson, "The Democratic Deficit in America," *Harvard Law & Policy Review*, December 2006; William Franko and Christopher Witko, *The New Economic Populism: How States Respond to Economic Inequality* (Oxford University Press, 2017).

44   Sanford Levinson, *Our Undemocratic Constitution: Where the Constitution Goes Wrong* (Oxford University Press, 2006); Nancy MacLean, *Democracy in Chains* (Viking Penguin, 2017).

45   Chrystia Freeland, *Plutocrats: The Rise of the New Global Super-Rich and the Fall of Everyone Else* (Penguin Press, 2012); George Packer, "We Are Living in a Failed State," *The Atlantic*, June 2020.

46   Lawrence Lessig, "Why the US Is a Failed Democratic State," *The New York Review of Books*, December 10, 2021.

47   Department of the Treasury, *Financial Report of the United States Government*, FY2021.

48   Kenneth Rogoff, "Government Debt Is Not a Free Lunch," *Project Syndicate*, December 6, 2019.

49   US Treasury, "Interest Expense on the Debt Outstanding," https://www.treasurydirect.gov/govt/reports/ir/ir_expense.htm.

50   Jerome Powell argued for a reduction of the deficit: "Putting the federal budget on a sustainable path when the economy is strong would help ensure that policymakers have the space to use fiscal policy to assist in stabilizing the economy during a downturn." Heather Long, "Fed Chair Powell Warns Congress that $1 Trillion Budget Deficits Are Unsustainable," *The Washington Post*, February 11, 2020.

51   St. Louis Fed, series GFDEBTN and GFDEGDQ188S; Congressional Budget Office "Budget"; https://www.cbo.gov/topics/budget.

52   Jason Furman and Lawrence Summers, "Who's Afraid of the Budget Deficits?: How Washington Should End Its Debt Obsession," *Foreign Affairs* 98 (2019), 2: 82–94.

53   Ibid.

54   Alan Auerbach et al., "If Not Now, When? New Estimates of the Federal Budget Outlook," *The Brookings Institution*, February 2019.

55   Mariana Mazzucato, "Capitalism's Triple Crisis," *Social Europe*, April 9, 2020.

56   US Department of the Treasury, "Total US Banking and Securities Liabilities to Foreign Residents by Type of Liability and Holder"; http://ticdata.treasury.gov/Publish/totalticliabs.txt.

57   Heather Boushey, *Unbound: How Inequality Constricts Our Economy and What We Can Do About It* (Harvard University Press, 2019).

58   Andrea Hasler et al., "Financial Fragility in the US: Evidence and Implications," George Washington University School of Business, November 30, 2017; https://www.nefe.org/_images/research/Financial-Fragility/Financial-Fragility-Final-Report.pdf.

59   NPR, "Paycheck-To-Paycheck Nation," December 16, 2020; https://www.npr.org/2020/12/16/941292021/paycheck-to-paycheck-nation-how-life-in-america-adds-up; Board of Governors of the Federal Reserve System. "Report on the Economic Well Being of US Households in 2018," May 2019.

60   Financial Health Network, "US Financial Health Pulse. 2019 Trends Report," 2019; https://s3.amazonaws.com/cfsi-innovation-files-2018/wp-content/uploads/2019/12/16161507/2019-Pulse-Report-FINAL_1205.pdf.

61   Jeffrey Sachs, *A New Foreign Policy: Beyond American Exceptionalism* (Columbia University Press, 2018).

62   Rana Foroohar, "How Big Banks Became Our Masters," *The New York Times*, September 27, 2017.

63   Andrew Fanning et al., "The Social Shortfall and Ecological Overshoot of Nations," *Nature Sustainability* 5 (2022): 26–36.

64   Popularized by Sarah Palin. Roger Ebert, "'Death Panels.' A Most Excellent Term," August 17, 2009.

65   Reema Patel et al., *Building a Public Culture of Economics* (RSA, 2018); https://www.thersa.org/reports/building-public-culture-economics.

66   Oxfam International, *An Economy for the 99 Percent* (Oxfam, 2017).

67   Edward Wolff, "Recent Trends in Household Wealth in the United States: Rising Debt and the Middle-Class Squeeze—An Update to 2007," Levy Economics Institute of Bard College Working Paper no. 589, March 2010; Edward N. Wolff, *A Century of Wealth in America* (Harvard University Press, 2017).

68   John Komlos, "GOP Tax Cuts Would Make the Rich Even Richer," PBS, Making Sen$e, October 18, 2017.

69   John Tomer, "Book Review of *Foundations of Real-World Economics*," *Society and Economy* 42 (2020), 1: 98–104.

70   Robert Reich, *The System: Who Rigged It, How We Fix it* (Knopf, 2020); Branko Milanovic, *Capitalism, Alone: The Future of the System That Rules the World* (Belknap Press, 2019).

71   Chris Benner and Manuel Pastor, *Solidarity Economics: Why Mutuality and Movements Matter* (Polity, 2021).

72   Luigi Zingales, *Capitalism for the People: Recapturing the Lost Genius of American Prosperity* (Basic Books, 2012).

73   George Akerlof, "Sins of Omission and the Practice of Economics," *Journal of Economic Literature* 58 (2020), 2: 405-418.

74   Tae-Hee Jo et al. (eds.), *The Routledge Handbook of Heterodox Economics: Theorizing, Analyzing and Transforming Capitalism* (Routledge, 2018).

75   Joseph Stiglitz, *People, Power and Profits: Progressive Capitalism for the Age of Discontent* (Norton, 2019).

76   Reich, *The System*, op. cit.; Andrew Cumbers, *The Case for Economic Democracy* (Polity Books, 2020).

Index

Printed in the United States
by Baker & Taylor Publisher Services